THE
CENTRAL AMERICAN
CRISIS
READER

EDITED BY

Robert S. Leiken
and
Barry Rubin

SUMMIT BOOKS
New York

Published by SUMMIT BOOKS
A Division of Simon & Schuster, Inc.
Simon & Schuster Building
1230 Avenue of the Americas
New York, New York 10020

SUMMIT BOOKS and colophon are trademarks of Simon & Schuster, Inc.
Designed by Irving Perkins Associates
Map by Ozzie Greif

Manufactured in the United States of America

1 3 5 7 9 10 8 6 4 2

Library of Congress Cataloging in Publication Data
The Central American crisis reader.

Includes index.
1. Nicaragua—Politics and government—1979–
—Sources. 2. El Salvador—Politics and government—
1979– —Sources. 3. Central America—Politics and
government—Sources. 4. Central America—Foreign rela-
tions—United States—Sources. 5. United States—Foreign
relations—Central America—Sources.
I. Leiken, Robert S., date. II. Rubin, Barry M.
F1528.C45 1987   972.8'053   87-1864

ISBN: 0-671-60058-3
0-671-60597-6 (pbk.)

We wish to thank the following publishers and authors for allowing their works to be quoted:

David Browning, *El Salvador: Landscape and Society* (1971), copyright Oxford University Press, by permission of Oxford University Press.
Bruce Marcus, editor, *Sandinistas Speak* (1982), copyright Pathfinder Press.
Gabriel Zaid, "Enemy Colleagues," permission from *Dissent Magazine.*

(continued at the back of the book)

Acknowledgments

Many people have helped in selecting, obtaining, editing, and typing the material in *The Central American Crisis Reader*. Much of Chapter 1 was prepared by Michael Clark and Chapter 7 by Eric Singer. Ivan Menjivar and Rhea Saab provided valuable research assistance on Chapters 3 and 4.

We would also like to express our particular gratitude to Thomas Hughes and the Carnegie Endowment for International Peace and to the following people: Adolfo Aguilar Zinser, Luz Maria Alvarez-Wilson, Bruce Cameron, Donald Castillo, Alfonso Chardy, Luz Maria Cortines, Robert Davis, Joseph Eldridge, David Jessup, Victor Meza, the National Security Archive, Dan Harris, Richard Millet, Murielle de la Porte, Janet Raimundo, Nina Serafino, Caesar Sereseres, Jorge Sol, Ricardo Stein, David Weiner, and others who assisted us in this project. Our editor Arthur Samuelson, provided invaluable help and encouragment.

*To our parents and in memory
of Raul Guerra and Ricardo Zuniga,
two brave Central American democrats.*

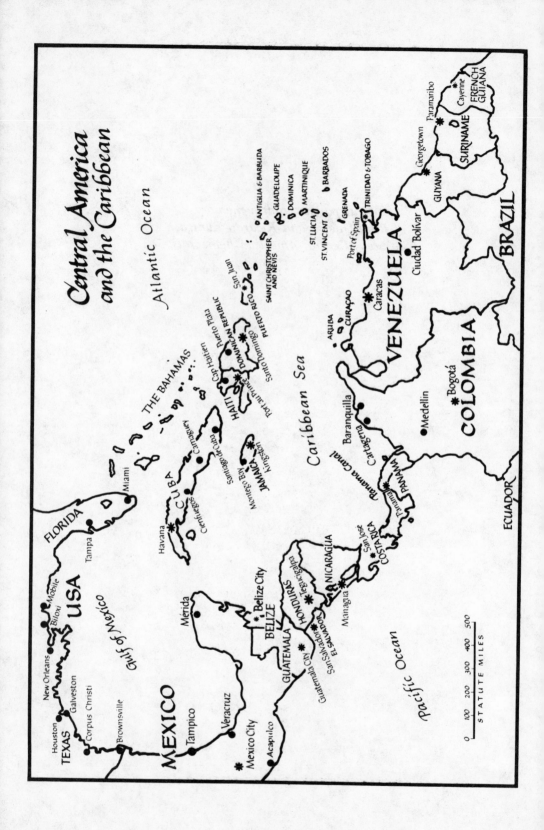

Contents

Contents

Contents

Chapter Two
REVOLUTION IN NICARAGUA

Contents

Chapter Three
THE SANDINISTAS IN POWER

Contents

Chapter Four

ORIGINS OF CONFLICT IN EL SALVADOR

Chapter Five
THE WAR IN EL SALVADOR

Contents

Chapter Six
U.S. POLICY

Contents

Chapter Seven
LATIN AMERICA, EUROPE, THE USSR, AND CUBA

Contents

Preface

The Central American crisis has generated a great deal of debate among Americans. We have selected statements, speeches, and documents that most fully reflect the positions and experiences of those directly involved in these issues in Nicaragua, El Salvador, as well as the United States, and other relevant countries. In general, we have sought to allow participants to speak for themselves rather than to present samples of commentaries and opinions by outside observers. Though the Central American crisis ultimately involves the whole region, we have chosen to provide the reader with an in-depth representation of the views of the major actors in the two principal countries of crisis, Nicaragua and El Salvador.

We have sought to provide many items hitherto either previously existing only in Spanish or completely unavailable to the general public. Many items have been specially translated; others have been obtained through trips to Central America or through the assistance of people from the region.

Chapter 1 provides an overview of the area's history, including translations of Gonzalo Fernández de Oviedo y Valdés's early view of the region, Augusto Sandino's political philosophy, and Salvador Mendietta's important analysis. The evolving view and involvement of the United States is presented, including a little-known, interesting essay by Walter Lippmann

16

and accounts by top U.S. officials and military officers.

In Chapter 2, much of the material on Nicaragua has been hitherto unpublished in English. This includes an extract from the novel of Xavier Argüello, a former official of the revolutionary regime and an outstanding young Nicaraguan writer, describing the Managua earthquake, which turned out to be a seminal political as well as a calamitous natural event. An extract from a book by Sandinista founder Carlos Fonseca Amador illustrates the movement's early pro-Soviet inclinations; their 1969 program states the organization's objectives. Other writings put into English for the first time include those of Sandinista leaders Henry Ruiz and Plutarcho Hernández as well as revealing internal Sandinista polemics. Perhaps the most revealing of these is Carlos Fonseca Amador's "Last Testament," considered the equivalent of Lenin's "Last Testament," disclosing the nature of the sharp antagonisms within the Sandinista leadership.

None of the authentic original documents from the anti-Somoza opposition in Section IV of Chapter 2 have ever been published in English before. Sergio Ramírez provides a fascinating account on the formation of the anti-Somoza united front. Two pieces by Pedro Joaquín Chamorro, the martyred editor of *La Prensa,* were also translated for the first time and give a sense of his thought. Cardinal Obando y Bravo's declaration against Somoza shows the Catholic Church's position during the revolution.

Chapter 3 provides insight into the goals and motives of both the Sandinistas and their emerging opposition. Particularly interesting is a previously untranslated article by Sergio Ramírez, now vice-president, and the secret internal Sandinista "72-hour" document. On the opposition side, material previously unavailable in English includes the position paper of the business association (COSEP), Chamorro's memorandum which caused a sensation when published in Nicaragua, and the platform of the Democratic Coordinator, along with Pablo Antonio Cuadra's moving account of the fate of Nicaraguan culture.

Turning to El Salvador in Chapter 4, we have translated and published for the first time two opposing position papers on land reform by a major revolutionary group and by the private-sector association ANEP. The sharp contrast illustrates the social contradictions that gave rise to armed conflict. Several FMLN documents never before published in English were obtained from guerrillas or from the university archives in San Salvador. These show the different ideological and strategic perspectives among the revolutionary groups and it is interesting to compare them to the internal Sandinista polemics presented in Chapter 2. A number of other documents are also published for the first time. Robert Leiken's interview with Fermán Cienfuegos is the most candid sample of the political views of a Salvadoran guerrilla leader we know.

In Chapter 5 we present for the first time several items found on captured FMLN leaders, authenticated by leading experts and journalists. They include revealing documents on Sandinista-FMLN relations and on the internal relations and personalities of radical cadre. The perspectives of President José Napoleón Duarte and of the right-wing leader Roberto d'Aubuisson are also presented.

Chapter 6 presents the views and policies of the Carter and Reagan administrations. Assistant Secretary of State Viron Vaky's testimony provides the most coherent presentation of the former; Jeane Kirkpatrick and the Sante Fe Report present some of the early intellectual inspiration of the Reagan administration policy. The secret correspondence between Assistant Secretary of State Thomas Enders and President Ortega in 1981 gives a sense of the inner workings and problems of U.S.-Nicaragua negotiations. Representative Michael Barnes' "Democratic Alternatives," never before published, summarizes what became the dominant Democratic Party position. The differing perspectives of President Reagan and the Congress is provided from a number of standpoints.

Chapter 7 includes many resolutions and communiqués never before published in book form that show the attitudes of Latin American leaders, the Contadora group's mediation efforts, and the role of the USSR and Cuba. The secret letter from the Soviet Communist Party to the FMLN, never previously published, was obtained from private sources in Central America and was verified as authentic by a leader of the recipient group. Yuri Andropov's comment on Nicaragua and Afghanistan, never previously published in English, illustrates an interesting aspect of the actual Soviet position on the issue.

The editors have tried to provide a full and fair selection of the points of view of governments and oppositions in El Salvador, Nicaragua, and the United States. We hope this book will increase understanding of the evolving situation and of the issues that are being debated—and fought over— at the cost of so many lives.

R.S.L.
B.R.

Introduction

I. The Burden of the Past

Crisis, and only crisis, brings Central America to the fitful attention of U.S. policymakers. Every few decades, like a wandering comet, the region wheels back into the American focus and then disappears in a vapor (or whiff of grapeshot), leaving neither Central America better off nor the United States more enlightened.

Central America's geopolitical stability over the past century explains why U.S. policymakers could afford to neglect the region despite its obvious strategic salience. No regime hostile to the United States or tied to a foreign power has been able to establish itself (outside of the limited British presence in Belize and Bluefields) since independence from Spain and the Monroe Doctrine were mutually proclaimed in the third decade of the nineteenth century.

This status quo came to rest on the pillars of a relatively static society, authoritarian military governments, the allegiance of the Catholic Church, economic dependency on the United States, and, in the last instance, recourse to U.S. military power. In the past, sparks of revolution were extinguished by U.S. covert or police actions. In the twentieth century, U.S. intervention became an integral feature of Central American political

19

life but did not require any special attention. Thus, though Central America is adjacent to the Panama Canal, two major oil exporters (Mexico and Venezuela), and the Caribbean Sea (a crucial commercial and military thoroughfare), the United States has paid less notice to the region than to the Middle East, Southeast Asia, or Western Europe. Yet, as the Kissinger Commission on Central America was not the first to note, "the ability of the United States to sustain a tolerable balance of power on the global scene at a manageable cost depends on the inherent security of its land borders."* Or as Soviet strategists recognize, "in military strategic terms [the Caribbean] is a sort of hinterland on whose stability freedom of U.S. action in other parts of the globe depends."†

Central America's geopolitical stability and the status quo have been shaken in recent years. As a consequence, Central America suddenly ascended to the top of the American foreign policy agenda, becoming the most passionately debated issue since the Vietnam War. Opinion leaders now assert frequently, and with enormous confidence, diametrically opposed views of the crisis. All assume that Central America is some place they have seen before: for conservatives, Cuba in the 1950s and Angola in the 1970s; for liberals, Vietnam in the 1960s. But we cannot grasp Central America with the blunt instrument of analogy. Policy has been predicated on unexamined premises and debate polarized in stereotyped positions. If Central America is small it is not simple. American policy has groped for decades in its "heart of darkness."

The journey to Central America passes through time as well as space. The region is not only poor, it is "underdeveloped." Step outside its capital cities and you encounter the Middle Ages, with its muddy thoroughfares, wooden plows pulled by draft animals or even humans, seasonal rhythms, local landlords, and feuding factions. Medievalism continues to cast a shadow over Central America's present.

One such legacy is Central America's condition as a "divided nation." In the sixteenth century, the isthmus was organized as part of New Spain in the "Captaincy General of Guatemala." However, political unity was beset by rivalries among the individual conquistadores, who each established their own governments, a system later institutionalized by the Spanish colonial "intendance" system. In this way, the Spanish colonial system institutionalized regional conflict.

These centrifugal tendencies soon were linked to international imperialist rivalries. By the sixteenth century the French, the Dutch, and later the English were already competing with the Spanish for hegemony in Central

---

**The Report of the President's National Bipartisan Commission on Central America* (New York: Macmillan, 1984, p. 109).

†*International Affairs,* Moscow, February 1967.

America. In the nineteenth century, aided by the British and the Americans, Central America won independence from Spain. But efforts to create a unified Central American nation ran foul of local factionalism and outside interference. Colonial and ecclesiastical jurisdictions hardened into national boundaries. These divisions were intensified by fighting between factions which, although often called "liberal" or "conservative," resembled Western European political parties only in name. They were more reminiscent of the retinues of a feudal warrior or caudillo.

Warlordism, or *caudillismo,* under the banner of "conservative" or "liberal" political parties, became a perpetual obstacle to national unity and Central American federation as well as an open invitation to foreign intervention. Factional rivalries transcended frontiers. Central American states customarily harbored exiles and habitually meddled in the internal affairs of their neighbors. These phenomena were the negative expression of Central America's condition as a "nation divided." Outside powers—Spain, England, and then the United States—took advantage of these divisions. Frequently one of the feuding factions would invite the intervention of a colonial power. By the early 20th century the United States had come to monopolize that role.

Militarism was another legacy of this past. While the establishment of national armies in the late nineteenth century was a step forward in the struggle for national unity and against outside intervention, the armies themselves became new arenas for factional and personal ambitions. Despite the drafting of constitutions and the founding of parties, coups, not elections, became the traditional means for transferring power.

Nonetheless, although Central American economies preserved their colonial character as food and raw material exporters and remained highly dependent on the advanced countries, after World War II the region underwent rapid economic growth, participated in the revolution in telecommunications, and felt the pressure of new ideologies. The Central American *campesino* lives at once in the dark ages and in the "global village." The clash of the old and the new is one of the key components of the Central American crisis.

From 1950 to the late 1970's the annual gross domestic product of Central American countries grew at a rate of over 5 percent. Employment rose steadily, per capita income doubled, and exports increased sixteenfold. Home and foreign markets broadened, a manufacturing sector developed, and productivity and output grew steadily. The urban portion of the population increased from 15 percent in 1950 to 43 percent in 1980. The export sector modernized in response to rising world prices for sugar, coffee, bananas, and cotton; roads, electricity, and telephone lines were extended to previously isolated areas. Irrigation made its appearance along with pesticides, improved seeds, fertilizers, and other new techniques.

Yet, while the medieval landscape acquired some of the appurtenances of the twentieth century and landlords and a new rural bourgeoisie prospered, many peasants fared badly. The very success and expansion of the export sector reduced available arable land. Land rents nearly quadrupled during the 1960s. By the early 1970s about 70 percent of the region's rural holdings were small plots of less than 10 acres. At the same time, 6 percent of rural holdings made up more than 70 percent of the total arable land.

Of the rural population of Central America, approximately one-half live on tiny plots. Rising rents meant that greater numbers of peasants were forced to join the growing class of landless laborers and that farm workers could no longer afford land on which to subsist during their off-season. Since small farms could not absorb even the natural growth of the population, younger sons and daughters constantly joined the new rural proletariat.

Many eventually migrated to rural towns and cities in search of factory or service jobs. Yet imported capital-intensive technology and the narrowness of Central American markets restricted employment. Inflation bit into wages. Real wages in Guatemala, for example, decreased by an estimated 25 percent between 1972 and 1977. Natural disasters like the earthquakes in Nicaragua and Guatemala and hurricane Fifi in Honduras exacted a toll paid mainly by the poor.

Despite their economic activation, Central American countries remained among the most inequitable in Latin America. In Guatemala, El Salvador, Nicaragua, and Honduras during the 1970s the poorest 20 percent of the population received only between 3 and 4 percent of the national income, the poorest 30 percent between 16 and 18 percent. On the other hand, the top 20 percent of the population received about 60 percent of the national income, the richest 5 percent about 30 percent. Most Central Americans lacked doctors (one to more than 2,000 people), hospital beds, and clinics while chronically suffering from eye diseases, malnutrition, and epidemics of malaria, dengue, hepatitis, and typhoid fever. Life expectancy was about fifty-five years, one of ten children died as infants, and only half of the survivors ever learned to read. In Honduras only 46 percent of the population had access to safe drinking water; in El Salvador the portion rose to 53 percent. Malnutrition was endemic in the Central American countryside. According to the United Nations, 96.6 percent of the rural homes in Honduras were without water; 89.4 percent had no toilet; 94.5 percent had no electricity.

With the paralysis of the Central American common market in the 1970s, regional economic growth slowed to a standstill and inflation soared. In the late 1970s and early 1980s, prices for Central American exports fell while those of oil and manufacturing imports skyrocketed. Monetary reserves fell, and external debt rose rapidly. Inadequate medical, sanitary, and educational services were cut back even as population continued to increase at an annual rate close to 3 percent. Shantytowns of landless migrants from the countryside now surrounded perilous cities where the wealthy sought sanctuary in armored cars behind guarded, electrified walls.

II. The Age of the Democratic Revolution in Central America

Pressure for agrarian reform began to build throughout Nicaragua, Guatemala, El Salvador, and Honduras during the late 1960s and early 1970s. Reform movements which emerged almost simultaneously in each of these countries suffered similar fates. In El Salvador the electoral coalition led by Christian Democrat Napoleón Duarte and Social Democrat Guillermo Ungo was robbed of victory in 1972 by fraud and a subsequent military coup. The populist reform movement led by young military officers that came to power in Honduras in the same year had been dispersed by 1975. In Guatemala a reform coalition led by General Efraín Rios Montt was deprived of victory by an electoral fraud in 1974.

Rising protests and demands for reform reflected deeply-rooted socioeconomic changes. Economic expansion had altered Central America's class structure, producing a middle class and an urban working class. The shock of earthquake and massive relief efforts heightened social awareness. In Guatemala Indians in remote villages learned that their welfare was now not only of national but of international concern. This awakening consciousness provided the necessary background for guerrilla groups, for the first time, to make major inroads among the Indian population.

The new activism in the Central American Catholic Church reflected the emergence of national bourgeoisies exposed to university educations, international economic institutions, and the Western media. The church has been deeply permeated by reformist currents which dominated the historic 1968 meeting of Latin American bishops in Medellín, Colombia. As a consequence, the centuries-old alliance between sword and church was broken. The church hierarchy often remonstrated against the military, even as lower-level clergy sometimes joined the guerrilla movements themselves. At the same time, military reform movements led by young socially conscious officers emerged in all the Central American armies.

But during the 1960s and '70s the economic, social, and ideological changes we have been describing were not followed by political reforms or by the kind of democratic revolutions that took place in the West during the late eighteenth and nineteenth centuries under similar pressures. Instead, political channels were blocked, agrarian reform stymied or paralyzed. Labor unions encompassed only a small minority of the working population, and labor was generally unable to defend its interests in an organized way in most of Central America. As a consequence, in El Salvador, Guatemala, and Nicaragua, left-led mass organizations and guerrilla movements, often significantly influenced by Havana, gained the leadership of mass opposition movements.

The tides of Central American affairs had ebbed and flowed in obscurity. But in 1979 the Nicaraguan revolution, like lightning over a darkened sea, disclosed unsuspected and deep turbulence. In that previous darkness, Central American society had undergone a sea change.

Nicaragua's popular insurrection against the Somoza tyranny was called "the beautiful revolution." It united virtually the entire population against the corrupt Somoza dynasty and won broad international support. Latin American democracies like Costa Rica and Venezuela, whose Social Democratic President Carlos Andrés Pérez was called "the godfather of the Nicaraguan Revolution," supplied arms and logistic and political support, as did Cuba. When international efforts to remove Somoza by mediation failed, a broad popular insurrection, now led by the Sandinistas, succeeded in toppling the dictator.

The last twenty-five years of the Somoza dynasty were a period of sustained but unequally shared economic growth. Landless peasants flocked to shantytowns around Managua, while the industrial proletariat expanded and labor activism mounted. A modernizing business and technocratic class grew up; the universities swelled with new students and political militants. The earthquake which leveled Managua in December 1972 set in motion the chain of events which would eventually lead to Somoza's downfall. Somoza pocketed international relief funds and used Managua's devastation as a pretext to confiscate property belonging to the new bourgeoisie. As businessmen, professionals and churchmen turned against him, the repression of labor unions and political parties engendered a broad movement against Somoza.

In 1973, the UDEL (Democratic Union for Liberation) was formed under the leadership of Pedro Joaquín Chamorro, the outspoken editor of Nicaragua's only independent newspaper, *La Prensa*. In late 1974, the Sandinistas seized the house of a leading Somoza follower and succeeded, through the intervention of the Archbishop of Managua, Miguel Obando y Bravo, in freeing leading Sandinistas from Somoza's prisons. Somoza's retaliation was harsh. The Sandinistas' daring action had gained them sympathy among Nicaragua's youth. By the second half of the 1970s, Somoza's National Guard treated all young people as Sandinista sympathizers. The reprisals broadened and radicalized the opposition to Somoza.

These events enhanced the Sandinista National Liberation Front (FSLN), but the group itself grew slowly until 1978. In the early 1970s, by the accounts of various Sandinista leaders (see Chapter 2), Sandinista combatants did not number more than two or three dozen, despite help from Cuba. A year before the revolution, the total number of Sandinista militants was probably less than 300. Meanwhile, Pedro Joaquín Chamorro's UDEL, with the support of the Catholic Church, was a broad alliance involving most Nicaraguan business and labor organizations, *La Prensa,* political parties ranging from the Marxist-Leninist Nicaraguan Socialist Party (PSN) through the Social and Christian Democrats, the traditional anti-Somoza Conservative Party, and even breakaway sections of Somoza's own Liberal Party. The insurrection against Somoza was detonated by the assassination of Pedro Joaquín Chamorro—not by the Sandinistas, most of whose forces had languished for years in the northern mountains.

As anti-Somoza sentiment sharpened, one faction of the feuding Sandinistas initiated an alliance with the growing, above-ground anti-Somoza coalition. Led by Plutarcho Hernández and Humberto and Daniel Ortega, the Tercerista faction considered the alliance "tactical and temporary," as stated in their 1977 "General Platform." But when Somoza foreclosed all peaceful options and international mediation efforts failed, the Sandinistas —promising pluralism, a nonaligned foreign policy, and a mixed economy —gained leadership of the anti-Somoza revolution. When Sandinista columns converged on Managua, on July 19, 1979, they were greeted by the jubilant populace as conquering heroes.

The rule of the Salvadoran oligarchy and military was more brutal than Somoza's tyranny, and that country's inequities more severe. After Salvador's military regime reportedly fixed the 1972 election, many young Salvadorans saw no option but armed struggle. During the 1970s, revolutionaries who had repudiated the Salvadoran Communist Party organized both guerrilla groups and "popular organizations" that included grass-root Christian communities, labor unions, and peasant and student associations. In 1979 and early 1980, the popular organizations mobilized tens of thousands of people in antigovernment demonstrations. After the triumph of the Nicaraguan revolution, the turmoil in El Salvador led reform-minded military officers, backed by the parties that supported Duarte in 1972, to engineer a military *coup* and to organize a reformist junta in October 1979. The new revolutionary organizations mostly boycotted the October junta. Some reformist military officers along with Social Democrats, Communists, and radical Christian Democrats sought a dialogue with these groups, but these efforts fell apart and so did the first junta. The autumn of 1979, when a broad-based ruling coalition seemed possible in Nicaragua and a reformist junta held power in Salvador, proved to be the high point of the democratic revolution in Central America.

III. The Contradictions of the Democratic Revolution

At that time, many Central Americans believed they were entering a new era. Democratic Costa Rica, reformist sections of the Honduran army, and one Salvadoran revolutionary group (the Armed Forces of National Resistance) had furnished arms, sanctuaries, and funds to the Sandinistas. Many of these Central American supporters saw the Nicaraguan promise of a "third way" between neocolonial capitalist exploitation and Soviet-style "real socialism" as the opening of a Central American epoch of democratic revolution, economic cooperation and development, national independence and regional unity.

But these aspirations were beset with enemies on the right and on the left. In 1980, sectors of the Guatemalan, Honduran, and Salvadoran military and security forces began covertly to assist former Somoza National Guardsmen seeking to overthrow the Nicaraguan Revolution. They had the blessings of the right wing of the U.S. Republican Party and the assistance of the Argentine military dictatorship. Also in 1980 the Salvadoran oligarchy began to regroup behind cashiered Major Roberto D'Aubuisson, the alleged mastermind of the Salvador death squads.

The doctrinaire left and its international allies were also bent on destroying the possibility of a "third way." Many of the leading members of the Sandinista National Directorate had strong emotional, political, and ideological ties with Havana and Moscow. The founder of the FSLN, Carlos Fonseca Amador, had written an artless apology for the Soviet Union which became a basic Sandinista text. Some FSLN leaders, like Henry Ruiz, were trained in Moscow; many more were educated and trained in Cuba. After the Sandinistas took power, Nicaraguans noticed that some leading members spoke with Cuban accents and used Cuban phrases. Some Nicaraguans were reminded of Somoza, who spoke English better than Spanish.

Within the Salvadoran guerrilla movement as well, there were strong affinities for Cuba and the Soviet Union. However, there were also groups such as the FARN (Armed Forces of National Resistance), led by Fermán Cienfuegos, and the ERP (Revolutionary Army of the Poor), who in the late 1970s were antagonistic to the Soviet Union as the "other superpower" which was, in their view, equally imperialist and at most a temporary and tactical ally.

Nevertheless, as the civil war widened and lengthened, the Soviet bloc and Cuba, which had supplied much of the guerrillas' arms and continued to supply their ammunition, steadily gained influence among the Salvadoran revolutionaries. As the Sandinistas established political and military ties to the Soviet and Cuban Communist parties, and with the ascendency of Ronald Reagan to the White House, Central America became the newest Third World arena of superpower conflict.

IV. The Superpowers in Central America

The United States

In 1927, with U.S. Marines occupying Nicaragua, Walter Lippmann remarked that "all the world thinks of the United States today as an empire, except the people of the United States. . . . To admit that we have an empire still seems to most Americans like admitting that they have gone out into a wicked world and there lost their political chastity (see document, Chapter 1)." The curious American ambivalence toward their unconscious empire is bound up with what the Mexican writer Octavio Paz has called "imperial democracy." The United States originated in an anticolonial struggle for "life, liberty and the pursuit of happiness"—what today are called "human rights." Yet as the United States grew into a great industrial and military power it acquired what the rest of the world, and certainly Latin Americans, regarded as an empire. The American expansion to the Pacific Coast was achieved through land grants but also by force. Our dominance in Central America was not usually achieved by direct force and military occupation, though we employed such methods in Mexico and Cuba in the nineteenth century and Panama and Nicaragua in the early twentieth century. In general, however, economic, political, and financial rather than military coercion was preferred. The invisibility of these methods, the American anticolonial heritage, and the relative openness of our political process made it both suitable and necessary to present the American acquisitions as something other than empire. Lippmann was certain that

> an overwhelming majority of our citizens do not wish to rule other people, and that there is no hypocrisy in the pained protests which rise whenever a Latin American or a European speaks of us as imperialistic. We do not feel ourselves to be imperialists as we understand that word. Foreigners pay little attention to what we say. They observe what we do. We on the other hand think of what we feel. And the result is that we go on creating what mankind calls an empire while we continue to believe quite sincerely that it is not an empire because it does not feel to us the way we imagine an empire ought to feel.

Secretary of State Philander Knox's review of the history of the Monroe Doctrine demonstrates the unconscious evolution of the United States from anticolonial to imperialist power in Central America (see Chapter 1). The Monroe Doctrine originated as a declaration against "further colonizations by any European powers and was understood at the outset by the newly enfranchised Latin American states as a defensive movement in their favor rather than a step taken by the United States in its own interest and for its own self-defense." As U.S. interests in the region expanded, a certain ambiguity arose. Knox acknowledges that "from aiding an embarrassed neighbor in doing the right, or in defending a right, to assuming vicarious responsibility for his wrongdoing, is a far cry." Nonetheless, this "heaviest and most matter-of-fact responsibility" led Knox to assert, "We should respond to the needs still felt by some few of our Latin American neighbors in their progress towards good government, by assisting them to meet their just obligation and to keep out of trouble. . . ." This policy took on the form of a U.S. financial and political protectorate over Central America.

By 1927, Under Secretary of State Robert Olds was declaring, as a principle established by the Monroe Doctrine and reinforced through "logic" and "long practice," that Central America was "a legitimate sphere of influence of the United States." He stated flatly that "Central America has always understood that governments we recognize and support stay in power, while those which we do not . . . fall. Nicaragua has become a test case. . . ." (See document, Chapter 1.)

Throughout most of the twentieth century, the United States exercised unchallenged hegemony in the region and monopolized foreign intervention. The route to dominance was nearly always smoothed by U.S. illusions of assisting "free elections," democracy, and the the formation of "nonpartisan armies." However, for Central America, the results were usually military dictatorships.

In the 1920s, on behalf of "free elections" and against a supposed "Bolshevik threat" emanating from revolutionary Mexico, the United States created in Nicaragua a "nonpartisan professional army" (the National Guard) and led it into battle against the Mexican-backed guerrillas of Augusto Sandino. The United States furnished military equipment, combat officers, and trainers as well as roads, medical care, and the inevitable electoral apparatus. The Marines were able to isolate but not vanquish Sandino, and casualties and discontent at home forced them to withdraw. Anastasio Somoza, the United States hand-picked chief of the National Guard, assassinated Sandino and cast aside elected government and democracy via a traditional Central American military coup and established a forty-year dictatorship. Nonetheless, in Frank D. Roosevelt's famous phrase, Somoza was "our son of a bitch." (Though the phrase was commonly associated with Somoza, the Roosevelt epithet originally referred to Rafael Trujillo, the military ruler of the Dominican Republic from 1930 to 1961.) Two generations of Nicaraguans drew the conclusion that America's talk of democracy and posture of innocence abroad was little more than a Trojan horse for U.S. hegemony.

For the State Department, our efforts were part of the struggle of "democracy vs. barbarism," as Olds put it. The mission of civilizing the savage was deeply rooted in our history. It was a tradition that ignored social and historical conditions of the "barbarians." As Octavio Paz writes, "When the United States abandons its isolation and participates in the affairs of the world, it does so in the manner of a believer in a land of infidels."*

U.S. military interference and political engineering left a legacy of distrust and anti-Americanism. The consequences have been twofold: an increasing desire on the part of Latin American countries to establish foreign policy agendas separate and even opposed to that of the United States; and a susceptibility in certain sectors of Latin America to Soviet influence under the initial assumption that "the enemy of my enemy is my friend." The emergence of the four-nation Contadora Group (Colombia, Mexico, Panama, and Venezuela) and the Lima Support Group (Argentina, Brazil, Peru, and Uruguay), which has sought a regional settlement for the Central American conflict, is a manifestation of the first tendency. The pro-Soviet proclivities of the Sandinistas are an example of the second.

Today the United States finds itself in the situation of the legendary boy who cried wolf. The Soviet Union and its Cuban allies have gained a foothold in Latin America and seek to spread their influence via Nicaragua. At the same time, as the Contadora countries have acknowledged, the United States has legitimate national security concerns in the region, interests which are jeopardized by Soviet/Cuban hegemonic ambitions.

U.S. Interests

Current U.S. economic interests in the region are few; our trade and investment there are slight. No strategic raw materials are presently obtained from Central America, and it is not a major petroleum producer.

Central America, along with the Caribbean islands and Mexico, constitutes the largest and fastest-growing source of immigration to the United States. The entrance of large numbers of men and women from the region is altering the composition of the United States' national minority population and is bound to affect the American economy in years to come. So, while Central America is not a major supplier or market, economic development would help to create general stability and prosperity in the region, thus contributing to American security and prosperity.

But, Central America is significant less for what it is than for where it is. Central America is part of the Caribbean Basin—a single geopolitical region which embraces the littoral states as well as the islands. While the northern tier of South America, Mexico, Panama, Central America, and the Caribbean islands are heterogeneous in their political histories, ethnic compositions, cultural traditions, and economic levels, from a geopolitical and strategic standpoint they form a unit. The Caribbean Basin connects both the Atlantic/Pacific and the north/south trade routes of the hemi-

*One Earth, Four or Five Worlds (San Diego: Harcourt Brace Jovanovich, 1985, p. 50).

sphere. It is the great crossroads of trade with the Middle East, Europe, Africa, the Indian Ocean, and Latin America. The Caribbean is a key transit and transshipment zone for imported oil coming from the Middle East, Africa, Venezuela, and Mexico. Its shipping routes presently carry half of U.S. oil imports. The Caribbean Basin contains several singularly important refineries as well as Mexico and Venezuela, world-level oil exporters. The United States Department of Commerce has forecast that imported raw materials will rise from 20 percent of total U.S. consumption to nearly 50 percent by the year 2000. The bulk of these raw materials enter the country via the Caribbean.

The Caribbean Basin is important to Western security, not only as the route to the U.S. southern flank, but also as the prospective passage for U.S. ship convoys essential in NATO contingency planning for the relief of Western Europe. In World War II, over 50 percent of the American supplies to Europe departed from U.S. ports in the Gulf of Mexico. In the early phase of the war, German U-boats destroyed considerable tonnage in the Florida Straits. The prospective entrenchment of a Soviet naval force able to attack convoys from Gulf ports or the Panama Canal would jeopardize the Western Alliance.

The Panama Canal itself has increased in strategic and commercial relevance in recent years. While supertankers and large aircraft carriers cannot pass through the Canal, its traffic has been growing as high fuel costs have rendered South American routes prohibitive. Only thirteen of the 475 U.S. naval vessels cannot transit the Canal.

Central America's revolutionary ferment has riveted the attention of U.S. policymakers. To the extent that Central American revolutions are linked to Soviet strategic objectives, they represent a major threat to United States security interests.

The Other Superpower

The crisis of the U.S.-backed Central American status quo offered Moscow an inexpensive opportunity to confound its superpower rival. Previously, Moscow had consigned Central America to the U.S. sphere of influence by geographic fatalism. When this region, like other "backyards" of the world, was swept into the vortex of revolution, Soviet interest quickened. Yet precisely because this is a U.S. zone of influence, Moscow's capacity to project power is clearly limited. These opportunities and limitations form the parameters within which Moscow has operated.

Between 1965 and 1979, the Soviet Union had achieved rough nuclear parity with the United States and widened its conventional advantages. Moscow's acquisition of a blue-water navy and a capacity to air- and sea-lift troops and equipment, combined with the U.S. repudiation of intervention, enabled the Kremlin to form a more effective "natural alliance" with many Third World national liberation movements.

During this period, Soviet tactics underwent major innovations. Moscow declared that "political-military fronts" modeled on Fidel Castro's July 26th Movement could play the role previously reserved for vanguard Marxist-Leninist parties. Economic ties with the Soviet bloc were no longer regarded as the main factor for the "noncapitalist road of development." Instead, in the mid-1970s the fundamental factor became the "political, military, strategic, and moral influence of the states of the Socialist community," which translated into growing Soviet military and security assistance to revolutionary movements and "national revolutionary" governments.

This shift reflected the widening gap between Soviet economic and military performance. Accordingly, in dealing with countries like Angola, Ethiopia, Vietnam and later Nicaragua, Moscow recommended the preservation of mixed economies and economic ties with the West. At the same time, the Kremlin sought overwhelming influence in the military, security, and intelligence spheres.

The favorable "global correlation of forces," proven success for the new strategy, and a compliant Cuba influenced the dramatic modification of Soviet policy toward Central America at the end of the 1970s. Nonetheless, no such shift would have occurred without compatible conditions in Central America. Indeed, one Soviet analyst has affirmed that before 1978 "none of us would utter an optimist phrase about the future of that struggle."

In the summer of 1978, Havana mediated differences among the Sandinista factions, helping to achieve a March 1979 reunification which pro-Cuban leaders dominated. As the uprising approached, Havana increased direct arms deliveries, organized and armed an "internationalist brigade" to fight alongside the FSLN guerrillas, and dispatched military specialists to the field. During the spring of 1979, Cuban military advisers from the Department of Special Operations accompanied FSLN forces into battle while maintaining radio communications with Havana. After the victory, key military advisory and intelligence positions were awarded to Cubans. That decision led Panama's nationalist General Omar Torrijos Herrera to withdraw Panamanian advisers in 1980 and to offer "friendly warnings" against overreliance on Cuba.

In the wake of the Sandinista revolution, Soviet-backed Communist parties in Latin America and Soviet Latin Americanists definitively discarded Khrushchev's policy of "peaceful transition to socialism" that had been pursued with singular dedication in Latin America. At the same time, Moscow urged local Communists to coordinate with groups carrying out armed struggle. Che Guevara's tactics, excoriated as "ultraleft adventurism" by Moscow in the 1960s, were rehabilitated.

In those Central American countries where the United States has been the backer and the perceived beneficiary of the status quo, anti-Americanism has often translated to pro-Sovietism. Nowhere has this been more true than in Nicaragua, where U.S. support for Somoza helps explain the original pro-Soviet bias of many Sandinista *comandantes*. The Nicaraguan government sought from the outset a special relationship with the Soviet bloc. Soviet generals paid a secret visit to Managua a month after the Sandinistas took power, and a major Soviet and Cuban military security and intelligence role emerged rapidly.

By July 1980, the Sandinista regime had signed economic, scientific, technical, and cultural accords with the Soviet Union, Cuba, East Germany, Bulgaria, and Czechoslovakia. Before President Reagan took office in January 1981, the familiar Soviet-bloc division of labor in the Third World was emerging in Nicaragua. The evidence is typically partisan and partial, but former Sandinista leaders, defectors, diplomats in Managua, and other sources draw a similar picture. The Cubans provide doctors, teachers, construction workers, military specialists, intelligence operatives, and advisers to the Sandinista party and to various government ministries; Soviets concentrate on state security along with Cubans and East Germans; the East Germans also assist in intelligence and communications; the Bulgarians handle finance, economic planning, and construction; and the Czechs provide some military advisers. Moscow equipped the Nicaraguan army during 1980 and Havana used Nicaragua to forward supplies to the Salvadoran guerrillas.

A reading of the founding documents, internal polemics, and private declarations of the FSLN demonstrates the Sandinistas' early ideological commitment to Soviet- and Cuban-style "socialism." Reacting against repeated American interventions in Nicaragua, many came to regard Moscow as their "natural ally" and harbored enormous expectations of Soviet economic and military support. In their view, concrete signs of fidelity were needed to assure such backing. Thus, in August 1979, the Sandinista delegation supported Soviet-Cuban-Vietnamese positions against Yugoslavia in the Havana meeting of the Movement of Nonaligned Countries. Later, in the United Nations, in the face of overwhelming Third World condemnation of the invasion of Afghanistan, the Nicaraguan delegation abstained.

Kremlin optimism toward Central America reached a peak in the winter of 1980–1981. In November 1980, for the first time, Central America was mentioned as a region where "socialist-oriented" states were emerging in an article in the official Soviet Communist Party organ *Komunist* by Boris Ponomarev, the leading Soviet Central Committee foreign policymaker. Two months later, Ponomarev alluded to Nicaragua's "taking the road of transition to socialism." Salvadoran Communist Party leader Shafik Handal was awarded an article in the same issue of the Soviet party organ, a rare distinction for a party leader not in power. Both *Pravda* and TASS featured triumphal reports on the Salvadoran guerrillas' "final offensive."

In retrospect, however, the failure of that offensive appears to have occasioned another reassessment of Moscow's Central American policy. Optimism disappeared from the Soviet-bloc media and a curtain descended on El Salvador. Brezhnev omitted mention of Central America in his assessment of the world situation at the Twenty-sixth Congress of the Soviet Communist Party.

By early 1982, Moscow and Havana were anxious to appear as peace-makers in the Caribbean Basin as the heady optimism of 1979–1980 gave way to a more guarded view of revolutionary possibilities. Soviet analysis no longer referred to a "regional upsurge" but stressed the "ebb and flow" of country-specific situations. Moscow pictured the revolutionary movements as reacting defensively to a revanchist U.S. foreign policy, characterized as a return to the "big-stick diplomacy" of the pre-Vietnam era. "The aggressive United States counteroffensive" in Central America was portrayed as one aspect of a resurgent United States "militarism" counterposed to the Soviet "peace offensive."

Soviet deliveries of military equipment to Nicaragua have increased substantially since 1981, reaching higher levels in 1984 as anti-Sandinista rebels mounted a serious challenge to the government. Moscow, now the world's foremost counterinsurgency power, supplies the overwhelming bulk of assistance to Nicaragua's modernized military and security forces.

Soviet authorities have frequently intimated to U.S. diplomats that the "Nicaraguan problem" can be resolved only in the context of U.S.-Soviet relations. Sandinista eagerness for close ties with Moscow has permitted the Soviet Union to pursue a virtually cost-free policy. Nicaragua could be a bargaining chip in Moscow's preferred "political settlement" in Afghanistan. Meanwhile, the United States support for Nicaraguan rebels diverts attention from Afghanistan, and Moscow exploits the intervention for propaganda purposes. If, despite United States pressure, the Sandinistas survive, a Soviet-aligned regime could gradually be consolidated.

Moscow appears to be pursuing a wait-and-see, long-term strategy in Nicaragua. By 1986 Managua depended on Moscow for most of its oil and on the Soviet bloc for most of its trade. The Kremlin encourages the Sandinistas to diversify trading partners and aid donors. Meanwhile, Soviet-bloc countries help train a new pro-Soviet technological, cultural, and political elite. The Soviet-bloc presence in the intelligence, security, communications, and military fields has deepened, but Moscow provides only enough military aid to make U.S. military intervention costly and save the Soviet "revolutionary" reputation, not enough to deter a U.S. invasion or risk a superpower confrontation. The tragedy for Nicaragua is that, taken together, Washington's legacy of interference, Moscow's cynicism, and Managua's imprudence have converted that tiny country into the newest arena of superpower contention.

V. U.S. Policy

Central America's crisis is rooted in the region's poverty and dependence. A bitter history of U.S. military intervention and political interference has made anti-Yankeeism a rallying point for revolutionary movements.

At the same time, Central America has become an element of our own very different crisis. Our Central American debate is awash in high-sounding phrases. Domestic politics have engulfed not only politicians but also journalists, academics, and public figures pronouncing on Central America. Conservatives close their eyes to abuses in El Salvador or Guatemala so as not to weaken President Reagan; liberals prefer to ignore abuses in Nicaragua so as not to strengthen him. As a result, public discussion of Central America has deteriorated into a frenetic but tedious and stereotyped propaganda war.

The dispute reflects the profound division of the U.S. elite, its increasing isolation from the American public, and its inability to forge a foreign policy consensus. The weakening of the conservative wing of the Democratic Party and the liberal wing of the Republican Party is one example of this. But we now also have liberal and conservative think tanks, foundations, and media.

But at the same time the elite and mass opinions are frequently in discord. While elite opinion tends to be ideological, polarized, and dogmatic, public opinion, according to recent polls, is centrist, pragmatic, and eclectic. There is an adversary politics of the elites, a consensus politics of the masses.

Surveys of American public opinion on Central America in general, and Nicaragua in particular, reflect a curious discrepancy between elite and mass opinion. Within the establishment and intelligentsia, funding for the Nicaraguan rebels or "contras" is the most divisive and passionate issue since the Vietnam War. The controversy reflects the current profound ideological polarization of the American political establishment. On either side of this ideological gap, opinions are held with absolute conviction and passionate intensity.

The mass public, on the other hand, has been generally apathetic and ignorant about Central America. In April 1981, CBS found that only half of Americans thought that El Salvador was in the Western Hemisphere, and only a quarter that it was in Central America. Polls by CBS and ABC in 1983 revealed that only 8 percent of Americans could identify which side the administration was supporting in both Nicaragua and El Salvador and that only 50 percent knew about the fighting between the Sandinista government in Nicaragua and the rebels. In January 1981, Americans ranked El Salvador last on a list of twelve concerns behind "what's going on in professional football" and "the shooting of John Lennon." Moreover, many Americans who had opinions appeared deeply ambivalent. Most agreed with President Reagan's assessment on the importance of Central America to United States national interest and the threat posed by a Soviet presence. Yet public opinion opposed virtually all of the president's military measures to check the threat—including support for the contras, joint military exercises in Honduras, military sales to El Salvador, and naval blockades.

Subsequently, the situation has changed somewhat. In 1983, according to an ABC poll (March 6), only 59 percent of the public had heard or read about fighting between the Sandinista government and rebels seeking to overthrow it; by 1986, this percentage had risen to 72 percent. In 1983, ABC found that only 29 percent thought the United States was backing the rebels rather than the Nicaraguan government and 47 percent had no opinion; by 1986, 50 percent knew the United States was backing the rebels and only 33 percent had no opinion.

The increased knowledge among the American public about the Central American situation had some bearing on policy choices. On June 5, 1985, the *New York Times* found that though a majority still opposed help for the anti-Sandinistas, "support for the administration policy is increasing especially among the growing numbers who know which side the United States backs. . . ."

All polls show significant opposition to the president's policy in Nicaragua. However, the pollsters' phrasing of the question strongly impacts on the response. In June 1986, a *Washington Post*/ABC poll found that 29 percent favored and 62 percent opposed "military and other aid to the Nicaraguan rebels known as the Contras." However, when asked in another poll about support for aid "to the Contras fighting the leftist government of Nicaragua," 35 percent favored and 44 percent opposed. A June 1986 Roper poll found that a majority favored humanitarian aid to Nicaraguan rebels and that the public divided about evenly on "military aid" for contras fighting the "Soviet-backed" Nicaragua government. Further information about the situation in Nicaragua appears to elicit a less unfavorable response. Moreover, in an increasing number, Americans find Nicaragua to be a threat to the United States. In April 1986, CBS found that 56 percent regarded Nicaragua as a threat and only 20 percent did not. CBS/*New York Times* in the same month found that 59 percent of the American public believed that Nicaragua will provide military bases for the Soviet Union while 16 percent did not believe so. Only 25 percent had no opinion.

There is a growing concern about the dangers posed by Nicaragua's ties to the Soviet Union. At the same time, the mass public is reluctant to choose either of the policy alternatives provided by the two sections of the American elite. This is consistent with general post-Vietnam foreign policy attitudes among the American people. On the one hand, Americans regard Moscow as a threat, but on the other, they are deeply concerned about a long-term U.S. involvement.

Because of the gap between elite opinion and the masses, the American foreign policy establishment has more difficulty in forming foreign policy than in the period between the Second World War and the Vietnam War. The elites which formed the Marshall Plan and the major tenets and policies of postwar internationalism had a popular consensus. The successful conclusion of the campaign for passage of the Panama Canal Treaty led by Sol Linowitz was perhaps the last expression of such an elite-led policy. But elite leadership had already eroded during the Vietnam period. Now often the public leads the elites in forming foreign policy. Two good examples of this are the public responses to the invasion of Afghanistan and to the Iran hostage crisis. As a result of this gap between the elites and the general public, elites have resorted to manipulation. Defense and arms-control policy has been managed in terms of "the nuclear freeze" and the MX as the "peace keeper." In Central America, all sides of the debate have presented the crisis as one between heroes on the one side and villains on the other. The Reagan administration presents the Nicaraguan rebels as "freedom fighters"; Thomas O'Neill, Speaker of the House, described them as "butchers and maimers." Recently the scandal caused by the reported diversion to a rebel supply network of money from U.S. arms sales to Iran has intesified the Washington and media debate. Though the scandal may well affect U.S. policy, the basic situation on the ground in Central America remains the same.

With respect to El Salvador, American policymakers have had some success in matching their policies to the seemingly contradictory sentiments of the American public. This has been far less true in the case of Nicaragua. Given the highly-charged rhetoric of the American elite over Nicaragua, it is unlikely that a bipartisan policy will be formed. Nonetheless, bipartisanship is probably a prerequisite to any solution for the Central American crisis. To the extent to which the public becomes more familiar with the complex realities of Central America and has the opportunity to hear Central American voices and read their words, the possibilities for the formation of a sober national policy may increase. We hope that the following documents will contribute to this educational process.

R.S.L.

The Historical Background

I. Landscape and People

A land bridge between North and South America and a narrow isthmus separating the Atlantic and Pacific oceans, Central America has been an economic and cultural crossroads and a battleground for foreign powers throughout its history. The line of volcanoes dotting its Pacific mountain chains and periodic earthquakes seem to mirror the unsettled nature of the land. Poets like Nicaragua's Paolo Antonio Cuadra (Document 1) often draw attention to the impact of geography and geology on Central American culture.

Pre-Columbian Central America contained two distinct Indian cultures. Hunter-gatherers lived to the north and east, in the inhospitable tropical interior and in the drenched lowlands on the Atlantic coast. Along the Pacific, the rich volcanic soils allowed more intensive agriculture—maize, beans, squash, cotton, and cacao—and the rise of small states culturally akin to the Indian empires in Mexico. Extensive trade took local merchants as far away as Mexico and Peru. But the region was never politically united: there were forty-seven different "languages" in Nicaragua alone at the time of the Spanish conquest.

Most of the people lived by farming in small settlements or on the outskirts of ceremonial cities inhabited by priests and the warrior aristocracy. Life was harsh for the vast majority, who lived subject to their rulers' whims. Warfare was constant; slavery and human sacrifice were widespread.

The report of Gonzalo Fernández de Oviedo (Document 2), an early Spanish chronicler, reflects the mixture of admiration and disgust on the part of the Spanish conquerors who began to establish themselves in the area in 1522. Yet their invasion was hardly civilizing. The Europeans fought against the Indians and among themselves for the next twenty years over power, slaves, gold, and silver. Their abuses were denounced to the Spanish crown by the friar, later bishop of Chiapas, Bartolomé de Las Casas in his famous *Devastation of the Indies* (Document 3). Incensed at the behavior of Pedro Arias de Ávila, the first Spanish conqueror, Las Casas refused even to mention his name.

Modern scholars like William Sherman (Document 4) have pointed out that most of the conquistadores' practices were in line with local behavior. Still, the invaders' ruthlessness upset a hitherto stable ecological and demographic balance. The Indian peoples were quickly reduced in numbers. They were almost totally wiped out in Nicaragua, where, according to a 1548 Spanish census, only 11,000 were left from a population previously estimated at between 500,000 and 750,000.

Having destroyed the labor force, the Spanish lost interest in the area. The colonizers who remained had to restore some Indian rights, including limited self-government and communal landholdings *(ejidos)*. Murdo MacLeod (Document 5) describes a system based on large ranches and grain-growing estates surrounded by satellite Indian hamlets engaged in subsistence agriculture. The Indians paid tribute from their crops and provided workers for the estates.

This basic pattern prevailed until the start of large-scale coffee production for export in the mid-nineteenth century. As described by David Browning (Document 6), the great landowners extended their holdings at the expense of the *ejidos* and peasant plots. Those who lost their land became dependent upon the large estates or had to migrate to the cities. Present-day Central America continues to depend disproportionately upon agriculture, especially for foreign exchange.

Central America's political division, into separate countries and among quarreling parties, has also been a persistent source of regional problems. The Spanish colonial administration had ruled the region, along with parts of present-day Mexico, under the captain-general of Guatemala. These provinces declared themselves independent of Spain in 1821, but unity quickly collapsed into civil war.

In the towns, the leading creole (locally born Spanish) families split into two parties. The Liberals favored trial by jury, separation of church and state, local autonomy, private enterprise, and free trade. The Conservatives wanted to protect against British economic domination, retain Spanish institutions including military and church privileges *(fueros),* and build a strong central government and public economic sector.

Contemporary observers, like U.S. Minister Ephraim Squier, attributed the struggle's ferocity to the irresolvable nature of these issues (Document 7). But "Liberal" and "Conservative" did not have the same meaning as they do in the United States. The two groups were often merely local factions based on personal or family rivalries and a desire for power. Both sides resorted to dictatorship, martial law, torture, and execution.

Although the Liberal-ruled Central American confederation broke up in 1838, the idea persisted that Central America was an artificially "divided nation" that could potentially become a single united country. Salvador Mendieta, a leading Central American historian and passionate exponent of unity, lamented in 1910 (Document 8) that the region's political fragmentation was at the root of its problems. Bitter factionalism brought instability and foreign intervention: Liberals and Conservatives turned to outside powers for help to gain power in one country and then in neighboring states. They also organized and assisted like-minded factions struggling to rule the other countries. While neither domestic politics nor the international environment allowed reunification, this theme continues to shape the ambitions, behavior, and foreign policies of Central American leaders.

II. The Imperial Dimension

The evolution of Central American politics cannot be understood apart from the nearly constant, frequently violent, intervention of external forces. The enduring allure of the region derives from its unique geographical position. Spain, later France and Britain, and finally the United States have all come to appreciate its strategic importance for both North and South America.

The idea of a strong confederated republic free of outside interference, expressed so idealistically by Simón Bolívar, leader of the continent's struggle against Spain (Document 9), has never been realized. The present crisis stems from the interplay of foreign and domestic influences, including the historic willingness of local political groups to seek foreign help and to intervene in other Central American countries.

U.S. interest in the isthmus was first expressed in the Monroe Doctrine, which declared that the Western Hemisphere was "not to be considered as subject for future colonization by any European powers." As U.S. power grew, so too did an urge to intervene. The United States must prevent, said Secretary of State Philander Knox, extra-hemispheric meddling arising from Central America's political instability or unpaid debts (Document 10).

The Clayton-Bulwer Anglo-American treaty of 1850 (Document 11) guaranteed both powers equal access to any future canal through Nicaragua. Nicaragua was not asked its view. Some Americans thought the United States' "manifest destiny" should go even further. When the adventurer William Walker, at the invitation of Nicaraguan Liberals, overturned the Conservative government and made himself president of Nicaragua, *Harper's Weekly* welcomed the event (Document 12). Walker was later expelled by a coalition of Central American armies with some help from the United States and Great Britain. After an attempted comeback, he was captured and executed in Honduras.

The U.S. role in the isthmus became more direct after the turn of the century when President Theodore Roosevelt built the Panama Canal. After Nicaraguan dictator José Santos Zelaya tried to impose Liberal hegemony and reunite Central America by force, the United States and Mexico established the Central American Court of Justice to settle disputes. Troubles between Washington and Managua continued, however, when Zelaya asked European states to construct a Nicaraguan canal to compete with the one in Panama and canceled the U.S. concession. When a revolution erupted against Zelaya in 1909, the United States worked to assure his overthrow.

In 1912, U.S. forces landed to aid the Conservative government of Adolfo Díaz, accountant of a U.S.-owned mining company, and a permanent Marine presence was established. Dana Munro, who served as U.S. chargé d'affaires in Nicaragua, considered this intervention as a turning point in U.S. relations with Central America (Document 13).

To guarantee that Zelaya's initiative would not be repeated, President Woodrow Wilson's administration negotiated the Chamorro-Bryan treaty with Nicaragua (Document 14) granting the United States "in perpetuity [and] forever free from all taxation . . . the exclusive proprietary rights necessary and convenient for the construction, operation, and maintenance of an interoceanic canal . . . by way of any route over Nicaraguan territory." When El Salvador and Costa Rica protested the treaty to the Central American Court of Justice, Nicaragua withdrew from the organization. The incident killed both the court and another generation's hope for Central American unity.

By 1927, with U.S. influence pervading the Caribbean, columnist Walter Lippmann observed that the proper name for this dominion was "empire" (Document 15). Lippmann argued that refusal to face the political facts prevented the United States from acknowledging and discharging responsibilities and obligations to its troubled neighbors.

III. The First Crisis: Sandino and Martínez

Once the U.S. Marines were withdrawn from Nicaragua in 1925, the country returned to its unstable politics. A Conservative general, Emiliano Chamorro, staged a coup that Washington refused to recognize. Successful U.S. maneuvering led to Chamorro's ouster and returned the dependable Adolfo Díaz to office. But peace proved more difficult to attain, and it soon became clear that without a larger U.S. intervention, the Liberals would take power.

Under Secretary of State Robert Olds (Document 16) argued that failure to act would undermine U.S. credibility—particularly given strong Mexican support for the Liberal opposition—and a small Marine force was landed.

Former Secretary of War Henry Stimson was sent as a special envoy to evaluate the situation. He offered the Liberals a deal. An immediate cease-fire and general amnesty would be proclaimed and the Liberals returned in a coalition government. Both sides in the civil war would be disarmed; the United States would train a National Guard and supervise elections. Until then, the Marines would keep the peace. All the Liberal generals, except one, accepted the agreement (Document 17).

The lone Liberal holdout, General Augusto Sandino, challenged Stimson's plan with a guerrilla war against the Marines. Although his military accomplishments were limited, Sandino became a folk hero and a potent symbol of resistance to the "Colossus of the North" throughout Latin America. A stubborn nationalist who resented foreign meddling of any kind, he also broke with his Marxist Salvadoran secretary, Agustín Farabundo Martí, who returned home to found the Communist Party of El Salvador. Sandino had his own brand of populist, anticolonial philosophy (Document 18).

The Liberal candidate, Juan Sacasa, won the 1932 elections and the United States withdrew. Sandino kept his promise to lay down arms when the Marines left. But in February 1934, the new director of the National Guard, Anastasio Somoza, ordered Sandino's arrest and execution. Two years later, Somoza ousted Sacasa and "won" election by 107,000 to 169 votes. Marine historian Bernard Naltz asked, "What had the two major interventions accomplished?" (Document 19).

In his rise to power, Somoza was encouraged by the U.S. failure to prevent the emergence of an even more brutal dictatorship in El Salvador. Central America's smallest but most densely populated nation was hit hard by the Depression. When coffee prices plunged in 1929, the economy collapsed, national income was halved, and the plantation workers' daily wage was cut from 30 to 15 centavos.

Conditions were ripening for revolution, predicted U.S. military attaché Major A. R. Harris (Document 20). In December 1930 a coup overthrew an ineffectual civilian government and brought to power General Maximiliano Hernández Martínez, the most notorious of Central America's dictators. Washington, reluctant to recognize the coup, was even more unwilling to intervene.

Within El Salvador, peasant leaders and the Communist Party (PCS) organized against Martínez. In his memoirs, Miguel Marmol, a Salvadoran Communist leader, recalls how the PCS first discovered and then supported growing sentiment for a popular insurrection (Document 21).

After several delays, the insurrection was set for January 22, 1932. The result was a bloody massacre by the army, described simply in Gregorio Bustamante's official history of the Salvadoran military (Document 22). These events, which Salvadorans call La Matanza ("the slaughter"), made Martínez popular with the oligarchy and kept him in power for twelve more years.

IV. Living with the Dictator

By this time, the United States was frustrated by years of apparently useless involvement in Central America and was preoccupied with its own economic crisis and growing war clouds in Europe. The result was President Franklin Roosevelt's Good Neighbor Policy, popular in Latin America for its noninterventionist principles.

Once Washington renounced military force in the region, however, the familiar pattern of Central American politics reasserted itself. Nonrecognition had once been sufficient to impose Washington's will because a threat of force lay behind it. Martínez's coup showed that nonrecognition without teeth was ineffective. In Guatemala, Jorge Ubico abandoned his democratic pretensions beginning in 1932 and ruthlessly consolidated power. Somoza waited until 1936 to follow suit.

With the coming of World War II and with the United States seeking hemispheric support against the Axis, Roosevelt began to close ranks with the Central American dictators despite those men's fascistic leanings. Pragmatically, if somewhat reluctantly, the dictators took advantage of the new mood in Washington.

The new relationships were short-lived. The wartime ideology of democratic struggle against fascism undermined the dictators and encouraged middle-class politicians, professionals, and students to overthrow Martínez in May 1944 and Ubico in July. In Costa Rica, a 1948 revolution and an ensuing land reform produced Central America's only pluralist political system. To prevent further coups, the army was dissolved and replaced with a small national police force.

Only Somoza survived, and even he stepped down after his presidential term expired in May 1947, though continuing to rule from behind the scenes. When he returned to office in May 1951, Somoza sought to appease the opposition by an arrangement with Conservative leader Emiliano Chamorro to allow the opposition 40 percent of the parliamentary seats.

Somoza benefited by being a reliable Cold War ally for Washington, noted Secretary of State Dean Acheson (Document 23). Many Americans, like Patrick McMahon, were effusive in their praise (Document 24). Most Nicaraguans were less enthusiastic. After numerous coup attempts failed, a young poet named Rigoberto López Pérez killed the dictator on September 21, 1956. Knowing he would die in the attempt, López Pérez, who was to become a hero for the Sandinistas, wrote a note to his mother explaining his action (Document 25). Somoza was succeeded by his son, Luis Somoza Debayle; another son, also named Anastasio, became head of the National Guard.

In El Salvador, civilian rule in 1944 lasted only a few months. Afraid that the post-Martínez regime's liberalism was leading to a repeat of the 1932 confrontation, the army staged a coup in October 1944, just five months after Martínez was overthrown. Another coup followed in 1948. As in Nicaragua, opposition was tolerated, even supported, but on terms acceptable to the governing authorities. Paul Kennedy, who covered the region for the *New York Times,* described a typical election of the period (Document 26). Only in Guatemala did a major political change occur.

V. The Guatemalan Episode

When the dictator Ubico was overthrown in 1944, power passed to a group of junior officers, including Jacobo Arbenz. To the surprise of many, the junta allowed free elections and the inauguration of the winner, Juan José Arévalo, as president in March 1945.

A wave of reform swept Guatemala. Arévalo stressed a "spiritual socialism" for the "psychological liberation" of people rather than a redistribution of wealth. Nevertheless, Guatemalans' lives improved dramatically as the regime instituted universal suffrage, spent one-third of its budget on social welfare, outlawed forced labor, adopted a progressive labor code, and raised workers' wages by 30 percent. Political parties were permitted across the spectrum from left to right, including a growing Communist Party.

Arévalo survived many attempted coups during his six-year term and handed over power to the victor of the 1950 elections, Minister of War Arbenz. President Arbenz went even further than Arevalo by instituting land reform, distributing over 1.25 million acres to about 56,000 families between June 1952 and the end of 1953. The peasants received access to the necessary training and credit.

This effort—aimed at creating a class of smallholders—was hardly Communist, but big landowners and the American-owned United Fruit Company (UFCO) were determined to stop Arbenz. UFCO had operated for decades in Central American countries as a virtual state within a state (Document 27), hence the term "banana republics."

The U.S. government responded to both UFCO claims and its own concern that Guatemala's "Red President" was spreading Communism in the hemisphere. After a meeting with the president and his wife, U.S. Ambassador John Peurifoy sent a secret cable to Washington concluding, "Normal approaches will not work" (Document 28).

Thereafter, the Eisenhower administration launched covert operations to weaken and discredit Arbenz's government while secretly paving the way for a coup. In March 1954, the United States asked the Organization of American States to condemn the intervention of international communism in the hemisphere. Guatemalan Foreign Minister Guillermo Toriello Garrido won great applause, but little actual support, with a defense of his government (Document 29). U.S. Secretary of State John Foster Dulles was delighted when the anti-communist resolution was passed almost unanimously and claimed it would help "preserve this hemisphere from the evils and woes that would befall it if any one of our American states became a Soviet Communist puppet" (Document 30).

The steady barrage of propaganda and destabilization left Guatemala in a state of crisis. Arbenz's supporters began to demand that arms be distributed to the peasants, but the president refused. The incident alarmed army officers, however, and they withdrew their loyalty from the regime. When the long-feared invasion began in June 1954, the U.S.-backed forces of Carlos Castillo Armas triumphed without a single battle being fought. Arbenz resigned and went into exile. Until 1985, power in Guatemala stayed firmly in the army's hands, despite several guerrilla movements, sometimes backed by Fidel Castro's Cuba.

VI. Heritage of Crisis

Among those attracted to Arbenz's Guatemala was a young Argentine doctor named Ernesto "Che" Guevara who drew important lessons from the Guatemalan experience. When Fidel Castro came to power in Cuba in January 1959, Che urged him to disband the army and other institutions and replace them with new organizations controlled by the revolutionaries.

The Cuban revolution's example sent tremors throughout the region. Flushed with their success, Marxist ideology, and the need to break out of isolation, the Cubans immediately began sending both encouragement and aid to the small guerrilla movements that sprang up almost everywhere in the region. Throughout the 1960s, as in his speech at the founding conference of the Organization of Latin American Solidarity, Castro called for armed revolt (Document 31).

Rightist dictatorships seemed most vulnerable to this campaign. Central American students were fascinated with the idea of a guerrilla-led revolution. In Nicaragua, journalist Marvin Alisky found that the close relationship between Somoza and the United States added nationalist fuel to the opposition's anger (Document 32).

Cuba's activities at first prompted the massive U.S. program of development aid and support for moderate democratic reform embodied in President John Kennedy's Alliance for Progress (Document 33). First results were impressive: civilian influence and reformist forces grew in El Salvador, Guatemala, and Nicaragua; the Central American Common Market brought unprecedented high rates of economic growth.

The Catholic Church was also changing. Historically, the church hierarchy had been one of the main pillars of the traditional order. In 1968, the Latin American bishops came out squarely for reform and said that a social system that made a decent life impossible was sinful. Although recommending nonviolence, they were reluctant to criticize those who confronted "institutionalized violence" with guns (Document 34).

Nevertheless, Washington worried that any break with the military rulers would foment instability and an opening for radical, anti-U.S. forces. Secretary of Defense Robert McNamara defended continued arms supplies to Latin American armies in the face of Senate criticism (Document 35). The U.S. stopped pressuring for reform and civilian democratic rule.

To make matters worse, by the end of the 1960s, war between El Salvador and Honduras and the uneven distribution of benefits spelled doom for the Central American Common Market. El Salvador's rapidly growing population, as Thomas Anderson points out (Document 36), has produced a demographic crisis, and the oil crisis of the 1970s contributed to economic stagnation. As World Bank statistics show (Document 37), the majority of people were still impoverished while literacy, living standards, and life expectancy were low. These statistics reflect only averages, however, and because gross inequalities of land and wealth are the norm in Central America, the actual impoverishment of the majority is understated.

The militaries also trampled civilian rule and civil liberties, again with the exception of Costa Rica. After permitting fairly free elections in 1972, El Salvador's military arrested, beat, and then exiled the winner, Christian Democrat José Napoleón Duarte. In Nicaragua, Anastasio Somoza Debayle, who took over when his brother Luis died in 1967, exploited the devastating 1972 earthquake to his own financial advantage. In Guatemala, the army unleashed waves of violence and death squads against guerrilla groups, Indian peasants, and reform-minded priests.

Together these difficulties compounded and deepened what Salvador Mendieta had called Central America's "infirmity." Central America's current crisis has emerged out of these political roadblocks, economic problems, international rivalries, and ideological battles.

I
LANDSCAPE AND PEOPLE

1.
PABLO ANTONIO CUADRA: THE NICARAGUANS

THE GEOGRAPHICAL BRIDGE

Let us begin with the land. In his *Geografía de América,* Oscar Schmieder says that a land bridge between North and South America was not yet present in the Tertiary. What is today our country did not exist. Like Botticelli's Venus, Nicaragua rose from the sea—young in comparison to the rest of America—lifted on the shoulders of that line of volcanoes— heraldic colossi that make up our coat of arms—which are pivots of our slender geographical bridge, land which from that time on was to serve as a pass and a link between the two Americas. Thus, the very geological formation of Nicaragua already presaged that the future inhabitants of such a place shall be transient.

THE EARLIEST TRACK OF EXODUS

As a sign of fate, it is interesting that the most ancient human footprint in Nicaragua should have been the track of a foot in flight. The tracks of Acahualinca tell us of primitive Indians who perhaps came down from the north in pursuit of the bison, wandering hunters who abandoned Managua —and since then how many other times was the Nicaraguan obliged to leave?—because another god, a raging volcano, spitting fire and lava, forced them to flee.

The prehistory of this land is covered with the tracks of Acahualinca. It cannot but astound to realize that there passed through the narrow corridor of Nicaragua the human seed of countless groups and human conglomerates of the Southern Continent coming from the north, as did

From his *El Nicaraguense.*

also countercurrents, recognized by archaeology, of many southern groups and tribes going north. Imagine those ancient tribes of hunters and gatherers desiring, perhaps, to settle, and being displaced, in turn, by new waves of emigrants. The probable history of the Indian tribes found here in apparently fixed abode by the Spaniards can serve us as a point of departure for conceptualizing those human ties shrouded in the dark of the centuries and millennia. The Maribios, or Subtiavas—a group that originated in California—had occupied a large part of Nicaragua, stealing land from the Indians who apparently came from the south and, dispossessed, moved on to occupy the interior and north of our country. The Subtiavas were "Hokanos" and established trade along the Pacific Coast introducing the use of metals and metallurgy all along it and from Panama or, at least, Nicaragua, as far as the U.S. Southwest. The Chorotegas, in turn, pushed and cornered the Subtiavas. Then the Nahuas arrived, pushing out the Chorotegas and taking over part of their territory. And Torquemada and Gómara further added an Aztec, or Mexican, invasion by sea in which the Nahuas were defeated and part of their lands seized. In the narrow isthmic corridor, all the groups found by Spain had wandered, moving spurred by an omen of peregrination. And the dispossessed and dispossessors, and those who came and moved on, and those who came and stayed, all implanted a vagabond restlessness, instilling in some the same "seaport" psychology of the transient, interested in what is happening outside, eager for news of afar, expectant of the unknown, and stamped by nostalgia.

EVER THE WANDERER DESTINY IN THE NEW HISTORY

Since that time, man in Nicaragua was of the "Mediterranean" type: man who lives at a crossroads. And this psychology graven by geography in the Indian world was scored even deeper in relief when Spain entered to shape our history. Nicaragua is exposed and formed into a bridge, no longer between the two Americas as in prehistoric times, but between the two seas. The needle of the compass of our destiny keeps spinning but always points the way. The principal discoveries and the founding of Nicaragua's most important cities were the outcome of the quest for a new navigational route. First, the search for a passageway to the West Indies. Then, the Pacific having been discovered, the search for imaginary straits called "the Doubtful Strait." And later, Lake Nicaragua having been discovered and the myth of the strait dissipated, the search for the outlet to the Atlantic of the Great Lakes, for the passage between the two oceans. These searches formed Nicaragua. Once formed, geography insisted on imposing its law of "exodus." The idea of a passageway was converted into the idea of a canal, and our policy (for how many years?) seems to hang on that fate.

A COUNTRY OF MEDITERRANEAN FERMENT

Let us go over our history moved by the forces of that "destiny": searches that signified voyages, questing that signified contact with the exterior and new voyages, sorties, returns, sails at sea, and armies that pass. Nicaraguan armies to Peru, to Costa Rica, the Conquest barely ended. Pirates attracted to that Mediterranean point and by that strategic "pass." Slavers. Walker.* Foreign interventions.

2.
CAPTAIN GONZALO FERNÁNDEZ DE OVIEDO Y VALDÉS: A FIRST VIEW OF CENTRAL AMERICA

The plains of Nicaragua are among the most beautiful and tranquil lands to be encountered in these Indies, being as they are so very fertile with cornfields and vegetables, with beans of divers kinds, many and divers fruits, and much cacao, a fruit that resembles the almond and that circulates among those people as money† and with which they purchase all other things of great price or small, gold as well as slaves and clothing, things to eat, and so forth. There is great abundance of honey and beeswax, and much hunting of pigs and deer and other such wild beasts, as well as rabbits and other animals, and good fisheries, of the sea and the rivers and lakes; great abundance of cotton, and much and good clothing is made from it spun and woven by the Indian women of the country; and it is an annual crop, for each year they sow and harvest it.

There is a great multitude of people in that province of Nagrando where the city of León is, as well as in others of that land, and many of them are not governed by caciques or a supreme ruler, but as communities by a certain number of elders elected by vote; and they created a captain-general for matters of war, and he and the others ruled their state, and when he died or was killed in any battle or encounter another was elected, and sometimes they themselves killed him if they found him disadvantageous to their republic. Afterward, in order to make use of the Indians and to deal with one head and not with so many, the Christians abolished that

---

*William Walker, an American soldier of fortune who became president of Nicaragua in 1856.

Document 2 from *Historia General y Natural de las Indias* (1530s).

†That is, the cacao bean, in parts of pre-Hispanic Central America and Mexico.

good custom and those councils or congregations of elders, and since they were chiefs and lords of divers places and of vassals who were of one mind and position among each other, they were separated by them and made caciques over the distributions and new subjugations into which the Spaniards placed them, but nevertheless there are also caciques in some of these parts and lords of provinces and islands.

They had books of parchment that they made of the hides of deer, a span in width and from some ten to twelve paces in length, that were shrunk and folded and reduced by the folds upon another to the size of a hand; and painted upon them in red or black ink were their characters or figures in such wise that even though they were not letters or writing, all had meaning and was understood very clearly by them in whatsoever was desired; and painted by them in those books were their boundaries and estates, and whatever they wished to be represented, and roads, rivers, mountains, and forests, as well, and whatever else, which in times of strife or dispute could be determined from them as decided by the elders, or *guegues* (meaning old men).

They had their houses of prayer which, as in New Spain, they call *orchilobos,* and their priests for those horrible diabolic sacrifices; and before each of those temples there stood a mound or heap of earth made by them, the height of a spear, narrow on the top and broad below, built as the piles of wheat or barley on a threshing field, and there were small steps cut into them by which that priest of the devil ascended together with the man or woman or youth to be sacrificed or killed there on top in the sight and presence of the people. These of Nicaragua have many rituals like those of New Spain, who speak the same language, as I have said. Those of the Chorotega tongue, who are their enemies, have the same temples; but in language, rituals, ceremonies, and customs they differ so that they do not understand one another. The Chontales are also different in their tongue and they do not communicate with each other, it being no more similar than Basque is to German.

There is one thing, of those that I will mention, in which they resemble one another and are in conformity, and it is that each group has its squares and marketplaces for its trading and goods in each main town; but only those of their same tongue are allowed into those fairs or markets, and if others should come, they are sold to be eaten or used as slaves; and they, likewise, conform in that all those mentioned eat human flesh and all are idolators and servants of the devil in various modes of idolatry.

There are prostitutes who earn their livelihood by giving themselves to whoever wants them for ten cacao beans, which has been mentioned is their money; and some have pimps, not to give a share of their earnings to but to use them in their service to accompany them or to guard the house while they go to the markets to sell themselves to whomsoever they please.

They have divers gods, and so, during the time of the corn harvest, or that of cacao, or cotton, or beans, with an appointed day and on different days they hold different prescribed and special fiestas, and have their dances and chants for that idol and the harvest of the crop or fruit they have obtained. All are archers but they do not herd.

In some parts there are lords or princes of much territory or many subjects, as is the cacique of Teocatego or he of Mistega, or of Nicaragua, or Nicoy, and others have principal vassals and *caballeros* (that is, over-lords with vassals who are heads of provinces or towns having suzerainty vested in them) whom they call *galpones,* and those generally accompany and guard the person of the prince and are his courtiers and captains; and these chiefs are very brutish in manner, and pitiless, and very deceitful, and have no compassion.

Their marriages are of many kinds, and it should be said of them that commonly each has one wife only, and few have more, except for the chiefs or whoever is able to maintain more wives; and the caciques who have as many as they wish.

They are great sorcerers and sorceresses and have much communion with the devil, especially those priests of Satan, who have a position superior to them and are held in great veneration.

They differ very much in their forms of government, and the word of messengers and chieftains is trusted in all that they say or order on the part of the lord, so long as they carry in their hand a feathered fly whisk (which, as among the Christians, is the staff of authority); and this fly whisk is handed over by the lord to whom he considers to serve him best, and for such time as he pleases for him to be his officer. On the islands of the Gulf of Orotiña and in other parts, they use long rods of very beautiful wood and in the top part of them there is a hollow or empty space with little sticks inside which, on shaking the staff while holding the tip fast to the ground, by moving or trembling the arm, sounds like those toys filled with pebbles for pacifying infants; and one of those messengers goes with that staff to the square of a village and the people come running forthwith to see what he wants; and he, with the staff held as described, cries out: "Come ye! Come ye! Come ye!" And this having been said thrice in their tongue, he states the orders of that lord in the form of a pronouncement, and then he goes off forthwith; and in peace or in war, or in whatever manner they are ordered, they obey completely what they were told, without fail in any way whatsoever. Those rods replace the fly whisks which, as was said, are carried by the others and are the insignia of authority; and in returning with a reply, they place the rod where another dozen, more or less, of them are near the prince, for this and other purposes; and he gives them out with his own hand as and when he sees fit.

3.
BARTOLOMÉ DE LAS CASAS:
THE DEVASTATION OF THE INDIES

In the year 1523, at the end of the year, this same tyrant [Pedro Arias de Ávila or Pedrarias] went into Nicaragua to subjugate that most flourishing province and a sorrowful hour it was when he entered that land. Who could exaggerate the felicity, the good health, the amenities of that prosperous and numerous population? Verily it was a joy to behold that admirable province with its big towns, some of them extending three or four leagues, full of gardens and orchards and prosperous people. But because this land is a great plain without any mountains where the people could take refuge, they had to allow, with great anguish, the Christians to remain in the province and to suffer cruel persecutions from them. And since these Indians were by nature very gentle and peace-loving, the tyrant and his comrades (all of whom had aided him in destroying other kingdoms) inflicted such damage, carried out such slaughters, took so many captives, perpetrated so many unjust acts that no human tongue could describe them.

He once sent fifty horsemen with pikes to destroy an entire province. Not a single human being survived that massacre, neither women nor children nor aged and infirm. And that province was larger than the county of Rusellón in Spain. This terrible massacre was punishment for a trifling offense: some Indians had not responded to a summons promptly enough when the tyrant had commanded that they bring him a load of maize (that grain taking the place of wheat in this region), or else had asked for more Indians to be assigned to serve him or his comrades. And there was no place where the Indians could take refuge from the tyrant-Governor's wrath.

He sent companies of Spaniards to open up other provinces—that is to say, to attack and pillage the peoples in those provinces. They were allowed to capture as many Indians as they liked in peaceful settlements, to become their slaves. And they put the captives in chains and made them carry heavy loads, weighing as much as three arrobas.* And they had to carry these cargoes on their backs for long marches. The result was that the number of captives soon dwindled, most of them dying from exhaustion, so that from four thousand captives there remained only six. They left the

---

*An *arroba* equals roughly 22 pounds.

dead bodies on the trail. They were decapitated corpses, for when a captive sank under the heavy load, the Spaniards cut off his head, which fell to one side while the body fell to the other while the captives chained together continued their march without interruption. When commanded to do similar labor, with this experience behind them, the surviving Indians went off weeping and saying, "These are the roads down which we went to serve the Christians. In the past, even when we worked hard we could return to our houses, our wives, and children. But now we go without hope of ever again seeing them."

This tyrant once took it into his head to make a new *repartimiento* (distribution of captives among the Spaniards), this being either a caprice of his or, as was rumored, to rid himself of some Indians he disliked and pass them on to someone else. This occurred at the time of year when grain should be sowed and it kept the Indians from their usual tasks at seed-time. Later on, as a result, the Christians lacked grain, whereupon they seized the stores of grain the Indians kept for themselves and their families. In the famine that followed, more than thirty thousand Indians perished of starvation and there were cases when a woman would kill and eat her own child, in desperation.

Since all the settlements of the Indians in this fertile land were situated in the midst of gardens and orchards, the Christians resided in them, each Christian taking over the houses of the Indians who had been allocated to him according to the royal grant known as the *encomienda*. The Indian who had owned the house now worked for the Christian as his servant, cooking his meals, tilling the soil, working without rest. Oh, the pitiful Indians! Men and women, the aged and the children all worked for this Spanish Christian. For the children, as soon as they could stand on their legs, were put to work. And thus the Indians have been used up and consumed, and the few who survive are still being wasted away. Nor are these hardworking Indians allowed to own a house or anything of their own, and in this respect the Spaniards in Nicaragua have gone beyond the excesses of injustice that have prevailed on the island of Hispaniola.

The greatest and most horrible pestilence that has laid waste the province of Nicaragua was the freedom given by the Governor to his subordinates in the matter of petitioning slaves from the caciques of the towns. They petitioned every four or five months and each time a new allotment. The Governor could obtain fifty slaves at a time by threatening the cacique with being burned at the stake or thrown to the fierce dogs if he refused. Since the Indians do not commonly have slaves, at the most a cacique may have two or three or four, he simply went through the settlement, taking to begin with all the orphans, then taking one son from those who had two, and two sons from those who had three. In this way the cacique completed the number demanded by the tyrant, with loud lamentations and weeping by the people, for it seems they most greatly love their sons. And since this act was repeated many times, that whole kingdom became depopulated during the twenties and until the year thirty-three.

For this transaction was aided by six or seven ships voyaging along the coast to take on board and sell the surplus requisitioned slaves in Panama and Peru. And all of those captives soon died for as it has been ascertained from experience repeated a thousand times, the Indians when uprooted from their native land very soon perish. Then, too, they are never given enough to eat and their labor is never lightened in any way, since they are bought and sold to do only heavy work.

Thus more than five hundred thousand Indians were torn out of this province and sold into slavery. And those Indians had been as free as I am. In the infernal wars waged by the Spaniards another five or six hundred thousand souls have perished up to the present time. And these ravages continue. In a matter of fourteen years this province has undergone these things. There must now be in Nicaragua four or five thousand Spaniards who kill, each day, through acts of violence, oppression, and servitude, numerous Indians, and they boast that they have established one of the great population centers in the world. It was more than enough what those Spaniards did in the province of Cuzocatán where the Villa San Salvador is situated, or is at least in the vicinity. It was a felicitous land bordering the coast of the southern sea, extending a distance of forty or fifty leagues,* and in the capital city of Cuzocatán the Indians gave the Spaniards a great welcome, more than twenty or thirty thousand coming out with gifts of live chickens and cooked foods. In response to this welcome, the captain-general ordered each of his officers to take as many Indians as they liked to serve them as cargo bearers. Each Spaniard then took one to five hundred Indians they needed to be well served, and the innocent Indians endured being allocated in this way and they served the Spaniards fault-lessly, wholeheartedly, revering them.

Meanwhile the captain-general commanded the Indians to bring him gold, much gold, for that was mainly what he had come there for. The Indians replied that they would gladly provide the Spaniards with all the gold they possessed, and they gathered together a large quantity of copper axes overlaid with a coating of gold, giving them the aspect of solid gold. The captain then had the gold assayed and when it was found that the axes were of copper, he exclaimed: "To the devil with this land! There is no gold here," and he commanded his men to put the Indians that served them in chains and branded as slaves. This was done and to all the Indians they could lay hands on, and I saw one of the sons of the ruler of that city being chained and branded. Some Indians escaped, and when the Indians of the

---

*A Sanish *legua* equals roughly 3 1/2 miles.

land heard of this great misfortune, they gathered together and took up arms and in the battle that followed, the Spaniards massacred and tortured a great number of Indians. Then they built a city which has now, by divine justice, been destroyed in three deluges, one of water, another of muddy earth, the third of stones larger than thirteen oxen.

When the Spaniards had killed all the chieftains and all the Indians capable of making war, they cast all the others into infernal servitude. And when the Spaniards demanded tribute-slaves, they gave them their sons and daughters, the only slaves they had. These the Spaniards sent by shiploads down the coast to be sold in Peru.

Thus, with massacres and other outrages they laid waste a kingdom extending for more than one hundred square leagues, a land that had been among the most flourishing and populous in the whole world.

4.
WILLIAM L. SHERMAN: SLAVERY AND FORCED LABOR

Slaves, *tamemes, naborías,* forced labor, and tribute all existed in Central America before the advent of the Spaniard. Pre-Hispanic times saw a stratified society in which a native aristocracy enjoyed status and luxury at the expense of the maceguales and the sub-macegual class. In a variety of ways some Indians were brutalized by others. When the Spaniards became the new masters, many of the native practices were retained with some adaptations, while new forms of labor were introduced. There were, however, surprisingly few changes in the basic labor structure, which continued much as it had for centuries. . . .

Spaniards were cautioned to exact no more tribute and labor than the Indians gave in heathen times, but those injunctions were frequently breached. Spaniards were at pains to point out that conditions improved with them because the Indians' souls were saved, that some were rescued from the sacrificial altars, and that there was a higher morality and better order. Although the new masters were unconscionable in their demands, they said the native principals were as bad or worse.

During the years of pacification many Indians were killed; however, Spaniards maintained that before they arrived there was almost constant warfare among many of the tribes. It is true that the conquerors did away

From his *Forced Native Labor in Sixteenth Century Central America* (Lincoln, Neb., 1979), pp. 328–29.

with cannibalism, human sacrifice, and frequent, if not continuous, warfare. Nevertheless, in other respects the lot of the Indians worsened under the Europeans.

5.
MURDO MACLEOD: COLONIAL CENTRAL AMERICA

The picture which emerges of Central American economic life during the sixteenth and seventeenth centuries is one of two great systems. Much of the countryside was filled with cattle and sheep and with Indian and Spanish staples such as maize, beans, and wheat. Largely for home consumption and prestige, or for local trade, this agricultural complex was primarily a phenomenon of the highlands, although cattle swarmed everywhere. The Central America of cattle and cereals had its eras of great expansion, prosperity, and decline, but the primary function of this agricultural system was a limited one—the feeding of local populations and the maintenance of the existing class structure. As a result, the declines in this economy were felt mainly by the poorer and less powerful sections of the populace, and had a correspondingly secondary impact on the immediate economic life of the masters of colonial Central America. The system of cattle and cereals was in effect a background economy, a continuing, relatively unobserved support to the other and more brilliant colonial economy of foreign trade, shipping, and quick wealth.

The other great system was the one of the "produits moteurs," the golden keys to wealth, which rose and fell for the first three centuries after the Spanish conquest. Except for the early days of silver and gold production, these products were agricultural and were mostly grown in the Central American "fertile crescent" which runs east and south along the Pacific coast from the isthmus of Tehuantepec to the plains of Guanacaste and Nicoya. Consisting of volcanic soils which were originally of high fertility, this strip was to undergo intensive cultivation in some areas and much of its soil and its peoples suffered damage as a consequence.

It is within this second great economic system, at once more dynamic and more fragile than the background one of extensive farming, that the great "booms" occurred which made fortunes for Central Americans or cast them into despondency. The patterns repeated themselves several times. A product would be discovered, would develop with an amazing

From his *Spanish Central America: A Socioeconomic History, 1520–1720* (Berkeley, 1974), pp. 48–49.

rapidity given the technologies of the time (Spanish could be the most singleminded of men), would enjoy a period of great prosperity in which it was squeezed for every last pound of production and profit, and would then go into profound decline or stagnation.

The disappearance of the boom would then set off a frantic but determined hunt for another dynamic export crop. These periods of depression often saw a fragmentation of the Central American area as different regions which were no longer able to look to the great money-earning product which had united Central America economically each sought new solutions in the most regionally appropriate directions. As a consequence it was normal to find minor booms in one or more small areas of the Audiencia of Guatemala during these depressions, while the rest of the area remained depressed in the aftermath of the last major boom. These minor booms occurred because some small sub-region had found a crop of sufficient dynamism to rescue it temporarily from the general depression, but not sufficiently profitable or in demand to rescue the area as a whole. Such secondary regional solutions rarely lasted for long. Concluding the cycle would be the rise of a new product which was sufficiently organized or commanded enough of an outside market to reunite economically much of the area under the Audiencia, even if only briefly and unequally.

This cyclical pattern was affected by dozens of outside variables. Population loss and soil erosion cut short some booms; lack of outside markets prevented some crops from becoming as profitable as was first hoped. Tastes, fashions, and fads kept some trades from disappearing entirely, and competition from other areas prevented Central Americans from asking high prices and quick profits for others. But the general pattern, even with these distortions, is quite clearly discernible.

6.
DAVID BROWNING: LANDOWNERSHIP IN THE NINETEENTH CENTURY

With the introduction of coffee came new attitudes that regarded man's use of the land in less tolerant terms. The land came to be viewed as the estate of the coffee planters. Above all else, the ways in which it was to be used, owned and settled, were to be determined by the desire for it to produce the maximum amount of coffee of the highest quality at the lowest price.

From his *El Salvador: Landscape and Society* (Oxford, 1971), pp. 174–7, 206–7, 220–21.

At first it was hoped that the systems under which man had used the land of El Salvador would be capable of achieving this: early coffee plantings were made by the villages on their common land as well as by the planter on his private estate. But the coffee planters quickly decided that such hopes were unjustified. Unlike the experience with cocoa and balsam, there was no need for the coffee merchant to rely on local production by small-scale cultivators. Unlike the slow and uncertain growth of plantation indigo, the rewards of coffee farming were great, immediate and available to those who could produce the greatest amount of fruit in the shortest time. After initial attempts to convert the existing structure of landholding for commercial purposes, the decision was taken, by a coffee planters' government, to abolish any aspect of man's ownership, use or settlement of the land that hindered the rapid establishment of coffee plantations.

The principal result of this decision was the abolition of communal land ownership in favour of individual proprietorship. In a series of decrees, passed over a short period, the government sought to dismantle an agrarian structure that had evolved gradually over four centuries and to replace it with a system based exclusively on individual private land ownership, and, more importantly, on a concept that regarded the land and its inhabitants as capital resources that should be employed efficiently in order to maximize personal fortunes. Such a concept was totally alien to those cultivators whose attitude towards the land and towards the recurring cycle of planting and harvest still remained rooted in their Indian past. Meanwhile the speed of the land reform and the impatience with which it was enacted prohibited consideration of the complex character of the system being destroyed or the problems that were created by its destruction. . . .

Historical evidence about the village of Juayua, in the centre of this western coffee district, indicates the transformation of a village surrounded by common land to one surrounded by privately-owned coffee plantations. By 1858 three private landowners had planted 40,000 coffee bushes near the village. One planter, a French immigrant, Luis Watallín, employed 100 workers on his plantation and demonstrated his rank and relative wealth in the village by the construction of a large and conspicuous mansion, the "Casa de Cristá." Another planter, General Francisco Salaverría, had expanded his coffee plantations so rapidly that in 1858 President Gerardo Barrios wrote to him "When the bushes that you have planted are in fruit, we are going to call you Count of Salcoatitán and Marquis of Juayua." In 1877, the village was renamed El Progreso in recognition of its "agricultural wealth and material improvement." But this prosperity was not shared by all the inhabitants, who became increasingly reliant on the plantations for a living and, according to a report of 1879, lost their traditional common lands to private landowners to such an extent that extension of the common land required purchase of ground from neighbouring properties: "If the Indians of this village are to grow permanent crops they cannot be expected to abandon their annual subsistence crops, and there are many who have no lands to cultivate and no money with which to buy them." In the case of Juayua, the 1881 abolition of *tierras comunales* merely legalized a process of alienation of their lands that was already well advanced. The ultimate reaction of the villages to this situation was demonstrated when, in 1932, Juayua became the headquarters of the largest peasant uprising Central America has experienced. . . .

The *tierra comunal* and the *ejido,* had by the end of the nineteenth century been abolished as recognized systems of land tenure and use. The government, and the coffee-planters that it represented, were satisfied that they had realized the potential of the land that had become apparent as a result of the political, economic and commercial changes that came with national independence and the introduction of coffee. Laws were passed that transferred the ownership of land to private lands. But this new appraisal of the land was shared by only a few of the people that lived on it. The concept of a *patria*—a land and its people operating as factors of production in the national interest—was not understood or accepted by all. To many, the intimate personal bond between the soil, the rain, the growth of maize and free access to land, remained a meaningful and indeed an essential belief. Though the legal concept of common land was destroyed, many individuals who had relied on the common land continued to act in accordance with their belief in the customary rights of access to land. In El Salvador, "common lands" had been the legal expression of an attitude of mind: though the legal recognition of this concept was destroyed, the attitude of mind that had created the concept remained. Faced with the disappearance of one way of expressing this concept, the subsistence farmer sought other ways of doing so. Thus the squatter family has come to regard the entire countryside as its "common land": it will settle where it may, it will resist eviction, it will use every means possible to assert its belief that it has as much right to land as have all other members of the community.

It is all too easy for the Anglo-American observer, whose view of land is grounded in a system based on definition and orderly conveyance of land ownership, to dismiss this point. Even within the completely different cultural context of land settlement in North America, however, there are examples of bonds between men and the soil that cannot be examined purely in terms of legal rights and economic analysis, but require interpretation within the full cultural context of the societies involved and the regard they have for the land they occupy. For example, the bond with the land felt by the tenant farmers of Oklahoma, as they were dispossessed by the large, mechanically-operated cotton farms, could surely have been the feeling of the *milpa* cultivator in El Salvador as he found his lands disappearing under the coffee estates.

"Sure," cried the tenant men, "but it's our land. We measured it and broke it up. We were born on it, and got killed on it, died on it. Even if it's no good it's still ours. That's what makes it ours—being born on it, working on it, dying on it. That makes ownership, not a paper with numbers on it."

In the early twentieth century no thought was given to such considerations. The remarkable development of commercial agriculture in El Salvador during this period was a great achievement and consumed the energies and attention of the government and the landowners. It was not until certain new factors appeared that those who had transformed the nation into a "large and well-kept garden" began slowly to realize that a garden, however well tended and organized, may by itself not be satisfactory if all those living in it do not agree with the way it is laid out and with the way it is run.

7.
EPHRAIM SQUIER: CENTRAL AMERICA'S FRAGMENTATION

It has been a subject of remark, with many perhaps of surprise, that the dismemberment of the Spanish empire, and the independence of its American colonies, were so easily accomplished. That it was, in great part, due to the weakness of the mother country, is indisputable. But there were other causes favoring that result, to which we shall briefly allude.

The aristocratic portion of the Spanish American population, by which is meant not only those who held places or derived importance from their connection with the government, but those also whose principles were monarchical and exclusive in their tendency, including the vast body of the richly endowed priesthood, were not only astonished at the spread of liberal principles at home, but feared that the sweeping reforms there effected would extend to America, and reach their own body. They trembled for their prescriptions and privileges. But self-confident and presumptuous, claiming to possess the education, and most certainly possessing the wealth of the colonies, and the power which it confers, they saw with less alarm the development and promulgation of liberal ideas in America. And when the cry of *"Separation from Spain"* was raised, they caught it from the lips of the people, and made it almost unanimous. In this separation they saw not only their present security, but the perpetuation of their cherished powers and privileges. The Viceroy hoped, from the reflex and

From his *Notes on Central America* (New York, 1971).

representative of an emperor, to become himself a king, to shine with
original not borrowed lustre; and the aristocracy to rise from a colonial
dependency to a national rank and independence. They looked forward to
the establishment of a political and priestly oligarchy, which should dominate over the ignorant masses, with more than their present powers and
distinctions. Thus the absolutism, the old intolerances, the prejudices, and
corruptions of Spain, born of priestcraft and tyranny, took refuge in America, and made their final stand against the progress of liberal sentiments.
The heterogeneous union thus effected, for the accomplishment of the
single object of separation from Spain, was successful. Except in Mexico
and Colombia, and some of the seaport strongholds of South America, this
result was achieved with scarce a struggle. Spain confided in her colonial
officers to maintain the integrity of the empire; and when these failed her,
she knew too well her own weakness to prolong a contest, which our own
revolution had shown her must be hopeless. Nowhere was the separation
effected with greater unanimity, and more easily, than in Central America;
and to that country do we more particularly refer, in the pages which
follow.

But no sooner was the separation effected, hardly had the mutual con-
gratulations upon that result been exchanged, when the people called, in
a voice of thunder, for absolute independence, on the basis, so far as they
could comprehend it, of the great Republic of the North.

And now commenced that deadly, uncompromising struggle between
the two grand, antagonistic principles which we have indicated; represented, on one side, by a rich and powerful aristocracy, and a jealous and
beneficed clergy, and on the other, by the people, sensible of their abstract
rights, rich only in their devotion, but enthusiastically attached to what
they understood to be Liberty and Republicanism; between, in short, what
in Mexico and Central America have been called the *Serviles* and *Liberals*
—names which we shall henceforth use, for the sake of easy distinction.
From a struggle for supremacy, it is easy to perceive, how this contest
became one of extermination; for there can be no compromise, no fusion,
between principles so implacably hostile as those which now divided the
Spanish American colonies. Hence has resulted, in great part, that fierce
intolerance which I have pointed out and deplored at the commencement
of this chapter; and hence that series of revolutions and counter-revolu-
tions, which have hitherto distracted the Spanish American States, and in
which the great mass of our people see only the rivalship of petty chieftains,
and partisan struggles for ascendancy.

8.
SALVADOR MENDIETA: THE INFIRMITY OF CENTRAL AMERICA (1910)

The separation was committed, as a crime is committed, in secret, stealthily, with the subsequent proffering of hypocritical explanations to avoid scandal.

None of the states declared that the separation would be forever, but that it was only temporary, until a Constituent Assembly could meet to reorganize the nation on a sounder basis. . . .

After Morazán was executed in 1842, the pro-union* ideal lacked a worthy representative to replace this greatest of Central Americans. Such apostles as Cabañas, Vasconcelos, and, to a lesser degree, Gerardo Barrios remained who continued confessing to Christ deep in the shadows; but none could take the master's place.

From then on, local politics, devoid of ideals, consisted of struggle for power as its sole end, using for the purpose the cruelest, foulest, most despicable means, and eschewing all noble concepts.

The epoch was ushered in of international humiliation; of the insignificance and ridicule of Central America beyond its borders; of loss of territory; of factions almost every month and sometimes permanently, headed by godless savages, without consciences, bound by no law; and of the unbridled dominance of foreign ministers and consuls.

Everything became demeaned by the paltry new milieu; the two federal parties degenerated into countless personal or local parties; and Morazán's soldiers themselves, dragged along by the whirlwind of nonentities and mediocrities, sometimes lost their union orientation and were drawn into the mire of local politics.

Guatemala and El Salvador became rival countries, countries of perpetual mutual hatreds, as did Nicaragua and Costa Rica. The first two and then the third assumed the right to impose governors in Honduras, and the state of chaos became chronic to the point where Napoleon III's remark seems apt: "Constantinople and Central America are the most interesting and beautiful parts of the globe; but it is a pity that they should be in the worst hands, those of the Turks and the Central Americans."

At this point, what I wrote in my first book, *Páginas de Unión,* published in 1903, is worth repeating:

From his book, *The Infirmity of Central America,* 5 vols. (Barcelona, 1910)

*Union of the Central American States.

"With the federation broken up, civil wars, the servile prophecy notwithstanding, continued loosing upon our radiant countryside the devastating breath of their never ending siroccos and, as a logical consequence, power fell to the strongest and most corrupt. The very smallness of the sections into which the former republic was divided could not but contribute to increasing this horrid centralism more and more, this frightful spread of the presidential 'I' that is strangling us day by day.

"These five most wretched provinces set themselves up as real nations and acquired the habit of much, much *patriotism,* which showed through as a senseless hatred of the neighbor. Each statelet had its own rival and marked out its historical events in number of revolutions, factions, riots, and foolhardy episodes that caused it to drop ever further below the concept of a civilized people.

"The primary requirement of all that exists is, without a doubt, the preservation of that very existence: unstable governments recognized the primordial need, and well was it justified, of preserving themselves at any cost. Out of this, as a natural sequence, came the most complete economic and administrative mess, since the entire attention of the governor was concentrated upon holding on to his post, under constant attack from buzzing swarms of pretenders. . . .

"And, finally, in punishment for that stupid fragmentation, that indescribable division, the scourge of God came, the shameful lash wielded by the conscienceless pirate, the brutal Anglo-American seeking to exterminate the native of these lands, the poor devil of a mestizo as he called him; and he came like a colossal avalanche and fell upon us, robbing, murdering, and laying waste.

"Then, the few great souls that still remained among us laid aside their local rancors, tried to forget the odious past to join forces and free the homeland, that poor, moribund, and abandoned homeland; then, in opposition to the base interests of the moment—always so positivist—the great Mora was to be seen, warming his peaceful, hardworking people to move upon Nicaragua, their torches of patriotism blazing, to redeem the scared rights of our nationality; then, great-hearted Jerez and Chamorro joined together for the common defense; then, El Salvador was to be seen, speedily lending its energies and its fervor to the patriotic conflict; then, finally, Guatemala and Honduras, at last—governed at the time by the most servile of separatists—were also to be seen marching on the scorched and mortiferous fields of the sister province to fire the shots brotherhood demanded.

"Gentlemen, I must stop here. And I will pause long enough to tell you that I am blinded by indignation, that I can feel myself trembling with anger beyond description to think that in these times, and after the black memory of the arrogant Yankees, there should be in this Central American land those who favor our annexation by the United States. Is it possible that that rare and bracing spirit called patriotism could be inspiring those who propose such a thing? You shall answer for me: NO! Nor could it have been otherwise: not until now have I recognized the newspaper scribblers, of widespread profound vileness, as annexationists and not just the prowlers of political corruption."

II
THE IMPERIAL DIMENSION

9.
SIMÓN BOLÍVAR: THE JAMAICA LETTER (1815)

The States of the Isthmus from Panama to Guatemala will perhaps form a confederation. This magnificent location between the two great oceans could in time become the emporium of the world. Its canals will shorten the distances throughout the world, strengthen commercial ties with Europe, America, and Asia, and bring that happy region tribute from the four quarters of the globe. Perhaps someday the capital of the world may be located there, just as Constantine claimed Byzantium was the capital of the ancient world.

10.
SECRETARY OF STATE PHILANDER KNOX: THE MONROE DOCTRINE AND THE CARIBBEAN (1912)

It thus appears that the Spanish-American States understood the Monroe doctrine to import a definite pledge by the United States to them of mutual support in its maintenance and to involve joining with them in some kind of specific alliance, offensive and defensive, for that purpose. The Senate responded to the proposal for a congress by confirming two commissioners, for whose expenses the Congress appropriated means; but one of them died, the other reached Panama too late to take part in the first session, and no second session was ever held. . . .

U.S. National Archives, Record Group 59, 817.51/297A, January 22, 1912.

To illustrate how the self-preservation features of the Monroe doctrine have been espoused and lived up to by all of our national administrations, whatever their party allegiance or political creed, as well as to show the association between the instinct of self-preservation and the idea of aiding our neighbors to guard themselves against invasive alien influences from which, in the end, we ourselves should suffer, the Venezuelan episode of 1895 may be pertinently cited. On its face, the issue between Venezuela and Great Britain was merely one of determining an undefined boundary line; in its essence it appeared to involve the setting up of expanded colonial domination by Great Britain over a large part of the historical territory of Venezuela. The dispute lasted nearly half a century. Mr. Evarts, Mr. Frelinghuysen, and Mr. Bayard successively urged upon Great Britain the acceptance of the arbitration asked by Venezuela. Mr. Blaine followed in 1889, after Barima, at the mouth of the Orinoco, had been proclaimed a British port. When Mr. Cleveland assumed office Mr. Olney renewed the appeal for arbitration with the alternative of conventional agreement upon a definite boundary. In February, 1895, Congress, by joint resolution, approved the President's recommendation of arbitration. On July 20, 1895, Mr. Olney addressed to Ambassador Bayard an instruction which has become one of the famous papers of our diplomatic annals. He asserted that the right of one nation to intervene in a controversy to which other nations are directly parties may be availed of "whenever what is done or proposed by any of the parties primarily concerned is a serious and direct menace to its own integrity, tranquillity, or welfare."

He elaborately analyzed the history and scope of the doctrine of Monroe, especially dwelling upon its noncolonization declaration, deducing "that the Venezuelan boundary dispute is in any view far within the scope and spirit of the rule as uniformly accepted and acted upon." He was careful not to link himself to the cause of either disputant. To quote only very briefly, he said that the United States "being entitled to resent and resist any sequestration of Venezuelan soil by Great Britain, it is necessarily entitled to know whether such sequestration has occurred or is now going on."

Mr. Olney's conclusion was that it appeared to be the unmistakable and imperative duty of the President to ask "for a definite decision upon the point whether Great Britain will consent or will decline to submit the Venezuelan boundary question in its entirety to impartial arbitration."

The dispute was eventually and happily ended by arbitration.

It was at this period of the development of the doctrine and in this very controversy that a new suggestion was made, in negative form, to the effect that if the Government of the United States had the rights which it claimed, it must take them *cum oncre* and so assume certain obligations and responsibilities. This was indicated by Lord Salisbury in answer to Mr. Olney's able presentation of the doctrine in the statement that—

"It is admitted that he [President Monroe] did not seek to assert a protectorate over Mexico or the States of Central and South America. Such a claim would have imposed upon the United States the duty of answering for the conduct of these States, and consequently the responsibility of controlling it. . . . It follows of necessity that if the Government of the United States will not control the conduct of these communities, neither can it undertake to protect them from the consequences attaching to any misconduct of which they may be guilty toward other nations."

In this relation I am disposed to emphasize the fact that our course in the Venezuelan incident, apart from obeying the instinct of self-preservation, was distinctly and mainly responsive to the appeal of Venezuela and in the direction of lending a helpful hand to a suffering neighbor to enable a just determination of her asserted claim of right. So far as Venezuela was concerned we imposed no burden upon that then feeble State; we simply assisted it to throw off a burden. It was surely zeal in the defense of a sister Republic and unaffected consciousness that our power was for beneficent use which called from Mr. Olney these vigorous words:

"To-day the United States is practically sovereign on this continent and its fiat is law upon the subjects to which it confines its interposition."

The spirit behind these words contemplated, I am sure, no arbitrary exercise of sheer power, but a determined zeal in magnanimous consideration for the rights of other American Republics, a sincere sympathy with them in their trials, an insistence upon the right, that good might come to them and that our own vital interests should not be menaced.

The first positive pronouncement, from which has grown in the lapse of fruitful years the great body of precept and precedent which is to-day called the Monroe doctrine, is found in President Monroe's annual message of 1823, in which he stated that—

"The occasion has been judged proper for asserting as a principle, in which the rights and interests of the United States are involved, that the American continents, by the free and independent condition which they have assumed and maintained, are henceforth not to be considered as subject for future colonization by any European powers."

This statement was designed as a politic declaration, made to fit a specific "occasion," namely, the claim of Russia, under the ukase of 1821, to exclude all alien commerce and industry from the coasts and waters of northwestern America down to the fifty-first parallel. John Quincy Adams, then Secretary of State, resisted this avid claim on the ground that no Russian settlement existed on the territory, to which the United States laid equal claim; and on July 17, 1823, more than five months before President Monroe's message, Mr. Adams gave notice to the Russian envoy to the effect that the flaw in the Russian contention could not be cured by making settlements, as an afterthought, to prop up an unjustified claim of title. What Mr. Adams said was—

"that we [the United States] should contest the right of Russia to any territorial establishment on this continent, and that we should assume distinctly the principle that the American continents are no longer subjects for any new European colonial establishments."

It was this categorical declaration that Monroe embodied in his message, with the verbal change that the original "settlements," which under Mr. Adams's pen became "territorial establishments" and "colonial establishments," was altered to "future colonization." Thus amended, the Adams caveat, directed specifically at the Russian claim, became in time merged in the Monroe doctrine proper and, a generation later, played its part in the negotiation of the Central American and Clayton-Bulwer treaties with Great Britain as a question of fact, resting on the assertion that the continent was "occupied by civilized independent nations" and was "accessible to Europeans and each other on that footing alone."

The Monroe doctrine proper, as enunciated in a different part of the celebrated message of 1823, was much more far-reaching. It was called forth by the menace of a combination of European powers with the purpose of interference in the political affairs of the recently enfranchised American Republics, whose sovereign existence had been acknowledged by the United States but not then by Europe. This movement, an outgrowth of the Holy Alliance of 1815 and originally confined to Europe as a league for protecting the principle of legitimacy as against revolution, for upholding the divine right of kings as opposed to the rights of the people, was extended, in the summer of 1823, to embrace intervention, in behalf of Spanish sovereignty, in America. France proposed to Great Britain that when the allies should have accomplished their task of restoring the Spanish throne they should propose a congress with the view to the termination of the revolutionary governments in Spanish-America; but England looked upon this proposal with disfavor, and Canning, late in the summer of 1823, sounded the United States as to the possibility of the two Governments taking a joint position against interference by the allies in Latin America. The opinion of Jefferson that—

"Our first and fundamental maximum should be never to entangle ourselves in the broils of Europe; our second, never to suffer Europe to intermeddle with cis-Atlantic affairs"—

was echoed by Monroe's advisers. The suggestion of joint action with Great Britain was not favored, but the coincidence of British policy with our own was not unwelcome. England, indeed, took the initiative in October 1823, by declaring that, while neutral as to the contest between Spain and her American colonies, the "junction" of any foreign power with Spain against the colonies would be viewed as constituting "entirely a new question upon which Great Britain must take such decision as her interests required." The Canning declaration was imminent and was soon rendered specifically effective by the utterance of Monroe; the fact that the two great maritime powers were moving in parallels toward the enunciation of a vital principle made impracticable the accomplishment of any project of American interference by the allies, and they were not slow to realize the force of Monroe's announcements when he said:

"We owe it, therefore, to candor and to the amicable relations existing between the United States and those powers to declare that we should consider any attempt on their part to extend their system to any portion of this hemisphere as dangerous to our peace and safety. With the existing colonies or dependencies of any European power we have not interfered and shall not interfere. But with the governments who have declared their independence and maintained it, and whose independence we have on great consideration and on just principles acknowledged, we could not view any interposition for the purpose of oppressing them or controlling in any other manner their destiny, by any European power, in any other light than as the manifestation of an unfriendly disposition toward the United States."

Like all general formulations of great principles the Monroe document has required interpretation and construction to apply its precepts to special cases.

It was understood at the outset by the newly enfranchised Latin-American States as a defensive movement in their favor rather than as a step taken by the United States in its own interest and for its own self-defense. In 1825 the southern republics proposed to convene a congress at Panama to form an alliance of all the independent American States for self-defense and to settle some principle of public law to govern their relation with each other. One of the measures scheduled for discussion was:

"To take into consideration the means of making effectual the declaration of the President of the United States respecting any ulterior design of a foreign power to colonize any portion of this continent, and also the means of resisting all interference from abroad with the domestic concerns of the American Governments."

It goes almost without saying that, from aiding an embarrassed neighbor in doing the right, or in defending a right, to assuming vicarious responsibility for his wrongdoing, is a far cry. Between these two extremes, as between all extremes, there lies a median zone where they touch or even overlap. That is the case when the question arises how far, in a given situation, this nation may go in helping another American people to avert any injurious consequences of wrongdoing.

In principle it is not the duty of the United States to prevent a foreign state from seeking redress, or to shoulder the wrong and assume its redress ourselves. But it is equally obvious that the measures to which a foreign state might ordinarily resort to enforce its claim might amount to political interference in the affairs of the American continents, as by occupation and administration of territory, or like extreme coercive steps. That is a contingency which the tenets of the doctrine, joined to the dictates of common prudence, authorize and counsel us to avert by all proper means, in fulfillment of a responsibility we owe to ourselves, even if not in the discharge of any conventional or moral obligation.

The point was well considered in President Roosevelt's annual message of 1905. He examined it in its tortious and contractual aspects. As to the former, he said:

"If a republic to the south of us commits a tort against a foreign nation, such as an outrage against a citizen of that nation, then the Monroe doctrine does not force us to interfere to prevent punishment of the tort, save to see that the punishment does not assume the form of territorial occupation in any shape."

As to the latter aspect, he said:

"On the one hand, this country would certainly decline to go to war to prevent a foreign government from collecting a just debt; on the other hand, it is very inadvisable to permit any foreign power to take possession, even temporarily, of the customhouses of an American Republic in order to enforce the payment of its obligations; for such temporary occupation might turn into a permanent occupation."

And upon both propositions he reached the conclusion that—

"The only escape from these alternatives may at any time be that we must ourselves undertake to bring about some arrangement by which so much as possible of a just obligation shall be paid. It is far better that this country should put through such an arrangement, rather than allow any foreign country to undertake it."

My distinguished predecessor, Mr. Root, voiced the same views in a speech made in 1904 at the annual dinner of the New England Society:

"And if we are to maintain this doctrine [the declaration of Monroe], which is vital to our national life and safety, at the same time when we say to the other powers of the world, 'You shall not push your remedies for wrong against these republics to the point of occupying their territory,' we are bound to say that whenever the wrong can not be otherwise redressed we ourselves will see that it is redressed."

These, gentlemen, constitute the more important announcements, with the elements involved therein, which have been made during our past history, and whatever particular phase of the Monroe doctrine you may choose to emphasize, it appears to me evident that there is one certain deduction from the premises, and that is that the best way to avoid the difficulties occasionally arising out of any responsibilities which this doctrine in certain of its aspects may seem to impose is to assist the less fortunate American Republics in conducting their own affairs in such a way that those difficulties should not be liable to arise. The most effective way to escape the logical consequences of the Monroe doctrine is to help them to help themselves. Assuming the correctness of Mr. Root's corollary, it is our duty, to ourselves and to them, to cooperate in preventing, where possible, specific conditions where we might have to become in too great a measure accountable. We diminish our responsibilities in proportion as we bring about improved conditions. Like an insurance risk, our risk decreases as the conditions to which it pertains are improved.

I most confidently assert that, under the Monroe doctrine in its ultimate analysis, the heaviest and most matter-of-fact responsibility that to-day rests upon the United States is that we should respond to the needs still felt by some few of our Latin-American neighbors in their progress toward good government, by assisting them to meet their just obligations and to keep out of trouble. We wish to see them prosper, and their prosperity, by reflex action, is felt not only by us but by all the members of the American family. . . .

Practically from the outset the Republics of Central America, especially Honduras and Nicaragua, have been torn with internal dissension and overrun with revolutions. In Honduras and Nicaragua these ills are still prevalent. Beset with strife these less fortunate Republics, although endowed by Providence with vast natural resources, have never been permitted to progress toward a normal and economic development. Early in their existence as independent States they found their treasuries depleted and their resources squandered in futile attempts to suppress internal disorder, and as a natural result they have been continuously compelled to borrow at exorbitant rates of interest from those willing to incur the disproportionate risk of lending them the moneys necessary for the temporary conduct of government, with the result that they now find themselves hopelessly entangled in the mesh of enormous and rapidly increasing national indebtedness. Their revenues have never been properly applied so as to meet the ever-increasing demands of their national creditors.

Because of the difficulty of communication in these countries the customhouses have ever been the objective point of the revolutionists and successive contests for their control have marked the national existence. Once having lost control of the customhouses and the revenues derived therefrom, the constituted authorities have found themselves confronted with a lack of funds and have ultimately been deprived of the means necessary to defend the capitals.

Control of the customhouses once obtained, it becomes necessary for the successful revolutionists to expend enormous sums, practically the entire national revenue, in the maintenance of an army adequate to continue them in control. Under such circumstances the payment of the interest on the national debt has been out of the question, and such governments fall into a state of hopeless default which deprives them of any further foreign credit.

Honduras and Nicaragua alike occupy a central position stretching from the Caribbean to the Pacific and separating the other Central American Republics. In Central America there are many rivalries as between the heads of the five Republics, but there has seldom been an open breach between them which has resulted in an international war. Rather than seek a direct means of redressing their grievances it has been found far more effective and less dangerous than open hostility for the president seeking to injure his neighbor to institute and set on foot a revolution of political malcontents against the government. For years the revolutions and internal commotions of several of these Republics have been caused by their neighbors who have taken advantage of their position to harbor political refugees from their neighbors and aid or permit them to foster a hostile movement against their native republic, which is fomented in security without the borders of the country at whose government it is aimed, and which is then permitted to cross the international line at some convenient location, thence to contend for supremacy.

Honduras, because it borders on three of the other Republics, Guatemala, Salvador, and Nicaragua, has for years been the hotbed of most of the internal disturbances of its neighbors, and in fact has been the cockpit of Central America. So great has been the abuse of the undefended central position occupied by Honduras that as long ago as 1907 all the Republics of Central America joined in a peace conference and signed at Washington, under our auspices, a convention one article of which had for an object the neutralization of the territory of that Republic so as to prevent its further use as a center of disturbance.

Under such conditions the Republics of Honduras and Nicaragua came to seek the counsel and assistance of the United States.

Provided the enormous waste on military establishments could be checked, the customs revenues of both these countries, properly administered, should be ample to meet the interest and sinking fund on their just national obligations, and it is in order to establish a system for the accomplishment of this end that the present conventions have been framed. . . .

In order to avoid the danger of further embarrassment with foreign creditors, the conventions provide (first) that a loan shall be placed in the United States; in order to provide that the bankers' contracts, which it will be necessary to negotiate to work out the details of their financial problems, may be equitable and just, and also that they may be properly executed, it is provided (second) that the signatory governments shall take due note of the terms and shall consult in case of any difficulties. That the loan may be properly secured, the conventions stipulate (third) that the customs duties shall be pledged; that this security may be adequate and may not be interfered with, it is agreed (fourth) that the customs duties shall not be changed without the consent of the Government of the United States. To assure the proper collection and administration of the customs by a competent person, it is provided (fifth) that a receiver general of customs shall be appointed by the Government of the country concerned from a list of names prepared by the fiscal agent of the contemplated loan and approved by the President of the United States. To insure the proper discharge of the duties of the receiver of general customs, it is agreed (sixth) that he shall be under obligation to report annually, and upon request, to both parties to the conventions. In order that he may effectively, conscientiously, and independently perform his functions, and to prevent customs houses continuing to be the goal of revolutionists, it is stipulated (seventh) that the Government of the country concerned will protect him and (eighth) that the Government of the United States shall afford him such protection as it may deem requisite, there being thus obtained just so much assurance of stable conditions and proper customs collections as will enable Nicaragua and Honduras to borrow the money necessary to rehabilitate their national finances at anything like a reasonable rate of interest. . . .

If these conventions are put into operation, . . . within a few years the revolutions which keep these countries in a state of constant unrest will be eliminated; the neutrality of Honduras and Nicaragua in Central American affairs will become an accomplished fact; and the peace of the rest of Central America will be immensely strengthened. . . .

Alone, these countries find it impossible to extricate themselves from the thraldom of civil strife, and they quite naturally look to their more prosperous and powerful neighbor for aid and guidance. Shall we refuse it any more than we refused to heed the cry of Cuba or that of the Dominican Republic?

With the Monroe doctrine as a tenet of our national faith, can we refuse to these Republics that measure of assistance which will render their Governments stable and keep them from foreign interference? These are the questions involved in these treaties which are now pending before the United States Senate.

The adoption of the present conventions is counseled not only by the humanitarian motive of preventing useless bloodshed (hundreds of lives having already been saved by the Dominican arrangement) and by the ever-increasing important political reason of avoiding the danger of European entanglement in the affairs of the countries surrounding the Caribbean, but is also more than justified from a purely material standpoint. In 1909 the total foreign trade of the Central American States, including

Panama, amounted to approximately $60,000,000, of which about one-half was with the United States. When we consider that the total commerce between Mexico and the United States is in the neighborhood of $117,-000,000 we can realize in some degree the trade possibilities with the Isthmian Republics, especially if it be understood that under the arrangement between the United States and the Dominican Republic the trade with that country has increased since 1903 (prior to the installation of American officials in the customhouses), when it was somewhat over $4,-000,000, to about $11,500,000 for the year 1910, and that the share of the United States in the total foreign commerce of the Dominican Republic has materially increased in the same period.

Several of the Republics of South America have grown great and powerful and enjoy the highest culture, fine political ideals, and stable Governments. These Republics, indeed, are, consciously or unconsciously, fellow sponsors with the United States of the Monroe doctrine as a Pan American idea as well as an American policy. The growth of such nations lightens our responsibility. The logic of political geography and of strategy, and now our tremendous national interest created by the Panama Canal, make the safety, the peace, and the prosperity of Central America and the zone of the Caribbean of paramount interest to the Government of the United States. Thus the malady of revolutions and financial collapse is most acute precisely in the region where it is most dangerous to us. It is here that we seek to apply a remedy.

It would not be sane to uphold a great policy like the Monroe doctrine and to repudiate its necessary corollaries and neglect the sensible measures which reason dictates as its safeguards.

11.
THE ANGLO-AMERICAN CLAYTON-BULWER TREATY

The United States of America and Her Britannic Majesty, being desirous of consolidating the relations of amity which so happily subsist between them by setting forth and fixing in a convention their views and intentions with reference to any means of communication by ship-canal which may be constructed between the Atlantic and Pacific Oceans by the way of the river San Juan de Nicaragua, and either or both of the lakes of Nicaragua or Managua, to any port or place on the Pacific Ocean, the President of

From William Malloy, *Treaties, Conventions, International Acts, Protocols and Agreements,* Vol. 1 (Washington, 1910).

the United States has conferred full powers on John M. Clayton, Secretary of State of the United States, and Her Britannic Majesty on the Right Honourable Sir Henry Lytton Bulwer, a member of Her Majesty's Most Honourable Privy Council, Knight Commander of the Most Honourable Order of the Bath, and Envoy Extraordinary and Minister Plenipotentiary of Her Britannic Majesty to the United States, for the aforesaid purpose; and the said Plenipotentiaries, having exchanged their full powers, which were found to be in proper form, have agreed to the following articles:

ARTICLE I.

The Governments of the United States and Great Britain hereby declare that neither the one nor the other will ever obtain or maintain for itself any exclusive control over the said ship-canal; agreeing that neither will ever erect or maintain any fortifications commanding the same, or in the vicinity thereof, or occupy, or fortify, or colonize, or assume or exercise any dominion over Nicaragua, Costa Rica, the Mosquito coast, or any part of Central America; nor will either make use of any protection which either affords or may afford, or any alliance which either has or may have to or with any State or people for the purpose of erecting or maintaining any such fortifications, or of occupying, fortifying, or colonizing Nicaragua, Costa Rica, the Mosquito coast, or any part of Central America, or of assuming or exercising dominion over the same; nor will the United States or Great Britain take advantage of any intimacy, or use any alliance, connection, or influence that either may possess, with any State or Government through whose territory the said canal may pass, for the purpose of acquiring or holding, directly or indirectly, for the citizens or subjects of the one any rights or advantages in regard to commerce or navigation through the said canal which shall not be offered on the same terms to the citizens or subjects of the other. . . .

12.
HARPER'S WEEKLY: WILLIAM WALKER AND THE WAR IN NICARAGUA

It has been heretofore the fashion to denounce the English progress in the East, and to hold it up as the advance of arrogance, violence, and injustice. We do not so regard it. Ever since the middle of the sixteenth century,

From *Harper's Weekly*, "The War in Nicaragua," February 27, 1857.

when Europe threw off its feudal slough of military barbarism, and ceased to occupy itself exclusively with brutal, preposterous, and internecine wars, the progress of civilization has been carried on by the bold spirits who, stimulated sometimes by love of adventure, sometimes by thirst for gain, sometimes by passionate desire of liberty, have derided danger, and scorned every consideration of prudence.

Spain furnished the grand filibusters of the first epoch—the Cortéz and Pizarros, who opened the way to the El Dorado of the West. England, a little later, sent out her Drakes, her Raleighs, and, in another century, her Clives and her Hastings; while on this side of the continent, from the Massachusetts Bay to the Great River discovered by De Soto, the whole coast was invaded by a swarm of adventurers from every part of the Old World.

That in this process—which has been now going on for centuries—dreadful sufferings have been inflicted on the primitive races, it is impossible to deny or to overlook. The hands that have been employed have been neither smooth nor pure. Fraud has been allied to force, and stratagem has joined hands with cruelty, to attain the aids of the superior castes. Both continents have been sullied by enormous crimes, and from the farthest east to the extreme west a cry has gone up to Heaven against the enormities of the invaders.

It must never be called sentimentalism to deplore or to denounce these crimes. . . .

But, on the other hand, while standing aghast at the commission of these abominations, let us not be misled into a misconception of their real results. Let us not shut our eyes to the manifest development of the scheme of Providence in regard to this world.

Does any one desire to roll back the planet to the sixteenth century? Shall Massachusetts and Connecticut make way for a new race of Pequods and Nipnucs? Shall India be re-surrendered to the rules of a fresh dynasty of Hyder Alis and Tippoo Saibs?

And he who runs may read that force is the necessary forerunner of civilization. The brute mind of the savage or the heathen must be reached by the manifestation of power—the only god he worships. How long would it take to open the gates of Heathendom by argument and persuasion, by protocols and diplomacy? What a geological cycle—an eocene or a plyocene period of peaceful efforts could not accomplish with the pagan savage, is done in the twinkling of an eye by a Cortéz at Mexico, or a Clive at Plassy. Such is the law of our existence. . . .

And this brings us by no violent transition to the question of Central America, which, recurring at frequent intervals, now again looms up before us, pregnant with mischief if met in a timid or a vacillating spirit, but fraught with no dangers that may not be conquered by a bold and honest policy.

We do not refer to Walker or his destiny. That chieftain seems to be endowed with quite as few scruples as any of his filibustering predecessors, from Drake or Cortéz to the present day, and to have far less than the sagacity which belongs to his class. His interruption of the Transit line was a brutal blunder; with a bullheaded fatuity that no Milesian ever outdid, he cut himself off from his own base of operations, and, in a sense very different from that of the Norman or the Roman invader, "burned his own boats." The consequences he has rued, and seems likely still more to rue.

Still—and it is certainly from no affection for him that we speak—we believe it is best that he should succeed, and we wish him success. Reckless and unscrupulous as he is, we can not see what is to be gained by returning the country to the possession of the mongrel banditti and native cut-throat ruffians who, for the last thirty years, have made that beautiful part of the world a mere den of thieves. We have no doubt that Walker, if once securely established, would be compelled, by the love of organization and discipline that marks our race, to establish a government which, though founded on fraud and violence, would in the lifetime of a single generation, give to that country a degree of tranquility and repose which it has never enjoyed even under the palmiest days of Spanish occupation. But these results are all now staked on the hazard of a die, and while we write, Walker may have shared the fate of Boulbon and many other desperate adventurers before him.

The Central American imbroglio presents another and probably much more important question—that, viz., connected with the Clayton-Bulwer and the Clarendon-Dallas treaties. The question, divested of diplomatic verbiage, seems to be this: The conquest of California in 1846, and the discovery of its treasures, opened a new world, and made Central America —which presents the shortest cut to our El Dorado—a matter of first-rate importance. The Isthmus is occupied by a mongrel race of Creole-Spaniards, negroes and Indians, divided into half a dozen wretched, half-organized governments. How shall the safety of the transit be obtained? How shall the works of internal improvements, railroads, or canals, called for by the wants of the age, be completed? These questions must be answered by England and America, the two great commercial powers which directly and indirectly are the most interested in the preservation and maintenance of a proper transit—and they are not easy of solution.

Out of this difficulty grew, in 1850, in, we believe, a very untimely hour, the Clayton-Bulwer treaty, designed to declare and define the rights of the two countries in the debatable land, and to extend their protection over the interoceanic communications. Whether illdrawn or ill-imagined, it is at all events certain that the treaty was satisfactory to neither party; its terms became the subject of angry debate, and the discussions that ensued have made our relations with Great Britain very precarious during the last three or four years.

To obviate these difficulties we have taken another step in the same direction, and the Clarendon-Dallas treaty has been concluded; the object of which is to remove the ambiguities resulting from the treaty of 1850, to make the terms of the contract more precise, and pretty substantially to take the Isthmus into the joint keeping of Great Britain and this country. The Clarendon-Dallas treaty is the completion of the general idea of the Clayton-Bulwer treaty.

Now we believe that the whole idea of this policy is wrong, and we think that the country so regards it. It is wrong for two obvious reasons: In the first place, John Bull and Jonathan are not at all the dogs to hunt in couples. It is in vain to attempt to organize a peaceful and harmonious co-operation between two great rivals, who have different, distinct, and independent interests. You can not yoke Sir Henry and Eclipse in the same harness.

In the second place, this policy admits the idea that the interests of England and the United States on the Isthmus are equal and identical. The notion is perfectly false. The country crossed by the interoceanic communication is almost part of our empire. We have a deep and direct interest in Panama and Nicaragua to which England can neither politically nor commercially pretend. For her to do so would be almost as absurd as for us to set up an equal interest in the question of the Punjab or Cabul.

We are no great sticklers for the Monroe doctrine, nor do we put it at all on that ground. The Monroe declaration was made about thirty-seven years ago, when all Europe was groaning under a despotic league which threatened to establish proconsular governments on this continent. To say that that declaration applies in its original meaning to the present state of the world is an absurd anachronism.

Our objection rests on general principles, which are as true now as they were in 1821, which are likely to be as true in 1875 as they are in 1857. We believe that an alliance between ourselves and England for the purpose of exercising control over the Southern Republics rests on an essentially false combination. Our interests are distinct, often hostile—our notions of government are diametrically antagonistic. Whatever may be the reciprocal feeling of the literary and commercial classes of the two countries—and we rejoice to believe it is one of growing respect and regard—the *governing classes* of the two countries—the democracy of the one and the aristocracy of the other—still look upon each other with mutual jealousy and mutual distrust. The manufacturer of Manchester and the banker of New York fraternize and hob-nob together, and hug each other *ad libitum,* but the American democrat and the English aristocrat, the hoosier and the feudal proprietor agree together like oil and vinegar, like fire and water.

Now we believe that this jealousy and distrust will not be diminished by any alliance or combination for joint operations in regard to a subject where our interests are clearly greater and stronger than those of Great Britain. Far otherwise. We believe that such a league can only lead to bickering, and perhaps to strife. If, therefore, the thing were to be done over again, we believe the good sense of the country would forbid any operation like that of the Clayton-Bulwer treaty, and prefer to trust the fate of the Isthmus to be decided by the current of events, by fortuitous Walkers and casual Spencers, leaving out of view all ideas of annexation or incorporation, in nowise at present desirable, simply relying upon the fact that our greater proximity, and the vastly greater enterprise of our population, would ultimately, in some shape or another, bring the country under the control of our race.

But the question is now a very different one, and must be decided on very different grounds. We must either go backward or forward. We can not stand where we are. We must either abandon the Clayton-Bulwer treaty, or complete it. In the present age of the world everything moves rapidly, and the Nicaraguan question has advanced half a century since 1850. The native government has fallen to pieces. Walker is heading Nicaraguans. Spencer is leading Costa Ricans. A triumvirate of New York merchants feeds or fans the flame; and what is more ominous than all, the omnipresent steam power of England is hovering over the scene, and everything is done under the muzzles of her guns. In such a state of things it will not do to stand still. "Masterly inactivity" is not at all the thing.

It will not do to kick the Clarendon-Dallas treaty out of the Senate, and then fold our hands and think we have done a great deed. Three lines of policy are before us. They are clear and distinct. The one is to renounce all combination with England; to break up the Clayton-Bulwer treaty, as by its provisions we have a right to do; leave each country to pursue her own course; and commit Central America to her fate, without interference direct or indirect. Another, to perfect and complete the Clayton-Bulwer treaty, and to regulate, conjointly with England, the affairs of the Isthmus. The third is, to assert the superior rights of this country in regard to Central America; to reject the alliance of England, and to mark out and pursue for ourselves a policy of bold, and, at the same time, wise control, which shall protect our citizens, and look to the future transfer of dominion, whenever, if ever, it shall become desirable and discreet.

Of these, the first is a policy of abnegation that, it may be pretty safely said, this country will never adopt. The second is a line of prudence, which avoids some present dangers, and will, peradventure, cause greater future perils. The third is a policy of audacity and enterprise—of audacity often the parent of safety. It must be backed by a powerful navy; and, above all, by a bold and determined front. It involves an immediate and sudden change in our foreign policy. Is the country ready for it?

13.
DANA MUNRO: U.S. POLICY TOWARD NICARAGUA

The intervention in Nicaragua in 1912 marked a turning point in American policy in the Caribbean. Before 1912, the navy had frequently made a show of force to prevent fighting which would endanger foreigners or to discourage revolutionary activities. Sometimes, as in Nicaragua in 1910, such measures had influenced, or decided, the outcome of a civil war, but there had been no case before 1912 where American forces had actually gone into battle to help suppress a revolution. American public opinion, as reflected in the press, seemed on the whole to approve what was done, but many voices were raised in protest. Senator Bacon, who had criticized previous actions of the State Department in Central America and had presented a resolution denying the right of the President to use the military forces in operations in a foreign country without the express consent of Congress, again spoke out when the marines first began to arrive in Nicaragua, pointing out that the State Department had gone ahead with its financial projects in spite of the Senate's refusal to approve them and that the power of the United States was being used to support private interests in profitable, speculative operations. The Senate unanimously approved his resolution for an inquiry.

The intervention intensified the already prevalent fear and mistrust of the United States in the other Central American countries. On the other hand, for several years after 1912 the recollection of what had happened . . . discouraged potential revolutionists throughout the isthmus. Except for a *coup d'état* staged by the Minister of War of Costa Rica in 1917, there was no case where a government was overturned by force in Central America between 1912 and 1919. When disturbances threatened, the appearance of an American warship was enough to restore tranquility. The belief that the United States would intervene to uphold constituted governments helped the groups in power in each country to remain in power with little regard for the rights of their opponents, but it at least gave Central America an era of much needed peace.

In Nicaragua, the continued presence of the legation guard was interpre-

From his *Intervention and dollar diplomacy in the caribbean, 1900–1921* (Princeton, 1964), pp. 215–16.

ted to mean that no revolution would be tolerated. This meant that the conservatives would stay in power, though everyone, including the State Department, knew that they were a minority party. The arguments advanced in defense of this policy: the assertion that the liberals included a large proportion of the "ignorant mob," and that most of their leaders represented the evil *zelayista* tradition, were perhaps put forward in all sincerity by officials who had little contact with any except the conservatives, but they made little sense to anyone who had friends in both parties. The support of a minority government was inconsistent with the principles that governed American policy in the Caribbean, but for more than ten years no Secretary of State wanted to assume responsibility for the revolution that would almost certainly follow the legation guard's withdrawal.

14.
THE CHAMORRO-BRYAN TREATY (1914)

The Government of the United States of America and the Government of Nicaragua being animated by the desire to strengthen their ancient and cordial friendship by the most sincere cooperation for all purposes of their mutual advantage and interest and to provide for the possible future construction of an interoceanic ship canal by way of the San Juan River and the great Lake of Nicaragua, or by any route over Nicaraguan territory, whenever the construction of such canal shall be deemed by the Government of the United States conducive to the interests of both countries, and the Government of Nicaragua wishing to facilitate in every way possible the successful maintenance and operation of the Panama Canal, the two Governments have resolved to conclude a Convention to these ends, and have accordingly appointed as their plenipotentiaries:

The President of the United States, the Honorable William Jennings Bryan, Secretary of State; and

The President of Nicaragua, Señor General Don Emiliano Chamorro, Envoy Extraordinary and Minister Plenipotentiary of Nicaragua to the United States;

Who, having exhibited to each other their respective full powers, found to be in good and due form, have agreed upon and concluded the following articles:

From William Malloy, *Treaties, Conventions, International Acts, Protocols and Agreements,* Vol. 3 (Washington, 1921), pp. 2740–41.

ARTICLE I.

The Government of Nicaragua grants in perpetuity to the Government of the United States, forever free from all taxation or other public charge, the exclusive proprietary rights necessary and convenient for the construction, operation and maintenance of an interoceanic canal by way of the San Juan River and the great Lake of Nicaragua or by way of any route over Nicaraguan territory, the details of the terms upon which such canal shall be constructed, operated and maintained to be agreed to by the two governments whenever the Government of the United States shall notify the Government of Nicaragua of its desire or intention to construct such canal.

ARTICLE II.

To enable the Government of the United States to protect the Panama Canal and the proprietary rights granted to the Government of the United States by the foregoing article, and also to enable the Government of the United States to take any measure necessary to the ends contemplated herein, the Government of Nicaragua hereby leases for a term of ninety-nine years to the Government of the United States the islands in the Caribbean Sea known as Great Corn Island and Little Corn Island; and the Government of Nicaragua further grants to the Government of the United States for a like period of ninety-nine years the right to establish, operate and maintain a naval base at such place on the territory of Nicaragua bordering upon the Gulf of Fonseca as the Government of the United States may select. The Government of the United States shall have the option of renewing for a further term of ninety-nine years the above leases and grants upon the expiration of their respective terms, it being expressly agreed that the territory hereby leased and the naval base which may be maintained under the grant aforesaid shall be subject exclusively to the laws and sovereign authority of the United States during the terms of such lease and grant and of any renewal or renewals thereof. . . .

15.
WALTER LIPPMANN: AMERICAN EMPIRE (1927)

EMPIRE: THE DAYS OF OUR NONAGE ARE OVER

All the world thinks of the United States today as an empire, except the people of the United States. We shrink from the word "empire," and insist that it should not be used to describe the dominion we exercise from Alaska to the Philippines, from Cuba to Panama, and beyond. We feel that there ought to be some other name for the civilizing work which we do so reluctantly in these backward countries. I think the reluctance is genuine. I feel morally certain that an overwhelming majority of our citizens do not wish to rule other peoples, and that there is no hypocrisy in the pained protest which rises whenever a Latin American or a European speaks of us as imperialistic. We do not feel ourselves to be imperialists as we understand that word. We are not conscious of any such desire for expansion as the Fascists, for example, proclaim every day. We have learned to think of empires as troublesome and as immoral, and to admit that we have an empire still seems to most Americans like admitting that they have gone out into a wicked world and there lost their political chastity.

Our sensitiveness on this point can be seen by an incident which happened recently in connection with that venerable book of reference, the "Almanach de Gotha." Here, in this social register of the royal and princely families of Europe, there appears, as of 1924, a list of American "protectorates." They are Cuba, Dominican Republic, Haiti, Liberia, and Panama. Now there can be no doubt that Washington exercises as much real authority in these countries, with the possible exception of Liberia, as London does in many parts of the dependent empire. Yet the "Almanach de Gotha's" innocent use of the word "protectorates" was immediately protested by Mr. James Brown Scott, Director of the Division of International Law of the Carnegie Endowment for International Peace. Mr. Scott pointed out, quite accurately, that the United States had never officially admitted the existence of any protectorates, and that Secretaries of State had again and again announced, as Mr. Hughes did in 1923, that "we recognize the equality of the American Republics, their equal rights under the law of nations."

I do not know what the "Almanach de Gotha" is going to do about this,

---

From his *Men of Destiny* (Seattle, 1927), pp. 215–21.

but it is certain that the rest of the world will continue to think of us as an empire. Foreigners pay little attention to what we say. They observe what we do. We on the other hand think of what we feel. And the result is that we go on creating what mankind calls an empire while we continue to believe quite sincerely that it is not an empire because it does not feel to us the way we imagine an empire ought to feel.

What the rest of the world sees is that after we had, in the years from 1803 to 1853, rounded out the territory of continental United States by purchase and by conquest, there was a pause in our expansion; that this was followed by the purchase of Alaska in 1867, the annexation of Hawaii in 1898, the obtaining possession of the Philippines and Puerto Rico, and, in a different form, of Cuba as a result of the Spanish War. From that time on the expansion of American influence in the Caribbean and the West Indies has widened until there is hardly a country in that whole region which has not seen an American intervention. In an article which was printed in *The New Republic* Professor Shephard of Columbia University has counted the following separate military interventions in the Caribbean between 1898 and 1927. In Cuba, four; in Panama, five; in the Dominican Republic, five; in Nicaragua, six (the last still in progress); Haiti, one, still in progress; Mexico, two; Honduras, six; Costa Rica, one; Colombia, one. Scattered all over the Caribbean are American High Commissioners and other officials, working under treaties, loan agreements and the like.

For all practical purposes, we control the foreign relations of all the Caribbean countries; not one of them could enter into serious relations abroad without our consent. We control their relations with each other, as was shown recently when the State Department thought it an outrage because Mexico recognized one President of Nicaragua when we had recognized another. We exercise the power of life and death over their governments in that no government can survive if we refuse it recognition. We help in many of these countries to decide what they call their elections, and we do not hesitate, as we have done recently in Mexico, to tell them what kind of constitution we think they ought to have.

Whatever we may choose to call it, this is what the world at large calls an empire, or at least an empire in the making. Admitting that the word has an unpleasant connotation, nevertheless it does seem as if the time had come for us to look the whole thing squarely in the face and to stop trying to deceive ourselves. We shall persuade nobody abroad by our words. We shall merely acquire a reputation for hypocrisy while we stumble unconsciously into the cares and the perils of empire. . . .

The refusal to recognize what we are doing in the Caribbean, the persistent use of meaningless, high-sounding generalities about "equality" in lieu of direct discussion of our increasing penetration and control, has prevented the formation of a body of intelligent and disinterested opinion.

When something happens in the Caribbean, the only voices heard are those of the oil men, the fruit men, mining men, bankers on one side, and the outraged voices of the Gladstone liberals on the other. The debate is conducted by the hard-boiled and soft-hearted. There is no opinion which is both hard-headed and far-seeing. The effect on policy is bad: the hard-boiled interest works continuously, and the rather amateurish officials in the State Department who are assigned to these duties are unable to cope with it. They do not know enough. They are not strong enough. They have no sufficient incentive to set themselves up against the powerful interests which are telling them what they ought to do. So usually the situation is developed without the check of public criticism until it reaches a climax where marines have to be used. Then the soft-hearted people roll over in bed and wake up. There is a great outcry about imperialism, and the policy of the government becomes confused and vacillating. After a while the soft-hearted clamor subsides, the normal relations are resumed between the hard-boiled interests and the ambitious young diplomats with a career to be made.

There can be no remedy for this until Americans make up their minds to recognize the fact that they are no longer a virginal republic in a wicked world, but they are themselves a world power, and one of the most portentous which has appeared in the history of mankind. When they have let that truth sink in, have digested it, and appraised it, they will cast aside the old phrases which conceal the reality, and as a fully adult nation, they will begin to prepare themselves for the part that their power and their position compel them to play.

III
THE FIRST CRISIS: SANDINO AND MARTÍNEZ

16.
UNDER SECRETARY OF STATE ROBERT OLDS: THE NICARAGUAN CRISIS (1927)

This Government indisputably has what may be designated a Caribbean policy which has never been definitely formulated and openly avowed. It rests upon irrefutable logic and has been enforced by long practice. Geographical facts can not be ignored. The Central American area down to and

U.S. National Archives, Record Group 59, 817.00/585, January 2, 1927.

including the Isthmus of Panama constitutes a legitimate sphere of influence for the United States, if we are to have due regard for our own safety and protection. That we can never be indifferent to what happens in this area is a principle of policy no less fully established than the Monroe Doctrine itself. The Panama Canal is a vital asset, and the effective control of the only other potential water route between the Atlantic and the Pacific, through the Republic of Nicaragua, is equally vital to our national interests. These considerations require no elaboration. If any country can ever be held to have a special interest in a given area it is the United States in its relation to all of Central America lying south of the Republic of Mexico. Until now the world at large has at least tacitly conceded this position.

[The issue] has been forced by Mexico, whose policy for many years has been progressively anti-American. Mexico has consistently attacked us by confiscation of the rights of our nationals on her own soil and is now delivering this flank attack upon us through Central America. . . .

Until now Central America has always understood that governments which we recognize and support stay in power, while those which we do not recognize and support fall. Nicaragua has become a test case. It is difficult to see how we can afford to be defeated.

The main thing we have at stake in this controversy is our prestige. If we permit the issue to be resolved against us we shall, at least for a time, take rank as a second-rate power so far as influence in Central America is concerned.

Moreover, it is to be expected that Mexico would capitalize her victory to the limit. The cancellation of our treaty rights covering the Nicaragua canal route would be one of the possibilities. The effect upon our interests in the adjoining republics would necessarily be disastrous. . . .

17.
HENRY L. STIMSON: AMERICAN POLICY IN NICARAGUA (1927)

I believe that the history of our recent action in Nicaragua . . . makes it clear that in no way have we transgressed upon the sovereignty and independence of the government of our sister nation. Every step which we have taken has been upon the earnest request of the Nicaraguan Government. More than that, the principal step which we propose to take—namely, to assist in the supervision of the national election of 1928—is one which we

From his *American Policy in Nicaragua* (New York: Scribner's, 1927).

have been formally requested to take not only by the government itself but by the opposition party to that government. General Moncada, who was formerly the commander-in-chief of the revolutionary forces and is now the duly elected political chief of the Liberal Party, has joined in the request of the government that we should so assist in this election, and his action has, I believe, the concurrence of the entire present directorate of that party in Nicaragua.

I believe therefore it is entirely accurate to say that our presence in Nicaragua today is for the purpose of taking an action which we have been requested to take by the government and which has the cordial concurrence of the opposition party in Nicaragua. Such an entire concurrence in any political object is a rare event in a Central American country.

In the next place, the purpose of our action, far from being in derogation of the rights and interests of Nicaragua as a sovereign and independent state, is to promote that independence and sovereignty in the most effective way. We are to assist her to hold for the first time in her history as a republic a free and fair election of her president. She has asked us to do this; her statesmen have freely admitted the prevalence of the ancient evil of government-controlled elections which has destroyed her democracy, and they have asked our president to assist them in eradicating this evil and starting them afresh upon the road of order and of peace. Can anyone say that this great constructive step is an impairment of her sovereignty?

18a.
AUGUSTO SANDINO: VIEWS ON POLITICS (1931)

All of Mexico was involved in the Sandino Affair, and the atmosphere of confusion was a thick fog that did not permit a very clear view. The most lucid of spirits, with no ideological ax to grind, saw Sandino's purity of heart in its precise configuration and affirmed his heroic stature; the interpretations of others were in accord with the color of their respective political lenses and some even vilified him. The masses expressed not judgments but the desire to know him, to see him appear in the capital city so that they might feast their eyes. Sandino recalled that moment in these words: "Meanwhile, the press contributed to converting the matter of who represented me into a cat-and-dog fight. . . . On the one hand, Farabundo Martí, and the Communists; on the other, Pavletich and the Apristas, and Paredes who turned out to be a loafer and a liar, even giving him the benefit of the

From Edelberto Torres, *Sandino y Sus Pares* (1931).

doubt, because it might have been the case that he acted mistakenly out of youthful enthusiasm but, in any case, he was the direct cause of the muddle.

"The truth of the matter is that President Portes Gil was not told that I was requesting military and financial aid from Mexico but that I was seeking asylum, and Paredes did not know this since he never saw President Portes Gil but dealt with him through third parties. I was so exasperated by the slander heaped on me because of the intrigues of the Communists, Apristas, and other revolutionary groups that I expelled Martí, Pavletich, and Paredes from my ranks, telling them that I never wanted to see them again."

A report sent by Martí to the central executive committee of the International Red Cross, dated February 22, 1931, in which he gives a detailed description of his strange exile aboard merchant vessels, contains a paragraph in which he expresses quite an unfavorable opinion of the great leader. This paragraph reads as follows: "In Nicaragua there is the power of Moncada, the agent of Yankee imperialism, whom we fought from the Segovias, when Sandino was being supported by the revolutionary anti-imperialist organizations, before he betrayed the world anti-imperialist movement to turn into a petit bourgeois liberal caudillo with aspirations of ruling Nicaragua in a semifeudal, semicolonial mold."

His deepest displeasure was caused by Paredes, who assured him that Portes Gil had indicated that he would help him with arms and money. Pavletich and Martí had good recollections of their relation with Sandino despite the fact that he did not accept the Aprism of the one or the Marxism of the other. He never swerved from his goal—expulsion of the invaders; nor would he change his tactic of struggle—war against them. It was impossible for him to accept political compromise with anybody in view of his iron-bound commitment to national liberation.

18b.
AUGUSTO SANDINO: INTERVIEW (1933)

We had seen General Sandino as he rode with several officers, inspecting his troops, when he said to me:

"See, we are not soldiers! We are the people. We are armed citizens."

Recalling these impressions of the social aspect of the Sandinista movement, I questioned the general one afternoon while we conversed, as he rocked himself in his rocking chair.

From *Conversaciones con Sandino,* interview with Ramón de Belausteguigoitia (1933).

"It has sometimes been said that your uprising had a definite social character. You were even branded Communists. This, I realize, was prompted by a tendentious smear campaign."

Sandino: "Attempts have been made at various times to twist this national-defense movement by converting it into more of a social struggle. I have opposed this with all my power. This is a nationalist and anti-imperialist movement. Ours is a banner of freedom for Nicaragua and all Hispano-America. It is a people's movement, in addition, in the social sense and we stand for a spirit of progress in social aspirations. Representatives of the International Federation of Labor, the Anti-Imperialist League, the Quakers have tried to see us here, to influence us. . . . We have always maintained our firm criterion that this was essentially a nationalist struggle. [Farabundo] Martí, the proponent of communism, saw that he couldn't put through his program and withdrew."

The General fell silent, lost in thought.

"In some countries, for example, Mexico, many have considered the Sandinista movement basically agrarian. I have had occasion during my stay in Nicaragua to see that land ownership is very fragmented and that this is a country of small holdings. There are barely any latifundios, and those are not very large. The agrarian movement, then, doesn't have much scope. The few that have no land do not starve to death, as had been said. In fact, I had the opportunity to bear out these impressions of a Promised Land in a way that was not very flattering, to be sure. There is a beautiful stand of mango trees near Granada that reaches as far as the lake. While a kind of caretaker who has the rights to the fruit picks it as best he can, two or three ragged fellows wait around for fruit to fall for their daily fare. It didn't pay them to work on the coffee plantations because they would earn fifteen centavos and so they preferred this simple pleasure. According to them, the country is ruined; there is no work anywhere."

I continue to insist with the General on the land question and ask him if he is in favor of abetting the country's small-property orientation by giving land to those who have none.

Sandino: "Yes, of course, and it's something that presents no problem for us. We have unoccupied lands, perhaps the country's best land. That is where we've been."

And the General explains his project for colonizing the Coco River zone, an extremely wild sector.

"Nicaragua imports many products it shouldn't—grain, fats, even meat —through the Atlantic Coast. All of that can be produced here. We will make the river navigable to begin with, then we will begin to open arable lands. The lushness of the vegetation is incredible. For the time being, the wild cacao alone would put them on a commercially profitable footing."

I: Do you believe in capital development?"

Sandino: "Unquestionably, capital may do its work and develop, but there must be no demeaning and exploitation of the worker."

I: "Do you believe immigration is advisable?"

Sandino: "There is a lot of land here to be distributed. They could teach us a lot. On the condition, however, that they respect our rights and treat our people as equals."

Then the General adds jokingly that if foreigners were to come there with other ideas, prompted by an inadmissible spirit of exploitation or political domination, they would put brambles in their path so that the going would not be so easy for them. Otherwise, all foreigners would be received as brothers, with open arms.

We recall at that moment the admirable disinterest shown at all times by General Sandino and the special clause in the agreement he had just signed which stipulated that his delegates express in his name "his absolute personal disinterest and irrevocable resolve to accept nothing that might reflect upon the motivations of his public conduct."

Then I asked him: "Have you no ambition to own a piece of land of your own?"

Sandino: "Ah, there are those who think I am going to become a latifundista! No, nothing of the kind. I will never own property. I have nothing. This house I live in is my wife's. Some say that is being foolish, but there's no reason for me to do otherwise."

Recalling that General Sandino is about to be a father, I ask: "What about your children, if you have any?"

Sandino: "No, that makes no difference! Let there be work and activities for everybody. Rather, I am in favor of the land belonging to the State. In this particular case of our colonization of the Coco, I favor a cooperative system. But that is something we have to go into more carefully.

"With respect to those things"—the General points out with a smile—"I had a case today of the many who come to tell me their trouble that illustrates the greedy spirit of some people who deal with money. This is a poor man with a big family who borrowed three hundred pesos a long time ago. Now, the man who lent him the money wants it back, and since he doesn't have it, the man wants to take his house, his cattle, everything, and even his children as slaves. I said to the lender, 'Do you think your money is worth the tears of this poor family?' Then I told the other man to go to one of those lawyers who they say obtain justice, and to come back another time. I hope to convince them. You see," the General adds, "what goes on here." And his face breaks into a broad smile that reveals his good nature.

I smile, too, at the recollection of this benevolent justice that displays his persuasive spirit rather than his guerrillero's sword.

I: "General, you are very fond of nature, aren't you?"

Sandino: "Yes."

I: "More than the city?"

Sandino: "Yes. Nature inspires and gives strength. Everything about it teaches us. The city wears us out and diminishes us. The country is not for selfishly closing yourself off in it, however, but to leave for the city to improve it.

"The sight of the plants, the trees, the birds and their ways, their life . . . are a constant education."

The General's clear and precise diction, the didactic intent of his explanations, even the gestures of his hand, which he moves continually showing his short straight fingers, reveal to us not the dreamer in the General but the man of searching, profound thoughts, in whom there burns the eternal desire to know.

Then, I ask him: "Is it true that you would like to study?"

Sandino: "Yes, I am interested in studying nature and the deepest relations between things. That is why I like philosophy. Naturally, I am not going to become a student at this point. But, to know, to learn . . . always!"

We then go on to talk about the military theme, about the aspects of killings in the campaign, and I ask him: "Were the Americans ruthless?"

Sandino: "Oh, I won't be the one to tell you that. Ask around and you'll find out."

I: "There is talk among your enemies, General, of unnecessary deaths, of crimes attributed to some of your troops."

Sandino: "If anything wrong is attributed, no matter what, I alone am responsible. Is it said that there were murders? Then, I'm the murderer. That injustices were committed? Then, I am the unjust one. It has been necessary to punish not only the invader but the one who is in complicity with him."

The General rises and speaks forcefully, his eyes burning with indignation.

I: "When people have spoken to me about such things, I have said that freedom is not won by smiling at the invaders. That is the price of freedom. But, naturally, I believe it sounds harsh when an outsider says it."

Sandino: "Oh, yes, the price of freedom!"

By association of ideas, General Sandino has turned to his strictness with his troops in maintaining discipline. Since there has been talk on this point, I ask him: "How many executions have you ordered among your troops?"

Sandino: "Five. Two generals, a captain, a sergeant, and a private. One of the generals because of offenses he committed. I was informed that he had raped several women. I got proof of the actions and ordered him executed. The other one was for treason."

And the General told how he was dubious about General Sequeira's loyalty from the time he arrived. One day, he was taken by surprise by planes that launched a furious bombardment. General Sandino remained motionless in a corner when, in the midst of the explosions of the bombs, he sensed somebody approaching stealthily. It was Sequeira, pistol in hand. "He wants to kill me!" Sandino thought. He immediately drew his gun and jumping on him forced him to put up his weapon. Sequeira was removed from his command but continued to take part in operations. The General caught him again in a situation similar to the foregoing. Just as he was about to be captured, he escaped toward the American camp. Sandino sent out a detachment to bring him back at once, dead or alive. They brought him back dead.

I: "Is it true that all your weapons, rifles or machine guns, have been captured from the enemy? What percentage do you estimate?"

Sandino: "You can say that all of them outside of a few rifles and the original 'Concons,' which don't work anymore. Those without rifles waited until the enemy was engaged or they went into action with bombs and pistols, or simply formed part of the reserves."

I: "General, did you have a feeling during the struggle that you would win a decisive moral victory?"

Sandino: "No, when I got into this undertaking, I believed I would never come out of it any way but dead. I considered it necessary for Nicaragua's freedom and to raise the banner of dignity in our Indo-Hispanic countries."

19.
BERNARD NALTZ: THE U.S. MARINES IN NICARAGUA

What had the two major interventions accomplished? The first, with its lightning swift campaign, had forestalled possible European intervention

From *The United States Marines in Nicaragua* (Washington, 1968), an official Marine Corps history.

and provided the republic with an opportunity to attain financial stability. Legitimate American investments, the lives and property of American citizens, all were protected. The Marine regiment had restored order quickly enough, but statesmen failed to arrive at a solution for the problems that plagued Nicaragua.

Less successful from a political point of view was the second intervention. True, the Marines had halted a bloody civil war; but they had not brought peace to the country, for Sandino's die-hards were never brought to task. Worse still, patriotic Latin Americans came to hate the United States because of its interference in Nicaraguan affairs.

Some estimate of this political failure may be gained from a glimpse at post-occupation Nicaragua. The American Marines and seamen killed in action during the campaign left behind them two great monuments, the Guardia Nacional to maintain order and an electoral law to insure honest elections. Neither survived for long.

Under the direction of its new leader, Anastasio Somoza, the Guardia became the decisive factor in Nicaraguan politics. In fact, it was the Guardia which was given the assignment of murdering Sandino after the rebel leader had been given amnesty by the Sacasa government. From Jefe of the Guardia, Somoza became President of Nicaragua in 1936. For two decades he was dictator of the country, naming Presidents, dismissing them at his whim, or ruling as Chief Executive himself. He died 29 September 1956 as a result of an assassin's bullet, to be succeeded in office by his son Luis.

20.
MAJOR A.R. HARRIS: REPORT ON EL SALVADOR (1931)

About the first thing one observes when he goes to San Salvador is the number of expensive automobiles on the streets. There seems to be nothing but Packards and Pierce Arrows about. There appears to be nothing between these high priced cars and the ox cart with its bare-footed attendant. There is practically no middle class between the very rich and the very poor.

From the people with whom I talked I learned that roughly ninety percent of the wealth of the country is held by about one half of one percent of the population. Thirty or forty families own nearly everything in the

U.S. National Archives, Record Group 59, 816.00/828, December 22, 1931.

country. They live in almost regal splendor with many attendants, send their children to Europe or the United States to be educated, and spend money lavishly (on themselves). The rest of the population has practically nothing. . . .

I imagine the situation in El Salvador today is very much like France was before its revolution, Russia before its revolution and Mexico before its revolution. The situation is ripe for communism and the communists seem to have found that out. On the first of December, 1931, there was in the Post Office in San Salvador over 3,000 pounds of communist literature emanating from New York City, which had been confiscated by the postal authorities during the previous month.

The authorities seem to realize that the situation is dangerous and are quite alert in their fight against communistic influences. One thing in their favor is that the people never go hungry. The poor can always get fruit and vegetables for nothing and they can steal [fire] wood. . . .

Also, since they never had anything, they do not feel the want very acutely of things they have never had. . . .

A socialistic or communistic revolution in El Salvador may be delayed for several years, ten or even twenty, but when it comes it will be a bloody one.

21.
ROQUE DALTON: MIGUEL MARMOL

A moment came when an emergency meeting was called to consider a series of secret reports that had come to the attention of the leadership of the Party which indicated that a coup against the Araujo government was in the offing, inspired probably by the Minister of Defense, General Martínez, himself. Several comrades and I declared ourselves in favor, in principle, of beating the coup to the punch by arousing the masses to a national insurrection, since a government headed by General Martínez, who was personally and directly responsible for most of the massacres and repression that I have described, would be a ferocious antipopular, terrorist dictatorship. I believe that the prospect of such a dictatorship removed any taint of adventurism from an uprising that would be proposed under those circumstances, and the truth of the matter is that we could count on sufficient popular strength to be optimistic about it. We would see later on

From his *Miguel Marmol, Los Sucesos de 1932 en El Salvador.*

what was lacking. Farabundo Martí, however, took our proposals coolly and said that it didn't matter all that much if General Martínez were to take power, that, in any case, our real possibilities of preventing it were very scanty, and a national uprising was too high a price for avoiding the advent of a dictatorial government. And he added, what is more, that the conditions for success of an uprising would be more favorable under a criminal government. Farabundo quoted copiously from Lenin and said that the Salvadoran Army was not sufficiently discredited yet in the eyes of the people while, on the other hand, a civilian government like Araujo's was already totally discredited. It was therefore possible that a coup by an army man like Martínez would be supported by large sectors. Farabundo said that we should direct not an uprising, but rather measures for a positive confrontation of the coup, the safeguarding of the organizations, the maintaining of mass influence under the new circumstances, and so forth. That same night, a worker by the name of Contreras, who was our candidate for mayor of Ahuachapán, came to the meeting. He arrived in an extremely agitated state to report that the Ahuachapán base was surrounded by a contingent of 900 peasants who had decided to settle accounts for the abuses they had been suffering at the hands of the military authorities. He reported that the admonishing of Colonel Escobar, the commander of the regiment, had gotten nowhere and that the local heads of the Communist Party had asked for a delegate from the Central Committee to come and calm the peasants down and try to get them to go back home before the massacre started. I was assigned the task and left at once. When I got to Ahuachapán, I talked to the besiegers and was able to convince them to go back to work. Colonel Escobar said, "Those sons of bitches can only deal with their own kind." A week later the same situation came up. Seven hundred peasants began a determined encirclement of the local military headquarters. This meant that the people in Ahuachapán and throughout the entire west were physically up in arms. Again, I was the one assigned to pacify the mob and again I was successful. However, now the peasants told me that this was the last time, and that I should tell the Party to take care not to send any more people to throw cold water on them, since the next pacifier who came around (even if it was me) would run the risk of "getting himself put to the machete before the class enemy." The people were boiling; they'd had it. The Party ordered me to remain in the Ahuachapán zone to continue the pre-election work in the countryside. The task was tremendous and under pressures of every kind. I worked in the city by day and in the mountains at night, eating when I could and sleeping once every three days. Around the time of the elections, I began having hallucinations because of weakness and overwork. I had gotten to the point where I was seeing the National Guard shooting at me and killing me and finally the time came when I fainted dead away. The Red Cross took me to Santa Ana and from there sent me to San Salvador, but I could not rest for even a week since the local leadership in Ahuachapán insisted on my being around. The prospect of a violent outbreak was no longer a remote possibility; it could be felt just around the corner. I was very much afraid of generalized violence being imminent, since I knew that the people would be the ones to suffer the worst, and because of that I tried in my work to channel popular anger in the direction of a general strike, a level somewhere between "electionism" and insurrection. The Party was not aware of this; it was purely my personal doing. The thing was that right then, those of us who were at the mass fronts were the ones who really understood the evolution of the struggle and our opinions had to prevail over the calculations being made by the Central Committee back there in the light of theory. I believe that it was because we didn't do that more thoroughly and in an organized manner that we lost the battle in 1932 so overwhelmingly. It was because, as we say in El Salvador, we were fighting with our pants down.

22.
GREGORIO BUSTAMANTE: THE MATANZA IN EL SALVADOR

Great popular uprisings broke out in the western departments of the Republic in December 1931, the principal organizers of which were the leaders, Farabundo Martí and the students Mario Zapata and Alfonso Luna. They were captured at their headquarters in the suburbs of San Salvador and executed on the spot without a trial of any sort. Lists of followers were taken from them that included the names of workers who lived in the capital. All of those were hunted down and executed the moment they were caught, including innocent working people who had been denounced for personal grudges, the gossip of any old woman sufficing to send many honorable men with large families to their death. Trucks loaded with victims of the police left nightly for the banks of the Acelhuate River, where they were executed and buried in great trenches that had been readied for them, without the names of the martyrs having even been recorded by those barbarous executioners. . . .

General Martínez mobilized forces to put down the uprisings, giving

From his *Historia Militar de El Salvador,* pp. 106–7.

highly drastic orders with no restrictions to the leaders of those troops. The machine guns began to sow panic and death in the regions of Juayúa, Izalco, Nahuizalco, Colón, Santa Tecla, the Santa Ana volcano, and all the coastal villages from Jiquilisco to Acajutla. Some villages were wiped out completely and the workers of the capital were barbarously decimated. One ingenuous group presented themselves voluntarily before the authorities to offer their services. They were ushered into the National Guard building, where they were lined up and machine-gunned to the last man. Panic spread throughout the business sector of the country and all levels of society. Nobody's life or property was safe. Various foreign businessmen sought the help of their respective countries. The British government sent warships to the port of Acajutla, where permission was requested from General Martínez to disembark troops to aid their countrymen, but the tyrant refused, alleging that his authority was sufficient to control the situation. As proof of this, he had a telegraphic report transcribed for them that had been transmitted by General Don José Tomás Calderón from the city of Santa Ana, which read: "As of this moment, I have liquidated over 4,000 Communists."

The slaughter was horrible, with neither children, women, nor old people spared. In Juayúa, all decent persons who were not Communists were ordered to appear at the Town Hall to receive safe-conducts. When the square was filled with men, women, and children, the streets leading from the square were blocked off and the innocent multitude was machine-gunned, leaving alive not even the poor dogs who always faithfully follow their Indian masters. A few days afterward, the official who directed the terrible massacre described in full detail the macabre deed committed in the parks and walks of San Salvador, bragging about being the hero of the operation. The slaughter was continued on a lesser scale by the infamous *"Cívicas,"* organized in all the villages by General Martínez. These were groups made up of depraved men who committed unmentionable abuses against life and property and the honor of innocent girls. Reports came in daily to the President on the number of victims during the previous twenty-four hours and the pillage was so great that even the poultry were nearly exterminated.

Reports published by various persons assert that the number of dead came to over 30,000. The actual figure, however, amounted to no less than 24,000 persons murdered. The black months of December 1931 and January, February, and March 1932 will never be forgotten.

IV
LIVING WITH THE DICTATORS

23.
SECRETARY OF STATE DEAN ACHESON: MEMO ON SOMOZA (1952)

CONFIDENTIAL

Subject: Visit of General Anastasio Somoza, President of Nicaragua

President Somoza of Nicaragua is having lunch with you at 1:00 P.M. on Friday, May 2. He is in Washington, accompanied by his wife, Salvadora De Bayle de Somoza, on route to the Lahey Clinic in Boston for medical treatment. His visit is entirely unofficial. President Somoza will come to the White House after calling on me in the morning.

President Somoza has two sons: Luis, a Senator, and Anastasio Jr., a graduate of West Point (1946) and Chief of the General Staff. A daughter, Lillian, is married to Nicaragua's present Ambassador to the United States, Guillermo Sevilla-Sacasa. He is proud of the fact that he has ten grandchildren, and also that one son is married to an American. As a young man Somoza lived in Philadelphia for six years and there met his Nicaraguan wife. He speaks fluent English and likes to recall your visit to Nicaragua when you toured Central America on a special mission as Senator.

Somoza is an able man with an engaging personality. He is informal, genial, energetic, persuasive and politically astute. He is also impulsive, vain and egocentric. His desire for personal gain is very great.

In 1933 he became and still remains Director General of the Nicaraguan National Guard which the American occupation forces had organized. In 1936 he ousted the president. In a subsequent vote he was overwhelmingly elected to the presidency. He served in this office from 1937 to 1947. His present term runs from 1950 to 1957.

While the Nicaraguan government is democratic and republican in form, President Somoza has run it largely as a one man show. His methods

Memorandum to the President, May 1, 1952. From *Foreign Relations of the United States 1952–1954,* Vol. 4, pp. 1369–70.

have often been criticized in the United States and Latin America. He has, however, restored order to Nicaragua and in recent years has been less repressive. Nicaragua now has a two party system and a free press. Recent delegations to international meetings have been bi-partisan.

Nicaragua has consistently supported United States foreign policy. The government and the people give every evidence of friendship to the United States and our prior occupation of Nicaragua has left no residue of ill-feeling. Somoza, himself, is a great admirer of this country and he considers his official visit in 1939 as guest of President Roosevelt a highlight of his career. The Fourth of July is celebrated enthusiastically throughout Nicaragua.

24.
PATRICK MCMAHON: SOMOZA OF NICARAGUA
(1955)

Of all the chiefs of state in the world today, the one who is the most friendly to the United States of America, one who has demonstrated his friendliness by actions as well as by words, is Anastasio Somoza, President of the Republic of Nicaragua.

No government cooperated more wholeheartedly during the war than did that of Somoza in Nicaragua. And no government has cooperated with us more firmly in the diplomatic wrangles of the Cold War period.

A typical illustration of Somoza's wartime attitude was recited by a former Air Force officer who, back in 1942, was instructed to grab a plane to Nicaragua and see if he could negotiate permission for the United States to build an air base in that territory. Since such negotiations are complicated, lengthy matters, he was ordered to pack for a stay of several weeks.

When the officer's plane landed at the Managua airfield, he was whisked by private car to the Presidential Palace and, to his surprise, immediately received by Somoza himself. The officer, who was selected for the job because of his excellent command of Spanish, addressed the President in his own tongue. He talked less than ten minutes when Somoza interrupted him and in perfect English, with only the slightest trace of accent, said:

"The United States wants to build air bases in Nicaragua? But, of course. Just tell me what you need. You shall have it."

And less than two hours after he had landed in Nicaragua, the dazed

From *American Mercury,* 1955, pp. 132–36.

officer was back in his plane, with a treaty in his pocket that was virtually a *carte blanche.*

The Nicaraguan Ambassador to Washington, Doctor Guillermo Sevilla-Sacasa, tells another story which is equally illustrative of Somoza's postwar attitude toward the United States. Don Guillermo has represented his country at more than fifty international conferences, including all major meetings of the United Nations and the Organization of American States during the past ten years. During eight of these years Somoza was President of Nicaragua. Before each conference, according to diplomatic custom, he asks his government for instructions.

"And each time the same reply comes back, signed by the President," the Ambassador says.

"Even the words are the same. Just one short sentence. 'Cooperate fully with the delegation of the United States of America.' "

As a result, Nicaragua is the only country in the world today that has supported the United States on every single dispute, at every international assembly.

This has meant much more to this country than just a single supporting vote from a tiny neighboring republic. On numerous occasions the Soviet Union, Britain, and even the Arab states have sought the support of the Latin American bloc in opposition to certain U.S. policies. And the firm support our policies have received from Ambassador Sevilla-Sacasa in the private consultations of the Latin American diplomats has had an invaluable effect in winning solid hemispheric support for the U.S. position.

But curiously, and ironically, Somoza's warm display of friendship to the United States has not always been returned in kind. From the time he first became President in 1937, he has been the target of unrelenting attack by an influential group of U.S. journalists who are more interested in jamming their own particular brand of ideology down the throats of other nations than in reporting facts to their own readers.

And their prejudices have been consistently reflected in the attitudes of a powerful group of policy-making officials in the Departments of State and Defense in dealing with the Nicaraguan government. As one U.S. diplomat remarked:

"We have not made one single request of the Nicaraguan government that has been turned down. On the other hand, we in return have not only refused to give them the small amount of military assistance they have requested, but our Department of State will not even allow them to buy arms in the United States—with their own money.

"Also, Nicaragua desperately needs more and better highways to continue its economic improvement. A modest, well-planned highway program in Central America, financed jointly by the U.S. and the local governments, would have a tremendous economic effect on the entire region, and strengthen it immeasurably against Communist infiltration. It would cost us less over a four- or five-year period than we spend in a single year in economic aid to Israel, 8,000 miles away. Yet the total amount of assistance we have given all of Central America and Panama, since the end of the war, has been less than that which we gave the little city of Trieste."

But what Somoza wants and needs most desperately—and has not received—is a firm U.S. policy toward the Communist conspiracy that already has firm control in Guatemala, dominance in Costa Rica, and which threatens to engulf all Central America. Failing this, he would like at least a free hand for his own government—and the friendly governments of Panama, El Salvador and Honduras—to deal with the menace in their own way without interference from Washington. Even this has not been granted.

The reason for our peculiar official attitude toward Somoza is not too hard to find. "Tacho," as he is known to his countrymen, is believed by our devout "ideologists" to be a dictator. He is said to have seized power twenty years ago by undemocratic means. He has suppressed democratic forces in Nicaragua, ruthlessly, they charge. He has looted the public treasury to enrich himself. He has used the force of his government to ruin his business competitors. Those are the charges so freely aired in the U.S. press against "Tacho" Somoza, and which account for the unfriendly attitude by our government to the country that has consistently supported us, in peace as well as in war.

This reporter, in a brief, recent visit to Nicaragua, does not pretend to have come up with the entire answer, or to have learned the entire truth about "Tacho" Somoza. But he did learn some very obvious facts which somehow seem to have escaped the attention of many of the journalists who visit there, as well as many of our officials in Washington. Facts which warrant considerable attention in judging the man and the country who have been so friendly to us.

Fact No. 1: There are fewer soldiers and police—the inevitable trappings of the true dictatorship—in Managua than in any other capital he ever visited, including Washington, D.C.

Fact No. 2: Somoza has brought peace and political stability to a country that for nearly half a century knew nothing but constant, bloody, political turmoil. The continuous warring of opposing factions for power had been so vicious that twice within twenty-five years we had to send the Marines to Nicaragua and occupy the country to stop the bloodshed and restore a semblance of order.

Fact No. 3: This alleged dictator was recently elected to the Presidency by an overwhelming majority in what U.S. residents there describe as "a freer election than many of our own, back home."

Fact No. 4: "Tacho" Somoza permits a vigorous opposition press to operate, without molestation, and to criticize his government freely.

Fact No. 5: Several members of the opposition party occupy seats in Somoza's cabinet.

Fact No. 6: During the past several years, only five men in Nicaragua have been jailed for political reasons—and these were Communists.

And Somoza's method of dealing with them provides an excellent object lesson to those interested in effective ways of handling Communists. For all the while these Communist leaders were in jail, two days each week they were escorted under armed guard to their places of employment and forced to earn enough money to support their families. "Why should our government have to support families of those traitors?" Somoza asks, reasonably enough. The story quickly went the rounds of all classes in Nicaragua, as it appealed to the keen Latin appreciation for irony. And when the Communist leaders were finally released from jail, they found to their intense chagrin that instead of being the "martyrs of the working class," as they had so fondly imagined, they had become the laughing-stock of all Nicaragua.

Probably the most effective way that has yet been found to deal with Communism is ridicule like this.

Fact No. 7: While it is true that Somoza has become a very wealthy man, even his more temperate critics agree that he has done so by risking his own, personal money in investments that were regarded as so speculative that most Nicaraguans would not touch them.

Fact No. 8: And while Somoza's investments have greatly enriched Somoza, they have also enriched all Nicaragua. He has pioneered new agricultural enterprises and methods, started new small industries, opened many lines of new business. He not only has given employment to thousands, but he has set an example for other Nicaraguan farmers and businessmen which has had a beneficial effect on the entire economy.

Fact No. 9: During the eighteen years since Somoza first became President, and particularly during the past four years, his government has achieved what U.S. Ambassador Thomas E. Whelan calls an "economic miracle." Twenty years ago when the Marines left Nicaragua, the country's entire holding of gold and foreign exchange was less than $400,000. Today it is nearly $30 million. As recently as 1940, the country's exports totaled only $3.7 million; its imports, $7 million. In 1952 its exports were $42 million, its imports, $39 million, and both are still increasing. Once a one-crop country—coffee—Nicaragua's agriculture has been expanded and diversified under Somoza, and it now exports, in addition to coffee, large amounts of cotton, cattle, sugar, cereals, and sesame seeds. As a result, the living standards, although still very modest, have risen from among the lowest in the world to among the highest in Central America. Nicaragua's credit rating, which up to a few years ago was virtually nonexistent, is now among the highest of any government in the world.

Fact No. 10: Unlike many governments in Latin America which are making every effort to kick private U.S. capital out of their countries, Somoza is anxious to attract it. He has a strong admiration for U.S. business methods, and particularly our technical ability. He, himself, obtained his business training in the United States. His two sons were educated here: Tachito at West Point; Luis at the University of California. (In fact, Somoza met his wife while he was living in Philadelphia.) Somoza not only wants to attract U.S. private capital, but he would like to have American farmers, engineers, technicians and businessmen come to Nicaragua and settle, and help him develop the country.

Those are just a few of the obvious *facts* about Somoza's government. There is one other which should be mentioned and which, to this writer, seems the most important of all.

Partly as a reflection of Somoza's personal feeling and partly as a result of the unceasing efforts of our popular Ambassador Whelan, the friendliness toward the United States has percolated through all classes of Nicaraguans.

One of the most pleasant experiences I have ever had in a foreign country was a ride with Ambassador Whelan from Managua to the Pacific Coast through rich agricultural lands, over narrow mountain trails, and through tangled jungle. Along the way we passed hundreds of farmers and farm laborers, plus gangs of engineers, surveyors and workmen engaged in building a new highway. And almost without exception, when those people spotted the American flag on the Embassy car, they smiled broadly at us, waved, and shouted something about "El Embajador Americano."

There's practically no place left in the world today where the sight of the American flag, or the American Ambassador, evokes such a warm response.

Perhaps that is the most important thing that our officials in Washington might consider in shaping their policies toward the friendly little neighboring republic of Nicaragua and its president, "Tacho" Somoza.

25.
RIGOBERTO LÓPEZ PÉREZ: FAREWELL LETTER TO HIS MOTHER (1956)

León, September 1956

My Dear Mother,

Though you have never known, I have always been involved in everything concerned with attacking the dismal regime which rules over our fatherland. In view of the fact that all attempts at making Nicaragua once again (or for the first time) a free country, without stain or dishonor, have failed, and even though my comrades disagree with me, I have decided to try to be the person who will begin the end of this tyranny.

If God wills me to die in the attempt, I do not want anybody to be blamed in the very least, for it has all been my own doing.

X, who knows us all very well, has remained in charge, as have all our fellow countrymen residing here, of helping you in whatever you may need.

As I told you once before, some time ago I took a life insurance policy for 10,000 córdobas, with double indemnity, which is to say 20,000 córdobas. Y will pull all the necessary strings for this money to reach your hands, as it is in your name. There is an exception to this: as you well know. I have always lived with the Andrade family, who have been so kind to me for such a long time, and I want 1,000 córdobas of that money to be given to Miss Dina Andrade so that she may finish her schooling, as she might be forced to abandon her studies for lack of funds. . . .

I hope you will take all this calmly and realize that what I have done is a duty that any Nicaraguan who loves his fatherland should have carried out long ago.

This is not a sacrifice, but a duty I hope I have been able to fulfill.

If you take things the way I wish you to, I assure you that I will be very happy.

So, no sadness, because a duty to the fatherland well carried out is the greatest satisfaction a righteous man, such as I have striven to be, can take with him.

If you take things serenely and in the absolute conviction that I have done my highest duty as a Nicaraguan, I shall be very grateful to you.

Your son who has always loved you so much,
Rigoberto

26.
PAUL KENNEDY: A SALVADORAN ELECTION

Long before the actual campaigning began for the 1956 elections, and that was fully a year before the change in administration, the various interest groups and prospective candidates began jockeying for position.

This premature activity could have been absorbed without too much difficulty, and, in fact, President Osorio* was even then preparing for any untoward trends, but the major preoccupation just then was evidence of a split developing within the armed forces. That was always a bad sign in El Salvador, the system being what it was. Entrenched colonels were being jostled by cliques of majors and captains who had caught a distant scent of power. Added to this was the clear indication that for the first time since 1931 a civilian was preparing to run for the presidency. This was Roberto Canessa, a brilliant young statesman and member of a wealthy coffee family. For a brief time there were five contestants, and then four, three of them military or military-diplomatic, and finally there was only one, after possibly the bitterest campaign in the country's history. Sr. Canessa, in addition to having been constantly harassed by attempts to disqualify him, was physically attacked by an obviously officially-inspired mob. Another candidate, Colonel José Alberto Funes, at the time an ambassador for his country, was charged with irregularities in the conduct of his office. And so it went.

Had it not been for the violence and the openly corrupt election practices, the campaign would have provided some humorous relief. Colonel José María Lemus, candidate of the administration's Partido Revolucionario Unión Democrático (PRUD), was challenged on the grounds that he was not born of Salvadoran parents, and his party forthwith displayed documents to show he was the illegitimate son of a Salvadoran schoolteacher and a Honduran woman. Sr. Canessa was challenged for allegedly falsifying his age on a birth certificate, and he produced his mother and father and the delivering physician to verify it. He was declared ineligible anyway. One of the more obscure candidates campaigned on a promise of an ox and six acres of land for every farmer. He was immediately denounced as a Communist. He escaped being jailed but lapsed into obscurity without a whimper.

From his *The Middle Beat,* Ed. Stanley Ross (New York, 1971), pp. 176–77.

*Osorio had been installed provisionally by a group of military officers following a coup. Two years later, in 1950, he was elected president backed by a party of his own creation.

Colonel Lemus, who in order to campaign had resigned his post as head of the Ministry of the Interior, which includes the national police, clearly had the advantage. To overcome this advantage the remaining candidates made a listless attempt at coalition, a classical gang-up strategy in Latin America which nearly always fails. The attempt to form an effective coalition failed for a number of reasons, including the fact that in the process some of the most promising of the eligible candidates were cancelled out.

Tension grew rapidly as the public learned that a blatant political fraud was underway. A virtual state of siege was invoked by President Osorio and along with it foreign press censorship, the latter being totally ineffective except for slowing down traffic while the correspondents found ways of getting copy out. Troops patrolled the streets throughout the nights and the rumors of revolt against Osorio and his disciple Lemus (whom Colonel Osorio was later instrumental in overthrowing) continued to proliferate so rapidly that very few persons left their homes at night.

The election, when it finally took place, was wholly farcical. Crowds of paid voters were openly hauled from one voting booth to another in government trucks. There was little or no control attempted at the various polling places. Foreign correspondents visiting the outlying voting stations were given ballots and told, amidst great jollity, to go ahead and vote. I kept mine for years as a souvenir.

V
THE GUATEMALAN EPISODE

27.
THOMAS KARNES: UNITED FRUIT IN CENTRAL AMERICA

United first entered Honduras on a large scale in 1913 when it purchased . . . the right to build a railroad and grow bananas. . . . In the same year other concessions gave United the right to the Trujillo Railroad. In this fashion United's two railroads, which also operated banana farms and purchased from local growers, dominated zones of influence. . . . Almost instantly the lush banana lands of Honduras became United's chief supplier and within a decade the company's Honduran investment and pro-

From his *Tropical Enterprise* (Baton Rouge: Louisiana State University Press, 1978).

ductivity tripled those of every other country where the company was located. The chief port was Tela. Thousands of workers were hired, many from various Caribbean islands. . . . United's subsidiary, Tela Railroad Company, built a hospital, ice plant, generators, and water systems, and in 1914 began construction of a one-thousand-foot wharf. Expending $200,000 a month on payrolls alone, United thrust its rail lines south and east from Tela, clearing jungle and draining fertile banana lands as the line grew. The company declared $7,250,000 net profit for the 1915 banana year, just 100 percent higher than the year before. The increase the next year was another startling 100 percent. In 1920 with its ships returned by the government, and shortages and strikes ending, the company announced payment of more than $6,289,000 in dividends and a profit in excess of $38 million. By 1921 the United States consul at Tela could report his belief that Tela had not only outstripped La Ceiba as Honduras' largest banana exporter, it probably ranked first in the entire world. In the week of his report 180,000 stems had been shipped from Tela at thirty cents gold per stem stateside. The division claimed two hundred miles of railroad, some fifty farms, five banana shipments each week, and two cruise ships from New York each month. . . .

One study concludes that in the 1920s and 1930s agricultural workers in Nicaragua were paid as poorly as any in America because of the great competition within labor's ranks. The first workmen's compensation act did not become effective until 1930 and provided only minimum assistance in accidents and illness; the employer was required only to pay thirty córdobas (at that time on a par with the United States dollar) in death benefits when a fatal accident occurred on the job. No general labor code was passed until 1945, but it was more a statement of goals than a series of obligations. As a result Standard and other foreign firms could provide just about what pay and services they wished in Nicaragua. . . .

In September of 1929 . . . a decree from the [Honduran province] of Atlántida [put] into effect a maximum work day of eight hours without any reduction in wages. The regular work day for Standard had been ten hours, however, and manager J. R. O'Connor informed the workers at La Ceiba that the company would put the reduced day into effect but would also reduce pay proportionately, leaving employees with only 80 percent of their former salaries. O'Connor contended that the governor had exceeded his authority, and that, in fact, the national act upon which Atlántida's law was based had said nothing about the workers retaining the same salary. The hourly workers at Standard went out on strike September 5. The cause of solidarity was weakened by the fact that the railroad and other workers on monthly payrolls did not support the strike, and the strikers were able to prevent the loading of only one ship and then by a threat of force. . . . The next morning the military commander of the district brought in reinforcements to the Ceiba garrison. . . .

By that evening a full crew was at work, although many of the nonstriking workers feared for their safety and crawled under the docks to avoid the pickets on the way to work. . . . Over the ensuing weekend the strike collapsed.

Although the American consul did not believe that the disturbance had been caused by communists, he concluded that they had taken advantage of the strike. The government of Honduras went further, however, and ordered the arrest by local commanders of all foreign communists found in their districts. Late in the following June the republic declared martial law in the four departments, including Atlántida, where American influence predominated. Some forty foreign-born were deported and others arrested for an alleged plan to destroy all private foreign property and bring about a general strike on the Fourth of July, a holiday in the American districts. The deportations succeeded in preventing the attacks, however, and Honduras' labor situation quieted once more.

28.
AMBASSADOR JOHN PEURIFOY: IMPRESSIONS OF ARBENZ (1953)

SECRET

Guatemala City, December 17, 1953—7 p.m.

154. President and Mrs. Arbenz entertained my wife and me privately at dinner last night and we had a frank six hour discussion of the Communist problem here lasting until two this morning. President showed depth of his feeling against United Fruit Company and his admiration for Guatemala's Communist leaders, leaving no doubt he intended to continue to collaborate with them.

I opened conversation by telling President I was interested in seeing what I could do to improve relations and asked if he had any suggestions. He began by saying problem here is one between United Fruit Company and his government. He spoke at length and bitterly on Fruit Company's history since 1904, complaining especially that now his Government has a $70 million budget to meet and collects only $150,000 in taxes.

I interrupted here to say I thought we should put first things first, that as long as Communists exerted their present influence in Guatemalan Government I did not see real hope of better relations.

President then answered that there were some Communists in his Government and that [they] had certain amount of influence, but they were "local." He described his friendship with Victor Manuel Gutiérrez, Communist secretary general of country's only national labor federation, and José Manuel Fortuny, head of Guatemala Communist Party. They were both "honest" and followed Guatemalan not Soviet interests. They went to Moscow (Fortuny is on trip there now) merely to study Marxism, not necessarily to get instructions.

I asked by name about several Communists and Communist suspects in National Agrarian Department, directorate general of Radio Broadcasting and Guatemala Institute of Social Security. Before translating, Mrs. Arbenz started in each case to deny [they] were Communists, but three times President contradicted her saying he was sure they were. I asked whether Government [advertising] helped support Communist *Tribuna Popular* and after Mrs. Arbenz again started to deny, President admitted that it did. Also asked about Guatemalan Congressional memorial observances for Stalin's death and Mrs. Arbenz explanation was Guatemalan people regarded Roosevelt, Churchill and Stalin as saviors of world. Communists presented no threat and his government was in full control.

Touching on the Caracas conference, I told President that since he has said Communists were of no consequence in Guatemala, I found it strange Guatemala had cast its vote against inclusion of the item on Communist infiltration on agenda. He said that this was interference in internal affairs, that they did not want outsiders coming in to investigate their country. I told him this was not a question of investigating, but discussing means and methods of combatting a godless ideology, but he reiterated views that Communism was not a threat. President took up agrarian reform, saying there had been much opposition from American circles and others in the country. I told him we had worked and were working with countries who had introduced land reform, citing my experience in Greece* and present situation in Bolivia. I said the difference seemed to lie in the administration, not in principle of assisting poor people to obtain land. I pointed out the explanation was perhaps in fact that National Agrarian Department was dominated by Communists. I said I was sorry he had had no concrete proposals to make to improve our relations. He then reverted to Fruit Company and said this was the stumbling block: It was a large American organization which dominated press in U.S. I explained Fruit Company was relatively small by US standards and no corporation as far as I knew dominated any of US press whose Guatemalan reports were based on

*Ambassador Peurifoy had been Ambassador to Greece, 1950–53.

on-the-spot investigation. At one point President stated if there were a choice, it would be for Guatemala to live under Communist domination than live for fifty years with Fruit Company.

Foregoing took place in atmosphere of frank and polite exchange of views, and on leaving I told President I was disappointed because we had not accomplished anything. He said after I had become familiar with country, I would probably come around to his way of thinking. I told him I did not believe anything would make me convert to Communism and feared situation would get worse because Americans had given blood and paid high taxes and would continue to do so as long as Communism threatened free nations. President ended by giving me private phone numbers, saying I should get in touch with him whenever I wanted without going through Foreign Office.

I came away definitely convinced that if President is not a Communist he will certainly do until one comes along, and that normal approaches will not work in Guatemala. I am now assessing situation in this light and expect to submit recommendations in a few days.

29.
FOREIGN MINISTER GUILLERMO TORIELLO GARIDO:
DEFENDING GUATEMALA (1954)

What is the real and effective reason for describing our Government as communist? From what source comes the accusation that we threaten continental solidarity and security? Why do they wish to intervene in Guatemala?

The answers are simple and evident. The plan of national liberation being carried out with firmness by my Government has necessarily affected the privileges of the foreign enterprises that are impeding the progress and the economic development of the country. The highway to the Atlantic, besides connecting the important productive zones it traverses, is destroying the monopoly of internal transportation to the ports now held by the Ferrocarriles Internacionales de Centro América (an enterprise controlled by the United Fruit Company), in order to increase foreign trade free of grievous and discriminatory charges. With construction of national ports and docks, we are putting an end to the monopoly of the United Fruit

---

Address at the Third Plenary Session of the Organization of American States, Tenth Inter-American Conference, Caracas, Venezuela, March 5, 1954. OAS Document 95, SP-23.

Company, and we will thus make it possible for the nation to increase and to diversify its foreign trade through the use of maritime transport other than the White Fleet, also belonging to the United Fruit Company, which now controls this essential instrument of our international commercial relations.

With the realization of the plan of national electrification, we shall put an end to foreign monopoly of electric power, indispensable to our industrial development, which has been delayed by the lack, the scarcity, or the distribution failures of that important means of production.

With our Agrarian Reform, we are abolishing the latifundia, including those of the United Fruit Company itself. Following a dignified policy, we have refused to broaden the concessions of that company. We have insisted that foreign investment be in accordance with our laws, and we have recovered and maintained absolute independence in our foreign policy.

All this is being done in Guatemala, and yet the American nations are not aware of it. The news that reaches them through the news agencies that serve the cause of the monopolies is distorted news, almost always defamatory. All these modest efforts to bring about changes in the interest of progress are called Communism.

These bases and purposes of the Guatemalan revolution cannot be catalogued within a Communist ideology or policy: a political-economic platform like that put forward by the government of Guatemala, which is settling in rural areas thousands of individual landowners, individual farmers, can never be conceived of as a Communist plan. Far from that, we believe that raising the standard of living and the income of rural and urban workers alone stimulates the capitalistic economic development of the country and the sociological bases of a genuinely Guatemalan functional democracy. . . . International reaction, at the same time it is pointing out Guatemala as a "threat to continental solidarity," is preparing vast interventionist plans, such as the one recently denounced by the Guatemalan government. The published documents—which the Department of State at Washington hastened to call Moscow propaganda—unquestionably show that the foreign conspirators and monopolistic interests that inspired and financed them sought to permit armed intervention against our country, as "a noble undertaking against communism." Let us emphasize before this Conference the gravity of these events. Nonintervention is one of the most priceless triumphs of Pan Americanism and the essential basis of inter-American unity, solidarity, and cooperation. It has been fully supported in various inter-American instruments, and specifically in Article 15 of the Charter of the Organization of American States. . . .

The government of Guatemala will never permit its internal politics to become the subject of discussion, much less of decision, in any international body. If by some absurdity, which we are sure will never happen, the governments of the American States, setting aside the principle of nonintervention and acting against their own national interests, go so far as to reach any decision contrary to the principles of the Charter of the Organization, the peoples of the hemisphere would, for a long time to come, be forced to renounce all possibility of economic and social progress.

The government of Guatemala has repeatedly denounced before the United Nations the systematic campaign of defamation that foreign interests, united with native feudalism, have waged against this republic, as well as the whole series of subversive acts designed to destroy the social advances of the Guatemalan Revolution, and the innumerable threats that have culminated in the most recent campaign in behalf of unilateral or collective intervention to destroy the democratic regime of Guatemala.

All the foregoing clearly explains the reasons why Guatemala opposed, in the meetings of the Council of the Organization, the inclusion on the Agenda of this Conference of the topic proposed by the United States on "the intervention of international Communism in the American Republics." We felt at that time, and today feel more strongly than ever, that such a proposal constitutes a maneuver against Guatemala, which has been unjustly and maliciously accused of being Communist, of being a beachhead of Communism, a threat to the Panama Canal, a bad example to the other peoples of the hemisphere, and of threatening the security and solidarity of the American Republics.

We feel this proposal was merely a pretext for intervening in our internal affairs. . . .

Allow me to analyze briefly the United States proposal, so that you may clearly see the danger it contains: First, it speaks of "International Communism" as an interventionist power, but, have we as yet reached an agreement on the meaning of this term? What is International Communism? Is it perhaps a doctrine or a philosophy? Is it an economic theory? Is it perhaps merely a political party, or is it supposed to be an instrument in the hands of the Soviet Union?

Because, Gentlemen, if Communism is a political doctrine, a philosophy, or an economic theory, no one needs to be concerned with the fact that it is international in character, since no doctrine, no philosophy, not even any scientific theory can be limited to a single nationality. All these concepts are obviously universal, as are all ideas; and it is not possible to assert that ideas are interventionist, nor accuse them of intervening in the internal affairs of States.

For if it is affirmed that ideas could be interventionist, it could also be logically asserted that the vehicle of intervention is man's thought, and therefore the basis would be laid for the persecution of ideas and discrimination for political reasons, an extreme condemned by the principles of constitutional and international law.

Now then if what the United States means is that the Soviet Union is intervening in the internal affairs of the American States, it would be desirable for them to say so.

"As for Guatemala," as President Arbenz stated in his message to the Congress of the Republic on the first of this month, "it is obvious even to the most perspicacious that the Soviet Union has not intervened nor is it intervening in the internal affairs of our country, nor does it threaten us with any intervention, contrary to what has happened to us from dominant interests in other countries. Besides, Guatemala is not disposed to permit intervention by any foreign power."

Anyone who looks at the chapters of the Charter of the Organization of American States will find a splendid code of guarantee of the integrity, sovereignty, and independence of the Member States, as well as a powerful obstacle to any kind of abuses by the powerful nations that have infringed upon those rights.

However, it is deplorable to observe that the peoples of America have shown little enthusiasm for the Organization and have little faith in the efficacy of its work. And the worst of it is that we must confess that such an attitude is reasonable and justifiable.

If we ask ourselves what Pan Americanism has done for the peoples of America, and we want to be sincere in our reply, we shall have to admit that those peoples have often been deceived. Pan Americanism can do nothing for the effective benefit of man in America so long as it does not face the real problems of the hemisphere and the tremendous fact of a majority of nations with an underdeveloped economy, the peoples of which are prisoners of ignorance and poverty, in comparison with other highly industrialized nations, in relation to which they are kept in a semicolonial dependent situation as suppliers of raw materials and cheap food, and as certain markets for their manufactured goods.

Pan Americanism has not been able to achieve a balance in this situation, and it has not even been able to obtain an adequate correlation between the prices paid for raw materials and foodstuffs, and the price charged for manufactured goods.

On the contrary, some of its actions have served to perpetuate that situation, and many times even agreements reached in good faith have resulted in tying the hands of these countries and favoring the political and economic hegemony of the strongest.

30.
SECRETARY OF STATE JOHN FOSTER DULLES: THE DECLARATION OF CARACAS (1954)

I returned last Sunday from Caracas after 2 weeks of attendance at the Tenth Inter-American Conference. . . . The Conference has made history by adopting with only one negative vote a declaration that, if the international communism movement came to dominate or control the political institutions of any American State, that would constitute a threat to the sovereignty and political independence of all the American States and would endanger the peace of America.

That declaration reflects the thinking of the early part of the nineteenth century. At that time, Czarist Russia was aggressive. Czar Alexander had made a claim to sovereignty along the west coast of this continent and had organized the so-called Holy Alliance which was plotting to impose the despotic political system of Russia and its allies upon the American Republics, which had just won their freedom from Spain.

In 1823, President Monroe, in his message to Congress, made his famous declaration. It contained two major points. The first related to the colonial system of the allied powers of Europe and declared that any extension of their colonial system in this hemisphere would be dangerous to our peace and safety. The second part of the declaration referred to the extension to this hemisphere of the political system of despotism then represented by Czarist Russia and the Holy Alliance. President Monroe declared that "it is impossible that the Allied Powers should extend their political system to any portion of either continent without endangering our peace and happiness. It is equally impossible, therefore, that we should behold such interposition, in any form, with indifference."

The first part of President Monroe's declaration against extending the European colonial system in this hemisphere has long since been accepted and made an all-American policy by concerted action of the American States. However, the same could not be said of President Monroe's declaration against the extension to this hemisphere of a European despotic system. It seemed to me, as I planned for the Caracas conference, that the threat which stems from international communism is a repetition in this

---

"The Declaration of Caracas and the Monroe Doctrine," press conference statement of March 16, 1954, in U.S. Department of State, *Intervention of International Communism in Guatemala* (Washington, D.C., 1954), pp. 10–11.

century of precisely the kind of danger against which President Monroe had made his famous declaration 130 years ago. It seemed of the utmost importance that, just as part of the Monroe declaration had long since been turned from a unilateral declaration into a multilateral declaration of the American States, so it would be appropriate for the American States to unite to declare the danger to them all which would come if international communism seized control of the political institutions of any American State.

That matter was debated at Caracas for 2 weeks and a declaration in the sense proposed by the United States was adopted by a vote of 17 to 1, with 2 abstentions.

I believe that this action, if it is properly backed up, can have a profound effect in preserving this hemisphere from the evils and woes that would befall it if any one of our American States became a Soviet Communist puppet. That would be a disaster of incalculable proportions. It would disrupt the growing unity of the American States which is now reflected by the Charter of the Americas and by the Rio Treaty of Reciprocal Assistance. . . .

It is significant of the vitality of our American system that no one of the American Republics, even the most powerful, wanted to deal single-handedly with the danger, but that it was brought to the Inter-American Conference table as a matter of common concern. Furthermore, the declaration, as adopted, contained in substance the words of President Eisenhower, expressed in his great peace address of April 16, 1953, that the declaration "is designed to protect and not to impair the inalienable right of each American State freely to choose its own form of government and economic system and to live its own social and cultural life."

VI
HERITAGE OF CRISIS

31.
PREMIER FIDEL CASTRO: A CALL TO ARMS (1967)

Whoever stops to wait for ideas to triumph among the majority of the masses before initiating revolutionary action will never be a revolutionary.

Address at the closing of the First Conference of the Organization of Latin American Solidarity, August 10, 1967.

For, what is the difference between such a revolutionary and a latifundium owner, a wealthy bourgeois? Nothing!

Humanity will, of course, change; human society will, of course, continue to develop—in spite of human beings and the errors of human beings. But that is not a revolutionary attitude.

If that had been our way of thinking, we would never have initiated a revolutionary process. It was enough for the ideas to take root in a sufficient number of men for revolutionary action to be initiated, and, through this action, the masses started to acquire these ideas; the masses acquired that consciousness.

It is obvious that in Latin America there are already in many places a number of men who are convinced of such ideas, and that have started revolutionary action. And what distinguished the true revolutionary from the false revolutionary is precisely this: one acts to move the masses, the other waits for the masses to have a conscience already before starting to act. . . .

And there is a series of principles that one should not expect to be accepted without an argument, but which are essential truths, accepted by the majority, with reservations on the part of a few. That Byzantine discussion about the ways and means of struggle, whether it should be peaceful or nonpeaceful, armed or unarmed: the essence of that discussion—which we call Byzantine because it is like the argument between two deaf-and-dumb people—is that it distinguishes those who want to promote the revolution from those who do not want to promote it, those who want to curb it from those who want to promote it. Let no one be fooled.

Different words have been used: if the road [of the armed struggle] is the only one, if the road is not the only one, if it is the exclusive one, if it is not the exclusive one. And the Conference has been very clear in this respect. It does not say *only* road, although it might just have well said only road: it says fundamental road, and the other forms of struggle must be subordinated to it: in the long run, the only road. To use the word "only," even though this meaning of the word be understood—the true meaning —might lead to errors about the imminence of the struggle.

That is why we understand that the Declaration, by calling it the fundamental road, the road that must be taken in the long run, is the correct formulation. If we wish to express our way of thinking, and that of our Party and our people, let no one harbor any illusions about seizing power by peaceful means in any country in this continent, let no one harbor any illusions. Anyone trying to tell such a thing to the masses will be completely deceiving.

This does not mean that one has to go out and grab a rifle, and start fighting tomorrow, anywhere. That is not the question. It is a question of ideological conflict between those who want to make revolution and those who do not want to make it. It is the conflict between those who want to make it and those who want to curb it. Because, essentially, anybody can tell whether or not it is possible, whether or not conditions are ripe, to take up arms.

No one can be so sectarian, so dogmatic, as to say that one has to go out and grab a rifle tomorrow, anywhere. And we ourselves do not doubt that there are some countries in which this task is not an immediate task, but we are convinced that it will be their task in the long run.

There are some who have put forward even more radical theses than those of Cuba; that we Cubans believe such and such a country doesn't have conditions for armed struggle, and that we're wrong. But the funny thing is that it has been claimed in some cases by representatives who are not quite in favor of the theses for armed struggle. We will not be angered by this. We prefer them to make mistakes trying to make revolution without the right conditions than to have them make the mistake of never making revolution. I hope no one will make a mistake! But nobody who really wants to fight will ever have differences with us, and those who do not want to fight ever will always have discrepancies with us. . . .

There are some who ask themselves if it is possible in any country of Latin America to achieve power without armed struggle. And, of course, theoretically, hypothetically, when a great part of the continent has been liberated there would be nothing surprising if, under those conditions, a revolution succeeds without opposition—but this would be an exception. However, this does not mean that the revolution is going to succeed in any country without a struggle. The blood of the revolutionaries of a specific country may not be shed, but their victory will only be possible thanks to the efforts, the sacrifices, and the blood of the revolutionaries of a whole continent.

It would therefore be false to say that they had a revolution there without a struggle. That will always be a lie. And I believe that it is not correct for any revolutionary to wait with arms crossed until all the other peoples struggle and create the conditions for victory for him without struggle. That will never be an attribute of revolutionaries.

To those who believe that peaceful transition is possible in some countries of this continent, we say to them that we cannot understand what kind of peaceful transition they refer to, unless it is to a peaceful transition in agreement with imperialism. Because in order to achieve victory by peaceful means, if in practice such a thing were possible considering that the mechanisms of the bourgeoisie, the oligarchies, and imperialism control all the means for peaceful struggle . . . [the media for influencing opinion]. And then you hear a revolutionary say: They crushed us, they organized two hundred radio programs, so and so many newspapers, so and so many magazines, so and so many TV shows, so and so many of this and so and so many of the other. And one wants to ask him: What did you expect? That they would put TV, the radio, the magazines, the newspapers, the printing shops, all this at your disposal? Or are you unaware that precisely those are the instruments of the ruling class to crush the revolutions?

They complain that the bourgeoisie and the oligarchies crush them with their campaigns, as if that is a surprise to anyone. The first thing that a revolutionary has to understand is that the ruling classes have organized the state in such a way as to maintain themselves in power by all possible means. And they use not only arms, not only physical instruments, not only guns, but all possible instruments of influence, to deceive, to confuse.

And those who believe that they are going to win against the imperialists in elections are just plan naive; and those who believe that the day will come when they will take over through elections are super-naive. It is necessary to have been present in a revolutionary process and to know just what the repressive apparatus is by which the ruling classes maintain the status quo, just how much one has to struggle, just how difficult it is.

This does not imply the negation of forms of struggle. When someone writes a manifesto in a newspaper, attends a demonstration, holds a rally, propagates an idea, they may be using the so-called famous legal means. We must do away with that differentiation between legal or illegal means, and call them revolutionary or nonrevolutionary means.

The revolutionary, in pursuit of his ideal and revolutionary aims, uses various methods. The essence of the question is whether the masses will be led to believe that the revolutionary movement, that socialism, can take over power without a struggle, that it can take over power peacefully. And that is a lie! And those who assert anywhere in Latin America that they will take over power peacefully will be deceiving the masses.

We are talking about conditions in Latin America. We don't want to involve ourselves in any other problems, which are already large enough, of those of other revolutionary organizations in other countries such as those of Europe. We are addressing Latin America. And of course, if they would only confine their mistakes to themselves . . . but no . . . ! they try to encourage the same mistakes in those who are already mistaken on this continent! And to such an extent that part of the so-called revolutionary press has made attacks against Cuba for our revolutionary stand in Latin America. That's a fine thing! They don't know how to be revolutionaries over there, yet they want to teach us how to be revolutionaries over here.

But we are not anxious to start arguments. We already have enough to think about. But of course, we will not overlook the direct or indirect, the overt or covert attacks of some neo-Social Democrats of Europe.

And these are clear ideas. We are absolutely convinced that, in the long run, there is only one solution, as expressed in the Resolution: the role of the guerrilla in Latin America.

32.
MARVIN ALISKY: OUR MAN IN MANAGUA (1960)

Even the location of the American embassy in Managua has become a hated symbol to the Nicaraguans. It is adjacent to the castle of General Anastasio Somoza, Jr., to the west and to the home of the father's widow to the south. Next to the general's castle lies the Presidential Palace atop the Loma de Tiscapa, the hill dominating Managua.

Other governmental offices are downtown, but the command post of the dynasty is the two Somoza brothers' homes high upon Tiscapa. In front of the Somoza mansions, to the north, the hill slopes to Avenida Somoza. Tiscapa bristles with machine guns, sentry posts, and artillery turrets. No other embassy lies within this inner circle.

JOURNALISTS AND ILLITERATES

The Somozas make much of the fact that token freedom of the press exists. But Nicaragua is eighty per cent illiterate, although official figures put the percentage at sixty-one. Because of the high illiteracy in the country the radio constitutes the major medium of communication, and radio stations are heavily censored. Two soldiers patrol each of the five Managua stations that broadcast news. The other seven stations and most of the provincial stations carry no news.

In 1959, the U.S. embassy's public-affairs officer, Stuart Ayers, began a writers' workshop, which prompted the rector of the National University of Nicaragua to ask the State Department to send a visiting professor of journalism under the Smith-Mundt program to convert the workshop into a school of journalism. Except for the dailies *La Prensa* and *La Noticia,* Nicaraguan newspapers mainly dispense opinion, and the country needs trained newsmen. I was therefore especially pleased when I was appointed an exchange professor last summer.

Late last June, journalism students met at the school to elect a representative to the university's student federation. University rules require that each college or school have such a representative. Unfortunately, among the anti-Somoza faction of the students there were a few vocal anti-Yankees. This threw Ambassador Whelan into a panic. He made a call on the Somozas.

Reporter Magazine, December 22, 1960, p. 27.

The journalism school was financed in part by the binational Nicaraguan-American Cultural Center, whose regulations forbid any type of political activity. With this rule as pretext, the school was thrown out of the National University. Dr. Fiallos Gil, the university rector, was held personally responsible by Ambassador Whelan when students on campus burned an American flag and an effigy of the ambassador to show their fierce opposition to the part the U.S. embassy had played in the expulsion. If he had not interfered, the pro–United States students might well have won the election.

I was still in Nicaragua last August when the United States finally broke with Dictator Trujillo of the Dominican Republic. For the first time I heard kind words for the United States on the streets of Managua. Ambassador Whelan immediately dissipated the good will: he was the only diplomat in Managua to go to the airport to bid a tearful good-by to Luis Logroño, retiring as Dominican ambassador to Nicaragua. A picture of Whelan embracing Logroño, which appeared in the August 27 issue of *La Prensa* of Managua, was widely circulated.

In July the U.S. government encouraged the World Bank to make a $12.5-million loan for a Nicaraguan hydroelectric agency. This multidam project to harness the Tuma, Viejo, and Matagalpa Rivers will benefit the Somoza dynasty, since the family owns most of the land involved. Although the loan was made in order to extend the country's electrical output for the Nicaraguan people, the Somoza-owned newspaper *Novedades* claimed that it "demonstrates United States moral approval of the Somoza administration."

Long before Whelan came to Managua, Nicaraguans were smarting under American support of conservative presidents. In 1912 the United States sent down Marines, and for more than two decades, Nicaragua remained a protectorate of Washington, with Marine-supervised national elections. The occupation ended briefly in 1925, but in less than a year the Marines were back to put down a new revolution. They did not leave for good until 1933. And even today an American, Thomas Downing, is Nicaraguan collector of customs. None of this has helped to make the Nicaraguan people our friends.

Anti-Somoza Nicaraguans range from Communists, rootless political adventurers, followers of Castro, and terrorists on one side to priests, Conservative Party landowners, idealistic students, and disgruntled businessmen on the other. The one thing they have in common at the moment, aside from hatred for the Somozas, is a dislike for the United States for what they think is our unquestioning support of the dictatorship. Every public utterance or action by Ambassador Whelan tends to reinforce their claim. He dismisses all these groups as Communists.

On July 23, 1959, four university students in León were shot down in cold blood for leading an anti-Somoza political rally. Ambassador Whelan issued a statement calling the young men Communists. An American priest, Father Mark Hurley of St. Paul's Catholic Church in San Francisco, gave the victims the last rites and declared that they were God-fearing practicing Catholics. In 1960 on the anniversary of the killings, students from high schools in various parts of Managua wore black ties. As police cuffed them with rifle butts, there were almost as many denouncements of Whelan as of the Somozas.

Dozens of students and young adults told me that as soon as arms can be obtained, the fighting will start. Already in recent years, several abortive revolts have erupted. One time it is the eastern jungle; the next time, the Honduran border; the next time, the Costa Rican border; the next—? Hardly a month passes without terrorist bombs exploding in the middle of Managua.

If the rebels are finally successful—and many Nicaraguans substitute the word "when" for "if"—the United States may well find itself as unpopular in Nicaragua as it is today in Cuba.

33.
PRESIDENT JOHN F. KENNEDY: THE ALLIANCE FOR PROGRESS (1961)

One hundred and thirty-nine years ago this week the United States, stirred by the heroic struggles of its fellow Americans, urged the independence and recognition of the new Latin American Republics. It was then, at the dawn of freedom throughout this hemisphere, that Bolívar spoke of his desire to see the Americas fashioned into the greatest region in the world, "greatest," he said, "not so much by virtue of her area and her wealth, as by her freedom and her glory."

Never, in the long history of our hemisphere, has this dream been nearer to fulfillment, and never has it been in greater danger.

The genius of our scientists has given us the tools to bring abundance to our land, strength to our industry, and knowledge to our people. For the first time we have the capacity to strike off the remaining bonds of poverty and ignorance—to free our people for the spiritual and intellectual fulfillment which has always been the goal of our civilization.

Yet at this very moment of maximum opportunity, we confront the same forces which have imperiled America throughout its history—the alien

Address at the White House, March 13, 1961.

forces which once again seek to impose the despotisms of the Old World on the people of the New. . . .

We meet together as firm and ancient friends, united by history and experience and by our determination to advance the values of American civilization. For this new world of ours is not merely an accident of geography. Our continents are bound together by a common history— the endless exploration of new frontiers. Our nations are the product of a common struggle—the revolt from colonial rule. And our people share a common heritage—the quest for the dignity and the freedom of man. . . .

. . . we North Americans have not always grasped the significance of this common mission, just as it is also true that many in your own countries have not fully understood the urgency of the need to lift people from poverty and ignorance and despair. But we must turn from these mistakes —from the failures and the misunderstandings of the past—to a future full of peril but bright with hope.

Throughout Latin America—a continent rich in resources and in the spiritual and cultural achievements of its people—millions of men and women suffer the daily degradations of hunger and poverty. They lack decent shelter or protection from disease. Their children are deprived of the education or the jobs which are the gateway to a better life. And each day the problems grow more urgent. Population growth is outpacing economic growth, low living standards are even further endangered, and discontent—the discontent of a people who know that abundance and the tools of progress are at last within their reach—that discontent is growing. In the words of José Figueres, "once dormant peoples are struggling upward toward the sun, toward a better life."

If we are to meet a problem so staggering in its dimensions, our approach must itself be equally bold, an approach consistent with the majestic concept of Operation Pan America. Therefore I have called on all the people of the hemisphere to join in a new Alliance for Progress—*Alianza para el Progreso*—a vast cooperative effort, unparalleled in magnitude and nobility of purpose, to satisfy the basic needs of the American people for homes, work and land, health and schools—*techo, trabajo y tierra, salud y escuela.*

TEN-YEAR PLAN FOR THE AMERICAS

First, I propose that the American Republics begin on a vast new 10-year plan for the Americas, a plan to transform the 1960s into an historic decade of democratic progress. These 10 years will be the years of maximum progress, maximum effort—the years when the greatest obstacles must be overcome, the years when the need for assistance will be the greatest.

And . . . if our effort is bold enough and determined enough, then the close of this decade will mark the beginning of a new era in the American experience. The living standards of every American family will be on the rise, basic education will be available to all, hunger will be a forgotten experience, the need for massive outside help will have passed, most nations will have entered a period of self-sustaining growth, and, although there will be still much to do, every American Republic will be the master of its own revolution and its own hope and progress.

Let me stress that only the most determined efforts of the American nations themselves can bring success to this effort. They, and they alone, can mobilize their resources, enlist the energies of their people, and modify their social patterns so that all, and not just a privileged few, share in the fruits of growth. If this effort is made, then outside assistance will give a vital impetus to progress; without it, no amount of help will advance the welfare of the people.

Thus if the countries of Latin America are ready to do their part . . . then I believe the United States . . . should help provide resources of a scope and magnitude sufficient to make this bold development plan a success, just as we helped to provide . . . the resources adequate to help rebuild the economies of Western Europe. . . .

Secondly, I will shortly request a ministerial meeting of the Inter-American Economic and Social Council, . . . [to] begin the massive planning effort which will be at the heart of the Alliance for Progress. . . .

A greatly strengthened IA-ECOSOC, working with the Economic Commission for Latin America and the Inter-American Development Bank, can assemble the leading economists and experts of the hemisphere to help each country develop its own development plan, and provide a continuing review of economic progress in this hemisphere.

Third, I have this evening signed a request to the Congress for $500 million as a first step in fulfilling the Act of Bogotá. This is the first large-scale inter-American effort—instituted by my predecessor President Eisenhower —to attack the social barriers which block economic progress. The money will be used to combat illiteracy, improve the productivity and use of their land, wipe out disease, attack archaic tax and land-tenure structures, provide educational opportunities, and offer a broad range of projects designed to make the benefits of increasing abundance available to all. . . .

Fourth, we must support all economic integration which is a genuine step toward larger markets and greater competitive opportunity. The fragmentation of Latin American economies is a serious barrier to industrial growth. Projects such as the Central American Common Market and free-trade areas in South America can help to remove these obstacles.

Fifth, the United States is ready to cooperate in serious, case-by-case examinations of commodity market problems. Frequent violent changes in commodity prices seriously injure the economies of many Latin American countries, draining their resources and stultifying their growth. . . .

Sixth, we will immediately step up our food-for-peace emergency program, help to establish food reserves in areas of recurrent drought, and help provide school lunches for children and offer feed grains for use in rural development. . . .

Seventh, . . . I invite Latin American scientists to work with us in new projects in fields such as medicine and agriculture, physics and astronomy, and desalinization, and to help plan for regional research laboratories in these and other fields, and to strengthen cooperation between American universities and laboratories.

Eighth, we must rapidly expand the training of those needed to man the economies of rapidly developing countries. This means expanded technical training programs, for which the Peace Corps, for example, will be available when needed. It also means assistance to Latin American universities, graduate schools, and research institutes. . . .

Ninth, we reaffirm our pledge to come to the defense of any American nation whose independence is endangered. As its confidence in the collective security system of the OAS spreads, it will be possible to devote to constructive use a major share of those resources now spent on the instruments of war. . . . Armies can not only defend their countries—they can, as we have learned through our own Corps of Engineers, help to build them.

Tenth, we invite our friends in Latin America to contribute to the enrichment of life and culture in the United States. We need teachers of your literature and history and tradition, opportunities for our young people to study in your universities, access to your music, your art, and the thought of your great philosophers. For we know we have much to learn. . . .

To achieve this goal political freedom must accompany material progress. Our Alliance for Progress is an alliance of free governments, and it must work to eliminate tyranny from a hemisphere in which it has no rightful place. Therefore let us express our special friendship to the people of Cuba and the Dominican Republic—and the hope they will soon rejoin the society of free men, uniting with us in our common effort.

This political freedom must be accompanied by social change. For unless necessary social reforms, including land and tax reform, are freely made, unless we broaden the opportunity of all of our people, unless the great mass of Americans share in increasing prosperity, then our alliance, our revolution, our dream, and our freedom will fail. But we call for social change by free men—change in the spirit of Washington and Jefferson, Bolívar and San Martín and Martí—not change which seeks to impose on men tyrannies which we cast out a century and a half ago. Our motto is what it has always been—progress yes, tyranny no—*progreso si, tiranía no!. . . .*

Let us once again transform the American Continent into a vast crucible of revolutionary ideas and efforts, a tribute to the power of the creative energies of free men and women, an example to all the world that liberty and progress walk hand in hand. Let us once again awaken our American Revolution until it guides the struggles of people everywhere—not with an imperialism of force or fear but the rule of courage and freedom and hope for the future of man.

34.
CATHOLIC BISHOPS: MEDELLÍN DECLARATION (1968)

The Latin American Church, united in the Second General Conference of its Bishops, has chosen as the central theme of its deliberations Latin American man who is living a decisive moment of his historical process. In making this choice she has in no way "detoured from" but has actually "returned to" man, aware that "in order to know God, it is necessary to know man."

The Church has sought to understand this historic moment in the life of Latin American man in the light of the Word, Who is Christ, in Whom the mystery of man is made manifest.

This assessment of the present naturally turns our scrutiny to the past. Upon examining it, the Church can verify with joy that the work has been carried forward generously, and she expresses her gratitude to all those who have laid the foundations of the Gospel in our lands; to those who have been active and present through charity to the different cultures, especially to the Indians of the continent; to all who have continued the educational work of the Church in our urban and rural areas. At the same time, she must acknowledge that throughout the course of history all her members, clergy and lay, have not always been faithful to the Holy Spirit. A glance at the present joyously confirms the dedication of many of her sons and also the frailty of her own messengers. The Church accepts

From Final Declaration, Second General Conference of Latin American Bishops, Medellín, Colombia (1968).

history's judgment on her chiaroscuro past and assumes the full historical responsibility that befalls her in the present.

It is certainly not enough to reflect, to be more discerning and to speak. Action is required. The present has not ceased to be the hour of the word, but it has already become, and with dramatic urgency, the time for action. It is the moment to exercise creativity and imagination in inventing the action that must be performed and brought to term with the boldness of the Holy Spirit and the balance of God. This assembly has been invited "to take decisions and establish programs only under the condition that we are disposed to carry them out as a personal commitment even at the cost of sacrifice. . . ."

In this General Assembly of the Latin American Bishops the mystery of Pentecost has been renewed. Together with Mary, the Mother of the Church, who by her patronage has aided this continent since its first evangelization, we have implored the light of the Holy Spirit and, persevering in prayer, have been nourished by the bread of the Word and the Eucharist. This Word has been the object of earnest meditation. The goal of our reflection was to search for a new and more dynamic presence of the Church in the present transformation of Latin America, in the light of the Second Vatican Council, which was the theme assigned to this Conference.

Three broad areas over which our pastoral care extends have been considered in relation to the process of continental transformation:

In the first place, the promotion of man and of the peoples of the continent toward the values of justice and peace, of education and the family.

Secondly, the need for an adapted evangelization to the need, and a process of maturation of the faith of the masses and the elites by means of catechesis and the liturgy.

Finally we touched upon those problems dealing with the members of the Church that require greater unity and pastoral action by means of visible structures, also adapted to the new conditions of the continent.

The following conclusions express the fruit of the work of the Second General Conference of the Latin American Bishops in the hope that all the People of God, encouraged by the Holy Spirit, commit themselves to its complete fulfillment.

1. JUSTICE

There are in existence many studies of the Latin American people. The misery that besets large masses of human beings in all of our countries is described in all of these studies. That misery, as a collective fact, expresses itself as injustice which cries to the heavens.

But what perhaps has not been sufficiently said is that in general the efforts which have been made have not been capable of assuring that justice be honored and realized in every sector of the respective national communities. Often families do not find concrete possibilities for the education of their children. The young demand their right to enter universities or centers of higher learning for both intellectual and technical training; the women, their right to a legitimate equality with men; the peasants, better conditions of life; or if they are workers, better prices and security in buying and selling; the growing middle class feels frustrated by the lack of expectations. There has begun an exodus of professionals and technicians to more developed countries; the small businessmen and industrialists are pressed by greater interests and not a few large Latin American industrialists are gradually coming to be dependent on the international business enterprises. We cannot ignore the phenomenon of this almost universal frustration of legitimate aspirations which creates the climate of collective anguish in which we are already living. . . .

Political Reform

16. Faced with the need for a total change of Latin American structures, we believe that change has political reform as its prerequisite.

The exercise of political authority and its decisions have as their only end the common good. In Latin America such authority and decision-making frequently seem to support systems which militate against the common good or which favor privileged groups. By means of legal norms, authority ought effectively and permanently to assure the rights and inalienable liberties of the citizens and the free functioning of intermediary structures.

Public authority has the duty of facilitating and supporting the creation of means of participation and legitimate representation of the people, or if necessary the creation of new ways to achieve it. We want to insist on the necessity of vitalizing and strengthening the municipal and communal organization, as a beginning of organizational efforts at the departmental, provincial, regional and national levels.

The lack of political consciousness in our countries makes the educational activity of the Church absolutely essential, for the purpose of bringing Christians to consider their participation in the political life of the nation as a matter of conscience and as the practice of charity in its most noble and meaningful sense for the life of the community.

Information and "Concientización"

17. We wish to affirm that it is indispensable to form a social conscience and a realistic perception of the problems of the community and of social structures. We must awaken the social conscience and communal customs in all strata of society and professional groups regarding such values as dialogue and community living within the same group and relations with wider social groups (workers, peasants, professionals, clergy, religious, administrators, etc.).

This task of "concientización" and social education ought to be integrated into joint Pastoral Action at various levels. . . .

20. It is necessary that small basic communities be developed in order to establish a balance with minority groups, which are the groups in power. This is only possible through vitalization of these very communities by means of the natural innate elements in their environment.

The Church—the People of God—will lend its support to the downtrodden of every social class so that they might come to know their rights and how to make use of them. To this end the Church will utilize its moral strength and will seek to collaborate with competent professionals and institutions. . . .

2. PEACE

I. THE LATIN AMERICAN SITUATION AND PEACE

1. "If development is the new name for peace," Latin American underdevelopment with its own characteristics in the different countries, is an unjust situation which promotes tensions that conspire against peace. . . .

The Problem of Violence in Latin America

15. Violence constitutes one of the gravest problems in Latin America. A decision on which the future of the countries of the continent will depend should not be left to the impulses of emotion and passion. We would be failing in our pastoral duty if we were not to remind the conscience, caught in this dramatic dilemma, of the criteria derived from the Christian doctrine of evangelical love.

No one should be surprised if we forcefully re-affirm our faith in the productiveness of peace. This is our Christian ideal. "Violence is neither Christian nor evangelical." The Christian man is peaceful and not ashamed of it. He is not simply a pacifist, for he can fight, but he prefers peace to war. He knows that "violent changes in structures would be fallacious, ineffectual in themselves and not conforming to the dignity of man, which demands that the necessary changes take place from within, that is to say, through a fitting awakening of conscience, adequate preparation and effective participation of all, which the ignorance and often inhuman conditions of life make it impossible to assure at this time."

16. As the Christian believes in the productiveness of peace in order to achieve justice, he also believes that justice is a prerequisite for peace. He recognizes that in many instances Latin America finds itself faced with a situation of injustice that can be called institutionalized violence, when, because of a structural deficiency of industry and agriculture, of national and international economy, of cultural and political life, "whole towns lack necessities, live in such dependence as hinders all initiative and responsibility as well as every possibility for cultural promotion and participation in social and political life", thus violating fundamental rights. This situation demands all-embracing, courageous, urgent and profoundly renovating transformations. We should not be surprised therefore, that the "temptation to violence" is surfacing in Latin America. One should not abuse the patience of a people that for years has borne a situation that would not be acceptable to any one with any degree of awareness of human rights.

Facing a situation which works so seriously against the dignity of man and against peace, we address ourselves, as pastors, to all the members of the Christian community, asking them to assume their responsibility in the promotion of peace in Latin America.

17. We would like to direct our call in the first place, to those who have a greater share of wealth, culture and power. We know that there are leaders in Latin America who are sensitive to the needs of the people and try to remedy them. They recognize that the privileged many times join together, and with all the means at their disposal pressure those who govern, thus obstructing necessary changes. In some instances, this pressure takes on drastic proportions which result in the destruction of life and property.

Therefore, we urge them not to take advantage of the pacifist position of the Church in order to oppose, either actively or passively, the profound transformations that are so necessary. If they jealously retain their privileges, and defend them through violence they are responsible to history for provoking "explosive revolutions of despair." The peaceful future of the countries of Latin America depends to a large extent on their attitude.

18. Also responsible for injustice are those who remain passive for fear of the sacrifice and personal risk implied by any courageous and effective action. Justice, and therefore peace, conquer by means of a dynamic action of awakening (concientización) and organization of the popular sectors, which are capable of pressing public officials who are often impotent in their social projects without popular support.

19. We address ourselves finally, to those who, in the face of injustice and illegitimate resistance to change, put their hopes in violence. With Paul VI we realize that their attitude "frequently finds its ultimate motivation in noble impulses of justice and solidarity." Let us not speak here of empty words which do not imply personal responsibility and which isolate from the fruitful nonviolent actions that are immediately possible.

If it is true that revolutionary insurrection can be legitimate in the case of evident and prolonged "tyranny that seriously works against the fundamental rights of man, and which damages the common good of the country" whether it proceeds from one person or from clearly unjust structures, it is also certain that violence or "armed revolution" generally "generates new injustices, introduces new imbalances and causes new disasters; one cannot combat a real evil at the price of a greater evil."

If we consider then, the totality of the circumstances of our countries, and if we take into account the Christian preference for peace, the enormous difficulty of a civil war, the logic of violence, the atrocities it engenders, the risk of provoking foreign intervention, illegitimate as it may be, the difficulty of building a regime of justice and freedom while participating in a process of violence, we earnestly desire that the dynamism of the awakened and organized community be put to the service of justice and peace.

Finally, we would like to make ours the words of our Holy Father to the newly ordained priests and deacons in Bogotá, when he referred to all the suffering and said to them: "We will be able to understand their afflictions and change them, not into hate and violence, but into the strong and peaceful energy of constructive works."

35.
SECRETARY OF DEFENSE ROBERT MCNAMARA: U.S. MILITARY AID (1966)

In 6 years, 1962 through fiscal 1967—the year during which I have been responsible for military assistance—we have supplied about $435 million worth of grant aid to 20 Latin American countries.

During that time, and of that $435 million, $13 million has been for combat aircraft, combat navy ships, and artillery. No tanks. It includes $200,000 worth of artillery, $10 million worth of ships, and $4 million worth of aircraft, which is very, very little. I can go into the individual items if you wish.

In addition to that grant aid we have entered into sales agreements with Latin American countries over that period of time. . . . The important point is this: That our small program of military aid to Latin America—$74 or $75 million in grant aid, plus the military sales—has resulted in our being able to help control a potential arms race and dampen it down to the point

Senate Foreign Relations Committee hearings, April 20, 1966.

where there are no other groups of countries in the world comparable to those Latin American countries, with a total population of 200 million, which have gross national products adequate to support military operations and have such small military forces.

Ten of the nineteen countries to which we give aid spend less than 10 percent of their governmental budgets on defense. Eleven of them spend less than 2 percent of their gross national product on defense. None of them, with one exception, has as many men in uniform per unit of population as does any nation in Europe other than Switzerland.

I don't think there is any question but what we have used our bargaining power, if you will, brought about by the military aid program to hold down defense forces, the defense expenditures and foreign exchange expenditures in Latin America. . . . Let me read to you from a memo of conversation that I had with an ambassador from one of those countries within the past 30 days.

> The ambassador used the first 15 minutes to lay out a case for additional military assistance to country E, a Latin American country. His points were that country E has a history of difficulties with her neighbors, although in recent years the difficulties have been limited to border incidents. That all guns in country E are for peace but that the power ratio of country E vis-à-vis her neighbors has gone from bad to worse and country E, being unable to obtain military ships and aircraft from the United States, plans to buy them from Europe. And Latin American countries have a history of buying them from Europe over the years. McNamara responded he was shocked that country E was expending her wealth on a basis such as this. He said he was aware of some of the proposals under consideration, and he said he thoroughly disagreed with them. He said he thought they involved much more than the population of country E desired and the strategic situation required. He added that he so far as he could affect the situation, he would not tolerate an arms race in E or country X.

And I stated they could not depend on our military grant aid from us if they were to misuse their resources as they proposed. . . .

Senator MORSE. You know, Mr. Secretary, that I have rejected that argument for years. It is nothing but an argument of international blackmail on the part of these Latin American countries. When they say "You either do it or we will go to Russia or to France, to someone else," our answer ought to be "Godspeed."

I don't think we have any justification being a party to either granting or selling to these Latin American countries this military equipment when the money ought to be spent to raise the standard of living of the people so they won't engage in Communist coups. That is why I made it clear at the beginning in my rejection of your major premise, that our military assistance program has not been a success.

36.
THOMAS ANDERSON: POPULATION PRESSURES

The question is whether El Salvador is in fact overpopulated in absolute terms or whether this overpopulation is in fact mythical. If the latter is the case, the blame must lie with the wicked oligarchs and their military henchmen, who have so distributed the land as to freeze out the small farmer. In this supposition all that is necessary to end the so-called overpopulation is a redistribution of the land and a deemphasis of cash crops in favor of food staples. This view was raised by Marco Virgilio Carías in 1971. If, however, the contention is true that El Salvador is absolutely overpopulated, it would suggest that radical measures must be taken to reduce the population. These would have to include some means of family planning. This view is gaining some acceptability in enlightened circles, although it is totally contrary to the entire culture and to the religion of El Salvador. Family planning runs into opposition not only from the clergy but from the entire spectrum of Salvadorean political factions, all of which see it as a Yankee imperialist plot to cut the number of Latin Americans.

The problem really lies with the Malthusian-sounding idea of "absolute overpopulation." Many thoughtful Salvadoreans claim that their country is not overpopulated, for other societies with far more than 570 persons per square mile do quite well. Carías and later Durham, in his careful study, seem to agree. Often the example of Holland is pointed to, a country with a population density of over a thousand persons per square mile that manages to skate along quite nicely. Such contentions overlook certain basic facts. First of all, the population of such industrial countries as Holland is stable. These countries do not have to contend with the problem of having every other person fourteen or younger. The more mature populations of such industrialized states provide a large pool of labor in proportion to the population as a whole. Further, the economies of such countries as Holland or Japan are based upon an infrastructure of highly technical education and a tradition of learning that is centuries old. El Salvador must deal with a population still half illiterate. Neither the government nor the society as a whole appears to have yet perceived that education is itself a natural resource of great importance, and even if a crash program were to be launched tomorrow to achieve such an education base, the results might

From his *The War of the Dispossessed: Honduras and El Salvador, 1969* (Lincoln, Neb. 1981), pp. 171–72.

not bear fruit for half a century. Countries with a high population and without great natural resources can achieve apparent miracles, but when the miracles are examined more closely, they are solidly based upon the conscious choices and extended histories of those countries.

El Salvador will be likely to remain a predominantly agricultural country for the foreseeable future and will not become another Holland. But could it be that, given the agricultural basis, a drastic redistribution of the wealth in land might solve the pressures of population? There are several observations which could be made here. First of all, those who have the land show scant indication of being willing to relinquish it gracefully. It will probably have to be torn from their grasp in an upheaval dwarfing that of 1932. The new junta may achieve such a miracle, but miracles are by definition highly improbable events.

Barring great strides in land reform, El Salvador will have to continue within the context of current landholding patterns, and in such a context there are indeed too many people. Even if the unlikely took place, it is hard to see that a diminution of export crops in favor of food crops would really solve the problems of the country. El Salvador, which produces so little of its nonagricultural needs, must export or perish as a modern society. Again, given an export economy, there are too many Salvadoreans for the land. This may not be absolute overpopulation, but it is close enough for all practical purposes.

37.
WORLD BANK: BASIC ECONOMIC INDICATORS

CENTRAL AMERICA: BASIC INDICATORS

COUNTRY	POPULATION	AREA	GNP PER CAPITA DOLLARS	GNP PER CAPITA AVG. ANNUAL GROWTH	ADULT LITERACY (%)	LIFE EXPECTANCY AT BIRTH	POPULATION WITH ACCESS TO SAFE WATER
Costa Rica	2.2	51	1,730	3.2	90	70	77
El Salvador	4.5	21	660	1.6	62	63	53
Guatemala	7.3	109	1,080	2.8	—	59	40
Honduras	3.7	112	560	1.1	60	58	46
Nicaragua	2.6	130	740	0.9	52[a]	56	70
Cuba[b]	9.7	115	—	—	96	73	—
United States[b]	227.7	9,363	11,360	2.3	99	74	—

NOTES: With one exception, all figures are for 1980; figures for adult literacy are for 1977.
a—Official government figure for December 1979.
b—Included for comparison purposes.

SOURCE: The World Bank *World Development Report 1982*.

CENTRAL AMERICA: STRUCTURE OF PRODUCTION

COUNTRY	GDP (millions of $)		DISTRIBUTION OF GDP (%)						PERCENTAGE OF LABOR FORCE IN:					
			AGRICULTURE		INDUSTY		SERVICES		AGRICULTURE		INDUSTRY		SERVICES	
	1960	1980	1960	1980	1960	1980	1960	1980	1960	1980	1960	1980	1960	1980
Costa Rica	510	4,850	26	17	20	29	54	54	51	29	19	23	30	48
El Salvador	570	3,390	32	27	19	21	49	52	62	50	17	22	21	27
Guatemala	1,040	7,850	—	—	—	—	—	—	67	55	14	21	19	24
Honduras	300	2,230	37	31	19	25	44	44	70	63	11	15	19	22
Nicaragua	340	2,120	24	23	21	31	55	46	62	39	16	14	22	47
Cuba[a]	—	—	—	—	—	—	—	—	39	23	22	31	39	46
United States[a]	506,700	2,587,100	4	3	38	34	58	63	7	2	36	32	57	66

a—Included for comparison purposes.

SOURCE: The World Bank *World Development Report 1982.*

CHAPTER
T W O

Revolution in Nicaragua

The 1979 Nicaraguan revolution was a tremendously important event in Central American history. The overwhelming majority of the nation rose up to overthrow the Somoza dynasty's decades-long rule. But the struggle over what will replace the dictatorship has not yet been resolved.

"I rob, you eat" was a famous slogan of dictator Anastasio Somoza. Unlike the military dictatorships in El Salvador, his regime generally survived by bribing the country with corruption rather than battering it with massive violence. There were no death squads. Yet, again in contrast to El Salvador, Somoza's stifling embrace stunted the development of mass organization and a politically sophisticated debate for many years.

Richard Millett (Document 1) describes how Somoza used corruption, U.S. support, and his National Guard army to stay in power. The 1972 earthquake was a turning point. On the one hand, as Millett and Jack Anderson (Document 2) point out, the devastation of Managua provided Somoza with a great money-making opportunity. But on the other hand, he encroached more and more on the economy. While the country underwent a sustained economic growth, Somoza's depredations led to the alienation of the middle class and the radicalization of many of its children. This anger is illustrated by Ernesto Cardenal, a leading Nicaraguan poet and future leader of the Sandinista National Liberation Front or FSLN (Document 3). The immediate effects of the earthquake on different types of Managuans are shown in Xavier Argüello's novel (Document 4) and in a telegram, published in the opposition newspaper *La Prensa,* that deflates Somoza's megalomaniacal style.

In the aftermath of the Cuban revolution, young would-be revolutionaries flocked to Havana. The FSLN was founded there in 1961. Somoza's provision of Nicaraguan territory for the training and launching of Cuban exiles for the abortive 1961 Bay of Pigs invasion made him a particular target for Fidel Castro. The Cubans provided some training and a good deal of ideological and political orientation for the fledgling FSLN. The credulous admiration of FSLN leader Carlos Fonseca Amador for the Soviet Union is demonstrated by his description of his stay there (Document 6). The FSLN's 1969 program (Document 7), published in the Cuban magazine *Tricontinental,* shows the organization's pro-Soviet and Leninist principles and its determination to follow the Cuban guerrilla example in waging "a prolonged people's war."

Despite these intentions, however, the FSLN remained a small, politically unsuccessful group for well over a decade. As FSLN leaders Henry Ruiz and Omar Cabezas show (Documents 8 and 9), the bourgeois students had great difficulties in reaching out to the workers and peasants it claimed to represent. The attempt at guerrilla war in the mountains was preoccupied with merely surviving in that hostile terrain. These events also shaped the psychological atmosphere of the FSLN. It saw itself as an elite group composed of the strongest, bravest, toughest, most macho, as a vanguard worthy of leadership and with the right to manipulate the masses, rather than as a segment of the people who only represented their wishes.

During the long years before the 1979 revolution, the FSLN was plagued and characterized by constant factional infighting involving personal rivalries as much as ideological arguments. Ultimately, there were three different strategies put forward for making the revolution. The "old guard," led by Carlos Fonseca Amador, Tomas Borge, and Henry Ruiz, continued to believe in "accumulating forces" and waging guerrilla warfare in the countryside. It became known as the Protracted Popular War (GPP) faction.

Another faction, led by Jaime Wheelock and calling itself the Proletarian Tendency, split off in the mid-1970s. This group adopted the most traditional Marxist-Leninist perspective, asserting that only the organized urban proletariat could spearhead a revolution. If the GPP tendency saw the Sandinistas as leaders and directors of a guerrilla army, the Proletarian Tendency wanted the FSLN to organize a "vanguard party" based on the workers.

As business, trade unions, and the legal political parties began to battle against Somoza, however, a third group, the Terceristas, would break off in 1977. They emphasized building a broad united front against Somoza and a mass uprising as the means for removing him. Its leaders were Humberto and Daniel Ortega. Yet even the 1977 Tercerista platform did not question the common Sandinista objective of seizing a monopoly on power but merely argued against announcing this "in an open way."

This internal crisis was sparked by the FSLN's most successful operation to date, the seizure of hostages in December 1974 at a party of the Managua elite. As described by one of its organizers, Plutarcho Hernández, the action was quite successful in itself and gained the FSLN worldwide publicity. But it also brought down vicious repression from the Somoza regime and harsh criticism from within the FSLN. Disagreement with the operation, which they viewed as "adventurous" (Document 11), led Wheelock and others to form the Proletarian Tendency. Carlos Fonseca Amador responded, just before his own death at the hands of the National Guard, with a sharp attack on Wheelock and his followers (Document 12). Both sides justified their position by references to Marxism-Leninism.

The divisions among the Sandinistas gave rise to fierce recriminations, and they accused one another of being "petit bourgeois," "capitulationist," and "CIA agents." Unlike the Salvadoran revolutionary groups during the 1970s, the Sandinistas steered clear of the fundamental ideological debates then taking place in the international communist movement. The Sandinistas argued about tactics for gaining power, not over what to do once they took power.

Meanwhile, other opponents of Somoza were organizing. These forces included businessmen, trade unionists, and a range of political parties including Social Democrats, Christian Democrats, Conservatives, and even a faction of Somoza's own Liberal Party. The Democratic Union of Liberation (UDEL) brought together many of these factors (Document 13), and the most widely accepted leader of these oppositionists was Pedro Joaquín Chamorro, scion of an old Nicaraguan political family and publisher of the opposition newspaper *La Prensa.* Somoza was increasingly isolated.

Recognizing the significance of this development, the Tercerista faction of the FSLN sought to build alliances with this much larger segment of the population. In 1977 Sergio Ramírez was assigned to work with a group of twelve prominent citizens, "Los Doce" (Document 15), who were prominent in mobilizing support for the revolution. What was not generally known then, even by some of the dozen members, was the group's role as an FSLN front. Several of the participants were secret FSLN members; others were cooperative fathers or brothers of FSLN leaders.

Chamorro proposed uniting everyone against the dictatorship (Document 16) and praised the FSLN. At the same time, however, he worried about the Sandinistas' ambitions and the radical rhetoric that labeled as "bourgeois" everyone who did not follow their lead. Chamorro pointed out that "the irrational outcry against the 'bourgeoisie' comes not from . . . the workers . . . but originates usually among those elements of the bourgeoisie [the FSLN] who wish to show off by talking like proletarians" (Document 17).

The murder of Chamorro in January 1978 (Document 18), which has never been solved, was widely attributed at the time to the dictatorship. It set off a wave of strikes and revolts (Documents 19 and 20) in which the FSLN played a marginal role. These mass actions, largely spontaneous, were directed by independent trade unions and UDEL. The Sandinistas' brave attacks on the National Guard added to their prestige and the FSLN grew quickly. Yet they still did not have cadre or cells in the mass organizations and never gained hegemony over the struggle. The three FSLN factions were only united in Havana, under Cuban pressure, in March 1979.

As the battle against Somoza and the National Guard escalated into a virtual civil war, the church leadership joined the anti-Somoza coalition in calling for the dictator's removal (Document 21). Somoza was surprised that the Carter administration called for his resignation and supported the opposition. But he also managed to outmaneuver Washington's mediation efforts (Document 22). U.S.-organized diplomatic efforts failed because the U.S. government did not push hard enough and Somoza successfully stalled for time (Document 23).

FSLN leader Humberto Ortega admitted the Sandinistas' lack of control over the insurrection (Document 24). The key elements of victory were the massive opposition to Somoza, U.S. refusal to assist the dictator, the FSLN's arms, and help from Colombia, Cuba, Costa Rica, Panama, and other countries. At the end, even the Organization of American States took the unprecedented step of calling for Somoza's resignation (Document 25).

The dictator finally fled the country in July 1979. A coalition of forces encompassing the vast majority of Nicaraguans had triumphed in rejecting dictatorship. But now the FSLN proceeded to use its prestige, arms, and discipline to carry out the two goals it had long envisioned: a monopoly of power for itself and the implementation of a second, Marxist-Leninist, revolution in Nicaragua.

I
SOMOZA IN POWER

1.
RICHARD MILLETT: THE SOMOZA REGIME

Graft was common in Nicaragua, but Somoza refined and systematized it. Emboldened by the example of their leader, the officers and men of the Guardia used their positions, especially in customs, immigration, and police, to enrich themselves. They even engaged in wholesale cattle smuggling. The corruption extended from the Minister of War, General Reyes, to the private on the street who would demand, "pay me five córdobas or be arrested." The rural population came to fear the Guardia, claiming that the local soldiers, who were also the rural police, could simply walk into their homes and take anything, leaving them no possible redress. All of this alienated the Guardia from the civilian population, making them a separate military caste, loyal only to their own leader, not to the nation as a whole. They did manage to maintain a high degree of internal order and stability, but the average citizen found himself paying an ever-increasing price for these benefits.

The preoccupation with graft cut sharply into efficiency and by March 1940 the American Legation felt that only the two companies of presidential guards had any potential for combat. Alarmed by this, Somoza began to seek possible American aid for a total reorganization of the Guardia. The American Minister informed the State Department that if we wanted "to maintain Somoza in power," or to "avoid the outbreak of revolution shortly within Nicaragua," we would have to provide such services. The State Department, however, was not anxious to bolster the Nicaraguan dictator's sagging prestige and instructed the American Legation to avoid "any intimation that such appointments would be desired by the United States."

Failing to secure American aid, Somoza set out to reorganize the Guardia on his own. In the fall of 1940, when General Reyes went to Washington to attend a meeting of Western Hemisphere Chiefs of Staff,

---

From his *Guardians of the Dynasty* (Maryknoll, N.Y.: Orbis, 1977), pp. 198–99, 237–38.

the shakeup began. Somoza burst into the Campo de Marte, searched various officers' desks, and transferred most of the arms in the Campo to the Presidential Palace. The General Staff was overhauled with Colonel Medina, hurriedly promoted from Major, replacing Reyes as Chief of Staff. Eight officers were arrested, four discharged, and twenty others suddenly transferred. General Reyes knew nothing about the affair until his return from Washington. He was met at the Managua airport by the Chief of Police. Somoza demanded and obtained his prompt resignation from the Guardia, reportedly telling Reyes that he should be court-martialed and shot. The dictator offered a variety of explanations for his actions, including charges that Reyes had tapped his phones, had failed to carry out orders, was influenced by pro-Nazi elements, and was guilty of graft and corruption, a rather odd charge for Somoza to make against anyone else.

These actions revealed two Somoza tactics which, with considerable success, he would employ repeatedly in coming years. First, any officer whose popularity or power made him seem a potential threat was quite likely to find himself suddenly transferred, retired, or discharged. Those who accepted this treatment without protest often found themselves later restored to a measure of favor. Prison and death were generally reserved for those who actually attempted to overthrow the President. The other tactic was the identification of all opposition, actual or potential with whatever foreign threat currently preoccupied the United States. In the 1940s, this was the Nazi movement; later it would be the Communists. . . .

In the aftermath of the earthquake the Guardia Nacional virtually disintegrated. Most soldiers left their posts to take care of their families or to try to salvage personal belongings. Others, often led by officers, occupied themselves with massive looting, at times using Guardia vehicles to remove the stock from damaged stores. For nearly two days, Somoza was unable to muster even a company of troops. As a result, his prestige and that of the Guardia had sunk to an all-time low and the nation seemed on the verge of anarchy.

Once again the United States, personified by Ambassador Turner Shelton, came to Somoza's rescue. The American Embassy was destroyed by the quake, but Shelton's lavish residence in the suburbs was virtually undamaged. From there the Ambassador conferred regularly with the Nicaraguan strongman, encouraging him to seize total power, allowing him to regroup his troops and other supporters under the United States flag, and even suggesting that United States troops be brought in to help restore order. This last suggestion was not followed by the State Department, but most of the others were. The pretense of a ruling triumvirate was shoved aside and Somoza ruled by decree. When the junta's Conservative member, Dr. Agüero, protested, he was suddenly removed and replaced by a complete puppet, again reportedly at Shelton's suggestion.

The widespread destruction removed some traditional areas of graft for the Guardia, but the massive amounts of foreign aid, from both government and private sources, which flowed into Nicaragua during 1973 more than made up for this. Initially, the Guardia profited by selling looted goods on the black market; later, sales of relief supplies and of smuggled luxuries provided major sources of income. In addition, Guardia families got first priority on those relief supplies which were distributed, with second priority going to other employees of the government and lowest priority being given to the public at large.

Shortly after the earthquake, the entire downtown area was sealed off by barbed wire and Guardia patrols. Approximately a quarter of a million of the city's inhabitants were evacuated to other Nicaraguan towns and hundreds of thousands of others were housed in temporary tent cities around the edges of the capital. Military courts took over some of the judicial functions within Managua. Despite widespread opposition and considerable evidence that the center of the city was permanently subject to the threat of further quakes, Somoza announced his determination to rebuild the capital on the original site. A number of reasons were advanced for this decision, but it was generally accepted that it was major, land-owning interests of the Somozas and of Guardia officers in the Managua area that doomed all proposals for relocation of the capital.

The earthquake destroyed more than property and human lives. It eliminated many traditional sources of Guardia graft and badly damaged the reputation of that force's strength and reliability within Nicaragua. Somoza could do little to counteract the increased public contempt and hostility that surfaced in the months following the earthquake, but he could and did strive to restore Guardia cohesion and loyalty through additional pay raises, expansion of the force, and opening up of opportunities to profit from the diversion of relief supplies. As usual, Guardia were given first priority in home repairs or in the construction of new homes. If officers needed materials for construction, they often simply took them from relief supplies, transporting them in military vehicles. Enlisted men were seldom free to employ such direct methods, but their interests were also carefully looked after with José Somoza, popularly known as "Papa Chepe," often dealing directly with them in the traditional patron-client relationship.

2.
JACK ANDERSON: WORLD'S GREEDIEST DICTATOR
(1975, 1976)

A terrible earthquake devastated Managua . . . on December 23, 1972. For the impoverished populace, it was the worse natural disaster of the century. . . . [F]or dictator Anastsio Somoza . . . [i]t was his most bounteous Christmas.

The great destruction . . . didn't spare hundreds of properties owned by the Somoza family. Many of them were in the name of the dictator's mother. . . . But Somoza quickly recouped the family losses by ordering the National Insurance Company to pay off his mother before any other clients.

While others were picking up the pieces of their wrecked homes, Somoza and his henchmen bought up some cotton plantations near Managua for about $300,000. A week later, the government purchased the land from them for $3 million ostensibly as the site of "housing for the poor." Few homes . . . have been built on the . . . fields, which are still planted in Somoza cotton.

The United States, meanwhile, made a generous contribution to the reconstruction of Managua. Of course, this requires a considerable amount of cement. Guess who produces the cement? The Somoza-owned National Cement Company. And . . . who sets the price of cement? The Somoza government.

Brazil . . . offered $5 million in low-interest export credits to help the earthquake victims. Somoza used most the credits to import Mercedes-Benz automobiles and trucks. He extracted a . . . commission on each vehicle because he happens to own the Mercedes-Benz franchise in Nicaragua. Even Managua's municipal garbage trucks are Mercedes-Benz.

Emergency items . . . donated by many other nations . . . were stashed in an Air Force hangar under the supervision of Somoza's son. Some of the . . . supplies were sold on the black market. . . . [S]ources have no proof that the profits went to Somoza, whose nickname is "Tacho." But . . . the hangar was known in Managua as "Tacho's Supermarket."

Anastasio Somoza . . . runs Nicaragua as if it were his private estate. Through his family and flunkies, he owns or controls virtually every profitable industry, institution and service in the country. He also owns most of the land they sit on.

Jack Anderson column, United Feature Syndicate, 1975, 1976.

His enormous wealth has been squeezed out of his impoverished subjects. . . . They lie in shacks and teeming slums and eke out a living as best they can while the Big Banana stashes his millions in foreign banks. . . .

Classified documents . . . gathering dust in government vaults . . . outline how the current dictator's father stuffed his personal coffers at the expense of his countrymen. The picture they paint reveals that the man who occupies the throne today . . . is a carbon copy of his father.

3.
ERNESTO CARDENAL: SOMOZA DEDICATES THE MONUMENT TO SOMOZA

Somoza Unveils the Statue of Somoza in Somoza Stadium

It's not that I think the people erected this statue
because I know better than you that I ordered it myself.
Nor do I pretend to pass into posterity with it
because I know the people will topple it over someday.
Not that I wanted to erect to myself in life
the monument you never would erect to me in death:
I erected this statue because I knew you would hate it.

4.
XAVIER ARGÜELLO: EARTHQUAKE IN MANAGUA

Juvenal awoke suddenly to a rough jolt and a long, ominous volcanic roar from the bowels of the earth. The lights of the cell went out. Weak and dizzy, he tried to sit up. The prisoners shrieked in the darkness, crowding against the bars. He felt the pressure of bare feet on his head. Sweaty and foul-smelling bodies trampled him. Someone grabbed him by the hair. The ground moved nearly half a foot three or four times a second and bounced upward perhaps eight times. The foot-thick stone walls groaned as the

From Steven F. White, *Poets of Nicaragua* (Greensboro, N.C., 1982), p. 155.

From his novel *Las Delicias del Volga*. Translation © 1986 by Gladys Segal and Robert S. Leiken.

tremor surged furiously toward its climax. Fighting the human avalanche, he got up, narrowly escaping being trampled. It was impossible to walk or even stand. The heavy clay-tiled supports could not withstand the pressure and as the walls gave way the roof collapsed. He shielded his head with his arms, instinctively seeking protection from the shower of stones.

An earthquake that started in the lake itself had torn through the city, the El Hormiguero penitentiary, after splitting the Chico Pelon hill in half and demolishing the Leche La Salud processing plant. From the path of destruction it was leaving along the way, it could be seen coming all the way from Ciudad Jardín. It progressed in rather shallow concentric waves, ripping out laundries and toilets, and launching the contents of dressers and closets. In its path the quake left in the earth cracks like broken mirrors. Sidewalk bricks shook out of place. Automobiles swerved out of control on the zigzagging road, undulating like the surface of a stormy sea. Lampposts swayed amid spark-spewing wires, and heavy transformer-bearing corner posts fell thunderously into a snarl of cables.

The street was still shaking when Juvenal reached it. The first thing he saw was an old multistory mansion collapsing into a huge cloud of dust. The Campo Marte stone wall had disappeared and the military installations no longer looked repressive in this newly opened space. High-voltage cables were strewn everywhere, making it difficult to move about. Hodgson jumped out after him. He had managed to escape through a gap, after fighting desperately to free his legs caught in the debris, digging himself out with his bare hands. After him came Luis Borge Aquino, convicted of robbing Mrs. Esperanza Centeno's house; Skinny Zamora, known as the country's best locksmith or lock buster; and Uriel Mendoza, arrested for the death of an elderly woman, brutally murdered when she was stabbed seventeen times.

Along with Hodgson he got to the corner of El Guayacán, and when they turned on Avenida Bolívar, they were confronted suddenly by a hysterical mob in the middle of the street. Some wore pajamas, others covered themselves with sheets; the rest were half-naked; all ran in different directions, bumping into each other. None of them could be recognized, even from close up, except for the few who carried flashlights. The lights of a Volkswagen car with Mexican plates, which had been squashed under the concrete platform of a gasoline station, still blinked intermittently.

Patrons from the Las Cazuelas Bar crawled out from under the aluminum awning that had covered the outdoor tables. Traffic moved freely in both directions on Calle Colón. But the city was in the dark.

"Honey, this is an earthquake," said a heavy small-headed white woman in pants. Next to her was a potbellied guy in a tight-fitting polyester coach's shirt, watching the cars pass, as if scanning for a familiar face.

"Baby don't get hysterical."

"Its an earthquake! Look at those houses on the ground!" bellowed the woman.

The bartender hastily put away the money in a paper bag, lighting her way with candles.

"Fucking earthquake!" she mumbled. "They all got away without paying."

Two guys tried to calm the curly bleached blonde who shook her head back and forth violently, as if about to lose it. The bigger man—a broad mulatto with a pockmarked face—whispered something in her ear, attempting to kiss her. The skinny guy with collar-length hair watched them, smiling, holding on to his drink.

"Erika, Erika!" shouted the bartender. "Where's that faggot waiter? Help me out! They're going to steal the money!" They heard the kitchen gas tank explode, starting a fire in the back of the house. Finally, the mulatto slapped the blonde. He walked with her toward the baseball field across the street. The other man followed them, refusing to stay alone.

"Forget the dough and save your life," said Juvenal to the bartender. "All this is going to burn, and it isn't even yours to keep". . . .

. . . They walked toward the street without saying a word, unconsciously going in the direction of the Plaza Restaurant. Perhaps they were attracted by the fire engine's flashing red lights. The streets overflowed with voices, moans, and recriminations as neighbors shared their misfortunes with acquaintances and strangers alike. Rapidly rumors spread that the cataclysm had been caused by the Santiago and Momotombo volcanoes, adding a new element of terror to the collective fear. Being outdoors had provided a certain sense of safety. But there was no escape from a volcanic eruption. Most terrifying of all was the imagined scope of the earthquake. It was feared that the whole country was sinking, or that Central America might have vanished. Many feared the great day of God's rage was upon them, the angel's voice heralding the Coming of the Lord Omnipotent as He appeared through heaven's opened doors to deliver the Last Judgment. There was a heaviness in the air, as if one single earthquake were not enough to soothe the earth's wrath. The hot waters of the great lake convulsed. There was no wind. In the streets, the crowds clad in white moaned and cried in repentance of their sins. Caught between nakedness and fear they jousted for space with animals and debris, humbled under the unforgiving black sky.

And then another earthquake. While standing at the corner, Juvenal saw everything around him falling. Whole walls collapsed thunderously amid thick, asphyxiating clouds of stale dust that burned the eyes. Juvenal saw another mansion collapse. On its facade was a sign advertising Quaker oatmeal. Amusing in its own macabre way, the Manzanares house shook like jelly, not quite ready to fall. Dr. Icaza's clinic spit tiles from its roof onto the street. The advertising signs were shaken out of place and stripped of their relevance by the earthquake. All these sun-dried clay-brick houses were overloaded upon weak foundations. Their interiors had been remodeled and their structural soundness had been eroded.

Juvenal held on to an electric pole and felt it vibrate. The woman next to him shouted at her husband, "The girl, the girl, the girl!" The people squeezed against each other, begging God's mercy. Men ran in all directions, often stepping on each other, dodging the falling eaves and roofs. Howls and noise of shattering wood and glass were everywhere. Women who came out of nowhere bellowed in terror. They hugged each other while they mumbled their prayers, imploring the Lord to halt the cataclysm. The first tremor disturbed the geologic faults along the outskirts of the city. A large readjustment was set in motion to reestablish balance. A 900-meter area of sedimentary rock, marine formations of different periods, miocenic and oligocenic strata and the Rivas formation—which was the deepest rock exposure—were shaken in unison. This area was five kilometers away from the underground epicenter. Managua's eastern block slid several inches sideways onto the western block, along the Tiscapa fault, which divides the city vertically in two, with a fall of six inches, and then the block slid in the opposite direction. The surface-level seismic waves spread at a rate of about three kilometers per second, causing other minor cracks, loosing its destructive power, and moving away from the epicenter under the city.

Then a brilliant, pure moon appeared from behind the clouds, and in the firmament appeared the Seven Lambs with the same Morning Star that once guided Wise Men to adore our Lord. People stood up silently, defeated by nature. Any prayers said were barely audible. All of December's chill suddenly descended upon Managua. The city mourned through the baying of thousands of dogs.

5.
ANTONIO GARCIA ET AL.: TELEGRAM TO SOMOZA (1973)

SENOR GENERAL ANASTASIO SOMOZA DEBAYLE
CHIEF OF THE NATIONAL GUARD
SUPREME COMMANDER OF THE ARMED FORCES
PRESIDENT OF THE NATIONAL EMERGENCY COMMITTEE

La Prensa, August 1973.

PRESIDENT OF THE AGRICULTURAL COMMITTEE
DELEGATE TO THE CENTRAL AMERICAN COMMON MARKET
LEADER OF THE NATIONAL LIBERAL PARTY
HEAD OF THE FOREIGN FINANCE COMMITTEE
CANDIDATE FOR THE PRESIDENCY OF THE REPUBLIC
EX-PRESIDENT OF THE REPUBLIC
GRAND MASTER OF THE ORDER "RUBEN DARIO"
SENATOR FOR LIFE
PROMOTER OF RURAL ELECTRIFICATION
PROMOTER OF AGRO-INDUSTRY
PRESIDENT OF LANICA AIRLINES
PRESIDENT OF MAMENIC SHIPPING LINE
CHAIRMAN OF THE NATIONAL CEMENT COMPANY
CHIEF EXECUTIVE OF "EL PORVENIR" PLANTATION
CHIEF EXECUTIVE OF "CENTRAL DE INGENIOS" REFINERIES
LEADER, FLAGBEARER, OUTSTANDING ONE, GUIDE, INSPIRED AND
ILLUSTRIOUS ONE, SAVIOR, SUPREME RULER, BENEFACTOR, UNIQUE
LEADER, GLORIOUS ONE, TALENTED ONE, MAN OF DESTINY,
COUNSELLOR, ILLUMINATOR, WISE, VIRTUOUS, UPSTANDING,
INSPIRING, INTELLIGENT, REGAL, SERENE, PRUDENT, BUILDER,
CREATOR, HURRICANE OF PEACE, NEGOTIATOR, FUTURE PRESIDENT,
REFEREE, ARBITER OF JUSTICE, SUPREME COMMANDER, GENERAL IN
CHIEF, FAMOUS ONE, MAGNANIMOUS AND GENEROUS ONE, HIS
EXCELLENCY, MOST EXCELLENT ONE, JUDGE, PREDESTINED,
DISTINGUISHED, RENOWNED, CHOSEN, VICTORIOUS, BRILLIANT,
STRONG PERSONALITY, CLEVER, FABULOUS, MAGNETIC, WEST
POINTER, STRATEGIST, ORGANIZER, PROTECTOR, STATESMAN,
COMFORTER OF THE AFFLICTED, STATISTICIAN, WINNER, SWORD,
PACIFIER, POLAR STAR, MORNING STAR, GENIUS, RESTORER,
EMANCIPATOR, LIBERATOR, IDEALIST, LIBERAL, PLANNER, SOLID
ACADEMIC BACKGROUND, MAN OF SCIENCE, ENGINEER, HELMSMAN,
PILOT, CAPTAIN, DIRECTOR OF INDUSTRY, BASTION, BULWARK,
FORTRESS, BEACON, THE MAN, PALADIN, PATRIOT, DEMOCRAT,
SAVIOR OF THE REPUBLIC, GIANT, FIRST TAXI DRIVER (AND ALL
"FIRSTS" EVER KNOWN OR IMAGINABLE), SACRIFICED TO HIS PEOPLE,
ALTRUISTIC, DOCTOR HONORIS CAUSA, BACHELOR AD HONOREM,
CHIEF OF CHIEFS, INDISPUTABLE CHIEF, SUSTENANCE OF DEMOCRACY,
SUPPORTER OF LATIN AMERICA AND GREAT FRIEND OF NIXON

SEÑOR GENERAL:

WE READ ALL THESE DESCRIPTIONS OF YOU IN YOUR OWN NEWSPAPER,
NOVEDADES, AND HAVE BEEN UNDERLINING THEM DAILY TILL LAST
MONDAY, AUGUST 12.

IN THE NAME OF ANY OF THESE OFFICES OR QUALITIES, WE WOULD
LIKE TO ASK YOU TO DO SOMETHING TO STOP THE PRICE OF CONSUMER
GOODS FROM RISING AND TO MAKE THE RAIN FALL.

YOUR HUMBLE SERVANTS, WORKERS OF THE CITY OF MANAGUA,
ANTONIO GARCÍA, F. CRUZ, H. MARTÍNEZ

II
THE FSLN'S FORMATIVE YEARS

6.
CARLOS FONSECA AMADOR: A NICARAGUAN IN MOSCOW (1958)

In Nicaragua I had heard many things about Moscow and Russia. One of
my sources was the free U.S. embassy movie presentations at Plaza Laborio
of Metagalpa. Other sources were Hollywood films, and radio broadcasts.
The image depicted by the media was of a Moscow fraught with blood, a
city of grim, suffering millions. I had been shown undernourished workers,
who had no justice system to protect them, in a Moscow full of tanks and
bayonets pointed at men and women who dared to protest. . . . This was
the image of Moscow depicted in songs and even in comic books available
to our innocent children. This disquieting image caused me grave concern
because, if these descriptions were accurate, I had made the biggest mistake
of my entire life when I accepted the airplane ticket. . . . Perhaps my rash
decision would yet cause my family great pain, if I suffered in Moscow the
alleged fate of political terror that those who did not obey the Kremlin
were said to have suffered. . . . Suddenly I felt relieved, when I remembered
the doubts I had in Nicaragua about anti-Soviet propaganda. The Yankees
were lying about Moscow, just as they had lied about criminal dictatorships in Latin America. According to them, Trujillo was the United States'
best friend, and we know that is not true. According to them, Moscow is
the city of death. That is probably false. They have lied about issues that
are right before our eyes. They are probably lying about faraway Moscow
as well. These thoughts gave me peace. . . .

In Moscow and on my way to the Ukraine and Leningrad, I saw dilapi-
dated housing. Yet, Sputnik research and development programs had cost

---

Published as a booklet in 1958 and republished in *Barricada,* the FSLN's organ,
November 8, 1980. Translation copyright © 1986 by Gladys Segal.

many millions of rubles. Those deadly weapons I had seen in Red Square on November 7 must have been very costly. They had spent millions to produce the long-range missile that might destroy New York. The 214 million Russians know well the high cost of bombs, missiles, and rockets. And had they not spent their rubles on this arsenal, they might have already solved their housing problems. . . .

I wish to make one more point about property ownership in the Soviet Union. Soviet leaders such as Nikita Khrushchev, Bulganin, and Mikoyan live in great modesty. Like all other Soviet citizens, they cannot own factories, farms, or businesses. They live off their salaries. Their wives—also known as their companions—work. Nikita's companion is a schoolteacher. The wives are not given media exposure because of their husbands' leadership.

There are many inventors in the Soviet Union. In 1954 there were 500,000 inventions recorded. This is the by-product of the people's level of culture. There is no illiteracy in the Soviet Union. Under the pre-1917 czarist regime, 60 percent of the people were illiterate. Libraries are very popular. Books are the items most sold in the Soviet Union. In the United States there are more telephones, automobiles, and televisions than in the Soviet Union, but there are no more books in the United States than there are in the Soviet Union. . . .

Religious life in Poland is exemplary. The Communist Party leads the government. The Catholic Church plays an educational role in its schools. Cardinal Wizinski, the church's highest prelate in that country, endorsed Communist candidate Gomulka in the elections.

Many people with devious intentions have attempted to conceal religious practices in Poland and in other socialist countries, where there are church-sponsored newspapers. This is also true for Czechoslovakia, where I saw stores that carried religious paraphernalia exclusively. . . .

In Poland there are other political parties besides the Communist Party, such as the Farmers' Party with their representatives in Parliament. These parties are legal, and they have their own publications.

7.
THE FSLN PROGRAM OF 1969

The Sandinist Front of National Liberation (FSLN) grew out of the Nicaraguan people's need for a vanguard organization, which through a direct

Tricontinental, No. 17 (March–April 1970).

struggle with its enemies, is capable of seizing political power and establishing a social system that will wipe out the exploitation and misery our country has suffered throughout its existence.

The FSLN is a political-military organization whose objective is the seizure of political power through the destruction of the bureaucratic and military apparatus of the dictatorship and the establishment of a Revolutionary Government based on a worker-peasant alliance and the support of all the anti-imperialist patriotic forces of the country.

The Nicaraguan people have suffered under the oppression of a reactionary and fascist clique imposed by Yankee imperialism since 1932, the year in which Anastasio Somoza García was designated chief director of the so-called National Guard (GN). The Somozaist clique has reduced Nicaragua to the status of a neocolony which the Yankee monopolies and the oligarchic national groups exploit.

The present regime is a politically unpopular and juridically illegal regime. Its recognition and aid from North Americans constitutes an irrefutable proof of foreign interference in Nicaraguan affairs. . . .

We have reached the conclusion that the people's Sandinist revolution and the destruction of the regime that is the people's enemy will come about as a consequence of the development of a hard and prolonged people's war. . . .

1) The Revolutionary Government. The people's Sandinist revolution will establish the Revolutionary Government of the People and will create a nation without exploitation, without oppression, without backwardness, a free, independent, and progressive country. The Revolutionary Government will undertake the following measures, of a political character:

a) It will liquidate the reactionary state structure based on electoral farces and military coups and will establish a system of full participation of all the people, on a national level and on a local level (departmental, municipal, regional).

b) It will deprive of their political rights those individuals who occupy high public positions as a result of the electoral farces and military coups that have taken place in the country, following the publication of this document.

c) It will establish the full practice of human rights and all individual safeguards.

d) It will guarantee freedom of expression of ideas which lead first of all to the energetic diffusion of people's rights and patriotic responsibilities.

e) It will guarantee freedom to organize the workers' trade union movement in the city and in the countryside; freedom to organize peasant, youth, student, women's cultural, and other movements.

f) It will guarantee the right of Nicaraguan emigrants and exiles to return to the country.

g) It will guarantee the right of asylum to citizens of other countries persecuted for engaging in revolutionary struggle.

h) It will severely punish the tormentors responsible for persecuting, informing on, torturing, or assassinating revolutionaries and the people.

2) A basic and independent economy . . .

   a) It will nationalize the assets of the mining and forestry companies, etc., and other such riches usurped by the Yankee monopolies in Nicaragua.

   b) It will nationalize the huge landholdings, factories, sugar refineries, means of transportation, and other assets usurped by the Somoza family.

   c) It will nationalize the huge landholdings, factories, transport, and other assets usurped by the politicians, the military, and all the other accomplices in administrative corruption sanctioned by the regime which is the enemy of the people.

   d) It will nationalize banks and place them exclusively at the service of the economic development of the country.

   e) It will establish state control over foreign commerce with ways to diversify it and make it independent.

   f) It will plan the national economy, thus eliminating the anarchy reigning in production under the present regime.

   g) It will control the exploration and exploitation of natural resources, for which it will create special state institutes. Electrification will occupy a special place in the integral development of the country.

   h) It will establish control and participation by the workers in the administration of industry and other nationalized assets (latifundia, factories, mines, etc.).

   i) It will protect the small—and middle—sized proprietors (producers, tradesmen). . . .

   m) It will refuse to acknowledge the usurious loans imposed on the country by the Yankee monopolies.

3) Agrarian revolution. . . .

   a) It will expropriate the capitalist agricultural industries and all aspects of the latifundia, with a view to liquidating the parasitic hold on the land by the exploiters.

   b) It will hand over the land to the peasants free of charge, in accordance with the principle that the land must belong to those who work it.

   c) It will stimulate and promote the organization of cooperatives in the countryside.

d) It will facilitate every type of aid to the peasant and will grant loans at low interest rates for the purchase of farm equipment and machinery, seed, fertilizer, etc.

e) It will cancel the debts contracted by peasants with the landowners and other usurers.

f) It will carry out a technical revolution in agricultural production. . . .

h) It will protect the small—and medium—sized landowners.

i) It will protect the landowners who collaborate with the armed revolutionary struggle; the lands of these owners which exceed the limit established by the agrarian laws promulgated by the revolution will be purchased from them for distribution among the peasants who need them.

j) It will liquidate the forced work stoppage that the peasant suffers during most of the year and will create sources of work for the peasant population.

k) It will guarantee markets for agricultural, meat, and dairy products.

4) Labor legislation and social security. The people's Sandinist revolution will put an end to the unjust conditions of life and of work that the workers suffer under the present regime.

a) It will promulgate a labor code and other laws of social security for the exclusive benefit of the broad mass of workers.

b) It will put into force full freedom of trade union affiliation and organization.

c) It will impose absolute respect for the dignity of the worker, prohibiting his unjust treatment in the course of his work.

d) It will liquidate the punishing unemployment.

e) It will extend social security coverage to all workers and employees in the country; the coverage will include illness, accidents, physical incapacitation, retirement, etc.

f) It will extend free medical care to the entire population; it will construct clinics and hospitals throughout the entire national territory. . . .

i) It will provide adequate housing for every family.

5) Special plan for the Atlantic Coast. The people's Sandinist revolution will put into practice a special plan for the Atlantic Coast and other areas of Nicaragua sunk in the most complete abandonment.

a) It will stimulate a special program to be applied to the Atlantic Coast, the region of the country that has continuously suffered the most cruel Yankee exploitation.

b) It will stimulate the mining industry, converting into a nightmare of the past the mining centers of the Atlantic Coast that have been nothing less than Yankee concentration camps.

f) It will stimulate the flowering of local culture on the Atlantic Coast, originating in the historic traditions of the region.

g) By the measures stated, it will wipe out the ignominious discrimination to which the indigenous Misquitos, Sumos, Zambos, Blacks, and all other sectors of the peoples of the Atlantic Coast have been subjected.

6) Liberation of women. The people's Sandinist revolution will abolish the odious discrimination that women have suffered compared to men, and will establish economic, political, and cultural equality between women and men.

a) It will establish the principle that woman is equal to man in political, economic, cultural, and social life.

b) It will put an end to the discrimination that woman has suffered and which is reflected in the abandonment of the working class mother.

c) It will extend special attention to mother and child.

d) It will establish two months of maternity care before and after birth for working women.

e) It will establish the right to equal protection from revolutionary institutions for children born out of wedlock.

f) It will establish nurseries and other centers for the care and attention of children.

g) It will promulgate progressive laws concerning the family and marriage.

h) It will eliminate prostitution and other social evils to raise the dignity of women.

i) It will raise the political, cultural, and vocational level of woman through her participation in the revolutionary process.

7) Administrative honesty. The people's Sandinist revolution will clean out traditional governmental administrative corruption and will establish strict administrative honesty.

a) It will abolish the criminal industry of vice (prostitution, gambling, the sale of alcoholic beverages, the sale of drugs, etc.) which the privileged National Guards exploit.

b) It will establish strict control of all taxes collected in order to prevent government officials from profiting,

d) It will put an end to the business by which military commanders appropriate the budgetary allowance earmarked for the care of common prisoners, and will construct care centers designed to rehabilitate delinquents.

e) It will abolish the contraband practiced on a large scale through the political and military clique

f) It will severely punish individuals who engage in crimes against administrative honesty (embezzlement, contraband, profit from the exploitation of vice, etc.). . . .

d) It will inculcate in the consciousness of the members of the people's army, the principle of relying on their own force to carry out the fighting tasks and to develop their creative initiative. . . .

13) Solidarity among peoples. The people's Sandinist revolution will practice a true combative solidarity with the peoples fighting for their liberation.

a) It will actively support the fight of the peoples of Latin America, Africa, and Asia against imperialism, colonialism, and neocolonialism.

b) It will support the struggle of North American Blacks to win human rights.

c) It will support the struggle of all the peoples against the installation of yankee military bases in foreign countries.

14) Central American people's unity. The people's Sandinist revolution will struggle for the true union of the Central American peoples within one country.

a) It will support an authentic unity with its brother peoples in Central America. This unity will begin with the cooperation of forces to achieve national liberation and establish a new social system, without imperialist domination or national betrayal.

b) It will liquidate the so-called integration which seeks to multiply Central America's subjugation to Yankee monopolies and the reactionary local class.

15) Veneration of martyrs. The people's Sandinist revolution will cultivate gratitude and eternal veneration for its martyrs

Free Fatherland or Death
Sandinist Front of National Liberation
Some place in Nicaragua

8.
HENRY RUIZ: THE GUERRILLA ERA

We never doubted that armed struggle was the way to victory over the dictatorship. . . . Our questions were along other lines: whether the underground practices were right, whether we were technically capable of carrying on the struggle, whether this was the proper moment for the emergence of armed activity. . . .

It must be recognized that [our defeat at] Pancasán saw the virtual annihilation of the Front's best cadres. . . . Nevertheless, a few were still left and with them we prevented that from being the final chapter [in the struggle]. . . .

The FSLN at that time was an organization of cadres, not a mass organization. It was necessary to find a way . . . to bring the mass and the vanguard into a closer relationship, to incorporate the people into the armed struggle. . . .

At one point, we intended to kill Somoza, but this was where Carlos Fonseca's great foresight came in. Carlos maintained that Somoza was an invaluable asset who personified all our country's contradictions: the line between national liberation and liberation from the dictatorship . . . [and] the economic contradictions of the bourgeois sector. In short, dictatorship and class oppression were clearly identified in the person of Somoza. . . .

By 1973, Somoza had alienated the rest of the Nicaraguan bourgeoisie. He was no longer satisfied with controlling the means of production and . . . became a threat to the . . . game that he and the rest of the bourgeoisie had created. . . . After the earthquake, Somoza broke the rules. His incursion created enmity and jealousy, making a political lineup against him. In this way Somoza tipped the balance against himself.

The church began conspiring and so did the bourgeoisie itself; we began making contact with different people and realized that something new had happened. In the mountains, we now formed relations not only with the peasants, but also with the small producers, cattlemen, and coffee growers. . . . By [1974], Somoza had a substantial group of opponents and the Front had become an important factor to whom the people were turning for an answer. Under these circumstances, we planned the assault on Castillo's house, even though the original idea was to take an embassy. . . .

We were petit-bourgeois in origin, of student background, and the

From *El Nicarauac*, Vol. 1, No. 1 (May-June 1980).

mountains were like a crucible. It was there that the cadre were really identified. Carlos Fonseca was obsessed with tempering the cadre under very difficult conditions. . . .

We maintained that the popular war would lead to a popular uprising despite the fact that at the moment we were few and—regretfully, I must introduce a fact on which I don't want to elaborate—divided and not receiving the support we needed. . . . We felt that if we were able to count on fifty well-armed men we could find a way to use the weapons well. . . . We were just living for that opportunity to come. . . .

9.
OMAR CABEZAS: A SMALL INSURGENCY

We put forward a program for university reform; we studied the reform of Córdoba and wanted to change our own university. We fought to change the content of the courses; and we were able to transfer large sums of money to the Frente out of the coffers of the National Union of Students. . . .

Our work in Subtiava took off like wildfire, but very quietly and out of the light. And we started presenting the image of Sandino in Subtiava. The Indians had a leader, a historical figure, who more than any other was representative of their people: Adiac. We presented Sandino as an incarnation of Adiac, then Adiac as an incarnation of Sandino, but Sandino in the light of the Communist Manifesto, see? So from shack to shack, from Indian to Indian, ideas were circulating: Adiac . . . Sandino . . . class struggle . . . vanguard . . . FSLN.

Gradually a whole movement was born in Subtiava. Here I want to make you see how these things were interrelated. We started penetrating other barrios in León, through the relatives of Subtiavans who had moved there when they got married or for whatever reason. We set about recruiting these relatives and this was how we made our initial contacts with the Subtiavans in other barrios. I'm talking about La Providencia, Reparto Vigil. There was a time when FER* was going to organize a special branch to deal with the barrios. Now our influence was not just in the high schools; we had grown not just in the university; FER was beginning to have a real presence in the barrios.

From his *Fire from the Mountain* (New York: Crown, 1985), pp. 29, 37–38, 45–46, 17, 63–65, and 86–87.

*FER: The Revolutionary Student Front.

Since it was always the Frente behind FER, when the work in the barrios reached a certain level the Frente said, "Fine, now FER can forget it. The underground network of the Frente will take over from here." . . .

The problem was, we didn't have any organic ties; we still didn't have any ideological or political ties to the people. Because the message we had for the people carried with it danger, expectation, strangeness, and fear. We had to be very persuasive. I discovered something then—I mean a personal political discovery; I'm not talking about figuring out that water boils if you heat it—I discovered that language identifies. I discovered for myself how language communicates.

Looking out over the faces of the people, I saw the workers in their caps. They didn't nod yes and they didn't nod no; fat women with aprons on who didn't laugh but didn't frown either; their faces were impenetrable somehow, impersonal. More than once we had the feeling we weren't getting anywhere, that the people didn't understand, that it didn't matter to them at all. And dammit you wanted to pick up a stick and beat what you were saying right into their brains. But you couldn't.

At the beginning that lack of communication was a block. And on top of that the Guard might come and start harassing them, or harassing us, or all of us together. I remember once when I was talking, a couple of swearwords slipped out; then ha, ha, ha! people smiled when I swore, and looked at each other. No doubt about it, they were communicating with each other; they were chuckling, but chuckling about something I'd said. I realized I was getting through to them. This is important, because it dawned on me then that a swearword or a crude word used in the right way can be explosive, very sharp politically. It's one thing to go into a barrio and start lecturing about the current historical juncture. It's something else to start talking about how the rich with their fat investments are off whoring in Europe, see? . . .

Even after six years of aboveground work, when I left for the mountains I went with the idea that the mountain was a tremendous power. We had this myth of the compañeros in the mountains, the mysterious, the unknown, where Modesto* was, there at the top. And in the city both the people in the underground and those of us working legally always talked about the mountain as a sort of mythical force. It was where our power was, and our arms and our best men; it was our indestructibility, our guarantee of a future, the ballast that would keep us from going under in the dictatorship; it was our determination to fight to the end, the certainty that life must change, that Somoza must not go on polluting every aspect of existence.

The mountain was our refusal to believe that the Guard was invincible.

*Henry Ruiz.

But sure enough, the reality hit. And you were right on the verge of demoralization when you got into the mountains and found nobody there but Modesto with fifteen other men divided into little groups. Fifteen or who the hell knows how many—what I do know is that there couldn't have been more than twenty guerrillas in the mountains at that time. It made you want to turn right around and go back. Mother-fucking son of a bitch! What is this shit? You are right at the point of saying to yourself, Holy Mother of Christ! this is the worst decision I've ever made in my life. You feel you've started out on something that has no future. . . .

All day as we went along I kept thinking about the camp; I was spurred on by the thought of the camp, remembering everything they had told me about the mountain. In the city the mountain was a myth, it was a symbol, as I told you before. I wondered what the camps would be like, and what Modesto looked like, how tall would he be, if I had ever met him—all these things. What I mean is the idea of getting to the camp and demystifying, that's the word, demystifying it, once and for all, finally seeing it from the inside, that's what I'd spent almost six years working for day and night, with no Christmas, no Holy Week, no vacations. All because of that mountain. Because of the FSLN, because of that mystery which was growing greater with every passing day. If anything in that hellhole of mud, in that nightmare of mud and raw blisters and exhaustion and discomfort made me happy it was this: finally, on my own two feet, I was approaching it—I was going to see those famous men in person, the guerrillas, people like Che. What would their beards be like, and the battles, and the work with the campesinos? How would they cook? I was going to be in the heart of the Frente Sandinista, in the most hidden, the most virgin part of the Frente, the most secret, the most delicate, the Frente of Carlos Fonseca and all of that. Carlos: I had never met him, never had a chance to meet him. And all of that propelled me forward. We transformed our loneliness into a brotherhood among us; we treated each other gruffly, but actually we loved each other with a deep love, with a great male tenderness. We were a group of men in a single embrace, as brothers, a group of men bound by a permanent kiss. We loved each other with blood, with rage—but it was a brotherly love, a fraternal love. I remember on one march a compañero came across a baby bird in its nest and carried it with him for six days. One of the compañeros farther down the mountain had mentioned that his mother loved little birds, so since he was going to take mail down to the city, he took that opportunity to take the bird with him, to go six days with a tender little bird. Savages like us, battling the vines, fording rivers, marching six miles through rivers, over stones, trying to keep from falling —to save that little bird. Watching out for your pack and thinking how any minute the Guard might come, and death, all of that, with the little bird; battling the environment, sleeping with the little bird. To take it to the compañero so he could give it to his mom. When the compañero received the little bird he just stared; they embraced, and I'm sure he didn't cry. Because he couldn't cry anymore or refused to. It's like that song of Carlos Mejía Godoy's about us always having a clear look in our eyes. There was no selfishness among us.

As if the mountain and the mud, the mud, and also the rain and the loneliness, as if all these things were cleansing us of a bunch of bourgeois defects, a whole series of vices; we learned to be humble, because you alone are not worth shit up there. You learn to be simple; you learn to value principles. You learn to appreciate the strictly human values that of necessity emerge in that environment. And little by little all our faults faded out.

That was why we said that the genesis of the new man was in the FSLN. The new man began to be born with fungus infections and with his feet oozing worms; the new man began to be born with loneliness and eaten alive by mosquitos; he began to be born stinking. That's the outer part, because inside, by dint of violent shocks day after day, the new man was being born with the freshness of the mountains. A man—it might seem incredible—but an open, unegotistical man, no longer petty—a tender man who sacrifices himself for others, a man who gives everything for others, who suffers when others suffer and who also laughs when others laugh. The new man began to be born and to acquire a whole series of values, discovering these values, and cherishing them and cultivating them in his inner self. You always cultivated that tenderness in the mountains. I took care not to lose my capacity for that beauty. The new man was born in the mountains, as others were born in the underground in the city, as the guerrilla was born in the brush.

III
DIVISIONS IN THE FSLN

10.
PLUTARCHO HERNÁNDEZ: INSIDE THE FSLN

The meeting [of October 1974] was one of the most important in the history of the FSLN. It took place . . . at an extremely critical moment for our organization. The previous year's losses and the growing demands of or-

From his "Inside the FSLN: Chronicles of a Combatant," published in Costa Rica in 1982.

ganizational work made the situation more complicated than usual. On top of everything else, we had just received a tape recording sent from abroad by comrade Humberto Ortega which admonished us to obey all the orders issued by the National Directorate that remained in the exterior and demanded, in a rude and threatening tone, total submission to his decisions. . . .

Among the main decisions reached at this meeting were . . . to deliver a letter to Carlos Fonseca from us in reply to Humberto's tape and concerning other important internal matters; to notify the comrades abroad that our National Directorate in the interior was no longer provisional . . . to advise them also that we would accept nobody but Carlos Fonseca from the National Directorate abroad as secretary general of the FSLN; and that Humberto would regain his status in the Directorate only after his return to Nicaragua. Other decisions taken at the October meeting were . . . to carry out a rescue operation to free the comrades in prison. . . . Plutarcho Hernández was placed in charge of training the participants, Tomás Borge of planning, and Eduardo Contreras of the direct execution of the plan. It was also decided that the comrades in the mountains should carry out actions in their area to divert the enemy's attention and facilitate the urban work somewhat. . . .

After [this] meeting, all of us returned to our respective regions and jobs with determined minds and hopes pinned on the great action that was to begin on the night of December 27 at José María Castillo's house, in one of the most exclusive residential sections of Managua.

We selected twenty comrades to go to a safe house in Las Nubes, close to Managua, where comrade Tomás Borge would conclude their special training and preparation for the action. . . .

And so, December 27 arrived, and by pure chance, Eduardo Contreras . . . and I happened to be listening to the radio news of *El Clarín* as we were talking in a safe house in Managua, when we heard the reporter Laszlo Pataky publicly thank Dr. José María Castillo for his kind invitation to attend a party he was giving that night at his house . . . "in honor of the distinguished Ambassador of the United States of America, Mr. Turner Shelton." Of course, many other Nicaraguan and foreign dignitaries were also invited. . . . The three of us jumped with joy in the realization that the long-awaited operation would take place that very night. It was 8:00 A.M. and we had sufficient time to notify Tomás Borge and the squad leaders to be prepared to go into action that day. With Eduardo Contreras we made a tour around Castillo's house and drew a preliminary sketch. . . .

The action was not launched until 10:50 P.M., unfortunately after the Yankee ambassador had already left. The assault was a complete success even though our comrades were not very well armed. . . .

The comrades in prison were set free and $1 million was obtained from the dictatorship plus $15,000 that was stashed away in a closet in the house and a small collection of firearms belonging to the doctor. . . .

Comrade Jaime Wheelock, abroad at the time, was quick to condemn the December 27 action, alleging that it was nothing but an expression of the marked petit-bourgeois inclinations that affected the National Directorate. Wheelock alleged that we had released fourteen comrades from jail only to put in 200 picked up during the crackdown that followed. This was how a comrade who was living abroad and who had never risked his life in defense of the ideas he claimed to uphold heaped insults on those of us who were working from day to day regardless of danger in seeking to overthrow the tyrant. This . . . clearly reflected the profound separation of many militants living abroad from the hard realities of the situation at home. . . .

We were being accused of "petit-bourgeois deviation" by those who set themselves up as the sole representatives of the proletarian ideology within the FSLN. . . . In an internal message addressed to the militants of the FSLN, Wheelock explained the break with Carlos Fonseca, at whom Wheelock leveled accusations that were so virulent and insolent that I do not believe they should be reproduced in this book. . . .

The "Proletarian Tendency" accused [us] of being "glory bound" and "anarchistic." They maintained that we could not bring the people to rebellion without first carrying out patient and prolonged efforts within the working class. They insisted on criticizing the conspiratorial nature of our work and called for methods unworkable given the concrete circumstances of Somozaism at the moment. . . .

In view of this situation of crisis and internal division in the FSLN, it became urgent for Carlos Fonseca to return. We were convinced that only he could introduce the necessary elements of discipline and harmony that would help put things in order. . . .

Carlos did all he could to explain and interpret the divisive attitudes within the FSLN and was particularly harsh in his judgment of the political behavior of Wheelock and Humberto Ortega. . . .

After the spectacular December 27, 1974, operation, the FSLN carried out no more actions of major magnitude and impact. It was not until October 1977, the date of the assault on the San Carlos base, that the FSLN recovered the initiative and launched the offensive in the final phase of the struggle to overthrow the dictatorship.

11.
FSLN-PROLETARIAN TENDENCY: THE INTERNAL CRISIS

There are two divergent ideological currents in the Nicaraguan revolutionary movement today: the proletarian and the petit bourgeois. The former, based on the theory of scientific socialism, is rooted in the proletariat and stresses its dominant role in the revolutionary process.

The latter is made up of two main factions. The first [Prolonged Popular Struggle] . . . seeks support in the peasantry and urban petit-bourgeoisie rather than in . . . mass struggle.

The second [Tercerista] faction represents the most retrograde positions of the petit-bourgeoisie. . . . They consistently resort to tactics of terror and putschist adventurism. . . . With financial support from one sector of the bourgeoisie and some military strength, they armed a group of patriotic citizens [in October 1977] and are throwing themselves into a senseless offensive which . . . dovetails perfectly with the malaise of the imperialists and domestic bourgeoisie. . . .

Like Lenin, we consider . . . that the only things that can have true and responsible agitational value . . . are events in which the masses themselves are the protagonists and which stem from their will and class interest. . . .

Members of petty-bourgeois groups in leadership positions in the FSLN . . . launched . . . a frantic series of disciplinary actions, dismissals, decisions by the "official" leadership to shift activists to isolated areas or abroad, expulsions, and other persecutions together with a . . . campaign and personal attacks to discredit, distort, and cover up the real issues at the core of the confrontation. . . .

The Front's first political platform recognized the proletariat as society's fundamental class, the vanguard of the revolutionary sruggle, and saw the peasants as their closest ally. . . . The enemy to be defeated . . . was the Somoza dictatorship and . . . the National Guard, while U.S. imperialism was recognized as the principal foe. The bourgeoisie and landowners were also considered enemies of the revolution. . . .

The central ideas of the [petite bourgeoisie's] ideology were: (a) Nicaragua is a semicolonial, primarily agricultural country with marked semifeudal features and the majority of its population were peasants; (b) because

From "La Crisis Interna y Las Tendencias," *Colección 4 de Mayo,* No. 1 (1978).

the Nicaraguan economy is predominantly agricultural, the working class is small; (c) the age-old backwardness of Nicaragua . . . explains the ebbing of popular struggle and the disorganization of the masses; (d) political power resides in a collusion of the sell-out Liberal-Conservative clique working hand-in-glove with the imperialist master. . . .

The assertion that Nicaragua is a primarily agricultural, semifeudal country is inaccurate . . . failing to take into account changes in economic and social conditions caused by capitalist development. . . . Arguing that Nicaragua is populated mainly by peasants will lead to assigning guerrilla struggle waged in the countryside . . . a central social and political importance. . . . To consider Nicaragua a peasant country also means assigning to that class the fundamental role as the basis of the revolution. . . .

A National Directorate has been in existence since 1969 which, however, never functioned as a political body in the country but rather through provisional delegates who generally imposed their own criteria and work style upon the organization. Some leaders sympathized with the insurrectional schemes, others with those that were guerrilla-oriented, and as long as a rather primitive structure was retained, a one-man administration mentality set in that gave rise to recurrent leadership disputes. . . .

Shortly before the 1975 crises, the FSLN was politically fragmented because of the confrontation of two leadership groups who had incompatible political strategies. . . . With one group advancing the strategy of "Prolonged Popular Warfare" (GPP), and the other proposing an insurrectional strategy [Terceristas], it was basically a case of struggle between the two factions for political hegemony. The strategies in this struggle . . . were advanced to define the differences between the factions and to obtain as many followers as possible. . . .

The GPP is a continuation of the "foci" approach . . . inspired by the guerrilla experience in Vietnam, it laid out a series of guidelines . . . which conceived of the revolutionary process as the preparation of social and technical conditions for carrying on guerrilla warfare throughout the entire country—mountains, countryside, and city. This line considers the FSLN as an organization for preparing the armed struggle while, at the same time, being a "front" through which the masses will join in the guerrilla struggle, an "army" for the attrition of enemy forces, and an underground apparatus with predominantly logistical functions. . . . Consequently, as far as this line is concerned, the FSLN link to the masses seeks not so much to strengthen the popular organizations as to reinforce its own internal infrastructure. . . .

The foolhardy rightist populist line of the Terceristas . . . goes back to the early years of FSLN activity when armed struggle was conceived of as the initiator and catalyst of the entire people. Basically, it was inspired by an idealist and somewhat romantic interpretation of the Cuban revolution. . . . More markedly petit-bourgeois, they resort enthusiastically to the methods—denounced by Lenin—of "stimulant terrorism" which supplants mass revolutionary action. The class lines of society do not even exist for the Terceristas: the vanguard of society is not a particular class but the FSLN which directs "our entire people from the poorest and most suffering to the well-off patriotic sectors. . . ."

The key positions of the Marxist-Leninist line may be summarized as follows:

1. To be revolutionary, any political action must be related to the concrete conditions of society. . . . A revolutionary action outside the class struggle is inconceivable.
2. In undertaking a revolutionary transformation, the classes involved in it must be the ones that wage a stubborn struggle for their emancipation. No party, no group, can take over the revolutionary role of the masses.
3. Nicaragua's economic conditions mark the proletariat as the . . . director of the revolution. It is the FSLN's function . . . to be the political vanguard . . . for organizing, educating, mobilizing, and directing the mass struggle for socialism and national liberation . . . by preserving the interests and viewpoint of the proletariat. . . .
6. The most immediate and bitterest enemy of our people is the Somoza military dictatorship, as the concrete expression of imperialism in Nicaragua and of the political-military support for bourgeois domination. The most urgent political task is the revolutionary overthrow of the military dictatorship . . . while at the same time the struggle is waged against the exploiters on the various battlefields of class exploitation. . . .
9. Combining armed struggle with political struggle and raising the level of class struggle to prepare the masses for implementing higher forms of revolutionary violence . . .

The breakdown of the petite bourgeoisie within the Front has been reflected in this process of struggle for unity through the following aspects, among others:

1. The narrow factional spirit that has characterized the opportunistic cliques and led them inexorably to recalcitrant sectarianism, personal allegiances, and even fanaticism.
2. The abandonment of political methods of internal struggle and the substitution of skillfully calculated manipulation . . . which has led each faction to lay claim to the legitimacy of the National Directorate in order to impose their criteria and the positions of isolated elements.
3. . . . Ideological struggle and confrontation of positions of principle are avoided or obstructed.
4. Continual swerving and vacillation . . .

5. Irresponsible and systematic personal attacks that have accompanied and often taken the place of political discussion in both factions.
6. The opportunism of their undermining tactics . . .

12.
CARLOS FONSECA AMADOR: LAST TESTAMENT
(MARCH 1976)

A point has been reached in the life of our organization at which Jaime Wheelock's defeatist attitude is finding sympathy among various comrades of the National Directorate in the exterior. . . .

Early last December, Eduardo Contreras, a member of the National Directorate, request[ed] authorization to meet with Wheelock and the other two who were expelled, adding that if refused such authorization he would go through with the meeting anyway even if it meant resigning his post in the National Directorate. . . . After the meeting was held he sent a new communication to the interior in his capacity as a member of the National Directorate expressing his agreement with Wheelock's position.

Humberto Ortega, a member of the National Directorate living outside the country . . . [also] met with Wheelock. . . . Ortega and Contreras, each on his own, have taken positions . . . lacking in revolutionary consistency. There is a substantial component in those attitudes that is at odds with Sandinista sense of honesty and responsibility.

It is our obligation to help these brothers overcome those liberal weaknesses. . . .

It should also be added that besides openly acknowledging that Wheelock was right, Ortega and Contreras, still uninterested in waiting for the views of the Directorate in the interior . . . went even further . . . and decided to bring the discussion before the rank and file of the organization in the exterior. . . .

Careful consideration should be given the message sent secretly by Humberto Ortega to Camilo Ortega, who was honest enough to pass it on to higher echelons. . . . The message . . . stated that Wheelock's position was correct. It also specified that . . . he might also keep it from the higher echelons if he deemed it advisable. . . .

In his letter to Camilo Ortega, Humberto Ortega called Tomás Borge ambitious. Such an accusation would be unjustifiable at any time, but it so

---

From his last political document before being killed by Somoza's army. In the original, all the FSLN leaders were referred to by their code names.

happened that the message reached us . . . just when we had learned about how heroically our brother Tomás had fought and also that he was . . . captured, wounded, having fired his last bullet. Naturally, it was really sickening to read an accusation against our brother Tomás under those circumstances. Our brother's unselfishness has been exemplary, and the very opposite of petty ambition.

Furthermore, while Humberto Ortega's letter tried to be careful about revealing the identity of members of the organization, Tomás' first and second names nevertheless appear in it, which is hardly indicative of a desire to protect him. . . .

We recognize that the brothers do, indeed, realize that the Sandinista Front, the Nicaraguan revolutionary movement, is having serious problems.

The fact of the matter is that these problems have caused them to lose their composure to the point where they have fallen into a state of veritable desperation.

We said that they see that problems exist.

However, they have not stopped to think that seeing problems is a far cry from solving them. They forget that our Directorate went through the experience of an inner struggle in which obstacles arose from another direction, such as lack of understanding, impulsiveness, disconnection from concrete reality. . . .

Frankly, this new polemic is no more than an updated and expanded version of the earlier one. At the same time that they came out on Wheelock's side, they refused to return to the country. Obviously, they do not wish to share responsibility for the adverse aspects of what is inevitably occurring at the present time. It must be said that, although understandable, this is unjustifiable.

It may also be, however, that the two compañeros believe that they should hold themselves in readiness for the time being as a reserve of leadership cadres to ensure continuity should serious losses be suffered in the interior of the country. This would also be understandable. The negative aspect of it is that they themselves would be the ones to decide who should stand by as a reserve in the exterior without consulting the rest of the compañeros of the Directorate. When the time comes to discuss the matter, other compañeros may be chosen. But this does not preclude the possibility that some of the compañeros in the exterior may carry on in that capacity. . . .

What is more, they have not bothered to evaluate properly the efforts of the brothers in the interior—efforts that made it possible to resolve basic problems. And those successes will be the basis for further advances. That is what is newest in the life of our organization. Nevertheless, the cadres in exile who support Wheelock consider that he represent something "new" in the organization's life. We find not a single word about the many compañeros who formed the backbone of the great mass mobilizations held in certain regions of the country recently; about the many compañeros who provided the support that made possible the continuity of our forces in the mountains. . . .

How can one not respect those who are devoting themselves to the work in the interior? . . . It is incomprehensible the time Humberto Ortega and Contreras have spent in the exterior. Is there not a certain measure of unproletarian vanity present in speaking disdainfully of the work of the interior when they have not been directly involved in that work? . . .

These most recent vacillations should not blind us to the proofs of staunchness that [Humberto] and Cantreras have both demonstrated on other occasions. Nor should it lead into the trap of polemics. We must remember that Marxism-Leninism has already been discovered.

It shows disrespect in the extreme to disregard the colossal contribution of Marx and Lenin to theory and praxis. In avoiding argumentation, we agree with the viewpoint now current in the mountains to the effect that "futile polemics" should be opposed. . . .

We can be optimistic about Sandinista unity. The authority conferred by devotion to the work in the interior of the country, in the underground, will not be used to denigrate the anxious compañeros in the exterior. We must be confident that this attitude on the part of the interior will succeed in counteracting the deviations that have arisen.

I do not think that the way in which J. S. Wheelock has been treated is entirely correct. . . .

What is involved is no isolated matter but rather the policy of cadre development. . . .

J. S. Wheelock took asylum in 1970 at a time when other compañeros who were running greater risks than he remained underground. In 1972, he applied for readmission to the organization. . . .

As for me, I am not so sure it was a good move to finally propose to him that he go into the mountains, which, as is known, he refused to do. Perhaps the right thing would have been to leave the door of the organization open to him to become a satisfactory sympathizer instead of remaining the halfhearted militant he almost always was. It must be realized, however, that he himself was in large measure responsible for impeding such a solution because of his insistence on provoking reprisals for his openly divisive attitude. Luis Carrion's case was that of a person of bourgeois extraction and non-Marxist ideological background who was assigned a highly responsible post in the Managua regional organization on the basis of a rather mechanical decision. On our part, we brought it up in our organization at one point that ideological vigilance was being neglected in certain aspects by giving prominence to groups which, although transitorily supporting our line, hold ideologies foreign to the proletarian ideology. . . .

As a matter of fact, when I was able to take up the matter with Humberto Ortega and Eduardo Cantreras, they said that I was overreacting and that the main and decisive point was the attitude of a person in practice. That, to be sure, is decisive but not the only thing, and ideology must be given consideration and not ignored. Of course, ideological rectification is worthless without corresponding practical behavior, yet without a Marxist ideological orientation positive practical behavior is insufficient.

The foregoing all provides important experience applicable to the treatment of our cadres. This point is highly significant because a correct cadre policy is indispensable in solving general problems whatever they may be. . . .

Nothing is more ridiculous than the complaint of alleged insults against Wheelock on the part of the Directorate in view of the fact that Wheelock was the first to launch not only insults but unfounded charges against the Directorate of the interior. . . .

There has been talk that the Directorate is "cliquish," "opportunistic," lacking in "moral standing." These were the terms used by persons who had not spent more than a few weeks in the underground to describe those who had devoted an entire lifetime to the revolution. . . .

The thing is that Wheelock remarked to a compañero whom he saw after the meetings at which it was decided to take reprisals against him that he "didn't understand" how he had managed "to come out of those meetings alive." He was practically saying that he had just met with murderers. Can a worse insult be imagined? Greater slander?

We recall the case of Roque Dalton in El Salvador.[1] We cannot believe that Roque Dalton committed worse breaches of principle than Wheelock did. Furthermore, with all due respect for the present revolutionary movement of El Salvador, the standing achieved by the Sandinista Front in its long struggle is undoubtedly more solid. The Sandinista Front can be proud of the composure with which it considered the Wheelock case, in contrast with the experiences of other places. . . .

Wheelock used other insulting epithets. At the end of last December, he went as far as to write that he wanted "to redeem the traditions of honesty and heroism" in the Sandinista Front. It was manifestly unfair for Wheelock to say any such thing to Federico and Tomás Borge. He also repeated the same remark in December that he had made in October, which was that the Directorate inside the country is cliquish. Even before he was expelled, but as that was about to happen, he stated that the Directorate wanted to make the mountains his "concentration camp." It is clear

---

[1]See Chapter 4.

that he used all the words at his command to cover up his open refusal to face the rugged life of the mountains; a ruggedness our brother Filemón Rivera described as "the soldier's ointment, the *comandantito's* purgative."

It is correct that we have to be partial, that is, to favor one party—the party that is right—but we must do so with discretion, keeping our emotions under control. Lenin said that a revolutionary must act with "a cool head and a warm heart." But if we are not careful, we make mistakes and act with a cold heart and a hot head.

Frankly, the outrageous accusation of security violations is the product of the panic that gripped those members of the petite bourgeoisie who were drawn into the struggle and ended up vacillating. It is noteworthy that Humberto Ortega and Contreras joined in this campaign before there was any intensification of the repression in Managua. . . .

One doesn't have to be very shrewd to realize that when halfhearted people harp on security violations, the purpose is to find a justification, a cover-up, for their indecisiveness, their lack of courage in the struggle. . . .

The fact of the matter is that Humberto Ortega, being out of touch with practical activity, thinks it is easy to adopt a whole series of security measures that in reality are not so easy (ultraleftism considers very easy what is not easy at all); Wheelock, on his part, is never satisfied by the security measures that are feasible. Thus, two extremes can meet in the present case. Careful attention should be given to the point because it tends to undermine the fighting spirit developed by the Sandinista guerrilla resolved to face the enemy at the risk of his life. Let us lose no time in recalling Lenin's writings in which he stressed the importance of this spirit in overthrowing antipopular power and winning revolutionary power.

The best refutation of the alleged gross security violations is the fact that the Sandinista Front is now in a position to carry on the struggle with the strength that it has succeeded in maintaining despite the colossal repression unleashed. . . .

IV
UNITED FRONT AGAINST SOMOZA

13.
UDEL'S MANIFESTO (1977)

The Democratic Union of Liberation (UDEL), a pluralistic opposition organization that includes political and labor sectors of all tendencies, addresses the Nicaraguan people in order to clarify its position with respect to the country's chaotic situation and to issue a call for the establishment of a NATIONAL AGREEMENT to immediately launch a democratization process. For this purpose, UDEL declares:

1. That the present violent situation is the outcome of the country's institutionalized violence, especially over the long years of dictatorial government that has shut off all civic and effective democratic pathways for solving Nicaragua's grave economic and social problems.
2. Because of the dictatorship's institutionalized violence, Nicaraguan homes continue being plunged into mourning, not only those of the youth who, moved by patriotic ideals and faced with the shutdown of democratic opportunities for contributing to the solution of national problems, find themselves obliged to take the desperate path of insurrectional action, but those of the officers and soldiers sacrificed in the fulfillment of a misplaced sense of duty, acting in defense not of the country's interests but of one who governs against the will of the citizens.
3. The violent situation rampant in the country cannot be corrected by government repression. That only produces more innocent victims and, indiscriminately exercised in the combat zones, increases the suffering of the people and lays the foundations for more violence in the future.
4. Violence can be controlled only by elimination of its causes. In that sense, UDEL ratifies the commitment set forth in its program to the effect that peace can be established only by initiating a process of political change that will convert Nicaragua into a truly democratic society, both pluralistic and independent, built upon administrative honesty, socioeconomic justice, and respect for all human rights.

"Manifiesto de UDEL," *La Prensa,* October 19, 1977.

In response to the concern expressed by the Archbishop of Managua, Monsignor Miguel Obando y Bravo, and shared by prominent citizens, UDEL considers that in order to immediately launch such a process of political transformation a broad NATIONAL AGREEMENT is necessary calling for and effectively insuring the fulfillment of five points:

1. Repeal of the Radio and Television Code and other repressive laws.
2. Amnesty and general pardon for political prisoners and exiles.
3. Appointment of a new head of the National Guard who will insure its professionalism and impartiality.
4. Effective enforcement of freedom of political and union organization.
5. Establishment of political statutes that guarantee pluralism and the participation of all sectors of the citizenry in the engendering of the public powers.

In demanding those points and others that may arise out of national dialogue that should be immediately launched, and in compliance therewith, UDEL is ready to join forces with all political and social sectors of the country whom it invites to a decisive national meeting on unity of action.

Managua, D.N., October 18, 1977.

NATIONAL EXECUTIVE COUNCIL

RAFAEL CÓRDOBA RIVAS. Partido Conservador. RAMIRO SACASA GUERRERO. Movimiento Liberal Constitucionalista. CARLOS ALVAREZ G. Confederación General del Trabajo (CGT Independiente). GUILLERMO BALTODANO SERRANO. Partido Socialista Nicaraguense. RODOLFO ROBELO HERRERA. Partido Liberal Independiente. DAVID OROZCO RAMÍREZ. Partido Socialcristiano Nicaraguense (PSC). LUIS SANCHEZ SANCHO. Partido Socialista Nicaraguense. AMADEO VANEGAS MONCADA. Central de Trabajadores de Nicaragua (CTN). EDGARD MACÍAS GÓMEZ. Secretario General del CEN.

14.
SERGIO RAMÍREZ: INTERVIEW (1977)

When the faction commonly known as the Sandinista Front's "Terceristas" conceived of the insurrectional strategy, the need arose to boost the

From Pilar Arias, *Nicaragua: Revolución* (Managua, 1979). Translation copyright © 1986 by Gladys Segal.

alliance with the democratic sectors of the national bourgeoisie through a group that seemed to give political backing to the Sandinista Front and might eventually join a government supported by a victorious Sandinista Front. This strategy began to develop in the midst of what was the FSLN factional conflict early in 1977.

At the beginning of 1977 I discussed these issues with Humberto and Daniel Ortega, and as an FSLN activist I was entrusted with recruiting and organization efforts for the group. Thus, in mid-June of 1977 we held a meeting with Humberto Ortega. I was joined by Joaquín Cuadra Chamorro, a prosperous lawyer with the Bank of America and the Nicaragua Sugar State Company. He was a man the bourgeoisie would find trustworthy beyond reproach. Also with us was Emilio Baltodano, manager of Café Soluble Inc., one of the country's most important industries. Others present were: Felipe Mantica, manager of a supermarket chain, member of the board of Bank of America, and associated with the highest echelons of private enterprise; Father Fernando Cardenal, professor at the Central American University; and Ernesto Castillo, who lived in exile in Costa Rica to escape a one-year prison sentence given to him by Somoza for having carried the book *Imperialismo y Dictadura* by Jaime Wheelock at his bookstore. Later we would be joined by Ricardo Coronel; Father Miguel d'Escotto, then communications secretary with the World Council of Churches in New York; and Carlos Tunnerman, former president of the National Autonomous University of Nicaragua (UNAN). It was a very productive meeting, and those who would later become "Los Doce" were very receptive to the Sandinista Front's approach and its strategy for an insurrection and an alliance with the democratic sectors of the bourgeoisie. . . .

That meeting and the following ones in Mexico were marked by great enthusiasm, in spite of the fact that we were discussing military action, but had no funds. In Mexico we were joined by José Benito Escobar; Casimiro Sotelo from California; Arturo Cruz, who worked with the Interamerican Development Bank in Washington, D.C.; Carlos Tunnerman; and Carlos Gutiérrez, who was living at the time in Mexico. . . .

The October offensive had great political impact on the country. It was the basis for the anti-Somoza bourgeoisie's launching of its own political operation. This bourgeois operation, based on the Front's military actions and on the pronouncements of "Los Doce," led to the request of a dialogue with Somoza. At this point, the church's intervention was sought. Also sought was intervention by INDE (the Nicaraguan Institute of Development) headed by Alfonso Robelo. The Liberal Constitutionalist and the Christian Socialist parties requested a dialogue that would attempt to stanch the nation's wounds and promote the healing process. But this might have been interpreted as a request for dialogue by "Los Doce." We made it clear that we had never requested a dialogue with Somoza. We had, in fact, requested a dialogue in alliance with the democratic forces and with the Front, but against Somoza. But since the bourgeoisie's motivation was using dialogue as propaganda, the whole issue was ignored.

In the meantime, we rapidly made diplomatic strides, establishing communication links with Carlos Andrés Pérez in Venezuela, José López Portillo in Mexico, and General Torrijos in Panama. Then, Miguel d'Escoto met in Mexico with Pedro Joaquín Chamorro, director of La Prensa, and leader of UDEL (the Democratic Liberation Union). A coalition of anti-Somoza groups and Pedro Joaquín agreed that UDEL not participate in the dialogue with Somoza, and for the first time they accepted a dialogue with the Sandinista Front. This first alliance, sought between the Front, "Los Doce," and UDEL, culminated in a meeting in the second half of January in Mexico. And it was then that Pedro Joaquín Chamorro was assassinated. . . .

15.
LOS DOCE: FIRST MANIFESTO (1977)

Presently, Nicaragua is experiencing a situation of intense drama. The clash between the dynastic government's repressive machinery and the unequivocal opposition to the dictatorship has become more acute, unavoidably leading toward an increase in acts of resistance to this oppression. Undoubtedly, the country is yearning for a substantial change, leading it on a path toward a new form of democratic and social organization. Armed clashes are on the increase, and if no other approaches toward a true solution are sought, the alternative will be war, with its grim and unpredictable consequences of loss of life and great damage to the national economy.

We think that any palliative or illusory solution to our problems will only exacerbate the sense of frustration and discontent that we are experiencing, because we are plagued by government-sponsored irrational violence, designed to quell dissatisfaction; by corruption, gnawing at the country's entire administrative system; and by total confusion of one family's private and public interests; by the fictions of the government that rules us. We live in a situation in which all decisions are delayed and hampered, and as the terrible aftermath of this overview, we have the tragic

Primer manifiesto de los Doce, October 18, 1977. Translation copyright © 1986 by Gladys Segal.

hopelessness that has plagued the Nicaraguan and his basic needs for work, shelter, health, education, and culture.

For a decade, the Sandinista National Liberation Front has selflessly fought for change in Nicaragua, and the lives of so many young people lost witness best the reality of the struggle carried out with an ever-increasing degree of political maturity.

We, the undersigned, do not hesitate to call upon all socially conscious Nicaraguans to solve our country's anguishing national problem *with the participation of the National Sandinista Liberation Front, so that a permanent and effective peace is guaranteed.*

FELIPE MANTICA ABAUNZA (businessman), JOAQUÍN CUADRA CHAMORRO (lawyer), MIGUEL ESCOTTO BROCKMANN (Roman Catholic priest), RICARDO CORONEL KAUTZ (farming engineer), CARLOS TUNNERMANN BERNHEIM (educator), FERNANDO CARDENAL S.J. (priest), EMILIO BALTODANO PALLAIS (businessman), SERGIO RAMÍREZ MERCADO (writer), ARTURO CRUZ (economist), CARLOS GUTIÉRREZ SOTELO (dental surgeon), ERNESTO CASTILLO MARTÍNEZ (lawyer), CASIMIRO SOTELO F. (architect).

16.
PEDRO JOAQUÍN CHAMORRO: SPEECH ON UNITY (1977)

[The people need] unity to fight for justice, unity to fight for freedom, unity to launch a democratization process that will lead the way to structural change and the basis for a system of political democracy, economic and social justice, and effective independence for our nation.

The unity of the people as a whole, of all the political, economic, and social sectors, [is necessary] to fight for the democratization of Nicaragua. . . . We now have greater possibilities than ever for choosing between . . . the dictatorship and the hope for democracy in Nicaragua's future.

Throughout the forty years of the [Somoza] dictatorship we have lived a legal fiction of democracy and a reality of dictatorship. Power has not resided in the people, not in the popular will, but in fraudulent electoral processes protected by the repressive force of arms . . . in the interests of a ruling minority. And in the same way, the popular will as a legitimate

---

Speech at La Cuesta Country Club during meeting in his honor, November 6, 1977.

source of political power has been misrepresented . . . all the institutions and procedures of democracy have been . . . corrupted. . . .

THE ARMY

The dictatorship converted the National Guard into a private army of the ruling family. Respect for professionalism and seniority has been supplanted by personal subordination, military discipline by authoritarianism. The pay of officers and soldiers has been kept at a very low level to force them to obtain their income through a network of illegal remuneration so that their loyalty is not to the law that determines their pay but to the person who pulls all the strings. . . . And what is worse, the idea that the people are enemies of the army was foisted on officers and soldiers when the truth is . . . that we are not enemies of the army but of the use to which it has been put in protecting a family that has perpetuated itself in power against the people's will. . . .

JUSTICE AND FREEDOM

The administration of justice is subordinate to partisan control and judges must decide a case according to political circumstances. . . . The convictions, abilities, and freedom of public servants are violated since their authority is vested not in these values but in an unconditional obedience or submission to blackmail and pressure. . . .

Freedom of speech, of conscience, of organization are eroded by repressive laws that limit liberty in a way compatible only with the dictatorship's security. The Radio and Television Code . . . legislation on slander and libel, freedom of speech, crimes against the economy, the exclusion by law of political organizations like the Communists, go beyond established patterns [and] are tailored to fit a political system that has no support other than that of repressive force. . . . The cost of the dictatorship's survival and its series of injustices touched more and more Nicaraguans and forces gathered to resist it. . . .

THE CRISIS OF THE SYSTEM

The dictatorial regime has been the political basis for an economic development process whose benefits have been withheld from the vast majority of Nicaraguans. The dictatorship's apologists frequently tell us of the high growth rates for gross domestic product, exports, investments, and the government budget. When we look behind all the jargon, however, we find ourselves facing a heartbreaking picture of an immense majority of Nicaraguans living under subhuman conditions. . . .

That type of development is in crisis. The short-term reawakening of the economy brought about by investment opportunities generated by the earthquake, the rise in coffee prices, and by the stimulus of growing external borrowing, cannot hide the basic trend toward crisis. . . .

The present crisis . . . has been hastened by the fact that the U.S. government's traditional support of the dictatorship has given way to the moral factor of human rights in its foreign policy. . . . The dictatorship is not an adequate framework for fostering just and balanced economic and social development. Furthermore, the exclusion of the majority of Nicaraguans from the benefits of economic growth has built up profound social and political tensions. Lastly, all democratic and civic opportunity is closed.

THE FSLN

The inability to solve the country's problems and the persistence of a regime of institutionalized violence has driven substantial contingents of our people to take the path of revolutionary insurgency.

The FSLN is not the product of foreign agents or exotic doctrines, as the government claims in its anxious search for international protection; the FSLN's violence is the harvest the regime has reaped. . . .

And so it has been expressed throughout the country: the church, the private sector, the union and professional organizations, and all opposition political sectors. The same was done by the Democratic Liberation Union (UDEL) in its declaration of October 17, 1977, in which it pointed out, "Because of the government's institutionalized violence, the homes of Nicaraguans continue to be plunged into mourning for the young men who, moved by patriotic ideals and in the face of a closure of democratic opportunities for solving national problems, find themselves obliged to take the path of insurrection. . . .

THERE IS NO SOLUTION WITH SOMOZA

There is no national solution within the framework of the dynastic dictatorship. . . . We want a peace based on a system which believes that economic, social, and political conditions should satisfy the demands of the people; a just and egalitarian society in which bread, education, health, and housing for all are not lacking; a national community united by brotherhood and not divided by hate. We want authorities elected by a fair and honest electoral process with the participation of all political sectors. This is the dream our people have fought for over long years. Their struggle and the blood they have shed obligate us. We are ready to honor that obligation. . . .

17.
PEDRO JOAQUÍN CHAMORRO: RHETORIC AND THE BOURGEOISIE

Anybody can make a big deal around here with words, and show off by looking to pick a fight, making a lot of noise. All just talk.

For example, we heard this gem over the local radio: "The bourgeois opposition and private initiative have no part to play in this affair [the revolutionary movement] and if they keep it up, their attitude should be considered suspect."

What is that supposed to mean . . . ?

To begin with, a huge percentage of Nicaragua's population belongs to the bourgeoisie, big, middle, or petit; such people, for instance, as shop-keepers, artisans, manufacturers of small articles, the grain merchant, those who have stalls in the markets, the lawyer who defends persons facing a court-martial, the medium-size and even the small farmer who forms part of what we could call the rural bourgeoisie, who owns a pasture lot and a few cows, those with a coffee crop, sugar cane, beans or corn to sell in the villages and cities. They are bourgeoisie, not proletarians.

Of course in the main, our population consists of peasants and workers, but the petite and middle bourgeoisie, people who earn their livelihood with the sweat of their brow, and whose contribution to the national production is considerable, cannot be relegated to the margins and much less be looked down upon, as certain sectors do every day with "proletarian" lingo that bears no relation whatsoever to the character or way of life of those who use it.

We call for reflection upon this matter because the daily speeches against the "bourgeoisie" have now come to constitute an integral part of a deca-dent, demagogic national vocabulary. And, actually, nobody listens except for the fabricators of the refrain themselves, making the tape-recording machines or the school yards resound. In so doing, they do not realize that they are swimming against a current that is not only real and strong but appreciable, because neither the man who works his parcel, nor the woman whose active business in the market supports an entire family, nor the professional whose studies have cost a thousand sacrifices, nor the medium landowner, nor the prosperous businessman with progressive ideas, are persons who should be abominated; they are estimable persons, part of the people, part of the very nation, and most essential, to be sure, to its reconstruction.

Secondly, why should the attitude of such working people be suspect when they wish to contribute to the country's democratization in some form . . . ? Why should they be denied that right—a duty at the same time —to make their contribution to a solution that all of us, proletarians, bourgeoisie, businessmen, professionals, women, and men alike, desire in Nicaragua . . . ? Who has the right to call the one person who seeks the country's democratization suspect . . . ?

It is curious and, at the same time, revealing to observe how the irrational outcry against the "bourgeoisie" does not come from the laborer, nor from workers who are struggling for the social advancement of their class, nor from the unionist (Socialist, Social Christian, or Social Democrat), but originates usually among those elements of the bourgeoisie who wish to show off by talking like proletarians.

A real contradiction, isn't it . . . ?

18.
LA PRENSA: THE MURDER OF CHAMORRO (1978)

THEY HAD HIM ASSASSINATED!
Martyr of Nicaragua and of Its Liberty

This morning, assassin's bullets cut short the life of Mr. Pedro Joaquín Chamorro Cardenal, director of *La Prensa.*

The cowardly and vile murder took place at about 8:20 a.m., on Second Street SW in Old Managua.

The precise location of the crime was a block and a half away from the former location of the Nicaraguan Bank on the well-known street El Trébol.

Mr. Chamorro Cardenal was driving his car to work in the direction of this newspaper. As usual, he was alone and unarmed.

The perpetrators of the murder were two individuals who used a sawed-off shotgun to kill the man who devoted his writings and his life to the continuous defense of the people of Nicaragua. . . .

A few minutes later, the halls of Hospital Oriental were filled with family members and friends. The sight of Mr. Pedro Joaquín Chamorro's bullet-

La Prensa, January 10, 1978. Translation copyright © 1986 by Gladys Segal.

ridden lifeless body brought tears to everyone's eyes. Even the hospital nurses cried openly when they found out what had happened.

At *La Prensa,* several military vehicles were parked at the entrance, giving the impression that the facilities had been occupied by the military. However, *La Prensa*'s personnel moved about normally, and undisturbed.

There were scenes of intense emotion at Hospital Oriental. A crowd of people poured into the streets around *La Prensa*'s office in search of information. The paper's editorial room was invaded by scores of journalists. . . .

Because his life ended in a patriotic martyrdom, because he was forever present in the first ranks of the fight to liberate Nicaragua, all of Nicaragua and all of its people mobilized immediately, inquiring about the criminal attempt, wanting to know details pertaining to his death. Hundreds of citizens from all walks of life practically ran to the hospital to ask about the tragedy with the hope that he might be saved. And when they found out about his death, they could not conceal the tears and profound sorrow caused by the unfortunate news, nor the deep sense of repulsion the murder awakened in them.

At the hospital itself, the nurses and nurses' aides cried bitterly when they found out that nothing could be done to save him from death. At Mr. Chamorro Cardenal's home and at the newspaper's offices the phones rang off the hooks with questions about the grim murder.

Similar calls were coming from all of Central America: from radio and television stations, from well-known newspapers, and from citizens, all wanting to know and inform their public about the vile attempt that cut short the life of one of Nicaragua's greatest citizens.

Mr. Pedro Joaquín Chamorro Cardenal died in ambulance number 11 of Managua's firefighter force, in route to the hospital. . . .

19.
LA PRENSA: STRIKE AGAINST SOMOZA (1978)

The country's two biggest trade unions, the General Federation of Independent Workers and Nicaragua's Workers' Union (CTN), have announced an open-ended strike within their ranks, as an act of mourning, and in protest of the vile murder of Mr. Pedro Joaquín Chamorro Cardenal, director of the newspaper *La Prensa.* Furthermore, the strike is declared in protest of the significant number of union leaders and union

La Prensa, January 13, 1978. Translation copyright © 1986 by Gladys Segal.

affiliates who have been jailed following the latest events. . . .

Leaders of the two workers' unions, which are known as the two most outstanding and combative organizations in Nicaragua, declared that this is the nation's organized workers' initial response toward the heinous crime committed against the champion of freedom of the press, and in view of the abuses and excesses seen lately in the country.

They ended by saying: "The working class is up in arms, and will play its important role in this moment of crisis as well as in the necessary struggle to end the harassment and social helplessness afflicting and anguishing the working class." . . .

20.
UDEL: SUPPORT FOR THE STRIKES (1978)

We wish to pay tribute to the private sector by demonstrating our heartfelt appreciation. The private sector has taught us an extraordinary civic lesson fraught with sacrifice. Together, businessmen, professionals, workers, and housewives have demonstrated what we knew from history: nothing can stop a people intent upon demanding that its dignity and its rights be respected.

We also give full value to the Catholic Church's contribution. In preaching its message of renewal, the church impressed upon the people the rallying cry that it is in this world that true Christianity, liberty, and justice must be practiced.

Essential to this movement has been the national press. With the sacrifice of its great leader, Mr. Pedro Joaquín Chamorro, the liberating forces unleashed themselves to perform the noble task of constructing a new Nicaragua. . . .

We reiterate to the National Guard and to public employees our belief that the struggle of the people, of the political parties, of the trade unions, and of private enterprise is against the tumbling and corrupt Somoza dictatorship, and in no way against the army, or the government workers, who must serve the country and the people. We thank our sister countries on the continent for their solidarity. We thank the world, which in one way or another backed the liberating struggle of our people.

We encourage all sectors to be firm in this struggle for dignity, justice, and liberty. . . .

"La Oposición Unida: Paro y Fuera Somoza," January 31, 1978. Translation copyright © 1986 by Gladys Segal.

V
MEDIATION AND INSURRECTION

21.
BISHOP OBANDO Y BRAVO: THE CURRENT SITUATION (1978)

The political antagonisms besetting the country, far from being resolved . . . have sharpened more than ever . . . in a spiral of violence that it now seems impossible to halt. Practically every day comes the tragic news of one or more deaths. Every day, the blood of brothers is spilled in a situation of virtual civil war where pity and love wither.

Violence has engendered violence as the hatred and resentment that produce this homicidal spiral shut the door to any rational solution ever more tightly. And so we look with stupor upon bands under different banners engaged in mutual destruction, increasing their arms, troops, and death plans. It is in the face of this threat of fratricidal extermination that we, as pastors of the Christian people, issue a call to reflection and to effective action for peace and justice.

We realize that those who chose violence do so often impelled by desperation and in the belief that, after the bitterness of the process, the desired good and justice will shine forth.

We believe, nevertheless, that violence not only threatens to make the possibilities of building the Kingdom of God based on brotherhood and justice more and more inaccessible but will end by being counterproductive for the very ones who resort to it.

What is there to expect today in Nicaragua if the present escalation of violence [and] repression continues. Each day brings more dead, more hatred, and more people demanding vengeance, and with this we are increasing the homicidal potential of society and creating groups which are motivated less and less by seeking the common good and more and more by blind desire for revenge. . . .

There is no doubt that those unjust structures still supported by . . . pretensions of legality and resting upon institutionalized violence must be rejected and countered by all the power of Christian commitment. But we

Message of August 3, 1978, from *Pensamiento Centroamericano,* No. 159 (April-June 1979).

must do this by seeking positive forms. . . . If Christian conscience has reservations regarding the use of violence for changing a given situation, there is all the more reason for rejecting the use of violence to maintain an intolerable and unjust situation. . . .

Broad sectors believe democracy is impossible if those who promise guarantees are the ones now in power, and those who hold power are distrustful of any solution not made by themselves, and, as a consequence, the solution that appears to be close and feasible, becomes more and more remote. . . . We see the obstacle and observe that instead of diminishing, it is growing, giving rise to a situation of rejection and impossibility for a dialogue with the catastrophic consequences already indicated.

22.
ANASTASIO SOMOZA: VIEW FROM THE BUNKER

After the elections of '78, the pressing problem continued to be our relationship with the United States. I needed the United States and I thought the United States needed me. Again I received a call from the U.S. Ambassador. He said he wanted to visit with me and I invited him to lunch. I did my best to convince him that the U.S. needed me and my constitutional government. It was a visit in which many of our problems were discussed. Then, in a cynical manner, he looked at me and said: "You know, there are some countries who want to overthrow you." My retort was, "What will it take to get them off my back?" He replied: "I think if you shorten your term of office, you will get them off your back." I looked at him in astonishment and said: "Are you trying to say I should resign?" His answer was a simple "Yes." This was a disturbing conversation.

I then pointed out to the Ambassador that I was duly elected to the presidency in an open, fair, and observed election. I reminded him that my election had been officially recognized by all the countries in Central America, and that I couldn't see the reasoning behind his views. I told him that possibly some kind of political arrangement could be made but that I didn't plan to resign.

My ire was rather obvious at that point and I decided it was time for frankness. I looked at him squarely in the eye and said: "Mr. Ambassador, whose brainchild is that? Your government's? Because I want to know officially!" He denied that such was the official position of the United States

From Anastasio Somoza, *Nicaragua Betrayed* (Boston: Western Islands, 1980), pp. 103, 106, 218–20, 223, 226.

and remarked that it was just a personal thought of his. Based upon the previous conversations which my friends had with the Ambassador, I was sure he was lying to me.

In retrospect, I went too far in my efforts to convince the United States that they should be working with me and not against me. Due to our long history of cooperation and mutual confidence, I continued to conduct my affairs in a manner which I thought would please the United States. The hope was always there that the U.S. would finally see the light. Another indication of my yielding to the desires of the U.S. relates to the "famous twelve" episode.

There were twelve men in Managua, of business, political, and religious backgrounds, who decided they wanted to oppose me openly. Their decision to take such action was made toward the middle of 1978. It wasn't the opposition factor which disturbed me. In reality, those men were preaching subversion, and this did disturb me. Also, I was upset because the international press always referred to these twelve men as "solid citizens" and "leading businessmen in Nicaragua." In truth, they were actually Sandinistas. We had intelligence information on all of them and we knew of their activities. . . .

After making subversive pronouncements, they suspected they might be arrested and incarcerated. Therefore, they decided to take refuge in Costa Rica. From that safe haven, they stepped up their campaign against me. I was ridiculed and attacked in advertisements, leaflets, and by other means. These twelve also had an excellent source through which they could attack me and that was the press. Their every word was given wide distribution. But they went too far. They wrote and signed a manifesto in which they called for an armed uprising against me. They told the people of Nicaragua that the only solution was to take up arms and overthrow the constitutionally elected government. In my books, that's treason.

The government of Nicaragua took legal action against these men and they were enjoined. This meant that if they returned to Nicaragua, they would be charged and tried for their subversive activities. The legal action, on the part of our government, caused a furor in the U.S. Embassy in Nicaragua. Immediately, the Embassy came to the defense of these men. Alan Riding, of the *New York Times,* took up the cause of the twelve and wrote highly critical articles about the action our government had taken.

If the Nicaraguan government had suddenly issued an order to arrest all Americans in Nicaragua, I don't think the U.S. Embassy would have been more irritated. Ambassador Solaun talked to different members of the Cabinet and applied as much pressure as was possible to get our legal order lifted.

This constant pressure on the part of the U.S. Embassy had its effect. The government of Nicaragua issued an announcement to the effect that since these men had made their subversive statements outside Nicaragua, no crime had been committed and they could, therefore, return. The order to enjoin had been nullified. . . .

My Cabinet and I knew that if we touched one of them, the U.S. Embassy would come down on us with full force. As a favor to the United States, we permitted these men to return. Had we stood firm against the U.S. pressure, we would have been better off.

Sometime in early February, 1978 the U.S. Ambassador called on me. I don't have the exact date because my date book, schedule of events, and list of callers were all left in Managua. The Sandinistas have those and I'm sure it has provided interesting reading for them. So, Ambassador Solaun came to see me and once again we went over the same problems.

Generally speaking, the Ambassador was expressing dissatisfaction with my government, and I was endeavoring to find out what it would take to satisfy the United States. Even Solaun would have to admit that I was always trying. I was never recalcitrant in my demeanor or spoken words.

At that meeting, I remember asking the Ambassador what kind of action I would have to take to create a different attitude in Washington. In calm voice and manner he told me the United States might be satisfied if I announced that I would get out of politics in 1981, and resign from the Army. My concern, and this concern possessed me, was for my country and the people of Nicaragua. If I lost in this battle with the Sandinistas, I knew the Communists would have Nicaragua. So, I told the Ambassador that his proposal met with my approval and that I didn't object to making such a public statement. . . .

I remember thinking that now, perhaps, I have some meaningful dialogue going with the United States and that we had established a common base from which we could work. I was not exactly in a state of euphoria, but I was happy that this meeting had proved to be productive. . . .

In the opinion of the negotiating team, with representation from the United States, Guatemala, and the Dominican Republic, there was only one solution to the political problems of Nicaragua. That solution meant that I, my son Tacho, my brother Joe, and our families would have to leave Nicaragua. I explained further that they were also involved in that solution, because after the departure of all the Somozas, they would have to turn the government over to a board consisting of three members, and that the Liberal Party would have one member on that board. Those respected leaders of the government were in a state of shock. They could imagine the opposition making such a preposterous proposal, but it seemed incomprehensible to them that the "good office holders" of the negotiating team could seriously do so.

I felt that all the military commanders should be advised as to the proposal, because they were certainly involved. So I called in the sixteen department commanders for a consultation. I explained to them that we had reached a crucial point in the negotiation process and that they needed to be informed as to the proposal which had been made. I then proceeded to explain to the military commanders what it would take to satisfy the negotiating team. Almost in unison, they said: "Those people are crazy."

It appeared a stalemate had been reached. I thought, however, there is one other possible solution that might satisfy the United States, and I say the United States because that country was calling the shots. That solution would be a plebiscite. I then called another meeting with the Cabinet, Congress, party leaders, and General Staff. The idea was explained to them and they thought it was more than fair.

The proposal was simply this: If I were the winner in an OAS-supervised election, I would reorganize the government, include the opposition party in significant governmental areas, and serve out my duly elected term. If I lost the election, I would resign as President and the opposition, principally the Frente Amplio de Oposición (FAO), would be in control of the government. I am oversimplifying the detailed plebiscite proposal, but I have stated the "guts" of the movement. To set forth the volume of official correspondence, proposals, and counterproposals, would require a book in itself. Basically, my position was that all the people in Nicaragua should have a say in such an important matter, so the fair approach was to hold an election.

The negotiating team had arrived in Nicaragua on October 6, 1978, and now it was nearing Christmas. The team ostensibly took a Christmas recess so that each representative could return to his respective country and receive further instructions. . . .

One member did return and that was the U.S. representative, William Bowdler. That should make it unmistakably clear that one person, Jimmy Carter, was calling all the shots and that the other members were on the multinational negotiating team in name only.

By that time, Ambassador Bowdler of the U.S. was aware of the unity which existed in Nicaragua. He came to visit with me and said: "I want to congratulate you, because you have the party, the Congress, the Army, and the government solidly behind you." I replied: "Mr. Ambassador, this should show you that I'm not telling lies to my people and they know what they are talking about." He then came back with a statement that enunciated perfectly the position of the United States. He said: "Nevertheless, I have instructions from the President of the United States and the Secretary of State of the United States to tell you that you have to leave." With that message of finality, I invited the Ambassador to lunch.

It was not what one could call an enjoyable luncheon. We reviewed the negotiation efforts, and I endeavored to show him the fallacy of the U.S. position. My words had no effect on the Ambassador. He pointed out that the President, the Secretary of State, the Secretary of Defense, and even Mr. Carter's Cabinet had concluded that I must leave. The Ambassador had laid all of his cards out on the table, face up, and I could read them clearly. . . .

Finally, the opposition forces came up with a counterproposal to my plebiscite plan, and their stipulations were submitted. They wanted the following:

• The removal of the Guardia Nacional from wherever they might be stationed in the country, and that the Guardia be confined to barracks during the election.

• The removal of designated policemen from any and all public duties and assignments in the country.

• The importation of three thousand foreigners to man all polling places and that they would determine who was eligible to vote.

• That on election day, I suspend the duties of all the justices of the peace in the entire country and transport them (around six thousand people) to Managua.

• I was to leave the country seventy-two hours before the election and take my brother, Joe, and my son, Tacho, with me.

• That new voting places were to be established throughout the country.

There were other ridiculous stipulations. Obviously, we could not accept those terms and conditions. The United States may not have learned about Communist promises, but I had learned. As a starter, I knew the moment the Guardia Nacional were confined to quarters, it would be a green light for all the revolutionaries to move in, and they would have. It would have been an open invitation to military disaster, and I knew it. Of course, that could have been the exact reason for the stipulation. But for the brashness of that requirement, we might have successfully negotiated the other stipulations. Even so, the Liberal Party leaders and I agreed to confine to barracks all military personnel except those on the frontiers and those engaged with the enemy.

I use the words "might have" advisedly. Obviously, we could not agree to terms and conditions which would have made it impossible for the Liberal Party to win. In retrospect, I don't believe Mr. Carter and Mr. Bowdler would have agreed to a fair and impartial election. I can see now that even if we had won an election which had been "rigged" against us, the United States would not have honored the results. . . .

There was no hesitation on the part of the Cabinet. They repeated that all of us were in this together. Their faces, their determination, and their loyalty will remain with me always. As a result of their decision, they would suffer and their families would suffer. This knowledge causes me grief and pain and these, also, will be with me always.

While the so-called negotiations were proceeding, Congressman John Murphy of New York had dinner with President Carter. The true purpose of the dinner was to discuss the problems in Nicaragua and, specifically, the plebiscite proposal which I had made. According to Murphy, they discussed Nicaragua for approximately forty-five minutes. In a later conversation with the Congressman from New York, he advised me that it seemed as though Carter's mind was set against Nicaragua and that he simply could not get through to him.

On another occasion, I tried to speak to Mr. Carter personally. I felt if I could talk to the man, there was just a chance he might realize that he was making a horrible mistake on Nicaragua. That conversation never took place. Carter's mind was made up, and he didn't want to talk to me.

My plebiscite proposal had been personally presented to Ambassador Bowdler, with the fervent hope that it would be acceptable to the United States. As it developed, the negotiating team, to their way of thinking, had completed their work. Before leaving Managua, Ambassador Bowdler came to see me. Bowdler said: "Mr. President, this paper which you have given me is unacceptable. I will leave Nicaragua and when, and if, you decide to accept the opposition's offer, I will be at your service." With that, he left. And that was the end of Mr. Carter's brainchild, the multinational consultation.

23.
INTERNATIONAL MEDIATION COMMISSION: REPORT ON CONCILIATION EFFORTS IN NICARAGUA (JULY 1979)

The members of the International Commission were Foreign Minister Ramón Emilio Jiménez, representative of the Dominican Republic; Ambassador Alfredo Obiols Gómez, representative of Guatemala; and Ambassador William G. Bowdler, representative of the United States of America. . . .

Upon the acceptance by the Government of Nicaragua and the Opposition of the offer of the three aforementioned States, the International Commission of Friendly Cooperation and Conciliation (CICAEC), was created. . . . In pursuing the goal of a negotiated settlement to the Nicaraguan crisis, the Commission decided to proceed in three stages: first, the

"Report to the Secretary of State on the Work of the International Commission of Friendly Cooperation and Conciliation for Achieving a Peaceful Solution to the Grave Crisis of the Republic of Nicaragua," July 1979.

achievement of a climate conducive to negotiations and identification of the position of the parties; second, evaluation of the situation and promotion of direct negotiations between the parties; and third, negotiation of a peaceful, democratic, and lasting solution. . . .

In the first stage . . . the CICAEC dealt directly with the President (Somoza), in a series of meetings which he granted upon request. It also met several times with the Broad Opposition Front (FAO), represented by its Political Committee, in the conference hall of the Curia in Managua. . . . Identification of the positions of the parties in the present crisis proved a difficult task. Strong emotions and deep resentments radicalized the positions of the parties to the degree that they were initially unable to think in terms of a compromise arrangement which was required in order to achieve a peaceful solution. Each of the parties regarded itself as the victor in the recent conflict, for although it was evident that government forces had won a military victory, it was not as clear whether this victory also represented a political triumph. . . .

Only after extended talks was the CICAEC able to convince the parties of the need to state realistically their assessment of the Nicaraguan problem and to engage in dialogue. . . .

The FAO's initial position . . . called for the President's immediate resignation along with that of his relatives in civil and military posts, the departure from the country of the Somoza family, the dismantling of the Somoza government and the National Guard, and the installation of a new government that would implement the 16 points of the FAO political program.

The position of the (ruling) Nationalist Liberal Party (PLN), on the other hand . . . insisted on General Somoza's continuance as the President of the Republic until the expiration of his term of office in 1981. At the same time it acknowledged the need for changes in the government, including opposition participation proportionate to the number of sympathizers that could be certified in an electoral census. . . .

In evaluating the situation the CICAEC took into consideration the views of the parties for achieving a settlement as well as the opinions gathered during . . . extensive consultations with persons and institutions . . . which recorded widespread and deep seated opposition to the government of President Somoza. This assessment led the CICAEC to conclude that agreement between the two contending forces in Nicaragua depended on General Somoza's willingness to consider resigning from his post for the purpose of facilitating a subsequent arrangement between the Liberal Party and the Broad Opposition Front.

In order to establish President Somoza's views on this point, the CICAEC asked to see him on November 7. At this meeting the CICAEC inquired, with all the respect due his high office, whether for the sake of peace in Nicaragua, he would consider the possibility of resigning from the

Presidency of the Republic prior to the expiration of his term of office.

Several days later the President responded negatively to the Commission's inquiry. . . . The Commission on November 21, 1978 submitted for the consideration of both parties the outline of a compromise settlement . . . based on an idea advanced by the PLN, calling for a simple and unambiguous plebiscite through which the people could express their view on whether or not President Somoza should continue in office.

The proposal . . . was received with suspicion both by the representatives of the FAO, who feared that the plebiscite might be manipulated in the manner of the past elections, and by those of the PLN, who considered such a process to be in violation of the Constitution. . . .

(Finally) the two parties agreed to begin talks on the terms and conditions for holding the proposed plebiscite. . . . The CICAEC drew up a draft agenda covering the points to be negotiated by the parties, prepared a set of proposed guidelines for conducting the talks, and sought a suitable location in which to hold them. . . .

In the belief that it would be especially useful to have delegates from two important sectors greatly concerned with the political process, namely the various private sector organizations comprising COSEP and the Church, the CICAEC also invited both groups to be represented at the talks by observers. . . .

The Political Committee of the FAO clearly stated that it would participate in direct talks with the PLN only after the following minimum guarantees were established:

> Full restoration of the constitutional guarantees and repeal of the martial law decree in force; general amnesty for all political crimes with a pardon for all persons already convicted of such crimes; dismissal of all pending cases; freedom to return to the country for all persons in exile or asylum; repeal of the Black Code and all other measures that restrict free expression of thought.

Considering such guarantees essential to creating a climate conducive to direct talks, and judging that the Nicaraguan people longed to see their constitutional rights restored with the approach of the Christmas season, the CICAEC asked President Somoza to lift the state of siege, declare a general amnesty, and revoke those portions of the Code of Radio and Television that were prejudicial to free expression of thought. The President responded favorably to the CICAEC request, thereby permitting the Commission to open the phase of direct talks.

[In] discussion of the second item on the agenda, "Consequences of the Plebiscite," . . . [d]isagreement developed immediately. The representatives of the FAO adopted a rigid stance to the effect that if the results of the plebiscite favored General Somoza, the FAO would maintain a position of responsible and peaceful opposition, but would not participate in the government. On the other hand, if General Somoza lost, the FAO wanted the following sequence of events to occur:

1. Resignation of the President.
2. Congressional acceptance of the resignation and the designation from among its members of a successor to the President.
3. Departure from the country of Somoza and his family.
4. Partial reform of the Constitution.
5. Installation of a Government of National Reconciliation for the implementation of the 16 points of the FAO.

The PLN representatives expressed their regret at the FAO position which they believed excluded the possibility of a government of reconciliation in the event that President Somoza should win the plebiscite. They also stated that they could not accept a solution that would be unconstitutional and rejected the notion of expatriating a Nicaraguan family.

Debate on the matter was suspended at that point. . . .

In an attempt to resolve the impasse and continue with the other items on the agenda, the CICAEC presented to the fourth session on the morning of December 18 a plan of action covering the two possible results of the plebiscite. After much discussion agreement was reached on this wording of the consequences of a victory by President Somoza:

> The Commission suggests that if the results of the plebiscite favor President Somoza, he organize his government as he deems best in order to achieve a national reconciliation, and the FAO pledges to maintain a position of civic, democratic, constructive, and peaceful opposition.

Immediately thereafter, and shortly before recessing, a discussion began on the consequences in the event that the results of the plebiscite went against President Somoza.

When the session resumed in the afternoon, the PLN delegation adopted an unexpected position. Despite the understanding reached during the morning, it once again insisted that the FAO participate in the Government of President Somoza in the event that he won the plebiscite. . . .

(T)he CICAEC concluded that the only way to overcome the impasse was to present a detailed draft of a (compromise) and to invite the parties to accept it. . . . The document sets forth in detail the conditions for the plebiscite and the steps to be taken to establish a government of national reconciliation, whatever the results of the voting. . . .

The sixth and final negotiating session was conducted at the Embassy of the United States of America at 6 P.M. on December 20. . . . Foreign Minister Jiménez presented the parties with copies of the draft . . . reading the proposal aloud for emphasis. During the reading some of the PLN delegates reacted in an inconsiderate manner, resulting in the adjournment of the session without further discussions.... The following day, prior to its departure from the country, the CICAEC received the reply from the Political Committee of the FAO indicating its acceptance of the draft, its willingness to participate in the immediate implementation of the plebiscite, and the advisability of effecting the necessary adjustments for its operation. A preliminary response from the PLN, also dated December 21, strongly criticized the actions of the CICAEC and the content of the draft. At the same time it indicated that a counterproposal would be forthcoming....

The CICAEC concluded that the criticisms raised in the December 21 document were groundless and could, if not refuted, lend themselves to misinterpretations. . . .

In its examination of the PLN counterproposal, however, the CICAEC noted a concept that merited careful study by the parties: the creation of a national plebiscite authority (NPA) to work in conjunction with and under the careful and systematic supervision of, the international plebiscite authority (IPA) on the basis of a definition of its responsibilities agreed to by the PLN and the FAO. Other changes suggested by the PLN, both in the process of the plebiscite and in its consequences, were not accepted by the Commission, which considered that they would be unacceptable to important sectors in Nicaragua whose support is essential to any peaceful solution.

On January 18, 1979, the PLN Negotiating Commission replied to the CICAEC communication of January 12. In its reply the PLN continued to oppose several portions of the December 20th proposal, relating both to the conditions for the plebiscite and basic elements of its consequences. The PLN note concluded that:

> For all of the foregoing reasons we reiterate the terms of our counterproposal of last December 26.

Given the impasse created by the PLN reply, the CICAEC concluded that for the moment the conditions were unsuitable for continued conciliation efforts on their part. The commission reached this conclusion with great regrets. . . .

GENERAL CONCLUSIONS

The Republic of Nicaragua is in every way experiencing a crisis of serious proportions.

The causes of this crisis are rooted in socioeconomic factors but the most obvious and tangible manifestation is the lack of free participation in the political process.

The absence of alternation in power of different political groups and the loss of confidence in existing electoral procedures, as a means of achieving that alternation, has brought about a growing discontent and frustration which has become so widespread that unless other opportunities or alternatives become available, they can lead to a growing tendency to seek or sympathize with violent solutions.

This prevailing crisis situation is creating a political polarization that fosters a climate of fear and insecurity.

The acute political polarization prompts the government to severely restrict personal freedoms which serves to produce violence that in turn engenders still more violence.

This vicious circle is the source of attitudes that seriously hamper the work of negotiation since the parties are reluctant to demonstrate the flexibility necessary to arrive at compromise solutions.

The foregoing conclusions, in addition to those which follow logically from this report, give cause to fear that in the absence of a negotiated solution there is a danger that escalating violence in Nicaragua may transcend the limits of an internal conflict and affect the peace and tranquility of the whole of Central America.

24.
HUMBERTO ORTEGA: THE STRATEGY OF VICTORY

Harnecker: What conditions were ripe for insurrection?

Ortega: The objective conditions of social and political crisis existed. But the conditions of the vanguard, in terms of the organizational level to lead the masses, and especially in terms of weapons, did not exist.

We didn't have the necessary weapons but everything else was ripe. . . . And we didn't have the experience of participating in a national uprising, the training such an experience gives the masses and the knowledge of the enemy, who showed up all his weaknesses. We didn't have enough weapons, but we did know that even if the uprising was not victorious it would be a blow from which the regime would never recover. We were absolutely convinced of this and so great was our conviction that a month later we were already calling for insurrection again.

There were some comrades on the left who held the view that September

Interview with Marta Harnecker, published in *Granma,* January 27, 1980. Translated in *Sandinistas Speak* (New York: Pathfinder Press, 1982), pp. 58–59, 61–62, 67–70, 73, 78–79.

practically negated all possibility of a short-term victory, that the operations had been a strategic mistake, a defeat, and they thus had delayed the day of victory. . . . it was an accomplishment, because we grew as a vanguard. One hundred and fifty men participated in that uprising and our forces were multiplied several times over: three- or fourfold, plus the potential for recruiting thousands of others. We grew in size and in firepower because we captured weapons from the enemy. The vanguard suffered very few casualties. There were people killed as a result of Somoza's genocide, but very few cadres were killed in combat. In other words, we were able to preserve our strength. . . .

Harnecker: When you planned the capture of the palace, did you consider the impact this would have on the masses?

Ortega: We knew the mass movement was coming to a head, but we preferred that it come to a head than that it not come to a head.

The important thing was to foil the imperialist plot which consisted of staging a coup in August to put a civilian-military regime in power and thus put a damper on the revolutionary struggle.

The palace operation had to do with the plot. We felt that since we didn't have a large-scale party organization, since the working class and the working people in general were not well organized, the only way to make ourselves felt in political terms was with weapons. That's why we carried out many operations that were military in form, but profoundly political in content. . . .

Harnecker: So, when some people ask why you called for the September uprising without having achieved the unity of the three tendencies, this is explained by—

Ortega: Conditions for unity did not exist then. First we had to strengthen the struggle, and all the tendencies were working on this.

Little by little we came to an understanding but around a line which was called for in practice; it was not our line but the one the people demanded. . . .

Harnecker: But didn't the fact that the emphasis was on urban insurrection as opposed to the guerrilla column lead to an unduly great loss of life and destruction? The fact that the struggle was centered on the cities makes it easier to repress, for example the bombing of the cities—

Ortega: That question is meaningless, because that was the only way to win in Nicaragua. If it had been otherwise, there would never have been a victory. We simply paid the price of freedom. . . .

What I mean by passive accumulation of forces is a policy of not getting involved in the conjunctures, of gaining strength while standing on the sidelines; a passive policy of alliances. It's a passive view which holds that it is possible to pile up weapons and gain in organization and number without fighting the enemy, while sitting on the sidelines, without involving the masses—not because we didn't want to do so but because we felt that if we showed our claws too much, they would come down hard on us and shatter the movement.

We knew we would be going on the offensive under difficult circumstances, but we knew we had the necessary minimum of resources to tackle this new stage.

By May 1977 we had drawn up a programmatic platform which outlined an insurrectional strategy that served to sum up the strategic viewpoint of insurrection which I, along with Carlos Fonseca, had prepared in 1975. This was in turn an outgrowth of the efforts made along these lines after the death of Oscar Turcios and Ricardo Morales in September 1973, following the Chilean coup. This marked the start of the debate within our ranks over the two strategies: guerrilla warfare centered in the mountains, on the one hand, and armed struggle focused on the masses, on the other.

That was the first debate. It was a bit immature and categorical: it's either the mountains or the cities. Raising this question as one or the other was not correct. . . .

The truth is that we always took the masses into account, but more in terms of their supporting the guerrillas, so that the guerrillas as such could defeat the National Guard. This isn't what actually happened. What happened was that it was the guerrillas who provided support for the masses so that they could defeat the enemy by means of insurrection. We all held that view, and it was practice that showed that in order to win we had to mobilize the masses and get them to actively participate in the armed struggle. The guerrillas alone weren't enough, because the armed movement of the vanguard would never have had the weapons needed to defeat the enemy. Only in theory could we obtain the weapons and resources needed to defeat the National Guard. We realized that our chief source of strength lay in maintaining a state of total mobilization that would disperse the technical and military resources of the enemy.

Since production, the highways, and the social order in general were affected, the enemy was unable to move his forces and other means about at will because he had to cope with mass mobilizations, neighborhood demonstrations, barricades, acts of sabotage, etc. This enabled the vanguard, which was reorganizing its army, to confront the more numerous enemy forces on a better footing. . . .

Harnecker: . . . Wouldn't your operations be considered a sign of adventurism, resulting only in even stronger repression against the people?

Ortega: Yes. Some sectors of the left that were engaged in setting up trade unions, etc., claimed that those actions had destroyed the organization and the resurgence of the mass movement, but this wasn't so. It is true that the repression would affect the open, legal organization of the masses, but it wouldn't affect their organization under really revolutionary conditions. To go along with such claims would mean falling prey to the big show the imperialists were mounting with all the talk about the bourgeois-democratic way out, in which the trade union movement was to participate. For us it was preferable that such a castrated trade union movement not be formed. . . .

The operations of October 1977 gave a big boost to the mass movement, but it wasn't until after the assassination of Pedro Joaquín Chamorro that they really came out in full force and made crystal clear their potential, their determination, and their Sandinista will to join in the armed struggle.

I would like to make clear that the uprising of the masses as an aftermath to Chamorro's assassination was not led exclusively by the FSLN. . . .

Harnecker: What made you issue the call for the insurrection in May?

Ortega: Because by then a whole series of objective conditions were coming to a head: the economic crisis, the devaluation of the córdoba, the political crisis. And also because, after September, we realized that it was necessary to strategically combine, in both time and space, the uprising of the masses throughout the country, the offensive by the Front's military forces, and the nationwide strike in which the employers, as well, were involved or in agreement. . . .

We always had a rear guard. The movement had direct experience with a rear guard dating back many years. Our country is not an island like Cuba, we have to rely on neighboring countries, and the revolutionary movement relied on support from the neighboring movements from the very beginning. . . .

We operated clandestinely in Costa Rica and Honduras. And in order to set up the rear guard at higher levels it became necessary—along with finding resources and setting up clandestine schools—to begin arousing— to begin arousing a feeling of solidarity with our cause among the main progressive political sectors in each country, without being sectarian, and not with the left-wing sectors alone, because that would have meant isolating ourselves. Nobody gave us a rear guard; we won the right to have one.

The alliances we achieved through our efforts were of vital importance in our obtaining heavy weapons and sophisticated equipment. . . .

We won the right to establish alliances, we imposed our right. If they hadn't seen us as a force to be reckoned with they wouldn't have approached us, but they realized we constituted a force and thus had to become our allies. And they did so due to our political program, even though ours was an armed movement with a revolutionary leadership.

The progressives realized that ours was a revolutionary movement and that we weren't totally in accord with their ideology, but they also realized that we had a political program that was, to a certain extent, of interest to them and that we had military power. Those three factors made it possible for us to establish true alliances, not paper ones. We made no agreement of any kind. We just set down the rules of the game and acted accordingly, and as a result we went on gaining political ground. . . .

It would have been very difficult for us to win by depending only on internal development. We realized that the internal gains had to be reinforced by the forces that existed abroad.

25.
OAS: REPORT ON HUMAN RIGHTS (JUNE 1979)

On June 23, 1979, the XVII Meeting of Consultation approved a resolution which, for the first time in the history of the OAS and perhaps for the first time in the history of any international organization, deprived an incumbent government of a member state of the Organization of legitimacy, based on the human rights violations committed by that government against its own population. The text of the resolution reads as follows:

WHEREAS:

The people of Nicaragua are suffering the horrors of a fierce armed conflict that is causing grave hardships and loss of life, and has thrown the country into a serious political, social, and economic upheaval;

The inhumane conduct of the dictatorial regime governing the country, as evidenced by the report of the Inter-American Commission on Human Rights, is the fundamental cause of the dramatic situation faced by the Nicaraguan people and;

The spirit of solidarity that guides Hemisphere relations places an unavoidable obligation on the American countries to exert every effort within their power, to put an end to the bloodshed and to avoid the prolongation of this conflict which is disrupting the peace of the Hemisphere;

THE SEVENTEENTH MEETING OF CONSULTATION OF MINISTERS OF FOREIGN AFFAIRS.

DECLARES:

From Inter-American Committee on Human Rights, "Report on the Situation of Human Rights in the Republic of Nicaragua," Seventeenth Meeting of Foreign Affairs Ministers, June 1979.

That the solution of the serious problem is exclusively within the jurisdiction of the people of Nicaragua.

That in the view of the Seventeenth Meeting of Consultation of Ministers of Foreign Affairs this solution should be arrived at on the basis of the following:

1. Immediate and definitive replacement of the Somoza regime.
2. Installation in Nicaraguan territory of a democratic government, the composition of which should include the principal representative groups which oppose the Somoza regime and which reflects the free will of the people of Nicaragua.
3. Guarantee of the respect for human rights of all Nicaraguan without exception.
4. The holding of free elections as soon as possible, that will lead to the establishment of a truly democratic government that guarantees peace, freedom, and justice. . . .

C. THE ESTABLISHMENT OF THE GOVERNMENT OF NATIONAL RECONSTRUCTION

1. On June 17, 1979, from San José, Costa Rica, the Sandinista National Liberation Front (FSLN) announced the formation of a five person Junta, or governing council, of the Provisional Government of National Reconstruction. Less than one month later, the FSLN appeared assured of a military victory; it controlled the cities of León, Chinandega, Estelí, Matagalpa and Masaya.

2. On July 13, 1979, at a press conference held in Costa Rica, the Junta announced that it was convinced that the "people's armed forces could take Managua and annihilate the National Guard." However, at the same time, the Junta put forward a "Plan to Achieve Peace." One day earlier, on July 12, 1979, the Junta, seeking OAS support, sent a copy of the Plan to the Secretary General of the Organization, Alejandro Orfila, to be transmitted to the member states. The text of this document is as follows:

Mr. Secretary General:

As we are doing with the Foreign Ministers of the member countries of that Organization, it is our pleasure to place in your hands the document that contains our "Plan to Achieve Peace" in our heroic and long-suffering homeland, now that the people of Nicaragua have established their political and military victory over the dictatorship.

We have developed that plan on the basis of the resolution adopted by the Seventeenth Meeting of Consultation on June 23, 1979, a Resolution that is historic in every respect, as it demands the immediate replacement of the genocidal Somoza dictatorship, which has now met its end, and backs the installation in our country of a broad-based, democratic government of the kind we ourselves are establishing.

Further, in stating that the solution to the serious problem is exclusively within the jurisdiction of the people of Nicaragua, that Resolution calls for hemispheric solidarity in preserving our people's right to self-determination.

In our "Plan to Achieve Peace," we are presenting to the community of nations in this hemisphere the purposes that have inspired our Government since its establishment and as set forth in our documents and policy statements, some of which we would like to ratify here:

I. Our firm intention to establish full respect for human rights in our country, in accordance with the United Nations Universal Declaration of the Rights and Duties of Man and the Charter on Human Rights of the OAS. . . .

STAGES OF THE PLAN:

I. Somoza submits his resignation to his Congress, which in turn accepts it and turns over the reins of power to the Government of National Reconstruction in recognition of the backing it has received from all sectors of Nicaraguan society.

II. Installation of the Government of National Reconstruction. This Government is made up of representatives of all sectors of Nicaraguan politics and has received the official support of all.

III. Immediately after the Government of National Reconstruction has installed itself in Nicaragua, the member countries of the OAS, especially those that sponsored or voted in favor of the Resolution, will then recognize it officially as the legitimate Government of Nicaragua.

IV. The Government of National Reconstruction will immediately do the following:

1. Repeal the Somoza Constitution.
2. Decree the Fundamental Statute which shall provisionally govern the Government of National Reconstruction.
3. Dissolve the National Congress.
4. Order the National Guard to cease hostilities and immediately confine them to barracks with the guarantees that their lives and other rights will be respected. The officials, noncommissioned officers and soldiers of the National Guard that so desire may join the new national army or civilian life.
   The Sandinista Army will enforce the cease-fire to facilitate fulfillment of these agreements by maintaining the positions won as of the time of the Decree.
5. Maintain order by means of those sectors of the National Guard which have honored the cease-fire and were appointed to these functions by the Government of National Reconstruction, a task which they will carry out in coordination with the combatants of the Sandinista Army.
6. Decree the organic law that will govern the institutions of the State.
7. Implement the program of the Government of National Reconstruction.

V. Those who have collaborated with the regime and who wish to leave the country, and who are not responsible for the genocide that we have suffered or for other serious crimes that demand trial by the civil courts, may do so with all necessary guarantees, guarantees which the Government of National Reconstruction will demonstrate now and henceforth. The departure of these individuals may be supervised by the Inter-American Commission on Human Rights and by the International Red Cross.

VI. The plan to call Nicaraguans to the first free elections that our country will have in this century, so that they may elect their representatives to the city councils and to a constitutional assembly, and the country's highest-ranking authorities.

Now, Mr. Secretary General the governments of this hemisphere have their opportunity to publicly declare their solidarity with the fight that our people have waged to bring democracy and justice to Nicaragua.

With the request that you convey the text of this letter to the foreign ministers of the OAS, we present our compliments.

JUNTA OF THE GOVERNMENT OF NATIONAL RECONSTRUCTION
VIOLETA DE CHAMORRO, SERGIO RAMIREZ MERCADO, ALFONSO
ROBELO CALLEJAS, DANIEL ORTEGA SAAVEDRA, MOISES HASSAN
MORALES.

PLAN OF THE GOVERNMENT OF NATIONAL RECONSTRUCTION TO ACHIEVE PEACE

Our premise is that while it is true that the solution to Nicaragua's serious problem is the exclusive competence of the Nicaraguan people, hemispheric solidarity, essential for this plan to take hold, will be accorded in fulfillment of the Resolution of the Seventeenth Meeting of Consultation of Ministers of Foreign Affairs of the OAS, approved on June 23, 1979.

The following steps will ensure the immediate and definitive replacement of the Somoza regime, already destroyed by the heroic and combative people of Nicaragua and their vanguard, the Sandinista National Liberation Front. Rejection of this plan in favor of a political solution would leave military destruction of Somocismo as the only recourse; this could go on for weeks and would lead, unnecessarily, to many more deaths and destruction.

8. Guarantee the departure from the country of all those military personnel, Somoza's functionaries who wish to leave and who are found not to have been involved in serious crimes against the people. . . .

3. On July 16, 1979, General Anastasio Somoza tendered his letter of resignation to the Nicaraguan Congress, the text of which reads as follows:

Honorable National Congress
People of Nicaragua

Having consulted the governments that truly have an interest in bringing peace to the country, I have decided to respect the decision of the Organization of American States and do hereby resign the Office of the Presidency to which I was elected by popular vote. My resignation is irrevocable.

I have fought against communism and believe that when the truth emerges history will vindicate me.

A. Somoza
President of the Republic

4. As a constitutional formality, in the early morning hours of July 18, the Nicaraguan Congress unanimously elected Francisco Urcuyo Maliaños, the President of the Chamber of Deputies, to replace Somoza and to facilitate the transfer of power to the Junta once it reached Managua from Costa Rica.

However, the newly elected President refused to relinquish the Office of the Presidency and announced that he intended to complete General Somoza's term, in other words, to serve until May 1981. Instead of arranging a speedy transfer of power, Urcuyo delivered an address in which he praised the National Guard and demanded that "all irregular forces lay down their arms." Next, he proceeded to fill all the key posts in the National Guard with young colonels and lieutenant colonels, following the departure, with General Somoza, of almost all the senior military officers. The new Director of the National Guard, Lt. Col. Federico Mejía González, called on the National Guard "to redouble . . . their efforts in the current fight."

5. Wednesday morning, July 18, three members of the Junta, Sergio Ramírez, Alfonso Robelo, and Violeta Chamorro, left San José, Costa Rica, for León, Nicaragua, where they joined fourth Junta member, Daniel Ortega, and declared León to be the new provisional capital. Interim President Urcuyo fled to Guatemala, leaving the new National Guard Director in charge. According to information received, Mejía, now promoted to General, began negotiations with a Sandinista representative and with Archbishop Obando y Bravo in the "bunker" of General Somoza, regarding the terms of National Guard surrender. In view of the posture that Urcuyo had assumed, the negotiations were no longer possible on the original cease-fire terms; as a consequence, the FSLN now demanded the unconditional surrender of the National Guard. After the meeting, one of the participants stated that the talks had reached an impasse because the

Sandinistas insisted on a surrender rather than a cease-fire in place. At approximately 2:00 A.M., General Mejía presented a list of the National Guard's demands, which included retention of all property belonging to individual officers in exchange for a surrender. The Sandinistas refused to accept these conditions and all communications broke off. Shortly before dawn on July 19, General Mejía, the General Staff of the National Guard, as well as most of the high-ranking officers, left Nicaragua by plane.

6. After a night of chaos, which some observers called "the worst night in the seven weeks of battle," the Nicaraguan civil war ended early on the morning of July 19, as Sandinista guerrillas took control of Managua and called for a cease-fire. At approximately noon that same day, the last of the commanders of the National Guard, Lt. Col. Fulgencio Largaespada Baez, ordered his soldiers to surrender. The text of his communiqué is as follows:

> Attention, Nicaraguans, attention: To the Commands and headquarters, officers, noncommissioned officers and enlisted personnel of the Nicaraguan National Guard:
>
> In the name of the General Staff of the Nicaraguan National Guard and with the approval of the Sandinista National Liberation Front (FSLN) and of the Junta of the Government of National Reconstruction, I, Lt. Col. Fulgencio Largaespada Baez, do hereby inform you of the following:
>
> **1.** The withdrawal of the General Staff of the National Guard, under the command of General Federico Mejía has led to the disintegration of our armed corps.
>
> **2.** The victorious position that the Sandinista Front has held and continues to hold throughout the entire national territory has brought an end to the war waged against the Sandinista Front and the defeat of the National Guard.
>
> **3.** To prevent further bloodshed and useless loss of innocent lives, National Guard noncommissioned officers and enlisted personnel are to obey the following orders:
>
> > **A.** Immediate cease-fire at all command posts and on all war fronts.
> >
> > **B.** Deposition of weapons in your respective headquarters or posts at the following shelters: Red Cross stations, churches and embassies. All these places will be respected by the victorious forces of the Sandinista National Liberation Front.
> >
> > **C.** White flags are to be displayed wherever armed soldiers are to be found; this will be regarded as a sign of unconditional surrender.
> >
> > **D.** Once the orders issued by the joint National Directorate of the Sandinista National Liberation Front and the Junta of

the Government of National Reconstruction have been carried out, the life and physical safety of every soldier who surrenders will be guaranteed.

This call does not constitute a betrayal of anyone or of anything. To the contrary, it represents the dignity invested in the National Guard, on behalf of the well being of our long-suffering people. This I swear before the altar of country and of God, our Lord.

The present communiqué has been drafted jointly and with the authorization of Commander Humberto Ortega Saavedra, on behalf of the joint National Directorate of the FSLN and of the Junta of the Government of National Reconstruction.

Effective immediately.

(signed) Fulgencio Largaespada Baez, Chief of the General Staff of the Nicaraguan National Guard.

7. On July 20, the Junta of the Government of National Reconstruction was installed in Managua.

The Sandinistas in Power

In July 1979, Nicaraguans were united in celebrating the "beautiful revolution." Somoza's dictatorship had been destroyed by a national coalition crossing class, political, and ideological lines. Nicaragua was admired around the world for its achievement; aid was forthcoming from all quarters. The future seemed bright. Within four short years, however, the nation was badly divided and facing civil war. It had become a focal point of conflict between the United States and the Soviet bloc. Many Nicaraguans felt that a new dictatorship had taken the place of the old. These were tragic events, coming so soon after the greatest achievement of Nicaraguan history.

Two issues were central in shaping these developments. First, the FSLN intended to maintain a monopoly on political power. Alliances with other sectors, mostly defined by it as "bourgeois," were merely tactical, a temporary expedient so that the Sandinistas could consolidate control and maximize foreign, noncommunist support. Using their Marxist-Leninist analysis, the Sandinistas concluded that the FSLN was the only true representative of workers and peasants while the "bourgeoisie" would oppose progress toward real socialism. Their expectation of an inevitable clash became a self-fulfilling prophecy.

Second, the FSLN sought to spread their revolution to neighboring countries. The priority placed on this policy and the resources devoted to it, however, would be determined by circumstances. Furthermore, as the "imperialist vanguard," the United States would be unwilling to accept Nicaragua's true independence. Again, conflict was inevitable and this analysis made the FSLN see an alliance with Cuba and the USSR not only as ideologically proper but also as a necessity for maintaining its political hegemony. By definition, they rejected the idea that such a relationship could ever compromise Nicaraguan independence.

These themes, and the alternative vision offered by the other elements in the anti-Somoza front, were visible from the very beginning. In his speech at the September 1979 Nonaligned Conference, for example, FSLN leader Daniel Ortega (Document 1) expressed the belief that "for the first time in their entire history, the Nicaraguan people can officially express their sovereign will." But he also made clear his government's support for a pro-Soviet position in the Nonaligned Movement, determination to move toward socialism, and expectation of U.S. hostility, although the Carter administration was still offering aid to Managua.

In a pastoral letter (Document 2), Catholic bishops extolled "the joy of a poor people, who for the first time in long years feel that their own country belongs to them." Yet these hopes would be disappointed if a socialism emerged that subordinated the people to a group that seized power over them. "We would be unable to accept such a dubious or false socialism." If, however, socialism meant that the interests of the majority came first, "We have nothing to object to."

FSLN leader Sergio Ramírez claimed (Document 3) that "deeper social change" could take place in Nicaragua only if it helped neighbors make a similar "transition." Despite the involvement of the middle class and businessmen in the anti-Somoza movement, he adds that Nicaragua had no "national bourgeoisie" but only "a group that acted as middleman for U.S. interests," though he acknowledges the cooperation of some elements.

The most important statement of FSLN policy emerged from the organization's first convention, which lasted seventy-two hours, in September 1979 (Document 4). Since "Sandinism had won the war, and the people acknowledged the total victory of Sandinism above all else," this was viewed as a mandate for FSLN rule and Marxist revolution. The alliance with "democratic segments of the bourgeoisie" was designed to isolate Somozism and strengthen the FSLN's forces, aiming at "domestic neutralization," and to avoid "Yankee interventionist policies." The revolution's first stage, Somoza's removal, was completed. The country was now in an "intermediate" era which would soon lead to a second stage that "will forever alter the balance of power between labor and capital." As for foreign policy, the revolution's objective was to consolidate itself at home.

Managua would give some aid to comrades elsewhere, but it would be cautious in doing so.

While the FSLN promised to hold free elections after Somoza's defeat, it defined this commitment in very particular terms. As Humberto Ortega explained at a mass rally (Document 5), elections would not be "a raffle to see who has power, because the people have the power through their vanguard, the Sandinista National Liberation Front and its National Directorate." At the 1982 May Day rally, Tomás Borge (Document 6) called for class struggle. While before the revolution "it was correct to form a broad national unity" to get rid of Somoza, the new phase required a struggle against the United States and "the capitalist sectors" who seek to gain power for themselves.

The idea that the FSLN was the sole legitimate representative of the workers and peasants was transmitted through all the organs of the state and the government-controlled media as shown by materials used in the 1980 literacy campaign (Document 7). As the business sector's organization, COSEP, charged, the FSLN was merging the government into itself. The emerging opposition complained about the postponement of elections and the FSLN's domination of the ruling executive (Document 8). In return, FSLN leader Sergio Ramírez (Document 9) attributed these complaints to the "bourgeoisie's" refusal to accept its status as a dying class.

Yet the non-FSLN forces—political parties, middle class, church, businessmen, and independent trade union leadership—were not the blind reactionaries portrayed by the Sandinistas. The church leadership was strongly influenced by the 1968 Medellín bishops' conference position of an "option for the poor" and by the ideas of Liberation Theology. In a position paper drafted before the revolution, but published only in 1981, Pedro Joaquín Chamorro (Document 10) criticized both laissez-faire capitalism and Marxism, proposing a democratic socialist state. Pablo Antonio Cuadra, a noted writer and an editor of *La Prensa,* describes the erosion of cultural and press freedom (Document 11) as the Sandinistas pursued a dogmatic Marxist-Leninist policy.

In light of the FSLN's determination to maintain complete control of the government and of specific political disagreements, an organized opposition emerged within Nicaragua. In its platform the umbrella Democratic Coordinator group (Document 12) called for "effective political pluralism," a "mixed economy," and "genuine nonalignment." It also advocated a regional peace solution and "dialogue" in El Salvador as well as in Nicaragua.

Two other opposition recruits are of particular interest. Edén Pastora was one of the best-known Sandinista revolutionary heroes and commanded the southern front in the struggle against Somoza. He broke openly with the FSLN in April 1982 (Document 13). After trying unsuccessfully to negotiate with the Sandinista government, he took up arms in 1983, forming ARDE, the Revolutionary Democratic Alliance (Document 17).

On Nicaragua's eastern, Atlantic coast, the Miskito Indians' demands for better treatment and some self-rule also led to clashes with the FSLN, and they furnished perhaps one-quarter of all antigovernment rebels. Although sparsely settled, the Indians' region has gold, lumber, fish, a long border with Honduras, and ports vital for receiving Cuban supplies. After the revolution, Sandinistas dispatched troops and scores of Cuban doctors, nurses, and teachers to help pacify the region. The independent indigenous population resented the soldiers' arbitrary behavior, political indoctrination, and the raising of Cuban flags. Miskitos also resisted the government's attempts to replace communal lands and tribal organization with state farms and block committees. Early in 1981 the government arrested about thirty Miskito leaders, setting off a wave of protest. In December 1981, the Sandinistas forcibly moved forty-two Miskito villages, about 8,500 people, into resettlement camps. Another 10,000 Indians fled to Honduras; 7,000 more were moved to state-owned coffee plantations in 1982. Brooklyn Rivera, leader of the Misurasata organization (Document 14), tried to stay independent of both the main "contra" group in Honduras and the Sandinistas. As a result, he was attacked by both sides. Sandinista leaders (Document 15) claimed the problem arose from Indian political backwardness and imperialist interference. Bernard Nietschmann, a specialist on Indian societies, testified about his visits to Indian villages to the OAS human rights commission (Document 19).

Former Panamanian vice-minister of health Hugo Spadafora (Document 25), leader of an international legion that fought against Somoza, also joined the battle against the Sandinistas, seeing the new struggle as "predominantly a peasant insurrection." He was murdered by the Panamanian army in 1985.

The Nicaraguan Democratic Force (FDN) is the largest rebel group. Its top military leadership has always consisted of former National Guard officers who originally organized themselves with Argentinian help and were taken up by the CIA in late 1981. Their commander, Colonel Enrique Bermúdez, was Nicaraguan defense attaché in Washington during Somoza's last years. Headquartered in Honduras, the FDN's soldiers were trained by Argentinian and U.S. intelligence operatives. Various anti-Sandinista émigrés joined the FDN, and the CIA organized some of them into a political directorate (Documents 16 and 18). Adolfo Calero, a Conservative Party leader who had been active in the anti-Somoza strikes and had a previous connection with the CIA, became the FDN's political leader in January 1983.

While the CIA controlled the FDN and gave funding to Pastora until

1984, the growing opposition within Nicaragua was fueled by Sandinista policies. As Arturo Cruz, a member of Los Doce and veteran anti-Somoza activist, pointed out in 1984 (Document 20), Nicaragua had reached a crossroads. The economy was suffering due to government mismanagement, U.S. pressure, and regional tensions. The Sandinista government's tightening links with the Soviet bloc and the Reagan administration's tough line had also proved mutually reinforcing in polarizing the situation. Only internal dialogue, negotiations, and a compromise solution could avoid an escalating conflict, Cruz concluded. The FSLN could not expect "the legitimate opposition to agree on unchallenged and permanent FSLN rule" and a "Marxist-Leninist system." The Sandinistas would have to recognize the rights of others to peaceful opposition.

Cruz hoped that the 1984 elections would provide a framework for compromise. The Democratic Coordinator (Document 21) formulated a set of guidelines to ensure a free and fair campaign and balloting. It nominated Cruz for president in July 1984. The Nicaraguan church (Document 22) also called for national reconciliation to avoid war and suffering.

The Sandinistas' policy in this situation was laid out in a secret speech by FSLN leader Bayardo Arce (Document 23) at a meeting of the leadership of the Nicaraguan Socialist Party (communist). "We see the elections as one more weapon of the revolution to bring its historical objectives gradually into reality," he told the meeting, by using them to consolidate the regime's political and ideological control.

Consequently, the Nicaraguan government refused to meet the Democratic Coordinator's main demands and Cruz withdrew from the election. Even Independent Liberal Party leader Virgilio Godoy, former minister of labor in the revolutionary government and now the main remaining opposition candidate, complained about the management of the elections (Document 24). In November 1984, the Sandinistas won almost two-thirds of the official vote count and Daniel Ortega was elected president.

Misgivings about the conduct of the election and the Sandinista government's direction led to a decline of support for Managua from Christian and Socialist Democrats in Europe and Latin America. In this regard, the decision of Carlos Andrés Pérez, former president of Venezuela and vice-president of the Socialist International, not to attend Ortega's inaugural took on special significance (Document 26). Within Nicaragua, Pérez was popularly known as "godfather" of the revolution, since he had provided more help and encouragement to the anti-Somoza forces than any other foreign leader.

Ortega himself used the occasion of his inaugural speech (Document 27) to cite the revolution's achievements and to claim that it supported pluralism and a regional settlement through the Contadora peace process. He expressed confidence that the government's military forces could defeat the growing challenge of the U.S.-backed, Honduras-based rebels. Opposition leaders abroad—including Cruz and Calero—replied with the "San José program" (Document 28) asking for negotiations mediated by the church.

Despite U.S. aid, the FDN guerrillas had only limited military success. Nevertheless, the military threat in northern Nicaragua forced a mobilization of government forces and the expenditure of half the budget on the war.

Domestic unrest was an equally serious problem. The economy continued to decline as the United States imposed an embargo and tried to block loans from international lending institutions. Western states cut back on aid; foreign debt grew to enormous proportions.

Alarmed by government policies and expropriations since 1981, the middle class had become reluctant to invest. Reluctant to sell for low official prices, peasants cut back production. Food shortages resulted, living standards fell precipitously, and government corruption damaged the regime's reputation. There was a growing harassment of legal opposition parties and groups. The church became more and more critical of the government. There were anti-draft demonstrations in a number of cities.

In the face of these problems, Daniel Ortega declared a state of emergency (Document 29), blaming it on "a mercenary war . . . imposed on us [and] financed, organized, and directed by the U.S. Government." Many civil rights were suspended in October 1985 (Document 30). An Amnesty International report (Document 31) documented human-rights abuses by the government as well as the FDN's kidnappings and murders of civilians.

Thus, Nicaragua stood at a new impasse. The Sandinistas could not, as it wished to do, establish a Cuba-type system because of internal dissent, U.S. leverage, and the limit on the willingness of Moscow and Havana to provide support. Neither the Reagan administration nor the FSLN was willing to compromise. On the military front, the government could not eliminate the "contra" rebels and the FDN forces were unable to come close to overturning a well-armed regime. While many democratic-minded oppositionists allied with the contras, control over the FDN was still in the hands of extreme rightists. The FSLN's attempt to hijack the anti-Somoza revolution and the U.S. effort to maintain control over Nicaragua's direction had made for a tragic deadlock.

I
SANDINISTA POLICIES AND IDEOLOGY

1.
DANIEL ORTEGA: NOTHING WILL HOLD BACK OUR STRUGGLE FOR LIBERATION (SEPTEMBER 1979)

The Government of National Reconstruction of Nicaragua and the Sandinista National Liberation Front salute the people of Cuba, their government, and the president of the Council of State, Comandante and Comrade Fidel Castro.

We also salute the peoples of Latin America, the Caribbean, Africa, and Asia for the solidarity they demonstrated in support of our cause.

On Saturday, September 1, in a Mexican newspaper, we read a dispatch datelined Havana that made reference to Nicaragua's position regarding the "problem" of Kampuchea. And we say "problem" because it is a problem for imperialism for *a people to be free.*

The dispatch in question noted that Nicaragua's delegation had aligned itself with the Soviet bloc by recognizing the government of people's Kampuchea. We all know what interests motivate the international press agencies of the so-called free world, so the deed does not surprise us.

We know that many of these press agencies, and with them the most reactionary sectors of the United States government and of Latin America, are waiting to pounce on our declarations at this meeting.

These are the same forces that gave rise to the Somozaist dictatorship. They are the same forces that defamed and assassinated Lumumba, that defamed and assassinated Che. These are the same forces that slandered and assassinated Van Troi, the same forces that slandered and assassinated Sandino.

Imperialism cannot conceive of a free people, a sovereign people, an independent people. Because, simply and plainly, for them *the people* is nothing more than an empty phrase. We just saw reconfirmation of this when our final offensive was launched.

They examined the war in mathematical terms. Somoza had a regular army. Somoza had more soldiers than the Sandinistas. Somoza had tanks,

Speech before the Nonaligned Conference in Havana, Cuba, September 1979.

planes, artillery, while the Sandinistas didn't. Somoza had more soldiers, more rifles, more communications than the Sandinistas. Therefore, Somoza had to win the war against the Sandinistas. But what was left out was that Somoza did not have the people, and that we Sandinistas were the people.

And when Somoza was losing the war, they were talking about Costa Rican intervention, Panamanian intervention, Cuban intervention, Soviet intervention—simply because they have never been able to understand, and are never going to understand, that people are capable of achieving their liberation, that people are able to solidarize themselves with people, and that therefore the free and sovereign people of Nicaragua today recognizes the right of Kampuchea to occupy this seat.

I repeat, imperialism cannot understand it because for them *the people* is nothing more than an empty phrase.

The Nicaraguan people have won, with their blood, the right to be here today, in this way breaking with a historic past of servility toward imperialist policy.

For the first time in their entire history the Nicaraguan people can officially express their sovereign will, joining this movement of the Nonaligned barely forty-one days after their triumph.

We are entering the Nonaligned movement because in this movement we see the broadest organization of the Third World states that are playing an important role and exercising a growing influence in the international sphere, in the struggle of peoples against imperialism, colonialism, neocolonialism, apartheid, racism, including Zionism and every form of oppression. Because they are for active peaceful coexistence, against the existence of military blocs and alliances, for restructuring international relations on an honorable basis, and are for the establishment of a new international economic order.

In the Sandinista revolution there is no alignment; there is an absolute and consistent commitment to the aspirations of the peoples who have achieved their independence and to those who are struggling to win it. That is why we are among the Nonaligned.

This transcendental step is part of the process of liberation that peoples are going through, peoples such as those in Grenada, Iran, Kampuchea, and Uganda, who won beautiful victories this year. . . .

Sandinismo is the incarnation of the nation. The Sandinista National Liberation Front, as the genuine vanguard of the great people's insurrection that defeated the dictatorship, is now pushing forward a process of national reconstruction whose first measures have been the massive expropriation of the property of Somoza and his civilian and military accomplices. So far more than 500,000 hectares, close to 50 percent of the entire arable area of the country, has been recovered by the people.

More than 180 industrial and commercial enterprises have passed into the hands of the people.

More than 400 mansions and homes have been expropriated in the interests of the people.

The banks have been nationalized.

We have begun to put an Integral Agrarian Reform Plan into effect. Agricultural exports have been nationalized.

The exploitation of natural resources has been nationalized.

By eliminating the 500 and 1,000 córdoba bills and retiring them from circulation, we are hindering the maneuvers of the defeated Somozaists to destabilize our country financially.

A real social thrust is being given to education, health, and housing.

A foreign policy of relations with all countries of the world has been established.

We have become part of the movement of the Nonaligned.

Sandinista Defense Committees have been organized as bodies of people's participation.

The Sandinista People's Army has been set up to fulfill the pressing need to guarantee the defense and advance of the revolution.

And this revolution has been expansive and generous toward its enemies. Thousands of captured soldiers have had their lives protected. Groups such as the International Red Cross were authorized to set up centers of refuge to give shelter to the Somozaist criminals who were fleeing.

The revolution is marching forward. The difficulties are great. The counterrevolution is a potential threat.

There are some who assert that we are assassinating the prisoners.

There are some who are trying to put conditions on international aid. The conspiracy is powerful and the most reactionary sectors of the U.S. government have already succeeded in stopping a small grant of $8 million that the U.S. government was going to give our country.

The most reactionary sectors of the Central American region are observing our process with trepidation. We have detected concentrations of Somozaist soldiers in neighboring countries. But just as we have been generous in victory, we will be inflexible in defense of the revolution.

To what has already been described, we must add the economic legacy of imperialist domination and the Somozaist war of aggression.

We find ourselves with a foreign debt of more than $1.53 billion. Of this amount, $596 million falls due this year, having been incurred as short-term loans at very high interest rates. The foreign debt is equivalent to three times the total annual exports of the country.

The loans obtained by Somozaism were misspent, squandered, and sent out of the country to personal accounts in the United States and Europe.

A study published August 14 by the Economic Commission for Latin

America (CEPAL) maintained that Somozaist bombing resulted in $580 million in material damage to the physical and social infrastructure in the agricultural, industrial, and commercial sectors. At present $741 million is needed to reactivate production.

To the losses cited above, we have to add the losses to the system of production that stem from the paralysis of economic activities. In addition we must add the resources required for restoring the country's economic apparatus at a time when it is also being transformed.

To give us a more graphic representation of the problem, CEPAL estimates that the situation we have described means that the Gross Domestic Product has declined 25 percent this year, 1979. In per capita terms, this puts the GDP back to the level that Nicaragua was at in 1962, meaning we have slid back seventeen years.

And to top it all off, our revolution found only $3.5 million in the state coffers. That is all that Somozaism was unable to loot.

Nicaragua's situation has provoked interest in the countries of Latin America and the rest of the world. Regional bodies have expressed their decision to aid us. Bilaterally we have close relations with many countries.

But we must be frank: The oppressive financial problem that confronts our process, which is directly related to restructuring the foreign debt and receiving financing in order to allow our economy to start up again, does not seem to seriously interest the developed countries. . . .

The people of Sandino are not going to step back from the ground already gained. Our integration with the peoples of Africa and Asia raises our morale in this great battle. The future belongs to the peoples.

The march toward victory will not be stopped!

2.
NICARAGUAN BISHOPS: PASTORAL LETTER
(NOVEMBER 1979)

We would like to begin with a word about what the Revolutionary process has accomplished, which prompts us to:

a) Recognize that over the years of suffering and being socially dispossessed, our people has been building up the experience necessary to transform it into a broad and profoundly liberating action.

Our people fought heroically in the defense of their right to live with

Letter signed by Archbishop Obando y Bravo and the six other Nicaraguan bishops, November 1979.

dignity, in peace and justice. This has been the profound significance of the action that was undertaken against a regime that violated and suppressed human, individual, and social rights. Just as in the past we denounced that situation as being contrary to the precepts of the gospel, we now wish to reaffirm that we take upon ourselves the deep motivation of that struggle for justice and for life.

b) Recognize that the blood of those who gave their lives in that prolonged struggle, the self-sacrifice of the youth who sought to forge a just society, and also the outstanding role played by the women—deferred since time immemorial—in all this process, signifies the unleashing of new forces in the construction of a new Nicaragua. All this underscores the originality of the historical experience we are now living through. Furthermore, the struggle of our people to be the creator of its own history has profoundly reflected the thought and work of Augusto César Sandino. This highlights the originality of the Nicaraguan Revolution by giving it a style of its own and a very clearly defined banner of social justice, affirmation of national values and international solidarity.

c) See in the joy of a poor people, who for the first time in long years feel that their own country belongs to them, the expression of revolutionary creativeness that opens broad and fruitful possibilities for the commitment of all those wishing to fight against an unjust and oppressive system and to create the New Man.

d) Duly value the decision to initiate the institutionalization of the revolutionary process upon a basis of law from the first day of victory. This, as demonstrated by the determination to retain the programs announced prior to victory, such as: the promulgation of the Law on the Rights and Guarantees of Nicaraguans, the effective enjoyment of freedom of information, of partisan political organization, religion, movement, nationalization to recoup the nation's wealth, the initial steps toward agrarian reform, etc.; as well as, the ability to take action at the very start of the process to plan and organize a national literacy campaign for ennobling our people's spirit, conferring upon them the capacity to better forge their own destiny, and to participate with greater responsibility and foresight in the revolutionary process.

e) Recognize that there are conflicting interests in the country arising from the agrarian reform, expropriation of large property owners, etc.; conflicts that may become aggravated by a process of change in economic, social, political, and cultural patterns.

f) Recognize, too, the risks, dangers, and errors in this revolutionary process, in the awareness that no process of absolute human purity has ever existed and, in that sense, to duly value freedom of criticism and of speech as a matchless means of pointing out and correcting errors and consummating the achievements of the revolutionary process.

TASKS

We believe that the present moment in the Revolution is a propitious time to effectuate the ecclesiastical option for the poor. However, we must remember that no revolutionary achievement in history has been able to exhaust the infinite possibilities of justice and absolute solidarity of the kingdom of God. Furthermore, we must assert that our commitment to the revolutionary process must not mean ingenuousness nor blind devotion, nor, even less, the creation of a new idol before which one must bow down unquestioningly. Dignity, responsibility, and Christian freedom are the irrevocable attributes of active participation in the revolutionary process. . . .

SOCIALISM

The fear has been expressed, at times with anxiety, that the present Nicaraguan process is heading toward socialism. We, the bishops, are asked what we think about that.

If, as some think, socialism becomes vitiated when it usurps from individuals and peoples their role as free protagonists in their history; if, it were to seek to submit people blindly to the manipulation and dictates of those who arbitrarily and unlawfully seize power, we would be unable to accept such a dubious or false socialism. Nor could we accept a socialism that seeks by overstepping limits to wrest from man the right to a religious orientation of his life or to publicly express such orientations and convictions, whatever his faith may be.

It would be equally unacceptable to deny parents the right to bring up their children in accordance with their convictions or any other right of the human individual.

If, on the other hand, socialism represents, as it should represent, primacy of the interests of the majority of Nicaraguans, and a model of a nationally-planned economy, fully and progressively shared, then, we have nothing to object to. A social project that guarantees a common destination of the nation's assets and resources and, on that basis, of the satisfaction of the fundamental needs of all, and permits the human quality of life to improve, seems fair to us. If socialism signifies progressive lessening of injustice and of the traditional inequalities between city and countryside, between the remuneration of intellectual and manual labor; if it signifies that the worker will share in the fruits of his labor, beyond economic norms, then, there is nothing in Christianity that contradicts this process. Rather, Pope John Paul II has just called to mind at the United Nations the concern evoked by the sharp division between labor and proprietorship.

If socialism stands for power wielded in the interests of the great masses and increasingly shared by the organized people in such a manner that there is progress toward a true transfer of power to the popular classes, it will find nothing in the faith but incentive and support.

If socialism leads to cultural processes that bring out the dignity in our masses and imbue them with the courage to assume responsibility and to demand their rights, then it can be said to constitute a humanization that merges with the human dignity proclaimed by our faith.

As for the struggle of social classes, we think that the dynamic factor of class struggle which should lead to a just transformation of structures is one thing, while class hatred is something else, aimed as it is against people and contradicting the Christian precept of guidance by love.

Our faith assures us that it is an urgent Christian duty to dominate the world, to transform the land and all other means of production so as to enable man to live and make of this Nicaraguan land a land of justice, solidarity, peace, and freedom in which the Christian annunciation of the Kingdom of God shall take on its fullest meaning.

We are also confident that the revolutionary process will be something original, creative, deeply national, and not in any way imitative since what we are seeking together with the Nicaraguan masses is a process that advances firmly on the way to a society that is fully and authentically Nicaraguan, not capitalist, not dependent, not totalitarian.

3.
SERGIO RAMÍREZ: SOCIALISM CANNOT BE INSTITUTED OVERNIGHT (JANUARY 1980)

How much importance do you attach to the geopolitical aspect in the current Nicaraguan process?

It must be admitted that deeper social change cannot take place in one country without a similar transformation in those that surround it. To be specific, a process of change in one Central American country requires that a similar process be in progress in the others. Naturally, this does not mean that we leave off pursuing our own course to its ultimate consequences, but we cannot neglect giving special attention to our immediate neighbors. We look upon America as a totality of which we are still-scattered segments,

From *Cuadernos de Marcha* (Mexico), January–February 1980.

but the first segments we must try to unify are those that compose Central America.

How would you characterize the U.S. attitude toward Nicaragua in these first months since July 19th?

Referring specifically to the Carter administration and to certain democratic sectors of the U.S. congress, I would say that, in general, they have a positive attitude towards Nicaragua. We have publicly declared that our purpose is to maintain stable, normal, and open relations with the United States. We spoke to President Carter in September and explained our position to him frankly. We told him that we were hoping for a new kind of relationship not characterized by dependency and servility as was the case with all previous Nicaraguan regimes. He replied that the U.S. government wished to draw a curtain over the past so that his administration would not be confused with the ones preceding it. On the basis of this approach we hope to build relations of a different kind despite the fact that the imperialist interests in the United States disapprove of what is happening in Nicaragua.

In the latter part of Somoza's regime, China became the principal buyer of Nicaraguan cotton. What effect has this had on the relations of the Government of National Reconstruction with that country?

We have not established relations with China so far nor has the government of that country proposed it. Within the formal framework of our foreign policy, we continue to have relations with Taiwan but this does not preclude seriously considering recognition in the future of People's China as the legitimate government of the Chinese people. As for our economic relations, it is impossible at this time to quantify them because we have practically no cotton crop, but when cotton production is resumed we believe that we will have no problem in disposing of it on the Chinese market. In the political aspect, it is well-known that we have publicly maintained a position of open repudiation of the Chinese invasion of Vietnam. However, we do not believe this is going to hurt our relations with China, just as we maintain stable relations with the United States despite the fact that we have been equally open on the question of Puerto Rican independence.

To what do you attribute the support the Revolution has received, and continues receiving, from certain sectors of the Nicaraguan bourgeoisie?

A distinction must be made between two types of bourgeoisie. On the one hand, there is the financial bourgeoisie that fled the country together with Somoza and from which we expropriated the banks and the entire financial system. That bourgeoisie never identified itself with national interests of any kind. In saying bourgeoisie, we apply the term broadly, since a true national bourgoisie never managed to establish itself here as it did in Argentina, Chile, or Uruguay. Ours was little more than a group that acted as middleman for U.S. interests. On the other hand, however, there is a democratic sector of the national bourgeoisie in the country today that is working on reconstruction and has a part to play in our process. We have elected the option of a planned economy because we believe there is no other way. Over 50,000 Nicaraguans died in the last two years fighting against the Somoza dictatorship and none of those young men could have conceived that their struggle would end in the enhancement of capitalist society in Nicaragua. They themselves were the ones who took the option —a bloody option. They chose a Sandinista project for a new society that calls for economic planning. What is more, the backbone of the new economic system is planning. It is within a planned economy that we have staked out a sector of production for the private sector. However, it is a sector assigned by the Revolution.

What made it possible to overthrow the Somoza dynasty in 1979 and why couldn't it have been done 10, 15, or 20 years ago?

It has to do with the process of political education and maturity of the masses in the country. The Somoza dynasty did not fall in 1956, for example, after the assassination of Somoza García, because the masses were not involved in the political process. It had been manipulated in the direction of the so-called "historical parallels," which were oligarchic factions—liberal or conservative—that received popular support activated through paternalistic, patriarchal mechanisms, but which signified no real popular participation at all. The authentic option of popular participation in the struggle against the dictatorship was put forward by the Sandinista National Liberation Front (FSLN). With the establishment of the FSLN in 1964, a slow process of education of the masses toward the option of armed struggle began. Why? Because the other option that had been offered it by the oligarchic factions was the option of elections, of civil struggle, which was slowly losing ground. In 1967, the Conservative Party, headed by Fernando Agüero, participated in rigged elections that were won by Anastasio Somoza and immediately proceeded to make a deal with him to form a farcical triumvirate. This episode completed the erosion of the electoral alternative while at the same time the armed-struggle option was taking shape. Then, after the 1972 earthquake, with the latter alternative having taken root in the popular consciousness, the opposition bourgeoisie found itself between two fires; its own option, which had fallen into disrepute, and that of armed struggle to which it had no choice but to bow because it was all that has proved effective for overthrowing dictatorship. There were, of course, sectors of the bourgeoisie which were betting that the armed struggle would lead only to getting Somoza out and putting in a moderate bourgeois-democratic government. Somoza's fall, then, came after a historical buildup of forces: the growth of popular support of the armed alternative; the development of an insurrectional strategy which, as of October, 1977, proved to be the most effective catalyst in the confrontation with the dictatorship; the activity of the Group of Twelve, a completely unprecedented experiment in Latin America, which made it possible to establish an effective alliance between the FSLN and the democratic sectors of the bourgeoisie; the decline of the dictatorship domestically and its isolation on the international plane, which led even to the withdrawal of the support the imperialists had been providing until then. It is thus a picture with many elements that is not a simple matter to reconstruct.

How do you feel personally when the world press calls you a Social Democrat?

Yes, I have seen that and it is now almost a stock phrase: "Sergio Ramírez, a German-style Social Democrat." I don't really know how the label originated. Even though this may seem a little strange, we Sandinistas are not very much concerned about being part of any of the main political currents of the world. In talking to European newspeople, I have explained to them that we are Sandinistas, we act like Sandinistas, and we have a Sandinista ideology. They answered that that was all very well but asked us to clarify whether we were Social Democrats, Eurocommunists, or followers of the Soviet, Chinese, or Albanian line. We reject that kind of a priori pigeonholing. We are building a revolutionary process very much our own and have, of course, a revolutionary ideology, but we want that revolutionary ideology to be identified as Sandinista. This does not mean to say that we think we are discovering the Atlantic Ocean and that we want to create a universal line of thought to be known as "Sandinista." Rather, we are perfectly clear in our minds about which currents of thought have moved history and are committed to them. We often hear sectors of Nicaragua, the traditional ones, to be sure—some well-intentioned, others not well intentioned—which insist that the Revolution must be original, that it must resemble no other, imitate no other, that it be truly Nicaraguan. Of course, a revolution that has no characteristics of its own is not a true revolution. Ours is going to be a Nicaraguan revolution to the degree in which it is the outcome of a particular historical process of foreign domination and of a no less unique historical process of internal domination. It has to do with an entire past with which we have broken or are trying to break. However, what happens is that sometimes when they say to us that this revolution has to be original, they are really thinking of something else: that this revolution should not break with the patterns of domination, not favor popular interests, and not be a revolution which, above everything, defends the interests of the workers and peasants, the only ones in the country who have never had anything. When the thinking is along those lines then, of course, we are on the other side. Only when it is recognized that this is a revolution that must defend such interests do we accept being told that it has to be an original revolution. That is the only originality it is capable of. The only context in which it is possible to judge the originality of this revolution is what kind of interests it defends.

4.
FSLN: "SEVENTY-TWO HOURS" DOCUMENT
(SEPTEMBER 1979)

Brothers:

The First National Assembly of Cadres of the Sandinist National Liberation Front was held in Managua on 21, 22 and 23 September. Although not all cadres and rank-and-file members were in attendance, the comrades who did attend were sufficiently representative to give a quite accurate idea of the situation in our country. . . .

We should underscore the far-reaching importance of this assembly in the history of our organization, inasmuch as it was, in fact, the first time that leaders, cadres and activists in our organization were gathered together. . . .

We would like this report to circulate among all our members, throughout the country and overseas as well, but for obvious reasons we cannot include, much as we would like to, the fundamental issues discussed at the assembly. . . .

The Reconstruction Government (which was born of an alliance of classes but which was mainly the political alternative that Sandinism had organized to neutralize Yankee intervention) entered Managua triumphant under conditions that were not at all like those that prevailed at the time it was created. Sandinism had won the war, and the people acknowledged the total victory of Sandinism above all else. It is true that in 1977 the main purpose of the alliance with the democratic segments of the bourgeoisie was to isolate Somozism and to expand the forces of the Sandinist Front. It was an alliance aimed at a domestic neutralization. However, the alliance that took the form of the National Reconstruction Government, the cabinet and, to a major extent, the FSLN's basic program, under the circumstances of the new offensive by the uprising, was *designed to neutralize Yankee interventionist policies in light of the imminent Sandinist military victory*. Organizing the government was a relatively easy task; it did not involve negotiations with the parties of the bourgeois opposition. Instead, it involved appointing patriotic figures who were somewhat representative. Thus, the Reconstruction Government took office under conditions different from the ones that gave rise to it. The presence of well-known Sandinist figures in the government compensated for the lack of consistency between the political blueprint that the government put together and the Sandinist revolution's overwhelming military victory. . . .

In a nutshell, the red and black flag covers the national territory. We can assert without fear of error that Sandinism represents the sole domestic force. We can assert that since 19 July the FSLN has exercised power on behalf of the workers and other oppressed segments of society, or to put in another way, the workers exercise power through the FSLN. In spite of its sweeping victory, however, Sandinism has not made radical moves to transform all of this power once and for all into the power of workers and peasants. This is because our political tactics are to develop conditions more favorable to the revolution and because our most urgent task at present is to consolidate the revolution politically, economically and militarily so that we can move on to greater revolutionary transformations.

Thus, after 2 months in power the revolution has actually taken very few measures that we could call sweeping. We Sandinists are engaged in military and political organization now, consolidating our revolutionary foundation. We have not yet put as much energy into in-depth economic and social transformations that this time will forever alter the balance of power between labor and capital. . . .

Another major economic measure that will benefit the masses is the rent freeze. This is designed to eliminate landlords so that negotiations can begin for the State to take over all of these rented houses and implement a rent adjustment policy under which tenants will pay the State a given percentage of their income.

The Agrarian Reform Institute will begin performing the revolution's first tasks in the countryside. There are currently two kinds of production units: the large units, which are directly run by the State, and the cooperative sector, which is run by the INRA and which consists of the various farm cooperatives that are being organized. . . .

We have already lopped off a strategic portion of the bourgeoisie's economic power by bolstering the material groundwork and strengthening the position of the exploited classes. Nevertheless, we can assert unambiguously that only a change in the relations of production, beginning with this sphere of the social economy of the government, will truly tilt the balance of power in favor of the oppressed, who already have behind them (and this is not to be made light of) the power of weapons and the Sandinist People's Army, which is there to assure that the progress so far is irreversible.

It is important to note here (and this is something on which the FSLN and the bourgeoisie agree, for differing reasons) that the dominant factor in establishing political guidelines is the international correlation of forces, more specifically the influence that imperialism and its allies exercise on the continental level. In other words, although it is valid to pursue a skillful policy of counteracting imperialism under the current circumstances, the FSLN seems to have adopted an instinctively rather defensive and more conservative posture instead of pursuing a clear-cut policy for this stage, whereas the bourgeoisie, in contrast to the conservative role it played in the past, is in an excellent position and can take better advantage than we can of the State's machinery, of its own economic base and of its opportunities to make more contingency policies available to imperialism for adversely affecting our revolutionary process.

Imperialism lost its armed vehicle in Nicaragua and lacks solid avenues for putting together any sort of reactionary plan in the near future. Because of the kind of military victory that we achieved over the dictatorship, the defeated National Guard cannot possibly organize an attack on us for the time being, especially since it would have to have strong backing from a bordering or nearby country. None of our neighbors could embark on such a chancy adventure, Honduras because it must remain neutral while in the midst of a quite complex domestic situation, and El Salvador and Guatemala because they have social upheavals to deal with. Some National Guard detachments that maintain ties with hard-core commands might gain the support of unofficial rightwing military groups or "White Hand–type" gangs and could possibly engage in terrorist activities or very limited banditry. A spontaneous counterrevolutionary uprising might also be helped by minor subversive acts organized by saboteurs on the Far Left or lumpen proletariat elements that have infiltrated our own ranks.

Though we do not wish to downplay the need for a strong army to take care of national defense, we would point out that at present there is no clear indication that an armed counterrevolution by Somozist forces beyond our borders is going to take place and jeopardize our stability. What merits our attention, instead, is domestic factors. Counterrevolutionary action from overseas will for some time most likely take the form of financial pressures by imperialism to undermine the economic and social foundation of the

Sandinist Revolution. The rousing momentum of our resounding, historic victory and the confidence of the masses in their vanguard, the FSLN, have so far enabled us to exercise a considerable power of leadership over our people. Moreover, the FSLN's political realism has won us overwhelming support from the middle-income strata of the population. We could say that the substance of the FSLN's policy since 10 July has appealed to the nation's patriotic sectors, thus reflecting the influence that several factors have had on our decisions, such as:

a) The need to gain ground to consolidate our army;
b) The need to maintain a high level of social cohesiveness, in particular with the bourgeoisie;
c) The expectation of financial aid from the Western bloc;
d) The need to detract from the legitimacy of imperialism's tactics of sabotage;
e) Our leadership body's political pragmatism. After all, it is a positive development that this "intermediate" situation is helping to further the desire to merge with the FSLN, a desire that has been voiced by "middle-of-the-road" political groups such as the Independent Liberal Party (PLI), Ramírez's Socialist Party (PS), the progressive wing of the MDN [Nicaraguan Democratic Movement], the PC [Communist Party] and the PSC. It is likewise positive that the reactionary bourgeoisie remains politically bankrupt. On the other hand, however, if this sort of approach becomes institutionalized, it is going to give rise to contradictions, manifestations of which are already beginning to surface. . . .

We have dealt imperialism an enormous political blow. It is in the economic sphere, however, that the bonds of domination remain and threaten to become the basis for a regeneration of an enclave of counter-revolutionary forces that could in the medium term pose a serious threat to our revolution.

Consequently, our revolution must make qualitative progress in the economic sphere as well, by seeking to transform the social relations of production in the entire area in which we have brought the bourgeoisie to bay and by incorporating urban and rural workers en masse into the struggle for sweeping changes in Nicaraguan society. . . .

The FSLN's position towards leftwing political parties is dictated by the attitude that they take regarding the revolutionary process. If their attitude poses a current danger, these parties will be treated as enemies of the revolution. This is the case with the Far Left groups that have taken sabotaging and counterrevolutionary stands, such as the MAP and its branches and the Trotskyite groups. These groups that oppose the process must be crushed! In contrast, leftwing organizations that show a willing-ness to work for the revolution's interests, whether by joining the FSLN, dissolving their own mass organizations or working closely under the leadership of the FSLN, should be encouraged to struggle tirelessly to preserve the revolution.

There are other sectors, however, that we also need to bring over to the revolution's side. The petty bourgeoisie presently acknowledges the FSLN as the vanguard of the revolutionary process. The same goes for small organizations of this sort and for the democratic segments of the bourgeoisie, who would rather work within an established framework than waste away. We must attract the petty bourgeois masses by giving them their own organizations and integrating them into the State's tasks. Furthermore, given the international situation, we must maintain the very small parties and try to absorb their most rational elements into the revolution. Our policy must be to preserve these small parties, which rather than representing the petty bóurgeoisie, are organized petty bourgeois groups. Specifically, our policy should be to change their notion of the Council of State, the real foundation of which ought to be the political activity of the organized working masses. We can be frank with some of these groups and explain the situation to them, whereas we have to be careful with others so as to achieve our aims.

In contrast, we must isolate the traitorous bourgeoisie, which is stubbornly trying to keep our country under imperialism's economic yoke, from the democratic sectors. Our tactics to achieve this aim must be in keeping with the circumstances surrounding the revolutionary process. We must attack it not as a class but through its most representative elements as soon as they give us the chance. By striking political and economic blows we will be able to greatly narrow its counterrevolutionary maneuvering room. This is also how we should seek to isolate the far leftwing groups that persist in engaging in sabotage and confusing the masses. This sort of policy will enable us to more easily pinpoint the enemies of the revolution and enable the masses to administer the main crushing blow against the counterrevolutionary enclaves of the traitorous bourgeoisie, the vestiges of Somozism and the Far Left.

We must strengthen diplomatic relations with the Catholic Church and, in general, pursue a careful policy aimed at counteracting conservative stands whenever possible, strengthening ties with priests who are sympathetic to the revolution and encouraging revolutionary sectors in the Church. We have to pursue a restrictive policy towards the Protestant Church, which consists mainly of American sects, undertaking intelligence work on them and, if they are caught doing something wrong, expelling them immediately.

Finally, our policy towards former National Guardsmen who sided with the FSLN in certain activities or who surrendered right away should be to seek a rapprochement, to keep a file on them and to prohibit them from serving in the Sandinist People's Army or the government. Exceptions are, of course, made for those individuals whose background is acceptable and who are indispensable at the moment because they possess certain technical skills.

2. Make the public sector the hub of the nation's economy and guarantee the active involvement of mass organizations.

To achieve our ends we must make use of Sandinism's political strength, the mass movement and the structure of government, while pursuing economic policies that benefit the working masses and the allied sectors nationwide that show a willingness to support the cause of the revolution. . . .

Our organizations must clearly distinguish between the forces that are on our side and the forces that are against us. The relations of production can no longer be viewed in the same way as before the overthrow of the dictatorship. In the first place, we must differentiate the state-run economy from the private economy. The state-run economy includes all of the confiscated Somozist properties in the city and countryside. Therefore, rather than regarding the State as an employer, the class organizations must strive to participate directly in production, in the reconstruction, in seeing to it that the government's economic programs are carried out, in eliminating the vestiges of Somozism from state-run institutions, in providing skilled workers for state-run enterprises and in finding jobs for workers in government production centers that offer new employment opportunities, etc. In other words, they must convince themselves that the public sector economy is there to serve the interests of the people and represents a production system that can rely on its own resources and sever the ties of economic dependence to imperialism. Secondly, we should pressure the progressive sectors of the bourgeoisie to bring their output levels in line with the standards of the new system and to produce mainly whatever is in the national interest. In contrast, we must not allow the traitorous bourgeoisie to ever take advantage of its ties with imperialism, because we know that rather than meet the most deeply felt needs of the masses and the entire country, they will produce goods to increase their wealth even if the people starve to death and remain permanently unemployed.

Moreover, the government should:

a) Pursue bolder educational, health care and housing programs that bring the revolution to the masses, giving priority to the peasant population and specifically the people living along the northern border and the Atlantic coast.

b) Effectively control the financial and banking sector, both by means of decrees and through politically trustworthy cadres, and prohibit foreign banks from channeling loans to the private sector.

c) Create state-run fishing, industrial and mining enterprises.

In addition, trusts must disappear, giving way to corporate enterprises to manage and run these enterprises. . . . The goal of the FSLN's foreign policy is to consolidate the Nicaraguan revolution, because this will help to strengthen the Central American, Latin American and worldwide revolution. We will consolidate our revolution by resolving our military and economic problems first and foremost; thus, on the one hand we will be preparing ourselves strategically to confront any aggression, and on the other we will be making headway in severing the ties of economic dependence on American imperialism. This will be our general approach to foreign policy, the guidelines for which are as follows:

  d) Develop the political and diplomatic relations that will further our military consolidation and economic independence.
  e) Chart and pursue a nationalistic, anti-imperialistic and democratic policy internationally, on the continent and in the Caribbean region in particular.
  f) Help further the struggles of Latin American nations against fascist dictatorships and for democracy and national liberation.
  g) The same principles apply to Central America, which has great strategic importance at present; we should underscore the need to counteract the aggressive policy of the military dictatorships in Guatemala and El Salvador by taking proper advantage of the internal frictions there, while stressing our differences with Honduras and the friendly conduct of Costa Rica and Panama. . . .

We have already heard of excesses committed by leaders of mass organizations. For example, they have practically nullified the authority of government representatives and are demanding measures that have nothing to do with the guidelines that have been charted and instead make the mass organizations the sole judges of how things should be run, without taking into account the nature of the revolution and the policy of alliances that we must pursue. In some cases, Sandinist leaders have attempted to become managers of enterprises and to establish administrative policy, which has caused political problems for us, instead of playing their proper role, which is to see to it that the government policy set forth by the FSLN is carried out in every respect. Mass organization policy must take into account the objective realities of the revolution. Economically speaking, we have state-run enterprises and private companies. Therefore, our policy must take these situations, these conflicts and these relations into account, because otherwise we will be promoting anarchy and getting bogged down in problems caused by our own actions, which will prevent us from tackling the fundamental problems that we must really solve. . . .

h) To see to it that most workers are channeled by their class organizations into state-run enterprises. In other words, the CST and the ATC should take care of unemployment problems under the country's new conditions through their ties with the government and thus guarantee a rebound in industrial and farm production. Private companies are a different matter, because labor relations are a factor there. Nevertheless, we must advise our organizations as to the sort of relations they should maintain, to turn to State bodies to clear up their problems, and to see to it that these companies produce what is in the national interest, and not to take radical action unless necessary, because any action that brings overall production to a halt is a severe blow to our efforts to overcome the economic crisis. . . .

Because of our revolution's triumph, the Sandinist People's Army has been acknowledged as the Constitutional Army of the Republic. It is therefore the mission of the FSLN to insure that its members are loyal to the revolution and to the leadership of the revolution's historic vanguard, the FSLN itself. The following mechanisms and tasks will guarantee this revolutionary loyalty:

a) Continual political education efforts within the Armed Forces.
b) The FSLN's vanguard structures will see to it that our organization's policies are communicated and pursued and that our members are politically involved in the Armed Forces.
c) The FSLN organizes its influence and political leadership through leadership committees and member groups within the Armed Forces. Through its military committee the National Directorate sees to it that its political education policy is transmitted throughout the military hierarchy, and it will be in charge of the FSLN's party groups within the Sandinist People's Army.
d) The mission of party groups is to respect and strengthen military structures and hierarchies.
e) The FSLN's task is to strengthen the political education section of the Sandinist People's Army; this section must consist of vanguard activists of recognized revolutionary qualities.

Other tasks within the Armed Forces are:

a) To strengthen the military leadership in strategic zones and to provide for the possibility that highly sensitive regions can be placed under the command of a member of our National Directorate. This applies to the northern, southern and Atlantic coast regions.
b) To purge the army at all levels, getting rid of elements who are not compatible with revolutionary measures.
c) To establish obligatory military service. . . .

For almost 4 years the FSLN was shaken up by the problems stemming from the political crisis it suffered in October 1975. During this period each faction had its own style, methods, tactics and strategy, and there was appreciable political mistrust among them as a result of the serious differences within the Sandinist Front. More than once we were in danger of not being able to carry forward our strategic plan for the uprising and of not being in a position to place the various factions under a single, monolithic leadership. Because of the imperatives of the political situation in late May, the urgent need to be as united as possible in confronting the enemy and our historic duty to lead our people to victory, we were in many places able to unite under a single leadership large contingents of forces, which in general observed the political and military instructions of our commands and fought tremendous battles against the Somozist National Guard and eventually ground it into dust.

Things are different today, however. Our organization, at the forefront of its people, has gained power and is thus in a position to implement the political blueprint that it proclaimed for so many years. This is a necessary condition for progressing towards a superior stage of struggle in which power will be in the hands of the people once and for all. To make sure that all forces are guided in a proper, revolutionary manner, to promote a wide range of organizations, to raise our people's levels of political awareness, to wage an effective battle against the traitorous bourgeoisie, which has started mobilizing to oust us from power and take hold of the country's economy and is trying to organize itself politically, in short, to discharge all of these responsibilities, we need a vanguard detachment that will first of all eradicate all of the vestiges of sectarianism from the Sandinist Front and place the organization under a single recognized political and military leadership and, secondly, rapidly begin building the revolutionary party. . . .

The major internal threat to the FSLN is the continuation of splinter groups or factions, which could sabotage its unity and greatly weaken any alliance that the FSLN might want to form with other revolutionary organizations. Organizational unity means eliminating once and for all the causes of political crises and striving to establish within the organization the party mechanisms for settling differences and thus strengthening the vanguard. Any organization that does not foster group debate, the education of its members and their involvement in resolving its burning problems, will wither rapidly, lose strength and vigor and die out politically.

We must realize that instead of aiming for an acritical approach, excessive democracy or excessive centralism, our organization should seek to function scientifically in accordance with revolutionary principles. Everyone realizes that we are currently devoting most of our efforts to efficiently redeploying our activists. Some of them still suffer from factionalism, political immaturity and ideological shortcomings. . . .

No one must divert efforts into factionalism or conspire against the organization's unity. This would be lowering our guard and providing fertile ground for divisiveness, while the enemy unites and works feverishly to set up his political machine and struggle against the revolution's dominance. We must realize that organizations usually have factions that cause strife. This is to be expected in any political organization. If the organization wages a proper revolutionary struggle against the factions that do not espouse a revolutionary ideology, it will gain greater political strength, and if it wages this struggle through organized political channels of involvement, then nothing can destroy the organization. . . .

Our highest aspiration as an organization is now to maintain revolutionary power, not to obtain it. Therefore, our goal is to have our people recognize their vanguard and undertake the tasks that it has set before them, the fundamental premise being that the FSLN is the legitimate leader of the revolutionary process. It is thus extraordinarily important to point this out to each politically and organizationally independent group and clearly explain the policy that the FSLN is pursuing to unite people around it, as well as the need for a single set of organizations of a clearly revolutionary stripe to make headway in the appointed tasks. . . .

5.
FSLN: STATEMENT ON THE ELECTORAL PROCESS
(AUGUST 1980)

1. For the Sandinista Front, democracy is not measured only in political terms, nor is it confined merely to participation in elections. It is more, much more. For a revolutionary, for a Sandinista, it means PARTICIPATION by the people in political, economic, social and cultural affairs. The more the people take part in these things, the more it will be democratic. And it must be said once and for all, democracy does not begin and end with elections. It is a myth to want to reduce democracy to that. Democracy begins in the economic order, when social inequalities begin to weaken, when workers and peasants improve their standard of living. This is the beginning of true democracy—and never before.

Once these objectives are achieved, it then moves into other fields: it

Read by Humberto Ortega at a ceremony marking the end of the National Literacy Campaign, August 23, 1980.

expands into the field of government, when the people determine their government, like it or not.

However, at a more advanced stage, democracy means participation by workers in the management of factories, farms, cooperatives and cultural centers. In sum, democracy is intervention by the masses in all aspects of social life. We have said this in order to state clearly, as a matter of principle, what the Sandinista National Liberation Front understands by democracy.

Despite this, the Sandinista Front believes that constructive criticism is the only kind of profitable criticism. Disagreement and pluralism will continue to be essential components of the SANDINISTA DEMOC-RACY. But it points out that the criticisms that ought to be taken into account are, fundamentally, the criticisms made by the workers, because these are the most disinterested, genuinely sincere and revolutionary, kinds of criticism.

2. The National Directorate of the Sandinista National Liberation Front reaffirms to the Nicaraguan people and to the world that the revolutionary process taking place in our country cannot go backward, and that it will continue onward to the ultimate consequences. There must not be the slightest doubt that it is A REVOLUTION that is underway today, and that it was to make a revolution that at the head of the Nicaraguan people, the Sandinista National Liberation Front took power on July 19, 1979, after 18 years of struggle and at the cost of almost 100,000 lives.

3. The responsibility we took on in conducting the war of liberation led us to examine the concrete realities of our country. We were thus able to assess the backwardness and the state of economic, social and moral destruction in which the victorious Revolution would find the country.

For these reasons, we seriously proposed that when victory was achieved, we should begin a PROCESS OF NATIONAL RECON-STRUCTION as the first great step in the Sandinista Popular Revolution.

4. Once in power, the Sandinista Front, as the true vanguard and leader of the Nicaraguan people, decided to install a Government Junta that would organize and head the work of the Government, supported by the work of the people to make national reconstruction possible.

5. One year after the Revolution, we can responsibly say that the country's backwardness and its economic, social and moral destruction are so profound and widespread that the nation cannot be expected to be reconstructed before 1985; the National Directorate of the Sandinista Front has therefore decided that the GOVERNMENT JUNTA must continue to lead the work of government until 1985.

6. Therefore, our worker people, our workers and peasants, our young people and women, professionals and businessmen, patriots devoted to national reconstruction, must be ready in 1985 to elect the government program and the country's best men to take charge of government and continue to push forward the work of our Revolution.

7. In January 1984, the JUNTA OF THE GOVERNMENT OF NATIONAL RECONSTRUCTION must, in order to make this victory of the people of Sandino a reality, begin the electoral process by which Nicaraguans will determine the Government that will continue to build the NEW NICARAGUA, the Nicaragua dreamed of by SANDINO, RIGOBERTO and CARLOS FONSECA.

LIBERTY OR DEATH!
SANDINO YESTERDAY, SANDINO TODAY, SANDINO FOREVER!

NATIONAL DIRECTORATE OF THE SANDINISTA NATIONAL LIBERATION FRONT

Commander Ortega then added:

As you will all have understood, the elections that we are talking about are very different from the elections sought by the oligarchs and traitors, the conservatives and liberals, the reactionaries and the imperialists, the "gang of villains," as Sandino called them.

These elections are different from those which Sandino spoke of when he was fighting against intervention: "do not obey a single order from the Yankee Marines in the farce of the election. No one is obliged to go to the ballot box and there is no law compelling them to do so. Be worthy of freedom, be deserving of it." Our elections will not be those elections imposed by the American gringos.

They are the elections imposed by you, by the working people, by the Sandinista youth, by the National Directorate of this Revolution. Such will be our elections. Remember that *they are elections to improve the power of the revolution, but they are not a raffle to see who has power, because the people have the power through their vanguard, the Sandinista National Liberation Front and its National Directorate. . . .*

6.
TOMÁS BORGE: SOCIAL CLASSES AND POLITICAL POWER (MAY 1982)

Under the bourgeois Somozist regime, every day you Nicaraguan workers witnessed how, when the workers staged strikes and took to the streets to demand better living conditions or the peasants forcefully demanded land, the National Guard, the bourgeoisie's instrument, did not stop to think whether the businessmen against whom the workers were struggling, or the big landholders against whom the landless peasants were struggling were Somozist or anti-Somozist, or whether they were members of the so-called opposition bourgeoisie. In order to defend the interest of the wealthy, the National Guard repressed the laborers in the rural areas, the workers in the cities and the peasants, even when—at times, in a vain effort to save themselves—the peasants would claim to be Liberal Party members.

As the businessmen and large landowners of the past had an army and a police corps like the National Guard and a security office at the service of their interests, today you, fraternal workers and peasants, the simple people of Nicaragua, have the Sandinist People's Army, the Sandinist police and the state's security bodies at your total service. [Applause, slogan "a single army," is chanted repeatedly.]

Frankly, one must be an idiot or must be easily deceived, or both, to ask for the people's support in giving the land back to the big landholders and the enterprises back to the Somozists. One must truly be an idiot, an evil person, or both, not to realize that our people have acquired revolutionary awareness; that they have become aware of their historic reality; that our workers have acquired class awareness. The proletariat does not acquire awareness spontaneously. Our workers, however, have already acquired this awareness. The proletariat is undoubtedly the most revolutionary class in history. However, it acquires awareness only when it comes into close contact with revolutionary theory and practice. At some point, the working class can become confused by the illusions which are created by bourgeois propaganda. The false aphorism—the false bourgeois principle that all men are equal in the eyes of bourgeois laws—can be disproven only through practice and the knowledge of revolutionary theory. . . .

On many occasions, however, the working class has fallen victim to

---

Speech at May 1 rally, Managua's Carlos Fonseca Amador Plaza of the revolution. *FBIS* vol. 6, May 3, 1982.

economy-oriented deformations. In other words, the satisfaction of certain demands has been presented as the final goal. In a society marked by exploitation, it is absolutely right for workers to fight for these demands. However, even under an exploitive regime, it can never be right for workers to forget their political demands and objectives.

In a society such as Nicaragua's where the power of imperialism and the bourgeoisie has been dealt a blow, it is just for the workers to continue making demands. But it would be against commonsense and against the advance of history to struggle for these demands while relegating the consolidation of their political power as a social class to second place.

This means that at this point in our history, when the control of bourgeois and imperialist exploitation has been eliminated forever here in Nicaragua, the working class' fundamental obligation is and should be the consolidation of their power within the revolution.

A revolutionary process has several stages; in the first phase of national liberation—which in Nicaragua was the war against the National Guard and Somozist bourgeois domination—the working class and the vanguard that represented its historical interests surrounded themselves with other social sectors and strata. At that point, it was correct to form a broad national unity in order to achieve a goal that was common to the entire nation: getting rid of the criminal Somozist regime, which also represented a great obstacle to Nicaragua's historical development. When the revolutionary victory occurred, a new phase began, during which there was still a need to unite the broadest Nicaraguan social strata in order to confront the common enemy of all Nicaraguans: U.S. imperialism. This means that the new phase, which follows the victory, places the greatest emphasis on the defense of our nationality; on the struggle on behalf of the national sovereignty; on the right of self-determination; and on the need to unite all Nicaraguan patriots to confront a cruel and colossal enemy: Yankee imperialism.

At this new stage, however, serious internal contradictions began emerging when the revolution was forced—as a result of its own dynamics and in accordance with the political tenets that had made it possible—to define which social sector would have priority in the revolution's political projects. Our people already know who the privileged ones were in the past, which were the privileged classes. Our people also know which are now the important classes for which this revolution was made.

Nevertheless, it is necessary to maintain the national unity among broad sectors of our society, including those bourgeois sectors which are willing to work alongside the workers in the areas of production and the defense of the fatherland. This new stage, however, is extraordinarily complex because on one side lie the interests of the workers and peasants, who are the backbone of the revolution. On the other side lie the capitalist sectors, which the revolution wants to keep on its side and which the revolution has even provided with fiscal incentives. But the capitalist sectors are torn apart over the denial of their political hopes and because the umbilical cord that tied them to imperialism as a result of their unpatriotic traditions, refuses to disappear. We ask: Is there a chance that some business or capitalist sectors which are connected with the agricultural production might cut that umbilical cord? Are those social sectors capable of understanding that the workers are the axis of the new society? Could they, we wonder, give up their political aspirations in order to dedicate their experience and capacity to production, that is concerned with the country's development as a whole?

Experience tells us that a certain number of elements in these social groups do not resign themselves to the new reality; and that even within the revolution there are those who thought that in the end, the dream of workers and peasants would end in a nightmare while the dreams of the businessmen as a class would lead to paradise.

But experience also shows that certain business sectors are willing to work alongside the revolution. Also, broad middle sectors and most of the small and medium-sized agricultural producers have joined the revolutionary process. Among the dominating sectors there are some who deceived themselves with false hopes about the nature of the revolution; those who finally realized that the revolution was not waged to satisfy their craving for power, their sad and miserable craving for power. Among them there are also those who failed to realize that real stars are not pinned on uniforms but shine up in the sky.

The people are free to love their leaders. But the leaders of the revolution are not squabbling over the love of the people. If there is any dispute, to put it this way, it is not over who is loved more by the people, but over who can love the people most.

When some people finally realized this, they simply turned their backs on the people and dug their own graves, so that today, 1 May, our working class with their strong muscles, will of steel, and firm and undaunting courage can fill them with shovelsful of dirt; with those shovelsful of dirt that are thrown on graves when the peoples decide to bury the traitors and scoundrels with silence and oblivion.

It is fitting that we should ask why we carried out this revolution. To exalt certain individuals? To maintain the privileges of the past? To maintain a regime of exploitation? Some people thought that we had defeated Somoza here to maintain exploitation in another guise, and want to describe such a change with the nickname of revolution. But this revolution was not carried out to pursue the goals of individuals. It was carried out to pursue the goals of the group; to fight the political contamination of the bourgeoisie and imperialism; to struggle against the philosophy of the wolves, and to do away with the philosophy of bites and toothmarks.

This revolution was not carried out to reinstate an old society, but to create a new society. This struggle, which basically belongs to the working class, has special characteristics determined by the specific conditions of Nicaragua.

When imperialism arose as the supreme form of capitalism, a struggle for markets began among the large capitalist countries. In that initial division of the world, Nicaragua and other Latin American countries suffered the terrible fate of falling into the hands of the Yankee imperialists. Our economy therefore became a dependent economy. This compelled our people to fight for their national liberation, and this fight took one specific form; that of nationalism.

This also explains why our country, subjugated by the United States, never produced a true national bourgeoisie. In our country the local bourgeoisie was never the ruling force. The ruling force was imperialism, through its local instruments.

The development of Nicaragua was achieved through administrative loans and investments, with Anastasio Somoza as foreman, just like Moncada and Chamorro had been in the past, to cite a few examples. When the army of workers and peasants under our general of free men (referring to Augusto César Sandino) kicked the Yankee invaders out of our land, the shrewd invaders formed a subservient army that played the role of an army of occupation, and provided the basis for not only the Somoza dynasty but also for the power of the oligarchy as a whole.

That is why our people's struggle became a struggle against the Somozist dictatorship, which, in essence, was a struggle against imperialism. It is here, in this dialectic confluence of national liberation and anti-Somozist struggle, that we find the essence of our victory. The form of our victory is the fall of the Somozist tyranny; the content of our victory is the triumph of national liberation.

And who was capable of interpreting this historic synthesis? The Sandinist national liberation front. It was Sandinism that was able to apply the theory of revolution to Nicaragua's specific reality. Therefore, the FSLN was the fundamental instrument for the workers' conquest of power, and the fundamental instrument for the consolidation of the workers' power.

What does this mean? It means that just like the human body needs vitamins and proteins to nurture and develop itself, the FSLN has to seek nourishment from the working class. The vitamins and proteins that the FSLN needs are the Nicaraguan workers and peasants. The intellectuals, professionals and other sectors of Nicaraguan society that would like to side with the Sandinist revolution have to support the interests of the workers and peasants. . . .

Businessmen, regardless of their ideological leanings, will have to share the patriotism of the Nicaraguan workers and peasants if they would like to stay in Nicaragua. The FSLN is the vanguard of the revolution. The FSLN is the vanguard of the Nicaraguan patriots. The FSLN is in the vanguard of national liberation. The FSLN—and it should be said now for once and for all—is the vanguard of the workers and the peasants, and as such it is the fundamental instrument of the revolutionary classes. The FSLN is the guide to a new society. . . .

Even though we have said that the probability of direct intervention has been averted, does this mean that imperialism has already given up on direct aggression against Nicaragua? It does not. It means that, perhaps, imperialism has given up on direct intervention for the time being. We would be dreamers and stupid if we thought that imperialism has given up trying to liquidate our revolution. Maybe imperialism finds it impossible for the time being—and I repeat; for the time being—to directly attack us. However, it has not given up on aggression.

So, what are the new forms imperialism is using and is going to use? It seeks to develop even further the destabilizing tactics against our revolution, for example, internal disarray within the ranks of the vanguard, fomenting of internal distrust and violence in Nicaragua, buildup in the technical capacity and firepower of the counterrevolutionary bands, particularly in the country's northern region. Imperialism seeks to expand sabotage, personal attacks and other types of terrorism. It is trying to confuse the people by promoting ideological deviations, manipulating the Nicaraguan people's religious feelings, exploiting the consequences of our economic difficulties. It is trying to unite all members of the counterrevolution and elements who have opposed the working class and the revolutionary process one way or the other.

All this explains the dilatory tactics in the negotiations. It is a sort of invasion with a different sort of soldier, the soldiers of misorientation, the soldiers of slander, the soldiers of ideological deviation who hold weapons which are sometimes even more dangerous than the rifles which are carried by the counterrevolutionary bands.

Sources of the counterrevolution and the rightist parties—many of whom, by the way, have already left Nicaragua—say that a government junta will be formed in exile. Do you know what they call it? The Supreme Directorate. They have suggested forming a junta. We even know that many of those who have been mentioned as probable junta members have not even been consulted. This should be clear, and also that most probably they will define their position. The junta proposed and approved by imperialism is composed of supreme directors, similar to the name I just gave you. The members are Alfonso Robelo, Edén Pastora, Monsignor Miguel Obando, Steadman Fagoth, Enrique Bolanos, Adolfo Calero Portocarrero, Col. Guillermo Mendieta, Col. Enrique

Bermúdez, José Francisco Cardenal, Fernando Agüero, and Fernando Chamorro Rapacciolli.

7.
THE LITERACY CAMPAIGN TEXTBOOKS (AUGUST 1980)

Carlos Fonseca showed us the way. He was the founder of the Sandinista National Liberation Front and fell in Zinica. Carlos lives on in the hearts of the people.
Sandino fought the Yankees. The Yankees will forever be defeated in our motherland.

> *The FSLN Anthem*
>
> *Forward march, comrades*
> Revolution-bound are we.
> Of our history we are masters,
> We are architects of our liberty.
>
> Forward march in tomorrow's quest,
> Sandinista front contenders.
> Under the banner of black and red protection
> Do or die for our country's redemption.
>
> Sandino's sons cannot be bought.
> Nor, alas, do they surrender.
> We will fight the Yankee,
> For he is the enemy of humanity.
>
> Forward march . . .
>
> Today's dawn is no longer tomorrow's temptation.
> A new sun will shine some day,
> Over the land to us bequeathed by our martyrs and heroes.
> A land fraught with deep rivers of milk and honey.
>
> Forward . . .
> Sandinista Front contenders . . .

Translation copyright © by Gladys Segal.

THE DEFENSE

The brave militia parades at the square with their rifles in hand. The militia is the people. The people are ready to defend us. The militia defends the country. Long live the militia!

SANDINISTA CHILDREN

Tono, Delia, and Rodolfo are members of the Sandinista Children's Association (SCA).

Sandinista children carry handkerchiefs. They participate in the revolution's labor and are very studious.

II
THE RISE OF THE OPPOSITION

8.
COSEP: ANALYSIS OF THE GOVERNMENT'S PERFORMANCE (NOVEMBER 1980)

There are political parties in Nicaragua. However, no law on political parties has been enacted to institutionalize their existence. . . .

The FSLN is in fact a political party, but it avoids defining itself as such, causing confusion between the Government, the party and the FSLN.

The FSLN unilaterally uses confiscated television, radio and newspapers, makes use of the economic and material resources of the state to campaign for the FSLN among the masses; quasi-State Sandinista organizations have been created with physical resources of the state such as buildings, and economic resources to conduct the propaganda activities of these FSLN organizations.

It is felt that the FSLN has imposed its idea of the elections on the Government Junta by ordering it to begin the electoral process in 1984, to culminate in 1985 with the election of "the best men and government programs," without specifying what these elections will be like; however, it was said that the elections would not be a raffle for power, because power is already in the hands of the people through its vanguard, the FSLN.

From OAS, *Report on Human Rights,* June 1981.

In its declaration of August 23, 1980, the FSLN stated its intention of remaining in power forever and of implementing an election system limited to changing people at levels of government that are not decisive in policy decision-making.

The operations of the Government Junta are predicated on the political will of the FSLN, which has three members on the five-member Junta.

The Junta has already accepted the supremacy of the National Directorate of the FSLN.

When two members of the Junta resigned, the FSLN National Directorate unilaterally and without consultation, replaced them by simply appointing people to the positions. This procedure confirms the supremacy of the FSLN National Directorate over the Government Junta, which in practice, has become the executor of its will.

This irregular situation of submission to the political will of the FSLN party makes a pluralist national unity Government into a Government of the FSLN party with a veneer of political pluralism.

The FSLN members of the Government Junta imposed their will and increased the number of members of the Council of State to 47, in violation of what all sectors had agreed on.

All the organizations that were added are controlled by the FSLN, which thus acquired for itself a majority on the Council of State.

The overwhelming majority on the Council of State of organizations controlled by the FSLN has consolidated the power block of the FSLN political party in the Council of State, enabling it to impose its political will at any time. . . .

9.
SERGIO RAMÍREZ: A SOCIAL CLASS BECOMES POWERLESS (AUGUST 1981)

When the bourgeoisie collectively understood that the Sandinista victory had rendered it powerless, depriving it of its historic might, it adopted an underhanded strategy, designed to weaken the new government politically and obstruct its consolidation. During the first few months after the victory, the bourgeoisie tried to penetrate quietly the newly emerging state's structures—pretending to be within the spectrum of the alliance but actually siting on the political fence, and attempting to modify the revolution's

From "Los Sobrevivientes del naufragio," in *La Historia Viva de Nicaragua* (Mexico, 2nd edition, 1984). Translation copyright © 1986 by Gladys Segal.

concrete results in its own best interests. They still hoped that those bold and brave boys would be naive and inexperienced enough to hand them the fundamental economic decision-making process. They also hoped that the aggressive private sector could exert enough pressure, and have its say, because of the lingering memory of its "active participation" in the struggle. However, at the outset, the traditional and neo-traditional parties took a more timid and hesitant attitude, thwarting the bourgeoisie's hopes of shared decision-making alongside the trade unions and the Sandinista Front.

Obviously, disenchantment set in within bourgeoisie ranks sooner than they had expected, because the new revolutionary state under Sandinista rule, according to the leadership's plan, quickly started implementing its changes. In view of banking, insurance, and foreign trade expropriations —as well as the efficient coffee harvest, the speedy reorganization of nationalized real estate, and the nationalization of the mining and fishing industries—the bourgeois political elite saw the need to recognize that the revolutionary leadership, although young, quickly became experienced and mature despite mistakes and blunders along the way. Unity, pluralism, and a mixed economy are based on revolutionary supremacy, and not upon division of power, or the deterioration of that supremacy. . . .

On July 31, 1979, a meeting with private industry leaders was held at government headquarters. For me, personally, this meeting was unforgettable. At the time, we had no regular army or police force. Many ministries and state agencies were without leadership, the various services had not been reestablished, and above all, there was no national or central command in power. Logically, the guerrilla forces carried out multiple functions where they were based. Their leaders not only implemented farm reform measures, they also carried out judicial functions. They performed marriages, set price lists, and punished usury and speculation.

At that meeting Mr. Jorge Salazar, who would later lose his life conspiring against the process, complained bitterly about production stagnation, about the guerrilla's confiscation of basic staples, about fuel rationing, and about the unnecessary state of emergency. He complained about food confiscation on farms by the military, about the indiscriminate killing of animals, and about trespasses on private property. As proof of these instances of highhandedness and excess, he presented the junta with a list, signed by the chief of a guerrilla squadron and embellished with a highly visible seal, quoting wholesale prices of basic staples and the retail price of these items to farmers.

It was only then that I comprehended the blind inability of a social class not only to understand that we were still at war, but also to comprehend the newly emerging revolutionary phenomenon. What they considered to be instances of highhandedness was no more than the expression of a people's wish to have justice, no matter how rudimentary and primitive this justice might have been. But, above all, I understood the long-range effect that this insensitivity would have on the rapport of the old leadership with the new revolutionary authority, because of the ousted leadership's incapability to see the revolution from within. Furthermore, the arguments expressed at that time . . . would later become systematic, and set in concrete: a refrain played to that same old tune of lack of confidence and security.

On the surface, that old tune was a tactical maneuver, because it served as a basis for demanding from the revolutionary state legal guarantees for production and for the financial stability of the private sector (constitutional guarantees for the protection of civil rights, laws against indiscriminate confiscation, etc.). At a deeper level, this meant a breach of historical confidence, because as a social class, it had lost its actual power, and was having difficulty accepting the alliance it was being offered. . . .

Because of all this, in April 1980, less than a year after the revolutionary triumph, the bourgeoisie decided to abandon its passive, underhanded attitude. This behavior had included trips to the United States to lobby for a $75 million grant, demands for concessions in the allowable extent of public questioning of the revolution . . . and the bourgeoisie's wish-list of further concessions, and all this according to the imperialists' advice. The purpose of these actions was to extract from the alliance political and economic power for itself. Therefore, the so-called "May Crisis," which included Robelo's resignation, the threat of trade unions and the traditional parties to leave the state council, and aggressive public statements, could only be interpreted as a bluff, because, obviously, the bourgeoisie had neither the strength nor the drive to replace the revolutionary hegemony and neutralize the Sandinista Front. The intention was merely to put us on the defensive, to undermine international unity, and reduce our domestic political scope, in order to force the leadership to make fundamental concessions as a prerequisite to the continuity of the alliance. . . .

For the Sandinista Front, the issue was to take advantage of the mixed economic system and political pluralism. The Sandinista leadership could maneuver to overcome the crisis . . . but there would be no compromise on fundamental issues. The bourgeoisie mistakenly played a game of all or nothing. . . . They misinterpreted the possibility of political participation as actual bourgeoisie participation in the revolutionary enterprise, and they continued to do so, because their participation in the production arena was the basis of their social contribution.

But actually, in May 1980 the bourgeoisie was confusing a political alliance with an outcome that would resolve the issue of power in their favor. Once the crisis was overcome, and their organizations became part of the council of state, the nature of the alliance changed to favor the revolution. . . .

The surge of the Salazar faction in October 1980 represented the rapid maturation of the bourgeoisie leadership's relentless armed-adventure option. Their traditional distrust in the process propelled them to attempt resolving the disagreement through a coup d'état, daringly and ingeniously seeking both an impossible hodgepodge of "disaffected" sectors within the Sandinista armed forces and the genocidal National Guard. No matter how the bourgeoisie glazes over this issue in the future, this was its most fatal step. . . .

At this point, the revolution favored a plan for a mixed economy which we did not envision including the same ruthless, capitalistic production system of yesteryear. The revolution could not allow free play for an archaic and out-of-touch system of private exploitation. We actually envisioned it as the harmonious and well-defined incorporation of the private sector within the great strategic flow of the people's proprietorship under whose political responsibility the whole national economic system was led toward change. . . . In other words, the whole national economic system was geared toward the Sandinista model of social reform. But a plan for a mixed economy such as we proposed did not depend only upon objective mechanisms made available to the private sector such as legal guarantees, foreign currency, credits, moratoriums, access to utilities. The major difficulties in achieving a viable and comprehensive understanding during these two years were ideological in nature, as part of the power struggle in the dominating class of yesteryear's determination to recover that power.

Maybe for a less backward or less primitive bourgeoisie, or should we say a more modern one, it would have been easier to understand the rules of the game in a country in which despite their permanent loss of power, there still was a guaranteed historic opportunity to participate in the process. . . .

10.
PEDRO JOAQUÍN CHAMORRO: FORGOTTEN MEMORANDUM (SEPTEMBER 1981)

Dear Arturo:

This paper contains some of my random thoughts and I ask you to work on it or, if it is worthless, to tell me so. . . . I submit it to you not just as

---

Letter to Arturo Cruz, published posthumously in *La Prensa,* September 8, 1981.

a friend but because you are an able man and, more than anything else, we must know what we want. . . .

THE PRESENT SYSTEM, paternalistic capitalism, has the following results:

1. The entire state system is concerned with the preservation, protection, and aggrandizement of big capital, including the foreign investor.
2. Society—health, sanitation, housing, education, land reform—is neglected. It is only given the leftovers from the banquet.
3. The state is supported by compulsive militarism that exploits vice and consumes most of the country's economic resources.

RESULTS:

It is unable to produce fewer underprivileged people but does turn out more rich ones and encourages the emergent middle class to ape the vices of the most wealthy.

LATIN AMERICAN SOCIALISM, in the case of Cuba, eliminated the wealthy class (the biggest producer), put an end to want but created overall poverty. What it achieved was the kind of gray equality in which development is possible only through the state, with a total absence of individual stimulation. It is characterized by being:

1. Stridently nationalistic in order to create the intoxication necessary to replace individual energy and to encourage the people to continue supporting the system.
2. Progress in the social areas—education, housing, health, sanitation, the land question—is its principal achievement and it has succeeded incomparably better than capitalist development.
3. It is supported by a messianic militarism fed by the idea that the homeland needs defense against external aggression by "imperialism."

RESULTS:

An extremely long stage of poverty and sacrifice with the elimination of freedom.

THE THIRD ALTERNATIVE can be attained by taking away the bad and leaving the good from the general guidelines discussed above. . . .

1. To leave the free enterprise area free but without special privileges and by seeking social evolution, not absorbent monopolistic growth. . . .
2. To utilize all the state's resources for the eradication of poverty, taking this as the goal of "social production." . . .

   To this end, it would be necessary to investigate thoroughly the possibilities of a state like ours developing a way to consume all the resources it is currently using for capitalist development to support "social production."

3. To utilize the military apparatus for social improvements. . . .

11.
PABLO ANTONIO CUADRA: NOTES ON CULTURE IN THE NEW NICARAGUA

In Nicaragua today a dramatic struggle is going on between ideology and culture. The ideology of the Sandinista Front has lost its utopian aspect, and what remains in its place is somewhat elemental and gray: a Marxism-Leninism which crudely apes the wretched Soviet notions of man and society, retailed second-hand by Cuba, and which—retailed once more by our own social realities—amount to nothing more than a complete and total failure, sustainable only through the mechanisms of totalitarian propaganda. This sounds strong—I know it—but is true nonetheless. From the point of view of culture, at least, our situation could not be worse. The reigning ideology, for its very survival, *requires* the negation of freedom and of the right to critical thought, elements which are, after all, indispensable for cultural work.

The ideology of the Sandinista Front has been presented to us, somewhat presumptuously, as the expression of "modernity": its Marxism is an advance, so it is said, in all areas, while the Nicaraguan culture that preceded it is represented as a tradition of failure. The "progressive" pyrotechnics of Sandinismo rather stupidly deny history: everything new is good, everything previous to it is bad. It is certainly true that the democratic tradition in Nicaragua, which is a substantial part of our culture, has nothing to point to but defeats. On the other hand, the germinal aspect of our history resides in the fact that the near-totality of our civil wars and insurrections have represented frustrated efforts to achieve democracy.

All our dictators disguised themselves as paladins of democracy, and began their governments by raising high its banners against the previous frustrated attempt. What we derive from our history is a tradition of *democratic aspirations.* There is nothing particularly "modern" about the effort to frustrate once more this secular desire of the Nicaraguan people by establishing instead some sort of new dictatorship, which offers what culture has always rejected, and presents in the guise of the new and the

From *Vuelta* (Mexico City), August 1984. Translated from the Spanish by Mark Falcoff.

modern, what is, in fact, the definitive defeat of these historic efforts. What is tragic is that this failure is essential to Marxism-Leninism: it is the failure of Marx who proposed a system intended to achieve the complete freedom of man, and only managed—thanks to the work of Lenin—to generate the most oppressive and totalitarian power in history. That failure is the result of a dialectic that, to our misfortune, functioned with the same brutal logic in Nicaragua, where the real movement of history was a heroic libertarian revolution against Somoza, a movement that was derailed by Marxist-Leninist interference, and brought us back to our point of departure—from dictatorship to dictatorship—which is to say, a reinforcement of the state machinery left behind by Somoza. A sad compensation for the rivers of blood shed by the thousands of Nicaraguans who fell in the struggle for liberty!

But the paradox is even deeper and more cruel than that: within that movement, the entire literary and philosophical production of our intellectuals expressed the same libertarian goal. We knew very well, from our own cultural tradition, what a highly admired novelist—Gabriel García Marquez—had said to us in a lapidary fashion: "When one reaches absolute power, one loses total contact with reality." Absolute power, the "progressive" ideal of Marxism-Leninism, means not only placing the state in opposition to culture, but sealing it off from the basic realities of our society. It is for this reason that the entire Nicaraguan literary movement, which played a vital role in the gestation of the revolution against Somoza, never contemplated the emergence of a totalitarian state, or even the enlargement of apparatus which was already too powerful, much less redeem the poor with the Communist formula "dictatorship of the proletariat."

For this reason "ideology" has had to impose itself slowly, operating, as it were, in various disguises, never calling things by their proper names, always denying and hiding behind false colors. Today the Sandinista leaders affirm and they do not affirm; another day they punish or insult those who call them Marxist-Leninists or Communists. For a long time the daily newspaper La Prensa was censured or operated under virtual siege conditions, because it persisted in documenting the totalitarian nature of certain acts or measures taken by the government. If we have learned anything in Nicaragua it is that Communism advances to the degree to which it can do so unobserved or unmarked. From the point of view of culture, this is a terrible, profoundly sterilizing attitude. Hypocrisy, false labels, can create slogans but not poems; propaganda but not life: there are no roots, there are no realities to nurture creative work, and this accounts for the fact that in six years of the revolutionary regime the literature production of Nicaragua has been astonishingly poor. This is all the more dramatic when we recall that it was the earlier effervescence of creative literary energy which first brought the Nicaraguan revolution to the attention of the world. Not only was that revolution betrayed on the political plane, but also on that of literature and art. The triumph of Sandinismo represents a crime against the spirit.

In November, 1979, when it was still possible to imagine that the Nicaraguan people were or could be united behind a single revolutionary project, we organized a symposium on "The Writer and the Revolution." To preside over it we invited the Minister of Culture, Ernesto Cardenal, and the Argentine writer Ernesto Cortázar. Seven Nicaraguan writers, representing the entire range of living generations, assembled before a numerous public made up of the intellectual, political, and university communities. Both Cortázar and the Minister of Culture ended by declaring themselves in favor of the absolute freedom of poetic creation, without any demands on the part of the state for political compatibility.

Those ideas, which were unanimously accepted by all who participated in the symposium, were the prelude to something truly original (and of course heretical for totalitarian ideologues). We thought it might be the single most important contribution of the Nicaraguan revolution to the world. I remember two Cuban poets, who had just arrived, expressing to me something more than their pleasure, their enthusiasm for those resolutions pertaining to creative liberty and intellectual independence. Inevitably, they suggested, such things eventually would influence developments in Cuba. Nonetheless, precisely the opposite occurred: two years later, in October, 1982, this commitment to freedom had been so completely abandoned that *Ventans,* the cultural supplement to the official daily *Barricada,* published on its first page the antique discourse of Fidel Castro, so reminiscent of Mussolini, entitled, "Everything Within the Revolution; Nothing Against the Revolution," the interpretations of which—made by political functionaries and police officials—have condemned a significant number of Cuban writers and artists to jail and exile.

Those empowered to outline the new official doctrine in cultural matters, or rather, to discard the first mask of freedom and to place over their faces another more severe (let us not forget that in Communist praxis all masks are ultimately designed to be discarded) were Commander Bayardo Arce, and novelist and Junta member Sergio Ramírez. The auditorium was packed by intellectuals from all corners of the country for the First Convention of Cultural Workers in February, 1980. In their speeches they began to reveal the Orwellian face of the supreme "commissary" whose job it is to define what revolutionary culture ought to be—what is permitted and what is not; which is to say, they proclaimed that by virtue of possessing power, they were converted into supermen, individuals of extraordinary talent, and therefore qualified to send all of the intellectuals and artists

of the country to a ramshackle schoolhouse, where they would be taught
how they ought to be and how they ought to work; and they believed
themselves competent as well to outline the parameters of future Nicaraguan culture. These were the first orders given to militarize our culture.

Arce expounded thus: "The artist *ought* to try to encounter the means
to represent the values we inherited from the heroic career of General
Sandino. *We* [referring here to the nine commanders; power, the revolu-
tion] should not like to see culture ever again assume the *decadent* forms
it has taken in the past." Hitler used the word decadent to exile an entire
vanguard school of art. What would be decadent for the State-Become-
Critic in Nicaragua?

Sergio Ramírez simply echoed the same ideas: "We never thought to
admit the existence of a culture isolated from the revolutionary process"
—words that reminded as of the words of Octavio Paz written in 1956,
"There is no more pernicious, barbarous prejudice than to attribute powers
to the state in the sphere of artistic creation. An artistic style is a living
entity, a continuous process of invention. It can never be imposed from
without; born of the profoundest tendencies within a society, its direction
is to a certain extent unpredictable, in much the same way as the eventual
configuration of a tree's branches. In contrast, official style is the very
negation of creative spontaneity. Power immobilizes; it freezes with a
single gesture—grandiose, terrible, theatrical, or finally, simply monoto-
nous—the variety which is life."

The negation of spontaneity in Nicaragua continued to be defined by
Arce: "*We want* to retain artistic quality, but remember, please, that art
is of no value if it is not understood by workers and peasants. *We want*
[a situation where, every time someone paints a picture or writes a poem,
publishes a book or arranges a song, that person asks himself, first, to what
degree is it going to assist our people in the process of self-transformation.
. . ." Wouldn't it be better, however, to educate people to understand art?
What Arce asks for is precisely what Cortázar called "a hateful personal-
ism." Moreover, his definitions completely ignore the astronomical difference between the voluntary choice of, say, a poet to write some verses, and
the imposition of the state which is, finally, the very essence of tyranny.

Sergio Ramírez continued the process of demolition: "Nicaraguan culture prior to June 19, 1979, was a failure," he said. But Ramírez forgets
that that very culture, with its edges badly charred by the drama of our
struggle, was never an attempt to produce a full-dress result, but rather,
the surviving fragments of a lengthy agony. Ramírez's fatuous remark
consigns, as it were, to the dust-heap of history an entire epoch in Nicaraguan history, whose leading figures include Rubén Dario, Alfonso Cortés,
Azarias Pallais, José Coronel, Joaquín Pasos, Carlos Martínez Rivas, even
Ernesto Cardenal himself. It puts the stamp of failure—much as one might

put an entire library to the revolutionary torch—upon a national tradition of painting, architecture, music, and other "bourgeois" artifices such as the novel. If our tradition were less valuable than in fact it is, there would be *even less reason* to discard the lot in the name of something which has yet to come into existence. Ramírez, like all Marxists who pretend to use a "scientific" method to analyze the past, falls into the realm of fantasy whenever the time comes to describe the future. "Revolutionary culture, just because it is revolutionary, *cannot fail to be* authentic, and cannot fail to be a culture of quality," Ramírez says in one speech, thus simply sweeping aside the entire history of a nation.

"Nicaraguan history begins with the Sandinista front." Such is the slogan of the regime—an attitude that might be, in the context of political liberty, nothing more than a case of understandable exaggeration, the pretentious boasting of some inexperienced young people suddenly come upon political power for the first time. In this case, however, it represents a statist ideology that seeks to abolish every cultural manifestation which is not fully coherent with it. The most dramatic and painful example was —and still is—the treatment of the Miskito Indians, an event which in all probability will have catastrophic consequences for our nationality. In this case, we are dealing with a cultural and historic problem which has been rendered virtually insoluble, pushed to the point of civil war, largely because those who sought to resolve it began by purposely denying the past.

At the time that the relationship between the Miskitos and the Sandinista Front began to break down (1981), I invited to the offices of *La Prensa* the representatives of Misurasata, the leaders of all of the political parties, and representing the FSLN and the government, the local authorities on the Atlantic coast. My purpose was to provoke a serious and sincere dialogue. The Miskito leaders explained their grievances, and in the process I learned something I had not previously known, namely, that they were asking for nothing that had not already been granted them in 1895 by legislative degree, at the time that the Mosquitia Reserve was formally incorporated into the Republic of Nicaragua. The conditions of that incorporation were: investment in the Atlantic Coast to encourage development; respect for local religion, language, and customs; the right of the Indian communities to elect their own authorities; respect for their communal forestlands; liberty for some of their political prisoners, etc. In spite of our efforts to persuade them to the contrary, the Sandinista *comandantes* insisted upon regarding these demands as "separatist"; in their view, the Miskitos were being manipulated by "imperialism," and the only response to their requests was a hard and unyielding refusal. To make things worse, instead of dispatching their own people to the Atlantic Coast, they sent Cubans. That produced a massive uprising on the part of the people of

Bluefields, followed by a chain of misunderstandings, violence, massive migration (into exile), repression, and other incidents that have done so much to damage the revolution's image abroad.

But Sandinista ideology has failed not only because it begins by rejecting or ignoring our culture, but also because of its specific philosophic content. Marxist collectivism—in the same way, be it said, as capitalist individualism—is incompatible with self-governing, self-sufficient communities. Let us recall that in Nicaragua it was the Liberal dictator José Santos Zelaya who decreed the dissolution of collective property in land and the Indian communities in 1906. Thus the "socialist man" turns out to be not so very different from his capitalist antecedent; the difference resides in the fact that Communism is statist, but not communitarian.

We have betrayed the two underlying currents of our long-suffering Nicaraguan and Hispanic-American culture: *calling ourselves enemies of imperialism, we mask from view a more fundamental loss of independence. Calling ourselves paladins of liberation, we have lost, in our conception of the state, the proper measure of man.* We insist upon this double paradox, for from it springs practically all of the danger which the Sandinista Front is likely to inflict upon us, and will in fact inflict upon us, if nothing is done to counteract it—and soon.

In the official version, Sandinismo is defending the independence of our culture. But under this rubric, to reject one model only to choose another —apart from being a contradiction in terms—is even more dangerous. At least in the prerevolutionary period we knew what it meant to surrender our sovereignty: now, however, we are not even permitted to call things by their proper names. In the days of Bolívar, after all, we often said that we did not fight for independence from Spain simply to fall under the tutelage of another colonial power. We said the same thing during the 1920s, when General Sandino was fighting the U.S. Marines. It seems to be the tragic destiny of tiny Nicaragua to represent the medular point of Spanish-America in its conflict with the United States. But, in that conflict, our strength (and in the final analysis, our victory) will consist in the reaffirmation of our Hispanic-American personality and the strengthening of an independent culture. Our anti-imperialism is meant to obligate the United States to act as a democracy in its relations with other American nations. We do not want war; we do not want to be allies in a war—nor satellites of the other superpower, so that it can win its victories with proxy forces; what we want is a Spanish-American alliance, the dream of Bolívar, and also, the dream of General Sandino. The purpose of that alliance would be to obligate the United States to behave towards our countries in a civilized manner, on a plane of equality and mutual respect. In this Fidel Castro has forfeited what might otherwise be his claim to continental leadership, since he legitimized the loss of his own country's (and ultimately our) independence to the Soviet Union. In 1979 the entire world believed that the new Nicaraguan revolution would rectify this Cuban error and that it would offer—in bringing about social change—the proper response of an independent nation. To date this has not been the case. The land of Dario is no more independent now than it has ever been.

In the same fashion, our sister republics of Latin America believed and hoped—wrongly, as it turned out—that our revolution would be not merely the autumn, but the definitive death of the Patriarch. The fall of Somoza was, symbolically, the end of an entire epoch in history of Spanish-American culture: the elimination of that aberrant, monstrous form of power, which appeared and reappeared throughout our collective history, thus frustrating what should have been our truer, more noble purpose as independent nations.

In Arce's speech cited above, he counseled thus: "The task of Nicaraguan intellectuals, whether they have or have not been committed thus far to the revolutionary process, to take their stand: those who are already with us, to reaffirm their commitment still further, and for those who were not involved, to do so now, so as to participate in this transition which is, of course, cultural, but at the same time and fundamentally political, economic, and social." In one fell swoop literature and art were converted into branches of the bureaucracy.

Slowly the pressures began to close in upon us. First came veiled threats. Then the purposeful exclusion of "uncooperative" writers and artists. Internal exile. A ban on the citation of books or articles by the nonaligned or the uncommitted. The Union of Cultural Workers began to threaten with sanctions those writers and artists who contributed to the literary supplement of *La Prensa*. It is painful to report that many young dissident poets have asked me, in my capacity as editor of that magazine, to publish their work under pen names—so as to avoid reprisals, and to be able to continue to work with some measure of tranquillity. This is how more than one writer or poet will eventually enter the anthologies of our national literature—under an assumed name!

In the much-discussed (and properly controversial) "workshops" sponsored by the Ministry of Culture, they teach one not merely how to sing, but what verses. Sergio Ramírez has said as much in one of his speeches: "The workshops on popular poetry which have been organized in Nicaragua since July 19 [1979], reflect the poetry of young combatants, a poetry often anonymous, spun of the experiences of daily life, of reality, which seems to me to be vastly more important than the poetry which is the product of elitist dilettantism, the poetry which, after all, is all we have produced thus far as a nation. This phenomenon—how to break with that tradition—is something to which we should focus all of our energies."

In truth, I wish that this enthusiastic critical judgment, made by Ramírez the politician, were the same as that made by Ramírez the writer. I shall only add that in a propaganda exercise for Sandinista Television, a young apprentice poet declared, "Before now I was in error: I went about writing love poems. In the workshop I have learned why my poetry was bad—it had no political message." Perhaps that poor lad was destined, nonetheless, to be the author of some very great love poems. We shall never know. What is certain is that from here on, he will be scratching out forced, pedestrian (or derivative) verses, unless his own genius comes to his rescue, if in fact he is so fortunate.

It is precisely because I believe our revolution possessed magnificent roots and our culture ample reserves to produce a really original, Nicaraguan response to the challenge of history, that I have remained at *La Prensa* to resist a dictatorial ideology which is increasingly totalitarian. After all, what is at issue is the destiny of an entire people. At times I close my eyes and contemplate the *via crucis* of that newspaper since the triumph of the very revolution to which it contributed with 45 years of struggle—not to mention the blood of its martyred publisher, Pedro Joaquín Chamorro, and the ashes of his enterprise, destroyed by the last dictator. What has been our fortune since then? Ceaseless pressures, threats to news agents and to reporters, death threats to some editors who have been forced into exile, mobs attacking our physical installations, jail sentences, violence, withdrawal of passports, tapped telephones, tampered correspondence, and—from official organs—insults and lies, employing a crude and obscene language never before heard in our country. Without any question, this kind of treatment does not announce the advent of a *new man;* instead, it repeats the barbarous practices which are, unfortunately, the warp and woof of Nicaraguan political history. Perhaps some sort of excuse could be made for it by calling it the characteristic conduct of a new militarism. What is intolerable, however, is the representation of censorship as some sort of culmination of a liberation movement; as the final "conquest" of that revolution which was, after all, ignited by the death of a newspaperman, of an intellectual whom even the hated regime felt obligated to officially proclaim "martyr to public liberties." To escape the clutches of three Somozas to merely to fall into the pit of censorship—really, for this there is no excuse! It amounts to crowning with fear the libertarian struggle of those who were not afraid to die.

Let us be clear: censorship is cowardice. On the part of the authorities it institutionalizes the abuse of power. It masks corruption. It is a school of torture: it teaches, and accustoms one to the use of force against an idea, to submit thought to an alien "other." But worst still, censorship destroys criticism, which is the essential ingredient of culture. The human condition, after all, is defined by the aspiration to always supersede oneself, which in turn requires nonconformity. As the Spanish poet Antonio Machado has his character Juan de Mairena say, "Even if we could teach a chimpanzee everything we know, he still would be unable to replicate the human condition, since that requires an essential willingness to question one's own nature, to desire to be other than what one is." What makes it impossible for the chimpanzee to mount the final scale in the animal kingdom is a lack of criticism, the only recourse that makes possible human and cultural progress. As I have told my Sandinista friends and former friends until I am blue in the face: any revolution which denies the right to criticize is bound to wallow in stagnation and backwardness. But in Latin America, something even worse will happen—the chimpanzee will become a gorilla.

For a writer there is nothing more depressing than to receive an editorial or an article mutilated by censorship—I leave aside an act of intellectual thuggery far worse, which is tampering with a poem! Nonetheless, a poet like the American Lawrence Ferlinghetti—I admit, a man of surpassing naiveté—was quite unmoved when I showed him mountains of censored manuscripts originally destined for *La Prensa.* They dealt with topics very far from the civil war or the particular themes proscribed by the Law of Emergency. Nonetheless, in due course his publishing house in San Francisco saw fit to bring out a piece of Sandinista propaganda entitled *Seven Days in Nicaragua Libre,* wherein Ferlinghetti, to counteract my complaints about censorship and also to wash his hands of the matter, asked Ernesto Cardenal, also a poet and Minister of Culture, for an official declaration on censorship. Among other lies, it affirms, "With respect to censorship, I don't believe there is a single important document by any of our leaders defending it. In fact, we don't like it, and we don't want it; we have imposed it only because we are at war. . . . The newspaper *La Prensa* openly defends the enemy, the actions of the CIA, and employs all of the arguments of the Reagan administration. . . . In any event, this censorship ended in May, 1984, when the electoral campaign began. Since then there has been no basis for attacking Nicaragua on this score, but of course they will find others."

With respect to this letter I should merely like to point out that (1) for Cardenal, whose status as a priest seems not to inhibit him from misrepresenting facts, to demand democracy and liberty is to somehow provide Reagan and the CIA with arguments to attack our country; (2) Cardenal lies when he says that censorship was imposed by wartime conditions. Censorship was established in Nicaragua—for the radio as well as for newspapers—long before. I refer Mr. Ferlinghetti to Decrees 511 and 512 of September, 1980; almost immediately thereafter, the Ministry of Defense began intermittently closing down my newspaper. In 1981 alone, between January and September, there were fourteen such incidents. (3) Censorship was not lifted in May. It was maintained before the electoral campaign, during it, and after it. It continues to this date. How it pains me to see an admired, even beloved poet—now drunk with power—repeating the same formulas and falsehoods as the Somoza dictatorship used to employ when it wanted to deceive *its* naive Yankee "friends." . . .

12.
DEMOCRATIC COORDINATOR: PLATFORM (MARCH 1982)

1. Effective political pluralism, based on an authentic equality of rights, duties and opportunities for all, stated by an equitable Law of Political Parties.
2. Mixed economy clearly defined by suitable laws which points out the limitations and regulations of both the state and private areas; showing, in an unequivocal manner, the types of legitimate ownerships within the Nicaraguan revolutionary process.
3. Genuine non-alignment in foreign policy, which should be expressed by real and effective independence from the hegemonic blocs and by keeping respectful relations with all the states in the world.
4. Definition of the characteristics of the coming elections—pinpointing concrete dates and proceeding to provide the proper juridic framework by means of an Electoral Law.
5. Restructuring of the legislative power, in such a way that its autonomy and the fair and effective participation of all sectors in the country are guaranteed in the making and supervision of government policy.
6. Revision of the Judicial Power to guarantee its autonomy and independence.
7. Restructuring of the Armed Forces, to give them a juridic framework which guarantees their national character, their professionalism, their non-partisan institutionality and their pluralistic constitution.
8. Revision of revolutionary laws and decrees in order to make their contents and application adequate to the exact fulfillment of the Government Program, the Charter, and the Statute of Rights and Guarantees of Nicaraguans.

In order to cooperate with this solution, the Democratic Coordinator takes the liberty to propose the following points:

1. The Central American Governments should commit themselves to a gradual disarming process in the region, having as a final objective the

reduction of military forces until only an established police force is left. This process will have to be finished by the end of 1984 at the latest. The sovereignty of the countries will be guaranteed on firm bases through— the O.A.S.

2. The Central American Governments should commit themselves to immediately start removing foreign military advisors and forces which are found in their territory.

3. The governments of Mexico, Venezuela, the United States and other developed countries should commit themselves to resume, or at least to continue the economic aid which existed in early 1980 and to offer to increase its levels for the coming year 1983.

4. In order to watch over the fulfillment of what has been agreed upon, we suggest the creation of an international committee formed by representatives of American countries which, with OAS assistance, carries out a function of mediator, warrantor and arbiter between the parties.

These negotiations between countries would be incomplete if, in a parallel manner, conversations between governments and opposition forces are not initiated in Nicaragua, El Salvador and Guatemala in order to search in every nation for democratic and permanent peace and stability.

In our Motherland, the Democratic Coordinator, which gathers important sectors of public opinion through democratic parties, independent labor unions and private sector organizations, demands active participation in every negotiation intent on searching for peace and national unity and, also, the necessary guarantees to insure democracy in Nicaragua. Consequently, it urges the FSLN Government to immediately start conversations with opposition democratic sectors. . . .

13.
EDÉN PASTORA: THE WATCHFUL EYE (APRIL 1982)

I will be the watchful eye to see that the revolution is never subverted or betrayed. This is what I declared on July 20, 1979, in the Plaza of the Revolution in Managua, Nicaragua. Historic circumstances assign responsibilities to men. Those circumstances oblige me to comply with my obligation as a Nicaraguan Sandinista. I was born in the obscurity with which *somocismo* dishonored and degraded my homeland, Nicaragua. At the age of seven I suffered the loss of my father, when he was assassinated by the oppressors of my people. When I grew up, I realized that many other

Statement made in Costa Rica on his break with the FSLN.

Nicaraguan families were suffering the same grief. Later, thanks to the opportunities for education that my mother offered me, I discovered the sad reality that U.S. imperialism had violated the sovereignty of my country many times and that the great majority of my fellow citizens were victims of the most degrading social injustice.

In the course of my education I also learned that there had been a patriot who loved Nicaragua immensely and that he gave his life in his fight for the liberation of us Nicaraguans. That man, Augusto César Sandino, is the fundamental inspiration of my civic life.

When I was very young I made the decision to be a revolutionary. I learned that it was necessary to take up arms to overthrow the tyrant and I abandoned my medical studies in Guadalajara, Mexico.

With the maturity brought by years of fighting, I became convinced that the only way to find real peace was through the establishment of democracy and the elimination of exploitation and all kinds of injustice.

Since I come from a family of working people, I alternated my periods of armed struggle in the mountains with periods of work in cattle raising, farming, commerce, and fishing. It may be to that experience that I owe my firm belief in the need for guarantees and incentives for production and investment as bases for economic development.

The despotism of the system that prevailed for more than forty years awakened in me the abhorrence of arbitrary rule and the love of individual liberty. Those principles form the basis of my revolutionary ideas, and I want to make clear once and for all that I have never concerned myself with doctrinaire labels. Guided by those principles, I was one of the founders of the Sandino Revolutionary Front in 1959, the first revolutionary movement that vindicated General Sandino as the immortal leader of our resurgence as a sovereign people.

Later, in 1961, I reaffirmed my Sandinista ideals—anti-imperialist, democratic, and popular—as one of those who forged the Sandinista Front of National Liberation, to which I have the honor of having given twenty-one years of discipline and loyal militancy. In 1976 I ended a period of tranquility and work at the side of my beloved wife and children in order to begin another chapter of struggle, responding to a call from my Sandinista companions. On that occasion I kept an appointment on the field of battle for what was the beginning of a transcendental crusade in the history of my people: the unification of all the national sectors in order to expel the dynastic tyrant from our homeland forever and establish a system of social revolution. An eminently just revolution, with the help of everyone, with hate for no one, motivated by justice and ready to defend the national sovereignty.

I must say with pride that the Sandinista Front of National Liberation, by taking up the glorious red and black flag of General Sandino as the historic vanguard in the war of liberation, has created the greatest epic in the national history. The Sandinista Front of National Liberation gave many martyrs and heroes to the nation. Many other citizens made sacrifices to support the fight for the liberation of our people. The biggest was that of Sandino, then his glorious generals and other companions, heroes whose names have been left in oblivion because of ingratitude and injustice. . . .

Together with other companions, I gave my contribution to the war of liberation, commanding the various missions that the revolutionary high command assigned to me, among them the taking of Rivas, the National Palace, and the political-military campaign of the Southern Front. I render respectful homage to the martyrs and heroes who made that glorious gesture possible, including the illustrious guerrilla priest Gaspar Garcia Laviana.

After the triumph I gave my services enthusiastically for the consolidation of the revolution, fulfilling whatever job the National Directorate of the Sandinista Front of National Liberation ordered me to do. Nevertheless, from the moment of the triumph I noted political and even moral deviations that endangered the revolutionary process and the very security of the Nicaraguan state.

I pointed out to my superiors the risk to which those imprudent acts and errors could expose the country. I did it in the interest of rectification and with revolutionary loyalty. After getting no response, I decided that the most appropriate thing was for me to separate myself from the government, channeling my revolutionary ideals into internationalism as a continuation of *sandinismo.* I made this decision with profound regret and without rancor. My dissidence and my cooperation have been, are, and will always be within the revolution.

I have kept silent, confident that patriotism would prevail among the leaders of the revolution. But my exhortations were never heard and, in response, I was attacked politically by those who considered themselves my brothers. Today, after ten months of prudent silence, I find myself obliged to break that silence and make public my attitude. At the same time I want to make clear my categorical repudiation of any aggressive action against my people and that I am disposed and prepared to combat from my trench any violation of the national soil.

Those Nicaraguans who truly love Nicaragua and who desire success for a just revolutionary process note with satisfaction the peace initiative of the president of Mexico, José López Portillo. I include myself among such Nicaraguans. The peace of our people is aided by the extent to which we are truly nonaligned. Contradictions and ambiguities have no place in *sandinismo.* Just as the invasion of Vietnam was imperialistic, so the invasion of Afghanistan is imperialistic. Just as a [country] that supports a fascist junta in El Salvador is imperialistic, so is that which supports a totalitarian regime in Poland. Our *sandinismo* cannot permit that we be caught up in the East-West conflict, since that is contrary to the national interests.

We know that injustice and class exploitation are the roots of the tragedy that Central America is living through and we must attack those roots with zeal. Today, just as yesterday, people have the obligation to liberate themselves from oppression and exploitation.

We must promote Central American fraternity, allowing each brother nation to seek social transformation by the way most suitable to its own reality and interests. In that connection, we must aspire for our revolution to be truly Nicaraguan, as the Mexican revolution is Mexican and the Cuban revolution is Cuban—to which I render homage of admiration. Both have positive aspects that could enrich our revolution, but we must preserve [our revolution's] genuine, Nicaraguan character.

I am an internationalist because I am a free man and I want to contribute to the liberation of all men. The total unselfishness of Commander Ernesto "Che" Guevara is, for me, a motive of inspiration. I am grateful . . . for the support that the internationalists of Panama, Costa Rica, Cuba, and other brother nations gave us during the war and are giving us now during the endangered peace. [But] in this moment, I express the sentiments of the majority of Nicaraguans when I say that the hour has arrived when they [the internationalists] should leave us alone—those who are not involved in activities that contribute to health and education. As someone who loves my people I take honor, like Sandino, in calling for all Nicaraguans to put themselves on a war footing as long as there is a foreign soldier on the native soil.

I know that the ranks of the Sandinista Popular Army and the Sandinista Popular Militia are filled by men and women of honor and love and that they constitute the only guarantee that the revolution is irreversible. Today I appeal to that honor and that love. The national economy, vital for the revolution, will recover only if we create a political climate that stimulates production and investment within a mixed economic system. A political system that generates internal and external peace can only be that in which democracy enjoys the status to which it is entitled, without omitting party pluralism, free elections, strict respect for individual rights, and the restoration of the rights of the worker.

The freedom of worship is not a simple declaration. It must be a reality that receives the most profound respect.

The revolution has no need to limit the freedom of press, since if it does, then the walls and fences, even in the prisons, will become newspapers.

The fundamental statute of the republic, the statute on rights and guarantees of Nicaraguans, is not complied with when, in the light of day or under cover of night, the seizures, confiscations, and expropriations overwhelm *somocistas* and anti-*somocistas,* counterrevolutionaries and revolutionaries, guilty and innocent. In the jails counterrevolutionaries rub elbows with Marxist revolutionaries, the latter being castigated for the serious crime of interpreting Marx differently than their comrades in power. With sorrow I have seen that intranquility reigns among my people, also anguish, fear, bitter frustration, personal insecurity. Our Miskito, Sumo, and Rama Indians are persecuted, jailed, or assassinated. And the press and radio are unable to denounce to the world this regime of terror that the feared State Security creates on the Atlantic Coast and in all of Nicaragua.

For all the reasons I have stated here I wish to make clear my disagreement with the conduct of the National Directorate, since to continue otherwise would force the people to pay a very high cost, even a return to the past, unless an armed people expels from power those whom the accusing and condemning finger of Sandino points to as traitors and assassins.

14.
BROOKLYN RIVERA: STATEMENT ON INDIAN RIGHTS
(APRIL 1982)

Our principal objective is a negotiated agreement between the Indians of Nicaragua and the government of Nicaragua. Such agreement would guarantee Indian property rights and Indian autonomy within the state of Nicaragua.

We are not calling for the overthrow of the government of Nicaragua. And we do not wish to slander the Nicaraguan revolution. Rather, we wish to present the facts about the problems facing the Indian peoples of Nicaragua and to look for responsible, peaceful solutions. We hope that the government of Nicaragua will be persuaded to begin talks with us soon.

We are making our case for Indian rights in our own behalf and without any alliance with Somocista or other counterrevolutionary forces. Our struggle for our Indian rights is our own Indian struggle and not part of the East-West political conflict or some other non-Indian conflict. We strongly oppose those who would manipulate the Indian rights struggle for their own ends, and we call on all American Indians, international organizations, human rights organizations and all the people of the United States to join us in opposing such manipulation.

The principal reason for the Indian rights crisis in Nicaragua is the antagonism created by the Sandinista government policy which denies the ethnic identity of our Indian peoples. It follows that the recognition of Indian rights to their territory and their autonomy are also denied. The government's policy requires assimilation of Indians to the philosophy and culture of those who control the government in Managua, thus converting us into peasants and mestizos without definition and aboriginal rights. Immediately after the revolution the Indian leadership had great faith in the Sandinista government and in the process of the revolution. We tried to walk as a people and as an organization with the current of the revolution and not against it. Later we learned that the Sandinista leaders never had good intentions towards our Indian peoples. Despite our efforts to work together as allies of the revolution, the Sandinista government consistently tried to impose its own will on MISURASATA and on the Indian people in general. We learned through experience that the government had no respect for our Indian customs and values, our traditional way of life and ancient rights. As for the traditional Indian organizations, in practice every effort was made to destroy them, to promote divisions and confrontations among Indian leaders, and to supplant Indian organizations, including MISURASATA, with organizations created and controlled by the Sandinista government in Managua. This was the case with ANCS (National Association of the Sumo Communities), an organization created by the government in May, 1981, to separate the Sumos from MISURASATA. But our Indian people refused to go along with the ANCS; proof of this refusal is a signed statement by all the leaders of the Sumo villages.

By February, 1981, the government exposed its intentions by systematically arresting all of the Indian leaders in the country and beginning a process of interrogation and overt intimidation which was clearly designed to put an end to MISURASATA and all other independent Indian leadership. Immediately after this February crackdown, several thousand Indians fled to Honduras. Stedman Fagoth and other MISURASATA leaders were among those who fled.

The February crackdown had prompted massive demonstrations and serious unrest among our Indian peoples. There was a great loss of confidence in the Sandinista government.

Several MISURASATA leaders, including myself, stayed in Nicaragua after our release from prison and interrogation. We and all Indian leaders other than Steadman Fagoth had been cleared of all allegations of Somocista and counterrevolutionary activities. Our hope was to find a peaceful solution to the growing crisis through negotiations with the Sandinista government. We were worried that Somocista or other counterrevolutionary forces would try to use our people for their own ends, and we believed that an agreement could be negotiated which would protect the rights of our Indian peoples and the security of the Nicaraguan government. We told the government in June that a solution to the dispute over Indian land rights would be the key to resolving the Indian crisis. The government agreed that we would present a written statement of our position in July, but while we were in the process of preparing that document the government decreed its Agrarian Reform Law which announced that the government would "give" to Indian peoples defined parcels or sections of land which each village would hold under an "agrarian title." This decree denied Indian ownership of all the lands of the Indian territory of the east coast of Nicaragua and set in motion a process which would promote confrontations between individual Indian communities. Once again Indian rights had been denied in a policy dictated by the government in Managua.

Shortly after the Agrarian Reform Law decree, we presented our own document which contained three principal points:

1) Indian land rights in Indian territory must be recognized as a whole and not as parcels or sections granted by the government.
2) Indians must be guaranteed their right to the natural resources of their territory.
3) The Indian right to self-determination or autonomy within their territory must be recognized.

These three points were flatly rejected by the Nicaragua government at a meeting in the first week of August.

15.
WILLIAM RAMÍREZ: THE IMPERIALIST THREAT AND THE INDIAN PROBLEM (OCTOBER 1982)

The liberation process was not the same in either depth or range in the various regions of Nicaragua. Revolutionary activity was not generalized on the Atlantic Coast as was the case on the Pacific. When the FSLN took power, a disparity in political consciousness was found to exist between the populations of the Atlantic and the Pacific.

The Government of National Reconstruction thus went into operation with a heritage of 400 years of colonialism and neocolonialism, and with marked discrepancies in development sharpened in the last 70 years by the

From *Nicarauac,* No. 8 (October 1982).

interests of North American imperialism. As part of this heritage, vestiges remained of prejudices in favor of white skin. The same kind of preference also prevails for blue-eyed blondes. Suffice it to look at the advertisements in the communications media to confirm these stereotypes. That is what imperialism has taught and continues to teach our people. Somocismo taught contempt for the Nicaraguan people in general and for our Indian and criollo brothers in particular. The ideology that evolved, which buttressed racist social stratification, became entrenched in the course of our history. Some people are conditioned by the idea that those with obviously Indian or Negroid features belong to the lower social classes. The dominant oligarchy of Nicaragua was mainly of white extraction. The groups in power under Somocismo were white.

However, the legacy of the past produced not only racial prejudice among the various sectors but ethnocentrism. The separate colonial developments on the Atlantic and Pacific created ethnic identities that were independently consolidated. A "Hispanic" identity emerged on the Pacific. On the Atlantic Coast, various identities crystallized into a sort of Anglo-Caribbean culture that retained strong ties with the Indian past.

The historic isolation of the Pacific and Atlantic ethnic groups led to a mutual lack of understanding which, combined with other factors, contributed to the creation of ethnocentric attitudes in the two populations.

Faced with this racist and ethnocentric situation, the Sandinista Popular Revolution, guided by democratic and popular principles, supported ethnic organization as a means of combating the differences of the past. And so MISURASATA, which stands for "Miskitos, Sumus, Ramas, Sandinistas United," was founded at the end of 1979.

Adhering to those principles and respecting the rights of the Indians, the government supported Misurasata by granting it representation in the State Council, as well as total freedom to organize with the status of a mass organization. For the first time, the problems of the Atlantic Coast were addressed with the participation of an ethnic organization of its own. The Indian population now knew that the Revolution offered the possibility of a solution to historic problems. And so Misurasata grew rapidly in its first year under the sympathetic eye of the government. Nevertheless, developments were contradictory. On one hand, there was cooperation, the outstanding example of which was the Indian Languages Literacy Campaign that gave 12,000 Indians the opportunity to learn to read and write their native languages. At the same time, however, this was used to consolidate themselves as an organization and so obtain better positions in the government from which to bring their influence to bear upon the unorganized rank and file. In that way, antagonisms arose out of this very objective situation for which the following factors were responsible:

•Relative lack of political awareness on the part of the coastal population, in view of the fact that revolutionary war was not waged on the same scale in that zone. Furthermore, there was no tradition of organization and struggle that might have rapidly brought the coastal people to an understanding of the revolutionary project.

•A high unemployment rate caused by the flight of North Americans and the consequent shutting down of industries. The large-scale nature of the mining, lumbering, and fishing enterprises, the difficult financial situation inherited from the former owners, and the financial blockade imposed by the United States against Nicaragua have made rehabilitation difficult for the Government of National Reconstruction.

•In addition to the foregoing, the strong ethnocentric tradition of the Pacific and Atlantic populations that aroused a feeling of permanent mutual distrust.

Misurasata grew in numbers, demands, and power. The demands pursued reached the point of open opposition to the development strategy being promoted by the Government of National Reconstruction. For example, Misurasata's action plan included the preparation of steps to be taken in January 1981 to demand exclusive rights over almost 45,000 square kilometers of the Coast which represent approximately 38 percent of the national territory. Jointly, they claimed political autonomy over that region. Those demands did not take local interests of thousands of mestizos and other criollo population into consideration who were not a part of the Misurasata organization. At the same time, they were obstructing the centralized control of the natural resources the exploitation of which would be for the benefit of the entire nation. And, lastly, in the political context, they presented a possibility for open manipulation by imperialism and consequent division of the national territory, thereby endangering the Sandinista Popular Revolution and the growth of the revolutionary process in Central America as a whole. That these suspicions were not unfounded was later demonstrated by the openly counterrevolutionary position assumed by the Misurasata leadership, supported by groups of former Somocista guardsmen in Honduras.

The Misurasata leaders were arrested in February 1981 in order to make them aware of the counterrevolutionary nature of the path along which they were leading the organization. Subsequently, all of them were set free except Steadman Fagoth, the head of the group, who turned out to have been a stool pigeon for the Somocista dictatorship's security office. Fagoth was granted conditional liberty in May. He decided to run away to Honduras, where he made contact with groups of former Somocista guardsmen, thereby demonstrating his true political orientation. At the same time, he incited the Miskito population to go over to the Honduran side for the purpose of heading an armed aggression against Nicaragua.

These positions on the part of the leading member of Misurasata created a climate of uncertainty among the coastal Indian population. Right after that, the other leaders of the organization issued a statement repudiating Fagoth's position and declaring their support for the revolutionary project. Nevertheless, in September of this year, a new document was issued that slandered the government, vindicated and legitimized Fagoth's actions and prior political direction, and ended with a call to the Miskito population to counterrevolutionary struggle.

This is why the Nicaraguan Government was obliged to withdraw official recognition of Misurasata, inasmuch as its demands had now turned into an attack upon national sovereignty, and also because a process of objective estrangement from the rank and file had taken place.

Imperialism fostered the separation of Miskito groups which are being given military training in Honduras and are making armed propaganda incursions throughout the Río Coco communities. They are seeking in this way to repeat the history of British colonialism. The British manipulated the Miskito leaders into attacking the Spanish population and enslaving their own Indian brothers.

Today, U.S. imperialism is manipulating the Miskitos in Honduras by pitting them against the Nicaraguans, utilizing for the purpose the Fagoth cabal and the dregs of the Somocista National Guard that remain in Honduras.

It is the obligation of this Revolution and this people to preserve revolutionary power and to continue the social transformation upon which we have embarked.

Territorial unity is above any other consideration and is not open for discussion of any sort.

Imperialism's dream is to separate the Atlantic Coast from the rest of Nicaragua. We will never allow this to happen. Our Indians are as Nicaraguan as the rest of the citizens and have the same rights.

16.
NICARAGUAN DEMOCRATIC FORCE: PRINCIPLES
(FEBRUARY 1983)

. . . we wish to precisely and clearly define the principles and short and longterm objectives of our struggle:

I. First of all, we declare that we repudiate any attempt to link us with the somocista past. The somocista dictatorship died in July, 1979 and, as the dictator himself, is politically buried in history.

II. We stand for the nationalistic and patriotic principles of the historic figure, Augusto César Sandino, and we stand against the deformation of these principles made by International Communism through the Frente Sandinista de Liberación Nacional (FSLN) whose leaders would have been repudiated by Sandino if he were alive, as he repudiated the Salvadorean communists, Farabundo Martí and so many others like them in his time.

III. We maintain that only the Nicaraguan people through free, just and honest elections have the right to decide the direction of their Revolution, its principles and goals, and within the framework of the widest possible democratic pluralism, to choose which political party should govern the nation.

IV. Once our country is liberated from communism, a representative provisional government will be installed, representing the various democratic groups now opposing the Sandinista regime.

V. We declare that we are not motivated by hatred or revenge. The honest public employees who have democratic convictions and who did not participate in the communist conspiracy will be able to continue serving in the administration of the country. Likewise, the members of the Sandinista army and Police who have not committed any crimes and who demonstrate democratic convictions will be able, if they so desire, to enlist in the national army and police. However, we will not tolerate the continued presence of thousands of the so-called "Internacionalistas," foreign invaders who are Marxist-Leninist agents and who collaborate with the Sandinista regime to oppress our people.

VI. It is our fundamental objective to fully guarantee the respect for human rights as they are stated in the Inter-American Convention for Human Rights. In establishing guarantee, it is essential to first review the injustices that have been carried out by the common and special tribunals, as recommended by the International Commission of Jurists. Also, review is needed in cases of expropriation of property, de facto or by virtue of decrees, in violation of civil rights. It is equally essential to restore complete religious freedom and the return of temples of worship to their respective congregations.

VII. We seek to reestablish the autonomous character of the universities and the reform of the educational programs at all levels, in accord with democratic tradition and fundamental national beliefs, based on our heritage.

VIII. We guarantee the establishment of free labor unions for laborers and skilled workers, and professional associations.

IX. We believe in the need for revision of the present Marxist agrarian reform law which allows the farmer to work the land but must sell his produce to government agencies. We propose that the law be changed to enable it to grant provisional titles to the farmers so they can enjoy the full benefits of the land until permanent titles are issued, and sell their produce on the open market.

X. We believe it is essential to have a publicly known, balanced national budget.

XI. A strict policy of fiscal austerity and incentives to increase production must be the basis for a healthy recuperation of the national economy.

XII. We believe that diplomatic relations must be maintained with all nations based on mutual respect for national sovereignty, strict reciprocity, and absolute respect for the principle of nonintervention in internal affairs. Our international policy should be based on our obligations within the inter-American community of states, without affecting our international commitments to other countries and to the United Nations.

XIII. We reiterate our proposal that municipal and National Constituent Assembly elections must be held within a year. The newly-elected National Constituent Assembly will be responsible for establishing the new constitutional system for Nicaragua as a true expression of the will of our people. In order to guarantee free and honest elections, the help of all democratic national sectors will be requested, as well as the technical assistance of international organizations such as the OAS.

17.
EDÉN PASTORA: PROCLAMATION (APRIL 1983)

Proclamation to the People of Nicaragua
Year of Sovereignty and National Dignity

Brother Nicaraguans:

Our Democratic Revolutionary Alliance (ARDE) has already proposed a meritorious and workable political solution for achieving peace in Nicaragua. We steadfastly maintain our devotion to peace and a political solution because we are convinced that it will be a guarantee of stability for all the brother nations of Central America. However, it is impossible to attain that goal in Nicaragua because history has repeated itself: my country is once again trespassed upon. It is our obligation in the name of national dignity to expel the interlopers from our soil and restore sovereignty and peace.

From Mountains of Nicaragua, April 15, 1983.

I write this proclamation now on Nicaraguan soil where I have decided to remain in order to carry on the struggle alongside my people and, if need be, to die for my steadfast ideals of freedom and democracy, as we were taught by Beledón, Sandi, and Pedro Joaquín.

I declare that if the Cubans who are today the instruments of intervention and death here in Nicaragua have not left this sacred soil within two weeks from today, they will end like all others who have dared trespass upon us: driven out or dead.

I repeat that this is a difficult struggle and that unity around a commitment to redeem our true and original Nicaraguan Revolution cannot be delayed and that it is the only road to freedom and democracy. I have complete faith that God will grant the clarity of vision and the fortitude to keep us from losing heart in this supreme commitment.

I feel that need in this simple countryman's heart of mine and urge my people to join together as one fist to drive out the interlopers and their puppets. There is, of course, no foreign master without a national servant.

I make a fraternal and revolutionary appeal to my comrades of the Sandinista Popular Army and the glorious Popular Militias to refuse to allow the National Directorate to involve them in this new war of liberation. The good soldiers and militiamen know full well who has betrayed our people and against whom they must turn their guns to save the country and the Revolution.

This is no more time for talk, no longer am I concerned with the eternal pharisees, the waverers, the opportunists, the envious, and the cowards, because those are never willing to die for the fatherland.

We must fight to put an end to praetorian armies and almighty soldiers, and so to stop fratricidal reprisals, and to see our people cast their votes freely; we must fight for the sovereignty of the civil power over the military, so that we may for the first time choose the path of justice, peace, and democracy.

In conclusion, I wish to declare that the only thing that concerns me is:

A Free Fatherland or Death.
Without Totalitarianism or Turning Back to the Past.

18.
EDGAR CHAMORRO: TESTIMONY ON THE CONTRAS

Toward the end of 1979 I began to work with a group of Nicaraguan exiles living in Miami who, like me, opposed the policies of the new government. In 1980 we constituted ourselves as the Union Democratica Nicaraguense (Nicaraguan Democratic Union), or "UDN." . . . The leader of our organization, with whom I worked closely, was José Francisco Cardenal. Cardenal had served briefly as Vice President of the Council of State, the legislature of the new Nicaraguan Government, but had resigned his post and left Nicaragua because of his disagreements with the new government's policies.

In 1981, the UDN underwent a transformation. During the first half of the year, Cardenal was contacted by representatives of the United States Central Intelligence Agency, and he began to have frequent meetings with them in Washington and in Miami. He also began to receive monetary payments from these people. He was told that the United States Government was prepared to help us remove the FSLN from power in Nicaragua, but that, as a condition for receiving this help, we had to join forces with the ex-National Guardsmen who had fled to Honduras when the Somoza Government fell and had been conducting sporadic raids on Nicaraguan border positions ever since. Cardenal was taken to Honduras by his CIA contacts on several occasions to meet with these Guardsmen. . . . We were well aware of the crimes the Guardsmen had committed against the Nicaraguan people while in the service of President Somoza, and we wanted nothing to do with them. However, we recognized that without help from the United States Government we had no chance of removing the Sandinistas from power. . . .

At that time, the ex-National Guardsmen were divided into several small bands operating along the Nicaraguan-Honduras border. The largest of the bands, headed by Enrique Bermúdez, a former Colonel, was called the 15th of September Legion. The bands were poorly armed and equipped, and thoroughly disorganized. They were not an effective military force and represented no more than a minor irritant to the Nicaraguan Government. . . . The merger of the UDN with the 15th of September Legion was accomplished in August 1981 at a meeting in Guatemala City, Guatemala, where formal documents were signed. The meeting was arranged and the

Testimony before the World Court, September 5, 1985.

documents were prepared by the CIA. The new organization was called the Fuerza Democratica Nicaraguense ("Nicaraguan Democratic Force") or, by its Spanish acronym, FDN. It was to be headed by a political junta, consisting of Cardenal, Aristides Sánchez (a politician loyal to General Somoza and closely associated with Bermúdez) and Mariano Mendoza, formerly a labor leader in Nicaragua; the political junta soon established itself in Tegucigalpa, Honduras, taking up residence in a house rented for it by the CIA. Bermúdez was assigned to head the military general staff, and it, too, was based in Honduras. The name of the organization, the members of the political junta, and the members of the general staff were all chosen or approved by the CIA.

Soon after the merger, the FDN began to receive a substantial and steady flow of financial, military and other assistance from the CIA. Former National Guardsmen who had sought exile in El Salvador, Guatemala and the United States after the fall of the Somoza Government were recruited to enlarge the military component of the organization. They were offered regular salaries, the funds for which were supplied by the CIA. Training was provided by Argentinian military officers . . . two of whom—Col. Oswaldo Rivero and Col. Santiago Villejas—I got to know quite well; the Argentinians were also paid by the CIA. A special unit was created for sabotage, especially demolitions; it was trained directly by CIA personnel at Lepaterique, near Tegucigalpa. Arms, ammunition, equipment and food were supplied by the CIA. Our first combat units were sent into Nicaraguan territory in December 1981, principally to conduct hit-and-run raids. The first military successes of the organization came in March 1982, when CIA-trained saboteurs blew up two vital bridges in northern Nicaragua— at Río Negro and Ocotal.

1982 was a year of transition for the FDN. From a collection of small, disorganized and ineffectual bands of ex-National Guardsmen, the FDN grew into a well-organized, well-armed, well-equipped and well-trained fighting force of approximately 4,000 men capable of inflicting great harm on Nicaragua. This was due entirely to the CIA, which organized, armed, equipped, trained and supplied us. After the initial recruitment of ex-Guardsmen from throughout the region (to serve as officers or commanders of military units), efforts were made to recruit "foot soldiers" for the force from inside Nicaragua. Some Nicaraguans joined the force voluntarily, either because of dissatisfaction with the Nicaraguan Government, family ties with leaders of the force, promises of food, clothing, boots and weapons, or a combination of these reasons. Many other members of the force were recruited forcibly. FDN units would arrive at an undefended village, assemble all the residents in the town square and then proceed to kill—in full view of the others—all persons suspected of working for the Nicaraguan Government or the FSLN, including police, local militia members, party members, health workers, teachers, and farmers from government-sponsored cooperatives. . . . During this period Cardenal grew increasingly unhappy over his lack of influence within the FDN. He had frequent conflicts with the CIA personnel who were supervising and directing the FDN's political and military activities and found that he had no control over Bermúdez or the other members of the FDN general staff, who answered only to the CIA. Eventually he quit the organization, returned to Miami and entered the insurance business.

In November 1982 I was approached by a CIA agent using the name "Steve Davis" and asked to become a member of the "political directorate" of the FDN, which the CIA had decided to create as a substitute for the "political junta." . . . I was glad to see that the United States Government was committed enough to our cause to be taking such an active role, and I agreed to join the directorate they were creating. . . .

The press conference was held the next day, December 8, 1982, at the Hilton Conference Center in Fort Lauderdale, Florida. We filed in and introduced ourselves as the directorate of the Nicaraguan Democratic Force (FDN) and then I read our statement of principles and goals. A CIA officer named "George" had rewritten our original version of the statement, and I had to read his words. In January 1983, at the instruction of CIA agent "Thomas Castillo," we put out a 12-point "peace initiative" drafted by the CIA, which essentially demanded the surrender of the Sandinista government. I thought this was premature, but "Castillo" insisted that it be done to get the FDN favorable publicity. Also at this time, another Nicaraguan civilian—Adolfo Calero—who had just left Nicaragua, was added to the directorate. Calero had been working for the CIA in Nicaragua for a long time. He served as, among other things, a conduit of funds from the United States Embassy to various student and labor organizations. . . . Despite these public relations efforts, the United States Congress enacted a prohibition on CIA efforts to overthrow the Nicaraguan Government, although it appropriated millions of dollars to the CIA for clandestine military and paramilitary activities against the Nicaraguan Government. Before this prohibition was enacted, the CIA agents we worked with spoke openly and confidently about replacing the government in Managua. Thereafter, the CIA instructed us that, if asked, we should say that our objective was to interdict arms supposedly being smuggled from Nicaragua to El Salvador. If any of us ever said anything publicly about overthrowing the Nicaraguan Government, we would be visited immediately by a CIA official who would say, "That's not the language we want you to use." But our goal, and that of the CIA as well (as we were repeatedly assured in private), was to overthrow the Government of Nicaragua, and to replace the Sandinistas as a government. . . .

Most of the CIA operatives who worked with us in Honduras were military trainers and advisers. Our troops were trained in guerrilla warfare, sabotage, demolitions, and in the use of a variety of weapons, including assault rifles, machine guns, mortars, grenade launchers and explosives, such as Claymore mines. We were also trained in field communications, and the CIA taught us how to use certain sophisticated codes that the Nicaraguan Government forces would not be able to decipher. This was critical to our military operations because it enabled various units, or task forces, to communicate with each other, and to coordinate their activities, without being detected by the Sandinistas. Without this communications capacity, our forces inside Nicaragua would not have been able to coordinate their activities with one another and they would have been unable to launch effective strikes at the designated targets. Even more critical to our military activities was the intelligence that the CIA provided to us. The CIA, working with United States military personnel, operated various electronic interception stations in Honduras for the purpose of intercepting radio and telephonic communications among Nicaraguan Government military units. By means of these interception activities, and by breaking the Nicaraguan Government codes, the CIA was able to determine—and to advise us of—the precise locations of all Nicaraguan Government military units. The information obtained by the CIA in this manner was ordinarily corroborated by overflights of Nicaraguan territory by United States satellites and sophisticated surveillance aircraft. With this information, our own forces knew the areas in which they could safely operate free of government troops. If our units were instructed to do battle with the government troops, they knew where to set up ambushes, because the CIA informed them of the precise routes the government troops would take. This type of intelligence was invaluable to us. Without it, our forces would not have been able to operate with any degree of effectiveness inside Nicaragua. The United States Government also made it possible for us to resupply our troops inside Nicaragua, thus permitting them to remain longer inside the country. Under cover of military maneuvers in Honduras during 1983, United States armed forces personnel constructed airstrips, including the one at Aguacate, that, after the CIA provided us with airplanes, were instrumental in resupplying our troops.

The CIA was also directly involved in our military tactics. The agency repeatedly ordered us to move our troops inside Nicaragua and to keep them there as long as possible. After our offensive at the end of 1982 was turned back, almost all of our troops were in Honduras and our own officers believed that they needed more training and more time before they would be ready to return to Nicaragua. The FDN officers were overruled by the CIA, however. The agency told us that we had to send our men back into Nicaragua and keep fighting. We had no choice but to obey. In 1983, the CIA instructed us not to destroy farms or crops because that would be politically counterproductive. In 1984, however, we were instructed to destroy export crops (especially coffee and tobacco), and to attack farms and cooperatives. Accordingly, we changed our tactics in 1984.

In September 1983, the CIA blew up the pipeline at Puerto Sandino. . . . The actual operatives were Agency employees of Hispanic descent, referred to within the Agency as "Unilaterally Controlled Latino Assets" or UCLAs. These UCLAs, specially trained underwater demolitions experts, were dispatched from a CIA "mother ship" that took them to within striking distance of their target. Although the FDN had nothing whatsoever to do with this operation, we were instructed by the CIA to publicly claim responsibility in order to cover the CIA's involvement. We did. In October, CIA UCLAs attacked Nicaragua's oil storage tanks at Corinto, also on the Pacific Coast. This was a combined sea and air attack involving the use of rockets. It was a complete success; all of the tanks were destroyed and enormous quantities of oil were consumed by fire. Again, the CIA instructed us to publicly claim responsibility, and we did. Later in October, there was another UCLA attack on Puerto Sandino, which again resulted in the demolition of the oil pipeline. We again claimed responsibility per instructions from the CIA. Subsequently, the UCLAs attacked Nicaraguan Government military facilities at Potosí and radio antennas at Las Casitas. We again were told to claim responsibility and we did. . . .

In May 1984 the United States Congress voted not to provide more assistance to the CIA for military and paramilitary activities against Nicaragua. Many of us became worried about receiving continued support from the United States Government and we expressed these concerns to our CIA colleagues in Tegucigalpa. We were repeatedly assured by the station chief and his deputies, in the strongest possible terms, that we would not be abandoned and that the United States Government would find a way to continue its support. At around this time we were visited by Ronald F. Lehman II, a Special Assistant to the President of the United States who was serving then on the National Security Council. Mr. Lehman assured us that President Reagan remained committed to removing the Sandinistas from power. He told us that President Reagan was unable at that time to publicly express the full extent of his commitment to us because of the upcoming presidential elections in the United States. But, Mr. Lehman told us, as soon as the elections were over, President Reagan would publicly endorse our effort to remove the Sandinistas from power and see to it that we received all the support that was necessary for that purpose. We received a similar assurance of continued United States Government support, notwithstanding the refusal of the Congress to appropriate more funds, from Lt. Col. Oliver North, another official of the National Security Council.

It was still important to these officials, and to the CIA, to obtain additional appropriations of funds from the Congress, and they had not abandoned hope that the Congress could be persuaded to resume funding our activities. Our CIA colleagues enlisted us in an effort to "lobby" the Congress to resume these appropriations. I attended meetings at which CIA officials told us that we could change the votes of many members of the Congress if we knew how to "sell" our case and place them in a position of "looking soft on Communism." They told us exactly what to say and which members of the Congress to say it to. They also instructed us to contact certain prominent individuals in the home districts of various members of Congress as a means to bring pressure on these members to change their votes. At various times Calero, Callejas, Zeledon, Salazar, Rodríguez and I participated in these "lobbying" activities.

A major part of my job as communications officer was to work to improve the image of the FDN forces. This was challenging, because it was standard FDN practice to kill prisoners and suspected Sandinista collaborators. In talking with officers in the FDN camps along the Honduran border, I frequently heard offhand remarks like, "Oh, I cut his throat." The CIA did not discourage such tactics. To the contrary, the Agency severely criticized me when I admitted to the press that the FDN had regularly kidnapped and executed agrarian reform workers and civilians. We were told that the only way to defeat the Sandinistas was to use the tactics the Agency attributed to "Communist" insurgencies elsewhere: kill, kidnap, rob and torture.

These tactics were reflected in an operations manual prepared for our forces by a CIA agent who used the name "John Kirkpatrick." I assisted "Kirkpatrick" in translating certain parts of the manual, and the manuscript was typed by my secretary. The manual was entitled: "Psychological Operations in Guerrilla Warfare." It advocated "explicit and implicit terror" against the civilian population, including assassination of government employees and sympathizers. Before the manual was distributed, I attempted to excise two passages that I thought were immoral and dangerous, at pages 70 and 71. One recommended hiring professional criminals. The other advocated killing some of our own colleagues to create martyrs for the cause. I did not particularly want to be "martyred" by the CIA. So I locked up all the copies of the manual and hired two youths to cut out the offending pages and glue in expurgated pages. About 2,000 copies of the manual, with only those two passages changed, were then distributed to FDN troops. Upon reflection, I found many of the tactics advocated in the manual to be offensive, and I complained to the CIA station chief in Tegucigalpa. The station chief defended "Kirkpatrick" and the manual, and no action was ever taken in response to my complaints. In fact, the practices advocated in the manual were employed by FDN troops. Many civilians were killed in cold blood. Many others were tortured, mutilated, raped, robbed or otherwise abused. . . .

When I agreed to join the FDN in 1981, I had hoped that it would be an organization of Nicaraguans, controlled by Nicaraguans, and dedicated to our own objectives which we ourselves would determine. I joined on the understanding that the United States Government would supply us the means necessary to defeat the Sandinistas and replace them as a government, but I believed that we would be our own masters. I turned out to be mistaken. The FDN turned out to be an instrument of the United States Government and, specifically, of the CIA. It was created by the CIA, it was supplied, equipped, armed and trained by the CIA and its activities —both political and military—were directed and controlled by the CIA. Those Nicaraguans who were chosen (by the CIA) for leadership positions within the organization—namely, Calero and Bermúdez—were those who best demonstrated their willingness to unquestioningly follow the instructions of the CIA. They, like the organization itself, became nothing more than executioners of the CIA's orders.

19.
BERNARD NIETSCHMANN: STATEMENT TO THE OAS (OCTOBER 1983)

I am a professor of geography at the University of California, Berkeley. My research and teaching specialties are indigenous peoples. . . .

Between 1968 and 1976 I spent 1/2 years in eastern Nicaragua in Miskito villages. . . .

I was supportive of the overthrow of the Somoza regime and the establishment of the new government and looked forward to a new and beneficial government policy toward the East Coast Indian peoples.

In 1980 I went to Nicaragua at the invitation of the Sandinista government to advise on and promote the possibility of establishing a national marine park off northeastern Nicaragua . . . to provide sustainable resources for coastal Miskito communities. . . . I heard again [in 1983] from some of my old acquaintances who called and wrote from Costa Rica. They were refugees and told me they had had to flee from their villages to seek safety in Costa Rica. They feared for their lives in Nicaragua. Some of these people were men of more than 60 years of age, others were women who came with children. . . .

I went to Costa Rica at the first opportunity to see these people and to learn what had happened to them and in their villages since I'd last visited the East Coast of Nicaragua. . . . I was also in a Miskito area in eastern

Nicaragua for several weeks. I traveled from village to village, staying for varying lengths of time depending on security considerations. I talked to hundreds of people, lived with them, ate what they were barely managing to live on, experienced the conditions, met many people I'd known from my previous visits.

HUMAN RIGHTS VIOLATIONS

It is with sadness that I report widespread, systematic and arbitrary human rights violations in Miskito Indian communities. These violations by the Sandinista government include arbitrary killings, arrests and interrogations; rapes; torture; continuing forced relocations of village populations; destruction of villages; restriction and prohibition of freedom of travel; prohibition of village food production; restriction and denial of access to basic and necessary store foods; the complete absence of *any* medicine, health care or educational services in many Indian villages; the denial of religious freedom; and the looting of households and sacking of villages.

ARBITRARY KILLINGS

In several villages I talked to people who had witnessed the arbitrary killing of Miskito civilians by Sandinista military forces. Many of these killings occurred during one of several Sandinista military invasions and occupations of Indian villages. Some of the villagers were arbitrarily shot when the government soldiers first invaded the villages; others were killed during the weeks of occupation, confinement, torture and interrogation. For example, it was reported to me by several different firsthand sources that one man was nailed through his hands and ankles to a wall and told he would remain there until he either confessed to being a "contra" or died. He died. His widow, dressed in black, and others in that traumatized village are filled with grief and anger over this and other atrocities committed during their forced confinement under a reign of terror by several hundred Sandinista soldiers. Other Miskitos were killed by forcing their heads under water to extract confessions of "counterrevolutionary" activities. Two older men—60 and 63 years of age—were threatened with death unless they confessed to involvement with "contras." They too were finally killed in the course of these same events.

Throughout my notes and tape recording are descriptions of such killings in village after village in the Atlantic Coast Indian region. Descriptions were given to me by wives, daughters, mothers, and other relatives and villagers. The occurrence of arbitrary killings of Miskito civilians appears to be widespread. A pattern is readily seen. Miskito men and women are accused of being contras, tortured or threatened with death unless they confess, killed, and then reported as having been contras, if, indeed, there is any report at all. . . .

Civilian Miskitos have been tortured in villages and according to reports which I consider to be very reliable, in jails. I received confirming reports and descriptions from reliable witnesses who saw beatings done by Sandinista military in many villages. I also talked to and photographed people who had been tortured. I was shown scars from what they said were bayonet wounds (a man of 60 years), fingernails pulled out (a man of 48 years), deep scars under fingernails from nails driven in (a man of 52 years). Several men reported that they had been held under water for long periods to extract confessions. . . . In each community that has experienced a Sandinista military invasion and occupation, women have been raped. Some were held down by soldiers, some were restrained with a bayonet under their neck and then raped. From what the villagers have observed and experienced, Sandinista soldiers are apparently given great freedom to do as they please when they invade an Indian village.

LOOTING, SACKING OF VILLAGES, CONFISCATION OF PROPERTY

One of the many things I noticed as being markedly different in Miskito communities was the absence of anything of value. Households had no radios, some had no dishes; more formal clothes usually worn to church on Sundays were absent. This was not the result of the people's poverty or the lack of clothes in stores—although these conditions prevail and are worsening—but are due to the theft of property by Sandinista soldiers. Radios, clothes, gold bracelets, necklaces, and rings had been stripped from the Indian villagers and looted from their houses. Again and again people reported to me that this happened to them when the Sandinistas occupied their villages. Furthermore, the soldiers killed their pigs, cows and chickens for food but did not pay for them.

In response to this policy many thousands of Indians have already fled Nicaragua to Honduras and Costa Rica. This flight is still continuing. While I was recently in Costa Rica the entire Miskito village of Set Net arrived and asked for protection from the U.N. High Commissioner for Refugees.

Others have stayed within the country and have struggled to survive under these harsh conditions or have actively joined in armed resistance. There has been terror and serious trauma in many villages yet the result has not been submission to Sandinista authority. . . .

The influence of the Indian warriors and the territory over which they have strong military control is growing. . . .

20.
ARTURO J. CRUZ: SANDINISTAS AT A WATERSHED
(SPRING 1984)

It is now clear that the revolutionary process is somehow irreversible—that Nicaragua will not return to its former feudalistic status which prevailed prior to July 1979. Yet, it is at least equally evident that the establishment, in its place, of communist rule will not remain unchallenged. Therefore, the leadership of *Frente Sandinista de Liberación Nacional* (FSLN) has a choice between social democracy, which would assure the viability of the regime, and Marxism-Leninism, which will provoke endless confrontation.

Revolutionary social transformation in Nicaragua is not questioned. Even the staunchest adversary of the Sandinistas—the *Frente Democratico Nicaraguense* (FDN)—pretends to justify its military stand on the ground that the revolution has been betrayed by the FSLN. The dissidents in arms constantly reaffirm their revolutionary vocation. This is true of *Alianza Revolucionaria Democratica* (ARDE). The array of dissident forces working inside Nicaragua through civic action—the Church hierarchy, business leaders, *La Prensa,* as well as other non-Sandinista media, independent political parties and labor unions—incessantly manifest their willingness for a democratic accommodation with the revolution.

What the dissidents (including elements within the Sandinista regime, who at this time cannot express their feelings publicly) adamantly oppose is the revolution's Sovietization. This writer acted as moderator at the meeting where ARDE's creation was decided. It was agreed that in order for any individual or group to be eligible for membership in the organization, two conditions had to be met—to be both revolutionary and democratic.

The concern is one that is openly shared by the Central American nations, and in various degrees by democratic governments in Latin America and Europe. . . . The real issue is not the number of guns from Cuba which Nicaragua has smuggled into El Salvador. The real issue, rather, is that in its present form the Sandinista regime is perceived as a source of political unrest and economic decline in Central America. Consequently, the crux of the matter lies in finding an effective and permanent solution —such as that being earnestly sought by the Contadora Group—which

From his "Nicaragua: The Sandinistas Regime at a Watershed," *Strategic Review,* Spring 1984, pp. 11–23.

would prevent the meddling of one state in the internal affairs of another and assure the respect by governments for individual rights within their borders.

The definitive removal from Nicaragua of Cuban and other Soviet Bloc military advisors, as well as an end to the Sandinista military buildup and to Managua's support of insurgency in neighboring Central American countries, must be part of the solution. Notwithstanding how important these conditions may be, they would achieve very little as a contribution to lasting peace and stability if they are not accompanied by a genuine FSLN decision finally to honor its unfulfilled 1979 commitment before the Organization of American States (OAS) to guarantee pluralism in Nicaragua. Central in such a formal decision should be a total separation of the Sandinista political party apparatus from the state.

Given the Sandinistas' predisposition to totalitarianism, this proposition may sound like a platitude to skeptical critics. Such critics may point out that this is foolishly asking a clique of hard-line ideologues to accept the failure of their project to establish a Marxist totalitarian regime—a doctrine which they consider as their gospel and departure from it as sinful. Nevertheless, it must by now be evident even to members of the Sandinista regime that the experience of the last five years corroborates the unsuitability of that regime's orientation to the objective conditions of Nicaragua and its people, of Central America and of the hemisphere—that the obsession of the most radical leaders and cadres of the FSLN with communism has undermined not only Nicaragua as a nation-state but also their own viability as a government. By now they must realize that they are in serious danger of being toppled from power. . . .

Having squandered their credibility, it is little wonder that the Sandinistas' overtures have been received, at home and abroad, with skepticism. Nevertheless, some "Sandinologists" suggest that a final judgment regarding the regime's ultimate intentions ought to be tempered somewhat by symptoms of pragmatism in its behavior. In fact, the FSLN has allowed more than a modicum of pluralism—albeit more formal than real—the remnants of which still linger in Nicaragua. Thus far, the Sandinistas have been testing the climate of geopolitical tolerance in order to determine how far they can go on the road to Marxism-Leninism. They must have learned by now that it is not an easy journey. . . .

Four factors were determinant in ensuring victory for the Sandinistas. In the first place, Somoza acted for them as their catalyst of turmoil. Hence he was their most reliable "ally," and therefore it was convenient that he remain in the presidential bunker until he was ripe to fall—and along with him the Liberal Party and the National Guard. Had Somoza resigned even as late as the spring of 1979, the Sandinista rocket would have fizzled.

Next, as was indicated above, the widespread popular indignation over

Pedro Joaquín Chamorro-Cardenal's assassination proved a windfall for the Sandinistas. Third, by enlisting the young, the FSLN assured a popular uprising. Finally, the business entrepreneurs were a source of financial support, and they along with labor could stop production—an essential step to make the government crumble. The Group of Twelve—which from its inception had at least four FSLN members—current Junta member Sergio Ramírez, Minister of Justice Ernesto Castillo, head of the Alphabetization Campaign Fernando Cardenal and Foreign Minister Miguel d'Escoto—acted in the final analysis only and actually as a Sandinista lobbying force. . . . By and large, the young have remained steadfast Sandinista supporters. Immediately after victory-day, businessmen started to act as a restraining force.

It should be noted at this point that Carlos Fonseca Amador, the Sandinistas' Mao, found in Marxism the answers he had eagerly sought. In his youth, he joined *Partido Socialista Nicaraguense* (PSN)—which had been formed in 1944—and subsequently traveled to the Soviet Union, where his enthrallment with communism was reinforced. Upon Batista's defeat by Castro in 1959, he began to develop ties with Havana, remaining a devout Marxist-Leninist until his death in 1976.

The FSLN was founded in 1961 by Fonseca Amador, together with Silvio Mayorga (now also dead) and Tomás Borge, adopting a much harder line than the PSN. In spite of abundant evidence that he was not a communist, the new organization was named after the legendary, anti-imperialist hero, Augusto César Sandino. This was also a shrewd political move designed to express nationalism. In fact, the FSLN has a monopoly on the term "Sandinista," which it uses as a brand-name for all the organizations it controls—e.g., *Ejercito Popular Sandinista* (EPS), *Central Sandinista de Trabajadores* (CST), etc. Non-FSLN political groups are strictly barred from using the designation.

In addition, the FSLN adopted Rigoberto López Pérez as one of its heroes. Rigoberto, as he is popularly known, killed Anastasio Somoza García five years prior to the appearance of the FSLN. His adoption for worship was also part of the Sandinistas' public relations strategy, with the objective of capitalizing on popular anti-Somocista feelings.

It is then quite clear that the hard core of the FSLN is Marxist from its origins. Their quest for power is a unique case in political history. Without gaining any status of consequence, the Sandinistas struggled for sixteen years with incredible tenacity and personal valor. They were merely an irritant for Somoza; the establishment looked upon them with apprehension but without immediate fear.

Coinciding with the heart ailments which afflicted Anastasio Somoza-Debayle, the turning point in the Sandinistas' political life began in 1977, when the *Tercerista* faction relaxed Marxist rigor and pressed for insurrec-

tion. The key element which really afforded the FSLN an historical opportunity was their foresightedness. Ironically, the other two FSLN factions
—the *Proletarios* and the *Guerra Popular Prolongada*—vehemently criticized them for their adventurism and lack of ideological purity.

Subsequently, a series of events took place in which there was an interplay of resolve, fate and opportunism: the initial, bold *Tercerista* attacks
in October 1977 against National Guard outposts and the first public
declaration of The Group of Twelve; mass protests against the killing of
Pedro Joaquín Chamorro-Cardenal in early 1978; the Indians' uprising in
Mobimbo; the daring seizure of the House of the Congress and the September insurrection; the unification of the three FSLN factions into a National
Directorate; and the final onslaught in 1979.

During the insurrectionary period, the FSLN showed its flair for mounting spectacular operations: outstanding among them was the assault
against the National Palace, site of the legislature. It is common knowledge
that this action provided the Sandinistas with newspaper headlines
throughout the world. Less known is the fact that at the same time they
began to give some first indications of their potential for absolutism, disquieting non-Marxists in the broad alliance, among them Alfonso Robelo.
One example was their persistent opposition to any solution, labeled as
"Somocismo without Somoza," which did not guarantee a position of
paramountcy for the FSLN. . . . It was for this reason that, as did Somoza,
they strongly rejected U.S. Ambassador William Bowdler's proposal for a
popular referendum. Neither did they rest until achieving the disruption
of the *Frente Amplio Opositor* (FAO), which they had originally joined in
order to secure for themselves a place in that pluralistic body formed by
legitimate opposition groups. Afterwards, however, when their own *Movimiento Pueblo Unido* (MPU) and *Frente Patriotico Nacional* (FPN) were
ready, they abandoned the FAO.

Nonetheless, with a great deal of political acumen—even if for cosmetic
reasons—the FSLN's leaders organized their first government with the
participation of non-Sandinistas, both on the Junta and in the Cabinet.
Such a timely flexibility contributed to assuaging the misgivings of erst-
while non-Marxist opponents to Somoza and disposed them to collaborate
with the Sandinistas. The difficulty for establishing effective and long-
lasting credibility rested in the fact that the Sandinistas' tolerance has been
ebb-and-flow all along. Edén Pastora's closest followers ascribe this lack
of consistency to the composition of the FSLN's Directorate by representatives of the three factions in equal numbers. Thus, they claim, the *Terceristas'* pluralist attitude is neutralized by the more radical elements. Based
on my personal experience, however, I do not totally share their views.

The assassination of Pedro Joaquín Chamorro-Cardenal is by far the
most relevant of all the circumstances which led to the Sandinistas' ascent

to power. One year before his unfortunate death, I met with him in Managua. During our conversation, I became aware of the genuine friendship which existed between him and the President of Venezuela. Thus, upon learning of his tragedy and amid my personal grief, the thought came to my mind that it meant Somoza's end—regardless of whether or not he was directly responsible. I also knew that this would have an impact on Carlos Andrés Pérez. The sequel proved my premonition to be correct: the Venezuelan President was filled with indignation. From then onward, he defiantly supported Somoza's ouster. . . .

Washington views Cuba's influence in Nicaragua with alarm, regarding it as a Soviet proxy in the Third World which presents a challenge to U.S. vital interests. Of particular concern to the United States is the knowledge that the effectiveness of the Cuban Air Force for action in the region can be enhanced with bases on Central American soil. The American press, as well as other international media, have extensively reported the swelling of the Nicaraguan Armed Forces to 70,000, with Cuban technical support. East Germans, Bulgarians and the PLO are among those who have helped the armed and security forces. . . .

Notwithstanding an unmistakable Cuban trait in the genesis of Nicaragua's revolutionary process, it might be an exaggeration to regard the Nicaraguan revolution merely as an offshoot of the Cuban revolution.

If one takes the rhetoric alone, isolating it from the unfolding events which may contradict it, Cuba sounds like a prudent counselor to the Sandinistas. For this reason, it is worthwhile to examine the speeches of Cuba's "maximum leader" in Managua and Ciego de Avila in July 1980 and, previously, in Holguín in July 1979. The prevailing tone of these speeches was that of advising moderation for the Nicaraguan process, recognizing that conditions in that country indicated that pluralism and the mixed economy constitute positive elements. In fact, while addressing his own people at Ciego de Avila, Fidel Castro repeated some of the concepts he had expressed a few days earlier before a multitude of Nicaraguans. He referred to the Sandinista revolution as a new revolutionary project in Nicaragua, implemented by the Nicaraguans, adapted to international circumstances and to the objective conditions of Nicaragua, in which businessmen are stimulated to participate. Fidel underscored a distinction between the two revolutions, pointing out that each should apply its own formula.

In their writings, several Sandinista defenders have contrasted Nicaragua with Cuba. They contend that polarized critics of the FSLN have eyes only for the similarities, while ignoring remarkable differences. Additionally, they often highlight the fact that the Sandinista model is not yet altogether Marxist-Leninist and that the internal debate concerning the speed required for reaching socialism still continues. . . . The Sandinistas' failure to define the revolution in pragmatic terms—categorically and in its earliest stage—could prove in the long run to be their own undoing. Worse still, coupled with the foregoing, their excesses of intolerance have filled dissidents, and by and large the nation, with unmitigated distrust. For much too long has the FSLN engaged in gamesmanship: stalling, scheming, it has emptied the bag of tricks. In order to survive, the Sandinistas must yield to reality and offer a forthright settlement proposal to both the United States and democratic opposition.

During their first four years in power, the Sandinistas have tried to act simultaneously on three separate stages—as in a three-ring circus performance—with distinctive behavior in each. A careful observer, however, detects contradictions among them. These contradictions, which have naturally impeded a smooth and well-coordinated performance, simply reflect the FSLN leaders' aims of achieving a revolution according to their own preconceptions, with little regard for other forces of society—except, of course, for tactical reasons. In more than one way, such a triple-staged approach is tantamount to the Sandinistas' wanting the best of all worlds.

On the domestic stage, the FSLN has demonstrated its disposition to reflect solely a seesaw tolerance for dissidence, keeping the private sector's future under the revolution in a state of uncertainty. Thus far, the Sandinistas' rule has been authoritarian.

On the second stage, the FSLN has endeavored to preserve normal relations with the international financial community: Sandinista Nicaragua has renegotiated an inherited foreign debt while retaining membership at the Inter-American Development Bank, the International Monetary Fund, the International Bank for Reconstruction and Development, the Central American Bank for Economic Integration and other Central American Common Market (CACM) institutions. This policy—in which the Nicaraguan regime has shown a sign of statesmanship, in sharp contrast to its narrow-minded style in domestic and foreign policies—is intended to reassure international financing sources that they should not be alarmed by the revolution.

On the third stage, Nicaragua implements a foreign policy with a sales-label of "nonalignment," while in reality it is based on an antagonism toward the United States and identification with the Soviet Union, Cuba and the PLO. Concurrently, friendly lines of communication and trade with the European and Latin American countries are being preserved. Special emphasis is given to Nicaragua's solidarity with Third World countries and liberation movements.

In summary, the FSLN seems determined simultaneously to exert authoritarianism inside Nicaragua, conduct business "as usual" with Wall Street and be a team-player of the Communist Bloc. . . .

Marxist dogmatic intolerance has undercut the base of the moral strength expected of the revolution. Such a totalitarian attitude is a child of the ill-fated decision of the FSLN's founders—continued by their followers—to choose Marxism-Leninism as their ideology. First and foremost, it reveals a lack of sophistication and a propensity for rigidity. Consequently, their ignoring, or failing to grasp, their long-oppressed people's yearning for true freedom is staggering. Those who combat them are driven by a deep-seated feeling that they were betrayed. . . .

The democrats' frustration regarding the revolution's Sovietization is twofold: it signifies both limitations of individual freedoms and the emergence of a new lifetime dictatorship. Admittedly, some of the elite's members are selfless, though fanatical, revolutionaries. However, there exist those who, lusting for sheer power, embrace communism as an opportunity and a means for becoming—as long as they are part of the "in" few—commanders or ministers. . . .

Political tensions are so polarized and intertwined with Central America's economic and social reality that economic development and social progress cannot take place unless violence is first ended. We are witnessing the waging of an ideological war, politically and militarily. Depending on who the victors in this struggle are, they will either impose a totalitarian model for all of Central America or they will open the way for a pluralistic society.

The Sandinistas committed a serious miscalculation in their inability to remain aloof from the Salvadoran insurrection, which broke out shortly after their own takeover in Managua. Their misguided and untimely involvement is perhaps one of the principal prods behind the difficulties which presently beset Nicaragua and hinder regional political stability and economic advancement. The intrusion into El Salvador made Nicaragua a controversial actor on Central America's political stage, arousing suspicions in the United States of a newly emergent regional threat. Moreover, from the moment of that intrusion a correlation was established between the radicalization of the Sandinistas and the economic deterioration in Central America. Consequently, unlike what democrats throughout the world—and particularly in Central America—had originally hoped, Nicaragua today is far from being a leader to be emulated, but rather is looked upon as a hotbed for subversion. Additionally, as a political institution, the FSLN has become hostage to constant scrutiny by its neighbors. In fact, in an atmosphere of brinkmanship, the Sandinistas have placed on themselves the responsibility for their own decision: *change or confrontation.*

The magnitude and complexity of the current Central American economic crisis is so alarming that its exacerbation for ulterior political motives cannot be anything but a crime against the people of the region. The five small, underdeveloped republics, with a combined population of 21 million, will need $23 billion in foreign capital inflows to recover by 1990 the standard of living they enjoyed in 1980. That figure exceeds total regional exports of the last four-year period or the aggregate gross domestic product of 1982.

The real rate of GNP growth has fallen from 8.1 percent in 1977 to minus 3.7 percent in 1982. Trade within the Central American Common Market has decreased in terms of value and of intraregional exports and imports as a share of total trade.

It is true that the largest countries with the strongest economic bases in Latin America, e.g., Mexico and Venezuela, have lately been in dire straits. Yet, Central America differs from them, in that political uncertainty— during these years of turmoil—bears an important share of responsibility for reductions in investment and production levels. This is largely due to "the ghost of communism looming on the horizon." It is equally true that external factors of a purely economic nature have seriously affected Central America, but there is a coincidence of rising social and political unrest with dwindling economic growth.

With the 1978 outbreak of open civil war in Nicaragua, the real growth rate of the regional GNP began to falter. By 1981, when Nicaragua's drift to the Soviet Bloc became more evident, and the guerrillas in El Salvador continued with renewed strength after the failure of their January "final offensive," this economic indicator had dropped to 1 percent.

One of the principal obstacles which the Sandinistas have encountered in the implementation of their Marxist-Leninist project in Nicaragua is the apprehension with which the other Central American countries have reacted. There is nothing strange about it. The capillary interlinking of the five republics renders it impossible for any one of them unilaterally to adopt an ideological model of society which is unacceptable and deemed a threat by the others.

Misgivings regarding Managua's regime are the more comprehensible in light of the Left's grandiose design for a unified Central America ruled by revolutionaries. A statement by the Honduran Government before the Organization of American States (OAS) is more than candid in denouncing the Sandinista government for what Honduras views as, inter alia: Nicaragua's breach of security terms in the Central American isthmus; Nicaragua's indifference to the tremendous consequences which may arise for all Central America from the creation of an "enormous" army (which is larger than the combined armed forces of all the other republics); and Nicaragua's role as a supplier of arms for subversion and terrorism.

By now, the Sandinistas must know that the days when their international prestige was founded on the image of heroic and dashing guerrilla commanders are gone. Nowadays their capacity to deserve international approval is proportionate to their respect for domestic pluralism and for human rights. For this reason, they attach great importance to public relations—and to all propaganda tools. Whenever they have applied restrictions on freedom of information or curbed the political activities of dissidents, they have faced international pressure. Subsequently, they relax their grip. Thus far, it has been akin to a trial-and-error period. However, they have gone through these political calisthenics so often that in the process their image in the Western World has been eroded, making Sandinismo appear as Somocismo revisited. Their disposition to assert their authoritarian rule is a reflection of their communist credo.

More recently, they have suffered two fiascos. One of them was the case of the Bishop of the Northern Zelaya Department. Managua publicly reported that the U.S.-born prelate had been kidnapped by Miskito counter-revolutionaries and that the government "feared for his life." A few days later the bishop appeared in Honduras at the head of more than a thousand Indians. He had voluntarily accompanied them there so as to give them spiritual comfort on their escape from Sandinista oppression.

The other case where the FSLN has seen its credibility impaired is the lack of seriousness in the decrees regarding both amnesty for dissidents and the electoral process. A close examination of those documents reveals that they are misleading, even devious. The exclusion of citizens responsible for committing acts against the state prior to December 1, 1981, leaves out the principals of the popular September 1980 Bluefields uprising against the Cuban presence in Nicaragua. Nor is it clear whether important heads of exiled political movements may return to Nicaragua to participate in the elections.

Upon my appointment as Ambassador to the United States in the spring of 1981, I was advised by the Government in Managua that relations with Washington were the keynote of our foreign policy. That parameter should have been faithfully observed. Common sense dictated that Nicaragua broaden the base of its international relations in order to achieve the wide interdependence which was imperative for its own viability as a nation-state and as a safeguard for its self-determination. Naturally, this implied retaining the respect and support of socialist governments. Wisdom also called for seeking ways to strengthen economic ties with Canada and the Arab oil-producing nations. A part of that policy might have been an adequate level of rapport with Cuba, and, to a lesser degree, with other members of the Soviet Bloc.

Notwithstanding the relevance of those ties, however, the center of Nicaragua's foreign policy continues to be the United States. Nicaragua cannot reach an effective political and security settlement with its Central American neighbors—so essential to Nicaragua—without some kind of U.S. guarantee. Furthermore, the economic and security factors are so overwhelmingly strong that it is unnecessary to discuss them.

The overriding issue in diplomatic relations between Washington and Managua is whether or not there is room for accommodation of the respective ideological beliefs. Above all, however, the issue is whether, in light of strategic considerations, an agreement will bring the two countries closer or conflict will separate them even more. From the beginning—given the misgivings of Washington about the new revolution—it was clear that the degree of tolerance on the part of the United States would be positively influenced if the revolutionary leadership appeared to be fundamentally nationalist, and negatively so if it behaved from a provocative "internationalist" posture. Unfortunately, the FSLN leaders have overlooked geographical realities and attempted, much too soon, to alter the course of Central American contemporary history. . . .

Let us call a spade a spade: There is sufficient tangible evidence that the FSLN is dominated by Marxist-Leninist influences. The Sandinistas have abundantly corroborated this by words and deeds. The ideological commitments of the leadership have a determinant bearing on the revolution's conduct, causing distress among Nicaraguans and concern among neighboring nations. There is, similarly, enough evidence concerning the Sandinistas' ties with the Communist Bloc, which are construed by the United States as a threat to regional security. Central American countries, on their part, have denounced Nicaragua for sponsoring subversion against them.

All this has boomeranged on the Sandinista regime, which is also subjected to insurgency supported by the United States, ostensibly to offset FMLN guerrilla actions against the Salvadoran reformist government, and by Honduras, which claims that it is so doing mostly as a "preventive" measure. More recently Washington justifies its backing of counter-insurgency as a pressure to bring the Sandinistas to the negotiating table. It is obvious that fear of communism's spread has reduced Central American economic activity to a state of near-paralysis. In Nicaragua, political uncertainty has divided the nation and constrained the national economy, thereby subjecting the people to deprivation.

At the present time, the FSLN is making gestures, expressing—at least formally—an intention to talk things over with its adversaries. The dissidents have manifested their willingness to hold a dialogue, in spite of their justified distrust of the Sandinistas. It seems only fair that they demand international guarantees.

Accommodation requires that both sides be willing to make some trade-offs. It would be an illusory perception of reality for the FSLN to expect the legitimate opposition to agree on unchallenged and permanent FSLN rule in exchange for some concessions. As a matter of fact, the entire initiative would be destined to fail if it is ideated solely on the basis of Sandinista "concessions." The key to the matter lies in the Sandinistas' recognition of the rights of others. The FSLN cannot hope to reach an agreement unless it is willing to accept that the perpetuation of a Marxist-Leninist system poses intolerable implications for Nicaragua as a nation and for Central America as a whole.

III
THE 1984 ELECTIONS AND AFTER

21.
DEMOCRATIC COORDINATOR: ELECTION PROGRAM
(DECEMBER 1983)

A climate of liberty and respect for citizens' rights is necessary so that the people may exercise their political rights without restrictions during the elections announced for 1985.

This electoral process can be characterized as authentic if it is carried out within the framework of guarantees that should exist before, during, and after the casting of votes. If the necessary guarantees are not granted, then the elections would be unjust, deceitful, and unfair—that is, phoney.

The current political situation requires:

I. State-party separation. A general restructuring of the state and parastate apparatus to put an end to the identifying of state and parastate organizations with the political party in power (the FSLN) and its ideology. This means transforming state organizations (such as the EPS [the Sandinist Peoples Army], PS [Sandinist Police], FAS [Sandinist Air Force], SSTV [Sistema Sandinista Television Network], etc.), which now have a political nature, into true national organizations removed from political or ideological sectarianism. It also means eliminating politics in education and other cultural activities controlled or financed by the state.

This also means breaking the economic and functional links between the state and FSLN organizations (such as the CDS [Sandinist Defense Committees], ATC [Farmworkers Association], AMNLAE [Luisa Amanda Espinoza Nicaraguan Women's Association], ANDEN [National Association of Nicaraguan Teachers], JS-19J [19 July Sandinist Youth], CST [Sandinist Workers Federation], etc.)

II. Repeal laws that violate human rights. Repeal, nullification, or reform —according to the case—of the laws that violate human rights, which were

Published in *La Prensa,* December 26, 1983.

pointed out in the studies prepared by the Permanent Committee for the Defense of Human Rights (CPDH) in October 1982 and later. Some of these laws are: Decree No. 48, the news media general law; Decree No. 1327, the Patriotic Military Service Bill; and those laws that violate the right to private property (Decree No. 759, on the confiscation of enterprises; Decree No. 760, on the confiscation of assets belonging to persons who are absent from the country more than 6 months; Decree No. 330, a law to prevent and combat decapitalization). Undue application of these decrees should be rectified and eliminated, and undue application of laws on expropriation for reasons of public utility should also be rectified and eliminated.

III. Suspension of the state of emergency. Suspension of the national state of emergency and full exercise of freedom of expression and information.

IV. Amnesty Law. Promulgation of an amnesty law pertaining to political crimes and related common crimes.

V. Respect for freedom of worship. Full respect for freedom of worship and the exercise of the churches' ethical and religious principles.

VI. Labor union freedom. Repeal, nullification, or reform—according to the case—of the laws that restrict full exercise of labor union freedom. The right to strike and to free collective contracts should be established, and the ILO agreements signed by Nicaragua must be respected.

VII. Autonomy of the judicial branch. The full return of jurisdictional function and independence of the judicial branch.

VIII. Habeas corpus on unconstitutionality appeals. To give to the fundamental statute and to the statute on rights and guarantees of Nicaraguans the unalterable importance appropriate to constitutions, and also to eliminate clause 1 of the habeas corpus law (Decree No. 417), to allow writs of habeas corpus on the basis of appeals of unconstitutionality.

IX. National dialogue on the call for elections. The holding of a national dialogue among all the political parties and movements, including those in arms, under the auspices and guarantees of the Contadora Group, for the purpose of agreeing on the form and content of a call for election of representatives to a national constituent assembly. These elections would be supervised by either the Contadora Group or the OAS.

Fundamental points of this call should be:

1. The fixing of the election date in January 1985.
2. Guarantees that the constitution to be promulgated will have a Western democratic nature, as conceived in the original program of the government of the revolution. This should also be expressed in the draft constitution that must be prepared by the State Council according to Article 18 of the fundamental statute, by means of a basic law that should function

as a mandate from the people to their representatives in that assembly, and which should list the powers of the assembly. For the purpose of guaranteeing the democratic nature of the new constitution, it is appropriate and necessary that the basic law and the draft constitution take into consideration the following points:

a. A republican, democratic, and representative state.
b. Independence of the legislative, executive, and judicial branches.
c. Election of supreme and municipal authorities every 5 years by direct and secret universal suffrage and through the electoral quotient system.
d. Full guarantees for human rights in accordance with the American Convention of Human Rights.
e. Full municipal autonomy.
f. Ensuring of an apolitical nature and professionalism in the Armed Forces, which must be subordinate to the civilian authority.
g. Separation of the army and the police.
h. Regulations pertaining to the administrative and judicial profession.
i. A prohibition on presidential reelection.

3. Deadlines for the promulgation of the new constitution and for the holding of elections for national and municipal authorities.
4. Another objective of the dialogue should be reaching an agreement that at the time of its installation the national constituent assembly will appoint a pluralist provisional government junta that will hold executive power during that interregnum with the powers established by the assembly.
5. There should also be dialogue on the provisions that should be included in the electoral law that will be in effect only for the election of representatives to the national constituent assembly and that should guarantee free operation of the political parties within the broadest spirit of democratic pluralism, free elections, effective suffrage based on trustworthy electoral lists, and the organization and operation of the electoral organization free from all pressure.

Some of those essential provisions would be the following:

a. A direct, secret, personal, and nondelegable vote (Article 20 of the American Declaration of the Rights and Duties of Man).
b. Minimum age of 18 to exercise the right to vote, and minimum age of 25 to be elected.
c. The right of parties to form coalitions for the elections and the obligation of parties to present, along with their lists of candidates, the lists of their national and departmental boards of directors elected democratically by the vote of their respective party assemblies or conventions.
d. Composition and powers of the Supreme Electoral Tribunal, departmen-

tal tribunals, and electoral directorates, and the qualifications of their members.

e. Cantonal division carried out by the departmental electoral tribunals.

f. Method of preparing the electoral registry and date for registration in it.

g. Equal guarantees for all parties in disseminating electoral propaganda in the state media.

h. Creation of an electoral police under the electoral directors during the electoral process.

i. Preparation of locations that will guarantee the casting of secret votes; supplying of appropriate and trustworthy ballot boxes and uniform ballots with clear distinction between the names of the parties, and their emblems and colors.

j. Control of the voters through indelible ink marks after identification is confirmed on the electoral list.

k. Regulations on the cantonal, departmental, and national vote count; an immediate telegraph report to the Supreme Electoral Tribunal; copies to all the parties of the proclamation of the results within a rational period of time; and a method to challenge the results.

l. General provisions, crimes against the exercise of suffrage and electoral freedom, and associated penalties.

We believe that implementation of these and/or similar foundations could create sufficient confidence in the electoral process that is to be initiated, even though we are aware that the topic is obviously not exhausted with these legal-political suggestions. We understand that a great deal of work must be undertaken to overcome resentment, impatience to win, and totalitarian temptation. We are also aware that no matter how many legal procedures are established, they will be of no use if the human heart and mind do not plan to honestly fulfill them.

May God illuminate and bless us all to enable us to achieve the longed-for peaceful solution to the national crisis.

FOR THE DEMOCRATIC UNIONS:

Central Organization of Nicaraguan Workers (CTN)

Confederation for Trade Union Unity (CUS)

FOR THE DEMOCRATIC POLITICAL PARTIES:

Democratic Conservative Party (PCD)

Social Christian Party (PSC)

Social Democratic Party (PSD)

Authentic Popular Social Christian Party

[Partido Popular Social Cristiano Autentico—PPSCA]

FOR THE COSEP:

Nicaraguan Chamber of Industries (CADIN)

Nicaraguan Chamber of Construction

National Confederation of Professional Associations (CONAPRO)

Confederation of Chambers of Commerce of Nicaragua

Nicaraguan Institute of Development (INDE)

Agricultural and Livestock Producers Union of Nicaragua (UPANIC)

22.
NICARAGUAN CHURCH: PASTORAL LETTER (APRIL 1984)

Our country, too, is plagued by a belligerent situation pitting Nicaraguan against Nicaraguan, and the consequences of this situation could not be sadder:

- Many Nicaraguan youths and men are dying on the battlefields.
- Many others look toward the future with the fear of seeing their own lives prematurely ended.
- A materialistic and atheistic educational system is undermining the consciences of our children.
- Many families are divided by political differences.
- The suffering of mothers who have lost their children, which should merit our great respect, is instead exploited to incite hatred and feed the desire for vengeance.
- Farmworkers and Indians, for whom the Church reserves a special love, are suffering, living in constant anxiety, and many of them are forced to abandon their homes in search of a peace and tranquility that they do not find.
- Some of the mass media, using the language of hate, encourage a spirit of violence.

One, albeit small, sector of our Church has abandoned ecclesiastical unity and surrendered to the tenets of a materialistic ideology. This sector sows confusion inside and outside Nicaragua through a campaign extolling its own ideas and defaming the legitimate pastors and the faithful who follow them. Censorship of the media makes it impossible to clarify the positions and offer other points of view.

Signed by nine bishops on the occasion of Easter, April 22, 1984.

Foreign powers take advantage of our situation to encourage economic and ideological exploitation. They see us as support for their power, without respect for our persons, our history, our culture, and our right to decide our own destiny.

Consequently, the majority of the Nicaraguan people live in fear of their present and uncertainty of their future. They feel deep frustration, clamor for peace and freedom. Yet their voices are not heard, muted by belligerent propaganda on all sides. . . .

The road to social peace is possible through dialogue, sincere dialogue that seeks truth and goodness. "That [dialogue] must be a meaningful and generous offer of a meeting of good intentions and not a possible justification for continuing to foment dissension and violence." (John Paul II, Greeting to Nicaragua, March 4, 1983)

It is dishonest to constantly blame internal aggression and violence on foreign aggression.

It is useless to blame the evil past for everything without recognizing the problems of the present.

All Nicaraguans inside and outside the country must participate in this dialogue, regardless of ideology, class, or partisan belief. Furthermore, we think that Nicaraguans who have taken up arms against the Government must also participate in this dialogue. If not, there will be no possibility of a settlement, and our people, especially the poorest among them, will continue to suffer and die.

The dialogue of which we speak is not a tactical truce to strengthen positions for further struggle but a sincere effort to seek appropriate solutions to the anguish, pain, exhaustion, and fatigue of the many, many people who long for peace, the many, many people who want to live, to rise from the ashes, to see the warmth of a smile on a child's face, far from terror, in a climate of democratic harmony. . . .

23.
BAYARDO ARCE: SECRET SPEECH ON STRATEGY AND TACTICS (MAY 1984)

Good morning, comrades. In the first place, I should like to convey the greetings of the Sandinista Front to this meeting of the central committee of the Partido Socialista Nicaraguense [Nicaraguan Socialist Party (PSN)].

Speech before the Political Committee of the Nicaraguan Socialist Party. From *La Vanguardia,* July 31, 1984.

In a recent meeting we had with the leaders of the PSN on the focus that we Communists should give the electoral process, the idea emerged that we could explain to you directly our idea of the electoral process and also advance a few of the more in-depth strategic ideas we have begun to discuss in the National Directorate of the Sandinista Front.

I believe that, in order to better understand our approach, it is important to understand our position. We believe that during the course of the Nicaraguan revolutionary process we have had the weakness, for a number of reasons, of still not having achieved the unity of our entire people, particularly of the revolutionary militants.

We consider that our country is living in a state of war, which though not formally declared, has been declared on a *de facto* basis. A war, furthermore, forced on us by the biggest imperialist power, which, since 1980, has been acquiring a series of characteristics, a series of manifestations governed by our capability of being able to influence its course.

Yesterday in a working meeting we tried to make a comprehensive assessment of our situation. We saw that U.S. military intervention, which is the strongest action the Reagan policy could take against us, would be possible if the United States succeeded in consolidating four factors.

First, if there were a large degree of domestic breakdown in Nicaragua. In other words, if the reactionary forces were organized, if substantial progress were made in sowing confusion among the people so that we would not be in a state of domestic discord, a civil war at home.

Second, we saw that the other factor was to see whether the regional countries, particularly our neighboring countries, Costa Rica, Honduras, and El Salvador, might offer optimum conditions for becoming a launching pad for aggression against Nicaragua. Indeed, just using the seas is not feasible, aircraft carriers are not enough, landing craft are not enough. All that is too limited.

Third, we looked at the international situation, which also includes the domestic situation in the United States. We therefore talked of four factors, because we make a distinction. Had the U.S. managed to have the international community, well, not support the policy of the Reagan government but just remain indifferent to the impact that policy is having in Central America, that would have had repercussions right away inside the United States in the way of greater indifference toward our problems. Naturally, that situation would have determined the likelihood of intervention, which is the most the U.S. can do to us after what it has already done.

Ever since we were confronted with this state of war, we have been following a two-way strategy. On the one side, confrontation with aggression of the type we are experiencing. On the other, the development of the construction of socialism consistent with the war setting we find ourselves in.

We believe that the fact that we are approaching the fifth anniversary of the triumph of the revolution free of the most effective means of destruction imperialism could bring into play, which is intervention, and the fact that we still retain strong international support, are still achieving some degree of domestic neutralization in the U.S., are still keeping the Central American countries from being converted into launching pads for aggression against our land, and, despite all the calamities brought upon us by the state of war, have still avoided any deep division from occurring among our own people (any other type of division does not interest us), this has been an important achievement of the revolution.

This interval has enabled us to move ahead in strategic ways. When we say move ahead in strategic ways, we mean that we have already turned over more than 700,000 *manzanas* [1 manzana equals 1.7 acres] of land to the peasants. We have turned rural credit around, we have successfully begun to promote cooperatives, and, coupled with that, are working in terms of an agro-industrial development which, in our judgment, is the hub of socialist transformation of our society.

Agro-industry for us is the same as metallurgy or energy for other countries. We have no choice but to process what we produce. And, as discussed a great deal by us, a number of agro-industrial investment projects will, within a few years, change the face of our country's economy.

But all of this is linked to the elections for one simple reason. We think the electoral process, which we announced and committed ourselves to as part of the program of the revolution, was and continues being an offensive tool from the standpoint of confronting U.S. policy. Intervention was at the point of occurring when we were struggling against the dictatorship. You are all aware that an American proposal to send a peace force here, to Nicaragua, was discussed in the Organization of American States in June 1979. Its purpose was to prevent a revolutionary triumph and to seek a manipulated triumph—in fact not even that, but a manipulated way out for the dictator. And, furthermore, we were directly threatened by the United States, which, as you will surely recall, began to establish bases in Costa Rica, surrounded our country with ships, and also began to establish bases elsewhere in Central America to give it the capability to influence the dynamics of our struggle against the Somoza dictatorship.

Against that background, we thus launched what we called the program of national reconstruction. As part of that program we spoke of bringing about revolutionary change based on three principles which made us presentable in the international context and which, as far as we were concerned, were manageable from the revolutionary standpoint.

Those principles were non-alignment abroad, a mixed economy, and political pluralism. With those three elements we kept the international community from going along with American policy in Nicaragua, in fact, we got a number of governments of various tendencies to back the position of Nicaragua, the position of the Sandinista Front and of the revolutionary forces.

Of course, once defined in specific terms, this imposed certain commitments. One was that we said we were going to elect a constituent assembly, that we were going to have elections. While we might view those commitments as negative, if we analyze our revolution in black and white, we still consider them to be positive at this time. Of course, if we did not have the war situation imposed on us by the United States, the electoral problem would be totally out of place in terms of its usefulness. What a revolution really needs is the power to act. The power to act is precisely what constitutes the essence of the dictatorship of the proletariat—the ability of the [working] class to impose its will by using the means at hand [without] bourgeois formalities.

For us, then, the elections, viewed from that perspective, are a nuisance, just as a number of things that make up the reality of our revolution are a nuisance.

But from a realistic standpoint, being in a war with the United States, those things become weapons of the revolution to move forward the construction of socialism. Furthermore, for us it is useful, for example, to be able to display an entrepreneurial class and private production in the mixed economy system we promulgated, while we move ahead in strategic ways. The important thing is that the entrepreneurial class no longer controls all the means to reproduce itself. It no longer controls the banks, foreign trade, or the source of foreign exchange. Therefore, any investment project in our country belongs to the State. The bourgeoisie no longer invests—it subsists.

In the future of our country, all change through development is in the hands of the revolutionary authority. That is well, just as it is well to be able to call elections and take away from American policy one of its justifications for aggression against Nicaragua, because the other two factors cannot be conceded.

Imperalism asks three things of us: to abandon interventionism, to abandon our strategic ties with the Soviet Union and the socialist community, and to be democratic. We cannot cease being internationalists unless we cease being revolutionaries.

We cannot discontinue strategic relationships unless we cease being revolutionaries. It is impossible even to consider this.

Yet the superstructure aspects, democracy as they call it, bourgeois democracy, has an element which we can manage and even derive advantages from for the construction of socialism in Nicaragua. What are those advantages, what was it we explained to the party leadership? The main thing about the elections, as far as we are concerned, is the drafting of the new constitution. That is the important thing. The new constitution will allow us to shape the juridical and political principles for the construction of socialism in Nicaragua.

We are using an instrument claimed by the bourgeoisie, which disarms the international bourgeoisie, in order to move ahead in matters that for us are strategic. On the one hand, it allows us to neutralize the aggressiveness of imperialism, while on the other it is going to provide us with a tool for moving ahead on substantive aspects of our revolution.

In saying this, we, the Sandinistas Front, are indicating that we cannot go into the elections with a pink flag in order to make a red constitution. That would weaken us and would create new international pressure on us. That means that the program the Sandinista Front is going to take into the elections is a more radical one—one that may be expressed in the constitution. But more so in implementing actions, which have their dynamics apart from whatever is said. We are getting things done.

This new juridical framework will enable us to move at a new, more dynamic pace, and that is the advantage we think we can get out of the electoral process. In that context—that the elections are going to enable us to be clearer in a number of things—we wondered what role the forces that have been called the allied forces were going to play. We cannot assess those forces with the same yardstick. For us, as we have told the leaders of the Nicaraguan Socialist Party and showed them in practice, our relationship with the Socialist Party is not the same as with the Popular Social Christian Party or with the Independent Liberal Party (PLI).

There is an ideological concept at the heart of the matter in such relations. Even the Independent Liberal Party, because of ideology, was gradually attracted and is virtually on the side of the right, regardless of the personal quality of some of its men.

The Popular Social Christian Party is a weak party and the Socialist Party a Marxist-Leninist party. We therefore have to approach each one from the angle of principles. We wondered what the purpose would be in encouraging the Socialist Party, for example, to run alone in the elections. But under what flag? That is one question we asked ourselves. To show there was pluralism; that is one factor that has been useful until now—to be able to say there are 11 parties here. Because we were operating in the absence of constitutionality, there was no law, nothing that allowed you to say, well, here is our revolutionary institutionality. All there was, was the determination of the Sandinista Front which was going to be expressed by the existence or non-existence of different political forces. But now the situation has changed.

[We propose] including a certain number of Socialist Party candidates for the national assembly on the ballot which the Sandinista Front is going to submit. We say to our colleagues that for practical reasons but most of all on principle—a more strategic perspective—we could not agree to having the ballot of the revolution bear the emblems of the three parties. And we told the Popular Social Christian Party the same thing, because if they run alone they will disappear.

For practical reasons and a little bit because this is the quickest explanation, our people would become confused by a three-flag notion (even though we have made progress in the political-ideological aspect and in the cultural aspect). With that business of putting three flags on the ballot people would not know who they were voting for. It is logical for them to vote for the red and black flag. Yet, more substantively—and we should discuss this strategically—what does a vote for Sandinismo mean under these circumstances? Imperialism is not attacking the Patriotic Front of the Revolution; it is not attacking parties. Imperalism says that Sandinismo means totalitarianism, Sandinismo means Marxism-Leninism, Sandinismo means the spread of Soviet-Cuban influence, Sandinismo is an imposition on the Nicaraguan people.

We believe that the elections should be used in order to vote for Sandinismo, which is being challenged and stigmatized by imperialism, in order to be able to demonstrate that, in any event, the Nicaraguan people are for that totalitarianism, the Nicaraguan people are for Marxism-Leninism. Contrary to what they did in Chile, here they are not going to be able to reverse the vote by force because the people also have the ability to exercise such force.

We are not the ones who, by international manipulation, converted Sandinismo into the symbol of those interests, of those factors in the world revolution. That was done by imperialism. We have not declared ourselves Marxist-Leninists publicly and officially, we get along without definition. The United States did us the favor of saying who we are and tried to frighten the whole world. But they failed. So now, what ideological value do we see in the electoral process?

The people will ratify, in a bourgeois-type exercise, this Sandinismo, which is totalitarianism, which is Marxism, which is the end of freedom, which means the spread of Soviet-Cuban influence, which is everything that gobbles up little children.

Hence, we contend that the ballot must be headed by one banner, the red and black emblem, that it should represent a vote for Sandinismo. Now, just what is Sandinismo, what has it been in the past and will actually be for a long time to come?

Sandinismo is not just militancy in the Sandinista Front. Sandinismo has been a revolutionary policy dominated by the Sandinista Front, because it has succeeded in maintaining a framework of national unity in order to move ahead in the transformation of this nation. We told our comrades that we would include on our ballot non-Sandinista entrepreneurs, because our ballot would stand for the hegemony of the Sandinista Front which will also guarantee the new constitution and national unity. We will include everybody. That is the reality of our revolution in coping with imperialism.

The comrades raised the point, quite properly, that this might dilute the image, even the identity of the Socialist Party, contending that for all practical purposes it would not appear as a separate entity. We suggested two ways to retain that identity. First, for the deputies who belong to the Socialist Party (or representatives, I do not know what they will be called, I call them deputies because that is their name everywhere, and there is no need to fear the word), for the candidates to the assembly who belong to the Socialist Party, the candidates on the ballot, to run as Socialist Party candidates. Moreover, in individual campaigning that will have to be done on their behalf—because there will have to be individual campaign advertising for each one—identify them as members of the Socialist Party.

But that is a short-term proposal. Here we get into a more substantive item, which in part was what led the political committee of the party to invite us here to talk. In November, a government will be elected in Nicaragua. Furthermore, an assembly will be elected that is going to write a new constitution, establish the political-juridical principles for progress in the construction of socialism. None of that is going to bring a stop to the U.S. war; that will go on, except that we will be given a new tool, for by then we will be legal.

The same thing is going to happen to us as to the couple who had been living together for 10 years and had a bunch of children, but it was not until they got married that their parents said, OK, you can come home to visit now. We are soon going to be legally married and gain a little more recognition. In that context, then, we ask, do we have strategic differences with the Socialist Party or does the Socialist Party have them with us? With that approach, we see that the matter is more substantive and we would ask our comrades whether the time has not come to make the Party of the Revolution stronger, to gradually form a single party. Why are we Communists going to be putting on different shirts if real, concrete socialism is being constructed through the strategy of power of the Sandinista Front?

We thus urge the party, for this is still not a decision for us to make (we have begun to discuss it), but urge you also to discuss the matter—whether we decide after the elections to drop the fiction of a Marxist-Leninist Socialist Party on the one side and on the other those of the Sandinista Front who have not yet changed labels. The problem of identity in the electoral process becomes absolutely secondary. What is the difference whether you have separate status or not in the electoral process if it is already perfectly clear what the strategic goal is from the viewpoint of the forces governing the society. We can [not] talk with the Eli Altamirano people [Communist Party of Nicaragua (PCdeN)] because our ideas are not the same. Nor can we talk with the Popular Social Christian Party because, in another area, our ideas are different. We cannot reach an understanding, strategically speaking.

We see the elections as one more weapon of the revolution to bring its historical objectives gradually into reality. Therefore, we intend to take advantage of them; first, to wage a political-ideological indoctrinary campaign among the people. We must raise the revolutionary consciousness of the people. Second, we are going to use the outcome to legitimize the revolution insofar as what it has done thus far, is doing now, and will continue to do in the future.

We are even trying to avoid changing appearances, let alone substance, in order to prevent confusion. Let the people vote for agrarian reform, which will continue. Let them vote for everything that has been done in the revolution, for literacy, adult education, confiscations, nationalization of the banks and foreign trade, free education, the Soviet and Cuban military advisers, the internationalism of the revolution. Let them vote for all that. That is the reality of our revolution and everything we have done has that dynamic behind it.

The most important thing, once again, is to be able afterward to write a constitution legitimized by the exercise of the ballot, which will allow us to say, "Here is our law." Up until now, with power exercised by decree, they come along and pressure us, even over a prisoner. The governing junta has issued some 100,000 decrees. A lot of ballpoint pens have been used for signing decrees.

There must be a continuing, stable legal framework. When we govern by decree, we are more subject to pressures, but when we have a legal framework nobody is going to tell a country to change its constitution. This will give us more stability, for what is vital to the revolution. It is vital to survive and advance. It is vital for us to defeat the anti-Nicaraguan policy of the United States.

The war will not end on November 4 or on January 10. The war will continue with or without Reagan; it may take on other forms but it will go on. What we are going to do is arm ourselves better in order to continue to develop and to cope with it.

From that angle, what then is important and strategic for the revolution? To be able to unite all forces and concentrate them on the primary considerations. We are a single force. Why use an activist of the Front and another of the Socialist Party on the same business? Why run an activist of the Front and another of the Socialist Party in the same district? We believe the elections compel us to think about these things.

We have a discussion pending with your political committee to work on three issues that will come up, as I understand it, in the meeting of the central committee. One, the idea of putting an end to all this artifice of pluralism—Socialist, Communist, Social Christian, Social Democratic parties, etc.—which has been useful thus far. That is over. And we are going to work to determine the direction of the revolution. That is one issue which would determine how we go into the elections, whether we run on the same ballot.

Even though still not valid, by common analysis, we insist that running together without alliances will have the least effect on the awareness of the masses. I still fail to understand what banner other than ours the Socialist Party could run under. If it becomes more radical it will be with Eli Altamirano; if less radical, with the Independent Liberal Party. That is our assessment.

Thus far in our discussions, held with their usual openness, we have no differences. Our strategic allies tell us not to declare ourselves Marxist-Leninists, not to declare socialism. Here and in Rome, we know, we've talked about this being the first experience of building socialism with the dollars of capitalism.

From that angle we do not see much difference. The other thing is that if, by your own decision, by the sovereign decision of the Socialist Party, you decide to run alone, we would then have to discuss the programs we are going to debate in order to avoid confusing the people.

We wanted to have that discussion with the Independent Liberal Party, but they actually believe they have 60% of the votes and have begun to place themselves in an integrated situation. . . . We have not yet started up our electoral machinery, we have other problems right now: patriotic military service [compulsory military conscription], the BIRs [reserve infantry battalions], the militias, the war. We have not begun to operate in terms of the internal political debate. This is causing a little friction, people who are reluctant but do not believe they are. . . . We still have not worked the *turbas* [Sandinista mobs], as they say, because it is not yet time.

Our job right now is to concentrate all our forces in the military effort, but later we will have to get into this as well. The important thing, if we are going to debate at all, is to clarify how we are going to debate. We believe that between the Nicaraguan Socialist Party and the Sandinista Front, strategically there is nothing to debate. We must take advantage of the change offered by the elections to gain other positive benefits: the unity of the Marxist-Leninists of Nicaragua.

24.
VIRGILIO GODOY: NICARAGUA, A COUNTRY OF
SHORTAGES (AUGUST 1984)

In his Saturday speech at La Trinidad, Godoy attacked the FSLN's monopoly on political information. "The government party has two newspapers, two television stations, and more than twenty radio stations subsidized by the Front." Perhaps, for the first time in five years, you will hear people in Nicaragua who think differently because, even at this point, there are weak spots in that monopoly, affirmed Godoy. Then he assured listeners that the Independent Liberal Party (PLI) advocates peace among Nicaraguans; but not the kind of peace advocated by others "while they arm themselves to the teeth." Godoy pointed out that Nicaragua "needs peace. But that peace does not require tanks or airports to be honored."

"Redefine your path," urged Godoy, addressing those who retain power unlawfully, "or there will be no choice but to return to exile someday when it will be said that it was the saviors who destroyed the country."

Subsequently, Godoy attacked Minister of Commerce Dionisio Marenco's Saturday statements that Nicaraguans face five more years of serious shortages.

Godoy added, "it is no longer possible to obtain painkillers and blood serum for hospitals. There are no shoe soles, no automobile spare parts, no rice, no beef, no beans. In fact, the shortages should be commemorated with a monument, because they have converted Nicaragua into a country of 'have-nots,' " said the speaker.

He stressed that the government dares not mention progress in the health field, because "presently fatalities due to lack of appropriate medical attention are on the rise, nor do they dare speak about education, because children have no school supplies. But they dare do other things." He then criticized the recently concluded 1984 Nicaragua Music Festival. "Not even the Romans dared go that far. They handed out bread at circus performances. Here in Nicaragua we only get the circus part. There is no money and no foreign currency," concluded Godoy. "But there are 450 guests, in top-rate Managuan hotels, living at your expense." . . .

La Prensa, August 28, 1984, p. 5. Translation copyright © 1986 by Gladys Segal.

25.
HUGO SPADAFORA: A PROBLEM OF IMAGE
(DECEMBER 1984)

Nicaraguans in exile, including some of those "leading" the war, residents of Nicaraguan cities and international public opinion have the idea that the war is not being won and that time is on the side of the communist dictatorship. However, those fighting within Nicaragua and the peasants in general hold a different opinion. How can this difference be explained? More importantly, who is right?. . .

[U]nlike the war against Somoza, this war . . . is predominantly a peasant insurrection. This is why the cities, at least in the initial stages, play a modest role.

Under a totalitarian regime of the left or the right, the cities are virtually turned into large concentration camps, with "state security," "defense committees," "turbas," etc., disguised as watchdogs. One needn't be very clever to realize why urban Nicaraguans don't share the same optimism of their campesino compatriots. When all that one sees and suffers is repression and fear, it is natural that discouragement grows.

The Nicaraguans in exile and international public opinion, on the other hand, are the victims of a double information block which keeps the urban people misinformed about the reality of the war inside Nicaragua. On one side, the propaganda, the misinformation and blockade, obvious and foreseen, handled by the communist dictatorship, which tries to lessen the nature and dimension of the real situation of the armed struggle that we democrats are carrying out in the plains and mountains.

Less obvious and predictable is the blockade and disinformation suffered by the war by the part of the great western media and by the same leaders, many in exile, which "lead" the war. . . .

The press seeks and covers the handful of top leaders, who can . . . easily be found, falling into the trap of believing that in that way they understand and catch the realities of the war. . . .

The result of the anomalous situation is disastrous. The fights within the leadership and between the organizations are known in detail, great emphasis is placed on the accusations of "betrayal" and on the reiterated commands—later revoked—of the "cease fires," etc.; all carried out in spectacular press conferences far removed from the theater of war. . . .

Open letter from Hugo Spadafora

It is understandable then, why the image of the war that Nicaraguans in exile and in the cities, as well as international public opinion have, is distorted.

It is also understandable, but not justified, why certain leaders are pessimistic and mistakenly believe in negotiations with the dictatorship or in a U.S. invasion, as more feasible means for resolving the political-military conflict.

26.
CARLOS ANDRÉS PÉREZ: REGRETS TO DANIEL ORTEGA (JANUARY 1985)

Mr. President Elect and Friend:

. . . As you and my other friends in the Sandinista Front directorate are aware, I have followed passionately, as a Latin American and a democrat, the process of the Sandinista revolution. I have continually expressed my unwavering satisfaction for and support of all the different stages of the process. My only aspiration and purpose has been to help free Nicaragua from the abominable Somocista dictatorship, and to win back the liberty and dignity of the Nicaraguan people, who have suffered so much shame and vexation throughout their martyred history.

We Latin Americans were jubilant in our celebration of the triumph of the Sandinista revolution. Two months after the victory I was invited by the national reconstruction junta and by the Sandinista directorate to deliver the Nicaraguan flag that Commander Eden Pastora had left with me, as I was then president of Venezuela. This flag was a patriotic trophy, taken during the heroic capture of the Nicaraguan Legislative Palace, a victory that freed valiant members of the Sandinista movement and, at the same time, demonstrated to the world the valor and drive of the Nicaraguan fighters.

My last visit to Managua was on Feb. 20, 1984, when I participated in the ceremonies marking the 50th anniversary of the death of General Augusto César Sandino. I was honored to be invited to the State Council's rostrum when an election date and plans to draw up electoral laws were announced. From that rostrum, I expressed my solidarity and confidence in the statements made by the Council's president. He reaffirmed the basic principles of the revolution: the pledge to carry out an electoral process

---

Letter from the former president of Venezuela and vice-president of the Socialist International.

with the participation—with equal conditions and opportunities—of all political sectors.

The next day, Feb. 21, in the Plaza de la Revolución, we heard from your own lips in the mass rally the most solid ratification of those goals. And that same day, at a private meeting that the European and Latin American guests at the ceremony held with you, we heard you state, in terms even more categorical than those expressed in public, your determination to carry out an electoral process with the broadest guarantees. These were pledges that we received enthusiastically, and repeated widely.

Without attempting to play down the importance of the electoral process of Nov. 4, 1984, in which you were elected president, those of us who believe we have done so much for the Sandinista revolution feel cheated, because sufficient guarantees were not provided to assure the participation of all political forces. Sadly, the limiting in this way of true political pluralism weakened the credibility of the elections.

These are the considerations that lead me today to decline your cordial invitation to attend the ceremonies on Jan. 10, 1985. Nevertheless, it concerns me that the public statement of my position could appear to justify the shameless intervention and the military aggression against Nicaragua.

I accept this clear risk because I sincerely believe that my gesture and my words are positive contributions. They are a call for reflection on the part of the Sandinista Liberation Front, and particularly on your own part now that you occupy the highest post in the republic. They are a call to reflect upon what the Latin American democracies and the rest of the world hoped for from that great revolution of all the Nicaraguan people: Political pluralism, a mixed economy and a nonaligned position—as the revolution pledged—conveying the true wishes of its people.

My conduct is not moved by any fear to face the criticism from those to whom we have been defending the Nicaraguan revolutionary process— those who wish to corral us into the false trap of communism and anti-communism. I protest and reject any attempted justification for another foreign intervention. Nor do I defend the Nicaraguan democrats who with the open support of the U.S. government, take the shortcut of armed violence when there still are possibilities for dialogue and understanding.

The electoral process is a positive development. The Nicaraguan people participated in an election, despite the limited options. It is one step toward a democratic system.

Wide possibilities are opening up for a political solution with the partici- pation of all the sectors of the Nicaraguan population. The example that President José Napoleón Duarte gave when he accepted dialogue in El Salvador is relevant to the current Nicaraguan picture. It is very significant that Nicaragua is about to draw up a proposed national constitution that could allow for open dialogue among all the representative sectors of the Nicaraguan nation.

I am confident that the efforts of the Contadora group will culminate in the coming months with the signing of the cooperation and peace accord. This will put an end to the disquieting Cuban-Soviet presence in Nicaragua and that of the U.S. armed forces in Honduras, which are both threatening to turn the Latin American process toward sovereignty and self-determination into an East-West war. In this way, Contadora will pave the way toward ending the war along the Nicaraguan borders and, at the same time, will create the right conditions for understanding and normalization of democracy for the fraternal and long-suffering Nicaraguan fatherland.

The Nicaraguan people, I am sure, do not want a North American intervention or an alliance with the Soviet bloc. I continue to express confidence that at this stage of the Sandinista revolution, under your presidency, you will follow paths that definitively and authentically clear up the confusion and doubts surrounding the goals of the Nicaraguan revolution, which fall within the framework that the revolution itself defined.

Your friend,

Carlos Andrés Pérez

27.
PRESIDENT DANIEL ORTEGA: INAUGURATION SPEECH (JANUARY 1985)

More than 40% of agricultural producers are organized in UNAG (Unión Nacional de Agricultores y Ganaderos—National Union of Farmers and Cattlemen). Young people, women, children, the handicapped, intellectuals, artists, journalists, professionals, technicians, artisans, the small and medium-sized industrialists are also organized into their respective unions and organizations. Today, the dreams of Sandino and Carlos[1] have been made a reality through the Literacy Campaign, the adult education programs, the multiplying of Popular Education Centers, with more than a million Nicaraguans studying. Also, 218 private educational centers—the majority religious in nature—have been subsidized. Today, the dreams of Sandino and Carlos[1] have been made a reality in the lives of the people who through intensive health programs have been able to reduce infant mortal-

---

[1]Carlos Fonseca Amador.

ity from 121 infants per thousand, in 1979, to 75.2 in 1984. This represents an increase in life expectancy at birth from 52.9 years in 1979 to 59.8 in 1985.

The implementation of the revolutionary program has meant supporting a system of mixed economy in the interests of the large majorities with an increasingly fair distribution of wealth, with 60% of the GNP in the private sector and 40% in the state sector. The private sector participates in primary activities with an average of 75% of the total, in secondary activities with 60% and in tertiary with 50%. Furthermore, 46 firms operate in our country with foreign capital from other Central American countries, Holland, the United States, Japan, Panama and the United Kingdom among others. At the same time, six large joint investment projects have been undertaken with capital from three countries.

Political pluralism has already been legally institutionalized through the Law of Political Parties, the Supreme Electoral Council and the Assembly of Political Parties. The right to pluralism was exercised by the people in the elections of November 4, 1984, when for the first time in Nicaraguan history, seven political parties of the most varied political and ideological strains participated. Human Rights are a specific concern of the Revolution and this has led it to establish, among other things, a prison system aimed at reintegrating the inmate in society. The modernization of the legal system is progressing, more than six major pardons have been granted and an amnesty has been decreed so that citizens who have been involved in counterrevolutionary activities can be reintegrated into society. More than 1,500 Nicaraguans have responded to this decree.

Freedom of the press has been demonstrated in Nicaragua by the access that workers have to the media which previously was the monopoly of the liberal-conservative oligarchy. This has not meant denying the existence of traditional means of communication, but has extended participation in the media to all sectors of the country.

The dreams of Sandino and Carlos have also been materialized in the efforts made on the Atlantic Coast where the Revolution has built the first highway linking Atlantic and Pacific coasts, simultaneously bringing improvements in infrastructure and social services to this region, respecting their culture and customs.

Nightmares have assailed these dreams; the same phantoms and the same horrors that have assailed Nicaragua since the last century and which enthroned oppressive regimes which had sold out to foreign powers. Once again, the attacks originated in the same country from which Walker's filibusters came to bloody Nicaragua in 1854 and from which the Marines came in 1912, until 1934 when they put Somoza in power, after assassinating Zeledón and Sandino. The nightmares keep coming to Nicaragua, sent by the U.S. rulers who were unable to foster democracy in more than a century of rule during which its neocolonial policies claimed more than 100,000 victims.

Since December 1972, when the earthquake occurred in Managua, until the end of 1984, as a result of the war of liberation, of the floods, of the present U.S. war of aggression and the earthquake itself, in twelve years our country has suffered the irreparable loss of 66,857 people among a total population that hardly exceeds three million.

During the same period and due to the same causes, we have suffered material losses in the sum of $3.9 billion; losses suffered by an economy that was hardly able to export an annual average of $400 million during these years.

More than $100 million have been appropriated by the United States Government to subsidize CIA-directed terrorist activities. The war of aggression alone which tries to destroy our people's just aspirations, has claimed a total of 7,698 victims in four years; 2,767 have been assassinated, including 132 children under 12 years of age, 48 women, 705 peasants and 152 technicians and professionals. Of the total of victims, 3,213 have been men and women younger than 21 years of age.

The North American people's money has been invested in order to incur material losses in the economy of the Nicaraguan people, amounting to more than $1 billion, with the mercenaries destroying centers of production, schools, health centers, bridges, fishing boats, fuel depots, machinery and construction equipment.

A truly dramatic situation has been inflicted on the people of Nicaragua by a war which the U.S. rulers promote militarily, politically and economically. These rulers today insist on demanding an even larger budget from the North American people to continue the bloodbath in Nicaragua. . . .

Since July 19, 1979, we have implemented a foreign policy within the framework of non-alignment and from this position we aspire to maintain good relations with all nations. For this reason, we will continue to make every effort necessary towards normalizing relations with all Central American nations. No Central American country should allow itself to be fooled into believing that Nicaragua represents a threat against them. Nicaragua will never be an aggressor.

Those who are determined to destroy the Nicaraguan Revolution are those who have conjured up the fallacy of the revolution without borders, of the alleged arms race and of the lack of democracy in Nicaragua. With these fallacies, they try to justify the imperialist policy which has been manifested in our region since the last century . . . a policy of domination which has left misery, exploitation, a lack of democracy, the people's genocide, the absence of dignity, independence and sovereignty. It is a systematically erratic policy that has forced peoples—such as the people of Nicaragua—into violently liberating themselves from tyrannies—such as that of Somoza—which were the product of this policy.

For this reason, we say that if there was a revolution in Nicaragua, it was the result of bad U.S. policy; if there is struggle and demand for justice and democracy in Central America, it is no more than the people's just response to this bad policy.

We have never hidden our interest in the changes that the Central American peoples demand be made, so that their realization can be peaceful, thus sparing peoples from suffering the painful consequences of violence.

We invite the Central American rulers to undertake a systematic dialogue to tackle the problems that overwhelm us and so that peace may exist between our nations.

We ratify our support for Contadora—this great Latin American effort supported by the International Community—which has placed its confidence in Mexico, Colombia, Venezuela and Panama's determined efforts towards peace.

Since 1854, we have been victimized by this policy which scorns the rights of peoples and proclaims itself international arbitrators with the right to militarily, politically and economically intervene. We are victims of this policy which considers it within its rights to overthrow governments, impose military bases, foment crime and terrorism—all in the name of democracy. . . .

But we are fully confident in the response of the people organized in the Militias, in the Reserve Battalions, in the Irregular Combat Battalions, in the Revolutionary Vigilance, in the Ministry of the Interior, in the Sandinista Police and in the other organisms for the defense of the country. . . .

28.
UNITY OF THE OPPOSITION: SAN JOSÉ PROGRAM (MARCH 1985)

We, democratic citizens, representatives of all sectors of the Nicaraguan Resistance, announce to the Nicaraguan people, to the governments and peoples of the Americas and of the world, the following manifesto:

Manifesto signed by Arturo Cruz, Alfonso Robelo, Adolfo Calero, and eighteen other opposition leaders.

THE PRESENT SITUATION OF NICARAGUA

In recent years, the Sandinista Front has submerged our people in a crisis without precedent in our national history.

At this time, the impact of this crisis is evident in the economic, political, social and moral spheres of the nation.

This situation is rooted both in the abandonment of the original Program of Government and the Fundamental Statute as well as in the interference of the Soviet bloc in our internal affairs. . . .

The solution to the national crisis can only be found through a genuine understanding among all Nicaraguans that might end the civil war and lead to the reconciliation of the Nicaraguan family.

We wish to emphasize that this initiative is not taken to search for a quota of power, but rather it seeks only to establish in Nicaragua the rule of law which will permit the people to live in peace and to go about resolving our problems within a new constitutional order. . . .

Therefore, in view of the gravity of the moment, and conscious of our civic responsibilities and of the urgent need to save our people from greater suffering, we accept the call of the Nicaraguan Democratic Coordinating Board and exhort the Sandinista Front, for the last time, and in definitive and absolute fashion, to participate in a national dialogue which will end the national crisis. This dialogue should follow these modalities:

CONVOCATION

The Nicaraguan Bishops Conference is the entity with the necessary moral authority to organize and coordinate the national dialogue. In this regard, we reiterate the petition made to it by the Democratic Coordinating Board to convene the national dialogue.

PARTICIPANTS

In order that the dialogue be efficient and produce the desired results, it is necessary to structure it in accordance with Nicaraguan reality. There are two political tendencies in Nicaragua: the totalitarian one which for the moment has accepted the Sandinista Front as its vanguard, and the democratic one which is divided into armed organizations and civilian organizations; therefore, the dialogue should be between these two political tendencies so that both can name their respective delegates, as many as the Bishops Conference feels is appropriate.

OBSERVERS AND GUARANTORS

We suggest to the Bishops Conference that it request the participation of the Central American governments in the dialogue as guarantors of the agreements which may be reached, given the fact that our fellow Central Americans are, in the final analysis, those which have been most directly affected by the Nicaraguan crisis.

The presence of these governments as guarantors in no way hinders the presence as observers or even as guarantors of other governments and democratic entities of the American continent.

MINIMUM REQUIREMENTS

We support fully the minimum requirements demanded by the Democratic Coordinating Board in order to initiate the national dialogue. They are: suspension of armed activities, with a ceasefire *in situ;* lifting of the state of emergency; absolute freedom of expression and assembly; general amnesty and pardon for political crimes and related crimes; entry into effect of the right of protective legal procedure (amparo) and *habeas corpus,* adding the granting of full protection of the physical and moral integrity of those members of the resistance who participate in the dialogue, in the event that it should take place in Nicaragua.

The application of these measures should be carried out under the supervision of the guarantor governments.

TEMPORARY PERMANENCE OF THE EXECUTIVE

If this dialogue is carried out, we pledge to accept that Mr. Daniel Ortega continue acting as head of the Executive Branch until such time as the people pronounce themselves in a plebiscite. . . .

29.
PRESIDENT DANIEL ORTEGA: STATE OF EMERGENCY (OCTOBER 1985)

A mercenary war has been imposed on us; a war financed, organized, and directed by the U.S. Government while U.S. troops and warships, in constant maneuvers and deployment around Nicaragua, constantly threaten us with a direct military intervention. The U.S. State Department openly sabotages our efforts before the international banking organizations. The threats, the false propaganda, and the political campaign to frighten, discredit, and isolate our homeland have not stopped for a minute. A criminal trade embargo has been imposed on us by the United States that further worsens the already difficult living standards of the Nicaraguan people in an attempt to force them to give up, because of hunger, their will for independence and freedom.

Despite this brutal aggression, the people of Nicaragua stand firm, and the Sandinist people's revolution advances. We have paid and continue to pay a high price for this. Thousands of patriots have given their valuable and irrecoverable lives fighting or have been murdered in the defense of the homeland.

Tens upon thousands of families have been forced to leave their land and homes. Huge amounts must be used for defense, thereby affecting production, consumption, and civilian investments. Hundreds of million of dollars in property and production have been destroyed by the direct action of the mercenary groups and CIA sabotage.

All these factors, the trade embargo, and the economic crisis that is affecting the developing countries have seriously affected the production and standards of living of our people. When all the patriotic sectors of the country are getting ready for new tours of voluntary work to pick coffee, cotton, and cut the sugarcane; when the government, amid the difficulties, is putting forth efforts to lower the price of the basic products that are distributed to the workers through the Rural Supply Centers [CAR] and other state supply centers thus firmly fighting the criminal speculation; when the agrarian reform projects are being increased for the peasants to own their own land and produce the necessary food; when the mercenary army, main instrument of the imperialist aggression has been seriously affected by the people and shows signs of its demoralization and defeat; precisely under these circumstances, the U.S. Government attempts to repair its weakened mercenary army and carry out other aggressive actions against the people and government of Nicaragua. . . .

The government and the heroic people of Sandino cannot allow this sabotage and political destabilization directed by the U.S. Government to continue to develop with impunity. The brutal aggression of the United States and of its internal allies has created a truly extraordinary situation. All efforts of the government and people should seek to defeat this aggression in the military, political, and economic fields. The life of the people and the defense of the national sovereignty demands this from us.

Therefore, the government of the Republic of Nicaragua announces the following decree:

[Unidentified announcer] State of National Emergency:

Article 1—the rights and guarantees provided for in Articles 8, 11, 13, 15, 17, Paragraph 2, 18, 20, 21, 23, 24, 31, 32, and 50 of Decree Number 52 dated 21 August 1979 and its amendments are suspended throughout the national territory . . . for the period of one year.

30.
THE OCTOBER 15 DECREE (OCTOBER 1985)

The following is a literal transcription of the rights which have been suspended:

Article 8: Every person has the right to individual freedom and personal security. No one can be submitted to arbitrary arrest or imprisonment or be deprived of his freedom, except for the reasons established by law and according to legal procedure.

Consequently: 1. Arrests can only be carried out with a written request by a competent judge or the authorities which have the legal power—except in the case of flagrante delicto.

2. Every arrested person will have the right to:

A. Be informed and notified without delay concerning the reason for his arrest and the accusations, charges, or case against him;

B. Be taken within 24 hours to a competent authority or be released;

C. Be allowed a writ of habeas corpus;

D. Be treated with the respect due a human being;

E. Be compensated in case of an illegal arrest.

Article 11: Every suspect has the right to equal conditions concerning the following guarantees:

A. Assumption of innocent until proven guilty.

B. Immediate notification, in a language that he understands and in a detailed way, of the nature of and reasons for the charges against him.

C. Trial, without delay, by a competent court. The trial must be public; however, in some exceptional cases the news media and the general public may be partially or totally excluded from the trial for moral, public order, or national security reasons.

D. Defense guaranteed throughout the process.

E. True and effective defense during the process, with adequate means and time for defense. If the prisoner does not appoint a

El Nuevo Diario, October 16, 1985. Translation in Federal Broadcast Information Service, Vol. 6, October 16, 1985, pp. 8–10.

lawyer, and if he is not a lawyer, defense counsel should be assigned to him immediately.

F. If a lawyer selected cannot be located, following a public summons, a defense counsel will be assigned.
G. Help, free of charge, from an interpreter if he does not understand or speak the language used by the court.
H. Participation in the presentation and acceptance of any kind of evidence before the final sentence is issued.
I. No forced self-incriminating testimony.
J. No prison sentence until all the evidence demanded by law has been collected; sentence should be issued within 10 days after arrest.
K. Right of appeal in accordance with the law.
L. No trial for a crime for which he has already been condemned or released through a definite sentence.
M. Right to a competent judge.

Article 13. Trial by jury is established for crimes which are specified by the law.

Article 15: Any person who entered Nicaraguan territory legally will have the right to circulate freely and choose his place of residence. Nicaraguans will have the right to enter and leave the country at will.

Article 18: No person will be subject to arbitrary or illegal interference in his private life, friends, home, mail, and communications, or attacks on his honor and reputation. He will have the right to be protected by the law against these interferences and attacks. In particular:

A. Homes or other private premises are inviolable and can be entered and searched only upon a written order by a competent judge, to prevent the perpetration of or impunity from crimes, or to prevent damages to people or property, in accordance with the law.
B. Private documents and communications are inviolable. The law will specify the cases and appropriate procedures to follow to examine or confiscate private documents, accounting books, and other related documents, whenever indispensable to clarify matters presented at justice tribunals or for fiscal reasons.

Article 20: Freedom of information is one of the principles of an authentic democracy. Therefore, it cannot be subject, directly or indirectly, to the economic power of any group.

Article 21: All people have the right to freedom of expression. This right includes the freedom to seek, receive, and disseminate information and ideas in a verbal, written, printed, or artistic way—or by another means of his choice. The exercise of these rights also includes some duties and responsibilities; consequently, they are subject to certain formalities, conditions, and restrictions established by the law. These could be deemed necessary to:

A. Safeguard national security and integrity, public security, and the national economy.
B. Defend public order and prevent crimes.
C. Protect the people's health, morale, dignity, reputation, and other rights.
D. Prevent the dissemination of confidential information or to guarantee judicial authority and impartiality.

Article 23: The right to participate in peaceful meetings is recognized. The right to demonstrate in public will be regulated by police laws.
Article 24: All types of propaganda against peace and all policies which advocate national, racial, and religious hate are hereby banned.
Article 31: Seeking to promote and protect the Nicaraguan's economic and social rights, the following are guaranteed:

A. The right to create and promote community, neighborhood, rural, and other organizations and labor and professional associations.
B. The right to create unions and join them, with members subject to the corresponding organizations' statutes.
C. Unions' rights to organize national federations and confederations and the latter's right to create or join international labor organizations.
D. The right to organize and promote labor and production cooperatives.

Article 32: The workers' right to organize a strike is recognized if exercised according to the law.
Article 50: All the people whose rights and freedoms—as recognized in the current statute and the fundamental statute issued on 20 July 1979—have been violated will be able to present a writ of habeas corpus, in accordance with the law.

31.
AMNESTY INTERNATIONAL: HUMAN RIGHTS IN NICARAGUA (MARCH 1986)

3. Amnesty International's principal concerns today

3.1 PRISONERS OF CONSCIENCE

Leaders and members of political opposition parties and their affiliated trade unions have been subjected to arrest and short-term imprisonment in what Amnesty International believes to be a pattern of intimidation and harassment. These arrests were carried out under the state of emergency in force since March 1982. Most of these prisoners were released before their cases were brought to trial, however, and those prisoners of conscience believed to have been wrongfully convicted of crimes have, with few exceptions, been released under the law of pardon, not long after sentencing.

However, some trade union and political party leaders who Amnesty International believes to have been prisoners of conscience have been detained repeatedly, sometimes for a year or more. They have also been required to present themselves at the State Security Service's public relations office "Casa 50" for further interviews and questioning by officials. Many short-term detainees have reported that interrogators threatened them with further, prolonged imprisonment without trial in the custody of the State Security Service, or trial under the Public Order Law, as a consequence of further independent trade union or political party activism. . . .

3.4 CONSCRIPTION AND CONSCIENTIOUS OBJECTION TO MILITARY SERVICE

. . . After the revolution the provisions of the previous constitution for compulsory military service were reflected in the new government's Fundamental Statute (Article 24). Only in 1983, however, was legislation introduced by which obligatory military service was to be implemented. A law of compulsory military service, the *Ley del Servicio Militar Patriotico,* Law of Patriotic Military Service (Decree 1337), was enacted on 13 September 1983 under which all men aged 18 (subsequently modified to 17) to 40 were required to register for military service, and were subject to call up for

From Amnesty International, "Nicaragua: The Human Rights Record."

active or reserve duty. Those aged 18 to 25 were subject to immediate recruitment for two-year periods of active service. Women aged between 18 and 40 are eligible for voluntary registration for military service under the law.

Exemptions from military service are provided under the law for illness or disabilities, as well as for men with certain specified family responsibilities. The law makes no provision for conscientious objection to military service, or for service to be performed as an alternative to military duty.

A series of penalties are established in the law for people who fail to register for military service, who do not present themselves when called for interviews or examinations, or who provide false information on registration. Those who fail to register or to report when called for active service may be imprisoned for up to four years.

Opposition to the conscription law was voiced by some sectors of the Roman Catholic clergy and by political opposition groups, which claimed that the new army was in the hands of a political party (the FSLN) and so was not a legitimate national army. In 1984 some parents' groups protested against the implementation of the law after high casualty rates were reported from Honduran border areas. They claimed that young recruits were sent into combat inadequately trained and armed. Further protests related to the manner in which conscription was enforced during the law's first year of application. In late 1983 and the first months of 1984 young people in some areas were reportedly picked up by army recruiters virtually at random in press gang operations, including many who were under or over draft age, or who were otherwise exempt under the law. An inter-ministerial commission was reportedly set up in mid-1984 to supervise a review of conscription procedures, and to investigate and remedy reported abuses. . . .

3.6 DETENTION AND INTERROGATION PROCEDURES: THE STATE SECURITY SERVICE

Since the creation of a new government in 1979 the Ministry of Interior's State Security Service has taken primary responsibility for the detention and interrogation of most suspects in political cases. Incommunicado detention is the norm for prisoners in State Security Service custody, with prisoners frequently held incommunicado for from 15 to 30 days and sometimes for several months. Although the State Security Service maintains offices and detention facilities in most major towns, the principal detention and interrogation facility is at its headquarters in Managua. Known as "El Chipote," it is located on the slope of the Loma de Tiscapa volcano behind Managua's Intercontinental Hotel. Most political detainees are reportedly brought for interrogation to "El Chipote" and held there pending indictment or release. . . .

In practice, the State Security Service's actions under the state of emergency and suspension of most civil rights appear to be largely unrestricted by the judiciary or any other civil authority. Optometrist Alejandro Pereira was detained on 6 June 1983 and taken to "El Chipote" on suspicion that on recent visits to Honduras he had contacted FDN and CIA officials, a charge he denied. Held totally incommunicado for 70 days, Alejandro Pereira was taken before a court only in January 1984. He was charged with violation of the Public Order Law Articles 1 b) and g), after he had signed a "confession" that he had provided political, military, and economic information to the FDN and CIA. During his seven months at "El Chipote," the State Security Service's Director refused to comply with a Supreme Court *habeas corpus* order to permit access to an examining magistrate to establish the condition of his health—he had previously had several operations for a duodenal ulcer and was hospitalized at the order of the court after his first court appearance in January.

While he was held incommunicado, an elaborate effort was made to convince Alejandro Pereira that his wife, too, had been detained, and that she would remain at "El Chipote" until he "confessed." Sra. Pereira had been taken to "El Chipote" on 9 June, dressed in a prison overall, and been walked past Alejandro Pereira as he stood in an open doorway; neither was permitted to speak. Sra. Pereira was then permitted to return to her home. For the next 70 days of incommunicado detention Alejandro Pereira was told his wife was also undergoing interrogation at "El Chipote."

After receiving a seven year sentence passed by the TPA court on 23 February 1984, based exclusively on his testimony while held incommunicado, Alejandro Pereira denied that his statement had been made freely, and claimed that he had been both psychologically and physically tortured. On appeal his sentence was raised to 15 years' imprisonment, the court rejecting his allegations out of hand. Amnesty International was given access by the president of the TPA court to the trial record, including the original copy of the "confession." The organization expressed concern to the authorities that the statement had been produced while the prisoner was incommunicado in the State Security Service's custody, and that his allegations of coercion had not resulted in any investigation of the State Security Service's procedures in the case. Further concern was expressed at the general failure of the Ministry of Justice (the public prosecutor's office) or the courts to challenge the validity of such "confessions" recorded by the State Security Service while prisoners were held incommunicado. In October 1984 Alejandro Pereira was released on health grounds through a pardon by the Council of State.

Amnesty International was concerned that in other cases the State Security Service appeared to have fabricated evidence and to have manipulated the government news media in order to denigrate political opponents, and justify to the Nicaraguan public their detention and prosecution. One such case was the prosecution and house arrest of Father Amado Peña, a priest well known for his outspoken criticism of the government in sermons in his Managua church, who is considered close to Cardinal Monseñor Miguel Obando y Bravo, a critic of the current government. On 22 June 1984 the State Security Service broadcast a video film which showed Father Peña leaving a car holding a bag, which, when opened by police officers, revealed a "terrorist kit" implicating the church in armed violence: several hand grenades, dynamite, and a white and yellow Vatican flag on which the letters FDN had been sewn.

According to Father Peña, however, who was interviewed by Amnesty International delegates in July 1984 while under house arrest, after celebrating mass on 22 June he had accepted a lift from a man at the service and, when the driver pulled up behind a parked car, was asked to hand a bag to a man in the other car. A video was recorded by the State Security Service as he stepped from the car holding the bag and shows the appearance of police officers on the scene and the opening of the bag in their presence. The drivers of the two cars were apparently neither questioned, detained, nor publicly identified by the State Security Service and Father Peña was told he could go home when the filming was completed. However, four days later, after the government news media denounced him as a terrorist accomplice, he was placed under house arrest, and confined to a Church seminary outside Managua. Ten foreign priests who had been critical of government policies, some of whom had been residents in Nicaragua for over 30 years, were summarily expelled from Nicaragua after protesting against the government news media's attacks on Father Peña. Amnesty International considered Father Peña a prisoner of conscience, falsely implicated in criminal activity by the State Security Service because of his expression of his political views. Although charges were brought against Father Peña before the Popular Tribunal the case never went to trial and the charges were dismissed by a legislative pardon in September 1984.

In a June 1985 letter to President Ortega, Amnesty International stressed its concern at the extraordinary *de facto* powers accorded the State Security Service under the state of emergency, and the consequent scope for abuse of these powers. The organization noted that the State Security Service routinely carried out detentions without apparent basis in law; that long periods of incommunicado detention subject to no known regulation were the norm for State Security Service prisoners in pre-trial detention; that in some cases even members of the judiciary were denied access to prisoners by the state Security Service and that State Security Service prisoners were routinely denied consultation with defense lawyers, or contact with families or doctors. Concern was also expressed about the lack of accountability of the State Security Service to the judiciary. State Security Service officers carrying out arrests and interrogations, who are responsible for determining the conditions and duration of incommunicado, administrative detention, are apparently accountable in practice only to the Minister of the Interior, and not to any court of law or other supervisory authority. . . .

3.8 ALLEGATIONS, INVESTIGATIONS AND PUNISHMENT OF OTHER ABUSE

Amnesty International has also received reports of other serious abuses of the rights of detainees. These have in past years included allegations of physical torture, "disappearance," and arbitrary killings. The organization has, however, welcomed a recent pattern whereby such allegations have been investigated and the police and military forces alleged to be responsible for such abuses have been brought to justice.

A number of cases of torture, "disappearance," and arbitrary killing were reported from the Pantasma area, in Jinotega department, near the Honduran border, in late 1983 and the first days of 1984. The reports followed a series of major attacks there by Honduran based troops of the FDN in which some 40 civilians were reported killed, some of them after capture. Nicaraguan army officers at Pantasma responded with a wave of human rights violations directed at individuals suspected to be supporters of the FDN. Abuses reported included the torture of detainees, at least six extrajudicial executions, and the apparent "disappearance" of four local people. In January 1984 a special prosecutor was appointed to investigate the Pantasma case and 41 military personnel were detained. In March 1984 a court martial in open session sentenced the region's army commander to 44 years' imprisonment (although a maximum of 30 years of the sentence can be served under Nicaraguan law), on two counts of murder, and for the torture of four captives; 12 subordinates received sentences of up to 14 years. The trial and convictions were widely publicized by the government inside Nicaragua. . . .

4.1 ALLEGATIONS OF TORTURE AND SUMMARY EXECUTIONS OF DETAINEES BY OPPOSITION FORCES

Since 1981 reports have been regularly received of detentions, torture and summary execution by armed opposition forces, with most reports coming from the areas of Jinotega and Matagalpa bordering Honduras, and the Atlantic Coast region. Victims of reported summary execution by forces associated with the FDN included a Miskito, José Cornejo, who was released in the December 1983 amnesty, and his wife. José Cornejo was reportedly accused by opposition forces of collaborating with the Nicaraguan authorities and as a consequence he and his wife were reportedly captured and killed in late January 1984 near the hamlet Yulo.

Others captured were reportedly taken to bases in Honduras or Costa Rica. Amnesty International appealed to the Honduran authorities in December 1982 after lay church leaders María Eugenia de Barreda and her husband Felipe Barreda were seized by FDN forces while working as teachers near the Honduran border, taken across the border, and reportedly transported by Honduran army forces to the town of Danli where they and other Nicaraguan captives were reportedly held and interrogated. According to detailed reports, from captives who escaped FDN/Honduran custody at Danli, the Barredas had been severely beaten. Other reports maintained that María Eugenia de Barreda had been repeatedly raped and was held bound and gagged. The bodies of the two were reportedly found near Danli several months later.

More recently, Amnesty International appealed to the Honduran authorities after the seizure by FDN forces in Nicaragua's Jinotega department of five student teachers on 28 September, 1984, and another on 5 October and their reported removal across the border to Honduras. In mid-November 1985 it was reported that one of them had escaped. She told a press conference in Managua that she had been held inside Honduras for part of her captivity, where she was raped and tortured. She believed that four of her colleagues may have been killed by the FDN. The detention of the fifth teacher remains unconfirmed and the Honduran authorities have made no response to inquiries about her fate and that of other captives reportedly taken to the FDN's Las Vegas camp.

In a similar case, forestry technicians Fausto Cristy and Jorge Canales, both Nicaraguans, and Regine Schmemann, a citizen of the Federal Republic of Germany, were seized on 14 June 1985 by forces of the largely Miskito Indian group MISURA while working north of Puerto Cabezas in Zelaya Department. They were subsequently taken into Honduran territory to the MISURA camp at Srum Laya. Following international protests, Regine Schmemann was removed from Srum Laya on 2 July by a delegation of three men, one whom was identified as a Honduran army officer. According to Regine Schmemann's testimony, the army escort was made aware that her two companions remained in custody at Srum Laya, but made no effort to assist them. She was subsequently taken first to a Honduran army command post in Gracias a Dios province, and then to the capital, Tegucigalpa, where she was handed over to a representative from her country's embassy and members of the International Committee of the Red Cross.

According to the account given to Amnesty International by Regine Schmemann, each of the three captives was threatened with execution while in MISURA custody. It is believed that her presence, as a citizen of the Federal Republic of Germany, may have provided some protection for her companions, and that there is now considerable danger to the lives of these Nicaraguan civilians. On 12 August 1985 Amnesty International telexed the president of the Republic of Honduras to welcome the reported steps taken by the Honduran army to secure the release of Regine Schmemann, and urged that similar measures be taken to ensure the physical safety of Fausto Cristy and Jorge Canales and to secure their immediate release.

While some prisoners were reportedly taken to bases outside Nicaragua by opposition forces, the forces of the FDN were more frequently reported to retain no prisoners, killing captives on the spot or after brief field interrogations. In some areas they reportedly killed their captives before the assembled residents of target communities. Witnesses of such killings of relatives and neighbors, and FDN personnel who have deserted the force, have described in detailed testimonies made available to Amnesty International execution-style killings in which captives were bound, tortured, and their throats slit by FDN forces. In some cases captives were shot dead or beheaded. The number of captives tortured and put to death by FDN forces since 1981 is impossible to determine, but is believed to total several hundred.

CHAPTER

F O U R

Origins of Conflict in El Salvador

The traditional pattern of Salvadoran society—political domination by military dictatorship and economic control by an oligarchy—broke down in the late 1970s. The country faced a simultaneous three-sided struggle among the old ruling groups, democratic reformers, and Marxist revolutionaries.

El Salvador's landowning elite was much larger than the "Fourteen Families" of local legend, but money and power were still extremely concentrated in a very small proportion of the population. In 1975, 41 percent of rural families had no land at all and most peasants remained at the subsistence level. The military, as in the massacres of the 1930s, was committed to maintaining the oligarchy's privileges.

El Salvador is considerably more industrialized and cosmopolitan than Nicaragua. Its working class is larger, and it has a history of political activism and trade unionism. The Salvadoran countryside is more polarized than in Nicaragua, where the existence of an agricultural frontier, among other things, has given a better chance for individual small farmers. In tiny El Salvador's countryside, patron-client relations prevail. This degree of class polarization and resulting political consciousness made the Salvadoran peasantry more accustomed to social organization and more radical than its counterparts elsewhere in Central America. Consequently,

319

Salvadoran society has been both more violent and better organized than that of Nicaragua.

The Salvadoran army was structured as a highly politicized body, as Professor Richard Millett shows (Document 2). The national military academy produced the senior officers, tied together by loyalty groups *(tandas)* based on their graduating class. Self-enrichment was an integral part of the system; corruption was merely the way officers received their share of the national bounty (Document 3).

In retrospect, the Salvadoran elections of 1972 were a political turning point comparable in some ways to the earthquake in Nicaragua the same year. A Christian Democratic engineer named José Napoleón Duarte led a left-of-center coalition against the army-oligarchy candidate, Colonel Arturo Armanda Molina (Document 1). Duarte clearly won the election, but fraud and military intervention deprived him of victory. Duarte was beaten up and forced into exile. The traditional pattern of politics was preserved again, but only temporarily.

The 1977 elections, like those of 1972, were marked by arrests, murders, a state of siege, and systematic miscounting. General Carlos Humberto Romero succeeded Colonel Molina, and the torture and killing of opposi- tionists, including trade and peasant union leaders, continued (Document 4). The National Association of Private Enterprise (ANEP) opposed even the mildest form of land reform, labeling it communistic (Document 5), while the Popular Revolutionary Bloc (BPR), one of the main mass organi- zations built by radicalized Christians and leftists, ridiculed the military regime's token 1976 land reform (Document 6).

After the "preferential option for the poor" was endorsed by Catholic bishops in their 1968 Medellín (Colombia) declaration, Salvadoran priests and laypeople formed local groups, Christian Base Communities (Docu- ment 7), that taught peasants and workers their rights and organized them to claim land and living wages. In reaction, the oligarchy and extreme right decided to suppress these protests, even setting up death squads to murder activist priests like Rutilo Grande (Document 8).

The Farabundo Martí Liberation Front (FMLN) has two main sources: radicalized religious activists and the Salvadoran Communist Party. The Catholic groups were rooted in the Christian base communities, and their ideas grew out of Liberation Theology.

In 1970, Salvador Cayetano Carpio, a former seminarian and secretary general of the Communist Party, resigned and organized underground the first cells of what would become the Popular Forces of Liberation (FPL). Shortly thereafter, other Communists left the party and joined young Christian Democratic dissidents, religious activists, and student radicals to form the People's Revolutionary Army (ERP). These groups criticized the Communist Party as revisionist (Document 9).

These organizations engaged in ferocious polemics in their newspapers, in the National University, and in the newly developing "popular organizations." Most important of the latter was the United Popular Action Front (FAPU), a broad coalition of peasant, trade union, teacher, and student organizations plus professors, radicalized clergymen, and members of the Communist Party, the FPL, and the ERP.

The ERP at that time viewed the revolution as a series of stages leading to mass insurrection. Like the Terceristas in Nicaragua, it also favored making alliances with all "democratic sectors," including workers, peasants, broad sections of the middle class, and "democratic army officers." It tended to be fiercely nationalistic and critical of the Cuban presence and influence in Nicaragua.

The FPL, like the Prolonged Popular War faction of the Sandinistas, considered the peasantry the key element in a "protracted people's war" and rejected the idea of a "united front" as "liquidating class contradictions." In later years, it was the group closest to Havana and Managua.

As a result of these conflicts (Document 10), FAPU split in July 1975 into groups controlled by the various leftist factions. The FPL formed its own popular organization, the Revolutionary Popular Bloc (BPR). But even as this split was developing, the ERP itself divided after its "Military Staff" tried and executed the group's leading intellectual, Roque Dalton.

The Dalton affair gives a great deal of insight into the Salvadoran left's internal politics. A poet and well-traveled radical activist, Dalton had written (Document 11) that "to be a communist is a beautiful thing" and in a poem entitled "OAS" that "the President of the United States is more the President of my country than the President of my country."

Joaquín Villalobos, commander of the ERP, murdered Dalton in 1974, accusing him of being both a Cuban and a CIA agent (Documents 12 and 13). Those critical of the ERP's behavior split to form the National Resistance Forces (FARN) (Document 14).

Despite these divisions among the radicals, their demonstrations and organizations grew steadily in size (Documents 15 and 16). But the Romero dictatorship was overthrown not by the opposition but by a revolt within the military's own ranks. In October 1979, a group of younger officers staged a coup (Document 17) and invited the cooperation of reform-minded civilians, including Christian Democrats, Communists, and Social Democrats (Document 18). A cabinet was established that included a number of veteran oppositionists.

Within a few months, however, some of them had become disillusioned by what they regarded as the slow pace of reform and by the recapturing of the army by traditionalist officers. The Communists and some Social Democrats, Socialists, and radical Christian Democrats, like Guillermo Ungo (Document 19) and Rubén Zamora (Document 21), resigned from the junta and went into exile. Later, they became leaders of the Revolutionary Democratic Front (FDR) allied with the FMLN.

The radical groups had reacted in different ways to the reformist military coup. The Communist Party welcomed the coup and prepared to join the government. The ERP called for an insurrection and set up barricades in San Salvador's suburbs. Later, in an about-face, it agreed to "study" any offer of participation in the junta. The FPL called the ERP's insurrections "suicidal" but opposed the junta as a U.S. plot.

The first half of 1980 was a turning point for El Salvador. In January 1980 the largest demonstration in Salvadoran history was fired on by security forces, leaving dozens dead and hundreds injured. Extreme rightists, probably associated with Roberto d'Aubuisson, assassinated Archbishop Oscar Romero, whose sermons (Document 22) had been stirring calls condemning human rights violations by the left and right and supporting popular grievances. These events and the outbreak of violence at Archbishop Romero's funeral in March ended the period of large street demonstrations. The junta marked its own break with the oligarchy by issuing its long-awaited agrarian reform program (Document 20). The revolutionary groups shifted to their mountain bases and began to unite under an umbrella structure that eventually produced the FMLN. The civil war began in earnest. The moderates split as some supported, others condemned the junta.

The FMLN-FDR members had far more political experience than did the pre-1979 Sandinistas. The Salvadorans had led labor and peasant unions, teachers' organizations, and broad political coalitions. Some of them had even been ministers of state and had campaigned in elections. Heated discussions in universities and political circles in the 1970s had exposed them to the full range of international leftist debates. Antagonism toward the pro-Moscow Communist party made some of the militants more willing to criticize Soviet and Cuban policy, although this background also meant that the FMLN was far more explicitly Marxist-Leninist than were the Sandinistas. Thus, Sandinista leaders complain of the violent, even fratricidal, nature of the Salvadoran guerrillas, while the latter speak with disdain of the "infantilism" of the Nicaraguan leadership.

In this atmosphere of confrontation, José Antonio Morales Carbonell, an FPL militant about to join the guerrillas, wrote his father, a leading Christian Democrat and cabinet minister (Document 23). His letter illustrated the agonies of a civil war which, as was the case in Nicaragua, divided families and close friends. The junta, he complained, had not implemented the promised reforms and the army continued its repression as if nothing had changed. Two months later, in June, Morales was captured and imprisoned by government forces.

Analyzing this polarized situation, State Department officials argued that unless rightist violence and military repression were curbed, the junta would lose its remaining support—at home, internationally, and in the United States Congress—and the Marxist left could triumph (Document 24). This pessimistic viewpoint seemed borne out by contemporary events. The leader of the radical right, d'Aubuisson, increased his attacks on the reformist junta (Document 25). His political forces, financed by the oligarchy, directed death squads as much against the center as against the left (Document 26). Leaders of the FDR were kidnapped and killed (Document 27) and American nuns were brutally murdered (Document 28). In none of these cases were the perpetrators punished.

Leonel Gómez, chief adviser to the president of the Institute of Agrarian Transformation (ISTA), had to flee the country in 1981 after a death squad murdered ISTA's president. The two men had exposed military corruption, which was, Gómez explained (Document 31), the system holding together the army. U.S. aid, he warned, would be devoured by this system. "The fundamental problem in my country is the army," he concluded, and while Duarte held the title of president it was the military that still held power.

The FMLN, explained the ERP, aimed at the establishment of a revolutionary government that would nationalize the economy (Document 30). Its ally, the FDR, composed of Christian Democrats, Social Democrats, and Communists who had split with the 1979 junta, presented a complementary program (Document 29). The FMLN would attack the economy; the right's atrocities and its subversion of the center would build support for the guerrillas.

The legacy of the FMLN's prehistory is one of lingering and sometimes bitter conflicts among the constituent groups and a linkage with several mass organizations. The FPL is the largest of the FMLN groups in membership but not in armed guerrillas. The ERP, with about 36 percent of the guerrillas, is by far the biggest and most effective fighting force. The FPL is next with 22 percent, followed by the FARN with 16 percent. Altogether, the FMLN has about 8,000 guerrillas along with a much larger number of militia members and sympathizers.

As the war escalated, the guerrillas consolidated their support system, but their reservoir of popular sympathy diminished. They consistently overestimated their military strength and the masses' readiness to support them. Their onslaught on the economy destroyed factories, stores, buses, cars, and public utilities, causing widespread disruption, suffering, unemployment, and misery.

Fermán Cienfuegos, leader of the FARN and in charge of FMLN foreign relations, commented in an 1982 interview, "All wars end in political settlements," and claimed that in this war "there are no winners and losers." The objective of FMLN military strategy, he insisted, is "not the defeat of the army but to bring about negotiations" (Document 33). But neither the 1982 elections nor the FMLN's own policy led to such a result.

Given the deadlocked, destructive civil war, was there a viable choice other than the traditional system and the triumph of a Marxist revolution? Bishop Rivera y Damas hoped for an alternative (Document 32). He called on the government "to purify its ranks of the administrative and military personnel who were impeding the progress of democracy and . . . human rights." At the same time, he condemned the left for "using weapons, . . . thus increasing the suffering of the people in general." The church favored dialogue between the government and the guerrillas.

I.
THE STRUGGLE AGAINST MILITARY DICTATORSHIP

1.
U.S. EMBASSY: REPORT ON THE 1972 ELECTION (1971)

To no one's surprise, the Government's *Partido de Conciliación Nacional* (PCN) on September 29 nominated Col. Arturo Armando Molina, Private Secretary to the President, as its presidential candidate for the forthcoming campaign. Over the past few months, the 44 year old career army officer rose to the top of the list of presidential possibles by a process of elimination.

Molina, a reserved, serious man, is reputed to be a good executive officer and extremely loyal to President Sánchez. While apparently held in respect by most military officers, he is not widely known in civilian circles and his skills as a campaigner have yet to be tested. Initial visits to some outlying Departments have elicited favorable comment that he listens rather than talks. . . .

B. DUARTE & UNGO

Equally unsurprising was the selection of PDC leader Napoleón Duarte as the candidate of the PDC-MNR-UDN coalition, the *Unión Nacional Opositora* (UNO). The three-term mayor of San Salvador (until 1970) was virtually the only national figure the PDC had at hand and the sole question was whether Duarte would accept the offer. He did so, but very much on his own terms. Aside from receiving assurances for various personal perquisites, Duarte took a very strong line with coalition leaders on questions of

Cable to State Department, October 22, 1971.

cabinet selections, platform, the role of the two minority parties, etc., so much so that he irritated some of his long-time friends within the party and aroused certain suspicions that he might have latent dictatorial tendencies.

Duarte, while known as an effective administrator and a good campaigner, tends to be somewhat irresponsible in his public pronouncements. He has long had many contacts with the official and non-official American community in San Salvador (he was educated at Notre Dame) but he is prone to complain about the exploitation of the less developed world by the developed states (read US), and reportedly has struck a fairly strong anti-American tone when among close Salvadoran friends. Duarte's running mate, Manuel Ungo, Secretary General of the small *Movimiento Nacional Revolucionario* (MNR), is regarded by some as one of the more intelligent men in the country. However, while he has friends and admirers in some intellectual circles, he is not widely known and his pensive, unimpressive manner would seem to lend little help to Duarte's campaign efforts.

Even before the campaign opened, it was obvious that the major parties are prepared to fight an essentially negative battle. President Sánchez, who has been travelling around the country inaugurating public works projects, has hit the leftist opposition on various occasions for its association with communists and "foreign ideologies" and has urged an "open battle" against this threat to the country at the ballot box. Not only is the PDC being attacked for its association with the PR-influenced UDN (cartoonists have portrayed the UNO as a trojan horse with "communists" creeping inside), but special stress is being placed on the PDC's support of the unpopular disorders that grew out of the recent teachers' strike. The theme of the danger from the left does not mean that the PCN will leave the rightist opposition (PPS, FUDI) untouched, however, and they have been chided for their "suicidal" refusal to recognize the need for evolutionary change.

There are indications that the PCN campaign will not be entirely negative. On the positive side, Molina can be expected to stress the accomplishments of the last two PCN administrations, especially in education. He will also hold out the prospect of additional reform, particularly in agriculture, public health, housing and government administration, and stress the extensive government experience of both himself and Mayorga Rivas. He will no doubt take special care in dealing with two questions that threaten to erode the parties' support from the right: agrarian reform and the unionization of rural workers. . . .

Equally disturbing to the right, especially among the coffee growers, is the revised labor code which is currently in committee in the legislative assembly and which would give rural labor the right to organize. The PCN itself is split on this question. In their nightmares, opponents to unionization can envisage a nation-wide communist-dominated rural union that would withhold harvest labor while the coffee rots on the trees. On the other hand, PCN moderates fear that if some limited form of rural organization (hopefully government controlled) is not allowed, extremists will go into the countryside and organize anyway. The Assembly is supposedly working its way through the massive revision to the labor code but has thus far avoided facing up to that section which deals with this sensitive issue and it is unlikely that it will do so before elections.

The tactics of the leftist opposition can also be expected to be essentially negative. In their declaration of coalition, the three parties claim that their main targets of attack are "two onerous realities—oligarchy and imperialism." However, once down to specifics, they have hit the government for *"oficialismo"* and *"continuismo"*—keeping itself in power "by fraud, imposition, and repression." The theme of repression will no doubt be heard frequently, with the contention that "terrorism and dictatorship are the answers of the government toward popular discontent." The opposition will hold that the "climate of repression" restricts their freedom to campaign and, in fact, leaders of the PDC, the MNR and UDN held a meeting with President Sánchez September 23 to seek his assurances that they will be guaranteed the freedom to campaign. But Sánchez did not take the bait entirely. He chided the opposition for its support of public disorders and held that a good electoral climate is the responsibility of all political leaders. However, he has since stated that the government will uphold the right of all legal parties to campaign.

The opposition charges of repression stem initially from the crackdown by security forces on the demonstrations resulting from the ANDES strike and have continued with such incidents as the detention by police of leftist leaders, the burning of *Radio Popular* (widely believed to be the work of ORDEN), and the disappearance of a Departmental Secretary General of the UDN. The opposition will no doubt latch on to any similar incidents that may occur during the campaign as further proof of their thesis. Concerning other issues, the UNO has said little to date but the PDC is known to favor extensive agricultural reform and a greater redistribution of private wealth. . . .

2.
RICHARD MILLETT: PRAETORIANS OR PATRIOTS

El Salvador's armed forces have expanded rapidly in recent years. In 1976 total military personnel numbered approximately 8,000, over half of which

From Robert S. Leiken, *Anatomy of Conflict* (Washington, 1984), pp. 73–76.

were assigned to the security forces (National Guard, National Police and Treasury Police). Only about 200 were assigned to the Air Force. By 1983 the Army had expanded to 22,000, the Air Force to 2,350 and the security forces to 9,500. The budget had grown from $50 million in 1978 to $139 million in 1982, plus an additional $82 million in United States military assistance.

The National Guard is a 3,500-man rural constabulary, created in the 1920s on the model of the Spanish *Guardia Civil.* The National Police, the only urban police force, has nearly 4,000 members; the Treasury Police, a body formally charged with controlling customs, borders, alcohol production and related tax matters, has nearly 2,000 individuals. These "security forces" are currently all under the control of the Ministry of Defense and are largely commanded by army officer graduates of the military academy. These forces, notably the National Guard and the Treasury Police, have been the principal perpetrators of indiscriminate violence against dissidents. They have been used by the traditional rural elite against peasant organizations, agrarian reform and potential "trouble-makers." The Treasury Police also maintains an extensive network of rural informers. These security forces do much of the "dirty work" of maintaining control and eliminating "subversives," leaving the Army free to concentrate on national defense, national politics and self-enrichment. Before 1980 the Army suppressed only extreme dissent, for example, after the fraudulent elections of 1972 and 1977.

The one-man military rule of pre-1944 El Salvador has given way to a trend towards corporate control by the armed forces, signaled in the 1950s by the rise to power of military academy graduates. While generally united in their determination to control the country, they are divided by ideology, personal loyalties and, most importantly, graduating classes from the *Escuela Militar.* Each year well over a hundred cadets are admitted to this institution, but just 10% graduate *four years later.* Brutal discipline, at times verging on sadism, weeds out those lacking strength, determination and ambition. The school admits boys of 15–18 and graduates hardened men, bound by lifelong loyalty to their classmates. Each class, known as a *tanda,* strives to protect and advance its members' fortunes. Success for one member means success for all and failure for any weakens the entire group. Hence they protect the less competent, more blatantly dishonest among them, viewing those outside the *tanda* system as unfit to judge the officer corps.

To advance their ambitions, *tandas* form alliances with other *tandas,* though rarely with the class one year ahead of them in *Escuela Militar* (which had brutalized them during their plebe year), nor with the class a year behind (which they had brutalized). Under this system, loyalty becomes incestuous, and group advancement, rather than defense of the national interest, becomes the ultimate goal. Officers in the security forces are bound to officers in the army through these *tanda* bonds, a tie which makes it virtually impossible to discipline an officer for crimes against civilians. In 1982 El Salvador's Defense Minister admitted to two United States Senators that "there is no formal system of punishment for abuses by members of the Salvadoran armed forces."

For this reason, the United States probably had less influence over El Salvador's military than over that of any other Central American nation. This *tanda* system made the military resistant to foreign influences. By law, Salvadoran army officers had to attend their own service schools, including the Command and Staff College. Given the post-1969 cutoff of arms sales and training of police forces it was not that difficult for El Salvador to respond to Carter administration human rights pressures in 1977 by abrogating the military assistance agreement.

During the 1970s, increased social pressures and the growing strength of the left made a major outbreak of domestic violence increasingly likely. The military's control was weakened by corruption and growing factionalism. The Sandinista victory in Nicaragua further encouraged the left and increased the military's fears and internal divisions.

When junior officers ousted General Carlos Humberto Romero's weak and corrupt administration, the Carter administration leaped at the chance to improve contacts with the military. A small amount of training funds (IMET) and authorization for $5.7 million in foreign military sales (FMS) were hurriedly included in a supplement to the fiscal year (FY) 1980 budget. Throughout 1980, however, civil conflict mounted and the military drifted back into the control of traditional senior officers. Human rights abuses escalated steadily, culminating in charges of military involvement in the December murder of four American churchwomen and two American agricultural advisers. Shortly thereafter, Colonel Adolfo Majano, leader of the "reformist" element within the armed forces, was dropped from the ruling junta. U.S. hopes for a moderate civil-military coalition were rapidly falling apart.

U.S.-Salvadoran military relations dramatically changed in January 1981. Military assistance, suspended following the December murders, was hurriedly reinstated when guerrilla forces launched a major offensive. In addition, emergency appropriations, ultimately totaling $25 million, were added to provide equipment and supplies for the Army. This was the first direct grant program for military hardware appropriated for Central America in several years. Even greater changes followed President Reagan's inauguration later that month.

The Carter administration's objectives were to persuade the army to curb human rights abuses, make basic reforms and ultimately permit civilian rule. The internal realities of Salvadoran military politics and the intransigent nature of the armed right confounded these efforts. The Reagan administration's priority was defeating the guerrillas. Restoring domestic order required creating a more effective military. Military assistance was raised to $82 million for FY 1982, and scores of U.S. military advisers were dispatched to El Salvador on missions lasting from a few weeks to a full year. This policy assumed that defeating the guerrillas was the Salvadoran military's top priority too, and it would increase military professionalism, which would decrease human rights abuses and enhance the armed forces' public image. All of these assumptions proved mistaken because, as those dealing directly with the Salvadoran military soon realized, the armed forces had their own agenda. Their top priority was *protecting* the military institutions from radical guerrillas, civilian politicians and foreign reformers. Next was promoting one's own *tanda* and excluding from the system those who had not passed through the *Escuela Militar.* Political ideology was low priority except for those officers linked to the extreme right such as former Major Roberto d'Aubuisson.

Under such circumstances, U.S. involvement with the military produced endless frustrations. It proved impossible to convict officers for human rights abuses, including those involving U.S. citizens. The war with the guerrillas was stagnating; economics and political costs rose steadily. To fill the expanding army's need for company-level officers, the United States began training Salvadoran noncommissioned officers in Panama. But the Salvadoran military refused to give graduates of this program regular commissions, keeping their status inferior to the *Escuela Militar* graduates'. U.S.-trained enlisted men often performed reasonably well, but a combination of high casualties and low reenlistment rates meant that the majority were out of the military a year after they were trained.

The January 1983 conflict between Defense Minister José Guillermo García and Colonel Sigifredo Ochoa disrupted the military command, paralyzed the war effort and resulted in the removal of the Defense Minister and the Colonel's departure for Washington. Part of this conflict stemmed from differences over strategy, with Ochoa and his supporters advocating a more sophisticated approach to counterinsurgency, emphasizing aggressive small unit actions and patrolling combined with political pacification. Traditional military rivalries, however, were at the heart of the conflict, with General García striving to maintain his supporters in key positions, despite their incompetence.

By late 1983, in part due to the change in Defense Ministers, the Salvadoran Army showed some signs of improved command and combat capability, although it was still insufficient to subdue the guerrillas. Widely publicized area offensives had limited results, casualties remained high and human rights abuses were again increasing. The military's low morale and the rural population's apathy were chronic problems. $136 million in military assistance for FY 1983 had done little to transform El Salvador's army into an efficient, modern force and there was little reason to think that the $86.3 million initially requested for FY 1984 would be any more effective. Despite three years of intensive U.S. efforts, the military still abuses its own citizenry, and responded more to its internal power struggles than to the civil conflict. U.S. officials feared that forcing the military to change might cause its collapse. But the military's failure to change increased the risk of a U.S. withdrawal. Disaster awaits for both the Salvadoran Armed Forces and the U.S. in Central America unless the officer corps is persuaded that its survival demands basic changes—including: removing incompetent officers, disciplining those involved in human rights abuses, abandoning some degree of power and privilege and, in all probability, supporting a political rather than a military solution to the current conflict.

3.
CHRISTOPHER DICKEY: "I OBEY BUT I DO NOT COMPLY"

On the stairway nearest the chief executive's office in the Casa Presidencial of San Salvador there hangs a large portrait of nineteenth-century Salvadoran hero Gen. Manuel José Arce in his full dress Napoleonic uniform. He holds a slip of paper on which is written the legend, "The Army shall live as long as the Republic shall live." It might as easily and truthfully say, at least as far as the nation's soldiers are concerned, that the republic is the army and the army is the republic.

   Given such a conception of the state, virtually any civilian institution— a legislature, a constitution, a civilian president—is likely to serve as window dressing for a government that is founded on force rather than laws. Democracy at best is an exercise. Certainly it is not coincidental that the only long-term conventional democracy in Latin America is in the one nation, Costa Rica, that has abolished its army. Yet U.S. policymakers continue to believe, and it is not clear why, that armies can be built or trained in Latin America which will guarantee democratic development rather than subvert it.

   The "establishment of nonpartisan constabularies in the Caribbean states" has been "one of the chief objectives" of U.S. policy at least since

---

"Obedezco pero no cumplo." From Robert S. Leiken, *Anatomy of Conflict* (Washington, 1984), pp. 36–43.

the 1920s. But as fast as the United States has "professionalized" an army, it has been converted to political ends. The most conspicuous example was Nicaragua's *Guardia Nacional.* Through the almost 20 years it occupied Nicaragua, the United States attempted to depoliticize its armed forces, first through training, then by building a new force, the Guardia Nacional, from the ground up. But even as Secretary of State Henry Stimson was warning Nicaraguan President José María Moncada in 1929 that Nicaragua's future was riding on "the establishment of an absolutely nonpartisan, nonpolitical Guardia which will devote its entire attention to the preservation of peace, law and order," Moncada was using it to round up his political enemies in the Conservative Party. By the time the U.S. Marines finally pulled out of Nicaragua in 1932, the force they had intended to be politically neutral served as the power base on which Guardia Commander Anastasio Somoza García constructed a family dictatorship lasting more than 43 years.

The idea that the most powerful institution in the country should *not* be politicized simply had no place in Nicaraguan tradition, just as, today, it has no place in the view of the Salvadoran officer corps. When Salvadoran officers say they are not involved and do not want to be involved with political parties, they are not removing themselves from the political arena, they are placing themselves squarely above it. The Salvadoran military may directly name a civilian president, as happened in April 1982, but no civilian president has the power to make even relatively minor changes in the military command structure.

Thus, for more than four years, ever since the October 1979 coup began the latest phase of El Salvador's relentlessly grim history, civilian politicians have said they were in a "process of control" over the army and security forces when in fact the reverse was true.

The young officers who had ousted Gen. Carlos Humberto Romero in 1979 were always strong on written ideals. They published a lengthy statement of principles the day of the coup in which they promised reforms and called for the establishment of truly democratic institutions. Many civilian politicians were brought into the newly formed government, including even members of the Communist Party, and the military took only two of the five seats on the five-man "revolutionary" junta. But as promising as all this might have seemed, when the civilians and some of the more radical young officers tried to gain effective veto power over the more traditionalist Defense Minister José Guillermo García, he and the commanders he had appointed forced the civilians out. Ten weeks after the new government was formed, the three civilians on the junta and every civilian in the cabinet resigned. García, of course, remained.

Then the Christian Democrats joined the government on the basis of a sweeping agreement that this time the military would abide by the promises of the coup. It was during this period—after the security forces slaughtered several leftist protesters occupying Christian Democratic headquarters, after a death squad probably connected with the security forces murdered one of the party's most charismatic leaders, as members of government farming cooperatives were being killed in wholesale lots and the national university was shut down—that Christian Democratic leader José Napoleón Duarte talked the most about the "process of control."

San Salvador Archbishop Oscar Romero, before he was assassinated in March of that year, described the Salvadoran reality much more accurately with one of those classic, anomalous-sounding Latin phrases: "Reform with repression."

After considerable prodding from the United States, in March 1980 the military finally did decree what were supposed to be sweeping reforms. But the only ones ever put into effect were aimed at the only group of civilians, the oligarchy, that had ever been able to share or subvert the military's domination of the country. None were meant to, nor did, touch the army's own power. Those that might have affected the holdings of some officers were never enforced.

And the repression. The U.S. press, prompted by the U.S. embassy, tended to explain it in circular terms. The murderers "of the extreme right" were simply political neanderthals. They killed all those people, presumably, just because they were there or because for some reason they were intent on destroying "the center." Certainly, they were out to stop the reforms.

In the complex netherworld of El Salvador's clandestine political violence all of the above may be true. Some murders were completely incomprehensible and much of the slaughter did grow out of vendettas so involved and so obscure that no one but the killers and, perhaps, the victims could be expected to decipher them. But a great deal of the murder in El Salvador was and is committed because the Salvadoran officer corps believes that on the most basic level, it works.

It is vital to remember this. The overall policy of repression, far from being the work of madmen who fail to understand the reality of their country, is carried out with cold calculation by officers who feel certain that Washington has no conception of where its demands are likely to lead. As they see it they are dealing with a logic—a reality, if you will—that Washington refuses to acknowledge. The human rights demands of Carter, of Reagan, of Congress are not enforced for much the same reason the *Nuevas Leyes* were not enforced four centuries ago: because to do so would very likely bring the whole structure of government crashing down. If Carlos V wanted gold, finally, he had to let the colonists get it by the means they chose; otherwise they would simply go home, leaving him with no gold and no colony. If Washington wants to stop communism, it has found itself obliged to let the Salvadorans do the job as they, not as it, sees fit. To do otherwise, it would have to be ready to accept revolutionary change in the region. That, Washington has made clear, it will not do. The result, the Salvadoran military realizes, is de facto acceptance of the means it chooses to employ.

Ironically, but in line with the classic pattern, Washington has multiplied its demands on El Salvador in proportion to their ineffectiveness. Every time the United States sets goals and they are ignored, then changes the definition of its goals to make it seem, for reasons of domestic political consumption, that they were obeyed, the gap between what it says it wants and what it gets grows wider. Disobedience—or, rather, non-compliance —is endorsed.

Again, consider the way Washington read the events of 1980 in El Salvador. It emphasized the efficacy of reforms that did not work and attempted to disavow or deny the effectiveness of repression which did.

The immediate goal of the Salvadoran army and security forces—and of the United States—in 1980 was to prevent a takeover by the leftist-led guerrillas and their allied political organizations. At this point in the Salvadoran conflict the latter were much more important than the former. The military resources of the rebels were extremely limited and their greatest strength by far lay not in force of arms but in their "mass organizations" made up of labor unions, student and peasant organizations that could be mobilized by the thousands in El Salvador's major cities and could shut down the country through strikes. The immediate goal of anyone interested in stopping the advances of the left had to be the elimination of the guerrillas' urban bases. This the government did. U.S. officials argued then and now that the land reform initiated in March 1980 played a major role in undercutting the guerrillas' popular support. They noted that the same organizations that were able to march hundreds of thousands of people through San Salvador's streets on January 22, 1980, could not mount a successful general strike by August of the same year, and showed virtually no major support by the time they staged their abortive "final offensive" in January 1981.

But if the reforms did in fact undermine popular support for the guerrillas, and this is far from certain, they would have had their greatest impact in the countryside—whereas today the rebels are stronger than ever in the countryside.

The great setback for the guerrillas in 1980 came not in their rural strongholds but in the cities, not as a result of the reforms but precisely because of the ruthless repression that killed almost 10,000 people in a year, among them many key members of the rebel organizations.

Washington repeatedly condemned the abuses as both morally wrong and politically counterproductive. U.S. Ambassador Robert White and his successors in the U.S. mission argued that right-wing death squads and the military's semi-clandestine slaughter ultimately benefitted the rebels; that people forced to choose sides by such violent tactics might be likely to choose the left; that on the international front the human rights issue was the most powerful weapon in the guerrilla arsenal. Yet this rather abstract reasoning, particularly at that point in the war, was difficult for many officers to understand. They did not see people flocking to the rebel banner as a result of the repression. Quite the contrary, they saw the rebel movement in the city dying. Literally.

As for the human rights "weapon" in the hands of the guerrillas, many officers probably underestimated its impact abroad in 1980 and 1981. But the certification process initiated by the U.S. Congress in 1982 to demand improvements on that front served after two or three instances to allay rather than aggravate the concerns of the most extreme officers. The certifications made it increasingly clear that the Reagan administration was not going to choose human rights over the fight against communism. The certification in the summer of 1983 drew little or no attention from the North American press and public, and by the fall the military could consider that whatever might have been lost on the human rights front was more than balanced by the elimination of the rebels' urban base. The high command wrote pages and pages of rules promoting the observance of human rights, so many pages that one must wonder what the semiliterate Salvadoran infantryman was expected to do with them. But the conviction remained among many officers that repression was not only useful, it was necessary, and that lip-service to human rights was all that the U.S. really demanded.

Events in the fall of 1983 suggest just how seriously Washington had been fooled, or had fooled itself about the Salvadoran army's response to its demands for improvements in human rights and improved "command and control." There had been embarrassments and anomalies all along. One example was the conduct of U.S.-trained battalions in the field. The commander of the first to enter combat, a generally capable officer of moderate politics by Salvadoran standards, was referred to around the embassy as "Thumbs-Behind-the-Back" Monterrosa because of recurrent reports about his units slaughtering civilians. But throughout 1982 and early 1983 the U.S. State Department was at least able to argue that "abuses" by the security forces were decreasing and the "death squads" disappearing. The embassy's regular reports known as "grim grams" cited statistics based on local press accounts and noted, accurately, a general reduction of tension in the capital. U.S. policy was working, U.S. officials said. Its demands on the Salvadorans were understood and were being complied with, they said.

In retrospect it is now apparent that the decline in urban slaughter came about less because of improved command and control than because the left had basically abandoned the capital after January 1981. With few suspects there were fewer killings. Murder in the countryside, meanwhile, was less frequently reported in the local papers and thus did not show up in the "grim gram" statistics. As soon as the left's efforts to renew operations and organizing in the capital became evident in mid-1983, the death squads and the "abuses" began to rise once again. The "process of control" over the armed forces, at least insofar as the slaughter of suspected rebel sympathizers was concerned, proved once again to be a paper promise.

Compounding the political problems raised by the revival of the death squads in the cities, from Washington's viewpoint, was the military dilemma provoked by the Salvadoran army's seeming inability to mount effective campaigns against any force capable of shooting back. At weekly background briefings in the U.S. embassy during 1982 and 1983, top U.S. advisers talked to the press about the ineptness of many Salvadoran commanders, especially those who had proved unable or unwilling to adopt the kind of search and destroy tactics the Pentagon recommended.

The advisers blamed the cliquishness of the Salvadoran officer corps for much of the problem. Men who had known each other since they were in their teens, who were bound by tradition, by *compadrazco,* in some instances by marriage, tended to cover for each others' abuses or incompetence in any case, and all the more so when the charges were coming from foreigners considered ignorant of Salvadoran realities. As this deeply imbedded cronyism proved virtually impossible for Washington to overcome there was increasing talk in early 1983 about what then-U.S. Ambassador Deane Hinton called "generational change": training virtually an entire new officer corps from the ground up. Salvadoran ninety-day wonders would not only emerge from their training at Fort Benning, Georgia, as better soldiers, they would be transformed overnight, as it were, from Latin American soldiers into North American soldiers.

Not surprisingly, the Salvadorans are remaining Salvadorans. The U.S.-trained second lieutenants and cadets are carefully watched by their superiors to make sure they conform to the traditions of the Salvadoran, not the United States army.

Meanwhile the most extreme right-wing clique of officers in the army has not only proved impervious to Washington's dictates, it has prospered and become ever more influential. This group, conspicuous for its fascist ideology and peculiarly tight-knit personal relationships, is dominated by Col. Nicolás Carranza and represented most publicly by Constituent Assembly President ex-Major Roberto d'Aubuisson.

Three years ago that group appeared to have been squeezed out of any significant role in the army or the nation's politics. Its senior commanders had been removed from positions of authority by then-Defense Minister García after their ties to the death squads had become embarrassingly public and their ultra-rightist ideology made them too intractable to control.

Since former Guardia Nacional Commander Gen. Carlos Eugenio Vides Casanova took over the defense ministry in April 1983, however, those officers have reemerged with more conspicuous power than they ever had before. A key element in their resurgence has been their adoption of Washington's language even as they ignore its principles. They have embraced the ideal of "professionalism," the latest Pentagon buzzword for a "nonpartisan constabulary." Senior U.S. advisers repeatedly have cited them as examples they wish the rest of the Salvadoran officer corps would follow. Yet these golden boys have a persistent way of becoming grave embarrassments; the very model of a modern lieutenant colonel proves either murderous or mutinous or both.

One of the most conspicuous examples is Lt. Col. Jorge Adalberto Cruz, commander of Morazán province. He was among those officers arrested with d'Aubuisson while plotting a coup against the Christian Democratic junta in May 1980. Papers seized with this group suggested links to the death squads and to the assassination a few weeks earlier of San Salvador's archbishop. Shipped off to the Chilean police academy for two years, Cruz is now back in El Salvador commanding the front-line garrison in San Francisco Gotera. In August 1983 he openly denounced El Salvador's political parties, said flatly that his country is not ready for U.S.-style democracy, and named several other commanders in the region as incompetent. As of December 1983, he was still in command in Gotera.

Lt. Col. Mario Denis Morán was head of the Guardia Nacional intelligence unit in December 1980 when four North American churchwomen were killed by members of that security force. When two U.S. labor advisors and the head of the Salvadoran agrarian reform agency were gunned down in the Sheraton Hotel a few weeks later, Morán was there. Although no conclusive evidence has implicated him in the crime, and he reportedly "passed" a lie-detector test, it is suggestive, certainly, that his personal bodyguard and that his second-in-command have confessed to being the trigger men. After that, Morán spent two years attached to various Salvadoran embassies in South America before Vides Casanova brought him back to command the garrison at Zacatecoluca—the same town, as it happens, where the alleged killers of the nuns are being tried.

The path to professional redemption for these officers was opened up by one of their old classmates, Lt. Col. Sigifredo Ochoa. As acting head of the notorious Treasury Police in the days immediately following the October coup, Ochoa had been implicated in the politically sensitive murder of a sacristan in one of San Salvador's working-class barrios. He was shipped off to diplomatic exile almost immediately. Then on his return to El Salvador he was given command of the rugged, poor, remote and guerrilla-infested province of Cabañas. In less than a year he had "pacified" his territory and established himself not only as the dominant military force, but the political leader of the province. U.S. Military Group Commander Col. John Waghelstein repeatedly lauded him as the most effective departmental commander in the Salvadoran army. But in January 1983, García, apparently irritated with Ochoa's increasing notoriety, and certainly aware of his close personal connections with d'Aubuisson and the ultra-rightists, ordered Ochoa to give up his command once again and accept de facto exile in Uruguay.

Ochoa's reported response was short and simple as he initiated a six-day mutiny that effectively ended García's authority and eventually led to García's removal, throwing the Salvadoran military into the renewed, relentless series of intrigues that increasingly crippled it through the course of the year.

"Obedezco," said Ochoa, "pero no cumplo."

4.
U.S. STATE DEPARTMENT: HUMAN RIGHTS IN EL SALVADOR (FEBRUARY 1979)

Human rights abuses, diminishing faith in the electoral process and underlying economic and social ills have led to growing terrorism from both extreme right and left. In reaction to the terrorism, a "Public Order Law" severely abridging civil liberties was passed in late 1977. A Government-sponsored para-military mass political organization, ORDEN, which operates largely in rural areas, has used violence in its conflicts with anti-Government peasant organizations and has engaged in active opposition to dissent in rural areas. Clashes in the countryside with anti-Government peasant groups have resulted in deaths. Salvadoran society is becoming increasingly polarized.

Recent elections in El Salvador have been marred by fraud. The present Government of General Carlos Humberto Romero came to power following the elections of February, 1977, in which fraud was again an issue. The Christian Democratic and allied opposition parties boycotted the 1978

Report on Human Rights Practices in Countries Receiving U.S. Aid, submitted to the U.S. Congress, February 8, 1979.

mayoral and National Assembly elections, leaving only token opposition from a small conservative party.

1. RESPECT FOR THE INTEGRITY OF THE PERSON, INCLUDING FREEDOM FROM:

A. TORTURE

There have been numerous detailed allegations of torture of prisoners by security guards, many of which are credible. Accusations against the National Guard and other security forces include denial of food and water, electric shock and sexual violation. Several apparently credible reports reaching foreign church and human rights organizations indicate that torture or the threat of torture were still being used by Government security forces in late 1978. There have been no public investigations of these charges.

B. CRUEL, INHUMAN OR DEGRADING TREATMENT OR PUNISHMENT

There is little doubt that certain elements of the security forces have subjected prisoners to "degrading treatment."

There have been conflicting allegations as to who fired first in some confrontations which resulted in deaths. In March, one police officer was killed and another severely wounded in a clash with protesters. Nine demonstrators were killed or wounded in that incident.

Several anti-Government peasants were killed by ORDEN or security forces and at least one member of ORDEN was killed during a major incident at San Pedro Perulapán. National Guard units occupied the area and arrested more than sixty anti-Government peasants but no members of ORDEN. Many of those arrested were physically mistreated. Allegations of serious abuses do not appear to have been investigated or targeted for Government corrective action.

Private violence has been endemic in El Salvador. In late September 1978 police began a campaign to confiscate the hand-guns carried by many citizens, a measure aimed at a reduction in that societal violence. The Department estimates that 150 politically related deaths occurred in 1978, including those killed by Government security forces, by ORDEN, by private unknown parties or by terrorists. Increasing terrorist incidents have produced growing fears within the business community leading to the departure of a significant number of businessmen and their families, exacerbating political and economic tensions.

C. ARBITRARY ARREST OR IMPRISONMENT

The Government passed the Law of Defense and Guarantee of Public Order in November 1977, in response to strong pressure to control the increase in kidnappings, assassinations and terrorist incidents. Elements of the Catholic Church and all major opposition parties and groups have condemned the new law as unconstitutional, maintaining it is tantamount to a State of Siege. The law gives Government officials authority to arrest and hold alleged subversives, terrorists or even critics for 72 hours without specific charges. It requires that detainees be turned over to the judicial system within 72 hours. According to credible sources, this 72-hour legal detention period itself has been exceeded in many cases, with the reports of capture being adjusted when and if the detained person is turned over to the courts. The Government admits the law is imperfect, but asserts it has provided a legal basis to combat a substantially increased terrorist threat. An International Commission of Jurists report, following a June visit by that organization's representative, stated that the law "results in serious infringements of the right of free speech . . . reduces the independence of the judiciary . . . and invites an abuse of power on the part of the security forces." Terrorist incidents have occurred more frequently since promulgation of the law.

Between December 15, 1977 and July 9, 1978, 715 persons were arrested under the law according to a report prepared by the socially-active Catholic Archdiocese of San Salvador. The report continued that of these, 590 were freed, most after being beaten, and stated also that two were assassinated and 21 "disappeared." In late August, the Salvadoran Commission on Human Rights said that the cases of about 200 persons detained under the Public Order law still were being adjudicated. However, Salvadoran government records in October indicated that 283 had been arrested to date under the law and that most of those had been released.

The Archdiocese, Amnesty International and other groups maintain lists of persons they believe to be political prisoners, "disappeared persons," and persons murdered while in official custody. The Congressional Research Service stated in a July report that "apparent arbitrary detentions," "disappearances" and "probably elimination" have become "an increasingly common pattern." The Archdiocese published in September 1978 a list of one hundred "disappeared persons" with dates of their reported capture by the security forces. Earlier, Amnesty presented a list to the Government of 62 persons allegedly detained who then "disappeared." The number of persons currently detained for political activities is unknown. Most estimates range between 100 and 200. . . .

D. DENIAL OF FAIR PUBLIC TRIAL

The judiciary is slow and over-burdened. After arraignment, long delays usually occur before trial. Trials are public and courts are believed to operate fairly and independently, at least in cases other than those involving security suspects or the wealthy.

In some cases involving those accused of terrorism, both judges and witnesses are alleged to refrain from guilty verdicts for fear of terrorist retaliation. On November 7 the chief judge of one of two civilian courts that administers the Law of Public Order was wounded in an assassination attempt which the leftist terrorist group, the Popular Forces of Liberation (FPL), claimed to have made. The police have been unable to apprehend the perpetrators of most of the kidnappings, assassinations and other acts of terrorism. In those few cases where alleged leftist terrorists have been apprehended and presented for trial, the prosecution has generally been unable to obtain a conviction.

E. INVASION OF THE HOME

Government security forces armed with the Law of Public Order have increased their searches of private homes. Under the new law, searches require neither court authorization nor search warrant. There are credible allegations that persons are taken from their homes by the security forces without a warrant or specific charge; this allegedly occurs most frequently in the interior of the country.

2. GOVERNMENTAL POLICIES RELATING TO THE FULFILLMENT OF SUCH VITAL NEEDS AS FOOD, SHELTER, HEALTH CARE AND EDUCATION

Some Government policies and actions indicate a growing awareness of the country's critical social and economic problems. However, no Government programs undertaken to date have changed the basic socio-economic structure with its problems and historic inequities. These include serious over-population, rising unemployment, highly skewed income distribution, widespread poverty and concentration of land ownership in the hands of the wealthy. Although the Government has asserted its desire to solve these problems, steps taken thus far have been modest and the rate of progress has been slow. Measures taken include action in 1978 to initiate a regional development program in small-scale irrigation, basic skills training and technical education focusing on the depressed northern area of the country. A new property tax law designed to encourage the break-up of unproductive large estates was passed and its implementation begun. The Government sells grain for less than the free market price. A recent across-the-board increase in the minimum wage was approved, but it did not fully offset the effects of inflation on lower income groups. Corruption involving public funds, though it does occur, is not notorious in El Salvador.

According to Government statistics expenditures for vital human needs (education, health, social assistance, social security and housing) represent approximately forty percent of the national budget, fifteen percent to eighteen percent being currently allocated to health-related expenditures. Elementary school enrollment is expanding at the rate of 4.6 percent per year and high school enrollment at 12.5 percent, both considerably higher than the population growth rate.

A natural population growth rate of 3.2 to 3.3 percent is El Salvador's most serious long-run problem. The Government formulated and recently strengthened one of the most progressive national family planning programs in the hemisphere.

3. RESPECT FOR CIVIL AND POLITICAL LIBERTIES, INCLUDING:

A. FREEDOM OF THOUGHT, SPEECH, PRESS, RELIGION AND ASSEMBLY

Freedoms of speech, press and assembly are sometimes restricted. An opposition newspaper *(La Crónica)* and several organs of the Roman Catholic Church are allowed to publish strong criticisms of the Government. Anti-Government commentary seldom appears in other newspapers, presumably because of the essentially pro-Government political beliefs and policies of their private owners. However, the Public Order Law provides up to three years' imprisonment for persons who disseminate, either inside the country or abroad, biased or false information designed to disrupt the constitutional or legal order or the country's peace and security.

While freedom of religion *per se* is not an issue in El Salvador, the Church's role in politics is. The constitution prohibits political activity by the Church or clergy. The Government continued throughout 1978 to denounce those Church statements and activities which it considered anti-Government and unconstitutional. The number of physical threats against the so-called progressive elements of the Roman Catholic hierarchy by right-wing groups decreased in 1978. The Church made credible charges that some lay workers in rural areas continued to be intimidated, beaten and harassed as "subversives" by local police authorities and Government supporters.

Some groups whose demonstrations previously have involved clashes with security forces have had their freedom of assembly selectively curtailed under the Law of Public Order. Government forces have forcibly broken up some of their meetings and arrested leaders. Permits have been issued for some anti-Government groups, however. The May 1 (Labor Day), 1978 demonstration was the calmest in many years.

Urban labor unions are authorized by law, but they are fragmented and dependent to a large degree on government and/or foreign assistance. Ideologically-oriented labor unions have been harassed, while those concentrating on trade union questions have operated more freely, though they too have encountered sporadic harassment. Peasant or rural mass organizations, with the exceptions of the *Unión Comunal Salvadoreña* (USC) and the Government-dominated ORDEN, are considered by the Government to be subversive and extra-illegal. The International Commission of Jurists noted in its June 1978 report that "violations of the rights of political and trade union opponents of the government are not isolated incidents...."

5.
ANEP: DECLARATIONS ON LAND REFORM AND THE GOVERNMENT'S RESPONSE (JULY 1976)

1ST DECLARATION OF THE ANEP

As a result of the latest decisions of the government which are causing grave discouragement and upheaval in the economic and social development of the country, we consider it our duty to place before public opinion the following considerations:

1. As the entity representing Salvadoran private enterprise, the ANEP has always supported the existence of an economic system responding to social justice, through the establishment of conditions appropriate to the development and stimulation of private activity. As a consequence of said philosophy we object to an economic policy inspired by the methodology and principles of centralized planning which has been preparing the basis for a regime with a tendency toward totalitarianism, covered with an apparent clothing of democracy.

2. The surprising and sudden procedure by which the latest legislation was imposed has destroyed the independence among the branches of government, nullifying parliamentary action, the solid rock of every democratic regime. . . .

5. Time has proven that our fears are not ill-founded. On establishing the first Agrarian Reform Plan, with purely political designs, an amazing

---

Statements by the National Association of Private Enterprise (ANEP) of July 8 and 9, 1976.

blow, lacking all justification, was struck at one of the best areas of Salvadoran agriculture. . . .

6. It is not possible to destroy the spirit of enterprise without creating more misery. Distributive justice cannot have as its basis the punishment of productive efficiency. Unless they have inverted all logic, or they are pursuing totalitarian objectives, the agrarian reform in El Salvador must have as one of its principal objectives the creation of more agricultural production for the benefit of a greater number of people within a regime of legality and respect for rights.

7. There exists a justified fear that the planning group is preparing additional projects that will further destroy the spirit of enterprise. . . . When the Constitution guarantees private property these fundamental principles cannot be thrown aside for purely political motives.

8. The NATIONAL ASSOCIATION OF PRIVATE ENTERPRISE (ANEP) reiterates that it does not oppose an agrarian reform, nor does it oppose national reform, if these concepts mean the incorporation of the vast majority into a more worthy life and a more just participation in national production; but it emphatically reaffirms that it cannot remain indifferent to an orientation that accentuates each day the insertion of the state, in a negative manner, into the economic and social life of our nation.

San Salvador, July 8, 1976.

3RD DECLARATION OF THE ANEP

WE DECLARE:

1. The ANEP is not a small group trying to direct the judgment of Salvadoran entrepreneurs. It is a federation of 25 associations representing the most productive sectors of the nation which uses its legitimate right to state its opinions. . . .

The ANEP rejects the demagogic and classist language of the latest publication of the government. This attempt to divide the citizenry is more appropriate to groups attempting to freeze relations, endangering social peace, than it is to the government of the Republic, whose primary obligation is to maintain a climate of tranquility and concord.

Such attempts to freeze relationships create a favorable environment for doctrinaire groups who, from their desks, try to impose foreign doctrines on the Salvadoran government, illegitimately using the influence that they have managed to acquire. The planning group uses the same doctrinaire, vague, imprecise, and therefore, dangerous language to which the demagogues of all latitudes are accustomed, especially in those nations where the liberties and rights of the citizens are endangered. . . .

5. The thesis of the group planning the Agrarian Reform, like any other, is a thesis worthy of study. What is not valid is that this academic focus, divorced from national reality, is adopted as a criterion of governance and

is imposed on the country without discussion, as a panacea allowing neither variation nor alternatives.

The ANEP rejects this totalitarian position and demands the right to state its opinion concerning a matter of such transcendent importance for the nation, in a manner free of pressure and shadowy threats.

The grave economic and social problems of the country will not be solved by attacking private property and other constitutional rights and freedoms, nor with efforts or experiments which have failed in other areas of the world. Instead there is needed a large dose of authentic nationalism, not merely of the word, but of thought and results, reforming what needs reformation, with the objective of creating better conditions for the more rational enjoyment of our natural and human resources. . . .

THE GOVERNMENT'S RESPONSE

1. What is truly surprising to the government and to the Salvadoran people is that the ANEP calls "surprising" a plan which has been announced over all the media of the nation by the President since January 14. On that date he said, "During the next weeks we will present to the Legislative Assembly the Plan for Agrarian Reform," which was published in the national press the following day. Moreover, this Plan, as has been done, could only put into practice the outlines and norms of the law creating the Salvadoran Institute of Agrarian Reform, which was published in the Diario Oficial, number 120, volume 247, June 30, 1975, that is to say, exactly one year before the President gave his sanction to the decree creating the First Plan. . . .

The Armed Forces are aware of the scope of this measure, whose purpose is nothing other than to bring justice to the sector that most needs it. This will be a new and magnificent opportunity through which the man who produces the agricultural riches of the nation can again prove to himself that his brother in uniform is always present to guard his conquests. . . .

2. The true productivity in the region of the Plan, categorically and repeatedly affirmed by the ANEP, is a totally unfounded and false claim. On the contrary, productivity in the area is one of the lowest of the nation's coastal zone, given that the indices of efficiency are as follows: in cattle-raising more than 55% is composed of uninhabited exploitations, worked on the basis of natural feed; in cereal there is only a 30% productive efficiency; and in cotton, which seems to support itself because of its importance, the index of efficiency is hardly 55%. . . .

The situation of these owners of small parcels of land inside the area of the Plan can be better clarified if one looks at the two extremes of land tendency in the area of the Plan in which 2,483 owners possess 5,006.43 blocks and five owners possess 17,318.73 blocks. For the good of the

nation, we hope that the ANEP did not know of these data before beginning to speak of the productivity in the area of the plan for private property
in a social function and, much less, of "social justice," which they mention
repeatedly in their thoughts. . . .

On the other side of the coin, even leaving aside the false supposition that
the entire area has the same very low average productivity of the small
landowners, 5 landowners have a daily income of 2,438.71 *colones* each,
that is to say that one landowner would have the income of 6,968 families.
Naturally the figures are larger as a result of the productivity derived from
ownership of the land. AFTER ALL, IT IS NOT A SIN TO HAVE A
HIGH INCOME, BUT NEITHER IS IT A SIN TO BE BORN. And
from this thought the writers of the ANEP's thoughts can draw whatever
conclusions they wish. . . .

The publication of the ANEP is a proof of the existence of freedom of
thought and freedom of expression in El Salvador, which constitute two
of the bases and guarantees of democracy. . . .

San Salvador, July 9, 1976.

6.
POPULAR BLOC: ATTACK ON THE JUNTA'S LAND REFORM (AUGUST 1976)

1. The First Agrarian Reform Plan is a counterrevolutionary economic-
   political measure of imperialism in our country, seeking the following
   goals:

   a) In the short term, to use demagogically the peasantry's desires to
   trick it into supporting the tyrannical regime's pro-imperialist
   policy and impede its incorporation in the revolutionary struggle.

   b) In the medium term, to guarantee the survival of the capitalist
   exploitative system, attempting to slow the final, mortal crisis of
   dependent capitalism in El Salvador.

   c) In the long term, to consolidate indefinitely its political and economic dominion over our country and to create a belt of imperialist penetration in Central America. . . .

2. The distribution of land within the Plan will be completed within three
   years (if it is ever completed) and involves only 4 percent of the land
   which will be awarded to only 12,000 families. This means that the

government believes the remaining 400,000 peasant families will continue to die with resignation of misery and hunger. . . .

3. The government, spokesman for imperialism, claims that in exchange for crumbs, the people will submit to their exploiters' designs to continue living off the sweat of workers and peasants.

4. . . . the government, following the orders of imperialism and its creole allies, is unleashing repression . . . killing humble peasants and workers, unleashing fear throughout the population, kidnapping, stealing, etc. This is designed to contain the advance of the popular revolutionary movement.

5. The government and its imperialist masters feel that the so-called "Agrarian Reform" is necessary as life insurance . . . precisely because the popular revolutionary struggle of our people is gloriously advancing. . . .

10. The contradiction between ANEP (spokesman for the creole bourgeoisie) and the government (the direct spokesman of imperialism) is fundamentally a difference of judgment over the best means to combat and exploit our people. While the imperialists and their puppet government think that it is now necessary to "concede a bit in order not to lose everything," ANEP states that it is necessary to defeat the revolution without having to sacrifice a thing. . . .

CONCLUSION

The Popular Bloc plans to undertake the following efforts to counter the counterrevolutionary plans pompously called the "Agrarian Reform":

1. . . . To unmask the plans of domination and exploitation of Imperialism and of the dominant creole classes. . . .

2. Specifically, to orient the field workers, laborers and poor peasants to the beliefs that:

   a) The land should belong to the workers of the entire nation.

   b) We must struggle to end every kind of monopoly over the land, be it of cereal, coffee, cotton or sugar-cane.

   c) The peasants . . . should struggle to obtain and use the land. . . .

   d) It is necessary to fight to improve the conditions under which land is rented.

3. To increase the combative, constant struggles of all the exploited masses for their immediate economic, political, and social demands.

4. To combat energetically the reactionary organizations created by the current regime (such as ORDEN, UCS, FOCCO, etc.), be they entities of repression or for generating its social base of support.

5. To fight for the incorporation of the working class into the revolutionary struggle and for the formation of a worker-peasant alliance.
6. To develop and consolidate the Popular Bloc looking forward toward
   the formation of the revolutionary front of the masses.

LET US COMBAT THE PLANS OF DOMINATION AND EXPLOITATION
OF IMPERIALISM, THE CREOLE BOURGEOISIE AND THEIR PUPPET
GOVERNMENT: THE FASCIST-LIKE MILITARY TYRANNY OF EL
SALVADOR!

FOR THE POPULAR REVOLUTION TOWARD SOCIALISM!
FOR A POPULAR REVOLUTIONARY GOVERNMENT!

7.
TOMMY SUE MONTGOMERY: CHURCH AND SOCIAL ACTIVISM

. . . The Second Vatican Council (Vatican II) convened in 1962 under Pope
John XXIII and closed three years later under Pope Paul VI. Prior to
Vatican II, national churches in Latin America presented a uniformly
traditional religious image, accompanied by sharply conservative social
and political attitudes. Virtually everywhere, including El Salvador, the
church was allied with the regime.

Vatican II changed this state of affairs almost overnight. The council,
strongly influenced by Pope John XXIII's social encyclicals, especially
Pacem in Terris, . . . asserted that the church is in and of the world, with
concerns well beyond the purely spiritual. They also emphasized that the
church is a community of equals by baptism. The prelates refused to
condemn communism per se, joining criticism of certain of its practices
with an equally strong critique of capitalism's abuses.

Three years after the end of Vatican II bishops from all over Latin
America gathered in Medellín, Colombia, for the Second Episcopal Conference (CELAM II). . . .

At Medellín the bishops called upon the church "to defend the rights
of the oppressed"; to promote grassroots organizations; "to denounce the
unjust action of world powers that works against self-determination of
weaker nations"; in short, to make a "preferential option for the poor."

The primary means of accomplishing these ends was the development

---

From her *Revolution in El Salvador* (Boulder, Colo., 1982).

of Christian Base Communities (CEBs). It can be argued that these communities are the most revolutionary development in the Latin American church because, for the first time in history, the masses of the people began participating in and taking responsibility for important aspects of their own lives and for each other; they were no longer merely observers at a ritual conducted for their benefit by a resident or visiting priest. This form of participation, however, has had social consequences. With a growing frequency that disturbs traditional members of the church, CEB members have moved beyond purely religious concerns to political issues. Nowhere in Latin America has this been more true or had more profound consequences than in El Salvador. . . .

AGUILARES AND RUTILIO GRANDE

Nowhere did the development of CEBs have a faster or more profound impact than in the small town of Aguilares, 35 kilometers north of San Salvador. There, in September 1972, Father Rutilio Grande and three fellow Jesuits arrived to take up pastoral duties. What happened in Aguilares in the succeeding four and a half years was replayed in many locales throughout El Salvador, sometimes with equally dramatic results.

Grande and his fellow priests divided Aguilares into ten mission zones and the surrounding countryside into fifteen other zones. They talked with residents of each zone about the best place to locate the mission center, then visited the families in each zone to learn about individual and community problems. In short, they conducted a socioeconomic survey of the parish, with many religious and cultural questions included.

Later, in each mission center, they conducted evangelizing sessions with children, then adults, the purpose of which was to give the people a basic outline by which they could continue celebrating the word of God on their own. In this way the priests were able to begin a process of "self-evangelization," of building a community, and of selection by the community of catechists and delegates of the Word. The delegates subsequently received additional weekly training and instruction from the priests. . . .

It cannot be emphasized too strongly that the work of Grande and his associates was consciously, deliberately, and exclusively pastoral, never political. At the same time the content of their evangelizing message, although always drawn from the Bible and the social doctrine of the church, was profoundly radicalizing in a political as well as a religious sense. . . .

Jesus' "preferential option for the poor," the message ran, did not mean that he hated the rich. On the contrary, he had many wealthy friends. In this sense, Grande continued, Jesus was the "liberator" of all people, poor and rich alike. This liberation results in a totally integrated human being, a person transfigured (converted) so that all aspects of one's life—family, business, pleasure—are a unified whole. Such liberation, Grande preached, would free the oppressed from their oppression, and their oppressors from oppressing.

It does not require much imagination to understand the impact of such a message on poorly educated *campesinos* for whom the biblical message until this time had been "accept your lot here on earth because your real reward will come in the hereafter." The *campesinos* lost little time relating the gospel message to their own "situation of misery and injustice. . . .

The results were electric. Eight months after the arrival of the priests in Aguilares, on May 24, 1973, 1,600 workers in the La Babaña sugar mill struck on payday for six hours because they did not receive an orally promised salary increase. The strike was peaceful and ended when management granted a raise, albeit less than that which was originally promised.

The strike was not organized by the parish, but many of the workers were members of the CEBs. . . .

By mid-1975 the priests of Aguilares were being called "subversives." . . . By Christmas President Molina was making public statements against what he termed "liberationist clerics." In the meantime, Father Rafael Barahona, a diocesan priest from San Vicente, was taken into custody and transported to National Guard headquarters in San Salvador. There he was severely beaten as his assailants "used profanity to insult me as a priest. One of them struck me and said mockingly: I am excommunicated, I am excommunicated." Barahona's bishop, Monseñor Aparicio, obliged not only the soldier, but all the other government officials responsible for Barahona's incarceration. "The torturer who clamored for excommunication now has it," a furious bishop wrote the national government. In one of his rare defenses of the pastoral work of his priests, Aparicio inquired if "the Constitution of El Salvador has two interpretations, one for the authorities and the other for the people? We would like a response, if it would not annoy you, Honorable Authorities, so as not to teach our students a mistaken lesson."

POLITICAL EFFECTS OF CHURCH ACTIVISM

President Molina's decree of a limited agrarian reform in March 1976 received strong support from the church.

In this period the right began looking for scapegoats on which to blame Molina's lapse and found one in the church, which, they decided, was "inciting the people to revolt." To appease the oligarchy, Molina and Minister of Defense Humberto Romero arrested five priests and expelled eighteen others, including two Jesuits from UCA. The climate was such that by May 1977 fliers urging Salvadoreans to "Be a Patriot! Kill a Priest!" were circulating in the capital. By then two priests had been assassinated, one of them Rutilio Grande as he drove with two parishioners from Aguilares to El Paisnal to celebrate mass on the afternoon of March 12, 1977. The three Jesuits who had been working with Grande were expelled. . . .

OSCAR ARNULFO ROMERO BECOMES ARCHBISHOP

The selection of Monseñor Oscar Romero, bishop of Santiago de María, as archbishop of San Salvador was greeted with widespread dismay throughout the archdiocese. . . .

Romero . . . had spent most of his priestly life in the eastern section of the country. He was considered to be quiet and noncontroversial. His detractors considered him an ally of the oligarchy and were extremely worried that he would halt or even try to reverse the process of evangelization that had been developed during the previous eight years. . . .

Romero stunned everyone by wasting no time declaring where he stood. But it was the assassination of Grande only three weeks after his installation that turned Romero into an unflinching prophet of the church. . . .

Romero understood well why this commitment would cause him and other priests to be labeled subversives; the moment the issue of defense of the poor is raised in El Salvador, he remarked shortly before the inauguration of President Romero, "You call the whole thing into question. That is why they have no other recourse than to call us subversives—that is what we are." Archbishop Romero declined to attend the inauguration of President Romero on July 1, 1977, reasoning that it was preferable to risk exacerbating hostilities than to appear and thereby bless a system characterized by fraud, corruption, and repression.

During Oscar Romero's three years and one month as archbishop, the role of the church in the political life of the country expanded with each succeeding crisis. At the same time, under ever-increasing difficulties brought about by waves of persecution against priests, religious, and CEB members, the church itself was growing and was having a greater and greater impact on the life of the average Salvadorean—which is to say, the poor. While Christian Base Communities multiplied, the focus increasingly was on the diminutive archbishop of San Salvador, both within and outside the country.

Romero's message reached into almost every corner of the country (as well as Guatemala, Honduras, and Nicaragua) via the radio station of the archdiocese, YSAX. Within a short time, the 8:00 mass on Sunday morning became the single most listened-to program in the nation. In second place were YSAX's commentaries, written by as many as twenty different people whose identities were a carefully guarded secret. In third place was Romero's weekly interview. All these programs were broadcast three times in order to reach the largest possible audience. . . .

All of these people were waiting for "Monseñor's" homily, which generally ran an hour and a half. Each sermon . . . began with a theological exposition—always with three points—on the scriptural readings of the day. Then he would relate the scripture to the reality of life in El Salvador. This was followed by church announcements, then a recitation of the events of the week just ended, including a reading of every documented case of persons who had been killed, assaulted, or tortured (by *any* group on the left or the right) or who had disappeared. The Salvadorean reality, however, ensured that the list of attacks at the hands of the government's security forces and the right-wing terrorist groups was many times longer than those by left-wing guerrillas. When an event, such as the coup of October 15 or the promulgation of the agrarian reform, warranted it, Romero would conclude with a "pastoral position" on the question.

These homilies, then, were not only religious instruction for the people, but they were oral newspapers as well. As such they were a potent force in El Salvador from 1977 onward. Just how potent can be measured by the fact that the YSAX transmitter or antenna was bombed ten times in three years. . . . The archdiocesan newspaper, *Tación,* was also the recipient of several bombs after Romero became archbishop. In spite of or perhaps because of the attacks, circulation almost tripled in the first half of 1977. . . .

Christian Base Communities were functioning; the number would grow to thirty-two in a short time. In February 1969 the priests began a two-month course in which the CEBs discussed biblical themes and the form of the CEBs. . . .

While these courses were going on the ubiquitous problem of land tenancy was coming to a head in Suchitoto. Roberto Hill . . . [one] of the country's wealthiest oligarchs . . . purchased the Hacienda La Asunción for $97 per *manzana* (1 *manzana* = 0.7 hectares), subdivided it, and put it back on the market for $280 to $680 per *manzana.* This so outraged the *campesinos* that they mobilized the entire town, and 3,000 people demonstrated in front of the *hacienda* to demand lower prices for the land. Receiving no response, 400 *campesinos* then demonstrated in San Salvador —the first such demonstration (not staged by the government) since 1932. . . .

The demonstration moved the National Assembly, where the opposition parties were just two votes shy of a majority, to pass a law obliging Hill to sell the land for $200 per *manzana.* Hill and the oligarchy were livid, but among the *campesinos* a "very positive atmosphere was created."

In April 1969 José Alas began a weekly course for the delegates of the Word on justice and peace, a major theme of Medellín. These sessions, Alas said, always began with "the Celebration of the Word and communion." Out of this and succeeding courses grew a recognition of "the necessity to form an organization of the people to deal with the state." During the next five years Alas, who was joined by his brother Higinio in 1972, continued to hold courses for the CEBs, primarily on biblical themes. But by 1973 they began to study systematically socialist and capitalist ideology. Alas has said that before 1973, explicitly political themes were occasionally addressed, as during the 1972 presidential election when they discussed agrarian reform, but there was never a systematic study of these issues.

In October 1972 the government announced its intention of building a second dam, the Cerrón Grande, on the River Lempa below Suchitoto, a project that would flood thousands of hectares. That, plus the blatantly fraudulent municipal and national elections in March 1974, served to convince the *campesinos* of Suchitoto that they needed a more formal organization to press their demands on the national government. . . .

The United Popular Action Front (FAPU) was formally established in April 1974 during a meeting of José Alas, a group of *campesinos,* and representatives of the Unitary Union Federation of El Salvador (FUSS), the Salvador Allende University Front of Revolutionary Students (FUERSA), the National Association of Salvadorean Educators (ANDES), the PCS, and others in the Basilica of the Sacred Heart in San Salvador.

Thus for the first time in Latin American history a popular mass organization came directly out of the evangelizing efforts of the Roman Catholic Church. . . .

8.
OAS HUMAN RIGHTS COMMISSION: THE DEATH OF RUTILO GRANDE

The death of Father Rutilio Grande, S.J. and of his companions Manuel Solórzano and Nelson Rutilio Lemus, on March 12, 1977, were denounced to the Commission . . . as follows:

> On the night of Saturday March 12, Father Rutilio Grande, S.J., 49 years of age, of El Salvador was driving to the town of El Paisnal to celebrate mass. He was accompanied by Manuel Solórzano, 72, and Nelson Rutilio Lemus, 16. While going by some sugar cane plantations, they were ambushed by machine-gun fire. All three died.

OAS report of November 17, 1978.

Father Grande had delivered a sermon on February 13 at an open-air gathering to protest the expulsion of Father Mario Bernal.

Some people feel that that sermon caused the death of Rutilio Grande. "We have only one Father and all of us are his sons . . . all of us are brothers, we are all equal. But Cain is the bad seed of God's plan; there are groups of Cains in this country."

Speaking of Mario Bernal and of the risk of being a Christian, he said the following: "Dear brothers and friends, I am fully aware that very soon the Bible and the Gospels will not be allowed to cross the border. All that will reach us will be the covers, since all the pages are subversive—against sin, it is said. So that if Jesus crosses the border at Chalatenango, they will not allow him to enter. They would accuse him, the Man-God, the proto-type of man, of being an agitator, of being a Jewish foreigner, who con-fuses the people with exotic and foreign ideas, anti-democratic ideas, i.e., against the minorities. Ideas against God, because this is a clan of Cains. Brothers, they would undoubtedly crucify him again. And they have said so!"

One month later, on Saturday March 12, Father Grande was driving past sugar cane plantations on his way to celebrate mass in El Paisnal, where he had lived as a child. The assassins riddled his body with more than ten bullets. . . .

There are a number of signs of Government complicity. One hour after the incident, telephone service in Aguilares was cut off, although it was not interrupted in the neighboring towns. At a point when few people knew of the murder, President Molina called Archbishop Oscar Romero to express his condolences (although the newspapers reported that the Archbishop made the call). . . .

The Archbishop published a bulletin, March 14, 1977:

The perpetrators of the vile murder of the priest from Aguilares are not common criminals. The true reason for his death was his prophetic and pastoral efforts to raise the consciousness of the people throughout his parish. Father Grande, without offending and forcing himself upon his flock in the practice of their religion, was only slowly forming a genuine community of faith, hope and love among them; he was making them aware of their dignity as individuals, of their basic rights as human beings and of their advancement as human beings. In other words, his was an effort toward comprehensive human development. This post-Vatican Council ecclesiastical effort is certainly not agreeable to everyone, because it awakens the consciousness of the people. It is work that disturbs many; and to end it, it was necessary to liquidate its proponent. In our case, Father Rutilio Grande.

9.
ERP: POLITICAL ANALYSIS OF THE PRESENT SITUATION (CIRCA 1973)

Until 1967 the Salvadoran Communist Party had unequivocally led the proletarian class. . . . The growth that the working class experienced during the 1960s was a factor in the emergence of revolutionary groups. . . .

Under the influence of revisionism, which is characteristic of all communist parties, the Salvadoran Communist Party started moving away from the radical tendencies of the revolution, and in its first movement toward the political right, it assumed the task of controlling the people . . . unavoidably causing division within the ranks of this young party, generating two clearly opposed approaches: a peaceful approach and the armed struggle approach, leading in 1969 to the first significant division within party ranks, and the loss of important leaders, who subsequently formed the Popular Liberation Forces. Several months later, the Salvadoran Communist Party's youth group experienced divisions within its ranks and the party lost gradually many young revolutionaries who joined radical elements in other sectors, forming the People's Revolutionary Army (ERP).

10.
FAPU: RESPONSE TO CRITICISMS (MARCH 1975)

Let's see what they say about the Unified Popular Action Front:

The popular liberation forces, which from the beginning questioned the alliance [with moderates], will continue to insist patiently, although continuously, upon the necessity of strengthening unity and advancing the revolutionary war which has as its premise the armed struggle for economic, social and political vindication."

Therefore, they maintain that unity must be "pure" and only at the revolutionary level. When they speak to us of such unity as a substitute for the popular front they show their misunderstanding of the popular front's

---

Boletín "Pueblo," Unified Popular Action Front (FAPU), Year 1, No. 1, March 1975.

role in the revolutionary party. If they were consistent, they would call on all revolutionary sectors to form a party, in which the various groups would dissolve and abide by one strategy, one tactic, one code of discipline, not contradicting the need to create a popular front, which would be the political expression of the alliance between workers and farmers, independent of the bourgeoisie ideology and the supporting political parties.

Their statement shows a lack of understanding of concrete conditions that make necessary the consolidation of the masses, gathering different political groups or organizations, as well as unaffiliated elements. In fact, members of such an alliance place the task of organization, propaganda, agitation, and nonarmed mobilization on a back burner. This stance only benefits the exploiters, since it does not allow isolating the enemy at all, isolating instead, through narrow-mindedness, ignorance or false radicalism, the exploited and oppressed masses. To think that the popular front is formed only by revolutionaries is a leftist utopia.

11.
ROQUE DALTON: ON HEADACHES

On Headaches

To be a communist is a beautiful thing,
though it causes many headaches.

And the problem with the communist headache
is, we assume, historical:
it will not cede to analgesic tablets
but only to the realization of Paradise on earth.
That's the way it is.

Under capitalism our head aches
and is torn from us.
In the struggle for the Revolution
the head is a delayed action bomb.

Under socialist construction
we plan the headache
which does not minimize it, quite the contrary.

Communism, among other things, will be
an aspirin the size of the sun.

12.
FARN AND FPL: RATIONALES FOR DALTON'S EXECUTION

A. FARN STATEMENT

It is evident that during this whole process of intense ideological struggle at the level of the ERP's National Command, the militarist elements, which are weak in matters of ideology and politics, start plotting various maneuvers by which they might obstruct or take over the mechanisms of ideological struggle. . . .

The militarists now undermine the political cadres, starting smear campaigns against those leaders who do not share their ideas. They show a police mentality in "recruiting" members of the cadre whom they entrust with tasks of "political vigilance" against their own comrades and cell leaders. They maintain and create networks of veritable "eyes and ears" in the organization who inform them as to the opinions expressed in the ideological struggle. At the same time they launch an intense campaign against "internal revisionism"—identifying that deviation with the political positions that seek closer contact with the masses and the combination of all forms of struggle useful to the revolutionary process. . . .

The role of "mastermind and conceptual coordinator" was assumed to belong to comrade Roque Dalton, in whom the militarists thought to find their "greatest adversary"—the only one "capable," because of his theoretical skills, of being the source and mainstay of conception.

A serious misjudgment on the part of the militarist clique. Isolated as its members were from the political development of broad sectors of the organization, they were unable to comprehend that while comrade Roque Dalton shared that conception, he had not, in his coordination of development and defense, played the fundamental role that they, in their deviationist minds, wished to assign him.

With the preconceived idea of "getting rid" (politically, for the moment) of comrade Roque Dalton as a step toward advancing in their positions, they increase their campaign of provocative acts aimed at eliminating him from the discussions and, in passing, at setting in motion a further scheme: the implication in the "frame-up" of certain members of the National

---

From Manlio Tirado's series in *Excelsior* (Mexico City), March 5–14, 1980. Official statements by the two groups on Dalton's death and the ERP's behavior.

Command, who would then have to consider Dalton as against the Military Staff of the ERP. . . .

April 13, 1980: A situation is provoked in which comrade "Pancho" is forced into behavior that the clique considers "military rebellion," and he is seized immediately in a crude and violent manner. Two hours later, comrade Roque Dalton is seized, accused of having incited Pancho to his rebellious stance. Arrest is also decreed for those members of the National Command who happened to be present at the time of the seizures, and in less than 24 hours a court-martial is called against the comrades.

Moments before convening the court-martial, which is to be run by the clique—which has instigated the provocation and arrests and whose members are about to enact the farce of setting themselves up as the judges—the other members of the National Command call an emergency session in hopes of heading off the irrational events now in progress. At this meeting one of the members of the clique designates himself "political chief of the organization," denies the authority of the fully seated National Command to prevent the court-martial, denies the National Command its right to appeal to the cadres in defense of the comrades, and raises direct threats of death against those members of the National Command who might attempt in any way to oppose the will of the Military Staff.

April 14: The "court-martial" takes place, and members of the militarist clique accuse Roque Dalton as instigator of Pancho's "rebellious" conduct and of plotting against the Military Staff, demanding his immediate execution. Dalton's defense is taken up by a member of the National Command, who succeeds in getting the Military Staff, constituted as self-appointed tribunal, to agree to hand down detention sentences against the accused comrades. . . .

April 17: The final meeting of the National Command of the old ERP is held, in which the clique seizes political power, dissolving the [National] Command organism on the pretext that certain of its members formed part of a right-wing opportunist faction supposedly headed by Roque Dalton, and arguing that the clique and its cadres constitute the "political majority" within the organization. They declare the ideological struggle as ended, announcing the triumph of their position and launching a new subjugation of those that oppose them. . . . They try to crush, under threats of expulsion, exile, and execution, all opposition and divergence from the line of the "political majority."

April 20: In an effort to preserve the organic unity of the ERP, those sectors among us that [did eventually split off and] now make up the [Armed Forces of the] National Resistance [FARN] send out a call to all cadres of the organization to hold a congress to determine once and for all the line and the strategic conception. This document is not even brought to the rank and file's attention.

The clique now embarks on a new phase of maneuvers: they reveal internally [to the ERP's membership] the identity of comrade Roque Dalton (who was known in the organization as Julio Delfos Marín), declaring him a right-wing revisionist and pro-Cuban agent who had infiltrated the ERP. Failing to alarm the rank and file with this accusation, they launch their cowardly accusation in the following days that he is a CIA agent, and they prompt the organization to declare a "military emergency." The [ERP's] army now assumes total control of the organization through its military staff so as to save the party; and they declare that under these conditions it is not possible to take up the ideological struggle, much less hold an extraordinary session such as the congress—until the [party's] army can guarantee the total purging of the infiltration effected, according to them, by comrade Roque Dalton.

May 1: It is under these circumstances that the leaders of what then becomes and now makes up the National Resistance [FARN], in full consultation with our cadres, hold an emergency meeting. The participants of that meeting agree on organizational separation from the militarist clique, which, having violated all Leninist principles, lacks the moral and revolutionary viability to continue in positions of leadership within our organization. The clique, however, keeps this declaration of separation secret from the cadres, and thus assumes responsibility for all the subsequent events.

May 8: The blind and irrational response of the militarist clique entrenched in the ERP was to try to assassinate the members of the new National Resistance [FARN] without the slightest warning. On this date, three criminal assaults are mounted, all of which, despite the ferocity with which they were carried out, end in failure, frustrating their criminal designs against members of the National Resistance.

May 9: Hastily and in order to justify their criminal actions of the previous day, they draft a communiqué, signed by the Military Staff, in which they condemn to death or exile all those they consider political leaders of the National Resistance [FARN].

May 10: Furious and impotent after the failure of the assassinations they had plotted against members of the National Resistance, the members of the clique turn their anger against the detained comrades and ruthlessly murder Pancho and Roque Dalton. . . .

B. FPL STATEMENT

Some of the peculiar facts surrounding Dalton were: his apprehension and interrogation by CIA agents and his subsequent and remarkable escape from the Cojutepeque prison; his disappearance for approximately ten days while on secret organization business; his possible links to the disappearance of comrade Mauricio in April 1974, who was in charge of counterespionage for the organization; and the fact that, according to statements by Sebastián Urquilla, Dalton "confessed" to him that he had been involved in the defection of his political superior (Lucrecio) in September 1974.

We do not point to these incidents as proofs, only as the framework that made it possible, by way of a scheme devised personally by Sebastián Urquilla, to support the charge that Dalton was a CIA agent. Naturally, they do not constitute any proof beyond establishing a series of puzzling incidents; each might well have its own explanation but together they warrant investigation. . . .

Dalton's execution touched off a furious campaign on the part of the petit-bourgeois "intelligentsia," which gradually settled into an effort to make a political banner of Dalton, to which rallied the most obscure and contemptible factions among the Latin American revolutionaries. These people—turning out their pronouncements, their essays and poems, from the safety of their parasitic exiles, from the banality of their existentialist lives or in academic positions—have come to see in Dalton something more than the simple opportunity of justifying themselves as petit-bourgeois intellectuals who consider themselves fathers and mothers of the leftist revolution. They have turned Dalton into a "revolutionary" of "great talents," ignoring the truth as to his role in the Salvadoran revolutionary movement and exalting his ephemeral militancy. Thus they hope to establish themselves as a sector under the banner of Dalton, poet and writer, this being [to them] what his death makes important, and making a hero of him, while the truth is that he was both victim and agent of his own death. . . .

In our country many humble men and women of the people have died setting valiant and heroic examples of combat, ideological solidarity, and revolutionary conviction. . . . But they weren't poets or writers, nor did they spend 10 years playing revolutionary tourist, serving among the bureaucracies of international revisionism, nor did they attend congresses and conventions to show off their leftist rhetorical accomplishments. Some of our comrades killed in heroic battles couldn't even read or write. Many have fallen in our land who were worth a hundred times more than Dalton; only poet and writer Dalton lived his life where publicity and the cult of personality were what counted, and now that he's dead everyone is rushing to condemn the "assassins" of such a famous poet, writer, good guy, and close friend.

Dalton's execution was a political ideological error; no petit-bourgeois adventurer deserves death for that fact alone. We admit this grave error because self-criticism is the ideological motor by which we advance. . . .

13.
GABRIEL ZAID: THE DALTON AFFAIR

Who is Joaquín Villalobos? Besides being "Secretary General of the Party of the Salvadoran Revolution and supreme military commander of the People's Revolutionary Army," he is no less than "the second most important figure in the joint command of the FMLN," the Farabundo Martí Front for National Liberation. This Front—through manifestos, demonstrations, meetings, drives, auctions, cultural events, donations of a day's wages, etc.—has received the generous support of diverse groups in Mexico, among others the Roque Dalton Cultural Brigade. But it turns out that Joaquín Villalobos, also known by his code name "René Cruz," is none other than Roque Dalton's assassin. In other words: the Roque Dalton Cultural Brigade invokes the name of the murdered poet in order to benefit his murderer.

What charges did Villalobos make in "executing" Roque Dalton? No less than that he was a CIA agent.

> The People's Revolutionary Army was the target of enemy infiltration in the person of the Salvadoran Roque Dalton, who served for a time in our revolutionary organization and who was collaborating with the enemy's secret services. . . . Roque Dalton was exposed, captured, and shot by the forces of the ERP. There exist countless proofs of his traitorous activity in the inner workings of the organization.

The "executioner"—has he withdrawn the charges? No. The other leaders, fellow comrades of both Villalobos and Dalton—have they brought Villalobos to justice? No. Have they at least shunned him? No. "He is the second most important figure in the FMLN."

But what did [FARN leader Ernesto] Jovel think, shortly before his death, of these "comrades" with whom he had again become allied? [After his death in late September] *Proceso* printed this interview with Jovel on October 6, 1980:

> Q. What is the current status of the matter of Roque Dalton's assassination? We understand that, in the interest of unity, it had to be laid aside, though accounts of the incident keep surfacing. What position will the FARN take concerning this assassination after the triumph of the revolution?·
>
> A: For the moment, both politically and within the pursuit of unity among the revolutionary forces, it is too delicate, too complex to explain. . . . The most important thing is the unity among all revolutionaries in the effort to overthrow the dictatorship. We'll leave it to history to investigate and to the revolutionaries as a body to judge. . . .

It was very hard for Jovel to sit down with a comrade who had murdered another, who had tried to crush the newborn Armed Forces of National Resistance and had issued orders (unsuccessfully) for his own liquidation. But he agreed to it. What finally became of Jovel, who was so accepting of political murder? A confusing death, which gave rise to ugly interpretations. . . .

Dalton began studying for a law degree at the National University of San Salvador, but quit school to devote himself to political and literary activities. He joined the Communist party while still very young. . . . He took part in the popular struggle against the tyranny of Colonel José María Lemus from 1956 to 1960, was persecuted and jailed, and just when he was about to be shot he escaped from prison . . . and traveled to his second country, Cuba, where he was an active contributor to the Casa de las Américas. He journeyed to Chile, Mexico, Czechoslovakia, Korea, and North Vietnam, and won numerous prizes and awards for his poetry. . . . He died on May 10, 1975, shortly before his 40th birthday and soon after joining the Salvadoran People's Revolutionary Army.

Dalton wanted to be a Salvadoran Che Guevara: a writer who sacrifices the writer for the sake of the revolutionary. He left Havana for El Salvador like Che for Bolivia; at approximately the same age (mid-life, two or three years short of forty) and with other similarities besides: being university-educated, interested in writing and making politics, with underground experience, with the experience of "having arrived" (though at very different levels); living in Havana as foreigners accepted into a second country, and not remaining to bask in it, but instead going off to make the revolution in another Latin American country, down an armed, clandestine, and backwoods path. That is: contrary to the normal preferences of Communist parties, which are for big cities, strikes, and the electoral process.

The anthropological error of Che and his followers is in not seeing that the revolutionary culture is an integral part of the culture of progress, and therefore opposed to the peasant culture. This is why Marxism catches on more readily in a "bourgeois boys' school" than among Bolivian Indians. It is easier to make university students aware of their right to grab for power than to convince the peasants to take up arms in order to cease being peasants. The true peasant guerrilla has always been conservative, defensive, on his home ground: not offensive, progressive, assaulting power. The student guerrillas go to the country in order to return to the city; to gain the experience, the credentials, the access to power that one must have in order to change things from the center and from above. For the students, guerrilla activity is the continuation of the rise to power by other means. . . .

If the Salvadoran government had allowed Duarte and Ungo to take over in 1972, blood would not now be running so freely. The Salvadoran Communist party would have been confirmed in its strategy, and the few guerrillas would have been left without that important urban connection. Today's guerrillas are break-aways from the capital up into the mountains (not peasant insurgents); break-aways from the Communist party, the university, the Church, who around 1970 began to take up arms. Cayetano Carpio ("Marcial"), ex-seminary student, founds the FPL:

> **Q:** You resigned from the Communist party?
>
> **A:** That's right.
>
> **Q:** Could you tell me why?
>
> **A:** Because of the Cuban Revolution.
>
> **Q:** How is that?
>
> **A:** I saw clearly, I understood that the transformation in Latin America is by the path of war. The Salvadoran Communist party held that the path was politics and that only at the end, when the final blow was to be aimed, should arms be used. . . .

This impatience with talk, this glorification of guns as the continuation of debate by other means, is what kills Roque Dalton. But it is there in his own argument: like Villalobos, like Jovel, Dalton assumes the necessity of assassination.

> There is not one good socialism and another bad. There is a historical, dialectical continuity, upward and positive, which displays many errors along the way. We cannot, without inspiring a useless measure of vanity that can only amount to impotence, *assume* the defeat of nazism, for example, and not *assume* the Stalin of the concentration camps. Or insist on emphasizing *the conditions that I as a lily-white intellectual attach to supporting the Cuban Revolution.* Who are we to go putting conditions on the power of the people, when this power never sent for us, never summoned us to support it! It has allowed us to support it, at any rate, and I for one feel grateful. The revolutionary's support of a revolution is, in essence, unconditional.

For Dalton, the errors and horrors of Stalin were supportable—unconditionally acceptable as part of something positive and upward. What he did not wish to accept but rather to violently reject was his being bourgeois. The open-mindedness of a progressive bourgeois was to be rejected as insufficient or as stealing from the proletariat. The least little thing that smacked of fascism (and what is there that hasn't smacked of fascism?) was as fascist as Hitler's crimes. A slaughter of innocents carried out by Hitler is in the evil, the sinister, the negative column; a slaughter of innocents carried out by Stalin is in the good, the upwardly positive column. Killing the Chief of Police is the highest achievement for a writer who truly wants to be a revolutionary. To write social criticism, form cultural brigades, put one's pen at the service of the first-class revolutionaries, while eating three meals a day, is for poor slobs who don't dare to take up arms.

> We are finally positive, at least I myself am—pardon the smugness—that our opportunity for social-revolutionary status is here at last, bright and clear, the possibility to stop being "second-class revolutionaries" as we have always been, and not always exclusively by our own fault.

Anyone familiar with Catholic culture will recognize in this moral urgency the theology of perfection. The Church Militant, in its battle against the devil, flesh and the world, rests on a sluggish base: first the unpracticing laymen; then come the second-class revolutionaries; then the secular clergy, the congregation, the most ardent believers, and other lay militants; and finally the perfect, who have renounced all and made an unconditional surrender of their lives to a rule of militant perfection: the monastic clergy (Jesuits, and so forth).

It is fitting to note that in the theology of perfection there is no mention of power struggles, nor is any advice offered as to how to get to be pope. Such matters, it is presumed, do not exist. If someone were to say that, in profound meditation, he'd heard a call to be pope, he would be ridiculed as a bad Christian. In the same way, to point out how, in revolutionary groups, parties, and regimes, there tends to be a greater turnover at the summit than at the base, to speak of power struggles at the top, or of possible successors—such matters are all indecent. God will provide. One must surrender unconditionally, not worry about who's on top.

In Dalton's urge for the perfection Che represents, he speaks of unconditional surrender but not of who should surrender to whom. He offers no advice as to how, once called to be a perfect revolutionary, a complete intellectual, a whole man, one is in fact to arrive at the power of a Castro or a Che. And what's to be done if the young economist Joaquín Villalobos hears the same call as Dalton, feels the same radical urgency for moral superiority, the same impatience with "starry-eyed poets" and aesthetes? Who's to surrender to whom?

From the perspective of those already armed, the desire for sacrifice on the part of a writer setting out in Che's footsteps could be seen as simply the desire for power of an upstart seeking the limelight: Che's leading role. Any combatant who is not content to be simple cannon fodder is a contender in the internal struggle for power—whether by hook (distinguishing oneself, winning over the leaders, the rank and file) or by crook. And who's right? How do you settle what's to be done (which in the final analysis is to settle who commands)? What direction do you take if there is no unified leadership (if nobody has secured power: taken charge of his comrades, like Castro)? What if there are no focal points of political-moral-doctrinal prestige like Castro or Guevara, and thus a conflicting array of principles, lines, and norms for the revolutionary struggle?

It is hardly surprising that those who renounce the force of arguments and choose the arguments of force in confronting oppression should use the same arguments in settling their differences. Roque Dalton was slain by a comrade who beat him at the use of his own arguments, in an internal power struggle. Terrible enough; neither the most thorough accord between thought and action, nor the most absolute and unconditional surrender, nor even taking to the mountains, strapping on arms and offering himself up to kill the Chief of Police saved Dalton from the final spit in the face at his death, accused by his comrades as a bourgeois. Just as if he'd remained a writer signing manifestos and eating three meals a day.

In the discourse of reason, the winner is the one with the reason. In the discourse of guns, the winner's the one with the gun.

14.
FARN: IN DEFENSE OF DALTON (FEBRUARY 1976)

NATIONAL RESISTANCE MILITANT:

We all know that the murderous faction of the ERP dared to say it was assassinating Roque Dalton because he was "an agent of the CIA, and betrayed our organization from within." This was no more than a fabrication by non-revolutionaries incapable of confronting the ideological struggle within the organization. They designed a web of lies claiming the organization was infiltrated, and Roque Dalton was labeled as the agent in order to create alarm, confusion and disorientation, therefore aborting "the ideological struggle because the organization is in danger." At the core, what was in danger was the militarist and reckless position they were

National Resistance Clandestine Release, "On Behalf of the Proletarian Cause," February 1976, No. 24, pp. 9–15. Translation copyright © 1986 by Gladys Segal.

trying to impose. The threat was in emerging less than successfully from a serious and profound ideological debate with the active participation of all of the organization's components. That is why they decided to fabricate that lie, even though the consequences might lead them to premeditated cold-blooded murder so the position of their choice would prevail. The true revolutionaries can demonstrate and scientifically prove what they say, more so in cases such as this one, in which the life of a colleague is at stake. A life fraught with revolutionary meaning.

15.
FAPU: HISTORIC MANIFESTO (MARCH 1976)

1. FAPU emerged as a nonelected political front, thus reiterating the exhaustion of the electoral struggle as the people's main instrument to achieve their most precious objectives: March of 1976 confirms the timeliness of our front, politically and ideologically.

2. FAPU proposed to consolidate popular forces to defeat escalating fascism through extraparliamentary antifascist struggle. Now, more than ever, the popular conscience feels intuitively that the time has come to rally to combat, directing the thrust of the popular struggle to avoid fascism.

3. FAPU initiated an armed mobilization against the fascists' military dictatorship, pointing out relentlessly the need to exercise this right on the part of the people. The popular sectors that followed this route have proved the effectiveness of the people's organized power. Those who depended upon the only mobilization they knew, electoral mobilization, allowed the dictatorship politically crucial time to consolidate the pro-fascist positions.

4. FAPU defined the position of the people and the unity of all the popular sectors through a healthy but firm ideological struggle. The few times in which sectarianism, opportunism, and wavering traditional positions have allowed the people this right are fraught with meaning: The military action which started on July 30, 1975, rallied the people and proved the popular sectors' ability to attain armed solidarity, to unite against the enemy's criminal attacks, towering above real differences and the leadership's conservative positions. . . .

There are no viable alternatives to marching forth in search of popular victories. A victorious retreat, forced participation, desperate clamor toward the army, or rash attacks upon the forces in power, desperately suggested by some, are no alternatives. . . .

16.
FPL: THE REVOLUTION IS THE BEST MEDIUM FOR THE COMPARISON OF STRATEGIC AND TACTICAL APPROACHES (1978)

1959 was a turbulent year in El Salvador, fraught with struggle against the government's fierce and repressive attack led by Colonel José María Lemus (who succeeded Oscar Osorio). Lemus tried in all ways to crush the popular struggle, which influenced the highest organizational ranks, leading the Communist Party to adopt a line favoring popular insurrection to overthrow that government. With this as a backdrop, the first paramilitary action groups within the popular sectors emerged. Such overrated popular agitation precipitated the downfall of Lemus' government to the military, serving bourgeois interests who wished to preempt the feared popular action, opening a way which they considered could emulate the Cuban example. . . .

Until 1964 the ranks of the Salvadoran Communist Party tried to pay attention to the struggle and to labor, in spite of acute ideological differences with the political right, which underestimated the role of the masses in the revolution. Unfortunately, the process of moderation was flawed, leading to the other extreme. This lurch was caused by the rightists' attempt to take advantage of the situation, making the turn a starting point for imposing the growing opportunism and revisionism, and bringing the party to the brink of its present abyss: a bourgeois island of sorts within the popular movement. This deepened the internal ideological struggle, especially in the Salvadoran Communist Party (within the conservative rightist opportunist stream), until it became irreconcilable and antagonistic, eventually leading to the establishment of new revolutionary organizations whose leadership gained increasing strength within the Popular Liberation Front.

Historically, we can see that the revolution's needs in El Salvador and in Central America, the level of achievement reached by popular organizations, the increasing intensity of social clashes, and the triumph of the Cuban revolution—which developed the dogmas that for years had supported the strategic and tactical approach of the Salvadoran Communist Party and of other popular organizations—were determining factors in a new stage of the ideological struggle, started within the ranks of those organizations in 1959, which throughout a period of ten years had improved with unsuspected historic repercussions and had given way to the establishment of revolutionary organizations whose reason for being was based on the application of an inappropriate political and military revolutionary strategy for drawn-out conflict.

During the 1960s, from the standpoint of the revolution, the most sensible sectors in these organizations established a growing internal ideological struggle against conservative opportunist nonproletarian sectors, whose thought and practice was of the petit-bourgeois type, and tried to give it life, colliding repeatedly with reality—with obsolete dogmas and approaches which, despite Marxist embellishments, failed to address the historic needs of the proletariat and its allies. . . .

After a heated internal ideological struggle, for a period of ten years, there was an unavoidable breakup between the dogmatic opportunist, revisionist petit bourgeoisie and the revolutionary current fighting to implement the military and political strategy of the people's revolutionary war.

This breakup crystallized in March 1970 with the loss of senior leaders of those organizations (Salvadoran Communist Party, Salvadoran Communist Youth, unions, etc.) and the direction toward the formation of a new truly revolutionary organization that would propel the people's struggle in all fields—pacifist and violent, legal and illegal—having as its axis the revolutionary armed struggle within the framework of a prolonged people's revolutionary war strategy.

The cornerstone of the revolutionary organization, which would later be called the Popular Liberation Forces, was laid on April 1, 1970, and the people started sensing a revolutionary path toward liberation. . . .

The Marxist-Leninist Popular Liberation Forces determine their political actions, both theoretically and practically, by the immediate and fundamental interests of the working class and other popular sectors.

Presently, our strategic goal is liberating the proletariat from imperialist domination, destroying the bourgeois state apparatus, and reinstating a popular revolutionary government based on the alliance between workers and farmers, toward the full realization of the popular revolution, and the establishment of socialism in our country. . . .

STRATEGIC TASKS IN THE REVOLUTIONARY PROCESS TOWARD THE ACHIEVEMENT OF A POPULAR SOCIALIST REVOLUTION

1. Develop and deepen the people's prolonged war, toward achieving radical proletarian revolutionary triumph.
2. Combine the armed struggle with other struggle tactics (legal, illegal,

peaceful, violent, etc.) as tactical and strategic measures toward the development of a people's war.

3. Organize and orient politically the industrial and farming proletariat, the farmer population—especially the poor or semi-proletariat—and other popular sectors that have been the prey of capitalist exploitation and oppression.

4. Recruit and mobilize all those popular sectors. . . .

5. Promote a revolutionary popular alliance between workers and farmers and the proletarian government.

6. Promote the revolutionary armed struggle and its military and paramilitary forces: urban and suburban guerrillas and popular militia. These are the foundation of the popular liberation army and all of them together constitute the popular liberation armed forces (FPL), which will wage the definitive battle against the imperialist reactionary forces and the Salvadoran and Central American bourgeoisie.

7. Strengthen the popular militia, in defense of the people and in support of the popular military armed forces liberation offensive, and politically awaken the popular conscience, promoting its organization and incorporation to the revolutionary war.

8. Consolidate the vanguard party.

9. Promote solidarity with other leading Central American organizations consolidating the revolutionary war at the regional level, and organizing a popular revolutionary army as well as regional alliances at all levels to defeat Yankee imperialism for the triumph of the revolution in Central America.

10. Promote solidarity with all the peoples fighting imperialism and capitalism, especially with revolutionaries in Latin America.

11. Promote friendship, solidarity and cooperation with socialist countries world-wide, mainly with socialist Cuba, the revolutionary leader in Latin America. . . .

VI. ABOUT THE ERP

A background comparison between the FPL and the ERP might be edifying. They both appeared almost at the same time. Why did the FPL develop firmly and consistently, maintaining great internal cohesion and growing political and military influence upon the people, while the ERP went from one polarization to another? Why did the FPL identify and develop strong ties with the people, and the ERP isolate itself from the people, falling into international and national disgrace? . . .

The ERP did not achieve the cohesion of one ideology, one theory, and one practice. It attempted to convert itself into a multi-ideology front—a spectrum of the new left made up of diverse groups that at times only seemed to share their irrational hate for communist parties. They maintained their own points of view and struggled to gain influence upon other members. This led to great changes of direction within the general strategic approach and to frequent divisions. In less than five years it suffered some six internal divisions when various groups formed or tried to form their own organization (Grupo de Occidente, ORT, RN, Escición Divergente, and others). Recently there was yet another division within the senior ranks; predictable damage was caused to this organization by the Trotskyists and the Maoists in leadership positions over the original organization's remaining shreds. . . .

The ERP's focus on the revolution was purely military. It was more concerned about technical combat aspects than about political military structure. It was oblivious of individual training. . . .

Harsh realities led the ERP to a new turning point, this time in the direction of crude adventurist militarism, and at the end of 1974 it developed the theory that "the masses' struggle was obsolete." However, the organization persisted in its belief that popular armed insurrection was imminent.

Such turns and strategic failures, as well as failures of circumstance, internally shocked the ERP, and all of its structure faltered under the pounding multisided internal militarist struggle, ending with the establishment of the "Militarist Camarilla" to rule over the leaders of the organization and the death sentence of more than a dozen ERP leaders. It was in this senseless militarist orgy that the poet Roque Dalton fell. The worker and carpenter, known by the pseudonym of Pancho (Armando), who survived an earlier massacre because of the timely intervention of the FPL, also succumbed. . . .

VII. THE NATIONAL RESISTANCE

From the onset, it was characterized by its wavering leadership, by its ambiguous and contradictory strategic character during what has become known as "the Period." . . .

Here in El Salvador a small Trotskyist core disseminated the theory that world revolution should be carried out by the working class and its allies (a) against imperialism, (b) against current socialist governments, and (c) against the local bourgeoisie. They used as their medium newspapers such as *Antidoto* and *Amanecera*.

They aimed their fire against socialist governments and communist parties with no exception. They disseminated their hate against the socialist bureaucratic leadership in the People's Republic of China (and never forgave Mao Tse-tung for having had respect and admiration for Stalin). They viciously attacked the Soviet Union, Cuba, and other socialist countries.

Their attacks on Fidel Castro were especially poisonous, and they were never sympathetic toward Ernesto Che Guevara. . . .

The decade of ideological struggle and the practical efforts of the masses made possible the cleansing of the revolutionary concept and made unavoidable the need for the formation of a true political military revolutionary organization to open the way for new phases of popular struggle. Therefore, the ideological struggle within the Salvadoran Communist Party and the traditional popular organizations had to go beyond the boundaries of the party, and emerge at the national level, in spite of the unrealistic rightist camarilla. . . .

The heroic popular struggle, which counteracted and overcame the cruel and bloody offensives of the counter revolution, was of great influence. The leadership showed the exploited of other sister nations that there is a place in Central America that is waging a prolonged revolutionary war strategy which can be of value in all of Central America, varying with political and economic differences, such as the place, the degree of development of the revolutionary forces, the correlation of internal forces, the various social classes. All these will determine the strategy of choice, as may already be seen in Guatemala and Nicaragua.

II
THE 1979 JUNTA AND THE TURN TOWARD WAR

17.
JUNTA: PROCLAMATION OF OCTOBER 15, 1979

In view of the anarchic situation being experienced by the country as a result of activities of the extremists which the current government could not curb, the lack of guarantees for the security and integrity of the citizens, noncompliance with the constitutional mandate and violation of basic principles such as:

1. Lack of participation by all sectors of the people in making great decisions affecting the national interest;
2. The use of violence as a means to solve the country's political problems, thus setting off a possible clash between the armed forces and the people; and
3. Allowing corruption in public administration, thus endangering the existence of the republic.

FBIS: Latin America, October 16, 1979, pp. 5–6.

Whereas the Salvadoran Armed Forces, responding to the general call and following strictly institutional duties, has overthrown the present government of the republic in order to restore constitutional order.

Citizens, the armed forces will conduct the country's affairs, allowing the participation of others for a prudent time which will permit: 1) Establishing the foundation and proper climate to establish a real and dynamic democracy; and 2) Holding free elections which represent the will of all Salvadorans.

We appeal to the extremist forces of the right and the left to end their attitude of violence because, in the future, they can participate peacefully in the country's democratic process by respecting the will of the majority, which, we reiterate, the armed forces will ensure is respected.

18.
CHRISTIAN DEMOCRAT–ARMY PACT (JANUARY 1980)

1. The Christian Democratic Party has been invited to offer an alternative solution in the present government crisis. The Party believes that, before there can be any restructuring of the government, the armed forces must define with unquestionable clarity the political, economic, and social policies to be followed by the new government.

2. For this reason, before starting any discussion on the composition of the junta and the cabinet, the Party proposes the following government platform as a necessary precondition for its acceptance of any government responsibility and asks that the Armed Forces adopt and publish it:

A. POLITICS

1. To define the current process as popular, directed toward national development, and aimed at changing the oligarchic structures of economic and social power.

2. To integrate into the government people who are representative of democratic and progressive parties and independent progressive people.

3. To exclude from the Revolutionary Junta and from the cabinet representatives of private enterprise and to outline for them the rules of the game enabling them to operate with certainty and security.

4. To restructure the Revolutionary Junta.

5. To have an urgent dialogue with all the popular organizations in order to achieve a peaceful means of living together with them and to outline clearly the norms of mutual behavior.

6. To decree a Constitutional law able to support the process of change.
7. To create a schedule for measures to be taken by the government to implement the ideas of this proclamation.
8. To expand the government's social base of support.

B. ECONOMIC AND SOCIAL POLICY

1. Agrarian Reform must be rapid and thorough, applying to the large landholdings and giving the land to those who work it.
2. To nationalize the export of coffee, cotton, sugar, and seafood.
3. To nationalize the country's financial system.
4. To reform labor laws, introducing peasant unionization.
5. To create a program of accelerated industrialization, supporting and giving incentives to national industrial capital.

C. THE MILITARY

1. To have the Revolutionary Junta exercise effectively the legal powers of the Presidency of the Republic.
2. To establish procedures for a politico-military team which will safeguard its implementation.
3. To accelerate the creation of security agencies which favor democracy and the respect for human and political rights.

19.
GUILLERMO UNGO: RESIGNATION FROM THE JUNTA (JANUARY 1980)

The insurrectional step taken by the Armed Forces on October 15, 1979, generated an alliance of that institution, as a real factor of political power, with the different opposition organizations and sectors—an alliance built on the Armed Forces Proclamation announced that day. On the basis of that alliance, the Military Movement accepted our inclusion in the Revolutionary Governing Junta on October 17, 1979.

The pronouncement of the Military Youth group and the presence of two of its heads in the Junta clearly denoted that in that alliance the Armed Forces as an institution was neither neutral nor apolitical. They had committed themselves together with the other political forces to encourage a process of democratization and profound structural change throughout the country.

This new national project clearly meant a break with the political-military framework which had prevailed for many decades. Further, it required the will to confront the minority interests of the right who would be hurt by the loss of their economic and political power.

Unfortunately, the circumstances have substantially changed. Those minority interests have been strengthened daily, planning, as they have been, to return to the previous frameworks of former governments, temporizing, creating obstacles and finally impeding the development of the objectives set out in the Armed Forces Proclamation.

Thus, the false notion of the neutrality of the military as an institution —used in the past to maintain a distance from the people—is being heard again. And that has generated a rightward turn in the process of democratization and social change.

Therefore, under these conditions, the Revolutionary Governing Junta has only minimal, and essentially formal, power. It lacks the capacity to lead the process of democratization and social change. Nor can it stop the development of the various mechanisms and activities which run contrary to the objectives of that process.

For that reason we support the resignations of the Cabinet ministers and the other government functionaries. And with this letter, we irrevocably submit our own resignations as members of the Revolutionary Governing Junta.

20.
JUNTA: AGRARIAN REFORM DECREE (MARCH 1980)

I. IT IS THE JUNTA'S OBJECTIVE TO ADOPT MEASURES INTENDED TO FOSTER AN EQUITABLE DISTRIBUTION OF THE NATIONAL WEALTH, AND THAT TO THIS END SOLID BASES MUST BE ESTABLISHED AT THE BEGINNING OF THE AGRARIAN REFORM PROCESS;

II. THE "AGRARIAN REFORM BASIC LEGISLATION" HAS BEEN DECREED ON THIS SAME DATE, WHEREIN THE GENERAL PROVISIONS GOVERNING SAID PROCESS HAVE BEEN ESTABLISHED;

III. IN ORDER TO GUARANTEE COMPLIANCE WITH THE OBJECTIVES OF THE LAW IT IS NECESSARY TO TAKE PRECAUTIONARY MEASURES THAT ALLOW THE TAKING OF POSSESSION OF LAND HOLDINGS INCLUDED WITHIN THE FIRST STAGE (OF THE PROCESS), IN ORDER TO

MAINTAIN NORMAL AGRICULTURAL PRODUCTIVE ACTIVITIES AND IMPLEMENT AN ORDERLY PROCESS OF ACQUISITION AND AWARDING OF LAND TO THE BENEFICIARIES;

THEREFORE:

BY VIRTUE OF THE LEGISLATIVE AUTHORITY CONFERRED (UPON THE GOVERNING JUNTA) THROUGH DECREE NO. 1 OF OCTOBER 15, 1979, PUBLISHED IN THE OFFICIAL GAZETTE NO. 191, VOLUME 265, OF THE SAME DATE,

DECREES:

ARTICLE 1. IN ORDER TO IMPLEMENT THE EXECUTION OF THE FIRST STAGE OF THE AGRARIAN REFORM THROUGHOUT THE COUNTRY, WHICH WILL INCLUDE LAND HOLDINGS IN EXCESS OF FIVE HUNDRED HECTARES, EITHER AS A WHOLE OR A COMBINATION OF SEVERAL UNITS BELONGING TO ONE OR MORE INDIVIDUALS, ESTATES OR ASSOCIATIONS. THE SALVADORAN INSTITUTE FOR AGRARIAN REFORM IS HEREBY AUTHORIZED TO PROCEED TO IMMEDIATE INTERVENTION AND TAKING OF POSSESSION OF LAND HOLDINGS INVOLVED, THROUGH DELEGATES OF THAT INSTITUTION OR OF THE MINISTRY OF AGRICULTURE.

SUCH DELEGATES WILL PREPARE A DOCUMENT ATTESTING TO THE TAKING OF POSSESSION OF LAND HOLDINGS (IN ACCORDANCE WITH THE LAW),

LAND HOLDINGS BELONGING TO AGRICULTURAL COOPERATIVES, PEASANT COMMUNITY ASSOCIATIONS OR OTHER CAMPESINO ORGANIZATIONS ARE EXEMPTED FROM THIS LEGISLATION.

ARTICLE 2. THE MINISTRY OF AGRICULTURE WILL COOPERATE IN THE IMPLEMENTATION OF THIS DECREE AND THE MINISTRY OF DEFENSE WILL ALSO ASSIST IN ITS IMPLEMENTATION, AS NEEDED. . . .

GIVEN AT THE PRESIDENTIAL HOUSE IN SAN SALVADOR.

(SIGNED)
COL. ADOLFO ARNOLDO MAJANO RAMOS
COL. JAIME ABDUL GUTIÉRREZ
DR. JOSÉ ANTONIO MORALES EHRLICH
DR. JOSÉ RAMÓN AVALOS NAVARREZO
OCTAVIO ORELLANA SOLIS, MINISTER OF AGRICULTURE

21.
RUBÉN ZAMORA AND OTHERS: RESIGNATION FROM
THE JUNTA (MARCH 1980)

. . . **I.** We believe that the conditions demanded publicly of the Armed Forces by the Party as prerequisite to participation in the Government—conditions publicly accepted by the Armed Forces—were meant to encompass, above all else, respect for the human rights of the peoples of the Republic. This respect for human rights is incompatible with the exacerbated and growing repression exercised against the popular organizations and against the people in general. In truth, the attitude of a sector of the Armed Forces, including those officers presently occupying key positions within the operative mechanism of the army and the public security bodies, implies not only actions contrary to even an elemental respect for the most fundamental human rights—such as the right to life and personal security—but even actions at variance with the traditional military discipline of obedience to the Commander in Chief of the Armed Forces which is presently constituted by the Revolutionary Government Junta. Continued toleration of this state of affairs by the Party and its high officials necessarily entails a measure of responsibility for those activities. The Party and its officials thereby render themselves morally-accountable accomplices to the repression unleashed daily against the Salvadorean people. Furthermore, the program of structural reforms, with which we have always been in agreement, loses all effectiveness if not implemented in a climate of freedom: which is to say, unless accompanied by the cessation of all repression and the democratic participation by the organizations representative of the people.

II. . . . It is a fact that both this Government's and this Party's attitude has been characterized by complacency. This includes the attitude towards the United States' offer to send a large quantity of military material and 36 counter-insurgency instructors to El Salvador to implement a "special, anti-subversive war." Failure to reject such proposals transforms us . . . into a battlefield for the struggles of the Superpowers, thereby exposing our people to suffer the attendant consequences. Lending oneself to a foreign intervention under any circumstances whatsoever is, plainly speaking, treason. This condemnation applies equally to all forms of foreign intervention, regardless of origin. We will equally condemn intervention by any country, capitalist or socialist, should such occur during the civil war today threatening to engulf our country.

III. Regarding the program of structural reforms proposed by the Party, we wish to make clear our complete agreement with and decided support for such reforms. Nonetheless, as we have also clearly stated, a program of "reforms with repression" runs contrary to the fundamentals of Christian Democracy. Agrarian reform must encompass not only the taking of lands from the major estate owners, but, above all, the economic and political participation of peasant organizations. . . .

How can the present process succeed if the peasants are repressed on a daily basis merely for organizing themselves? How can this process hope to reach fruition when the organizations representing thousands of peasants have not even been consulted while, to the contrary, the daily and growing repression against those organizations renders impossible any dialogue with them? How can this process serve democracy if, far from the democratic framework in which the Party envisioned it taking place, it is carried out under a state of siege? It is because of these inconsistencies that we have struggled within the Party for an end to the repression and to reject the special war of counter-insurgency. However, given the present Party leadership, none of our pleas has been accorded any importance.

IV. The two criticisms we have made concerning the actions of the Government in which the Party claims to participate—the maintenance of repression and complacency in the face of interventionist foreign plans—constitute the gravest accusations of behavior absolutely contradictory with the posture our Party has maintained throughout twenty years of struggle on behalf of the Salvadorean people. To accept this course of action in return for a share of the power—more formal than real—constitutes unacceptable lameness which allows the governmental process to degenerate into something neither democratic nor Christian. . . .

For all the reasons set forth in this letter, and with an energetic condemnation of both the continuous repression and the proposed foreign intervention, we hereby inform the Christian Democratic Party of our irrevocable resignation from its ranks. We wish to make clear that we continue believing in the principles of democracy and the social teachings of Christianity and will continue to support those principles for the remainder of our lives; but we take leave of this political body because we cannot accept the behavior of a lame and subservient leadership.

Respectfully,

Roberto Lara Velado
Fernando Diaz Rodríguez
Héctor Dada Hirezi
Rubén Zamora
Alberto Arena
Francisco Paniagua
Héctor R. Silva H.

22.
ARCHBISHOP OSCAR ROMERO: THE LAST SERMON
(MARCH 1980)

Let no one be offended because we use the divine words read at our mass to shed light on the social, political and economic situation of our people. Not to do so would be un-Christian. Christ desires to unite himself with humanity, so that the light he brings from God might become life for nations and individuals.

I know many are shocked by this preaching and want to accuse us of forsaking the gospel for politics. But I reject this accusation. I am trying to bring to life the message of the Second Vatican Council and the meetings at Medellín and Puebla. The documents from these meetings should not just be studied theoretically. They should be brought to life and translated into the real struggle to preach the gospel as it should be for our people. Each week I go about the country listening to the cries of the people, their pain from so much crime, and the ignominy of so much violence. Each week I ask the Lord to give me the right words to console, to denounce, to call for repentance. And even though I may be a voice crying in the desert, I know that the church is making the effort to fulfill its mission. . . .

Every country lives its own "exodus"; today El Salvador is living its own exodus. Today we are passing to our liberation through a desert strewn with bodies and where anguish and pain are devastating us. Many suffer the temptation of those who walked with Moses and wanted to turn back and did not work together. It is the same old story. God, however, wants to save the people by making a new history. . . .

History will not fail; God sustains it. That is why I say that insofar as historical projects attempt to reflect the eternal plan of God, to that extent they reflect the kingdom of God. This attempt is the work of the church. Because of this, the church, the people of God in history, is not attached to any one social system, to any political organization, to any party. The church does not identify herself with any of those forces because she is the eternal pilgrim of history and is indicating at every historical moment what reflects the kingdom of God and what does not reflect the kingdom of God. She is the servant of the kingdom of God.

The great task of Christians must be to absorb the spirit of God's

---

The Church and Human Liberation, March 24, 1980.

kingdom and, with souls filled with the kingdom of God, to work on the projects of history. It's fine to be organized in popular groups; it's all right to form political parties; it's all right to take part in the government. It's fine as long as you are a Christian who carries the reflection of the kingdom of God and tries to establish it where you are working, and as long as you are not being used to further worldly ambitions. This is the great duty of the people of today. My dear Christians, I have always told you, and I will repeat, that the true liberators of our people must come from us Christians, from the people of God. Any historical plan that's not based on what we spoke of in the first point—the dignity of the human being, the love of God, the kingdom of Christ among people—will be a fleeting project. Your project, however, will grow in stability the more it reflects the eternal design of God. It will be a solution for the common good of the people every time, if it meets the needs of the people. . . . Now I invite you to look at things through the eyes of the church, which is trying to be the kingdom of God on earth and so often must illuminate the realities of our national situation.

We have lived through a tremendously tragic week. I could not give you the facts before, but a week ago last Saturday, on 15 March, one of the largest and most distressing military operations was carried out in the countryside. The villages affected were La Laguna, Plan de Ocotes and El Rosario. The operation brought tragedy: a lot of ranches were burned, there was looting, and—inevitably—people were killed. In La Laguna, the attackers killed a married couple, Ernesto Navas and Audelia Mejía de Navas, their little children, Martín and Hilda, 13 and seven years old, and 11 more peasants.

Other deaths have been reported, but we do not know the names of the dead. In Plan de Ocotes, two children and four peasants were killed, including two women. In El Rosario, three more peasants were killed. That was last Saturday.

Last Sunday, the following were assassinated in Arcatao by four members of ORDEN: peasants Marcelino Serrano, Vincente Ayala, 24 years old, and his son, Freddy. That same day, Fernando Hernández Navarro, a peasant, was assassinated in Galera de Jutiapa, when he fled from the military.

Last Monday, 17 March, was a tremendously violent day. Bombs exploded in the capital as well as in the interior of the country. The damage was very substantial at the headquarters of the Ministry of Agriculture. The campus of the national university was under armed siege from dawn until 7 P.M. Throughout the day, constant bursts of machine-gun fire were heard in the university area. The archbishop's office intervened to protect people who found themselves caught inside.

On the Hacienda Colima, 18 persons died, at least 15 of whom were peasants. The administrator and the grocer of the ranch also died. The armed forces confirmed that there was a confrontation. A film of the events appeared on TV, and many analyzed interesting aspects of the situation.

At least 50 people died in serious incidents that day: in the capital, seven persons died in events at the Colonia Santa Lucía; on the outskirts of Tecnillantas, five people died; and in the area of the rubbish dump, after the evacuation of the site by the military, were found the bodies of four workers who had been captured in that action.

Sixteen peasants died in the village of Montepeque, 38 kilometers along the road to Suchitoto. That same day, two students at the University of Central America were captured in Tecnillantas: Mario Nelson and Miguel Alberto Rodríguez Velado, who were brothers. The first one, after four days of illegal detention, was handed over to the courts. Not so his brother, who was wounded and is still held in illegal detention. Legal Aid is intervening on his behalf.

Amnesty International issued a press release in which it described the repression of the peasants, especially in the area of Chalatenango. The week's events confirm this report in spite of the fact the government denies it. As I entered the church, I was given a cable that says, "Amnesty International confirmed today [that was yesterday] that in El Salvador human rights are violated to extremes that have not been seen in other countries." That is what Patricio Fuentes (spokesman for the urgent action section for Central America in Swedish Amnesty International) said at a press conference in Managua, Nicaragua.

Fuentes confirmed that, during two weeks of investigations he carried out in El Salvador, he was able to establish that there had been 83 political assassinations between 10 and 14 March. He pointed out that Amnesty International recently condemned the government of El Salvador, alleging that it was responsible for 600 political assassinations. The Salvadorean government defended itself against the charges, arguing that Amnesty International based its condemnation on unproved assumptions.

Fuentes said that Amnesty had established that in El Salvador human rights are violated to a worse degree than the repression in Chile after the coup d'état. The Salvadorean government also said that the 600 dead were the result of armed confrontations between army troops and guerrillas. Fuentes said that during his stay in El Salvador, he could see that the victims had been tortured before their deaths and mutilated afterwards.

The spokesman of Amnesty International said that the victims' bodies characteristically appeared with the thumbs tied behind their backs. Corrosive liquids had been applied to the corpses to prevent identification of the victims by their relatives and to prevent international condemnation, the spokesman added. Nevertheless, the bodies were exhumed and the dead have been identified. Fuentes said that the repression carried out by the

Salvadorean army was aimed at breaking the popular organizations through the assassination of their leaders in both town and country.

According to the spokesman of Amnesty International, at least 3,500 peasants have fled from their homes to the capital to escape persecution. "We have complete lists in London and Sweden of young children and women who have been assassinated for being organized," Fuentes stated. . . .

I would like to make a special appeal to the men of the army, and specifically to the ranks of the National Guard, the police and the military. Brothers, you come from our own people. You are killing your own brother peasants when any human order to kill must be subordinate to the law of God which says, "Thou shalt not kill." No soldier is obliged to obey an order contrary to the law of God. No one has to obey an immoral law. It is high time you recovered your consciences and obeyed your consciences rather than a sinful order. The church, the defender of the rights of God, of the law of God, of human dignity, of the person, cannot remain silent before such an abomination. We want the government to face the fact that reforms are valueless if they are to be carried out at the cost of so much blood. In the name of God, in the name of this suffering people whose cries rise to heaven more loudly each day, I implore you, I beg you, I order you in the name of God: stop the repression.

The church preaches your liberation just as we have studied it in the holy Bible today. It is a liberation that has, above all else, respect for the dignity of the person, hope for humanity's common good, and the transcendence that looks before all to God and only from God derives its hope and its strength.

23.
JOSÉ A. MORALES: A SON'S LETTER TO HIS FATHER
(APRIL 1980)

José Antonio Morales Carbonell, a militant of the Popular Liberation Forces (FPL), writes to his father, Antonio Morales Erlich, member of the second junta. (On June 13, José Antonio was captured and imprisoned in the jail of the National Police.)

Dear Father,

On May 30, 1979, I had to leave the country with a group of *compañeros* to visit the Embassies of France, Venezuela and Costa Rica, to demand freedom for our captured leaders. . . . Today, on my return after a long trip through various countries of Europe, I want to tell you that the entire world is exasperated. From every corner you hear *¡Basta Ya!*— Enough!—to the repression against the Salvadorean people.

It is inconceivable that after so few months in government, your seemingly good intentions . . . have been converted into such enormous compromises and complicities with the number one enemy of Humanity: Yankee Imperialism.

Compromises that seem to know no limits!

Compromises that have taken more lives than the last years of the Military Tyranny!

I remember that some time ago you told me . . . that the enormous crisis of imperialism in our country, caused by the uncontainable rise of the revolutionary movement, had to be used to present a more favorable alternative to U.S. interests and, at the same time, to carry out genuine changes in our country. . . .

But in the end, what are those promised changes?

The famed Agrarian Reform?

Or the permanent state of siege . . . ?

The famed nationalization of banks and foreign trade?

Or the growing and shameless intervention of Yankee Imperialism, that sends personnel trained in counter-insurgency techniques and other specialties; that sends a permanent and constant stream of arms and war supplies to strengthen the puppet armies and the para-military bands of assassins. . . .

It is really dishonorable to be in your situation, and still try to hide from the world the reality of violence and repression that our people suffer daily, crudely attributing it to the supposed provocations of the revolutionary organizations.

I am certain that you yourself don't believe that!

You should follow the example of the other Christian Democrats who decided to stop supporting the repressive regime, to stop serving as a "progressive" cover in exchange for a few crumbs of power, and to stop cynically attributing these desertions to merely "sentimental" motives.

At this point there are no longer intermediate positions, things are totally clear: one is either on the side of the oppressed, or on the side of the oppressors. To stay on their side makes you responsible as well for the crimes committed against the people—crimes committed by your very colleagues.

The least you can do at this moment is to be loyal to the principles you taught me.

Do it for your family, your children. . . .

Do it for the thousands of workers and peasants and for all our people who suffer hunger, misery, exploitation and oppression.

Do it for a minimum sense of human compassion, which I cannot believe you have lost.

It is lamentable to me that you find yourself in this situation, but I remember that you taught me to be clear, a clarity that obliges me to tell you . . . that I am ready to give the last drop of my blood for the liberation of our people; I have faith in the power and creativity of the people's forces and I am convinced that the only way to defeat the enemy is with arms in hand, destroying completely the repressive apparatus and creating a more just society, free of misery and exploitation. . . .

Your son,

José Antonio Morales Carbonell
El Salvador, April 19, 1980

24.
U.S. STATE DEPARTMENT: ANALYSIS OF THE VIOLENCE (APRIL 1980)

Most Salvadorans believe that the bulk of the violence in this country comes from the right, and that the security corps are killing large numbers of people in death squad-style operations. The victims are often teenagers, mostly boys who might possibly be leftist sympathizers. Parents of all political persuasions are urgently concerned about the safety of their children. This violence is destroying the reputation of the JRG [the junta] abroad.

The latest surge in rightist violence is imperiling the PDC-military alliance. Participation of the PDC in the government is essential to foreign and domestic belief in the reform program of the JRG.

We are actively aware that fear is impeding the development of a democratic center because centrist political and labor organizations are being victimized by the left and the right; they live in constant fear and are afraid to hold meetings. Key leaders of the centrist groups have been attacked or killed lately, allegedly by members of the security corps who do not understand the difference between leftist extremists and moderate reformers who support the JRG.

The high level of rightist repression is the glue that binds the contending factions of the Democratic Revolutionary Front (FDR) together. The moderate non-Marxist groups (such as the socialists) within the FDR are

---

Internal memorandum of April 28, 1980.

disenchanted with their radical companions. Their major objection to the present government is its failure to control rightist violence.

Although we know that the leaders of the church sympathize with the JRG's reforms and are increasingly fearful of the left, the rightist killings of peasants, teenagers, priests and nuns and the failure of the security corps to protect innocent people have forced them to take a neutral position between the government and the FDR and increasingly to criticize the JRG and Armed Forces.

Internationally, the left has made effective use of these killings to destroy support for the government. The leftists are exulting over the death of the Catholic women because it has caused the USG to suspend assistance.

CATHOLIC WORKERS

The government and people of the United States are shocked and dismayed by the deaths of four Catholic women who were raped and murdered on the night of December 2 by unknown assailants.

This brutal act has raised a storm of protest in the United States and allegations are heard on all sides that the Security Forces of El Salvador participated in the killings or hastily buried the bodies to protect rightist death squads from exposure or covered up evidence of the crime to avoid criticism from abroad.

These are grave charges that threaten the good relations between the United States and El Salvador. The President has sent a special mission here to work with governmental authorities in investigating the circumstances of the Catholic workers' murder and subsequent burial.

We have supported the reform program of the JRG with the largest economic assistance program in the Western Hemisphere and have supplied over $45 million in military assistance to the Armed Forces to help defend the JRG against attacks from leftist guerrillas and terrorists as well as to restore public order and end the depredations of rightist death squads.

The reforms have been implemented; popular support for the left has diminished to the vanishing point; the struggle against leftist guerrillas is being carried out successfully; the critical harvest is underway with our planning support for its protection; a decision to send the helicopters had already been made when the six FDR leaders were killed in highly questionable circumstances.

On the contrary, the circumstances surrounding the kidnap/murder of the FDR leaders and the hasty secret burial of the Catholic women suggest that the security forces were implicated in these atrocities; it is alleged here and abroad that the work of the death squads goes unnoticed by reason of a policy decision at high levels of the armed forces.

It is impossible for the USG to continue to cooperate in the various assistance programs we have offered to the JRG until this issue has been resolved and steps have been taken to restrain and punish those implicated in rightist violence.

We recognize that there is a hard core of rightist sentiment in the military and business community who believe a military coup is the only alternative to a "communist victory" and many among them believe a systematic campaign to kill all suspected leftists will succeed.

Some exhausted people in the upper and middle classes see the present security-political-social situation worsening and are tempted to support this alternative, and many of the urban and rural poor also would be happy to see an end to uncertainty.

We are convinced that a military coup would at best be a poor short-term solution. The right wing violence it would unleash in an effort to end the threat from the left would be terrible, and that plus efforts to reverse the reforms would, at some point, call forth a new, stronger and probably ultimately successful wave of leftist agitation and terror.

If a government of the left would be dangerous and unviable for the country, so would one of the right. A purely right wing military government would be completely isolated in the world, forced to rely on the uncertain help of the few other right wing military governments of the hemisphere.

If its only purposes were to kill dissidents and reverse internal reforms already in place, it would quickly dash hopes among all but the wealthiest classes of a democratic, just society. A right wing military government would face significant and effective opposition within the country and be swept away in a year or two perhaps in a civil war.

25.
ROBERTO D'AUBUISSON: REACTION TO THE FDR LEADERS' ASSASSINATION (OCTOBER 1980)

To the Salvadoran People and Armed Forces:
In light of the latest events, we wish to clarify the following:

1. There have been attempts to accuse the military or mysterious rightist forces of responsibility for the violent, traitorous attack in the San José

High School where six leaders of the Marxist subversion in this country were killed. Such charges are the Marxist leaders' strategy to justify their attack on the Salvadoran nation and attempt to seize power violently.

— The FDR is totally unmasked as being the leading group directing the violent seizure of power. . . .

— The repeated failure to form a government in exile or in those portions of the country they call "liberated" has brought serious difficulties within the political leadership of the Marxist revolution.

— Thus, what better chance for those who would sell out the country than to traitorously assassinate those leaders of the FDR who are in their way, blame the armed forces and the right, gain prominence in the international press and, most importantly, create conditions for launching their final offensive against the Salvadoran people.

— There is proof—which at the right time will become known—of who is really responsible for the assassination. Based on the information we have in our possession, we assign responsibility for this outrage to the United Revolutionary Directorate, which acted on the direct orders of Colonel Majano, member of the Revolutionary Committee of Government.

2. The Marxist plan for seizing power [includes the following points]:

— Create a popular revolutionary government that would be headed by Colonel Majano, Dr. Ungo. . . .

— Add the support of the Sandinista Front. . . .

— Achieve the recognition of neighboring states and claim international recognition of a state of war.

— Initiate military actions, which the Armed Forces know about and are ready to defeat.

3. We also know that U.S. Ambassador Robert White knows of these activities and is helping the Marxist plan, having offered about a million dollars to the new government which is attempting to direct the violent seizure of power.

26.
CRAIG PYES: THE SALVADORAN RIGHT

This alliance of both military and civilians was established to be a highly organized counterforce to the revolutionary organizations of the left. Its methods were to fight terror with terror, organization with organization, intelligence with intelligence.

"If Americans think this is a war with one army fighting another army, they are wrong," explained coffee grower Alberto Bondanza, one of ARENA's founders. "This is not a conventional war. The only way to fight it is the way they [the left] have fought us. Once you identify your enemy, probably he will die. Luckily, the army is not against us. The death squads, they are fighting the war."

The death squads were at first groups of highly motivated civilians aided by a few sympathetic soldiers. But later, as the right re-established its dominance in the military, the actual killing was carried out more by members of the security forces, with the knowledge of the highest levels of the Salvadoran military. . . .

The most visible member and the primary organizer of this paramilitary party is current Salvadoran Assembly President Robert D'Aubuisson. Elected in 1982, he is a former intelligence officer who has made a dramatic bid to be El Salvador's savior from communism . . . .

By D'Aubuisson's recollection a year ago, the summary executions had begun in government forces even before the 1979 coup, due at least in part to the deterioration of the Salvadoran justice system.

D'Aubuisson told the *Journal* in a long interview that when he was in the security forces, "we began to act incorrectly and not take them [those they picked up for interrogation] to the judge, but make them disappear instead, so the same chain [of having them set free after leftist threats] wouldn't continue."

D'Aubuisson's climb to public prominence came primarily after the 1979 coup.

His financial backing came from the families of El Salvador's monied elite, an oligarchy whose grip on the government and the military was severed in the 1979 coup. . . .

Some members of ARENA's leadership collaborated with the national security forces in the planning and operation of a "dirty war" of counterin-

Albuquerque Journal, December 19, 1982.

surgency to physically eliminate their political enemies. ARENA members said this meant polarizing the country and eliminating their enemies from the left to the political center.

This war "by assassination," which was made to appear the random violence of independent groups of fanatical rightists, was in many cases organized with high-ranking regular army officers and operated out of the intelligence offices of the National Guard, National Police and Treasury Police, as well as out of many military garrisons. . . .

"[There is] one man in particular, very strong—who is over him [D'Aubuisson] and lets him risk himself," explained a foreign military expert close to the National Guard.

The "one man," the highest ranking officer in the network mentioned by insiders, was former Vice Minister of Defense Col. Nicolás Carranza. Carranza was the number-two man in the Salvadoran military until December 1980, when U.S. concern about human-rights abuses helped to pressure him from his post.

The other primary agency of counterterror with which D'Aubuisson had worked was the National Guard's G-2 central intelligence office while the Guard was headed by Gen. Carlos Eugenio Vides Casanova, currently minister of defense.

During the time Vides commanded the guard, active-duty military officers working with the G-2 were linked in State Department cables to the March 1980 assassination of Salvadoran Archbishop Oscar Arnulfo Romero and to the January 1981 killing of two American labor leaders. . . .

ARENA insiders describe a theory of counterinsurgency (anti-guerrilla) warfare which parallels the development of the party.

The theory explains El Salvador's epidemic of death-squad killings as the implementation of a philosophy of selective and mass assassinations carried out in an organized manner.

D'Aubuisson is perhaps only the most public figure in ARENA, a political movement that contains others more powerful than he. The party organization spans all of El Salvador's 14 departments (provinces). It is divided into sectors that correspond roughly to the traditional divisions of Salvadoran society, such as youth, peasants and farmers.

But the party also embraces local military officers, security-force operations and a broad vigilante network of civil defense units suspected of being used to eliminate the party's political opposition.

Current U.S. intelligence indicates that ARENA may be connected to a single countrywide death-squad network, consisting primarily of three loosely knit regional organizations which in total do not exceed 50 persons. . . . When the returns of the March 1982 Salvadoran elections came in, it was clear the violent right had completed its transformation from an illegitimate, clandestine force to a strongly entrenched power in the Salvadoran government. ARENA captured 25 percent of the vote and D'Aubuisson the presidency of the Constituent Assembly.

With these electoral successes, party members had accomplished at least some of their goals: they had forced out the U.S.-backed Christian Democrats and completely disarmed and dismantled the progressive sectors of the army. . . .

"This emerging middle class has a greater fear of communism than anything even our ideologues can imagine," explained one member of the U.S. National Security Council, who, like most officials, refused to be quoted by name on El Salvador. "D'Aubuisson is not an isolated case. He's not a power seeker for himself or for 14 families. He symbolizes a new development. There's a hell of a lot more here than we [U.S. policy-makers] ever talked about."

ARENA Vice President Hugo Barrera, who bears a bullet scar inflicted by a labor agitator in his factory, experienced such an outpouring of emotion after joining D'Aubuisson that he composed a war hymn, still sung by ARENA faithful, called "Tremble, Tremble *Communista!*" . . . The plan, explained one D'Aubuisson aide, was to establish a three-tiered organization containing a "political or propaganda level . . . to encourage and protect the military level; . . . a financial system where we would always have money to attack; and a military level—what the United States called right-wing death squads—people who go out and kidnap and kill the communists the way they were doing it to the rightists."

"We divided into a Salvadoran group and a Miami group," said the D'Aubuisson aide. "The Miami group was finances."

In the Miami group were members of El Salvador's oligarchy. They felt dangerously exposed after the 1979 coup broke its hold on the military and upset the old power structure.

At the beginning, said a D'Aubuisson associate, "everybody [on the right] was jockeying for position. The people who had money were putting up the money, and the people who had the guts were doing it by putting themselves up."

Those who put up the money at first, and who later became key financial backers of ARENA, which emerged later, were primarily planters with agribusiness and banking interests and who live in condominiums in Miami. . . . Those who knew D'Aubuisson in ANSESAL, El Salvador's executive intelligence agency, where he worked until a few months before the coup, described him as an eager, energetic political policeman, whose photographic memory contained the information from file cards, computer printouts and dossiers on the political opposition.

In 1978, fresh from special training courses in Taiwan, D'Aubuisson composed a 64-page intelligence report for the National Guard which became *the* text on the relationships between social reformers and Marxist guerrillas for the various Salvadoran governmental intelligence services.

D'Aubuisson was assigned to the elite of those services, the Salvadoran National Security Agency, ANSESAL.

ANSESAL was formed of the heads of the military services and internal security forces and answered directly to the president. From its offices in the Presidential Palace, it functioned as the brain of a vast state security apparatus that reached into every town and neighborhood in the country. By conservative estimate, at least one Salvadoran out of every 50 was an informant for the agency.

In addition to gathering intelligence, ANSESAL was used to carry out death-squad activities before the coup, according to Salvadoran and U.S. officials.

After the coup, ANSESAL was ordered disbanded. . . . In addition to abolishing ANSESAL, when the young officers came to power in their bloodless 1979 coup, they retired or transferred nearly 60 senior officers and ordered the disbanding of the controversial rural paramilitary National Democratic Organization, known by its Spanish acronym, ORDEN.

They also established a commission to investigate the fate of political prisoners and the "disappeared.". . . Before the coup, almost 200 people a year were being killed, allegedly by government security forces. El Salvador was known in the international community as one of the world's worst violators of human rights.

After the coup, the rate of killing rose steadily to 800 a month.

Both U.S. and Salvadoran officials attribute most of the increased post-coup violence to "independent anti-communist death squads" financed by the oligarchy and directed by the right-wing paramilitary underground. The Salvadoran military leadership said that D'Aubuisson was running these paramilitary operations from Guatemala and that they had issued an arrest warrant to be served should he re-enter El Salvador.

D'Aubuisson said that, after he left the army, his activities were directed toward building a network, both within and outside the armed forces, which he said had been compromised by pro-Marxist elements supporting the coup.

Initially, he said, he met with former intelligence operatives and right-wing political leaders to salvage the intelligence system of the pre-coup regime. . . . D'Aubuisson said he considered the civilians in the new government communists or their "useful fools," and wrote that conclusion in an intelligence report for the army high command a few months after his ostensible resignation from the military.

In December 1979, only 11 weeks after joining the government, virtually the entire civilian Social Democratic opposition resigned over the question of death squads tied to senior military officers. The Social Democratic moderates had been viewed by many as the last chance to avert a violent revolution.

Within five months, government resignations from center-left democratic parties protesting the violence surpassed 30. Many subsequently allied themselves with leftist guerrillas.

D'Aubuisson's "new ANSESAL" was moved under the army general staff and, until late 1981, operated as a political police against the Christian Democrats then in power and did little else, according to military officials from the United States and El Salvador.

Rightist insiders involved with the paramilitary underground said that D'Aubuisson remained in contact with about 100 mostly low- and mid-level officers from the security forces, working closely with 15 to 20.

These sources pointed out the National Guard and Treasury Police, particularly their intelligence units, as the rightists' two main bases of support in 1980, which they called "a big paramilitary year." Both agencies have been accused by U.S. officials of conducting mass assassination campaigns.

The biggest target was the Christian Democrat Party (PDC). . . . more than 260 of the party's leaders, including 35 Christian Democratic mayors, have been murdered in the past three years. . . .

27.
AMBASSADOR ROBERT WHITE: MURDER OF THE FDR LEADERS (NOVEMBER 1980)

ON NOVEMBER 27 A MEETING OF THE DEMOCRATIC REVOLUTIONARY FRONT (FDR) WAS INTERRUPTED BY ARMED MEN AND KIDNAPPED SIX OF ITS TOP LEADERSHIP. LATER IN THE DAY THE BODIES OF FOUR OF THOSE LEADERS (INITIALLY IDENTIFIED AS JUAN CHACÓN, SECRETARY GENERAL OF THE POPULAR REVOLUTIONARY BLOC-BPR; HUMBERTO MENDOZA, LEADER OF THE POPULAR LIBERATION MOVEMENT-MLP; ENRIQUE ESCOBAR BARRERA, IN-COUNTRY LEADER OF THE NATIONAL REVOLUTIONARY MOVEMENT-MNR; DOROTEO HERMANDE, OF THE UNION OF SLUM DWELLERS-UPT, A MEMBER OF THE BPR) WERE DISCOVERED ON THE OUTSKIRTS OF SAN SALVADOR. ON THE MORNING OF NOVEMBER 28 RADIOS ARE REPORTING THE DISCOVERY OF THE BODY OF ENRIQUE ÁLVAREZ CORDOV, TITULAR HEAD OF THE FDR. THE WHEREABOUTS OF

Cable to Secretary of State Alexander Haig. Includes the statement of the Salvadoran junta and of a rightist death squad.

MANUEL FRANCO, HEAD OF THE NATIONAL DEMOCRATIC UNION (UDN)
IS UNKNOWN. BELOW ARE STATEMENTS RELEASED BY THE GOVERN-
MENT AND BY THE RIGHTIST GROUP WHICH HAS TAKEN CREDIT FOR THE
KILLINGS.

2. JRG COMMUNIQUE:

"TODAY THE GOVERNMENT LEARNED OF THE KIDNAPPING OF SOME
POLITICAL LEADERS, A FACT WHICH AT FIRST SOME OF THE MEDIA
WRONGLY CALLED A CAPTURE. THE ABOVE MENTIONED INCIDENT TOOK
PLACE IN THE EXTERNADO OF SAN JOSÉ (COMMENT: A CATHOLIC HIGH
SCHOOL) IN THIS CAPITAL.

TODAY THE AUTHORITIES BEGAN A THOROUGH INVESTIGATION OF
THE CASE AND THE FIRST RESULTS ARE THE FOLLOWING:

CONCERNING THE ABOVE MENTIONED KIDNAPPING THE RECTOR OF
THE COLEGIO EXTERNADO SAN JOSÉ, THE JESUIT PRIEST JOSÉ SANTA-
MARIA, THE ACTING HEAD OF SOCORRO JURISCO OF THE ARCHBISHOPRIC,
BORIS MARTÍNEZ, AND THE WATCHMAN JOSÉ ABDULIO TORREQUEAR-
TÍNEZ WERE QUESTIONED.

THE INCIDENT TOOK PLACE APPROXIMATELY BETWEEN 9:00 A.M. AND
11:40 A.M. THE POLITICAL LEADERS HAD CALLED A PRESS CONFERENCE
IN THAT PLACE WHICH IT IS SAID THEY HAD AGREED TO MOVE TO THE
METROPOLITAN CATHEDRAL.

AT 11:30 APPROXIMATELY 13 ARMED INDIVIDUALS ARRIVED IN TWO
VEHICLES: A RED DATSUN PICK-UP AND A LARGE BLUE TRUCK. ALL THE
INDIVIDUALS, WHO ARRIVED ARMED, HAD THEIR FACES COVERED. IN
NONE OF THEIR DECLARATIONS DID THE WITNESSES MAKE REFERENCE
TO HAVING SEEN UNIFORMED PEOPLE.

IT IS CERTAIN THAT THIS ACTION WAS CARRIED OUT WITH THE OBJEC-
TIVE OF WORSENING THE CLIMATE OF VIOLENCE THAT THE COUNTRY IS
EXPERIENCING, AGAINST THE WILL AND DESIRE FOR PEACE OF THE
SALVADORAN PEOPLE.

THE REVOLUTIONARY GOVERNING JUNTA DEMANDS THAT THE PLAN-
NERS AND EXECUTORS OF THIS CRIME RESPECT THE HUMAN RIGHTS OF
THOSE KIDNAPPED AND THEIR MORAL AND PHYSICAL INTEGRITY.

FINALLY, THE GOVERNMENT CALLS ON THE MAKERS OF PUBLIC OPIN-
ION AND THE CITIZENS IN GENERAL, IN ORDER TO AVOID COMPLICATING
THE SITUATION, TO ABSTAIN FROM SPREADING RUMORS OR SPECULA-
TIONS ABOUT THIS MATTER."

3. RIGHTIST COMMUNIQUE. ACCORDING TO THE NEWSPAPERS, THE FOL-
LOWING MESSAGE WAS RECEIVED FROM THE MAXIMILIANO HERNÁNDEZ
MARTÍNEZ ANTI-COMMUNIST BRIGADE:

"WE MAKE KNOWN TO THE CITIZENRY IN GENERAL: TODAY WE, A

SQUADRON OF THE GENERAL MAXIMILIANO HERNÁNDEZ MARTÍNEZ AN-
TI-COMMUNIST BRIGADE, MAKE KNOWN OUR RESPONSIBILITY FOR THE
JUST EXECUTION OF THE COMMUNISTS OF THE FDR: ENRIQUE ÁLVAREZ
CORDOVA, JUAN CHACÓN, ENRIQUE BARRERA, MANUEL FRANCO AND
HUMBERTO MENDOZA, FOR BEING MATERIALLY AND INTELLECTUALLY
RESPONSIBLE FOR THOUSANDS OF ASSASSINATIONS OF INNOCENT PEOPLE
WHO DID NOT WANT TO BE COMMUNISTS. WE ALSO WARN THE PRIESTS
WHO HAVE AN AFFINITY FOR THE TERRORIST MARXIST BANDS THAT
THEY WILL HAVE THE SAME FATE IF THEY INSIST IN THEIR SERMONS ON
POISONING THE MINDS OF SALVADORAN YOUTH. THE BRIGADE WILL
CONTINUE THE JUST EXECUTIONS OF THE TRAITORS *TO OUR COUNTRY.*"

28.
WILLIAM BOWDLER AND WILLIAM ROGERS: REPORT ON THE MURDER OF THE AMERICAN NUNS (DECEMBER 1980)

Sister Ita Ford was an American citizen and a member of the Maryknoll order. She had been requested by the Apostolic Administrator of San Salvador to assist in the work of refugee resettlement in Chalatenango in July, 1980. She worked under the supervision of Father Efraín López distributing food, clothing and medicine to the poor and the dispossessed, and lived in a modest parish house.

Chalatenango is an area particularly marked by competing violence between the left and right. During the latter part of November, it is reported that a sign appeared over the door of the Chalatenango parish house stating that all who lived there were Communists and anyone who entered would be killed. Neither Sister Ita nor local clergy gave the sign any special attention.

All the Maryknolls of the Central American region meet in assembly every year. Sister Ita Ford, together with Sister Madeline Dempsey and Sister Teresa Alexander, two other Maryknoll sisters who work in the Diocese of Santa Ana (and whom we interviewed), left El Salvador by plane on November 26 to go to the annual meeting, held in Managua, Nicaragua. At this meeting it was decided that a second sister should be assigned to assist Sister Ita in Chalatenango. This person was to be Sister Maura Clarke, also an American citizen, who had been working among the

Report to the Secretary of State.

poor of Nicaragua for the past fourteen years. She therefore packed her belongings and made preparations to accompany Sister Maura to El Salvador.

The four Maryknolls could not obtain reservations on the same plane back to El Salvador. Accordingly, Sisters Madeline and Teresa returned on a TACA flight arriving at the El Salvador International Airport at about 4:30 p.m., Tuesday, December 2. There they were met by two other American citizens, Ursuline Sister Dorothy Kazel and Jean Donovan, a lay volunteer, both of whom were engaged in similar parish work in the city of La Libertad. Sister Dorothy and Jean Donovan drove Sister Madeline and Sister Teresa to La Libertad, then returned to meet Sisters Ita and Maura at the airport. Sisters Madeline and Teresa understood the four intended to sleep at the Ursuline parish house in La Libertad, and that Sisters Ita and Maura planned to drive to Chalatenango the following day.

Sister Ita and Sister Maura arrived at the El Salvador International Airport from Managua on a COPA flight at approximately 6:30 p.m. the evening of December 2. Sister Dorothy Kazel and Jean Donovan arrived in their white 1978 Toyota van at approximately the same time to pick them up.

The airport was filled with foreigners arriving to attend the funeral the next day of the leaders of the leftist Democratic Revolutionary Front (FDR) kidnapped and murdered on November 27. The level of tension was high throughout El Salvador. Security forces patrolled the airport and its access roads.

The four Americans met and, while waiting for their baggage, chatted with a group of Canadian Churchmen. The Canadians left the airport first, at approximately 7:00 p.m.

We have not identified anyone who saw the four American Churchwomen alive after the Canadian group left them at the airport baggage pickup station.

The next morning, Wednesday, December 3, between 10:00 and 11:00 a.m., Father Schindler of the La Libertad parish called the U.S. Consul in El Salvador and said that Sister Dorothy and Jean Donovan had not appeared at a meeting they were to attend, and that he could not locate them. The Consul immediately called Col. López Nuila, Chief of the National Police, and told him of the disappearance. Col. López Nuila asked if the nuns were wearing habits. He was advised they were not. The Colonel promised to institute a nationwide search. A few hours later the Ambassador arranged to have the Minister of Defense advised. The Minister promised to do everything in his power to find them.

Father Schindler evidently spent the rest of Wednesday, December 3, searching for the missing women. (We were unable to talk with him in El Salvador; he was in the U.S. for the funerals.) At about 8:00 p.m. that night, he found their Toyota van on a road about ten miles northwest of the airport, in the direction of the City of San Salvador. The license plates had been removed and the van was burned so badly it had to be identified by the engine number. When he arrived at the airport, at about 9:30 a.m., on Thursday, December 4, the Ambassador was advised by radio that the Embassy had been called by the Vicar of the Diocese of San Vicente. The Vicar had been told that the bodies of the "American nuns" were buried near Santiago Nonualco, a remote village some 15 miles northeast of the airport, and about 20 miles from where the van had been found northwest of the airport.

The Ambassador and the Consul drove there immediately; the trip into what is a rugged and mountainous part of the country took some time. After several inquiries, a local villager directed them to the grave, which he called that of the "American women," beside a back road some way out of Santiago Nonualco. When they arrived at the site, at about 1:30 in the afternoon, Father Paul Schindler was already there. He too had received word from the parish priest. Reporters from San Salvador and foreign media representatives began to arrive. Some villagers started to open the grave. No authorities were present when they began. About 3:00 p.m., the secretary of the Justice of the Peace, who performs the functions of a county coroner, arrived from Santiago Nonualco. He gave permission for the bodies, already uncovered, to be removed from the grave. Shortly thereafter the Justice of the Peace, Juan Santos Cerón, appeared.

All four women had been shot in the head. The face of one had been destroyed. The underwear of three was found separately. Bloody bandanas were also found in the grave. After the disinterment, the Ambassador and Consul drove the Justice of the Peace and his secretary to San Salvador. In the course of the drive, the Justice of the Peace said that about 8:30 a.m. the previous day, December 3, the Commander of the Militia of Canton Hacienda San Francisco had notified him that there were four dead women on the road near Hacienda San Francisco. The Justice of the Peace and his secretary had then cooperated in the burial, following procedures they said had become standard at the direction of the security forces. They told the Ambassador that two or three such informal burials of unidentified bodies occurred every week.

29.
DEMOCRATIC REVOLUTIONARY FRONT: PLATFORM
(1980)

The economic and social structures of our country—which have served to guarantee the disproportionate enrichment of an oligarchic minority and the exploitation of our people by Yankee imperialism—are in deep and insoluble crisis.

The military dictatorship is also in crisis, and with it the entire legal and ideological order that the oligarchic interests and the U.S. imperialists have defended and continue to defend, oppressing the Salvadorean people for half a century. Victims of their own contradictions, the dominant classes have failed due to the decisive and heroic action of the people's movement. It has been impossible to stave off this failure, even with the more and more brazen intervention of the United States in support of such efforts against the people.

Unswerving commitment to the interests and aspirations of the Salvadorean people by the revolutionary organizations has led to the deepening and strengthening of their roots among the vast toiling majority and the middle sectors. Being so rooted in the people, the revolutionary movement is now indestructible. It constitutes the only alternative for the Salvadorean people, who can be neither stopped nor diverted from their struggle to gain a Free Homeland in which their vital desires will be made real. . . .

The revolution that is on the march is not, nor can it be, the work of a group of conspirators. To the contrary, it is the fruit of the struggle of the entire people—of the workers, the peasants, the middle layers in general, and all sectors and individuals that are honestly democratic and patriotic.

The most conscious and organized ranks of the Salvadorean people, now multitudinous, are fighting in a more and more broad and united way. The worker and peasant alliance through its combativity, level of consciousness, daring, organization, and spirit of sacrifice for the sake of the people's triumph has proven to be the most solid basis for guaranteeing the firmness and consistency of the entire Liberation movement. Expressing the unity of the entire people, this movement unites the revolutionary forces and the democratic forces—the two great torrents generated by the long struggle carried out by the Salvadorean people.

The decisive task of the revolution on which completion of all its objectives depends is the conquest of power and the installation of a *democratic revolutionary government,* which at the head of the people will launch the construction of a new society.

TASKS AND OBJECTIVES OF THE REVOLUTION

The tasks and objectives of the revolution in El Salvador are the following:
1. To overthrow the reactionary military dictatorship of the oligarchy and Yankee imperialism, imposed and sustained against the will of the Salvadorean people for fifty years; to destroy its criminal political-military machine; and to establish a *democratic revolutionary government,* founded on the unity of the revolutionary and democratic forces in the People's Army and the Salvadorean people.
2. To put an end to the overall political, economic and social power of the great lords of land and capital.
3. To liquidate once and for all the economic, political, and military dependence of our country on Yankee imperialism.
4. To assure democratic rights and freedoms for the entire people—particularly for the working masses, who are the ones who have least enjoyed such freedoms.
5. To transfer to the people, through nationalizations and the creation of collective and socialized enterprises: the fundamental means of production and distribution that are now hoarded by the oligarchy and the U.S. monopolies, the land held in the power of the big landlords, the enterprises that produce and distribute electricity and other monopolized services, foreign trade, banking, and large transportation enterprises. None of this will affect small or medium-sized private businesses, which will be given every kind of stimulus and support in the various branches of the national economy.
6. To raise the cultural and material living standards of the population.
7. To create a new army for our country, one that will arise fundamentally on the basis of the People's Army to be built in the course of the revolutionary process. Those healthy, patriotic, and worthy elements that belong to the current army can also be incorporated.
8. To encourage all forms of organization of the people, at all levels and in all sectors, thus guaranteeing their active, creative, and democratic involvement in the revolutionary process and securing the closest identification between the people and their government.
9. To orient the foreign policy and international relations of our country around the principles of independence and self-determination, solidarity, peaceful coexistence, equal rights, and mutual respect between states.

10. Through all these measures, to assure our country peace, freedom, the well-being of our people, and future social progress.

THE DEMOCRATIC REVOLUTIONARY GOVERNMENT—ITS COMPOSITION AND PLATFORM OF SOCIAL, STRUCTURAL, AND POLITICAL CHANGES

The *democratic revolutionary government* will be made up of representatives of the revolutionary and people's movement, as well as of the democratic parties, organizations, sectors, and individuals who are willing to participate in the carrying out of this programmatic platform.

This government will rest on a broad political and social base, formed above all by the working class, the peasantry, and the advanced middle layers. Intimately united to the latter forces will be all the social sectors that are willing to carry out this platform—small and medium-sized industrialists, merchants, artisans, and farmers (small and medium-sized coffee planters and those involved in other areas of agriculture or cattle raising). Also involved will be honest professionals, the progressive clergy, democratic parties such as the MNR [Movimiento Nacionalista Revolucionaria —Revolutionary Nationalist Movement], advanced sectors of the Christian Democracy, worthy and honest officers of the army who are willing to serve the interests of the people, and any other sectors, groups, or individuals that uphold broad democracy for the popular masses, independent development, and people's liberation.

All these forces are now coming together to make up a revolutionary and democratic alliance in which the political and/or religious beliefs of all are respected. The organized form to be taken by this voluntary alliance at the service of the Salvadorean people will be the result of consultations among all those who make it up.

IMMEDIATE POLITICAL MEASURES

1. A halt to all forms of repression against the people and release of all political prisoners.

2. Clarification of the situation of those captured and disappeared since 1972; punishment of those responsible (be they military or civilian) for crimes against the people.

3. Disarming and permanent dissolution of the repressive bodies—ANSESAL, ORDEN, National Guard, National Police, Treasury Police, and Customs Police, along with their respective "Special Sections"; of the Gotera "Counterinsurgency School" and the so-called Armed Forces Engineering Training Center in Zacatecoluca; of the cantonal and suburban military patrols; of the oligarchy's private paramilitary bands; and of all other kinds of real or nominal organizations dedicated to criminal action or slander against the people and their organizations. The current misnamed security bodies will be replaced by a civilian police force.

4. Dissolution of the existing state powers (executive, legislative, and judicial); abrogation of the Political Constitution and all decrees that have modified or added to it.

The *democratic revolutionary government* will decree a constitutional law and will organize the state and its activities with the aim of guaranteeing the rights and freedoms of the people and of achieving the other objectives and tasks of the revolution. In doing so, the *democratic revolutionary government* will adhere to the United Nations' "Universal Declaration of Human Rights."

The constitutional law referred to above will remain in force while the Salvadorean people prepare a new Political Constitution that faithfully reflects their interest.

5. Municipal government will be restructured so as to be an organ of broad participation by the masses in managing the state, so as to be a real organ of the new people's power.

6. The *democratic revolutionary government* will carry out an intense effort of liberating education, of cultural exposition and organization among the broadest masses, in order to promote their conscious incorporation into the development, strengthening, and defense of the revolutionary process.

7. The People's Army will be strengthened and developed. It will include the soldiers, noncommissioned officers, officers, and chiefs of the current army who conduct themselves honestly, reject foreign intervention against the revolutionary process, and support the liberation struggle of our people.

The new army will be the true armed wing of the people. It will be at their service and absolutely faithful to their interests and their revolution. The armed forces will be truly patriotic, the defenders of national sovereignty and self-determination, and committed partisans of peaceful coexistence among peoples.

8. Our country will withdraw from CONDECA [Central American Defense Council], from TIAR [Rio de Janeiro Inter-American Defense Treaty], and from any other military or police organizations that might be the instruments of interventionism.

9. The *democratic revolutionary government* will establish diplomatic and trade relations with other countries without discrimination on the basis of differing social systems, on the basis of equal rights, coexistence, and respect for self-determination. Special attention will be paid to the development of friendly relations with the other countries of Central America (including Panama and Belize), with the aim of strengthening peace and upholding the principle of nonintervention. Close fraternal relations with

Nicaragua will especially be sought, as the expression of the community of ideals and interest between our revolution and the Sandinista revolution.

Our country will become a member of the Movement of Nonaligned Countries and will develop a steadfast policy toward the defense of world peace and in favor of detente.

STRUCTURAL CHANGES

The *democratic revolutionary government* will:

1. Nationalize the entire banking and financial system. This measure will not affect the deposits and other interests of the public.
2. Nationalize foreign trade.
3. Nationalize the system of electricity distribution, along with the enterprises for its production that are in private hands.
4. Nationalize the refining of petroleum.
5. Carry out the expropriation, in accord with the national interest, of the monopolistic enterprises in industry, trade, and services.
6. Carry out a thorough agrarian reform, which will put the land that is now in the hands of the big landlords at the disposal of the broad masses who work it. This will be done according to an effective plan to benefit the great majority of poor and middle peasants and agricultural wage workers and to promote the development of agriculture and cattle raising.

The agrarian reform will not affect small and medium landholders, who will receive stimuli and support for continued improvements in production on their plots.

7. Carry out an urban reform to benefit the great majority, without affecting small and medium owners of real estate.
8. Thoroughly transform the tax system, so that tax payments no longer fall upon the workers. Indirect taxes on widely consumed goods will be reduced. This will be possible not only through reform of the tax system, but also because the state will receive substantial income from the activity of the nationalized sector of the economy.
9. Establish effective mechanisms for credit, economic aid, and technical assistance for small and medium-sized private businesses in all branches of the country's economy.
10. Establish a system for effective planning of the national economy, which will make it possible to encourage balanced development.

SOCIAL MEASURES

The *democratic revolutionary government* will direct its efforts in the social arena toward the following objectives:

1. Create sufficient sources of jobs, so as to eliminate unemployment in the briefest possible time.
2. Bring into effect a just wage policy, based on:

    a. Regulation of wages, taking into account the cost of living.
    b. An energetic policy of control and reduction of the prices charged for basic goods and services.
    c. A substantial increase in social services for the popular masses (Social Security, education, recreation, health care, etc.).

3. Put into action a massive plan for construction of low cost housing.
4. Create a Unified National Health System, which will guarantee efficient medical service to the entire population (urban and rural). Preventative care will be the principal aim.
5. Carry out a literacy campaign that will put an end to the social defect of illiteracy in the shortest possible time.
6. Develop the national education system so as to assure primary education to the entire population of school age and substantially broaden secondary and university education. Quality and scientific-technical diversification will be increased at all levels, and free education will be progressively introduced.
7. Promote cultural activity on a broad scale, effectively supporting and stimulating national artists and writers, recovering and developing the cultural heritage of the nation, and incorporating into the cultural assets of the broad popular masses the best of universal culture.

It is the unanimous opinion of the popular and democratic forces that only through realization of the measures contained in this platform can the profound structural and political crises of our country be resolved in favor of the Salvadorean people.

Only the oligarchy, U.S. imperialism, and those who serve their anti-patriotic interests are opposed to and are conspiring against these changes. Since October 15, 1979, various parties and sectors have vainly attempted to use the government to carry out a large part of the measures we propose without first overthrowing the old reactionary and repressive power and without installing a truly revolutionary and popular power. This experience has confirmed with full clarity that only the united revolutionary movement in alliance with all the democratic forces can carry out such a work of transformation.

The moment is approaching for this historic and liberating victory, for which the Salvadorean people have struggled and heroically shed so much of their blood. Nothing and no one will be able to prevent it.

For the unity of the revolutionary and democratic forces!

Toward the conquest of the *democratic revolutionary government!*

30.
PEOPLE'S REVOLUTIONARY ARMY (ERP): STATEMENT ON FMLN UNITY (MARCH 1980)

The Salvadorian people are at present confronting a crucial moment in history, in search of their final liberation. The struggle that is now taking place in our country expresses a people's right to be the author of its own destiny. For this reason, in order to exercise this right, we must not be deterred by the manipulation, the traps and even the direct intervention of American Imperialism, declared enemy of a country's right to self-determination and a firm ally of the oppressors of the world.

It is in this general context that our country, El Salvador, has suffered almost half a century of criminal and pitiless repression at the hands of murderous military dictatorships, which have protected the interests of American Imperialism and of the Salvadorian Oligarchy, while keeping our people submerged in a terrible drama of poverty which ranks us among the countries with the highest indices of illiteracy, malnutrition, lack of housing, infant mortality, etc., in the world.

The existence of this situation of permanent oppression has made the Salvadorian people become unyielding in its effort to achieve an alternative which offers real liberty, democracy and self-determination, and to this end it has developed its own means, evolving its popular organizations and strengthening its armed revolutionary movement.

The struggle, rapidly accelerating in this most recent stage, has provoked setbacks and superficial changes in government policy, in which American Imperialism has been the principal promoter.

It was in this situation that our convulsed nation heard all the fascist talk about "Dialogue and Free Elections" during the Romero era. The failure of this formula gave way to a "coup d'état" in order to avoid the almost certain international isolation of the dictatorship of General Romero.

This coup, promoted by the Americans, did not signify, nor could it signify the solution to the problems of our people, since the intent was to impede construction by the people of a true democratic and popular alternative.

The perseverance and combativity of the Salvadorian people in its struggle, and the honesty of the democratic sectors who had naively believed in the viability of structural reforms in our society, made it impossible to consolidate the initial attempt at forming a governing junta, bringing to a noisy conclusion the first American maneuver to this end.

There was no lack of opportunities, fencesitters and reactionaries to offer themselves for a second imperialist maneuver, and a second pact, this time between the Christian Democrats and the most reactionary sections of the military, was achieved.

The basis of this new pact was total acceptance of a demagogic plan of pseudo-reforms combined with cruel repression against the people. But some oligarchic groups and the army, in their voracity and tremendous criminal deformations, have not even accepted this scheme, and are looking for one that doesn't speak at all of reforms, and that uses repression as the only solution to the problems of the country.

Therefore, it is clear that the more reactionary sector of the Christian Democratic Party; the Oligarchy; Imperialism and the majority of the army are in agreement over one thing: to subjugate our people and destroy its organizations, since this is the fundamental prerequisite for any solution in their terms.

The Christian Democrats have been unmasked. The case of Mr. Duarte has clearly shown that he is a rabid "anti-communist," enemy of popular participation, who prefers to align himself with fascists before having to accept that this country has long since transcended his level of political consciousness, and will not accept the false guidance of petty politicians.

The maintenance in power of the Christian Democrats, or whatever other centrist formula, is a result of the need of the most murderous and reactionary sectors of the army not to remain alone in power, because as such they would become isolated on an international level, and that would obstruct the American plans for military, political, and economic intervention, and they would run the risk of being condemned by all of the democratic governments and nations of the world.

This is the reason why the government finds it necessary to give the appearance of being centrist, facilitating a deep and criminal repression, and making it appear on the international scene as the result of confrontations between rightist and leftist groups.

For this reason all nations of the world should be aware of what is really happening in our country, and of who is really governing El Salvador.

American Imperialism is directing the destiny of our country through the enormous control that it exercises over an army which is essentially murderous; which has in its ranks officials and troops who are bloodthirsty psychopaths, enemies of any form of popular organization; accustomed to making an entertainment out of the butchering of our people.

While this army exists in our country, a faithful servant of imperialism, and while the Oligarchy holds the economic power, there will be neither peace nor justice for our nation, and any government that does not have the popular sectors as the fundamental base for military, economic and political change, is a government condemned sooner or later to defeat.

We announce to the democratic movement all over the world that our nation is the victim of a murderous rightist military force, associated with a group which lacks popular support: the Christian Democratic Party, which allows itself to be used voluntarily to give the appearance of a moderate government, when it is in fact an extreme rightist one. . . .

The argument about violence and the evils of war, which for the poor and exploited have always existed, is now being used to condemn the just and heroic struggle with which the Salvadorian people have begun to defend themselves against so many years of oppression.

The war which is in fact taking place was not started by the people. However, the people are acting in their legitimate defense against the imposition, the permanent repression and the tremendous poverty with which they have finally lost patience, and which has obliged them to prepare themselves and devise new tactics, in an accelerated and creative way, including the organization of their own military forces.

There are those who argue that it is the strikes and the organized activities that are responsible for the fact that there is no work and that the economic crisis is growing worse. What has in fact happened is that this organized action on the part of the people has destabilized the economic situation to such a degree that the oligarchy is destroying everything by withdrawing all the money from the country, closing down factories, selling property and creating economic bankruptcy.

But it should be asked whether the solution is to accept the peace of exploitation and death that they wish to impose by eliminating the popular organizations.

There is only one solution: that the people take in their hands what legitimately belong to them, the huge plantations of coffee, sugar, cotton; the huge factories, the banks and all the properties of the oligarchy; this is the definitive solution and no other that would keep us subjected to poverty and permanent repression is acceptable.

Now, the sectors of the murderous and reactionary right wing attribute all the problems to communist subversion. They say that everything that is happening is part of a plan carefully prepared by International Communism. But we who they call subversives have not invented 50 years of military dictatorship, nor have we invented the tortures nor the electoral fraud, nor the massacres, nor the exiles. Nor have we cheated the poor by making them believe that they are poor, and that they are hungry and needy.

If we have made careful plans, they haven't been made in order to cheat anybody. They have been made so that the truth be known and so that the people prepare themselves for the conquest of their legitimate rights.

The reactionary and fascist right is accustomed to seeing the workers as sheep and slaves to whom they do not give the right to think and to organize. And so they invent the story about subversives who want to cheat the people. They are mistaken. The workers are no longer the same submissive people who used to put up with these humiliations, not saying anything and bowing their heads. Now they are getting ready to take what is rightfully theirs.

Those people who, from the comfort of the residential suburbs, of multiple economic resources, have not sensed the grave problems of unemployment and misery; don't know what it is to live in a village with the ever-present fear that the National Guard will arrive and rape the women, kill the men and steal what little they have; do not understand that the war is not just now beginning, but the war against the people began a long time ago, and that for that reason the only path open to the people is to defend themselves with all their strength.

The assassins of the Right raise the banners of Fatherland, Liberty, God and Work, talking about the Democratic and Representative Republic. But the Fatherland they defend belongs to fourteen families; their Liberty, the exploitation and humiliation of the workers; their God, the god of money, to buy consciences and corrupt the work of slavery and misery. These are not the values of our people. They are the values of a handful of oppressors and reactionaries. . . .

The Christian Democratic Party in our country is a group of corrupt petty politicians that does not have the least amount of popular support. . . . The People's Revolutionary Army (ERP) constitutes part of the most advanced sectors of the population that are struggling for liberation of our country, and that have resolutely taken up arms in this war of legitimate defense against the oppressors of our people.

In recent months our military forces have intensified their actions, taking towns, villages, cantons, suburbs and sections of cities, preparing the people for the tasks of insurrection.

More than 75 military operations have been carried out in recent days, and dozens of persons responsible for repression in different parts of the country have been executed; patrols of the National Guard, the National Police and the Treasury Department Police have been attacked, resulting in casualties which are later hidden from official bulletins of the Press of the Permanent Advisory Council of the Armed Forces (COPEFA), in order to avoid demoralization of the troops and to keep from raising the morale of the people with the news of the increased effectiveness of their military forces.

As part of our military activity we have captured elements of the oligarchy in order to oblige them to pay War-Tax in exchange for their freedom. Regarding this, the reactionary right has tried to discredit the revolutionary organization by constantly asking, "What do the subversives do with the money from the kidnappings?" and they make accounts over what they have paid to the organizations, trying in this way to say that it has been squandered. The answer to this question is simple: the people also need money in order to wage war, and what we have done is to recuperate part of the money that belongs to our people—which for the moment is in the hands of the oligarchy—in order to convert it into better organization, more arms, more propaganda, and in this way cover all the costs implied in the process of the People's Revolutionary War. The money that we recuperate is not used for luxury, nor is it wasted, nor is it spent for mercenary assassins. It is used for the people's conquest of justice and peace. . . . . The changes implemented by the Popular Democratic Government will embrace every aspect of the social, political and economic structure.

ECONOMIC CONSIDERATIONS:

- Expropriation without right to indemnization of all properties in the hands of the Oligarchy in the different economic levels, and their subsequent re-distribution as collective, communal, or state properties. This measure infers the realization of Agrarian, Industrial and Urban Reforms, without affecting the small and middle businessmen to whom incentives and support are offered.

- Expropriation of all Imperialist enterprises, and the abandonment of all treaties which subject our country to economic dependence.

- Management of the national economy on the basis of a system of national planning which embraces all branches, sectors and regions.

- Organization of an economic system based on collective property, communal property, state property, and private holdings of small and medium size.

- Nationalization of the export of coffee, cotton, sugar and other products.

- Nationalization of the financial and banking system.

- Nationalization of the production of electrical energy and the refinement of petroleum. . . .

Any effort in this struggle would be in vain if it were not directed towards a real, legitimate process of revolutionary unity. This necessitates the full and total concurrence of all forces which in these past few years have consolidated the organic, political and military structures of the Salvadorian revolutionary struggle. In this regard we welcome the process of unity which has begun to take place among the popular and revolutionary organization.

We firmly believe in the necessity for unity as a historical requisite in this moment, and for this reason we are opposed to any proposal which excludes unity. We are also opposed to expressions of immaturity and subjectivity that could obstruct a real process of unification. . . . . We greet the heroic comrades of the Popular Forces of Liberation (FPL) Farabundo Martí, and we applaud the maturity and profound conviction they are showing in this moment; likewise we greet the comrades of the Salvadoran Communist Party, PCS, who for a long time have tried to promote a unified process. . . .

GENERAL HEADQUARTERS OF THE PEOPLE'S REVOLUTIONARY ARMY (ERP) COMMANDER JOAQUÍN VILLALÓPEZ HUEZO, COMMANDER IN CHIEF

31.
LEONEL GÓMEZ: THE ARMY (MARCH 1981)

The fundamental question . . . is the nature of the Salvadorean army and the 500 or so officers who lead the Salvadorean army, the national guard, the national police and the treasury police. Your left says they are an instrument of the oligarchs. The State Department says they are people willing to learn, who want to do what is best for the country. Your right-wing says they are anti-communist and pro-American.

While you will find individual Salvadorean army officers who fit one or another of those descriptions, the Salvadorean army, in essence, is none of those things. Traditionally, and still today, men join the army in order to get rich.

Young men enter the officer corps to acquire the power and the spoils military service provides. Over 90 percent of the officers have attended the El Salvador military school; very few officers come up through the ranks. By law, graduates from this school may remain in the army for thirty years. Each officer comes from a graduating class, called a *tanda,* and each *tanda* has a president.

Loyalty to the *tanda* is generally greater and more commanding than loyalty to the institution in which they serve. During their thirty year careers, the officers of a *tanda* seek contacts, form alliances with other *tandas* and otherwise prepare for their goal of political power.

Every five years, in the past, elections were held. No matter which party had the most ballots, the army won. The winning President had been chosen by the previous President. Together they assembled a coalition of

Testimony before the House Foreign Affairs Committee, March 11, 1981.

officers from one major *tanda* and several allied *tandas* which were to enjoy the spoils for the next five years.

Let me give you an example of what kind of corruption I am talking about. It was an attempt to expose this corruption and bring about a small measure of justice in El Salvador that caused the army to have Rodolfo Viera, the first campesino President of the Institute of Agrarian Transformation (ISTA), killed, and to send 60 thugs to kill me.

When Viera and I took our offices in ISTA, we found that there was no bookkeeping system. We quickly discovered that ISTA had a building that did not exist. But more important, we began to look at the 106 properties already in ISTA's possession. Some were acquired in 1976–79 at the time when the government had a lot of money because of high coffee prices.

The first thing we discovered was that these properties were losing $20 per hectare. That is ridiculous when you realize how fertile the land in El Salvador is. But then we found one of the major reasons.

We discovered that these properties had been overpriced by at least $40 million. Some properties were already in the government's possession and had been sold to the government for a second time. Others were just grossly overvalued.

What happened to the excess? Some went to the sellers, but probably more came back to the government in kickbacks. ISTA at that time was run by a Colonel. I am not saying that he received $40 million. Rather he would have the kickbacks delivered to the office of President who would spread the graft among his and allied *tandas*.

Forty million dollars sounds like a minor matter, at least that is what the American State Department tells me. But it is not minor in El Salvador. It is particularly a matter of grave importance to the campesinos who now work these properties and have to pay the extra cost.

Viera and I went on national television in El Salvador in mid-year 1980 and exposed the $40 million overpayment. We also initiated charges against the Colonel who had been in charge of ISTA for a specific fraud of $40,000. The government in both cases did nothing. There was to be no justice for the campesinos, no punishment of army officers who had stolen from them.

On January 5, Viera had planned to resign. He was frustrated by the unwillingness of the government to confront corruption. He was tired of all the killings of the campesinos by the army. He was disgusted by the continuing efforts by President Duarte to force him to join the Christian Democratic Party and bring the UCS with him. He would not have joined the guerrillas or the *Frentes*. He would have continued to fight for land reform and against corruption. Instead, he was assassinated along with two American technicians.

In sum, this tells the story of another myth, a myth of your right-wing and your State Department. The Salvadorean army is not held together by an ideology of anti-communism. It is held together by a vast network of corruption.

Now the banks, 15 percent of the best lands, and all export-import activity have been nationalized by the government. Further, your government and others are pouring in vast amounts of economic aid. And, you do not think that the army doesn't see both of these developments as opportunities for further corruption?

I ask you this. If this government in El Salvador was serious about corruption, would Viera be dead and the former head of ISTA still be a free man? And the same goes for whether that government is serious about controlling violence against civilians. If it were, who would be under arrest —Colonel Majano, the progressive member of the junta, or Colonel Moran, head of the Treasury Police? After three government reorganizations, Majano is now in jail and Colonel Moran is still free and directing the Treasury Police, which your State Department describes as the Gestapo of El Salvador.

I have said that the army discarded the oligarchy when it no longer needed them. I have said that the army has supported the reforms because it needs to enlarge its base of support. However, the army is not willing to share power with any other elements of the society and most certainly not with the poor majority.

That takes me to another myth, one propagated by your State Department. They say there is a difference between the army, which is good, and the security forces, which are bad. This is a lot of bovine intestinal effluvia.

The primary institution of the armed forces is the officer corps: five hundred men, most all of whom attended the same military school. In many cases an officer will be rotated from one service to another. The factors that bind officers together from different services, especially the *tandas,* are greater than those which separate them. In summary, there is an integrated officer corps. If its leadership truly wanted to eliminate substantially the abuses now occurring it could. But remember it doesn't. The army is bent on a war to exterminate all possible challenges to its power.

In each military region, the army commander is responsible for the activities of the army. Through the chain of command and the informal ties, he knows which forces are doing what and which soldiers are a part of formal or informal death squads. I have no doubt that many people in the cities have been killed by death squads, who owe their allegiance to the oligarchs, now residing in Miami or Guatemala. But those kinds of killings are very few.

The vast majority of killings are made in sweeps in the countryside by the armed forces engaging in indiscriminate killings or by death squads that operate under the formal or informal direction of the regional or local army commanders. Let me be clear. I am talking about the majority of the army officers now in charge. There are some, especially younger officers, who are revolted and shocked by what is going on.

If these types of killings were to be brought under control, there would still be scores of death squad killings, ordered by the radical right in the oligarchy. But, there would not be over 5000 innocent deaths at the hands of the army, as there were last year in my country.

The fundamental problem in my country is the army, an army which presides over a military dictatorship. The problem is not the oligarchy; ten years of kidnappings and a year and a half of reform have fatally weakened it. Nor is the problem the so-called security forces or the death squads: both trace back to and are commanded by the army. The army officer corps is one institution which now holds the power and will use whatever means to keep that power.

How then does one explain the presence of the Christian Democrats, one of whom, Napoleón Duarte, is President? That is the wrong question. The real question is what have they been able to do in power? The reforms? With exceptions, the army supports the reforms in any case. Controlling violence? It has not happened. Secretary Bushnell points to the fact that unlike a year ago, Christian Democrat mayors in towns in Salvador are no longer being killed. I agree that is true. But, it is not because the army has changed. It is because the mayors have ceased to do anything but shuffle papers. A year ago they would receive complaints about violence and report them to the local military. Now they know better. Your Mr. Bushnell has taken a tragic situation and twisted it for progaganda purposes.

I have esteem for many of the Christian Democrats in government as people and I give them credit for their motives. But, they have accomplished nothing for the people of El Salvador. They have only given a facade to a military dictatorship. President Duarte is a 1981 version of Hindenburg.

A MEDIATION SOLUTION

At present, there is a military stand-off. The left clearly failed in its final offensive. But, it also showed the capability of mounting a coordinated country-wide offensive. The danger is that the government, encouraged by your military aid and advisors, will try to achieve a total military victory.

Let me tell you why it cannot. I agree with your State Department that neither the left nor the government enjoys popular support. A myth propagated by the left in my country and picked up in this country is that the left has broad popular support. That is not the case. I estimate that at best the left has 100,000 active supporters and 500,000 passive supporters. It has been badly divided in the past and has used tactics, including killings, which have alienated the people. It is also true that the most extreme part of the left is the military element. It is also the strongest.

But, it is also the case that the government enjoys even less popular support; it just has more guns and more trained soldiers. And, it has been very willing to use both. The killings by the army have traumatized the Salvadorean people. One is very cautious about rising up against the government when one has seen bodies of people sawed in half, bodies placed alive in battery acid or bodies with every bone broken.

32.
BISHOP RIVERA Y DAMAS: SERMON (MARCH 8, 1981)

... The extreme right, the true cause of all the social and political ills that are currently causing a crisis in our country—this extreme right, which has done little or nothing to resolve the political and military crisis that El Salvador is living through today—now wishes to save the situation by proposing what it has always proposed: the undemocratic solution of a coup d'état. We are sure that the Salvadoran people, with the same firmness and assurance with which they have said "No" to violence and Marxism-Leninism, will say a resounding "No" to any plan by the extreme right to seize power that would make pointless the sacrifice of so many lives. By the coup d'état of the military youths on October 15, 1979, the root of the evil was removed, and we hope that the extreme right and their foreign supporters, particularly certain prominent persons in the United States, understand that this root cannot be planted again in the soil of our homeland.

It is true that the leftist groups have maximized violence and their adherence to Marxism, and for this reason the majority of the people have turned their backs on them. It is undeniable, however, that much of that [violence] is in response to the oppression from which the people have suffered for many years. If the U.S. Government and its political representatives in this country have grasped that, then they are beginning to understand something of the true history of our country, and we are glad of it.

In fact, the extreme right has always been on the lookout for the best opportunity to seize power. Within the military ranks it has always had its unconditional orders from capitalism to frustrate attempts to institute social reforms. That is one of the major reasons why a great many of the

Salvadoran people have not yet been persuaded of the good will of the government which is currently presiding over the future of the country, and that is also the reason why many people who have joined the leftists without being radicals or extremists are opposed to the just reforms which the current government is undertaking as best it can.

More than once the Church has raised her impartial voice to tell the government to purify its ranks of the administrative and military personnel who were impeding the progress of democracy and following practices that were inconsistent with respect for human rights.

But now the Church is raising her voice more insistently with the extreme leftists, telling them not to insist on using weapons as a solution, since obviously there is no advantage to it. It is regrettable that the only road being left open to them is one of destruction of property and public services, thus increasing the suffering of the people in general.

. . . all Salvadorans must be aware that, although the armed conflict has not been capable of arousing enthusiasm and resulting in a seizure of power, yet it has the power to continue its devastation for many long years, and, furthermore, we must recognize that the regular military cannot do much against such a strategy. Contemporary history shows that in places where terrorism becomes established, the police force is unable to control it. Therefore, it is imperative to make the conflict more rational and humane and to seek an outcome that is more in keeping with our status as brothers and children of God.

For this reason, the Church of this archdiocese looks favorably upon the Junta's desire to find a political solution to the problem. We are very pleased that our current government and the United States are becoming convinced that the problem of El Salvador is not fundamentally a military problem, but a social, economic, and political problem. The weapons which should be used in this political conflict are the weapons of reason, expressed in words, and listened to in a dialogue; therefore, we are pleased that Mr. Duarte is convinced that a dialogue is necessary. We encourage him in his intention. As a pastor, we say that a dialogue is absolutely necessary, both to lessen or eliminate the power of terrorism in our country and to restore all that is good, noble, and just in the most troubled sectors of our country.

The political and military measure of amnesty establishes a standard for us. Many Salvadorans who joined the leftist groups did so because of evolving circumstances. For this reason, amnesty and its extension have been a very sensible way of giving all men and women an opportunity to return and to participate in building the nation in a civilized way.

Likewise, I am convinced that, within the ranks of the FDR (Revolutionary Democratic Front), there are some worthwhile people who cannot be simply excluded, but who should be given an opportunity, through dialogue, to participate in the responsibilities of public affairs, in peacemaking, and in the moral and physical reconstruction of the nation. Consequently, we declare that we are encouraging those who are seeking such a dialogue. It is clear, however, that we must draw a line on the blank page of the dialogue and exclude from the discussion certain matters about which there can be no dialogue.

We believe that those matters which must be excluded from the discussion include the reversal of the political and social reforms that have been undertaken, and the radical ideologies and practices of both the right and left. The key point of the discussion is the elections. We believe that this is the route which we all must seek. The Salvadoran people are anxious for things to return to normal, for a truly free opportunity to vote and to express their will, which is now silenced by doubt, fear, terror, and panic. We are sure that these elections, if they are truly free and democratic, as we are promised, will show the whole world that the Salvadorans are a moderate people; that they want changes, but changes that respect the highest values of mankind: life, the property necessary to support life, the dignity of the human person, and the freedom for the Catholic Church of our forefathers to carry out its mission.

I should like to end these remarks by saying a few words to the military, so that they will not be tempted to let power go to their heads and revert to old patterns of domination and military obstruction of the political life of the country. A few days ago the Minister of Defense said that, "The Army could not have succeeded in obtaining all it has without the cooperation of the people." True, the people said "No" to a violent solution, but these people have had almost no opportunity to say "Yes" and to express their political will in truly free elections. The few times that they have, they have been cheated and deceived. The situation must be corrected, so that the people in their sovereignty may decide, and justice and peace may triumph. Amen.

33.
FERMÁN CIENFUEGOS: THE NATURE OF THE WAR
(MARCH 1982)

R.S.L.: On the basis of past Nicaraguan experiences, it seems to me that you expected a popular rebellion in conjunction with the general offensive of January 1981.

Interview with Robert S. Leiken, in Managua, March 19–21, 1982; translated by Gladys Segal and Robert S. Leiken.

F.C.: No, we expected a general strike . . . concurrent with the military efforts. But, it was impossible to coordinate the calling of the strike because each zone was in a state of partial insurrection already. In other words, as of January 10, there were partial and local uprisings rather than a general insurrection.

R.S.L.: Why wasn't there a general insurrection?

F.C.: The people favored insurrections, but murder and fascist terror took their toll. On January 10 the masses were out of control. We have learned from the January 10 experience. . . .

R.S.L.: There is talk in El Salvador that election-related actions need to be taken in urban areas during the coming week . . . [elections in El Salvador were held March 28].

F.C.: There is talk about taking action to coincide with the elections. However, we are not going to touch a single voting booth, or a single voter. We will not disturb the voting process. We will not carry out assassination attempts against candidates. . . .

Generally, each military barracks has its own power backup. This causes problems. City blackouts knock out whole neighborhoods, forcing the enemy to cancel patrols. Therefore, there is an inventory of blackout-related military repercussions.

R.S.L.: Why do you burn buses?

F.C.: This has a political explanation. We are capable of bringing the country to a halt through strikes, which are nonviolent acts . . . but, we were answered with a massacre. We turned to a different method. We were not going to bring transportation to a halt. . . . The next step was a drivers' strike. They were organized, but they were fired. Apparently, the companies went bankrupt, and co-ops were organized. . . . For six years we endeavored to bring public transportation to a halt. But, the dictatorship destroyed our system, and we were forced to use other methods which are violent. These methods affect state co-ops, and businessmen, but this is the political price that must be paid. . . .

R.S.L.: You say this is your response to violence, but where will this response lead?

F.C.: Let me to explain: bus routes 13, 14, 15, and 30 transport workers to factories. Therefore, the workers do not get to work and can justify their absence by guerrillas' bus-burning. Therefore, the workers are not reprimanded . . . this is an indirect way of allowing the worker to go on strike, without making him assume the responsibility or bear the punishment.

R.S.L.: So called "advanced workers" might support this [type of action], but what about average or "backward" workers who already are experiencing difficulties in getting to work because of you. . . .

F.C.: Well, they might blame us, because they do not wish to lose their jobs. . . . The strike is linked to insurrection because, if instead of going to work, they stay in their neighborhoods, the usual mobilization is unnecessary even as striking in the traditional manner is impossible. . . . Therefore, the worker stays in his neighborhood and participates in neighborhood activities without assuming responsibility for the strike.

R.S.L.: Are these political activities?

F.C.: The worker joins neighborhood self-defense and weapons production efforts. . . .

R.S.L.: Thus you believe that you have calculated correctly the workers' reaction. . . .

F.C.: We are running out of options. There are two methods of demolishing an old building: with machinery or with dynamite. If dynamite is the method chosen, the whole building collapses, and this is a problem. If on the other hand violence is used methodically, the price to be paid in lives decreases. This is of utmost importance. . . .

R.S.L.: Are you sure of your calculations? They were not accurate in January 1981. Then a general strike was called, and you made a mistake. Now you are telling me that the negotiation opportunity has unleashed a crisis and elections will be followed by a U.S. intervention. Are these predictions accurate?

F.C.: If there were closer relations with the U.S., it might be different. But, as we stand, we must prepare for the worst. . . .

R.S.L.: Do you consider the Soviet Union an ally?

F.C.: At least, the Soviet Union is not an enemy who needs to learn to respect our uncompromisable sovereignty. . . .

R.S.L.: What is your view of Moscow's role in Poland?

F.C.: I do not know, nor do I wish to meddle in their affairs. The Poles must solve their own problems.

R.S.L.: Was there Soviet intervention in Poland's martial law?

F.C.: Honestly, I have not followed the developments very closely, but I believe that there must have been a dialogue between the Solidarity Movement and the army. In my opinion, the Poles must be allowed to solve their own problems and even though Solidarity represents a segment of the population . . . the Polish army stepped in . . . on behalf of the Party. . . .

This is a time of crisis in a society which needs to put an end to the current situation, bringing in a new constitution, a new democracy. I do not know what they are going to do, because they cannot continue like that. Otherwise, why would they have sent the army into the streets against the working class? I do not understand. I do not want to imagine the scenario of the army versus the working class. This is unacceptable. . . .

R.S.L.: What about Afghanistan?

F.C.: In that case, our opinion is that even though we do not support the invasion, the Soviet Union seems to be motivated by security-related considerations. . . . But, we cannot accept this line of reasoning. . . .

R.S.L.: Because the U.S could present a similar argument to support an intervention in El Salvador?

F.C.: Of course. I'll give you a hypothetical example: We were very concerned by the Soviet Union's intervention in Poland, and we would have to take a stance. . . . We were not going to condemn the Soviet action. I admit that up front. We would have had to consider our protest very carefully.

R.S.L.: Was this "concern" your personal opinion or the general consensus among all of you?

F.C.: It was the opinion of the majority.

R.S.L.: But, it was not unanimous?

F.C.: Some would be more hard pressed than others in assuming that position.

R.S.L.: Who would these be?

F.C.: It would be more of a problem for the Communist Party to take that stance. The FPL would be quicker to condemn the action. The others would have very few reservations in condemning it.

R.S.L.: Have your groups had a lot of experience with other countries in the past few years? Specifically, what have been their impressions of socialist countries?

F.C.: I visited Yugoslavia, Algeria, the Soviet Union, Cuba.

R.S.L.: What did you think of Yugoslavia?

F.C.: I was there for a short time. But, I consider it a unique socialist democracy. It is a highly democratic system, because everything from the smallest to the largest is independently negotiated. The economic system captured my attention: There is a system of industrial self-management by the workers, as is the case in private enterprise. . . . But, there are economic problems, as in all other parts of the world. Not even socialism is problem-free. This system of government also seemed to have its own logic in response to Yugoslavian needs. Algeria appears to be the political leader in Africa due to its geographic location, its foreign policy, and its role in the Middle East conflict. Algeria functions independently vis a vis social-ism as well as capitalism. . . .

CHAPTER
F I V E

The War in El Salvador

Three key developments shaped Salvadoran politics in the first half of the 1980s: U.S. military aid, the erosion of support for the Marxist guerrillas, and the emergence of President José Napoleón Duarte as the country's civilian leader. The moderate government enjoyed some success in weakening the right, army, and oligarchy but could not dismantle their influence. The regime made some gains in the war without being able to defeat the FMLN and FDR or force a negotiated solution on them.

The FMLN launched an all-out offensive in 1981 (Document 1) in an attempt to gain a quick victory before the government could consolidate its forces and before Ronald Reagan took office and presumably stepped up U.S. aid. In a secret analysis of guerrilla strength (Document 2), the U.S. military attaché concluded, "The guerrillas . . . can attack when and where they want" but the government could contain any offensive. "Consequently, there is no military end in sight to the war of attrition. . . ."

The FMLN presented a proposal for negotiations (Document 3), although its leaders also said this was mainly a tactical move, and sent an open letter to Reagan (Document 4). "Trying to define the Salvadoran conflict in terms of [U.S.-Soviet conflict] seems to us totally detached from reality"; internal causes produced the rebellion. They rejected the March

1982 elections: "How can a democratic process be guaranteed amid indiscriminate repression?"

Nevertheless, in retrospect, the elections marked some progress toward civilian rule and relative stability. The official U.S. observer team concluded that they were free and fair, at least for the participating parties (Document 5). The fact that the FMLN-FDR—which at the time appeared to represent at least 20 percent of the public—did not take part stirred uncertainty over the process even in Election Commissioner Rodríguez Rivas (Document 6) and in some foreign observers (Document 7).

The FMLN-FDR argued that they could not participate in elections because the right would have killed leftists who tried to campaign. Dozens of Christian Democratic activists as well as labor and peasant leaders had been murdered in past years. But the FMLN's anti-election stand also stemmed from a belief that power-sharing or even outright military victory was still within its grasp.

In fact, the 1982 election could not even resolve the deadlock between the Christian Democrats and extreme right. Electoral gains by the right, which considered even the 1979 junta's reforms to be excessive, allowed d'Aubuisson's ARENA party and the traditional army-backed party to control Parliament and block land reform despite Duarte's election as president. The FMLN could argue that nothing had really changed and that the military and oligarchy still ran the country. The church criticized both sides and called for negotiations (Document 8). In June 1983, the FMLN issued a five-point program (Document 9) calling for talks that would include the United States, a stance unacceptable to the Salvadoran government.

The Salvadoran army was slow to adopt more effective tactics despite warnings that its performance must improve or the war would be lost. American trainers and advisers were only partially successful in convincing the military to adopt small-unit patrols and night operations, rather than the large clumsy sweeps which the guerrillas easily dodged. Dr. Charles Clements, a doctor who worked with the FMLN, describes (Document 13) how military operations—particularly indiscriminate bombing—continued to kill, injure, and displace peasants—the main victims of the fighting.

Pressures in the U.S. Congress and from the executive branch demanding political and military reform benefited Duarte (see Chapter 6). The army, long associated with d'Aubuisson and the death squads, had to rethink its position. The new chief of staff and former military attaché in Washington, General Adolfo Blandon, later acknowledged, "We knew that public opinion in the United States and the view of many senators and congressmen opposed to military aid for El Salvador were largely due to our bad image because of the [death] squads."

The army did not want to risk losing congressional support and the continued high levels—$1.7 billion between 1981 and 1985—of U.S. aid. The death squads were weakened when denied help and recruits from the military, although killings of peasants continued and ARENA slowed implementation of the 1980 land reform. Blandon was also willing to see informal talks with the guerrillas. The officers knew they needed Duarte for political purposes, but the extreme right was still unwilling to accept economic reforms or yield control of the military to him.

The winning of a parliamentary majority by the Christian Democrats in the 1984 elections was another key development. In his inaugural speech (Document 10) Duarte stated, "The immense majority of the people have chosen the democratic solution by means of the vote, and this obviously makes it impossible for the guerrillas to seize the country." He also made a "social pact" guaranteeing cooperation from the leading trade union federation (Document 11).

Duarte's improved leverage and Blandon's cooperation allowed the president, in an October 1984 UN speech (Document 12), to propose negotiations with the FMLN. "I am offering the safety and security of a political place within a pluralistic, constitutional, democratic system" to those who had taken up arms, Duarte explained. Moreover, the military situation was also turning in the government's favor as the army's limited reforms (Document 14), the weight of U.S. aid, and the interdiction of supplies to the FMLN (Document 15) were damaging the guerrillas.

Another problem for the FMLN was the declining assistance received from Nicaragua's Sandinista government. FMLN leaders tried to convince Managua (Document 16) that continued support would be a better defense against U.S. pressure or the contras and that promoting revolution was a better option than any Contadora agreement. But in a meeting between the Salvadoran guerrillas and Nicaragua officials (Document 17) the Sandinistas were not persuaded. The FMLN was bitter about the Nicaraguan decision (Document 18).

Although Rubén Zamora, leader of the FDR, still expressed confidence (Document 19), the FMLN's expectation that the Salvadoran government would quickly collapse proved to be wishful thinking. Despite the guerrillas' continued claims that nothing had changed, the elections and shifts in power had brought about real, if limited, changes. Far fewer people supported the guerrillas, whether because of confidence in the Duarte government, exhaustion, repugnance at the FMLN's forced recruiting, or disapproval of the guerrillas' attacks on the masses' livelihood, buses, and electricity. FMLN documents reflected concern over the revolutionaries' isolation and lack of progress (Documents 20 and 21).

The FMLN also had internal problems. The FPL's second-in-command was murdered for allegedly being too soft-line; the organization's founder and commander, Cayetano Carpio, was forced by Nicaraguan leaders to commit suicide after being found responsible for the assassination. The FDR politicians expressed public concern about the FMLN's turn to terrorist tactics.

The long-awaited meeting at La Palma between government and guerrillas took place on October 15, 1984 (Document 22), but produced no progress. Unlike the rightist ARENA party, the army supported Duarte's exploratory diplomacy (Document 23).

There was little for either side to cheer about. The war was far from over. On the defensive, the FMLN had to break its forces into smaller units. It forcibly drafted peasants, and some elements turned to urban terrorism, including the kidnapping of Duarte's daughter and of many mayors. ARENA criticized Duarte for negotiating for their release (Document 24); Duarte criticized the FMLN for its new tactics (Document 25).

Popular discontent with the government was stirred by complaints from business groups, some bitter labor strikes, the hardships of austerity, and Duarte's personal accumulation of authority coupled with his inability to punish past human-rights violators or carry through major social and economic reforms. He was caught between pressures from the army and the right on one hand and the declining economy and the left on the other. The government seemed far from ending the war. More than 50,000 Salvadorans were dead, the country was in economic crisis, and the small degree of stability and progress it had achieved rested on a slender thread.

I
THE FMLN OFFENSIVE AND THE 1982 ELECTIONS

1.
FMLN: CALL FOR A GENERAL OFFENSIVE (JANUARY 1981)

The United Revolutionary Directorate of the Farabundo Martí Front for National Liberation, (FMLN—which has taken the General Command of all the Revolutionary Armed Forces of the five Organizations that make up the FMLN), addresses itself to all the Heroic People of El Salvador: Workers and Peasants, Revolutionary Men and Women, Democrats and Patriots.

The decisive hour has come to initiate the decisive military and insurrectional battles for the seizure of power by the People and the constitution of the Revolutionary Democratic Government.

Decades of suffering, more than 50 years of military dictatorship, are at the point of *being destroyed* forever by the upsurge of the popular struggle.

In this crucial and historic moment in the destinies of the Salvadorean and Central American Peoples, the *Unified Revolutionary Directorate* of the Farabundo Martí Front for National Liberation, which is the *General Command, calls upon all the People,* on the Workers, Peasants, Students, Teachers, Employees, Democratic Sectors, Soldiers and Progressive Officers; Religious Sectors, *to all:* men and women—to the *Struggles of the Regular and Guerrilla Revolutionary Units,* to *the Militias of the Revolution and to the Fighting Masses,* to *immediately initiate* the military actions of the Popular Insurrection *to win the victory of the Revolution.*

We call upon all the people to rise up as one man with all the means of combat, under the orders of their immediate leaders, in all the war fronts and throughout the length and breadth of the national territory, to fight valiantly for the definitive overthrow of the regime of repression and genocide of the criollo oligarchy and of imperialism.

EVERYONE TO THE STRUGGLE!!

We call upon all the patriotic and progressive officers and soldiers to join the ranks of the People.

This is the moment to place yourselves with your brothers, the workers!

Turn your arms against the cruel and bloody chiefs of the high command and commanders of the counter-revolutionary army!

The hour of the Revolution has arrived! The hour of Liberation has arrived!

The definitive triumph is in the hands of this Heroic and Valiant People, who have shed their blood for so many years to win the right to be free, to partake of Democracy, true Independence, Social Progress, Sovereignty and Self-Determination!

2.
COLONEL BOSCH: GUERRILLA STRENGTH (FEBRUARY 1981)

(1) THE CURRENT GUERRILLA SITUATION IN EL SALVADOR IS AS FOLLOWS: (A) THE SO-CALLED "FINAL OFFENSIVE" FAILED, BUT THE INSURGENTS ARE NOT DEFEATED.

(B) THE INSURGENTS ARE CURRENTLY CONDUCTING A CAMPAIGN OF

Cable to Secretary of State Haig, February 18, 1981.

HARASSMENT (*HOSTIGAMIENTO*) FOR THE FOLLOWING PURPOSES:

I. MAINTAIN THE INTERNATIONAL AND DOMESTIC IMAGE THAT THEY ARE STILL A VIABLE FORCE.

II. RESTRUCTURE THEIR INTERNAL ORGANIZATION.

III. RESUPPLY FROM EXTERNAL SOURCES.

(C) GUERRILLA ELEMENTS CAN ATTACK IN SMALL, WELL ARMED BANDS (APPROXIMATELY 40 MEN) WHEN AND WHERE THEY CHOOSE.

(D) THE INSURGENTS WILL PROBABLY HAVE THE CAPABILITY OF LAUNCHING COORDINATED ATTACKS SIMILAR TO 10 JANUARY IN THE APRIL 1981 TIME FRAME WHEN THEIR LOGISTICAL STOCKS ARE BACK TO THEIR PRE-"FINAL OFFENSIVE" LEVELS.

(E) IT IS ESTIMATED THAT THERE ARE 3,700 FULL TIME GUERRILLAS IN EL SALVADOR. THEY HAVE, IN ADDITION, APPROXIMATELY 5,000 PART-TIME SUPPORT PERSONNEL. RECRUITMENT OF NEW INSURGENTS APPEARS TO BE ON THE DECLINE AT LEAST FOR THE MOMENT.

(F) INSURGENTS EFFECTIVELY OCCUPY THREE DISPUTED *SOLSONES* (POCKETS) BETWEEN EL SALVADOR AND THE HONDURAS BORDER WHICH THE GOVERNMENT IS POWERLESS TO DISRUPT. . . .

(G) THE INSURGENT INFORMATION GATHERING SYSTEM, A RUDIMENTARY INTELLIGENCE NET, CONTINUES TO BE EFFECTIVE.

(2) THE CURRENT SALVADORAN ARMED FORCES SITUATION IS AS FOLLOWS: (A) THE ARMED FORCES CAN PREVENT THE GUERRILLAS FROM DEFEATING THE GOVERNMENT MILITARY.

(B) THE ARMED FORCES CAN COPE WITH A LOCAL SALVADORAN GUERRILLA EFFORT, BUT IF MORE SOPHISTICATED WEAPONS SEEN RECENTLY CONTINUE TO ARRIVE IN-COUNTRY, THE MILITARY'S CAPABILITY WILL BEGIN TO DECLINE.

(C) THE TOTAL SALVADORAN MILITARY ESTABLISHMENT NUMBERS NO MORE THAN APPROXIMATELY 17,000 (INCLUDES ADMINISTRATIVE AND SUPPORT PERSONNEL). THIS STRENGTH FIGURE GIVES THE GOVERNMENT NO MORE THAN A FOUR-TO-ONE RATIO OVER THE GUERRILLAS, AN IMPOSSIBLE PERCENTAGE TO TERMINATE THE INSURGENCY MILITARILY.

(D) THE GOVERNMENT CANNOT REPEAT CANNOT CONTROL INFILTRATION OF ARMS AND PERSONNEL FROM HONDURAS ON THE GROUND, FROM NICARAGUA BY WATER, AND FROM BOTH COUNTRIES BY AIR. THERE IS NO IMMEDIATE HOPE FOR THE SALVADORAN MILITARY TO CHANGE THIS SITUATION WITH THE RESOURCES CURRENTLY AVAILABLE.

(E) MILITARY OPERATIONS PRESENTLY BEING CONDUCTED BY THE GOVERNMENT ARE CHARACTERIZED AS FOLLOWS:

I. OBJECTIVES FAR EXCEED THE RESOURCES ALLOCATED.

II. MOBILITY CAPACITY IS NOT SUFFICIENT TO ENGAGE THE GUERRILLAS

DECISIVELY. (THE INSURGENTS ALWAYS CAN ESCAPE ENCIRCLEMENT.)
III. LOGISTICS STRAIN CAUSES OPERATIONS TO "GRIND DOWN" OR "FIZ-
ZLE OUT" PREMATURELY.
IV. ORGANIZATION FOR COMBAT IS NOT SUITABLE FOR COUNTER-GUER-
RILLA ACTIONS. (THE STRUCTURE OF THE SALVADORAN MILITARY ES-
TABLISHMENT IS NOT EVEN ADEQUATE FOR CONVENTIONAL WAR: IT
CURRENTLY RESEMBLES A 19TH CENTURY CONSTABULARY RATHER
THAN A MODERN ARMED FORCE.)
(F) THE MILITARY INTELLIGENCE SERVICE OF EL SALVADOR IS PRACTI-
CALLY NON-EXISTENT. INTER-AGENCY RIVALRY AND THE LACK OF AN
EFFICIENT ORGANIZATION PLACES THE GOVERNMENT IN AN INFERIOR
POSITION TO THE INSURGENTS IN THE GATHERING OF INFORMATION.
(G) THE CESSATION OF CENTRALIZED TRAINING IN EL SALVADOR RE-
SULTS IN RAW RECRUITS ENTERING COMBAT ALMOST IMMEDIATELY
AFTER INDUCTION. THE RESPONSIBILITY FOR PREPARING SOLDIERS FOR
THE INSURGENCY WAR RESTS WITH DEPARTMENTAL COMMANDERS
WHO ARE BURDENED WITH OTHER NUMEROUS TACTICAL, ADMINISTRA-
TIVE, AND POLITICAL RESPONSIBILITIES.
(H) THE MORALE OF THE SALVADORAN MILITARY REMAINS GOOD DE-
SPITE POLITICAL DIVISIVENESS IN THE OFFICER CORPS AND LACK OF
TRAINING IN THE ENLISTED RANKS. THIS SITUATION EXISTS PRINCI-
PALLY BECAUSE YOUNG OFFICERS ARE HIGHLY MOTIVATED AS A RESULT
OF THEIR MILITARY ACADEMY TRAINING AND BECAUSE THE PEASANT
SOLDIER HAS EXCEPTIONAL STAMINA AND WILL POWER.
    . . . THE ATTEMPTED OFFENSIVE OF JANUARY 10, 1981, AND THE
ARMED FORCES' RESPONSE RESULTED IN BOTH SIDES FIGHTING TO A
DRAW. THE RESOURCES CURRENTLY AVAILABLE TO THE GOVERNMENT
AND TO THE INSURGENTS INDICATE THAT THERE IS VERY LITTLE THAT
WILL CHANGE THIS SITUATION. THE GUERRILLAS HAVE THE INITIA-
TIVE ON THEIR SIDE—THEY CAN ATTACK WHEN AND WHERE THEY
WANT—AND THE GOVERNMENT HAS THE CAPACITY TO CONTAIN IN-
SURGENT ASSAULTS ON A CASE-BY-CASE BASIS. CONSEQUENTLY, THERE
IS NO MILITARY END IN SIGHT TO THE WAR OF ATTRITION IN EL SAL-
VADOR.

3.
FMLN-FDR: PROPOSAL TO THE UNITED NATIONS
(OCTOBER 1981)

. . . If today our people are waging an armed struggle under the leadership of its organizations, the FMLN and the FDR, this is because oppressive and repressive regimes have closed all peaceful avenues for change, thus leaving our people with only armed struggle as the sole and legitimate means to attain its liberation, thereby exercising the universal and constitutional right to revolt against illegal and repressive authorities.

Our struggle is, therefore, a just and necessary struggle to build peace and equality among all the Salvadorean people.

However, our desire is peace. To attain it we propose a political solution whose objective is to put an end to the war and establish a new political and economic order that will guarantee the Salvadorean people the full exercise of their rights as citizens and a life worthy of human beings.

All this entails our expressed willingness to start a dialogue with the civilian and military representatives that the Junta may appoint through a process of peace talks.

We propose that these peace talks which reaffirm our commitment to seek and implement a political solution be based on the following principles:

1. The talks should be carried out between the delegates appointed by the FMLN-FDR and representatives of the Government Junta of El Salvador.
2. They should be carried out in the presence of other governments that as witnesses will contribute to the solution of the conflict.
3. The nature of the talks must be comprehensive and include the fundamental aspects of the conflict. They must be based on an agenda established by both parties.
4. The Salvadorean people should be informed of the entire process.
5. They should be initiated without pre-established conditions by either party.

In an effort to establish a basis that will guarantee a political solution, the FMLN-FDR hereby express our willingness to discuss the following points:

Read by Nicaraguan leader Daniel Ortega before the General Assembly.

A. Definition of a new political, economic and judicial order that will allow
   and stimulate the full democratic participation of the different political,
   social and economic sectors and forces, particularly those that have been
   marginal. Elections will be an important element as a mechanism of
   popular participation and representation.
B. The restructuring of the Armed Forces, based on the officers and troops
   of the current army who are not responsible for crimes and genocide
   against the people, and integration of the hierarchy and troops of the
   FMLN.

Our Fronts consider elections a valid and necessary instrument of expression of the people's will whenever conditions and atmosphere exist that
allow the people to freely express their will. In El Salvador today we do
not have those conditions to carry out an electoral process, inasmuch as
the regime's repressive apparatus which assassinates political and labor
leaders and activists remains untouched; it persists in persecuting the
progressive sectors of the Church and is responsible for the daily physical
elimination of dozens of citizens, likewise the regime has currently in effect
a state of siege, martial law and press censorship and is escalating the war
against the people with arms and advisers sent by the Government of the
United States.

A political solution is necessary for our people for the stability of the
region, and for the maintenance of peace and security among nations. This
implies that governments should scrupulously observe the principle of
non-intervention in the internal affairs of other peoples. This is why we are
directly addressing the Government of the United States and demanding
an end to its military intervention in El Salvador, which is against the
interests of both the Salvadorean and American peoples and endangers the
peace and security of Central America.

Our proposal responds to the demands for justice which are in line with
the purest principles of international law, and of the interests of the nations
and peoples of the world searching for peaceful solutions to points of
tension. To this effect, the Salvadorean people express their confidence in
the understanding, participation and support of the international community in the attainment of its right to peace, freedom and independence.

Unified Revolutionary Directorate of the Farabundo Martí Front for National Liberation (FMLN)

Executive Committee of the Democratic Revolutionary Front (FDR)

4.
FMLN: LETTER TO PRESIDENT REAGAN (JANUARY 1982)

El Salvador, January 18, 1982

Mr. Ronald Reagan
President of the United States of America

Mr. President:

We have carefully read your new year's message to the American people in which you mention the measures you have taken to achieve world peace and in which you specifically say: ". . . our hearts feel anguished for those who suffer oppression . . . and we, the American people, begin the year with renewed commitment to our ideals and with the faith that peace shall be preserved and that liberty for all men must prevail."

We would like to point out, Mr. President, that we Salvadoreans have suffered centuries of oppression and at present we are suffering the repression perpetrated by the military dictatorship which has been in power for over fifty years. Our struggle is against that dictatorship, and if your heart is truly anguished by oppression, we see no sense in the fact that precisely your Administration has become the chief supporter of the military–Christian Democratic regime in El Salvador and that far from contributing to the freedom of the Salvadorean people, your Administration has decided to support a regime which is responsible for the death of over 30,000 people in a short period of two years.

What kind of world peace are you searching for if at the same time you are providing military assistance to an oppressive government? The military and political assistance your government provides the Salvadorean Junta has caused, among other things, that the war be long and that the most repressive elements of the Salvadorean army enshrine themselves in power; these people do not even hold any respect for U.S. citizens, as demonstrated by the assassinations of the four churchwomen. The recent decision to train 1,600 members of the Junta's army in U.S. bases confirms to us that your objective is not peace but war against our people. . . .

Trying to define the Salvadorean conflict in terms of the confrontation between your government and the Soviet Union seems to us totally detached from reality. It is misery and the repression imposed by the oligar-

Diario el Mundo, San Salvador.

chy and the military which makes thousands of Salvadoreans involve themselves in the struggle. We are not fighting with arms in our hands because we want war, but because successive regimes have closed all democratic channels for change and have forced us to exercise our legitimate right to insurrection.

It is us, the Salvadoreans, and only the Salvadoreans which are fighting every day against the dictatorship in order to change old and unjust structures. The 30,000 people killed are not Russians, nor Cubans, they are Salvadoreans who strive to live in peace and dignity. The only foreign forces that participate in the conflict are the U.S. advisors sent by your government. Therefore, to see our war as part of the East-West confrontation can only lead to the regionalization of the war and to the increasing intervention of your country, thus bringing more suffering to the Salvadorean people and also to the American people.

Furthermore, to claim that the March 1982 elections are the solution to the Salvadorean conflict is also far from reality. How can a democratic process be guaranteed amid indiscriminate repression? If you can decide the destiny of the United States it is because you are in power as a result of free elections. U.S. citizens participated in elections in time of peace, an indisputable condition for the people to elect its government. The Salvadorean government, far from creating the necessary conditions to achieve peace, is launching a war of extermination against our people. Thus, the March elections are not the solution to the Salvadorean conflict. They are yet another farce like those that the military dictatorship is accustomed to impose on our people. . . .

We hereby make a respectful request as a result of the aforementioned considerations, for the need of a change in your policy towards El Salvador. We are only demanding our right to solve our problems on our own without foreign intervention. If this new year your government has the interest and the will to bring about world peace, you have the opportunity in El Salvador not only to contribute to peace by not opposing a political settlement, but to establish worthy and friendly relations among our peoples.

Sincerely,

Salvador Cayetano Carpio
Joaquín Villalobos
Fermán Cienfuegos
Jorge Shafik Handal
Roberto Roca

5.
U.S. OBSERVER TEAM: CONDUCT OF THE ELECTIONS
(MARCH 1982)

On March 28, 1982, 1,551,687 Salvadorans went to the polls to vote. This turnout represented approximately 80 percent of the estimated electorate and surpassed all predictions of turnout made in the final days preceding the elections. The strong message that the Salvadorans seemed to wish to send with their participation in the election was one of desire for peace and progress in the social and economic development of their country.

The Salvadoran elections were held to choose deputies to a Constituent Assembly that would have the responsibility for selecting an interim government, writing a new constitution, and fixing a date for Presidential elections. According to the law established for the conduct of the election, the Constituent Assembly was required to convene 8 days following delivery of credentials to the elected deputies. The Assembly did convene on April 14, 1982. A President was sworn in on May 2, 1982, and a cabinet sworn in beginning the following week.

In preparation for the vote, six parties participated in the 2-month election campaign that began on January 28, 1982. Additional parties that had indicated an early intention to participate apparently were not able to mobilize sufficient support to meet the registration requirements. Some parties that had participated in previous elections in El Salvador declined to campaign. No party stood for the leftist opposition represented by the FMLN.

The observer team of Senator Nancy Landon Kassebaum and Dr. Clark Kerr made its first stop in the city of Santa Tecla, a suburb of San Salvador. The delegation arrived at 9 a.m., and already approximately 10,000 people were in line waiting to vote at one of the three locations established in the town. The lines stretched for blocks, but people stood quietly and patiently. The delegates asked randomly how long people had been standing in line. "Since 6:30" or "since 7" was the answer. At 9 a.m., the mood of the crowd was jolly and the temperatures still moderate. However, the delegation worried whether so many people would have the patience to stand in line the day long to vote. Those who were asked about this answered uniformly that they would wait until they could vote—all day if need be.

On learning that the observers were from the American delegation, the

---

Report of a delegation led by Senator Nancy Kassebaum.

crowds appeared pleased that so many people had come to see the elections and to "see how El Salvador really was." When asked why they came to vote in such numbers, they responded that they were voting for "an end to the killing, for peace and the future of our country."

Over and over again we heard the people say, "We are voting for peace and an end of the violence. We believe this election can be a new beginning for this country."

It is difficult to express the patience and purpose with which the Salvadoran people turned out to vote, enduring long hours in line to cast their ballots and, in some instances, attempts by the insurgents to scare them off. The election clearly is a repudiation of the guerrillas' claim that they represent the will of the Salvadoran people.

In general the election process itself was orderly and peaceful. The voting procedures adhered to rules established by the Central Elections Commission. There were poll watchers from at least two parties at each table we visited, and the election officials worked seriously at their responsibilities, both in processing the voters and later in counting the ballots. We did see some minor technical problems during the day, but we saw no indication of fraud. We believe they had no influence on the outcome of the elections.

The team arrived at its second stop, the city of La Libertad, on the coast and the furthest point it would travel from San Salvador, at about noon. As the delegation entered the village, they heard members of the crowd announcing, "we are going to form two lines, one of men and one of women, to establish better order." They became worried on seeing groups of people walking away from the polling place. It was noon, and they feared that might mean that people had become tired of waiting in lines to vote. Instead they learned that the local election officials had decided to move some of the voting tables from the confined areas of the schoolyard, where hundreds of people were waiting, to a second, more open place, thus dividing the crowd and relieving pressure in the schoolyard.

Of the 20 tables originally in the schoolyard, at least four were removed to a second place while the delegation watched. The ballot boxes, voting tables and registration books were carried by the three elections officials with observers from each of the parties accompanying them. A number of the prospective voters moved along with them too in order to be first in line at the new polling place.

The delegation stepped into one of the tiny school rooms where one election commission and one ballot box were installed. They counted 62 people packed front to back in line in stifling heat waiting to vote. Some 600 more waited in the small playground in front. Senator Kassebaum spoke with the waiting voters. They told her that they had walked some 8 kilometers to the polling place and that it had taken 2½ hours. They said that buses were not running, so they could not take the bus, and therefore had to walk. The bus owners reportedly had been afraid to put their vehicles on the road because of the threats to blow up all buses taking voters to the polling places.

The delegation recalled Father Hesburgh's report the night before that Acting Archbishop Rivera y Damas had told him that the "people have made up their minds to vote. They are going to speak with their feet."

From La Libertad, the delegation went to the much smaller municipio of San Juan Talpa, a village with only five voting tables. Again, though it was later in the day, there were still lines of hundreds of people long. In San Juan Talpa, the women stood in one line, the men in another, the two lines single file and side by side, waiting to enter the church where they would vote. One very pregnant woman waited on the sidelines. She indicated that she could not stand in line because of her condition, but that she would wait, hoping that the lines would thin so that she could vote, too. En route to San Juan Talpa, the group passed a man on the main road who was ferrying people to the polling place in his truck. He said he had begun about 6 in the morning and reported that he had made 10 trips already, carrying about 20 in his truck at a time. The delegation talked to the people in the truck and asked why they were making this tremendous trip just to vote. "If we all vote," they said, "we will show the subversives that we want liberty, justice, work and peace." A woman told the delegation that she felt this election was a base for a new society—a change in this country.

6.
RODRÍGUEZ RIVAS: COMMENT ON THE ELECTIONS

Q: Do you believe the Salvadoran people will support the elections?

A: The people want peace and reform. If they see the elections as the road to peace and reform, they will support them.

Q: How would you characterize politically the parties preparing to participate in the elections? Do they represent the whole of the Salvadoran political spectrum?

A: They represent the right and the center-right.

Q: Do most people consider these parties parties of reform? What has been the attitude of these parties toward reforms?

Interview with Robert S. Leiken.

A: Some of them have supported reforms but they have not been able to implement them when in power. Others are opposed. Others have said nothing one way or the other.

Q: Do you feel that the election is giving the people an opportunity to express their views, particularly the majority who you say support reforms?

A: That will depend on whether the left participates.

Q: If it doesn't, would the elections provide expression to all the major currents of popular opinion?

A: No.

7.
LORD CHITNIS: OBSERVER'S REPORT ON THE ELECTION (1982)

It rapidly became apparent that neither the guerrillas nor the government forces could hope for a military victory in the short term. It was from this date that the Junta, encouraged by Washington, mapped out the strategy that culminated in the elections a year later. Elections were the last element in the formula—which I characterize as reform-plus-repression—designed to win international support and keep open the vital lifeline of military and economic aid from the United States. . . .

A number of parties did not participate in the electoral process. . . . There is less general awareness of the corollary, that the holding of elections was itself a partisan political act. This is amply borne out by the background material published by the Central Electoral Council, which . . . is largely a defense of the policy of the governing junta and includes frequent attacks on the non-contending parties. Their refusal to take part was described as "an attack on the right of Salvadorans to freedom of choice." . . . The 700 Christian Democratic Party workers who were killed in two years put into perspective the refusal of the non-contending parties to go through the process of registering for the election. . . .

In general, the proceedings at the polling stations I visited, however chaotic, provided no evidence of [im]personation or double voting. The role of the army seemed to be confined to crowd control, and I gained the impression that (whatever attitudes to them in other circumstances may be) on this occasion and in this role they were accepted by the population.

Report of the Parliamentary Human Rights Group.

A relaxed atmosphere was quite widespread among the queues waiting to vote. . . . If the electors were going to have to vote to obtain the mark on their cards, they came to the sensible conclusion that they might as well enjoy it. . . .

Certainly the electorate had a choice before them. But there is much more to an election. . . . My conclusion is that the election in El Salvador was so fundamentally flawed as to be invalid for the following reasons:

Limited choice. . . . First there was the refusal of all parties to the left of the Christian Democrats to participate in the election, on the understandable grounds that had they done so they would have been butchered. . . .

Second, and more important, the electorate was given no choice on the question most of them cared about—how to end the war and the murderous violence. Every party which stood favored the military prosecution and even intensification of the war. None openly favored a negotiated settlement.

The pressure put on those Salvadorans eligible to vote. . . . I do not suggest that soldiers herded voters grimly to the polls. But the well-publicized . . . provision that a voter's ID card would be stamped with "indelible and invisible" ink, and that a record would be kept of his name, his signature or his fingerprints, were all the pressures that the authorities needed to ensure that a large number of Salvadorans, whatever they thought of the election and the good it was likely to do them, cast their votes. . . .

ARENA certainly did not win: it only got 29% of the vote. The Christian Democrat party can indeed be said to have lost, but only because after polling day was over all parties opposed to it suddenly . . . coalesced. . . .

It is clear to me that the result of this strange, foreign-inspired election cannot be said to represent what in normal circumstances would be a free and unfettered choice of the people of El Salvador about their future. All historical evidence suggests that their real preference would have been for a Christian Democratic/moderate left coalition. But that is not the worst charge which can be made against this irrelevant and bungled exercise. . . . The election complicated the political problems of the country [and] made life worse for the people in it. . . .

II
THE DUARTE GOVERNMENT

8.
UNITED NATIONS: HUMAN RIGHTS (JANUARY 1983)

With regard to economic, social and cultural rights, the Special Representative . . . takes into account the difficulties stemming from the economic crisis through which the country is passing and the fact that there can be no substantive improvement in those rights from one day to the next, but only through a gradual process of reforms, including agrarian reform, which requires, among other things, a genuine climate of social peace. The Special Representative considers, however, that the Salvadorean people still do not enjoy economic, social and cultural rights of any particular significance. In the same context, he wishes to add that the attacks on the country's economy carried out systematically by the guerrilla opposition, although presented as aimed at military targets, seriously compromise the future enjoyment by the people of El Salvador of very important economic, social and cultural rights.

With regard to civil and political rights, the Special Representative is morally convinced that during 1982 serious, massive and persistent violations of human rights have continued in the country and in many cases have ended tragically in attacks on human lives, precisely because of the continuing serious civil conflict taking place in El Salvador. While it is true that the information received shows that the number of assassinations has dropped to approximately half what it was in 1981, nevertheless the size of the figures given for 1982 clearly indicates that the situation with regard to respect for human life is still very serious. In the opinion of the Special Representative, responsibility for the violations of civil and political rights lies both with members of the State apparatus and violent groups of the extreme right, which seem to have acted in collusion with or been tolerated by the former, and with armed groups of the extreme left, although there are indications that the violations of human rights involving attacks on the life, physical integrity, liberty and security of persons are in the majority —but not solely—perpetrated by members of the State apparatus and

United Nations Economic and Social Council, Minutes, January 20, 1983.

violent groups of the extreme right, while terrorist acts against public and private property are mainly due to guerrilla groups.

With regard to the activity of the judiciary in El Salvador, the Special Representative considers that the situation is still unsatisfactory and that it calls for considerable improvement. Although he has observed signs of a slight increase in the punishment of violations of human rights, he has not heard that any of the proceedings initiated have resulted in a sentence. The Special Representative realizes, however, how difficult it is for the Salvadorean judicial system properly to investigate and to punish such a large number of offences as are at present being committed in the country in the prevailing atmosphere of generalized violence, and he notes the concern of the authorities of the Republic to encourage the activity of the judiciary.

The elections have produced a regression to a form of government which is similar to or worse than the regime ousted in October 1979. Although this regression has been blatant, it has not produced a strong public response. Public opinion has been neutralized by the impact of what has been portrayed as a high level of popular participation in the elections and by the concealment of true electoral results.

The measures of El Salvador's Constituent Assembly/Provisional Government against the agrarian reforms have been instrumental in helping public opinion begin to realize that a step backward has been taken in the country's "process of democratization." Public opinion is beginning to realize that the Salvadorean people has not increased its level of participation in the government and that instead the government has again come under the entire control of the Salvadorean oligarchy responsible for the exploitation and repression of the Salvadorean people for decades. . . . The FMLN-FDR refused to participate in the elections because if negotiations did not take place prior to elections, there would not have been conditions for the elections to develop as an exercise of free expression of the people's will. Among other things, the leaders of the progressive sectors could not participate in the electoral process because they had received a death threat from the Armed Forces, or had been "disappeared" or imprisoned. . . . The fundamental issue raised by the elections, however, is not how many people voted, but their real end result. Some people have tried to interpret the elections as a rejection of the FMLN-FDR, or at least as a symptom indicating that the FMLN-FDR does not have the majority support evidenced in the past.

The FMLN-FDR believes that in the March 28 elections the Salvadorean people behaved in a manner similar to that registered in the elections of Zimbabwe in 1979, where under similar circumstances 64 per cent of the electorate participated in elections and 67 per cent of the voters cast their ballots for the "moderate" Muzorewa. In the case of Zimbabwe as in the case of El Salvador, the electoral event was incorrectly interpreted as a defeat of the national liberation movement. This interpretation does not take into account that an election carried out under conditions of civil war in which the people are made to participate by means of coercion, fear, desperation or distortion, an effect which social scientists refer to as an "optical illusion" occurs which deforms the true expression of the people's will. The "optical illusion" was detected in Zimbabwe ten months after the 1979 elections when another election took place under peaceful circumstances and with broad-based participation. In these conditions the people voted for ZANU candidate Robert Mugabe, who received 57 per cent of the seats in parliament. . . . In El Salvador the most eloquent fact confirming that the FMLN-FDR has the support of the majority of the people is that only due to this support the FMLN-FDR has been able to resist, develop and advance, despite the constant large-scale offensives that the government's Armed Forces have launched against it with the advice and logistic support—worth millions of dollars—that the U.S. has provided.

9.
FDR-FMLN: FIVE POINTS (JUNE 1983)

The FDR-FMLN reaffirms our willingness to continue struggling until we achieve national independence, justice and peace for our people. At the same time, we maintain our policy of dialogue and negotiations, and propose the following points as a basis for achieving a solution to the conflict through political means:

1. The main goal is to recover national sovereignty and to achieve a just solution that enables us to overcome the current state of imposed war, guaranteeing all Salvadorans an independent, democratic and just society, as well as peaceful coexistence among the Central American people.

2. The aforementioned goal can be achieved through a direct dialogue, without pre-conditions among the parties to the conflict, in which all the problems our society confronts can be discussed comprehensively; and where all sectors interested in the search for peace and justice can contribute.

3. We define the parties directly involved in the conflict to be, on the one hand, the Governments of El Salvador and the United States, and on the other, our Fronts, the FDR-FMLN. While our conflict has its roots in the injustice and repression suffered by the people, the increasingly militaristic and interventionist role of President Reagan's Administration demonstrates that in El Salvador there will be no peace, no justice and no independence as long as this policy continues.

4. To achieve a political solution, the alliance between the democratic and the revolutionary forces represented by the FDR-FMLN is inseparable and indispensable. Attempts to solve the crisis by excluding one of our Fronts not only are infeasible but are rejected by the FDR-FMLN as divisive maneuvers.

5. We consider it necessary that third parties participate so that they provide their good offices to and witness the process of dialogue. Therefore, we believe it convenient that dialogue be held within the framework of a forum where the parties to the conflict can meet in an environment that ensures security and trust.

10.
PRESIDENT JOSÉ NAPOLEÓN DUARTE: INAUGURAL ADDRESS (JUNE 1984)

The achievement of democracy has never been easy for any people throughout history. El Salvador, all of its people, have paid a high price for it. . . . I wish to address all who kept their faith in democracy in the most adverse conditions, and who went to vote in the three democratic elections that we have held in the 80's. . . .

The significance of this unique, unprecedented, and new historic moment in our fatherland is that it is the product of the unmistakable and iron will of all of the Salvadoran people, who on two consecutive occasions— 26 March and 6 May 1984—went massively to the polls to freely elect their legitimate rulers. . . .

Why did we vote? When over 80 percent of the Salvadoran people turned out to vote, it was not only because of their profound faith in the democratic system and in freedom. At the bottom of their hearts, each Salvadoran has also expressed, in voting, his profound desire to achieve peace and to create the necessary conditions for all of us to have work, the means for a decent life, and access to products in accordance with the potentials of each of us.

Salvadorans, we must bravely, frankly, and realistically acknowledge the fact that our homeland is immersed in an armed conflict that affects each and every one of us; that this armed conflict has gone beyond our borders and has become a focal point in the struggle between the big world power blocs. With the aid of Marxist governments like Nicaragua, Cuba, and the

From *FBIS: Latin America,* June 4, 1984.

Soviet Union, an army has been trained and armed and has invaded our homeland.

Its actions are directed from abroad. Armed with the most sophisticated weapons, the Marxist forces harass our Armed Forces and constantly carry out actions intended to destroy our economy, with the loss of countless human lives and the suffering of hundreds of thousands of Salvadorans. For its part, our Army has been considerably enlarged, it has received better training, and it is imbued with a profound patriotic commitment to defend the people and to keep us from falling into the hands of Marxist subversion, which seeks to establish a totalitarian dictatorship in our homeland.

In the face of these realities, many Salvadorans have wondered why our Armed Forces have not yet managed to defeat the guerrillas. Many foreigners ask themselves the same question. Others, overwhelmed by international Marxist propaganda, wonder why the guerrillas have not yet managed to seize the country. The response to this is very simple: It has been clearly seen that the immense majority of the people have chosen the democratic solution by means of the vote, and this obviously makes it impossible for the guerrillas to seize the country. Then there is another truth. This is that many of us Salvadorans view the conflict as spectators, concerned only about our own interests, without contributing to the economic recovery, our national defense, or the solution of our social conflicts. This is the gist of the matter. So far, the people have rejected the violence and the war, but have not taken dynamic action, alongside the Armed Forces, to defend democracy, even though the situation has changed drastically. This is why it is important to point out our position on dialogue and the negotiation.

I have often said that if dialogue and negotiation are taken to mean a discussion of power quotas with weapons on the table, this would be denying the very essence of democracy, distorting the very essence of civilian power, and making a mockery of the mandate that the people have bestowed upon us. It is tantamount to accepting and admitting that power on both sides is exclusively in the hands of those who wield weapons. I have often said that differences should not be settled through violence and death, but through reason. I wish to recall my own words when, speaking to the nation, I said: If they were capable of taking up weapons, they should now be audacious in laying them down.

I receive the presidency of the Republic directly from the people, because democracy has triumphed and the Constitution prevails. Therefore, the Armed Forces are fulfilling their specific mission with upright discipline, changing the course of history, leaving behind the sad past when the Armed Forces were used as a tool of repression by the political groups that controlled power while the opposition that struggled for justice and freedom was subjugated.

This achievement, which was well explained by President Magaña, contrasts with the subjugation that leftist political sectors find themselves in with regard to the military guerrilla sector. The truth is that they have fallen under the authority of the guerrilla commanders, whom they must obey, and have not demonstrated so far that they are the leaders of the subversive movement. For this reason, to achieve credibility, they must demonstrate their authority over the armed sector, because in this way, any decision like that made by the subversive groups in Colombia would be heeded by the entire subversive movement. This would be an important signal, and one which the entire nation and all of our people expect, so that dialogue is not held with weapons on the table, but serves instead to find the political paths necessary to bring all Salvadorans into the democratic process. Since this is of momentous importance, allow me to repeat this: This would be an important signal, and one which the entire nation expects, so that dialogue is not held with weapons on the table, but serves instead to find the political paths to bring all Salvadorans into the democratic process.

For its part, my government will make efforts to promote a climate of security and confidence that will permit us, as a prior step, to begin as soon as possible a national dialogue among all democratic forces and majority sectors so that together we can draw up a formula of peace that will be the faithful reflection of the real feelings of the Salvadoran people and that will be vigorously supported so that no one can doubt that such a formula is a genuine decision and an expression of the will of all of the people and that should be turned into a common, energetic, and supreme effort capable of overcoming all obstacles and of achieving the great objective of peace. For this purpose, we will appeal to the law, international solidarity, patriotic responsibility, and, when circumstances demand, to the legitimate right of defense.

The structural crisis: The crisis we currently face has its origins in the unequal structures that have characterized our political, economic, and social process. But we have also recognized our weaknesses and errors so as to implement adequate reforms and begin to build democracy, social justice, and respect for human rights, and to achieve the peace that we need and desire so much. In the face of this reality, El Salvador does not need foreign ideologies. It does not need to hear the deafening language of sophisticated weapons or the materialistic clamor of an alleged specific destiny. It does not need to be an area of international dispute.

However, we need to build a new fatherland, free of an unjust past and in whose foundations there will be a predominant place for human development and freedom within a context of participatory institutions that will guarantee respect for the rights of all individuals without regard to their political position, economic condition, or social situation. . . .

These in turn can offer us the common good and the participation of the majority, values for which these great Salvadoran people have always fought; values on which misguided, impatient, and frustrated sectors even claim to support themselves, and which they have used as the primary reason for their struggle to obtain by means of blind and irreconcilable violence that which we are achieving peacefully as a majority. Those sectors do not realize that they are being treacherously used to establish an all-embracing dictatorship at all levels of the social structure, a totalitarian and atheist dictatorship in which the human being is stripped of his most elemental rights. These minority sectors are joined by others which, also by means of terror, stubbornly seek to return to a system of privileges which no longer have either a place or a reason for being in this new and emerging society, which has been called upon to grow deep roots.

For this reason I urge both sectors to abandon their violent stands and adopt the social pact so that together we may create a suitable climate so the peasants, the workers, the artisans, the small businessmen, in short, the sectors traditionally excluded from economic, social, political, and cultural development in El Salvador, may find and enjoy the betterment they yearn for in their lives and their work and for their descendants. Only in this way can we overcome the crisis. Only in this way can we achieve peace, the peace for which the people voted bravely, the peace that the innermost recesses of our nationality claim, the peace that the people conceive of not as a mere absence of armed violence but as an environment resulting from a system where there is no room for structural violence based on anachronistic forms of participation in the economic, social, political, and cultural life of our country. . . .

At the regional level, we now have all the moral solvency to endorse and give our support to the Contadora Group's efforts in the search for a political solution leading to levels of detente which smooth the way to peace, democracy, and social transformations with all the forces seeking these objectives.

Economy and development. Our major commitment is the promotion of our domestic development and economic recovery. . . .

One of our great objectives will be to strengthen the national cooperative movement, because we feel that it is one of the most efficient mechanisms for giving participation and opportunity to all the majority sectors and for achieving economic democracy and political stability in the country. We believe that along with the qualitative changes initiated in our economic structure, a necessary and unavoidable way to increase wealth and create new jobs in accordance with the social model that we plan to establish is to protect and encourage a strong private sector with opportunities for small, medium-sized, and big businessmen, within the framework of harmonious relations and cooperation with the public sector. . . .

The establishment, enforcement, and overall respect for human rights is inherent in the pacification and democratization of our homeland. It is for this reason that my government will endorse all the actions, initiatives, and mechanisms needed to achieve the overall betterment of our citizens so that, through the activities of the state, the individual is recognized as the origin and end of the common good. For this reason I will fight openly and tirelessly to control abuses of authority and violence of the extremes. I will fight tirelessly to eradicate from our homeland the death squads and all the problems of injustice and arrogance. No one—because I shall not permit it—will be able to say that this administration has violated the fundamental rights of my people. And whoever tries it will feel the full weight of the law. . . .

In 5 years, when I turn the presidency over to my successor, I aspire to have him receive a different country. I request your support and aid in these 5 years, which will be crucial. I ask you not to judge my government in advance or to deprive me of the chance to confront problems, because any delay may mean the death of a human being, the suffering of a mother, or the hunger of a child. The poverty and the problems are real, but together we can resolve them. The people's will elected me; their hope and faith will sustain me. When my people demand that I put an end to the death squads, to the violence, and to the foreign intervention, these demands are a challenge for me. I ask you to give me your support and strengthen our decision to work together, not apart. Let us all join the social pact. Let us seek the common points, let us plant the seed of faith, and we will harvest the fruits of democracy.

11.
CHRISTIAN DEMOCRAT–UPD UNION FEDERATION: SOCIAL PACT (MARCH 1984)

The undersigned, in representation of the Christian Democratic Party (PDC) and Popular Democratic Unity (UPD), agree to accept and enter into a Social Pact that contributes to the establishment of peace, democracy, and social justice in El Salvador, which the Government Plan for 1984–1989 bases on a scheme for the participation of all sectors making up our society; and which will contribute to the victory of the campaign of José Napoleón Duarte and Dr. Pablo Mauricio Alvergue for the presidency and vice-presidency of the Republic, respectively.

OBJECTIVES

I. The PDC and UPD will fight resolutely to improve the living and working conditions of the peasants, workers, and tradespeople and, in general, for the unity of the sectors traditionally bypassed by socioeconomic and political development in El Salvador.

II. The PDC and UPD will work unrelentingly to achieve national conciliation.

III. The PDC signs this Social Pact with a will to surmount the widespread crisis and form a democratic, multifarious, collaborative, just, and egalitarian society.

IV. The PDC and UPD will fight specifically for the following aspects:

1. Support of the efforts of the Contadora Group to find a political solution that will give us peace, democracy, and social change, with the participation of all social forces seeking those ends.

2. Achievement of a democratic society in which there is true freedom for the workers and people, in general.

3. Seeking the appropriate mechanisms to guarantee the freedom and security of the citizenry, which will affect equally those who contravene public order or violate human rights, regardless of ideology or membership in any public or private organization.

4. Attainment of effective status and respect for human rights.

5. Concrete and effective economic and social measures for establishing social justice in the nation.

6. Commitment to finding suitable machinery in the near future to enable reopening the University of El Salvador.

7. Struggle to attain full sovereignty and self-determination of the people of El Salvador.

8. Commitment to guarantee the structural social and economic reforms initiated in 1980, particularly Agrarian Reform, through such measures, among others, as amendments to Articles 105 and 106 of the present Political Constitution, aimed at fully favoring the interests of the workers and the people in general.

9. Joining forces with other democratic Latin American governments to restore peace and democracy in the hemisphere.

10. Granting representation to workers of the city and countryside through their organizations in all bodies that make decisions and implement government policies that directly affect them.

11. Commitment to the right of free unionization for all sectors and respect for its exercise.

12. Support of the necessary instruments to bring about an upsurge of all-embracing humanism of which man will be the center and apex of all created things.

13. Introduction of mechanisms for the gradual achievement of the political, economic, social, and cultural union of Central America.

14. Commitment to establish effective measures for freedom of transit, abode, residence, work, study, and trade for Central Americans; and, thereby to improve and strengthen the mechanisms of Central American economic integration, including its humanization and the free circulation of capital.

WITH ALL WORKING TOGETHER, EL SALVADOR DOES HAVE A SOLUTION

12.
PRESIDENT JOSÉ NAPOLEÓN DUARTE: SPEECH TO THE UNITED NATIONS (OCTOBER 1984)

I am convinced that the historic path of mankind is not one of violence but of democratic revolution.

It is understandable that those compatriots who left El Salvador years ago cannot or refuse to understand that things have changed; however, I know that the great majority of Salvadorians, and even the guerrilla commanders and fighters roaming about in the mountains of our homeland, are aware of this new situation. . . .

In El Salvador the terrorists have committed excesses but have failed, because the people do not support them and because we have the political will to build a united, pluralistic and democratic society. By persisting in their anti-historical obstinacy, they have dedicated themselves to the oppression of the simple farmers who are the victims of their reign of terror; they are robbing and killing people; they are leaving citizens without any means of communication because they are blowing up bridges and railroads; they are destroying electrical power lines and water systems; they are setting fire to plantations producing coffee, cotton and food crops. That leaves the poorest element of our population without work or hope.

It is so easy to destroy services which are needed by people and which took so many years to build up; the infrastructure that is part of our national heritage and that was established by the efforts and sacrifice of our people can be destroyed in an instant by the criminal hand of the terrorist, who uses dynamite and is financed by nations that have in mind only world domination and are perhaps laboring under a misunderstanding of history.

Unfortunately, the Revolutionary Democratic Front does not understand that we are experiencing a new reality, and therefore it is still trying to change things that no longer exist: a medieval agrarian structure, a financial structure at the service of the interests of a minority, an army at the service of a political system dominated by an economic elite. All those things no longer exist. In 1979 a profound process of change began, and it has been consolidated. Today we have a new agrarian structure which has placed our best lands at the service of the farmer. We have a new financial structure which supports and strengthens the new agrarian structure. We have a new trade structure for the products that we traditionally have exported, and this makes available to the country the hard currency thereby generated. We now have an armed forces that works for the people. And we have a people that has demonstrated its unshakable faith in democracy and has elected a Government by its own free will; we have a people that is working, suffering and dying to achieve peace and justice.

From this rostrum I ask those who advocate the ideology of armed subversion in El Salvador to change their strategies because of the new reality in my country. The El Salvador that they left in 1979 is not the El Salvador that exists in 1984. Today our country is breathing the air of freedom. Political parties are respected and encouraged. The people freely chose their leaders. Abuses of authority and violations of human rights have been reduced to the very minimum, and those who commit them are prosecuted and punished. Banks are lending large sums to farmers, who are actively participating in the social and political struggles. There is a very different society in El Salvador today. . . .

For all those reasons, I address the Salvadorian guerrillas and ask them to accept the new reality, to stop killing our brothers, to stop destroying bridges, to stop destroying the infrastructure of the nation, the public transport services, the plantations and the railroads. In a word, I ask them to stop killing and destroying and, together with all the rest of our people, to engage in the building of a new country, a free and democratic country in which peace will be the basis for our development.

I now wish to make an offer of peace.

Ever since I became President, by the freely expressed decision of the citizens of my country, I have been aware that my principal task is to work for the achievement of social harmony and internal peace in the Republic, which has been convulsed by a conflict with both internal and external causes. The time has come to put an end to that conflict. I am more convinced today than ever before that the existence of this conflict not only affects the life of my compatriots but is an element of friction that threatens the peace and security of other nations of the world, and particularly of our brother nations in Central America.

Hence, there could be no more appropriate time than this, when I am at this rostrum, to make before the peoples of the world an offer of peace, which would ensure for all Salvadorians—without any distinctions flowing from political or ideological position—social harmony and security. This offer is made within the framework of the Salvadorian Constitution, which has established the system of democracy and political pluralism, under which the most varied ideologies can coexist. . . .

Quite naturally, it is hard to convince those who up to now have viewed weapons and violence as the only way to ensure their political space that there can be a climate in which they can express their own thoughts without thereby suffering reprisals from adversaries.

But I have come here to affirm that as President of the Republic and Commander of the Armed Forces I am in a position to maintain those measures which, within our constitutional process, make it possible for them to abandon an attitude that runs counter to the history of the political evolution of the people of El Salvador. Furthermore, in due course I shall propose to our Legislative Assembly a general amnesty for political crimes. We are exercising control over abuse of authority and eliminating all the methods of repression that have existed in our country in the past and have in part been at the root of a rebellion for which there is no longer a need.

This means that I am offering the safety and security of a political place within a pluralistic, constitutional, democratic system which the Government is defending. As part of those efforts I invite the heads of the guerrilla movement now in our mountains to come without weapons to the village of La Palma, in the Department of Chalatenango, at 10 a.m. on 15 October, the anniversary of the insurrection movement of 1979, and in the presence of the representatives of the Church and the world press to discuss with us the details and scope of this proposal for their incorporation into the democratic process and the establishment of an atmosphere of freedom for the next election. I am convinced that our people, tired of violence, will take this proposal as sign of hope emanating from its lawful Government.

III
THE SALVADORAN CIVIL WAR

13.
CHARLES CLEMENTS: WITNESS TO WAR

Copapayo and its peninsula jutting north into Lake Suchitlán were cut off. Escape was blocked by a government garrison visible to the northwest on the opposite shore. To the south, the elite Ramón Belloso Battalion was advancing steadily upon us, pushing our few defenders back toward the village.

The soldiers had been trucked thirty miles north from the capital, San Salvador, and then deployed to sweep the hills and ravines of "subversives." With little resistance, they had ground their way to a ridge overlooking the neck of the peninsula. Around five o'clock that afternoon, the battalion set up its 81s and began firing down on us.

Whump! whump! whump! We listened as the mortar rounds left their cannisters. For a moment we heard nothing as the shells sped to the top of their arc. Then they came whistling down and exploded with concussions that shook the earth and sent shattered adobe in every direction.

The young children of Copapayo—several of whom I'd delivered—were my gravest concern. They were hysterical with fright. They screamed each time the mortar clusters began their descent. They clawed and tore at their mothers, desperate to escape the explosions.

There was no choice but to quiet them.

I crushed my store of tranquilizer tablets and mixed them with orange juice and brown sugar. Then, as each three-*whump!* salvo was over, I began zigzagging my way from trench to trench.

Sitting still in the trenches, the women were as impassive during the bombardment as stone figures from a Mayan relief. None of the mothers questioned what I was doing; they knew death too well. Each cooed, *"Dulce, dulce"* (candy, candy) as I dosed their terrorized infants according to my best guess of individual weight. By dark, there wasn't a conscious child under three years old in Copapayo.

From his *Witness to War: An American Doctor in El Salvador* (New York, 1984), pp. 3–6.

Then the *guinda* (evacuation) began. A single-file column of three hundred Salvadoran *campesinos* (peasants), and a few lightly armed rebel militiamen, snaked its way up out of the trenches and wound along the peninsula toward the government lines. In the ribbons of moonlight that broke through the cloud cover, I could see the stooped *campesinos* carrying their few belongings and comatose infants up a narrow trail leading them straight through a mile-wide zone held by the government troops.

There were still the stretcher cases to see to, as well as the women who were too old, too sick, or too many months pregnant to risk an all-night march past the Belloso Battalion. In the dark, they would leave by boat. My assistant was Miguel, seventy-five, by far the oldest man in Copapayo, a *campesino* gnarled by arthritis. Miguel was no stranger to fright and flight; his memory stretched back to the great *matanza* (slaughter) of the 1930s when 30,000 Salvadoran Indians and peasants were killed by the government. He had endured at least a dozen nights such as this and had declared he would flee no more.

"I'm tired," he told me, "and the enemy doesn't care about toothless old men."

We took the remaining women to two small boats. Some of the grandmothers were partially deaf and couldn't hear the *whumps!* The younger, pregnant women held on to them and pulled them to the ground before the explosions came.

Miguel dropped, too, and then heaved himself up ungainly as a camel. First he made it to all fours, then using his twisted hands and strong forearms, he pushed his rump skyward. Another shove, and he was balanced again on his spindly legs.

My maternity cases, their bellies distended, could hunker down only so far. Shielding their fetuses and their own aged mothers, they formed three-generational hills in the mortar flashes. Many of them had watched their children leave with the column. They knew they might never see them again.

"Hasta mañana," I whispered to the women in my poor Spanish. "Yo voy a cuidar a sus niños." (Until tomorrow, I'll take care of your children.)

They tried to believe me.

I left Miguel at the boats with the warning that if he didn't evacuate with the women, I'd send a stretcher for him and force him to go up the peninsula with the rest of us.

"All right, amigo, I will go," he lied.

We carried the stretcher cases and the children past the enemy positions. I'm not one to pray much. If God is truly all-knowing and all-powerful, it isn't for me to point out opportunities for divine intercession. But I did pray that whole long night of silent marching. I prayed for Miguel, and I asked that if any of the children were to die, that it be from an overdose at my hand—not because they awoke, whimpered, and were smothered into silence by their frightened mothers.

I knew peasant mothers who'd killed their infant children that way. Their agony never ceased. It was worse than the loss of a brother, husband, or father to the enemy, worse, even, than watching their children die of hunger and disease. It made them murderesses.

When dawn came, we were safe. Not a child made a noise that night and not a one had succumbed to the drugs. Thank you, God, for that.

We could hear the Belloso Battalion completing their siege of Copapayo, and later in the day we listened to a government radio report of the battle. The guerrillas, it said, had been vanquished to the last man.

Old Miguel.

We found him in the plaza when we returned. As a warning to the rest of us, his frail old arms had been nearly twisted from their sockets before he was shot in the stomach and left to die, slowly.

14.
EDWARD KING: THE SALVADORAN MILITARY
(SEPTEMBER 1984)

THE REFORMIST OFFICERS

Meetings with high-ranking members of the Salvadoran General Staff and field commanders confirmed that numerous officers within the Salvadoran armed forces, particularly those who have held combat positions during the past three years, are quite concerned about their poor professional image. They are ashamed of the military's involvement in death squads, tolerance of massive corruption and past political control of the country, all of which violate the Constitution they are sworn to defend.

These reformers are determined to remove from command positions officers who have financially profited from the war or become morally corrupted through participation in death squads as well as to remove inefficient and ineffective combat commanders who advanced in rank only because of personal and family contacts. They intend to professionalize the Salvadoran armed forces and, in as much as possible, separate the military from all political activities. They believe that the armed forces should subordinate themselves to civilian control and respect the Constitution and the duly elected government of El Salvador.

From Unitarian Universalist Service Committee, "U.S. Military Policy in Central America."

However, there are other groups of officers who are wedded to the past practice of running the country for personal profit and as they see fit. These officers have long had strong ties to the wealthy families and large business companies. They oppose efforts to take the army out of politics and subject it to real civilian control. They are also against any dialogue with the rebels. In many cases this resistance to reform is based on selfish reasons, but many of these officers believe that civilian leadership will inevitably lead to even greater corruption and become pro-communist. . . .

IMPROVING COMBAT EFFECTIVENESS

Salvadoran Army field commanders have been performing much more effectively, which has improved morale within the combat units and increased pressure on FMLN units. Increased Salvadoran training programs have improved combat capability in the battalions.

The recent lull in large scale FMLN military activity is not an indication of weakness or a loss of the will to fight. Instead, it reflects the rebels' need to recruit and train new troops, adopt new tactics to counter the Army's changed tactics and build ammunition stockpiles. The Salvadoran Army is doing much the same thing, but at the same time it has attempted to maintain pressure on the FMLN forces.

Constant tactical pressure by the Salvadoran Army has kept FMLN units on the move and has restricted their ability to conduct the set-piece battles they prefer in fighting a war of attrition. In part because of its difficulty in setting up and conducting strong offensive operations, the FMLN has returned to its past practice of striking at key parts of the civilian economy, interdicting main highways and indiscriminately burning buses and private cars. . . .

THE WAR IN MORAZÁN

Col. Domingo Monterrosa, commander of the Third Military Region, believes the FMLN units in the Morazán region have lost strength over the past year and now number around 3,000 in his zone. He said the morale and will to fight in the FMLN units in his sector is not as high as a year ago.

According to Col. Monterrosa, the guerrillas do not fight as hard as they once did, break contact sooner and withdraw much more quickly. He thinks that veteran FMLN fighters are becoming disillusioned by the length of the war. These experienced guerrilla soldiers, Col. Monterrosa says, are wondering how much longer they will have to fight to achieve the victory their leaders have promised. Meanwhile, green recruits join their ranks and the veterans wonder when these troops will become experienced enough to take some of the daily battle pressure off their hands.

Several officers said that FMLN units are receiving small amounts of arms and ammunition directly from Nicaragua, but other supplies—arms, ammunition, uniforms and equipment—are being purchased from black marketeers in Honduras and Guatemala. . . .

CIVIC ACTION: INEFFECTIVE

Col. Monterrosa thinks the military's current civic action program is ineffective. He cited the refugee problem in his zone to illustrate his argument. A number of refugees arrived in the city of San Miguel from Honduras and became the responsibility of his command. U.S.-style civic action programs call upon the armed forces to administer refugee programs, but Col. Monterrosa, while concerned about the refugees, thought that they should be the responsibility of a civil government agency. Army-run refugee programs frighten the *campesinos* because they present too much military presence, he said. He also pointed out that he did not have the resources to care properly for those voluntary refugees fleeing the FMLN-controlled zone.

The United States Agency for International Development (USAID) could help the Salvadoran government by taking refugee assistance programs out of military civic action channels and making them the responsibility of a civil agency. In July USAID increased its assistance to refugees who have left FMLN areas to live in government-controlled areas. But several visits to refugee camps indicate that these efforts are still not sufficient.

SENIOR U.S. MILITARY ADVISORS: TOO MANY AND TOO EXPENSIVE

I discussed the role of U.S. advisors with several general staff officers and some field commanders. They unanimously agreed that there are more senior U.S. officer advisors in El Salvador than tactical requirements justify.

The general staff officers thought that some senior U.S. officer advisors are no longer necessary and cost too much. (Each U.S. officer advisor costs the Salvadoran government approximately $10,000 annually, reducing the funds available for military equipment.)

The field commanders also believed that the two to three U.S. officers stationed at each regional command headquarters are not a justifiable cost to the Salvadoran government. Some regional commanders suspected that these advisors act as spies and report to the Embassy and the U.S. military group commander on activities at their headquarters. These officers prefer that the advisors be withdrawn.

The Salvadoran Army wants to increase the number of junior U.S.

officers and noncommissioned officers who are now training Salvadoran troops. It also wants to retain some of the advisors who assist in intelligence, logistics and maintenance functions. But it was quite clear that the Salvadoran Army believes that it does not need nor want to continue paying for those advisors to assist with staff and command duties. The Army considers its own field-grade officers quite capable of carrying out these assignments. . . .

SALVADORANS SEEKING A SALVADORAN SOLUTION

Some military officers are realizing that continued heavy fighting in support of a U.S.-backed East-West ideological anti-communist crusade in Central America is doing little for their country beyond hastening its destruction. One more frequently hears the observation that all Salvadorans must now come together to find a political, not a military solution to their own problems.

Increasingly, both the Salvadoran armed forces and elements of the FMLN are beginning to understand that neither side has much to gain from a prolonged continuation of an attritive war. As one FMLN combat leader said, "It serves no purpose for us to fight to win a desert that we will then have to come to you *gringos* to get the money to rebuild." Whether this sentiment will be allowed to act toward dialogue and political exchange remains to be seen.

There is an enlightened body of opinion within the Salvadoran armed forces that favors contacts with the FMLN. These officers recognize the futility of a prolonged war that will destroy what remains of the country's already weakened economic infrastructure. They agree about the need for talks with the FMLN about ways to reduce the human costs of the war and perhaps find an opening leading to the resolution of political differences among Salvadorans by Salvadorans. Both sides are tired after four years of war.

15.
GENERAL PAUL GORMAN: EXTERNAL SUPPORT FOR SALVADORAN GUERRILLAS (AUGUST 1984)

I propose to discuss four specific cases, or series of events, which illustrate the problems faced by President Duarte and his armed forces.

News Briefing by Department of Defense.

First: Infiltration across the beaches of Espino, Cuco, and Icacal, and up the Lempa River and Juquilisco Bay in southeastern El Salvador.

Second: Overland infiltration, using way stations and camps in areas dominated by guerrillas.

Third: Dispersed stores or caches. And,

Fourth: Well-guarded headquarters or base areas for control of guerrilla operations and logistics.

I believe each of these cases, or instances, demonstrates the validity of President Duarte's judgment that his country is the victim of a pernicious form of aggression by Nicaragua.

First, I direct your attention to the Jucuarán area, which is identified on the map as the green area right at the base of the map. . . .

We know from a man who participated in the event, a defector, that on April 28, at night, a shipment of assorted munitions arrived via these cayucas, to which the Ambassador made reference, on the beach, in the vicinity of Playa El Espino near the town of Boca de Botoncillo.

The shipment was there met by a guerrilla reception party and backpacked to a point just to the southeast of the village of Jucuarán. At that point, the shipment was transferred to mules and carried to the vicinity of the town of El Brazo.

Earlier the same evening, trucks were hijacked near the town of El Transito and moved to El Brazo where they rendezvoused with the mule shipment. This was on the evening of May 1. At that time, the shipment was transferred to trucks and moved north toward the city of San Miguel.

Intelligence analysts in El Salvador, and in my command, believe that this shipment was probably involved in logistically supporting the May 6 attack, by that faction of the guerrillas known as the "ERP," on the city of San Miguel—an attack which the Ambassador witnessed, since he was fired on by these ERP troops south of the city as he attempted to bring in the election observers on the morning of May 6.

That attack was thwarted by the Salvadoran Armed Forces, which had been alerted by intelligence not only to its timing but its location.

The U.S.-trained ARCE Battalion of the Salvadoran Armed Forces, reacting to that attack from the south, pursued the guerrillas south of San Miguel, and on May 10 a company of the ARCE captured, near El Transito, Bulgarian ammunition. . . .

Bulgaria operates a factory which produces identifiable NATO-standard ammunition. The United States intelligence services have seen this particular type of round only three places in the Western Hemisphere: south of the town of San Miguel, in El Salvador, just this year; several times in recent years in the hands of the Sandinista army in Nicaragua; and in 1973 and 1974, in the Dominican Republic in the hands of a group of insurgents known to have been supported by the Cubans.

In the continuation of that operation, on May 11, the ARCE Battalion captured a Vietnamese mortar, this time near the town of San Carlos. This is the box in which the mortar sight was contained. The markings here, in Vietnamese, are instructions to use with the 81 millimeter mortar. This is the sight; it was manufactured in North Vietnam in the late 1970s. And in the box there is an inspection or factory clearance chip, which would indicate that it was shipped from the factory probably circa 1978. . . .

About 10 to 12 days ago, the Salvadoran armed forces began what they called Operation Guazapa 13. During this operation the Salvadoran army successfully acquired intelligence from campesinos and from defectors.

As the army moved into the guerrilla stronghold, a guerrilla turned himself in and offered to lead Salvadoran armed forces units to an arms cache which he had helped create.

The Salvadoran Tigre Battalion immediately followed the guerrilla and located the arms. Among the items seized were some 44 U.S.-manufactured AR-15s, some seven M-16s, some six Belgian-manufactured FAL rifles, one U.S. M-1 rifle, one U.S. M-1 carbine, one U.S. .45 caliber Thompson submachine gun, three U.S.-manufactured light anti-tank weapons, and a substantial amount of TNT, Soviet-manufactured fuses, and other material.

In the U.S. Southern Command, we make a practice of tracing all reported weapons' serial numbers from whatever source, as long as we are certain that the serial numbers are accurate.

In this case, concerning the 44 U.S.-manufactured AR-15s, 33 have been traced, using the computers of the United States Army: 85 percent, or 28 of those weapons, were manufactured in the 1960s and shipped from the United States to Southeast Asia.

For the remaining 15 percent, or 5, there are no records for the serial numbers listed. None of those weapons were shipped to El Salvador. We still have 11 that we're concluding tracing action on.

Let me enlarge on this picture. The U.S. country team in El Salvador and Southern Command have traced the serial numbers on AR-15s and M-16s which the Salvadorans have captured from the guerrillas in recent months. We have also traced serial numbers of such U.S.-made weapons from lists or records in documents captured from the guerrillas in recent operations.

In this sample, 73 percent of the 214 weapons, as of July 21, were manufactured in the 1960s and shipped by the United States to Southeast Asia; 19 percent, some 40 weapons, were shipped to El Salvador.

Of 239 weapons, for which we could find serial numbers listed in guerrilla records, 57 percent were traceable to Vietnam, and only 5 percent traceable to shipments to the Salvadoran armed forces.

This evidence suggests to me that the guerrillas are not primarily armed with American weapons captured from the Salvadoran army, but with American weapons supplied by Vietnam through some transshippers— Cuba and Nicaragua. . . .

16.
FMLN: APPEAL FOR SANDINISTA HELP (NOVEMBER 5, 1983)

SANDINISTA NATIONAL LIBERATION FRONT COMRADES:

We are pleased to have received your message of solidarity and interest in the Salvadoran revolutionary process.

We strive to achieve a higher level of unity, aimed at correcting mistakes and strengthening the victories of the Farabundo Martí Liberation Front forces.

As part of the preliminary results of our meeting, and knowing the enthusiasm and interest with which our process is followed, we allow ourselves as revolutionaries and brothers to reflect upon the draft treaty presented by Nicaragua to the United States and to the governments of Central America.

We wish to make the following points:

1. Unity and full understanding between the Sandinista National Liberation Front and the Farabundo Martí Liberation Front is of the essence. Therefore, we reiterate our respect for the Sandinista National Liberation Front leadership and our firm commitment to unite Central American revolutionaries confronting the perils of aggression.

2. We are deeply concerned that we were not consulted about the treaties and the six-point proposal to the Contadora group, in spite of the fact that both plans include aspects that affect us directly.

3. The present U.S. policy is fraught with ominous aggression. We must be careful that our diplomatic plans and actions do not stimulate the aggressive tendencies of our enemies or confuse the masses with the expectation of achieving peace through anything other than combat.

4. Although there is no indication that an agreement with the imperialists can be reached through anything other than surrender and humiliation, this does not mean that we should give up the diplomatic struggle to isolate the main enemy and enlist allies to our cause. But we must analyze carefully the substance and timing of our diplomatic actions.

5. Our representatives were informed that the Sandinista National Liberation Front leadership was confronted with the choice between strategic negotiations and genocidal war. It opted for strategic negotiations involving our country. We take exception to this because there is no will to negotiate on the part of the United States and also because presently El Salvador has the upper hand in the conflict, thus maintaining the Central American revolutionary offensive. Also, the treaties are along the lines of an interventionist offensive and imperialist blackmail encouraging Reagan to persevere in his efforts.

6. Your assessment of the Salvadoran process is flawed. We will forward a broad document aimed at explaining our struggle, and helping to improve the regional strategy.

7. We consider that within the framework of the present U.S. interventionist offensive and the progress of El Salvador's revolutionary forces, there are political conditions for the development and implementation of more daring support plans to accelerate the process.

8. Foremost among our concerns is our inability to discuss the treaties, therefore deepening the differences between the Sandinista National Liberation Front and the Farabundo Martí Liberation Front, which could be used by the imperialists in their attempt to divide us in order to accelerate their plans of aggression.

9. We have recently discovered preparations for aggression against Nicaragua and El Salvador. In light of this, we wish to know Nicaragua's position in the event that this aggression were initiated only in El Salvador. These issues are the basis of our political and military plans to confront the intervention, and we are already working on them. In the event of an aggression against Nicaragua, we would intensify military action against the puppet army in solidarity with the Sandinista revolution. Finally, these issues are presented with the intention of establishing a dialogue between the Sandinista National Liberation Front and the Farabundo Martí Liberation Front and improving communications between us. We also wish to reiterate our firm commitment to respect and maintain unity with the Sandinista National Liberation Front political and military leadership.

Farabundo Martí National Liberation Front Command:

Commander Roberto Roca
Commander Leonel González
Commander Shafik Handal
Commander Joaquín Villalobos

San Salvador, Morazán, November 2, 1983

17.
MINUTES OF FMLN-SANDINISTA MEETING
(NOVEMBER 7, 1983)

Minutes of a meeting between the Farabundo Martí Liberation Front and DRI [Department of International Relations] (Sandinista National Liberation Front).

ITEMS PRESENTED:

a) Possibility of supply renewal for El Salvador and DRI.
b) Demand list of all supplies to be sent by EPS [Sandinista Army] to the border.
c) They say they are preparing for war.
d) Indications are that the aggression will be against Nicaragua.
e) Those who are not going to fight should leave.
f) The leaders remain alone with the committee and under the control of an officer.

EVALUATION:

a) Simplistic exposition.
b) Chauvinistic, irresponsible and historically boorish attitude.
c) Our position is loyal, mature and broad.

PRECEDENTS:

1) Nicaragua's non-consultation policy regarding the U.S.'s proposed treaties and agreements with El Salvador.
2) Other precipitate and non-consulted actions such as the International Solidarity Front initiative. Examine inconsistencies and difficulties.
3) Inefficiency, disorder and lack of attention toward the problems of El Salvador and problems in Central America.
4) Immobilization and near obliteration of our supply lines and confiscation of independently acquired supplies.
5) Farabundo Martí Liberation Front requested meeting with the Sandinista National Liberation Front which was held today at 17 hours. DRI represented by López and Gustavo.
Present were Hugo, Rodrigo, Venancio, Andrés and Valentín.

THE SANDINISTA NATIONAL LIBERATION FRONT'S EXPOSITION:

1. This is not a time for analysis, it is a time for action.
2. Great regional dangers—indications of imminent aggression.
3. Every day there is more open aggression against Nicaragua's air and naval space as well as its borders. . . .
6. They are preparing a Contra offensive.
7. No progress in the Contadora effort. Attempt to evade the regional problem.
8. We are unavoidably headed toward war. . . .
9. The leadership has issued the following orders: Prepare Nicaragua for self-defense. This is our contribution to Central America. We are concerned about doing away with CONDECA and about U.S. imperialist invasion of El Salvador. But all indications are that the aggressive build-up is against Nicaragua and we must act accordingly.
10. The treaty did not achieve its objective.
11. Tito and Daniel: Undermine Chief of State, Contadora and Spain attempts to formulate initiative as a general treaty thus disqualifying the Nicaragua treaties.
12. Friends abroad fear the worst for Nicaragua.
13. There is no negotiation possibility in sight.
14. We envision special measures concerning Central American residents. They can not continue functioning and living as they have up to date. They need to participate in the defense of the country.
15. We shall wage war with what we have and on our own. We do not expect assistance from our allies.
16. Our suggestions are based on fact and not on speculation.
17. If Nicaragua is attacked, the borders will dissolve.
18. You can count on us for assistance. We have always been inextricably linked.
19. The proposal arises from the imminence of war.

FARABUNDO MARTÍ NATIONAL LIBERATION FRONT'S VERBATIM STATEMENT:

1. The U.S. is experiencing today the most overt and aggravated interventionist tendency of the past few administrations.
2. The interventionist tide is aimed mainly toward Grenada and Central America.
3. Washington has no inclination toward seeking agreements. Imperialism and its policy of force and blackmail effectively aim to triumph, weaken and defeat us (the Farabundo Martí National Liberation Front has expressed the need to combine diplomatic efforts and other forms of struggle).
4. Today, as never before, the imperialist strategy reveals itself in all its crudeness as a confrontational regional action, becoming a strategic prob-

lem shared by our people and all revolutionaries in the isthmus. This is a crucial and highly dangerous time for El Salvador and for Central America.

6. There is no doubt that such an intervention will affect all of us. Therefore, not only do we need to face reality, we must also take precautions and study imperialistic logic. They always use the smoke screen approach as a means of distraction. Aggression to one of us will always be considered a dramatic and concrete aggression against all of us, El Salvador, Nicaragua.

7. Following the tragic Grenada invasion, the targets of choice for enemy attack are El Salvador, Nicaragua, Cuba.

8. Closely observed preparations for war by U.S. imperialists and their allies in the region.

9. However, we do not intend to base our policy on a unilateral prediction of assured intervention targeted against one country (Nicaragua and El Salvador). Such a narrow outlook could cause unpredictable conditions. It would be unadvisable to adopt one scheme only.

10. Options of intervention in the region:

a. El Salvador

b. Nicaragua.

c. A simultaneous or continuous intervention. We recognize each option in all its variations against El Salvador. It could be accompanied by the taking of strongholds in Nicaragua.

FARABUNDO MARTÍ NATIONAL LIBERATION FRONT'S (FMLN) PROPOSAL TO THE SANDINISTA NATIONAL LIBERATION FRONT (FSLN):

1. We consider that El Salvador's war has strategic importance for the Nicaraguan revolution and for the region. Nicaragua is the revolutionary leader.

2. Now more than ever, El Salvador, Nicaragua and all of Central America share objectives and interests.

3. The FMLN has as its loftiest goal the fulfillment of its duties.

4. The revolutionaries of El Salvador consider the time ripe for the FMLN and the FSLN to share strategic and historic responsibilities fundamental to the revolution.

5) Logically then, the FSLN has the responsibility to study El Salvador's war problems.

FMLN INITIATIVE TOWARD THE FSLN:

a) We propose the joint, continuous and systematic probe of the situation in the region with the participation of Nicaragua and El Salvador.

b) Joint efforts in all areas: political, military, public relations, diplomatic etc.

Finally we reiterate our understanding of Nicaragua's domestic situation as the broadest front in the struggle against U.S. imperialism and hence the need to view El Salvador as another target in the confrontation.

FSLN POSITION:
LÓPEZ: [Julio López, general secretary of DRI]

1. We share your values.
2. Up to date we have not cut off aid.
3. For practical purposes our approach has not changed, but if there is war, the situation will not be the same.
4. We will forward your proposal to the leadership.
5. We have no indications that the main thrust of aggression will be against El Salvador.
6. Our best contribution is to preserve power in Nicaragua. . . .

GUSTAVO'S PARTICIPATION (FSLN) . . . :

2. We do not want you to be caught off guard.
3. It is necessary to take concrete action:
a) Long-term working relationships will affect your ranks.
b) We have been given a list of comrades to be headquartered close to the border. There they will be trained and they will depend on the military.
  Deadline: they need to leave by Friday, Saturday. Staying here would be dangerous. One month of intensive training.
c) If the war broke out, they would act in EPS units.
d) Your units will occupy a Honduran strip between Nicaragua and El Salvador.
e) The others remain under the command of an intelligence officer for communication purposes, which are by no means guaranteed.
f) If you need to fight, it will be to protect your lives.

LÓPEZ:

1. Whether there is war or not, everything will be difficult for you: movement, communication with the outside.
2. Political cadres must be withdrawn immediately before Saturday. After that date we do not guarantee their safety.
3. After Saturday there is no guarantee that you will find us, since Salvadoran and DRI cadres will be transferred to other tasks such as neighborhoods, fronts or abroad.
5. All the logistics will zero in on defense. . . .

FMLN'S LAST COMMENTS:

Are there logistic contingencies for El Salvador? There was no answer.
We reflected: It seems appropriate to prepare for war in Nicaragua, but we must also foresee all other variables in the region.

18.
LETTER BETWEEN FMLN LEADERS (NOVEMBER 1983)

November 9, 1983

Commander Roberto Roca:

The latest messages (from Hugo and Valentín) make clear that the Sandinistas have decided to expel us. Maybe this was a concession agreed upon
with the imperialists or some intermediary. We, in turn, should send a
message to Fidel and make an assessment as to what we should expect. I
propose that we meet at noon (at my house). I will have a draft of that
message.

R.O.M.V

Simón

19.
RUBÉN ZAMORA: INTERVIEW (SEPTEMBER 1984)

Señal de Libertad: *Is the FMLN-FDR, the Salvadoran revolutionary movement, after more than three years of war, ready to seek an understanding
with its enemies to end the war? And with whom, other than those enemies
with whom you have fought to the death and who are now in power, do you
intend to negotiate and form a provisional government?*

Rubén Zamora: To understand the proposal, we must rise above the level
of understanding that pictures Salvadoran society in black and white
terms. Salvadoran society is much more complex. There are two main
parties to the conflict: on the one hand, the oligarchy with the support of
the army and the North Americans, and on the other hand, the forces of
the people, represented by the FMLN-FDR. But these two alone do not
comprise the entire society. Around the two principal poles of the conflict
revolve a number of forces which can go one way or the other.

Translation copyright © 1986 by Gladys Segal.

Radio Venceremos, No. 2 (August–September 1984).

This is the "ABC's" of a scientific conception of social reality. There is a central conflict, but in addition to this principal contradiction there is a series of secondary contradictions which favor one side or the other. On this basis our proposal for a Government of Broad Participation hopes to influence this series of secondary contradictions in Salvadoran society.

Until now, a group of forces, because of the polarization of the country, has tended to lean toward, let's say, the reactionary pole of the conflict. In order to advance the struggle of our people, the triumph of our people, it is necessary to neutralize these forces, or to attract them to the revolutionary camp, to the progressive and democratic sectors of the country. These forces won't be attracted by offering them death, by offering punishment, by offering bullets, but rather by understanding what some of their immediate needs are, and addressing those immediate interests.

At the heart of the problem is the question of reformism. The fundamental question, in my opinion, is this: with the proposal for a Government of Broad Participation, do we become reformists and thereby give up our revolutionary character? Yes or no?

If we answer this question solely on the basis of analyzing the proposals and the concrete measures outlined in the document, the conclusion is yes, our front has become reformist.

But this would be a completely idealistic analysis of Salvadoran reality, a formal analysis which forgets that the determining factor in whatever social situation, in whatever process of social struggle, is the social forces which move relative to the different proposals. I believe this is where the analysis should begin.

If the organized strength of our people, the majority of our people, was in the hands of the petite bourgeoisie and its reformist position, then the proposal of the front would become, essentially, a reformist policy. But if the fundamental strength of our people, that is, the organized workers and peasants, is directed by the revolutionary forces, the FMLN-FDR, then the proposal for a Government of Broad Participation contributes by attracting intermediate forces, but the fundamental direction of the process is assured by the camp in which the most important forces are found.

Therefore, it is not the same to make the same proposal in a European country as it is in El Salvador. In the European countries, important sectors like the organized working class are in the hands of parties like the Social Democrats or the Christian Democrats, so the significance of the proposal is determined by the control the Social Democrats or the Christian Democrats exert on these forces.

In contrast, in El Salvador the fundamental forces, the organized peasants and working class, are not with the Christian Democrats or with the army; they are with the FMLN-FDR and, therefore, they give fundamental direction to the process. . . .

Señal de Libertad: *Could you elaborate on the proposal for a Government of Broad Participation, perhaps on two or three of the more controversial aspects? What causes many questions is the point about restructuring the armed forces. It is realistic, and on what is it based? Is it possible to clean up and restructure the armed forces and combine them with the FMLN forces? On what do you base the claim that this will guarantee the best interest of the people?*

Rubén Zamora: Our confidence is based on two elements, one primary, and one secondary. The principal element is the development of the military strength of the people. Our position is clear: until the integration of the two armed forces is achieved, each side will retain its weapons. In other words, at no time will the FMLN lay down its arms. The military strength our people have attained is the fundamental guarantee that the integration of the two armies will be favorable to the interests of the people.

But there is a second element to take into account as well—the internal composition of the Salvadoran armed forces. The political development of the Salvadoran army over the past 50 years clearly shows the existence of two political tendencies: one which we can call "gorilla" has been the repressive tendency linked to the oligarchy and servile to the United States. Historically, this tendency has predominated.

But within the armed forces there has always been an alternative tendency. It is a tendency with a clear vision of social change, with something of a democratic character, with a vision of professionalizing the armed forces. This constitutionalist tendency has been able to predominate within the armed forces for short periods during moments of acute political, social, and economic crisis. What has been the problem, historically, for the constitutionalist tendency within the army? Whenever it has become dominant, which it has done through coups d'état, it has been without important links to the democratic, progressive, and revolutionary forces of the people. This was the case in 1944, 1948, 1960, and 1979, when its progressive aims were defeated and it rapidly lost control of the armed forces.

On what is our proposal based? On the concrete possibility that the constitutionalist tendency within the armed forces might have a real link with the progressive and revolutionary forces of our people.

Señal de Libertad: *To conclude, let's talk a little about the platform of a Democratic Revolutionary Government, which calls for changes in the economic structure which are more radical and more fundamental than what you are now proposing. Let's compare the main functions of the two proposals, for a Democratic Revolutionary Government and for a Government of Broad Participation. How are they related?*

Rubén Zamora: The platform for the Revolutionary Government and the proposal for a Government of Broad Participation are not the same for a simple reason. They are proposals with different characteristics.

The Platform of the Democratic Revolutionary Government is the basis of the FMLN-FDR alliance and is a longer-term proposal. The Proposal for a Provisional Government of Broad Participation is, as its name implies, a proposal for negotiations and for a provisional government. That is, a short-term proposal. This implies, then, that we must remedy the immediate problems of the country. So if we compare the two, the Proposal for a Provisional Government emphasizes political aspects, civil liberties, human rights, and not the structural aspects of profound socio-economic change. The latter proposal is a longer-term question. In this sense, the FMLN-FDR is not retreating from its position. Rather, they are proposals of two different natures.

The proposal for a Democratic Revolutionary Government is not a betrayal of the revolution. Although the final and worldwide objectives of the revolution can only be accomplished by a socialist society, the FMLN-FDR's proposal for a Democratic Revolutionary Government is not a proposal for socialism, but rather a means to move along the road to socialism. In the same way we are making a short-term proposal, a proposal for a provisional government. This in no way changes our goals or compromises our struggle for these goals.

20.
FMLN: PROPOSAL FOR POLITICAL WORK (MAY 1984)

Taking into account the fact that Duarte will try to politically isolate the FMLN-FDR both at the national and the international level, and will call on us to enter into a dialogue for the purpose of participating in the municipal elections, but with the condition of laying down our arms, the FMLN-FDR must develop and present a proposal for dialogue and negotiations in a remote area of the country without prior conditions, and consequently the FMLN must deal with three elements; (1) the military advance, (2) the pressure of the mass revolutionary movement and (3) the contradictions in the enemy ranks.

Planning Document for Meeting of the General Command of the FMLN, May 25, 1984.

OUTLINE FOR THE PLATFORM OF THE DEMOCRATIC OPENING

The political line of the FMLN is dedicated to disputing the social base of the Duarte-USA project and to the search to create political space in the democratic sectors that consequently fight for the revolution.

This political line rests upon the following considerations:

a. That the Duarte social project has a social base made up of forces and people that have been directly affected by the war.

b. The elements of that base have been identified as a result of the repercussions of the serious social crisis.

c. That the "social pact" project has limitations; it will not resolve the crisis of the country because such a crisis has come about from the profound structural crisis of a dependent capitalist system.

d. Contradictions within the ranks of the ruling classes.

e. The trade union organizations clustered under the UPD: the majority of its leaders are influenced by the imperialist trade union line of the AFL-CIO, which responds to the imperialist project. Many of these leaders formerly had positions in the administrative apparatus, suffering under a process of bureaucratization which alienated them from the base. . . .

21.
LETTERS ON REVOLUTIONARY CADRE (1984)

A

Dear Comrade Hilda:

Receive a brotherly salute and my wishes that you are well and contributing a lot to our party and to our process. I was frustrated and sorry because I was not able to complete the letter that I sent you in the mail that went out July 21st. Please forgive me for the disorder. My only excuse is that I had very little time to prepare what I had to send and write to you. With this letter we are sending you C40,000 in the following contain-

A: Letter from a Member of the Metropolitan Front to a member of the Political Commission of the Central American Revolutionary Workers Party, a member of the FMLN, July 22, 1984.
B: Letter from "Lara" to "M. G. and members of the Regional Committee of the Metropolitan Front" of the same group, October 18, 1984.

ers: one small package of instant powdered chocolate *(milo),* one box of instant coffee and one box of oats. I also sent a few things and a short note that Ester sends to Federico. The note that I wrote you I put it into a box of L&M cigarettes. I hope that you have already received all of this. I am writing this letter beforehand. I think that comrade M. G. could carry it and have it brought to you.

In this letter I will not send any specific information concerning the work that I have to do, since comrade M. G. will bring this in detail. Rather, I would like to send you some personal ideas of a general nature which I have had for some time now and which I believe will be of some help in giving you a clear picture of our situation in the front. It is obvious that our party is consolidating itself and making a significant contribution to our revolutionary process. The last Resolutions of the Political Committee denote the significant advance which has been made in that direction. The document provides us with clear-cut guidelines based upon which we can undertake our daily tasks. Although sometimes, perhaps owing to problems of communication, we have not been receiving a response as quickly as we would have wished to some of our proposals, it appears to me that our higher governing bodies are giving a clear and opportune response to our needs.

In general, despite the attacks of the enemy, the work in the front is progressing quite effectively. Qualitative and quantitative advances have been made. It has been possible, to some extent, to impact politically and militarily on several occasions. We have been able to acquire a presence in the metropolitan front and at the international level. I believe that this is unquestionable. However, we still have a lot to do, since as revolutionaries we must better our achievements and give more and more each day.

We have encountered some situations of an external and internal nature which are making it difficult to carry out the work in the front.

First of all, we are facing the situation of the very characteristics of the front which you are well aware of. We are working in the rear of the enemy. For this reason, we cannot overlook security measures, the facade, legend, etc. The fact that we have to work clandestinely and that we have to plot a lot force us to devote a lot of time and effort to tasks which under other circumstances we could perform very quickly. We know about the difficulties that we are having, even for three or more of us just to get together, and the difficulty in mobilization that some of our comrades are facing. The blows of the enemy cost us the loss of comrades and infrastructures that are necessary for our work. The difficult communications with the PMC and other fronts is another situation which has a negative impact on the performance of the work. As regards the situations of an internal nature which in my opinion can have a negative impact on the performance of the work, I could mention the following to you: In the political area, the little solidity of the partisan within the framework of the worker sector; there are facts which I believe confirm this statement: the capture of Mario in a situation which is not very clear, the desertion of Catarina, both of whom were pillars of ours in that sector.

The capture of Genaro is a fact that denotes the little capacity that we have had in the management and political control of a comrade who is militant and is a member of a governing body of the SO. We have been uttering statements and making queries on the attitude of the comrade. Nevertheless, the agreement was not fulfilled of sending him to a rural front, since he was considered necessary for the development of the work in that sector. Our own limitations made us vacillate and we are now suffering the consequences of that. The complexity of the work in the political structure, as well as the shortage of solid cadres in the worker sector, the difficulty of reproduction and a style of work that is quite scattered, are factors which, in my opinion, contribute to having such situations and to achieving concrete objectives. As regards the military structure, I believe that now we are enjoying the fruits of an effort at internal organization and consolidation. What would have to be ensured is the plan for the political military training, which is what will assure for us, in part, that this structure will continue its quantitative and qualitative advance.

As concerns the support structures, such as propaganda and training, administration and projects, we have the following situation before us: In the field of propaganda and training, with the means that are available to us at this time, what is needed is greater penetration and to regulate the frequency of the meetings of training and work, as well as to make efforts to set up or make use of infrastructures which enable us to reproduce the propaganda.

Because of the distinctive qualities of some members of the Propaganda Committee and their inclusion within the university student movement, it appears feasible that they be converted into our pillars for carrying out the work in that sector.

In regard to projects, we still have not been able to achieve the political control of the institution that could represent us in D . . . , although we have been able to establish relations with some institutions that make up that organization, which has enabled us to obtain a significant increase in funds raised.

Concerning other areas all that I could say is that the problems of communication and coordination still persist and sometimes all or at least three members of the CR are involved in personnel and supply tasks. This is my opinion; the following is the situation of the metropolitan front, looked upon perhaps from a negative point of view, but seeking to be as objective as possible, and with the intention that measures be taken that would help overcome these situations:

WITH REGARD TO THE DYNAMICS AND CONSOLIDATION OF THE CR

As you know, we are a group that is quite heterogeneous as regards our personal characteristics. However, our identification with the proposals of the party, our willingness to work, and our revolutionary conviction are elements that overcome that heterogeneity. We are in a process of consolidation, as a collective of management of the party in the region. With our limitations, we are trying to make the greatest contribution to solve the problems and difficulties that we are facing. It is a natural thing, as you say, that problems appear. In my opinion, these problems are secondary, but they could result in the consolidation of the collective. There are situations that occur within the framework of all of the problems that I have described to you which sometimes make us feel exhausted and impotent.

As you are aware, comrade Rodrigo is very conscientious and has great potential, but sometimes he displays attitudes that denote political immaturity. Sometimes he has shown a bitterness and resentment that have caused me considerable concern. I do not find him to be logical. It appears that he has not been able to recognize, with revolutionary humility, that there are comrades with greater ability and training. It seems to me that the course that he was given has confused him. He requires from the FMLN and from all of his comrades an excessive perfection. In my opinion, this denotes a romantic and idealistic conception of the process. I believe that this is a crisis that can be overcome. The comrade has been showing signs of overcoming that crisis. I assure you that all of us have been making an effort, in a brotherly manner and with a spirit of comradeship, to help him overcome that situation.

I have been quite involved with Lety. You know that she has a high level of identification with the party and that she has a great capacity for dedicating herself to work. You know better than I do that Lety has quite a lot of difficulty in materializing proposals and ideas. She is quite scattered. She finds it difficult to put things into the proper organization and to analyze things objectively. I have noticed that she is making a great effort to overcome that limitation. Her need for attention is great, perhaps because of the fact that she feels that vacuum. You may also rest assured that all of us, to the extent that we are able to do so, are trying to help her overcome that limitation.

As regards Lara, you already know her and you are aware of what her great limitations are and her tendency to walk on a single straight line. Comrade Mario Gonzales has earned my respect and in my opinion he is carrying out efficiently his role of conductor and person responsible for the front. He has shown ability, responsibility and revolutionary decision to raise his capacity as a militant of the party to the ultimate consequences.

The style of work of M. G. is perhaps somewhat, although not basically, different from yours. He gives concrete replies to proposals, without entering into the details with regard to the implementation of the proposals. He is also exacting with regard to concrete results of practical work. He has shown signs of considering ideas that differ from his own, if they are well founded and contain concrete proposals.

It is obvious that he has a great overload of work. The various areas that he has to deal with and the limitations of the team mean that his workload is burdensome.

He makes a great effort to accomplish his responsibilities efficiently. Personally, I have not had any difficulty in working with him. Quite to the contrary, I believe that we have achieved a rather high level of mutual understanding and harmony.

I think that we realize that the requirements placed upon us are great and that consequently the need to make a great individual and collective effort to overcome our limitations is great.

Well, dear comrade, these are my critical evaluations of our situation in the front. You can rest assured that in expressing these evaluations I have no other intention than to help you, as well as the other comrades who are members of the CP, to have a complete picture and one that is as objective as possible of our situation at the front.

Brotherly greetings.

B

THE POLITICAL-DIPLOMATIC STRUGGLE

There has been a loss in the balance of power at the level of the political-diplomatic struggle. The elections in El Salvador represent an important gain for imperialism: they legitimate the government and encourage expectations at the international level and especially among the North American people. Duarte creates expectations with regard to respect for human rights, with regard to a political solution to the conflict, and with regard to the achievement of reforms, etc.

Duarte makes concessions which are contradictory to the promises he has made (concessions to the oligarchy, promises to the UPD, promises to imperialism, concessions to the army).

At the international level the achievement of the expectations created by Duarte are coming to be doubted (sectors of the army which made commitments to North American Congressmen demand fulfillment of the promises).

In Europe, in spite of the expectations Duarte created in some governments, the FMLN has achieved some positive gains in the diplomatic struggle. On the recent trip representatives of the FMLN-FDR were received by five European governments (France, Holland, Spain, Italy, and Germany).

Regarding Contadora

The governments that have committed themselves to the proposals continue in spite of North American opposition to present their resolution to the Security Council. The position of the United States is revealed in relation to the Central American situation. This requires the FSLN to be more objective in its grants policy. The signing of the Contadora resolution favors them but damages the FMLN. It is reasonable to predict that the resolution will not be signed because imperialism is not willing to fulfill the agreements.

Solidarity

Although solidarity at the international level has also suffered a decline, at this time it is on the rise.

Cooperative Work

Cooperative work has been increased and very good results have been obtained. Work of this kind has been done with European and Latin American governments, and with institutions such as the Church, the International Red Cross, etc. The exchange of prisoners achieved through the mediation of the Church and the International Red Cross, the commitment to give asylum to disabled fighters, etc., are the facts that show that the FMLN is being recognized as a belligerent. The progress made in cooperative work is considerable.

Internal Political Struggle

The reactivation of the mass movement is a fact. Basically it has been generated by the economic crisis. It is possible to have greater influence of the FMLN among the masses. Steps have been taken for that purpose.

In the cooperation area work has been done with the Church and the Army. This type of struggle is advancing in a positive way.

Propaganda

Steps have been taken, but a vacuum is still noticeable.

In general, on balance there is a vacuum when it comes to combining the various forms of struggle.

Finances

The financial situation of the Party at this time is very bad. There has been no possibility of covering the September quota with the fund earmarked for "projects." Steps were taken to cover it through the strategic fund. Comrades have been detached for work in the "unity" organisms for economic recovery: C . . . and . . . D . . . Although there are problems, it is foreseen that for 1985 there will be an improvement in the situation. The agreement made by the CG at the FMLN has not been finalized in regard to the distribution of the unity funds.

22.
FMLN: ANALYSIS OF LA PALMA MEETING (OCTOBER 1984)

La Palma reflects the recognition of the existence of two powers in our country. On the one hand, the Salvadoran government has control over the central administration of the State, is in charge of the Armed Forces of El Salvador, maintains control of the principal cities and part of the national territory. On the other hand, the Farabundo Martí National Liberation Front and the Democratic Revolutionary Front (FMLN-FDR) maintain control of a third of a national territory, have significant popular support in the cities and the countryside, maintain their own Armed Forces, and enjoy important support and recognition from the international community.

The FMLN-FDR delegation maintained that the essential causes of the conflict in El Salvador remain the same: the systematic violation of human rights on the part of the Salvadoran Armed Forces and the death squads; the oppression and misery of our people as a result of domination by the oligarchy; the growing, open and massive intervention of the United States government in violation of our national sovereignty; and the right of our people to self-determination. Our delegation also put forth that the political-military and diplomatic capacity of the FMLN-FDR has grown considerably and has given rise to the existence of two real powers in El Salvador. . . .

Mr. Duarte maintains that profound changes in the national situation have taken place between 1979 and 1984. Duarte maintains that there currently exists a process of democratization that is bringing the violation

Political-Diplomatic Commission, FMLN-FDR, November 1984.

of human rights of the people of El Salvador under control, that has changed the antidemocratic and repressive nature of the Salvadoran Armed Forces, that has limited the power of the oligarchy, that has initiated profound reforms and guaranteed free elections with the participation of numerous political parties.

For this reason, according to Mr. Duarte, the causes that gave rise to the war no longer exist, thus making possible and necessary the surrender of the FMLN-FDR: laying-down of arms, general amnesty and participation in elections—in short, the acceptance by our Fronts of the 1983 Constitution, which was approved by the Constituent Assembly that was presided over by Roberto D'Aubuisson and dominated by the extreme right, and the result of elections that were partial and nondemocratic.

The first step toward dialogue has produced positive results. It was agreed to create a joint commission or mechanism between the Salvadoran government and the FMLN-FDR. This commission will be responsible for continuing the process of dialogue between the two parties involved. The limits initially imposed by Mr. Duarte regarding the nature of the dialogue (the FMLN to lay down its arms as a precondition to dialogue, attemps to exclude the FDR from the talks, a dialogue aimed exclusively at FMLN-FDR participation in elections, etc.) were surpassed at La Palma because of the true strength and justness behind the FMLN-FDR's position on dialogue.

The Salvadoran people and the majority of governments in the international community have given full support to the process of dialogue which began in La Palma. However, the road to a political solution to the conflict will most likely be arduous, complex and prolonged due to the intransigence of the Salvadoran oligarchy and some sectors of the Armed Forces, but principally due to the growing political, military, economic and diplomatic intervention by the Reagan Administration in our country.

23.
ARENA AND ARMY: RESPONSES TO LA PALMA
(OCTOBER 1984)

ARENA

There is a suspicious process that has resulted in the offer made by President Duarte to the subversive organizations. . . . This dialogue must not result in any arrangement or negotiations that betray the authentic and true interests of the Salvadoran nation in order to award a share of power to those who have systematically refused to participate in procedures outlined by our constitution.

GENERAL VIDES CASANOVA, SPEECH AT THE MILITARY SCHOOL

Our Armed Forces are militarily stronger. So now, more than ever, we maintain our firm determination to win. . . . The Armed Forces accordingly supports the steps taken by the President of the Republic and the Commander-in-Chief of the Armed Forces toward obtaining peace for our people, secure in that these steps follow the new constitution in effect in our country.

24.
ARENA: CRITIQUE OF DUARTE (OCTOBER 1985)

As a group of Salvadoran citizens, and because it is the main opposition political forum, ARENA cannot but voice its pleasure over the success of President Duarte in obtaining the release of his daughter, Inés Guadalupe, her friend, and the Christian Democratic mayors who were all kidnapped. The latter were favored in a circumstantial manner.

However, it is sad to admit and remember that the negotiations carried out with the subversive delinquents ceased being a point of honor since 1980, when the respect for the laws, nationalism, and patriotism became mere words, with no meaning at all for the subsequent Christian Democratic administrations.

Never before in the history of our fatherland had we endured such a deplorable situation, in spite of the fact we have been enduring the accelerated deterioration of the same. We will continue struggling to prevent further problems, because we believe our political group is on the side of truth. Therefore, and now with renewed willingness, our patriotism encourages us to take another step forward and cry: "At the service of the fatherland."

The interests of the fatherland should be sacred to all citizens, but for a ruler whose responsibilities go beyond any effort to define these interests, there cannot be anything above his patriotism nor can there be any personal interests that will replace the national interest, the interests of the people and of the country. History is filled with examples of persons who

El Diario de Hoy, October 26, 1985.

placed their duty, their responsibility, and national interests above their own private interests and were filled with glory and made many sacrifices, as they realized that to be in command is not a privilege, but an honor and a very heavy burden. . . .

However, El Salvador, like the phoenix, will emerge from its current chaos, because it has great and valuable resources. It has professional Armed Forces, which defend our flag with high patriotism, and abide by its slogan: "God, Union, and Liberty." It also has an efficient productive sector, of which there are few in the world, that only need to have their security protected in order to give all they can. We also have an exemplary people, noble and hard-working, who aspire to live in peace in order to work with dignity and freedom, but not with that liberty that the Christian Democracy claims and only serves to remind us of Madame Roland when she said before being killed at the guillotine: "Liberty, what crimes are committed in thy name."

In view of the aforementioned, ARENA will propose to the Salvadoran people, through the National Assembly, the following:

1. A draft bill that will prohibit all types of negotiations in cases of kidnappings, as it is believed that such negotiations, such as the one we now comment on and others, have been severe blows to the fighting morale of our Armed Forces inflicted by those whose main responsibility is to maintain it unharmed and which threaten national security, which is the right of the entire people.

2. A recommendation to the Executive Branch that it break relations with the Sandino-Communist Government of Nicaragua, as this government is the instrument of international communism in the area which encourages subversion and terrorism in our country.

25.
PRESIDENT JOSÉ NAPOLEÓN DUARTE: TERRORISM AND DEMOCRACY (NOVEMBER 1985)

Events of the past years have led to brutal actions of the past weeks, making it crystal clear that in El Salvador a battle is being fought between diametrically opposed principles: Humanism and terrorism.

Terrorism has grown as a world wide cancer. With few exceptions democratic nations have been unable to eliminate or significantly reduce its criminal consequences and disastrous effects.

Speech at National Press Club, November 1, 1985.

I must make clear here today something that no well-meaning individual can dare reject. There is a symbiotic relationship between totalitarianism and terrorism. This is possible thanks to those who promote, use, protect and guarantee its impunity. Moreover, totalitarianism feeds endlessly on terrorism.

As a counterpart to totalitarianism, there exist in open societies laws and principles based in humanism: A frame of reference within which the human beings can develop as individuals and as members of society. Nonetheless, open societies are susceptible to threats, to danger and to the thirst for power of those who profess totalitarian doctrines. To attempt against these rights, is to attempt against humanity.

The language used by totalitarians and terrorists, who are one and the same, may at times sound suggestive, but I invite you to bear in mind at all times that those who preach and practice hatred and violence cannot or will not ever be champions of justice. . . .

To better understand the process that has brought my country to the present confrontation between humanism and terrorism, let me remind you that the extreme left in El Salvador has gone through three different easily identifiable stages.

In the first stage, it publicly declared war against what the subversives termed the "national oligarchy," and the extreme left expressed its intent to fight for a democratic and representative government. These positions won them the support of leaders of parties within the Socialist International and of some free-thinking intellectuals around the world. However, when the Salvadoran Government enacted the land reform which turned over large land holdings to campesino cooperatives and the rented land to the tenant farmers, when it nationalized the banks and foreign trade, the extreme left turned to assassinations of campesino leaders, to burning crops picked by the cooperatives. When the first free elections in national history were held, the guerrillas shot against civilians who were in line to cast their ballots, burned ballot boxes and put fire to city halls and schools where balloting was taking place.

The people of El Salvador confronted the threats of the Marxist guerrillas and in the midst of bullet fire turned out to cast their votes in larger numbers than ever.

In the second stage, faced with the will of the Salvadoran population, the extreme left changed its objectives and stated that its fight was against the armed forces and the Government, who it considered "puppets of Yankee imperialism." The guerrillas then, besides their military operation, committed themselves to the merciless destruction of our infrastructure— blowing up bridges, schools, health care centers, city halls, railroads, electric pylons, water reservoirs, roads and anything in their path—that, to a poor nation like mine, required the efforts of generations to build. In indiscriminately denying the population the basic services such as water, education, health, electricity and telephones, the Communists, saying that these were military objectives, were damaging the majority of the Salvadorans, who not only have turned their backs on subversion but have defied it openly in the elections. During that period, the violent actions of the extreme left, in their alliance against democracy, joined with the violence of the extreme rightist individuals who brutally and in the name of Nazi inspired anti-communism and fascism tortured and killed civilians through their infamous death squads.

Two facts altered the strategy of the extreme left and of their foreign allies. The people of El Salvador enacted a new Constitution, elected freely a President and a new Congress in an electoral contest that gave a resounding victory to the Christian Democratic Party, to which I am proud to belong. At the same time, the armed forces increased its capacity through unprecedented technical improvement and demonstrated its commitment to law and the Constitution.

As the air we breathe and the freedom we enjoy, peace can only be appreciated in its full context when it is missing, when it is lost. The fight for national peace was not only the result of my devotion for the human being but a mandate that the people had given me at my election. Because of that mandate, on October 15, 1984, as the world witnessed our fervent desire for peace, I called in the United Nations for a serious and honest dialogue with the subversives to serve as a vehicle for them to become part of the democratic process and to compete for power through elections.

I left our meeting at the church in La Palma feeling optimistic and satisfied that my idealism had been vindicated. Among other factors, had the dialogue continued only among Salvadorans, if the guerrillas had not had so many commitments to their patrons in Cuba, Nicaragua, Bulgaria, the Soviet Union, Libya, the PLO, and others, then, even in the midst of the storm, we would have found a rainbow of peace.

Criticized by national and international opinion, stunned by the improvement of our soldiers and weakened by the will of the people, the Salvadoran guerrillas accepted Yasir Arafat's thesis of terror as submitted to the Palestinian leadership. In this third stage they have joined the criminal fanatics who believed they could obtain their goals by murdering a handicapped old man aboard the *Achille Lauro,* those who kicked to death a young sailor on the TWA flight, and those who have placed bombs in airports.

This is not different from what is happening in El Salvador. The guerrillas have begun this third stage by spraying bullets on innocent people in a sidewalk café and by terrorizing families, including my own. They kidnapped many Salvadorans, among whom were 33 mayors and municipal employees of small villages, young Ana Cecilia Villeda Sosa and my daughter Inés Guadalupe, mother of three young children, arguing that they too were military objectives. I will not speak today about my suffering. I have vivid memories of the tears in my grandchildren's eyes when they asked about their mother.

Obviously, these kidnappings were not only a declaration of war. They had a well-defined objective: to provoke repression, introduce disagreement within the armed forces and my government, and frighten the civilian population by showing that no one, not even the President, was safe from terrorism.

I rejected the idea to capture the families of the guerrilla commanders, because of my Christian and humanitarian convictions.

The spontaneous solidarity nationally and internationally in rejecting the condemnable act of kidnapping was so overpowering that the ex-guerrillas and now terrorists at first even denied the act, as PLO terrorists initially denied the murder of Mr. Leon Klinghoffer.

This crime against helpless individuals underscored the irrelevancy of the FMLN's political arm, the "Democratic Revolutionary Front" (FDR). The president of the FDR, when interviewed by reporters and members of the Socialist International, answered that he did not know anything about the kidnapping and later that he could not order or propose the release of the kidnapped. But a year ago, on October 15, 1984, in La Palma, the same president of the FDR maintained that the guerrillas and the FDR were the same thing, indivisible.

To prove that their crime was not an isolated case but a new stage of terrorism, the FMLN-FDR in El Salvador kidnapped last Saturday Colonel Omar Napoleón Avalos, the Director of Civil Aviation, when he was with his children, and thus unable to defend himself without endangering their lives.

In Central America, in my own country, countless persons from all walks of life, and in the case of my family, my daughter Inés Guadalupe, would not have been victims of the merciless violence of the terrorists if terrorists did not have the support, direction, approval and timely protection of the terrorist dictatorship in Nicaragua. Nicaragua is the Central American source for totalitarianism and violence, and is the sanctuary for terrorists.

The Salvadoran guerrillas, whose headquarter is in Managua, have been trained, sheltered, armed, helped by the totalitarian governments of Nicaragua and Cuba with the support of the PLO and countries such as Libya.

I ask if terrorism could be possible without the assistance given by governments that, like Nicaragua, show total disregard to all the principles and rules of international law. . . .

The FMLN/FDR have ironically claimed a victory for the kidnapping and murder of innocent women, children and civil authorities. Ladies and gentlemen, this is not the case. If these criminal acts were to change my commitment to establish in El Salvador a pluralistic democracy with a full participation of all political ideologies, then the terrorists could claim victory before the world.

If these actions from terrorists of the extreme left and the violent right were to decrease our love for the poor and our will to reduce to a minimum social injustice, then, and rightly so, they could consider us defeated.

If we were to abandon our efforts to achieve peace, to reestablish brotherhood among Salvadorans and respect for our ideological differences as part of democracy, then the terrorists and their allies in the FDR would have the right to consider themselves the winners. . . .

I declare to you today that terrorism in El Salvador is being defeated by humanism. Building schools, health centers and creating employment is superior to sabotaging the economic infrastructure and destroying existing schools and municipal buildings. Promoting cooperation and brotherhood is greater than kidnapping and assassination. The vast majority of the Salvadoran people and my government are committed to establishing firmly our system of constitutional democracy and to improving the living standards and welfare of our people. We are winning our battle. Humanism and love for mankind will triumph over terrorism. I invite all the nations on Earth and all men of good will to join with us in this struggle so vital for freedom and prosperity.

CHAPTER

S I X

U.S. Policy

Since 1979, El Salvador and Nicaragua, two tiny Central American countries once regarded as of secondary U.S. concern, have worked their way
to the very top of the American foreign policy agenda. During the tenure
of two U.S. presidents, Jimmy Carter and Ronald Reagan, policymakers,
legislators, and public opinion leaders engaged in heated debate over the
degree and significance of outside involvement in Central America;
whether to provide, condition, or withdraw assistance, both to the Salvadoran government and to anti-Sandinista rebels; and whether, indeed, American interests there were vital or not.

Traditionally, U.S. leaders have been most concerned about limiting
foreign influence and supporting reliable anti-communist allies in the region. Carter and his Latin American policymakers took a different approach from that of his predecessors or successor. They saw problems in
U.S.–Latin American relations in "north-south" terms, viewing poverty
and underdevelopment as the chief sources of tension. They were highly
sensitive to Latin American countries' demands that the United States
respect their sovereignty. For this reason, the administration strongly supported the Panama Canal Treaty (ratified in 1981).

To the delight of Latin democrats, the Carter administration spoke out
on human rights violations in Argentina, Brazil, Chile, and Guatemala,

leading to a breakdown of military aid relationships with these countries. The Carter administration, perceiving inequity, underdevelopment, and repression as the main engine of Central American instability—not Cuba or the Soviet Union, as was later contended by the Reagan administration —considered political and economic change as necessary and inevitable.

The unfolding Nicaraguan revolution of 1978–79 would provide the administration with the first test of its philosophy. The Carter administration neither disengaged from Somoza's Nicaragua nor made an all-out effort to bolster the dictator in power. Instead, it tried, albeit fitfully, to foster a transition to a moderate post-Somoza regime. The main U.S. effort was the formation of an international mediation commission, including Guatemala and the Dominican Republic, that sought a negotiated settlement in Nicaragua (see Chapter 2). In testimony before Congress, then Assistant Secretary of State for Inter-American Affairs Viron Vaky justified the administration's effort, saying, "This is fundamentally a Nicaraguan crisis and Cuba is not the only or even the most important of the supporters of the anti-Somoza rebellion" (Document 2). By opposing Somoza and promoting a peaceful transition, he argued, the United States could win the Nicaraguans' gratitude and future friendship while keeping the Sandinistas from monopolizing power.

Somoza proved stubborn and skillful at manipulating the United States; the Carter administration was slow and uncertain in pressuring Somoza. When in June 1978 Carter wrote a letter to Somoza noting some progress on human rights (Document 1), the dictator portrayed this as an endorsement of his policies. The moderate opposition was often disunited, and the Sandinistas were determined to win predominant power. Mediation efforts consequently failed, and in July 1979 the United States had no choice but to recognize the emergence of a new Nicaraguan government (Document 3). Vaky argued that Somoza "deliberately sought to polarize and radicalize the situation [to force] the moderate opposition (and the U.S.) . . . to support his continuance in power" (Document 4). He warned of a continued "polarizing dynamic of pressure for change, terrorism, and political radicalization" in Central America, a classic statement of the liberal position that internal problems would inevitably produce further revolutionary upheavals and that the United States should accommodate them. The new Nicaraguan government, he said, was "not distinguishably Marxist or Cuban in orientation" (Document 5).

In a September 1979 statement (Document 6), Deputy Secretary of State Warren Christopher stressed the administration's intention "to develop a positive relationship with the new government of Nicaragua based on the principles of nonintervention, equality, and mutual respect." In this way, the United States hoped to strengthen moderate elements in the regime and persuade the new government to moderate its domestic and foreign policies. By providing an alternative to dependence on the USSR, by discrediting the idea the United States was the inevitable enemy of Nicaraguan progress, the administration thought it could limit Soviet-bloc influence in Nicaragua. In September 1980, therefore, President Carter certified Nicaragua as eligible for U.S. aid (Document 7).

Meanwhile, the Carter administration welcomed the October coup by reform-minded officers in El Salvador. To help the new regime weather the outbreak of violence by right and left in subsequent months, the administration prepared to send $50 million in economic aid and $6 million in nonlethal military aid, and also considered sending U.S. Army personnel to help train Salvadoran security forces. In February 1980, Salvadoran Archbishop Oscar Romero wrote President Carter, criticizing the conduct of the Salvadoran military and warning aid would "sharpen the injustice and repression" (Document 8). Then in December 1980, following the murder of four American nuns in El Salvador, all U.S. aid was suspended. A State Department memorandum that preceded a U.S. investigative mission to El Salvador recognized death squad activities by "elements of the army and security forces" and asserted that "right-wing and official violence must be contained or . . . El Salvador will fall into the hands of right- or left-wing extremists with whom the U.S. cannot cooperate" (Document 9). In the last weeks of Carter's administration, economic and military aid to El Salvador was restored, and in his last days as president, Carter approved $5 million in military aid to El Salvador from his own contingency fund.

Conservatives were critical of the Carter administration's Central America policy, advocating increased support for the Salvadoran regime and a harder line against Nicaragua. In "The Hobbes Problem" (Document 10), Professor Jeane Kirkpatrick suggested that the "primacy of order" and the slow pace at which "political tradition and cultures change" required that the Salvadoran insurgency be defeated before reforms were sought. In "U.S. Security and Latin America," she argued that Carter's activism in Nicaragua brought down "an American ally . . . confronting an opponent well armed by the Soviet bloc" (Document 11). The platform of the Republican Party (Document 12) and the Santa Fe report (Document 13), both of which focused on Cuba's role in regional instability, also urged a turnabout in U.S. policy toward Central America. Several drafters of the Santa Fe report were rewarded with government posts in the Reagan administration.

Ronald Reagan came to office in January 1981 riding high on a wave of conservatism and public disenchantment with the perceived weakness of Carter's foreign policy. Impressed by her writing and her conclusions, Reagan selected Mrs. Kirkpatrick as U.S. ambassador to the UN and included her in his cabinet. The tone and substance of U.S. policy toward Central America shifted abruptly.

Now it was the Soviet-Cuban threat in Central America that was the main concern. An early State Department "white paper," disclosing military ties between Moscow, Havana, and the Salvadoran rebels, presented El Salvador's civil war as a "textbook case" of Soviet indirect aggression. "The situation in El Salvador," read the report, "presents a strikingly familiar case of Soviet, Cuban and other Communist military involvement in a politically troubled Third World country" (Document 14).

While the State Department supported large-scale aid for the Salvadoran government to counter the Marxist guerrillas, it remained open to negotiating its differences with the Sandinistas (Document 15). After having met with Nicaraguan leader Daniel Ortega, U.S. Assistant Secretary of State Thomas Enders promoted a secret exchange of letters proposing ways of resolving bilateral differences (Document 16).

In early 1982, concern over stability of the whole Caribbean Basin, heightened by the establishment of now two Marxist regimes—one in Nicaragua, one in Grenada—prompted President Reagan to answer petitions for a Caribbean "Marshall Plan." In a speech before the OAS, President Reagan unveiled his Caribbean Basin Initiative (Document 17). Following the administration's preference for private-sector solutions and for trade rather than aid, the CBI sought to grant major trade concessions for several Basin states, excluding Nicaragua and Grenada.

In Congress, Democrats tried to reorient U.S. policy in line with their own view of the Central American crisis, a view more akin to the Carter administration's. They succeeded in making U.S. aid to El Salvador conditional upon presidential certification of progress on elections and human rights there (Document 18). A House Intelligence Committee staff report (Document 19) criticized the CIA's failure to gather "firm information about . . . violence by the right and the security forces" in El Salvador, although Congress did accept the same committee's conclusion that Nicaragua was providing training, supplies, and logistical support to the Salvadoran guerrillas (Document 20). In December 1982, eighteen congressional Democrats, led by Representative Michael Barnes (D—Ind.), chairman of the House Subcommittee on Western Hemisphere Affairs, presented a comprehensive "Democratic alternative" to administration policy (Document 21). They questioned whether economic assistance, without "meaningful social development or reform," could produce regional stability.

Responsive to these critiques and aware that a failure to curb death squad activity and restructure the Salvadoran military would undermine the counterinsurgency effort, some elements in the administration began to put more stress on criticizing human-rights violations in El Salvador. U.S. Ambassador to El Salvador Dean Hinton, for example, strongly attacked Salvadoran death squads in October 1982 (Document 22). Six months later, Secretary of State George Shultz stated that military efforts and reform must go hand in hand (Document 23). Vice-President George Bush's trip to El Salvador in December 1983 marked a turning point. He met privately with Salvadoran military commanders and warned publicly that extreme rightists who favored military rule and used death squads against their opponents "are the best friends the Soviets, the Cubans, the Sandinista comandantes, and the Salvadoran guerrillas have" (Document 24).

The administration stood firm in its opposition to the Salvadoran insurgency (and the Nicaraguan government). In his April 1983 speech to a joint session of Congress, Reagan warned that public opinion would hold Congress responsible if it stood "by passively while the people of Central America are delivered to totalitarianism" (Document 25). He signaled a new offensive against Nicaragua, which he accused of masterminding regional subversion. Under Secretary of Defense Fred Ikle made it clear that military victory was the objective in both Nicaragua and El Salvador (Document 26).

To encourage a bipartisan consensus supporting its controversial Central America policy, the administration appointed in the summer of 1983 a "national bipartisan commission," headed by Henry Kissinger, that would explore the Central American question. The commission's report (Document 27) called for a major economic aid program to the region. A majority of the commission's members held that "existing incentives and pressures" (i.e., support for Nicaraguan rebels) should be sustained, but also supported certification of progress on human rights in El Salvador.

Due to congressional pressures and administration reappraisals, a bipartisan consensus on El Salvador was beginning to take shape. But critics like former U.S. Ambassador to El Salvador Robert White continued to argue the administration was ignoring death squad activity in El Salvador (Document 28). The election of José Napoleón Duarte as president of El Salvador in April 1984, however, and the Salvadoran military's ability to force the guerrillas into retreat made political support and aid for the Salvadoran government more acceptable in the United States, as congressional debates on Salvadoran aid in 1984 demonstrated (Document 29). Liberal Democrats like Representatives Gary Studds and David Obey and conservative Republicans like Robert Lagomarsino and William Broomfield differed over U.S. regional policy, but each side emphasized that in its own way it sought to help Duarte.

In the spring of 1984, public attention shifted from El Salvador to Nicaragua, specifically to U.S. aid for anti-Sandinista rebels, usually referred to as "contras." As early as November 1981, Reagan had approved covert operations against the Sandinistas employing these paramilitary forces, and over the next year the plans were implemented. Congress passed laws limiting the funding and extent of these operations, beginning with the Boland Amendment (Document 30) and in May 1984, following the mining of Nicaraguan harbors by an elite CIA unit, Congress suspended funding.

The administration worked hard to reverse Congress's position and to maintain aid to the contras. Assistant Secretary of State Langhorne Motley argued that U.S. support for the anti-Sandinista rebels could help prevent what most Americans wished to avoid in Nicaragua: both another Cuba and another Vietnam (Document 31). Secretary of State George Shultz put U.S. policy into a global context, portraying Nicaraguan rebels, like those in Afghanistan, Cambodia, and Angola, as part of an "international democratic revolution" fighting Soviet domination (Document 32).

The battle over aid to the rebels came to a head in the spring of 1985 when the administration tried to persuade Congress to end the ban on contra funding. Reagan himself offered a "peace plan" (Document 33) to demonstrate that he was seeking a negotiated settlement in Nicaragua. Representatives Barnes and Hamilton (D—N.Y.) proposed an alternative plan that emphasized negotiations and barred money for contra funding altogether (Document 34). The issue was fiercely debated in April 1985 (Document 35), and aid was voted down even when the administration limited its request to "nonmilitary aid." President Reagan's pledge to seek a political settlement and contra respect for human rights and not to support the return to power of former supporters of Somoza—together with Nicaraguan President Daniel Ortega's trip to Moscow—helped win passage for "humanitarian aid" in June (Document 36). The statement by Oklahoma Representative Dave McCurdy (Document 37) showed the willingness of some Democrats to hammer out a compromise with the administration.

The Reagan and Carter administrations had many points of difference and some areas of continuity concerning their Central American policy. Both wanted to avoid pro-Soviet states in the region, but the Carter administration thought the best way to achieve this end was by pressing reform upon military regimes, including El Salvador's, in order to remove the sources of instability. To prevent a Marxist guerrilla victory in El Salvador, however, the Carter administration gave aid to El Salvador in 1981. It also believed a conciliatory U.S. policy might moderate the Sandinista regime.

Originally, the Reagan administration stressed a Soviet-Cuban role in fomenting rebellion in El Salvador, but over time, internal debates and public pressure led it to adopt some of the Carterite notions of reform, in coordination with increased aid. On Nicaragua, the administration believed that the Carter policy of conciliation was no longer useful, if it ever was. After failing to exact commitments from Nicaragua to refrain from supporting Salvadoran guerrillas in exchange for a U.S. nonintervention pledge, the U.S. exerted military and economic pressure on the Sandinistas to induce them to meet U.S. concerns. Many Democrats continued to believe that the administration in fact sought nothing less than the over-throw of the Sandinista regime.

American political leaders had reached a consensus on Salvador policy. They agreed that the Salvadoran government should be supported in the struggle against the guerrillas while encouraged toward greater democratization and respect for human rights, although they put different priorities on these two factors.

No such basic agreement was reached on U.S. policy toward Nicaragua, over which heated controversy continued. Some liberals still opposed support for the contras and favored a rapprochement with Nicaragua. Other Democrats and some Republicans were willing to back the contras and take other measures against Nicaragua as a means of pressuring Managua toward a diplomatic settlement.

I
THE CARTER ADMINISTRATION

1.
PRESIDENT JIMMY CARTER: LETTER TO SOMOZA (JUNE 1978)

THE WHITE HOUSE
Washington

Dear Mr. President:

I read your statements to the press on June 19 with great interest and appreciation. The steps toward respecting human rights that you are considering are important and heartening signs; and, as they are translated into actions, will mark a major advance for your nation in answering some of the criticisms recently aimed at the Nicaraguan government.

I am pleased to learn of your willingness to cooperate with the Inter-American Commission on Human Rights. I believe that multilateral institutions can be a most appropriate and effective means of protecting human rights and alleviating concerns expressed about them. I sincerely hope that your government can rapidly reach agreement with the Commission on a date for their visit.

The Commission will be favorably impressed by your decision to allow the members of the so-called "Group of Twelve" to return to peaceful lives in Nicaragua. The freedoms of movement and of expression that are at stake in this case are among the central human rights that the Commission seeks to protect.

You have spoken about a possible amnesty for Nicaraguans being held in jail for political reasons. I urge you to take the promising steps you have suggested; they would serve to improve the image abroad of the human rights situation in Nicaragua.

I was also encouraged to hear your suggestions for a reform of the electoral system in order to ensure fair and free elections in which all political parties could compete fairly. This step is essential to the functioning of a democracy.

I would also like to take this opportunity to encourage you to sign and ratify the American Convention of Human Rights. I have signed this agreement and am working hard to have my country ratify the Convention.

I look forward to hearing of the implementation of your decisions and appreciate very much your announcement of these constructive actions. I hope that you will continue to communicate fully with my Ambassador, Mauricio Solaun, who enjoys my complete confidence.

Sincerely,

JIMMY CARTER

His Excellency
General Anastasio Somoza Debayle
President of the Republic of Nicaragua
Managua

2.
ASSISTANT SECRETARY OF STATE VIRON VAKY: TESTIMONY ON NICARAGUA (JUNE 1979)

Nicaragua is today the scene of a war of national destruction. Thousands of Nicaraguans have died and thousands more have left their homes or fled

Given before the House of Representatives Subcommittee on Inter-American Affairs.

to neighboring countries. The economy is in shambles. Political extremisms are rising. Hatred and fear have replaced order. . . . Nicaragua's tragedy stems from dynastic rule. Times have changed, Nicaragua has changed, but the Government of Nicaragua has not.

Whereas other countries in Latin America have developed modern systems of government and at least partially institutionalized military establishments, the Nicaraguan Government and armed forces have remained inherently the personal instruments of the Somoza family.

Over the past 20 years, a widening breach has opened between the Somozas and Nicaraguans in all walks of life. The actions necessary to keep power in a growing country in changing times have steadily widened that breach. Today, the failure of trust between the people of Nicaragua and their President is fundamental and irreversible.

Although some antagonisms go back 40 years and more, the current breakdown began in 1972, when an earthquake virtually destroyed Nicaragua's capital city of Managua. International relief efforts were exploited for personal gain. Corruption became so pervasive that it strangled freedom of initiative.

Rising middle class and business discontent was not allowed political expression. Nine out of ten opposition parties, including a dissident group from Somoza's own party, were kept from participating in the 1974 presidential elections, which were run according to procedures that Nicaragua's Roman Catholic bishops warned were the equivalent of "legal war."

Shortly thereafter, the FSLN, then a small radical band with a record of unsuccessful guerrilla skirmishes dating to the early 1960's, carried out a spectacular coup. Several key officials were captured at a Christmas party, then released in exchange for political prisoners.

Somoza instituted press censorship and a state of siege. The national guard launched a campaign against the FSLN. Little distinction was made between criticism and subversion. Such widespread and arbitrary abuses took place that citizens and institutions across the entire political spectrum turned against the regime.

The assasination of Pedro Joaquín Chamorro in January 1978 fanned tension into open conflagration. Chamorro, a leader of the Conservative Party, was publisher of the daily *La Prensa*. Over the years, his integrity and eloquence, although not effective in dislodging the Somozas from power, had made him a symbol of principled, legitimate opposition.

I believe this assassination, more than any other single factor, catalyzed opposition to the regime. It resurrected the ghost of the political assassination of Sandino in 1934—and with it the fears and outrage of a frustrated people. It led to an unprecedented outburst of popular revulsion. Private businessmen and professional leaders joined with political parties outside the Government in what later came to be known as the "Broad Opposition

Front." This organization, known by its Spanish initials as the FAO, united the many hitherto amorphous strands of moderate opposition to the regime. A general strike was called to force President Somoza's resignation.

Somoza remained unyielding. He would relinquish the presidency when his term ended in 1981, he said, but not before.

The failure of the peaceful general strike was followed by violence. Last August, FSLN guerrillas captured the entire Nicaraguan National Assembly. Applauding crowds lined the streets to the airport as the Sandinistas departed with some freed comrades. The dramatic photographs and reports accompanying this bold feat won the FSLN an international reputation.

In September a general insurrection began. The business community renewed the general strike. FSLN cadres, supported by large numbers of youthful civilian irregulars spontaneously adhering to their cause, gained control of substantial areas in many of Nicaragua's major towns. The superior firepower of the National Guard, including air attacks on urban areas, finally suppressed the revolt. Thousands of casualties, tens of thousands of refugees, and untold destruction and economic disruption marked Nicaragua's agony.

In an effort to head off the growing violence and radicalization, the Dominican Republic, Guatemala, and the United States offered to help search for a peaceful solution. Both the Government of Nicaragua and the FAO accepted the offer, made within the framework of an OAS resolution late last September. . . .

In our view, the mediation temporarily attenuated the climate of violence, and identified a number of procedures by which a process of reconciliation might develop. But Somoza's fundamental rigidity also demonstrated the tenuousness of hopes for compromise. Intransigence then fed intransigence with the relentlessness of a self-fulfilling prophecy. Week by week, Somoza's position deteriorated and his opposition became more radicalized.

The last three lines of the Report of the Mediation submitted to the Secretary of State concluded that "in the absence of a negotiated solution, there is a danger that escalating violence in Nicaragua may transcend the limits of an internal conflict and affect the peace and tranquility of the whole of Central America."

The mediator's fear that the conflict would soon cease to be a purely Nicaraguan matter was amply justified.

For more than 40 years, the Somozas have symbolized personal power in a region of the world whose modern history could be written as the struggle to overcome abuse of authority.

Opponents of the Somoza dynasty thus have great sympathy throughout

Latin America. Over the past year, sympathy has turned into support in neighboring democratic countries, particularly Venezuela, Mexico, Costa Rica, and Panama.

Last summer, when the national guard entered Costa Rica in pursuit of FSLN raiders, Venezuela and Panama rallied strongly to Costa Rica's support. Earlier this month, Colombia, Ecuador, Peru, and Bolivia—the remaining members of the Andean Pact—moved with Venezuela to seek Somoza's departure.

Classically, Cuba sees Nicaragua's agony as a chance to advance its own interests. Cuban support for the Sandinista cause has been indirect, but has recently increased. The possibility that the particular guerrilla factions Cuba has supported and helped arm could come to exert significant political leverage is cause for concern.

Cuban involvement increases support for Somoza within the national guard and alarms those who fear it could lead to the imposition of communism in the guise of democracy. Unless the crisis is settled rapidly, the fighting could thus increase ideological tensions and involve other countries in Central America.

But we cannot lose sight of the basic issue. This is fundamentally a Nicaraguan crisis. And Cuba is not the only or even the most important of the supporters of the anti-Somoza rebellion. Nicaraguans and our democratic friends in Latin America have no intention of seeing Nicaragua turned into a second Cuba, and are determined to prevent the subversion of their anti-Samoza cause by Castro. We join them in that important objective.

Where then do we stand?

Our actions are based on three fundamental principles. First, we are firmly convinced that the Nicaraguan people should be allowed to work out a political settlement to their internal crisis without outside ideological or military imposition.

Second, we are not rigid and do not seek to prescribe forms of government for other people. But we do firmly adhere to what the Andean Chiefs of State called "the democratic values of the American countries."

Third, we do not presume to dictate events or to play the role of arbiter in Nicaragua or elsewhere in Central America. The joint action of the nations of the hemisphere is required to help Nicaraguans find a way out of their agony.

There are two fundamental dimensions to the Nicaraguan crisis. The heart of the crisis is the domestic political question of a people's desire to end dynastic rule and the consequent issue of political succession—by whom and how this is to be accomplished. The other dimension is the resulting conflict, the violence that has become civil war and taken on a life of its own, that has brought in foreign involvement and partisanship

—all of which is in turn converting the domestic political succession issue into a wider issue of systemic order.

These two dimensions interact on each other. It is not possible to deal with one to the exclusion of the other. No political solution to the succession issue is possible as long as war continues; on the other hand, it is not possible to end the fighting, or to achieve an end to arms supply, without clear evidence that a satisfactory political solution has been achieved.

Our conclusions thus have been: No end to or resolution of the crisis is possible that does not start with the departure of Somoza from power and the end of his regime. No negotiation, mediation, or compromise can be achieved any longer with a Somoza government. Too much blood, too much hate, too much polarization have occurred for this to be possible. The solution can only begin with a sharp break from the past.

The departure of Somoza without a clear and viable structure, process or sequence to take his place, risks continued internecine political struggle, prolonged disorder, or the advent of extremism. That, too, is to be avoided.

The longer the war continues, the greater the likelihood that the conflict will spread, evolving into a complex crisis of international proportions, and the greater the problems any future government must face. The killing must stop.

Finally, the mounting human tragedy requires a major international effort to extend humanitarian assistance and to end the fighting.

With these thoughts in mind, we determined to reconvene the 17th Meeting of Foreign Ministers of the OAS to consider what we believe to be a legitimate threat to the peace and an issue of grave concern to the hemisphere.

Our proposals were outlined by Secretary Vance in his initial statement to the OAS. He called for a prompt replacement of the Somoza regime in a way that would mark a clear break with the past; formation of a broadly based transition government; negotiation thereafter of a cease-fire to end the war; and humanitarian aid. We asked for an OAS effort to foster and support these steps, and suggested that an OAS presence might be necessary to assist in their realization.

The reactions are worth noting.

Overwhelmingly, the nations of the hemisphere believe a change must occur. They favor an interim government, broadly based to reflect all groups in Nicaraguan society, to lead a transition to democracy based on self-determination.

A majority of OAS members clearly and openly sympathize with the opposition now fighting Somoza, and are increasingly showing it—by breaking relations with the Somoza Government and supporting the Sandinistas. Major states—Mexico, Colombia, Venezuela, Peru, Brazil, Argentina—all made clear they would approve no action that tried to save the status quo or prevent change.

The member states were plainly not prepared to approve an OAS peace force at the present time—an idea we had suggested as one way to deal with the danger of prolonged disorders after a Somoza departure. This reflected how deeply the American states were sensitized by the Dominican intervention of 1965, and how deeply they fear physical intervention.

The consequence was a revised resolution, which we supported, approved by 17 states. This resolution called for change and a return to democracy, and authorized member states to take such steps as they could to achieve these objectives. We would have preferred more specificity, but we believe the resolution is a good one and provides a basis for measures to resolve the crisis.

The proper role for the United States in this situation is not to add to the partisan factionalism. It is, rather, to work with other countries to create conditions under which the Nicaraguans themselves can resolve their agony. The tragedy will not end until a government emerges that is capable of earning the trust of the Nicaraguan people. The hatreds now dividing Nicaragua suggest such a government will take time to establish itself.

We are actively consulting with other nations to see what can be done. While we do so, we must remember that human suffering in Nicaragua is increasing day-by-day, hour-by-hour. We have taken steps to make food available to the Red Cross for distribution in Nicaragua, and we are consulting with other governments and international agencies on the provision of medical supplies and shelter to the victims of the fighting.

Assisting the refugees from civil strife, however, is but part of the massive humanitarian and reconstruction effort we believe will be required. This effort should also include bilateral and multilateral assistance to enhance integration and help regenerate a sense of progress and confidence throughout Central America.

3.
STATE DEPARTMENT: ON NICARAGUA'S REVOLUTION (JULY 17–18, 1979)

We hope the resignation this morning of Anastasio Somoza Debayle as President of Nicaragua will end that country's tragic civil war and will enable Nicaraguans to begin the process of reconstructing their country in peace and freedom.

From the beginning of the violence that set Nicaraguans against each other, the Organization of American States and its member nations, including the United States, have worked to facilitate a peaceful and democratic solution to the civil strife in Nicaragua.

After the bloody outbreak of violence and insurrection last September, we joined with other friendly governments to encourage a negotiated solution. The suffering and abuses documented by the Inter-American Human Rights Commission had already then made clear that the alternative to a negotiated peaceful settlement would be even worse violence.

A three-nation mediating group, in which the United States joined with the Dominican Republic and Guatemala, worked with both President Somoza and his growing opposition. The mediators succeeded in obtaining the agreement of major opposition forces to an internationally supervised plebiscite that would have permitted Nicaraguans to determine their future by secret ballot. President Somoza rejected the mediators' proposed formula for a plebiscite, despite warnings that rejection would likely lead to renewed violence.

Over the past several months, President Somoza became increasingly isolated. Nicaraguans of many persuasions cast their lot with the armed insurrection against him and against his family's domination of Nicaraguan life. In June, the nations of the Americas, assembled in the OAS, overwhelmingly called for the "immediate and definitive replacement of the Somoza regime [with] a democratic government."

The result this morning is the end of the most prolonged remaining system of personal rule in the modern world. To facilitate the transition, we will receive Mr. Somoza in this country, where he will join his wife, who is an American citizen. While in the United States, Mr. Somoza will have the protection of U.S. law; he will also be subject to its obligations.

Today's events will not end the suffering in Nicaragua. The war has created hundreds of thousands of refugees, both within Nicaragua and in neighboring countries. There is a great need for food, medicine, and emergency shelter. In the last few weeks, we have made nearly 1,000 tons of food and a large supply of medicine available to the Nicaraguan Red Cross. Now more can be done.

With the prospect that the hostilities that hindered the administration of humanitarian assistance will be ending, we can expand the emergency airlift to feed the hungry. This effort will be coordinated with the efforts of international agencies and with other nations throughout the hemisphere and the world.

A caretaker regime is in place to begin the process of national reconciliation. A government of national reconstruction, formed initially in exile, will assume power from the caretaker regime. It has pledged to avoid reprisals, to provide sanctuary to those in fear, to begin immediately the immense tasks of national reconstruction, and to respect human rights and hold free elections. The Inter-American Human Rights Commission and leaders from throughout the hemisphere, many of whom, like the members of the Andean group, took the lead in assisting the resolution of the conflict, will be present to offer their support.

Throughout this long and difficult period, we have repeatedly consulted with countries in the region. These countries have played an active and important role in facilitating the transition in Nicaragua. We will continue to seek their counsel in the days ahead, as we prepare to work with the new government.

We wish to look to the future and to build a new relationship of mutual respect with the people and Government of Nicaragua.

4.
ASSISTANT SECRETARY OF STATE VIRON VAKY: LETTER TO REP. LEE HAMILTON (JUNE 1979)

Somoza's refusal to engage in any meaningful dialogue with opposition elements and his rejection of the peaceful general strike of mid-summer 1978 led to the violent insurrection of September 1978. By then it was clear that an extraordinary effort to find a peaceful transition was urgently needed to head off further violence and bloodshed. We consequently joined in the tripartite mediation effort, pursuant to the OAS call in its resolution of September 23, 1978, for member states to extend their cooperation and good offices for such an effort.

In retrospect, the decision to attempt a mediation effort aimed at persuading Somoza to step down and facilitate an orderly transition to an interim government made up largely of moderates was, in my view, a sound one. It tackled the succession crisis at a time when it was still possible to achieve a moderate outcome and hold the radical elements of the Sandinista movement in check. Indeed, the mediation effort attenuated the climate of violence and forced the Sandinista guerrilla activity into the background and into virtual suspension. Recognizing the fragility of the opposition coalition, the mediators, without making special concessions to them, were nevertheless able to bring them along to direct talks and still

In U.S. House of Representatives, "United States Policy Toward Nicaragua" (Washington, 1979).

preserve the essential unity of the group. Thus the effort in effect catalyzed the moderate opposition elements into a relatively cohesive group capable of functioning. The mediation also identified procedures for effecting a viable transition and reconciliation, and secured full opposition support for them.

What was not foreseen was the obduracy of Somoza in negotiating his resignation and departure. It is now evident, looking back, that Somoza used the mediation to gain time in the belief that he could strengthen the National Guard and simply hold on. Somoza's fundamental rigidity shattered any possibility for compromise and a peaceful end to the Somoza dynasty.

The failure of the mediation effort was clearly a watershed. That failure came close to destroying the moderate opposition, leaving it with no alternative but withdrawal or radicalization. When the U.S. Government failed to react to Somoza's rejection of the mediators' last proposal, the opposition, the Sandinistas and the opposition's supporting patrons in Venezuela, Costa Rica, Panama and elsewhere concluded that either the U.S. was not serious or in any event that there was no solution to the crisis except by force of arms. It is from this period that the heavy buildup of the Sandinistas took place, and it was only after the mediation's failure and the beginning of the civil war in May 1979 that Sandinista elements became in effect legitimized as the main opposition leadership. And interestingly enough, although Cuba had supported the Sandinista movement from the mid-sixties, it was not until May, when chance of military success suddenly became real, that Cuban material support jumped to significant levels.

From May onward it became clear that Somoza could not survive until the oft-proclaimed end of his term in 1981, and that a military collapse was entirely likely. It was our view that a purely military solution would provide the least auspicious prospect for true self-determination and an enduring democratic outcome to Nicaragua's agony. The growing power of the Marxist leadership in the Sandinista army also raised increasing concerns that the final outcome might be determined by these elements on the basis of their control of coercive military power. We therefore again sought ways to promote an end to the conflict, and a transition that would maximize the possibility for all elements of the opposition to have a say in the transition. A pluralistic set-up appeared to be the best bet for avoiding an "ideological or military imposition" of a final outcome.

One is tempted to believe that throughout the last years Somoza persistently frustrated attempts for a moderate solution, and deliberately sought to polarize and radicalize the situation in the belief that if he could make his prophecy of "après moi le déluge" self-fulfilling there would be no choice for the moderate opposition (and the U.S.) but to support his continuance in power. Support for Somoza, however, was never, I believe, a viable option for us. A lid could not be kept indefinitely on the instability and the deep alienation and opposition to his rule which existed in Nicaragua. To "hold one's nose and support an unsavory dictator" as Evans and Novak recently argued was never a prudent or wise course. It would have ignored the depth and the widespread make-up of the opposition to Somoza, and would have missed the true essence of the problem itself.

The tragedy in the Nicaraguan situation may in historical perspective lie in the perhaps unknowable answer to the question of whether we should have—or could have—exerted greater pressure and leverage to secure agreement to a peaceful transition when that was relatively easy to accomplish.

5.
ASSISTANT SECRETARY OF STATE VIRON VAKY: TRENDS IN CENTRAL AMERICA (SEPTEMBER 1979)

Much of Central America—particularly the northern tier—is gripped by a polarizing dynamic of pressure for change, terrorism, and potential radicalization. These wrenching instabilities are rooted in basic underlying structural problems and vulnerabilities. The impact of recent events in Nicaragua is assuredly a factor in the internal politics of all countries in Central America. But even without Nicaragua the situation would be volatile.

The nations of the region face a number of common, interrelated social and economic problems, most of which produce direct pressures for political and systemic change.

- With the exception of Costa Rica, and to some extent Panama, societies in the region are characterized by deep class and, in some cases, ethnic divisions, endemic violence, political atomization, and distrust. Inequalities of opportunity mark the social, political, and class structures in varying degrees. The demands of new middle class entrepreneurs and professionals—an educated, informed, articulate, and generally ambitious group —for a greater national role and share of political power have frequently not been accommodated. The minimal needs of workers and peasants, whose ranks have been swollen by the population explosion, have also remained unmet in varying degrees. Growing social tensions and defeated aspirations have, therefore, become natural breeding grounds for alienation, opposition, and violence.

Department of State Bulletin, January 1980.

- With the possible exception of Costa Rica and Panama, virtually all of these countries are characterized by unequal and inequitable economic growth, national poverty, and maldistribution of income. While statistically many of these nations show respectable growth, the benefits of progress have, in most cases, accrued to traditional elites; the masses of the people find their situation little changed. Malnutrition and illiteracy rates remain high among the poor majority. Unemployment and underemployment are high and growing.

- Again with the exception of Costa Rica, and to some degree Panama—although the system there is not yet fully open—political institutions have, in the past, tended to be authoritarian and resistant to change. As pressures build up, governments have tended to rely on repression of dissent. Movements expressing pressures for modernization or more basic demands for equity have too often been frustrated by electoral manipulation and violence, censorship of the media, outlawing of political parties, and suspension of constitutional guarantees. Where legitimate channels of redress are choked off, the political situation tends to polarize to the extremes and the likelihood of peaceful evolution and change is reduced.

- Institutions of all kinds—from public order and social services to press and political parties—are being undermined by socioeconomic strains, human rights violations, and terrorism. These dynamics in turn produce obsession with survival and a temptation to blame external causes for the region's difficulties.

- Economic stress in the form of world inflation, fluctuating commodity prices, and recession have decreased real incomes and lessened the ability of governments to meet popular needs. Petroleum costs have quadrupled, with increasingly severe cumulative effects.

- New political lines and new economic challenges have been drawn in the region. Sandinista Nicaragua, Costa Rica, and Panama will not communicate easily with the passionately antileftist governments of the northern tier. Yet if communication is imperfect, regional tensions will grow, and the cooperation necessary to sustain a strong regional economy and Central American common market will be impeded. Fortunately, indications are that these potential costs are recognized, and tentative but significant efforts at "bridge-building" are in train by all national actors.

In sum, deep grievances; legitimate needs for reform, growth, and modernization; and basic demands for equity are all coursing through the region. These give rise to equally deep pressures for political and systemic change. As in other parts of the world, those aspirations and demands are so fundamental that change cannot be avoided. Defense of the status quo cannot prevent it or cap instability for long; it can only radicalize the dynamics at work.

A complicating factor is that Castroist/Marxist and extreme insurgent groups have seized upon these legitimate aspirations and unstable situations to advance their own objectives. Thereby, they may exacerbate the tensions and the violence, but they do not cause them. The upsurge of terrorism and subversion unfortunately often confuses perception of the realities and strengthens tendencies by those benefiting from the status quo to misidentify the issues and focus on insurgency rather than on the underlying core problems.

If there is any one central motif that characterizes Central America today, it is this intense—and essentially inevitable—pressure for change which has swept into the region. The central issue, in turn, is not whether change is to occur but whether that change is to be violent and radical—or peaceful and evolutionary and preserving individual rights and democratic values. . . .

Initially formed in exile, the new Nicaraguan Government is a coalition comprised of former guerrilla and civic leaders. . . .

. . . The Sandinista National Directorate, made up of guerrilla leaders, some with close ties to Cuba, wields major influence.

Since the GNR formally took office July 20, the following have become clear.

- Nicaragua's humanitarian and reconstruction needs are immediate and too great to be met by Nicaraguans alone.

- Administrative confusion and improvisation remain widespread, but the change of government is popularly accepted, and there is definite movement toward restoration of public order.

- The GNR has shown generally moderate, pluralistic tendencies in its initial policies. It is not distinguishably Marxist or Cuban in orientation, although Marxist figures are present in key positions. It has restrained reprisals, promulgated a decree guaranteeing individual rights, and permitted an independent press and radio. It has promised free elections. In foreign affairs the GNR has indicated a desire for friendly relations with all countries including their northern neighbors. Nicaraguan leaders have denied any intention of "exporting revolution."

- Nevertheless, the political situation remains very fluid, with heterogeneity, confusion, and flux in the power dynamics. The country's political and economic future thus remain unclear, and many outcomes or scenarios are still possible within the framework of the Sandinista revolution.

The central issue in the Nicaraguan situation, therefore—whether in terms of its internal system, its relations to Cuba, its attitude toward its neighbors—is the extent to which a moderate, pluralistic, and equitable democratic order can emerge in a country with few democratic traditions and whose new and inexperienced leaders could resort to authoritarianism to cope with the enormous tasks facing them.

The course of the Nicaraguan revolution will thus depend in part on how the United States perceives it and relates to it. Indeed, Nicaragua's future internal policies and relationships with the outside world will, in fact, be determined by those Nicaraguans who best define and meet the country's needs during the reconstruction period. . . .

El Salvador—the smallest and most densely populated country in Central America—presents a classic setting for social and political unrest. Its population density—at 565 persons per square mile—is the highest of any country in the Western Hemisphere. Population growth of 3.2% and agricultural land pressures have pushed the unemployment-underemployment rate above 30%. New jobs in industry absorb less than one-sixth of labor force entrants, and agriculture provides jobs for only one-half of new job seekers. Many Salvadorans, faced with poverty and lack of opportunity, have chosen to emigrate.

The export-oriented economy is characterized by a highly skewed distribution of income, wealth, and land. In agriculture, for example, 2% of the population owns almost 60% of the land. A small oligarchy controls much of industry and agriculture and has great influence on the quasimilitary government. The class structure is one of the most rigid in Latin America. Human rights violations have been serious, as noted in the Department's report on the human rights situation submitted to the Congress last January.

Under a constitutional system in place since 1962, military candidates have been regularly elected to the presidency under the banner of the official *Partido de Conciliación Nacional.* The political system has not accommodated dissent and demands for change well.

Political, economic, and social rigidities under successive regimes have not allowed a sufficient outlet for rising frustration and dissatisfaction. This atmosphere has spawned a dramatic increase in leftist terrorism, and terrorist movements have flourished, their actions accelerating a drift toward revolutionary violence.

The country has thus been caught in a chronic national crisis; antigovernment activity is rampant, often begetting violence, and trust is lacking on all sides. In these circumstances polarization is far advanced, and the prospects for avoiding insurrectional violence are rapidly dimming.

Fortunately, however, there are signs that President Romero, the moderate opposition, and the private sector are crucially aware of this spiraling polarization and some evidence of a desire to find some reconciliation. In mid-August President Romero announced a series of significant electoral measures, which, if they can be effectively implemented, hopefully would go far to end the spiraling violence, frustration, and polarization. Halting human rights abuses against the integrity of the person will also be crucial to allowing an atmosphere to develop which will permit these reforms a realistic chance of success.

President Romero's commitment to free municipal and legislative elections in March 1980 and to measures to reform and open up the electoral system is particularly encouraging. He also invited all political exiles to return, has asked the Organization of American States (OAS) for observers and advisors to assist in electoral reform, and has invited the International Red Cross to visit the prisons to judge conditions there. . . .

The Governments of El Salvador, Guatemala, and Honduras tend to see the world through a different lens than that used in the "south." They are apprehensive over the Nicaraguan revolution and what its impact will be. Anxiety over their future pervades these governments, which expect to have to contend with a new rash of insurgency.

Although circumstances vary among them, all three societies are relatively closed. Political systems and processes are relatively restricted. Economic development is at varying levels, but a small elite is the main beneficiary in each country, and opportunities for upward mobility remain limited. The incidents of violence, repression, and human rights violations are high in Guatemala and El Salvador.

With limited channels of redress or free political flow, dissent tends to back up into pressure and instability. Political and social tensions, instabilities, and polarization are considerably higher here than in the rest of the region, although domestic circumstances vary. El Salvador is the most volatile, given conflict between activated and polarized political and social groups, while Honduras is the most tranquil with optimistic prospects for social and political modernization.

EXTERNAL FACTORS

CUBA

The most important single factor governing possible Cuban involvement in subversive activities in the northern tier will be its perception of opportunities.

Profiting from its experience in the 1960's, Cuba has generally followed a policy of cultivating and maintaining contact with leftist rebel movements, in some cases providing subsistence-level support, safehaven as needed, and various types of training; urging disparate opposition forces to unite; counseling recipients of their aid to expand grassroots support; and waiting for the development of objective conditions propitious for additional support.

Given events in Nicaragua, Cuba is certain to increase its attention to Central America. Cuba, however, may now seek a period of assessment and digestion of the results of Nicaragua. Thus, we should not be surprised if the Castro regime carefully weighs the pros and cons of each situation as it arises and, rather than trying to force events to happen, should decide to react to events as they occur. In assessing opportunities Castro is very likely to consider such factors as the internal dynamism in each country, the U.S. reaction, the impact on members of the nonaligned movement, the degree of support or tolerance from other Latin American countries, the complexities of logistical problems, the extent of Cuban influence with the insurgent groups, and, ultimately, the chances of success.

The major question in the minds of interested neighbors is what kind of ultimate relationship with Cuba Nicaragua will develop. While Havana certainly has the gratitude of the Sandinista leadership for the assistance it provided, and considerable ties with key figures in the revolution, it is not automatic that—whatever Havana's intentions—the interests of the Sandinistas as the Government of Nicaragua will become identical with those of Cuba. There is, indeed, every reason to suppose that Nicaraguans would prefer independent development.

Certainly there are significant forces at work to produce something better than a worst-case model in Nicaragua. Practical considerations may work to constrain radical impulses within the Sandinista movement: a period of relative calm needed to rehabilitate the country; the diplomatic shelter that a broad-based policy affords in contrast to a provocatively Communist tilt; the potential for growing power and authority of moderate elements in the government and the society; and the support and cooperation of non-Communist countries and international financial institutions in and outside of Latin America.

OTHER LATIN AMERICAN COUNTRIES

Moderate governments of Latin America, especially the Andean group, have shown a keen interest in Central America. Venezuela, particularly, has chosen to play an active role of assistance and contact with these governments, and an official Venezuelan mission recently visited the northern tier countries. Mexico, too, has a major interest in developments in this geographically close region.

These governments have indicated their goal of fostering peaceful change in the region generally and supporting pluralism in Nicaraguan domestic and foreign policies. It can be expected that these nations will play an increasingly significant and constructive role.

U.S. POLICY RESPONSES

Central America's geographic proximity creates special U.S. interests in Central American peace, prosperity, and cooperation, enhanced by the symbolism from deep past involvement. Our interests embrace:

- The existence of reasonably stable and friendly governments free from domination by outside powers;
- Security against use of the region by forces hostile to us;
- Human rights, including the development of viable democratic institutions; and
- Economic and social development through domestic reform and increased regional cooperation and integration.

Given the volatile circumstances and vulnerabilities described, the inevitability of change, and the dangers of polarization and radicalization, we would hope to see those vulnerabilities reduced by peaceful change consistent with individual liberties and democratic values and more open, pluralistic, and equitable societies.

To help assure peaceful and evolutionary change, we want to work with the nations of Central America and with other hemisphere countries to achieve:

- An evolution toward more open, pluralistic political systems, maintaining contact with all elements in Central America, including labor and youth organizations, the media, private sector groups, and public officials;
- Social and economic development through bilateral and multilateral assistance programs;
- Positive relationships with the region's governments on a basis of nonintervention, equality, and respect for human rights; and
- Regional cooperation in dealing with common economic problems. . . .

NICARAGUA

We seek to develop positive relationships with the Government of National Reconstruction on the basis of nonintervention, equality, and mutual respect. I am confident that our new relationships will reflect efforts to foster respect for human rights and democracy.

We support a humane and pluralistic evolution, based on Nicaragua's own needs, without outside intervention from anyone. We plan to maintain contact with all elements in Nicaragua, including the church, the media, and the private sector, as well as public officials.

We will encourage Nicaragua and its neighbors to build bridges, to dampen tensions, to remove the possibility of involvement in each other's domestic political affairs, and to promote regional cooperation and security.

We are already helping alleviate human suffering and hope to assist concretely in the massive reconstruction task facing that nation, thus ensuring the best possible climate for the establishment of a normal democratic order with respect for human rights.

We plan to cooperate with other nations and public and private institutions in assisting Nicaragua's economic recovery and progress. . . .

6.
UNDER SECRETARY OF STATE WARREN CHRISTOPHER: U.S. POLICY AND THE SANDINISTA REGIME (SEPTEMBER 1979)

When the new Government of Nicaragua assumed power July 20, the country's political, economic, and security institutions had all ceased to function. Almost half of Nicaragua's population was displaced, hungry, or unemployed.

The new government, which was initially formed in exile, is a coalition of former guerrilla and civic leaders. It consists of a five-member junta as the executive authority, a 19-member Council of Ministers, and a 33-member National Council, still in the process of formation. While the Sandinista National Directorate, made up of guerrilla leaders, wields significant influence, so, too, does the Cabinet, which includes many moderate leaders. Lines of authority within the government are still unclear, and there is considerable administrative confusion.

The government's orientation, as revealed in its initial policies, has been generally moderate and pluralistic and not Marxist or Cuban. The government has restrained reprisals—indeed, I believe it has been more successful in doing so than any other recent government which has come to power in the wake of a violent revolution. The government has also promulgated a decree guaranteeing individual rights and has permitted an independent press and radio.

The leadership of the government is very diverse. While there are influential figures who espouse positions with which we strongly disagree—as at the recent nonaligned conference in Havana—the government as a whole has expressed a desire for close and friendly relations with us. Over time, we hope that Nicaragua will find a balanced foreign policy. We are encouraged by indications that the Nicaraguans are making a genuine effort to establish friendly relations with their neighbors in Central America.

The situation in Nicaragua today is in a process of evolution. With the support of the democratic countries in the hemisphere, Nicaragua will have an opportunity to revitalize its shattered economy and to continue on a moderate and pluralistic path. Without adequate support for reconstruction, the Nicaraguan Government might resort to authoritarian measures to expedite economic recovery. Our relationship would doubtless become more strained as a result. We believe that the best approach to the situation in Nicaragua is for us to adopt an attitude of friendly cooperation, including the provision of effective and timely assistance.

U.S. interests will be best served by the development in Nicaragua of a truly democratic government, within a flourishing, pluralistic society. We recognize that some elements of the present government might prefer a closed, Marxist society. We recognize as well that Cuba is already providing substantial advice and assistance to Nicaragua. But the situation in Nicaragua remains fluid.

The moderate outcome we seek will not come about if we walk away now. Precisely because others are assisting Nicaragua and may seek to exploit the situation there, we must not turn our backs.

We want to help alleviate human suffering in Nicaragua, speed reconstruction, foster respect for human rights and democracy, and promote regional development and security. These goals can best be achieved by working with the new government and with other nations and international institutions which share our basic objectives.

The basic tenets of our policy are therefore:

- To develop a positive relationship with the new government in Nicaragua based on the principles of nonintervention, equality, and mutual respect;

- To support the development of a democratic, pluralistic government in Nicaragua, by maintaining contact with all elements of Nicaraguan society, including the church, the media, and the private sector, as well as public officials;

- To cooperate with other nations and public and private institutions in assisting Nicaragua's economic recovery; and

- To help directly with the reconstruction effort by interim aid such as we are proposing today and by assessing and seeking to assist in the longer term effort. . . .

While the United States has taken the lead in averting famine in Nicaragua, we have not been alone in this effort. Private voluntary agencies operating in Nicaragua and in the United States have provided some $3.3 million in cash contributions to the relief effort. Other nations and international organizations have also participated generously. Seventeen nations have contributed so far, and a number of these countries are considering additional assistance. Venezuela, for example, has made available $20 million of its trust funds administered by the Inter-American Development

Bank (IDB) for essential imports. Costa Rica and Panama have provided food and technical advice. The Central American Common Market countries have made available $10 million in loans. Spain has pledged up to $7 million for relief and recovery. West Germany is providing $1.75 million for relief.

Looking to the future, we understand that three Central American countries are arranging a revolving export credit fund of up to $75 million to assist Nicaragua within the Central American Common Market. We also understand that the European Economic Community is providing special credit for $9 million for grain exports to Nicaragua and that Germany is arranging an assistance program totaling some $19 million.

We now need to begin to shift our efforts from relief to recovery—to assist the Nicaraguan people to meet their own basic needs of food, shelter, and medical attention. After reviewing the status of our assistance accounts and analyzing all possibilities, the Administration has concluded that the only immediate way to assist is to reprogram: (1) $8 million of Economic Support Fund (ESF) funds which had been planned for the Maqarin Dam but which were not required this fiscal year, and (2) $500,-000 from AID development assistance. These reprogrammed funds will enable us to put together an interim repair and rehabilitation program to help meet Nicaragua's needs. We are now completing an assessment of Nicaragua's longer term needs, and we will shortly be consulting with Congress on the feasibility of a longer term recovery program for the country. . . .

7.
PRESIDENT JIMMY CARTER: CERTIFICATION OF NICARAGUA AID (SEPTEMBER 12, 1980)

As required by Section 536(g) of the Foreign Assistance Act, the President is transmitting to the Congress a certification to release funds for aid to Nicaragua. The specific finding required by the law was that the Government of Nicaragua has "not cooperated with or harbored any international terrorist organization or is aiding, abetting or supporting acts of violence or terrorism in other countries."

The certification is based upon a careful consideration and evaluation of all the relevant evidence provided by the intelligence community and by our Embassies in the field. It also takes into account the Government of Nicaragua's repeated assurances that it is not involved with international terrorism or supporting violence or terrorism in other countries. Our intelligence agencies as well as our Embassies in Nicaragua and neighboring countries were fully consulted, and the diverse information and opinions from all sources were carefully weighed. The conclusion was that the available evidence permits the President to make the certification required by Section 536(g) of the Act.

This certification to the Congress permits the administration to proceed with disbursement of economic assistance urgently required to further U.S. national interests in this critical area. The administration does not intend to abandon the vital Central American region to Cuba and its radical Marxist allies. To the contrary, the assistance made available by the President's certification will enable us to give effective support to those moderate and democratic Nicaraguans who are struggling to preserve individual freedoms, political pluralism, the democratic process, and a strong, free enterprise participation in their economy. Sixty percent of the total $75 million in assistance will go to the private sector in Nicaragua.

8.
ARCHBISHOP OSCAR ROMERO: LETTER TO PRESIDENT CARTER (FEBRUARY 17, 1980)

Dear President Carter:

In the last few days, news has appeared in the national press that worries me greatly. According to the reports your government is studying the possibility of economic and military support and assistance to the present junta government.

Because you are a Christian and because you have shown that you want to defend human rights, I venture to set forth for you my pastoral point of view concerning this news and to make a request.

. . . I am very worried by the news that the government of the United States is studying a form of abetting the army of El Salvador by sending military teams and advisers to "train three Salvadoran battalions in logistics, communications, and intelligence." If this information from the newspapers is correct, instead of promoting greater justice and peace in El Salvador, it will without doubt sharpen the injustice and repression against the organizations of the people who repeatedly have been struggling to gain respect for their most fundamental human rights.

The present junta government and above all these armed forces and security forces unfortunately have not demonstrated their capacity to resolve, in political and structural practice, the grave national problems. In general they have only reverted to repressive violence, producing a total of deaths and injuries much greater than in the recent military regime, whose systematic violation of human rights was denounced by the Inter-American Commission on Human Rights.

The brutal form in which the security forces recently attacked and assassinated the occupiers of the headquarters of the Christian Democratic Party, in spite of what appears to be the lack of authorization for this operation from the junta government and the party, is an indication that the junta and the party do not govern the country, but that political power is in the hands of the unscrupulous military who know how to repress the people and promote the interests of the Salvadoran oligarchy. . . .

In these moments we are living through a grave economic and political crisis in our country, but it is certain that it is increasingly the people who are awakening and organizing and have begun to prepare themselves to manage and be responsible for the future of El Salvador.

It would be unjust and deplorable if the intrusion of foreign power were to frustrate the Salvadoran people, or to repress them and block their autonomous decisions about the economic and political form that our country ought to follow. It would violate a right which we Latin American Bishops, meeting in Puebla, publicly recognized when we said: "The legitimate self-determination of our people that permits them to organize according to their own genius and the march of their history and to cooperate in a new international order."

I hope that your religious sentiments and your feelings for the defense of human rights will move you to accept my position, avoiding by this action worse bloodshed in this suffering country.

Oscar Romero
Archbishop of San Salvador

9.
U.S. STATE DEPARTMENT: EL SALVADOR POLICY OPTIONS (DECEMBER 1980)

The principal problem facing U.S. policy is to hold open a "middle option." Although the prospect of the emergence of a leftist government has for the moment declined into insignificance, prospects of a government of the far

---

Secret memo entitled "What Could Be Accomplished by the Rogers/Bowdler Mission."

right are greater than they have been since last May, when ex-Major D'Aubuisson was arrested. . . .

The principal dangers for the "middle option" are the worsening economic situation, the surge of rightist violence and the polarization of Salvadoran society. Economic desperation, prolonged and increasing lack of personal security plus waning hopes for the survival of a "moderate" government are all contributing to this frustration and the accompanying polarization. It has reached the point that an overwhelming number of Salvadorans have had to make their choice. . . . In a choice between far left and far right, an unknown percentage of Salvadorans might opt for a "rightist" solution, whatever the brutalities, but the mass of the people would become sullen and rebellious as the rightist course picked up steam.

Reviving immediate middle and upper class belief in the "middle course" will revolve around punishing and curtailing the activities of criminal elements of the army and security forces. . . . Assuming there are army officers who can be made to stand up for discipline and order, they could at least try to impose total integration on the security services with their large quotients of officers and non-coms who are thugs and mobsters.

The worst danger for the "middle course" is the fact of a military establishment answerable to no one. Even the vaunted "military code of conduct" announced on October 15 is enforceable only to the extent that the Ministry of Defense chooses to act. It has not acted and will not so long as the present leadership remains. Creation of a "Distinguished Investigations Commission" that would include ranking military officers as well as civilian politicians and church leaders might offer genuine redress to genuine grievances against military members' depredations. But who would dare sit on such a Commission?

We do not see that a mere analysis of the incident of the murder of the Catholic women would accomplish what should be the real objectives of the Rogers mission. Something must be done to dismantle the whole structure of repression which struck these Catholic women as only four more victims among the thousands claimed this year by rightist death squads and security forces participants. Obviously, little can be done about left-wing violence, but right-wing and official violence must be contained or the "middle option" will disappear and El Salvador will fall into the hands of right- or left-wing extremists with whom the U.S. cannot cooperate.

10.
JEANE KIRKPATRICK: THE HOBBES PROBLEM (1981)

El Salvador's political culture does not help with the problem of legitimacy. Like the broader culture, its political culture emphasizes strength and *machismo* and all that implies about the nature of the world and the human traits necessary for survival and success. Competition, courage, honor, shrewdness, assertiveness, a capacity for risk and recklessness, and a certain "manly" disregard for safety are valued. There is a predictable congruity between the cultural traits and political patterns in El Salvador, a congruity expressed in the persistent tendency to schism and violence within the political class. Intermittent disruption and violence make order the highest value in such political systems.

Order, as John Stuart Mill emphasized, is the "preservation of all kinds and amounts of good which already exist." It is also the precondition for all other public goods, as Mill understood better than is generally realized. And, as always, heroes are people who make a special contribution to highly valued goods.

Hernández Martínez is such a hero. General Maximiliano Hernández Martínez, who governed El Salvador from 1931 to 1944, was minister of war in the cabinet of President Arturo Araujo when there occurred widespread uprisings said to be the work of Communist agitators. General Hernández Martínez then staged a coup and ruthlessly suppressed the disorders—wiping out all those who participated and hunting down their leaders. It is said that 30,000 persons lost their lives in the process. To many Salvadoreans the violence of this repression seems less important than the fact of restored order and the thirteen years of civil peace that ensued. The traditionalist death squads that pursue revolutionary activists and leaders in contemporary El Salvador call themselves Hernández Martínez Brigades, seeking thereby to place themselves in El Salvador's political tradition and communicate their purposes.

There is, inevitably, an arbitrary quality about governments which can reform themselves only by force or intrigue. And there is an inevitable brittleness about a polity in which political loyalty means loyalty to particular individuals—not to individuals who have been institutionalized in the fashion that kings and presidents are institutionalized, but to individuals whose claim to power rests ultimately on the fact that they have it.

AEI Public Policy Papers (Washington, D.C., 1981), pp. 133–36.

Where there is no legitimacy, there is also no authority. There is only power, and the habit of obedience to whoever successfully claims the power of government. Under these circumstances, a government's status depends, even more than usually, on its capacity to govern, to secure obedience, to punish those who disobey—in sum, to maintain order. Such a government can command obedience only insofar as it can secure acquiescence in its policies, can rely on habits of obedience, or can impose its commands by force and fear. . . . There are few grounds for thinking that Americans who have shaped U.S. policy toward El Salvador have been aware of the distinctive characteristics and problems of such political systems. Had they understood them, then some aspects of our policy would surely have been different.

What would have been different?

The administration would have been inclined to greet the coup of October 1979, which toppled President Carlos Humberto Romero, with mixed feelings. Instead, Assistant Secretary of State William C. Bowdler greeted it as the dawn of a new era, a "watershed date," in which "young officers broke with the old repressive order" and along with "progressive civilians" formed a government committed to "profound social and economic reforms, respect for human rights and democracy."

A more prudent appraisal of politics in Central America would have left policy makers a little less enthusiastic about the destruction of any constitutional ruler, not because they approved the ruler but because they understood that authority in such systems is weak, stability fragile, and order much easier to destroy than reconstruct.

Second, a fuller understanding of the political system of El Salvador would have left U.S. policy makers a bit less sanguine about the short range contributions of reform to political stability not because reforms are not desirable but because political traditions and cultures change slowly, not rapidly.

Third, clear comprehension of the problem of order in El Salvador would make U.S. policy makers more sympathetic to the inability of the government to control the situation, and less anxious to inhibit the use of force against violent challengers. . . . More than 9,000 persons have been slaughtered in El Salvador during the year since the new day dawned. The reforms that were counted on to provide social justice and vaccinate the masses against communism have been stalled by administrative inefficiency and the sabotage of both communitarians and defenders of the *status quo ante*. The harvests counted on to help El Salvador's acute balance of payments problems are being menaced and destroyed by revolutionaries for whose cause worse is better. Meanwhile violence perpetrated by communists, anticommunists, and simple criminals continues.

What is to be done? It is not a problem to which the American temper is well suited. The problem confronting El Salvador is Thomas Hobbes's problem: how to establish order and authority in a society where there is none.

In *Leviathan,* an essay first published in 1651, are found an accurate identification and insightful discussion of the essential elements involved in El Salvador's turmoil, laid out in marvelously lucid prose.

First, Hobbes insists on the primacy of order as the basic value of a political system without which no other value can be enjoyed.

> Whatsoever therefore is consequent to a time of Warre, where every man is Enemy to every man; the same is consequent to the time, wherein men live without other security, than what their own strength, and their own invention shall furnish them withall. In such condition, there is no place for Industry; because the fruit thereof is uncertain: and consequently no Culture of the Earth; no Navigation, nor use of the commodities that may be imported by Sea; no commodious Building; no Instruments of moving, and removing such things as require much force; no Knowledge of the face of the Earth; no account of Time; no Arts; no Letters; no Society; and which is worst of all, continuall feare, and danger of violent death; And the life of man, solitary, poore, nasty, brutish, and short.

Second, Hobbes predicts that to escape such pervasive insecurity and fear of death, men will eventually voluntarily submit themselves to a ruler in whom they will vest sovereignty, to whom they will swear obedience on condition that he maintain the civil peace required alike for survival and for civilization.

Third, Hobbes emphasizes that allegiance to a sovereign depends on his ability to maintain the order required to protect life, secure property, and cultivate virtue.

Fourth, Hobbes recognizes the importance of both legitimacy and fear in reinforcing the polity. He insists that the covenant establishing government is to be based on an oath sworn by God and enforced by fear of "some coercive Power."

Fifth, Hobbes argues that the war of each against all, which characterizes a society with no sovereign, grows finally out of the competition for power rooted in the nature of man.

Sixth, Hobbes argues that civil war and anarchy, being political problems, require political solutions. Autocracy is that solution he foresees. It is hardly an ideal one, surely not one acceptable under our human rights program, but wholly in keeping with the priorities stated by that most eloquent of El Salvador's democratic leaders, Napoleón Duarte:

> I think it is not important who is in or out. The most important thing is how can we solve the basis of our problems—the violence. Whoever has the capacity to do this should have the power.

Duarte hopes, as we all hope, that El Salvador can still be brought back from the verge of a civil war which promises only destruction and dictatorship. Helping would require a broader understanding of the context and the problem than our policy makers have shown so far.

11.
JEANE KIRKPATRICK: U.S. SECURITY AND LATIN AMERICA (JANUARY 1981)

... Nothing is as important as understanding the relationship between the recent failures of American policy—in Latin America and elsewhere—and the philosophy of foreign affairs that inspired and informed that policy. ...

The repudiation of our hegemonic past was symbolized by the Panama Canal Treaties, to which the Carter administration—from the President on down—attached great importance and of which it was inordinately proud. As Vice President Mondale put it in Panama City, the treaties symbolized "the commitment of the U.S. to the belief that fairness and not force should lie at the heart of our dealings with the nations of the world."

Anastasio Somoza's Nicaragua had the bad luck to become the second demonstration area for the "fresh start" in Latin America. Just because the regime had been so close and so loyal to the U.S., its elimination would, in exactly the same fashion as the Panama Canal Treaties, dramatize the passing of the old era of "hegemony" in Central America and the arrival of a new era of equity and justice. ...

Incorporating the nations of Latin America into a "global framework" meant deemphasizing U.S. relations with them. Especially, it meant reducing U.S. assistance to the area, since from the perspective of North-South relations, Latin America's claim to assistance was not nearly as impressive as that of most other nations of the so-called Third World. And, once the strategic perspective was abandoned, there was no reason at all for military assistance.

The global approach involved deemphasizing Latin American relations, not destabilizing governments. But other aspects of the Carter doctrine committed the administration to promoting "change." "Change," indeed, was the favorite word of administration policy-makers. In speeches with titles like "Currents of Change in Latin America," Carter, Vance, and their associates reiterated their conviction that the world was in the grip of an extraordinary process of transformation which was deep, irresistible, systematic, and desirable. Administration spokesmen reiterated in the fashion of a credo that "our national interests align us naturally and inescapably with the forces of change, of democracy, of human rights, and of equitable development" (Philip Habib). And the belief that the whole world was caught up in a process of modernization moving it toward greater democracy and equality subtly transformed itself into an imperative: the U.S. should throw its power behind the "progressive" forces seeking change, even if they "seemed" anti-American or pro-Soviet.

If commitment to "change" was the rock on which Carter's Latin American policy was built, his human-rights policy was the lever to get change started. Two aspects of the Carter approach to human rights are noteworthy. First, concern was limited to violations of human rights by governments. By definition, activities of terrorists and guerrillas could not qualify as violations of human rights, whereas a government's efforts to repress terrorism would quickly run afoul of Carter human-rights standards.

Secondly, human rights were defined not in terms of personal and legal rights—freedom from torture, arbitrary imprisonment, and arrest, as in the usage of Amnesty International and the U.S. Foreign Assistance Acts of 1961 and 1975—but in accordance with a much broader conception which included the political "rights" available only in democracies and the economic "rights" promised by socialism (shelter, food, health, education). It may be that no country in the world meets these standards; certainly no country in the Third World does. The very broadness of the definition invited an arbitrary and capricious policy of implementation. Panama, for instance, was rather mysteriously exempt from meeting the expansive criteria of the State Department's human-rights office, while at the same time the other major nations of Central America were being censured (and undermined) for violations. . . .

Ignoring the role of ideology had powerful effects on the administration's perception of conflicts and on its ability to make accurate predictions. Although Fidel Castro has loudly and repeatedly proclaimed his revolutionary mission, and backed his stated intentions by training insurgents and providing weapons and advisers, Carter's Assistant Secretary for Inter-American Affairs, William Bowdler, described Cuba as "an inefficient and shabby dictatorship"—a description more appropriate to, say, Paraguay, than to an expansionist Soviet client state with troops scattered throughout the world. The refusal to take seriously, or even to take into account, the commitment of Fidel Castro or Nicaragua's Sandinista leadership to Marxist-Leninist goals and expansionist policies made it impossible to distinguish them either from traditional authoritarians or from democratic reformers, impossible to predict their likely attitude toward the

United States and the Soviet Union, impossible to understand why in their view Costa Rica and Mexico as well as Guatemala and Honduras constituted inviting targets. . . .

The Central American countries also share a good many social and economic characteristics. All are "modernizing" nations in the sense that in each, urban, industrial, mobile, "modern" sectors coexist with traditional patterns of life. In each, a large portion of the population is still engaged in agriculture—most often employed as landless laborers on large estates and plantations that have long since made the transition to commercial agriculture. Economic growth rates in Central America have been above the Latin American average and per-capita income is high enough to rank these nations among the "middle-income" countries of the world. But in all of them wealth is heavily concentrated in a small upper class and a thin but growing middle class, and large numbers live as they have always lived—in deep poverty, ill-nourished, ill-housed, illiterate.

Things have been getting better for the people of Central America— infant mortality rates have dropped, years in school have increased—but they have been getting better slowly. It has been easier to break down the myths justifying the old distribution of values in society than to improve access to education, medical care, decent housing, good food, respect, and political power. . . .

The boundaries between the political system, the economy, the military establishment, and the Church are often unclear and unreliable. Weak governments confront strong social groups, and no institution is able to establish its authority over the whole. Economic, ecclesiastical, and social groups influence but do not control the government; the government influences but does not control the economy, the military, the Church, and so on.

A Democratic facade—elections, political parties, and fairly broad participation—is a feature of these systems. But the impact of democratic forms is modified by varying degrees of fraud, intimidation, and restrictions on who may participate. Corruption (the appropriation of public resources for private use) is endemic. Political institutions are not strong enough to channel and contain the claims of various groups to use public power to enforce preferred policies. No procedure is recognized as *the* legitimate route to power. Competition for influence proceeds by whatever means are at hand: the Church manipulates symbols of rectitude; workers resort to strikes; businessmen use bribery; political parties use campaigns and votes; politicians employ persuasion, organization, and demagoguery; military officers use force. Lack of consensus permits political competition of various kinds in various arenas, and gives the last word to those who dispose of the greatest force. That usually turns out to be the leaders of the armed forces; most rulers in the area are generals.

Violence or the threat of violence is an integral, regular, predictable part of these political systems—a fact which is obscured by our way of describing military "interventions" in Latin political systems as if the system were normally peaceable. Coups, demonstrations, political strikes, plots, and counterplots are, in fact, the norm. . . .

Cuba stands ready to succor, bolster, train, equip, and advise revolutionaries produced within these societies and to supply weapons for a general insurgency when that is created. The U.S. is important as a source of economic aid and moral and military support. Traditionally it has also exercised a veto power over governments in the area and reinforced acceptable governments with its tacit approval. Thus, to the objective economic and political dependency of nations in the area has been added a widespread sense of psychological dependency. When aid and comfort from the U.S. in the form of money, arms, logistical support, and the services of counterinsurgency experts are no longer available, governments like those of Nicaragua, El Salvador, and Guatemala are weakened. And when it finally sinks in that the U.S. desires their elimination and prefers insurgents to incumbents, the blow to the morale and confidence of such weak traditional regimes is devastating.

The case of Nicaragua illustrates to perfection what happens when "affirmative pressures for change" on the part of the U.S. interact with Cuban-backed insurgency and a government especially vulnerable to shifts in U.S. policy.

At the time the Carter administration was inaugurated in January 1977, three groups of unequal strength competed for power in Nicaragua: the President and his loyal lieutenants—who enjoyed the advantages of incumbency, a degree of legitimacy, a nationwide organization, and the unwavering support of the National Guard; the legal opposition parties which had been gathered into a loose coalition headed by Joaquín Chamorro, editor of *La Prensa;* and several small revolutionary groups whose Cuban-trained leaders had finally forged a loose alliance, the FSLN (Sandinist National Liberation Front).

From the moment the FSLN adopted the tactics of a broad alliance, the offensive against Somoza was carried out on a variety of fronts. There was violence in the form of assassinations and assaults on army barracks. When the government reacted, the U.S. condemned it for violations of human rights. The legal opposition put forward demands for greater democracy which had the endorsement of the FSLN, thus making it appear that democracy was the goal of the insurgency.

Violence and counterviolence weakened the regime by demonstrating that it could not maintain order. The combination of impotence and repression in turn emboldened opponents in and out of the country, provoking more reprisals and more hostility in a vicious circle that culminated finally in the departure of Somoza and the collapse of the National Guard.

What did the Carter administration do in Nicaragua? *It brought down the Somoza regime.* The Carter administration did not "lose" Nicaragua in the sense in which it was once charged Harry Truman had "lost" China, or Eisenhower Cuba, by failing to prevent a given outcome. In the case of Nicaragua, the State Department *acted* repeatedly and at critical junctures to weaken the government of Anastasio Somoza and to strengthen his opponents.

First, it declared "open season" on the Somoza regime. When in the spring of 1977 the State Department announced that shipments of U.S. arms would be halted for human-rights violations, and followed this with announcements in June and October that economic aid would be withheld, it not only deprived the Somoza regime of needed economic and military support but served notice that the regime no longer enjoyed the approval of the United States and could no longer count on its protection. This impression was strongly reinforced when after February 1978 Jimmy Carter treated the two sides in the conflict as more or less equally legitimate contenders—offering repeatedly to help "both sides" find a "peaceful solution."

Second, the Carter administration's policies inhibited the Somoza regime in dealing with its opponents while they were weak enough to be dealt with. Fearful of U.S. reproaches and reprisals, Somoza fluctuated between repression and indulgence in his response to FSLN violence. The rules of the Carter human-rights policy made it impossible for Somoza to resist his opponents effectively. As Viron Vaky remarked about the breakdown in negotiations between Somoza and the armed opposition: ". . . when the mediation was suspended we announced that the failure of the mediation had created a situation in which it was clear violence was going to continue, that it would result in repressive measures and therefore our relationships could not continue on the same basis as in the past." When the National Palace was attacked and hostages were taken, Somoza's capitulation to FSLN demands enhanced the impression that he could not control the situation and almost certainly stimulated the spread of resistance.

Third, by its "mediation" efforts and its initiatives in the Organization of American States (OAS), the Carter administration encouraged the internationalization of the opposition. Further, it demoralized Somoza and his supporters by insisting that Somoza's continuation in power was the principal obstacle to a viable, centrist, democratic government. Finally, the State Department deprived the Somoza regime of legitimacy not only by repeated condemnations for human-rights violations but also by publishing a demand for Somoza's resignation and by negotiating with the opposition. . . .

Since the "real" problem was not Cuban arms but Somoza, obviously the U.S. should not act to reinforce the regime that had proved its political and moral failure by becoming the object of attack. Because the State Department desired not to "add to the partisan factionalism," it declined to supply arms to the regime. . . .

In June 1979, after the U.S. and the OAS had called for Somoza's resignation, and U.S. representatives William Bowdler and Lawrence Pezzulo had met with the FSLN, the State Department undertook to apply the final squeeze to the Somoza regime—putting pressure on Israel to end arms sales, and working out an oil embargo to speed the capitulation of Somoza's forces. They were so successful that for the second time in a decade an American ally ran out of gas and ammunition while confronting an opponent well armed by the Soviet bloc.

The FSLN were not the State Department's preferred replacement for Somoza. Nevertheless, from spring 1977, when the State Department announced that it was halting a promised arms shipment to Somoza's government, through the summer of 1980, when the administration secured congressional approval of a $75-million aid package for Nicaragua, U.S. policy under Jimmy Carter was vastly more supportive of the Sandinistas than it was of the Somoza regime, despite the fact that Somoza and his government were as doggedly friendly and responsive to U.S. interests and desires as the Sandinistas have been hostile and non-responsive.

The Carter administration expected that democracy would emerge in Nicaragua. Their scenario prescribed that the winds of change should blow the outmoded dictator out of office and replace him with a popular government. Even after it had become clear that the FSLN, which was known to harbor powerful anti-democratic tendencies, was the dominant force in the new regime, U.S. spokesmen continued to speak of the events in Nicaragua as a democratic revolution. In December 1979, for example, Warren Christopher attempted to reassure doubting members of the Senate Foreign Relations Committee that "the driving consensus among Nicaraguans" was "to build a new Nicaragua through popular participation that is capable of meeting basic human needs."

The expectation that change would produce progress and that socialism equaled social justice made it difficult for Carter policy-makers to assess Nicaragua's new rulers realistically, even though grounds for concern about their intentions, already numerous before the triumph, continued to multiply in its aftermath. . . .

II
THE REAGAN ADMINISTRATION

12.
REPUBLICAN PARTY: PLATFORM (1980)

Latin America is an area of primary interest for the United States. Yet, the Carter Administration's policies have encouraged a precipitous decline in United States relations with virtually every country in the region. The nations of South and Central America have been battered by the Carter Administration's economic and diplomatic sanctions linked in its undifferentiated charges of human rights violations.

In the Caribbean and Central America the Carter Administration stands by while Castro's totalitarian Cuba, financed directed, and supplied by the Soviet Union, aggressively trains, arms, and supports forces of warfare and revolution throughout the Western hemisphere. Yet the Carter Administration has steadily denied these threats and in many cases has actively worked to undermine governments and parties opposed to the expansion of Soviet power. This must end.

We deplore the Marxist Sandinista takeover of Nicaragua and the Marxist attempts to destabilize El Salvador, Guatemala and Honduras. We do not support United States assistance to any Marxist government in this hemisphere and we oppose the Carter administration aid program for the government of Nicaragua. However, we will support the efforts of the Nicaraguan people to establish a free and independent government.

Republicans deplore the dangerous and incomprehensible Carter Administration policies toward Cuba. The Administration has done nothing about the Soviet combat brigade stationed there or about the transfer of new Soviet offensive weapons to Cuba in the form of modern MIG aircraft and submarines. It has done nothing about the Soviet pilots flying air defense missions in Cuba or about the extensive improvements to Soviet military bases, particularly the submarine facilities in Cienfuegos, and the expanded Soviet intelligence facilities near Havana.

Republicans recognize the importance of our relations within this hemi-

---

Pp. 68–69.

sphere and pledge a strong new United States policy in the Americas. We will stand firm with countries seeking to develop their societies while combating the subversion and violence exported by Cuba and Moscow. We will return to the fundamental principle of treating a friend as a friend and self-proclaimed enemies as enemies, without apology. We will make it clear to the Soviet Union and Cuba that their subversion and their build-up of offensive military forces are unacceptable.

We pledge to ensure that the Panama Canal remains open, secure, and free of hostile control.

The reservations and understandings to the Panama Canal treaties, including those assuring the United States of primary responsibility of protecting and defending the Canal, are an integral part of those treaties and we will hold Panama to strict interpretation of the language of the treaties, clearly established by the legislative history of Senate adoption of amendments, reservations, and understandings at the time of Senate approval of the treaties.

We would remind the American taxpayers that President Carter gave repeated assurances that the Panama Canal treaties would not cost the American taxpayers "one thin dime," and we emphasize the fact that implementing the Panama Canal treaties will cost them $4.2 billion.

13.
THE COMMITTEE OF SANTA FE: A NEW INTER-AMERICAN POLICY (1980)

Given the Communist commitment to utilize every available means to overthrow the capitalist order and to transform the world, internal and external security become inseparable. Destabilization through misinformation and polarization is the first step. As the subverting assault proceeds into the terrorist and then the guerrilla phase, external (usually Cuban) support and involvement which was originally only ideological merges into logistical support and even recruitment of foreign volunteers to fight the war of national liberation. . . .

The war begins with the establishment of a subversive apparatus. The second phase consists of terrorism and anti-government activity in the name of human rights and liberation; the third phase is guerrilla war. The fourth phase is full-scale war leading to the final offensive, such as occurred in Nicaragua in 1979 and will very probably be the case in El Salvador in

Published by the Council for Inter-American Security (1980).

1980. Throughout the entire campaign a mounting barrage of propaganda is directed at the United States.

The principal goals of the subversive and urban guerrillas who wage war against existing society are threefold:

1) to demonstrate to "the people" that the authorities are powerless to protect them, or even themselves, against the terror;
2) to finance escalating levels of violence, propaganda and terror by kidnapping, murder and robbery;
3) to provoke the authorities into overreacting (The aim here is to radicalize individuals who might sympathize with the revolution but probably would not themselves assist if it were not for the overreaction which leads to hatred and polarization, and the loss of U.S. support);
4) to overthrow the established government by combining the first three goals with "propaganda of the deed." As a major step to the ultimate goal, the terrorists create chaos.

The Sandinista triumph in Nicaragua clearly followed this pattern, but it also involved a new element—external aggression by troops with operational bases in Costa Rica that were equipped with arms imported via Panama from Cuba and the United States.

The Sandinistas included Communist cadres from other countries. In spite of all this international aid, when Somoza left the country, the insurgents had not even achieved their objective of liberating the town of Rivas, close across the Costa Rican border, where they intended to proclaim a provisional government. Somoza and the Nicaraguan Guard abandoned the fight because the United States had curtailed re-supply of ammunition.

The Nicaraguan base on the American continent will now facilitate a repeat of the new Nicaraguan revolutionary model. Already U.S. arms previously sold to Nicaragua have been sent to guerrillas in Guatemala. Guatemala is the strategic prize of Central America, adjoining as it does the vast Mexican oil fields. . . .

An ideologically motivated and selectively applied policy of human rights is detrimental to human rights properly conceived. It has cost the United States friends and allies and lost us influence in important Latin American countries. It has even contributed to the destabilization and loss or prospective loss of countries like Nicaragua, El Salvador, Guatemala and Costa Rica.

Nowhere are the human rights of life and property and civil liberty more secure now than they were before the selective initiation of the human rights campaign in 1977. The reality of the situations confronted by Latin American governments that are under attack by domestic revolutionary groups assisted by the Soviet-Cuban axis must be understood not just as a threat to some alleged oligarchy but as a threat to the security interests of the United States.

If the United States will content itself with a foreign policy that promotes peace and stability and the exclusion of Communism from the Americas, there will be ample opportunity to promote respect for concrete civil liberties and actual economic betterment for all the people of the Americas.

14.
STATE DEPARTMENT: WHITE PAPER (FEBRUARY 1981)

The situation in El Salvador presents a strikingly familiar case of Soviet, Cuban, and other Communist military involvement in a politically troubled Third World country. By providing arms, training, and direction to a local insurgency and by supporting it with a global propaganda campaign, the Communists have intensified and widened the conflict, greatly increased the suffering of the Salvadoran people, and deceived much of the world about the true nature of the revolution. Their objective in El Salvador as elsewhere is to bring about—at little cost to themselves—the overthrow of the established government and the imposition of a Communist regime in defiance of the will of the Salvadoran people.

Before September 1980 the diverse guerrilla groups in El Salvador were ill-coordinated and ill-equipped, armed with pistols and a varied assortment of hunting rifles and shotguns. At that time the insurgents acquired weapons predominantly through purchases on the international market and from dealers who participated in the supply of arms to the Sandinistas in Nicaragua.

By January 1981 when the guerrillas launched their "general offensive," they had acquired an impressive array of modern weapons and supporting equipment never before used in El Salvador by either the insurgents or the military. Belgian FAL rifles, German G-3 rifles, U.S. M-1, M-16, and AR-15 semiautomatic and automatic rifles, and the Israeli UZI submachinegun and Galil assault rifle have all been confirmed in the guerrilla inventory. In addition, they are known to possess .30 to .50 caliber machineguns, the U.S. M-60 machinegun, U.S. and Russian hand grenades, the U.S. M-79 and Chinese RPG grenade launchers, and the U.S. M-72 light antitank weapon and 81mm mortars. Captured ammunition indicates

U.S. Department of State, Special Report No. 80, "Communist Interference in El Salvador."

the guerrillas probably possess 60mm and 82mm mortars and 57mm and 75mm recoilless rifles.

Recently acquired evidence has enabled us to reconstruct the central role played by Cuba, other Communist countries, and several radical states in the political unification and military direction of insurgent forces in El Salvador and in equipping them in less than 6 months with a panoply of modern weapons that enabled the guerrillas to launch a well-armed offensive.

This information, which we consider incontrovertible, has been acquired over the past year. Many key details, however, have fallen into place as the result of the guerrillas' own records. Two particularly important document caches were recovered from the Communist Party of El Salvador in November 1980 and from the People's Revolutionary Army (ERP) in January 1981. This mass of captured documents includes battle plans, letters, and reports of meetings and travels, some written in cryptic language and using code words.

When deciphered and verified against evidence from other intelligence sources, the documents bring to light the chain of events leading to the guerrillas' January 1981 offensive. What emerges is a highly disturbing pattern of parallel and coordinated action by a number of Communist and some radical countries bent on imposing a military solution. . . . From June 2 to July 22, 1980, Shafik Handal visits the U.S.S.R., Vietnam, the German Democratic Republic, Czechoslovakia, Bulgaria, Hungary, and Ethiopia to procure arms and seek support for the movement.

On June 2, 1980, Handal meets in Moscow with Mikhail Kudachkin, Deputy Chief of the Latin American Section of the Foreign Relations Department of the CPSU Central Committee. Kudachkin suggests that Handal travel to Vietnam to seek arms and offers to pay for Handal's trip.

Continuing his travels between June 9 and 15, Handal visits Vietnam, where he is received by Le Duan, Secretary General of the Vietnamese Communist Party; Xuan Thuy, member of the Communist Party Central Committee Secretariat; and Vice Minister of National Defense Tran Van Quang. The Vietnamese, as a "first contribution," agree to provide 60 tons of arms. Handal adds that "the comrade requested air transport from the USSR."

From June 19 to June 24, 1980, Handal visits the German Democratic Republic (G.D.R.), where he is received by Hermann Axen, member of the G.D.R. Politburo. Axen states that the G.D.R. has already sent 1.9 tons of supplies to Managua. On July 21, G.D.R. leader Honecker writes the G.D.R. Embassy in Moscow that additional supplies will be sent and that the German Democratic Republic will provide military training, particularly in clandestine operations. The G.D.R. telegram adds that although Berlin possesses no Western-manufactured weapons—which the Salvadoran guerrillas are seeking—efforts will be undertaken to find a "solution to this problem." (Note: The emphasis on Western arms reflects the desire to maintain plausible denial.)

From June 24–27, 1980, Handal visits Czechoslovakia where he is received by Vasil Bilak, Second Secretary of the Czech Communist Party. Bilak says that some Czech arms circulating in the world market will be provided so that these arms will not be traced back to Czechoslovakia as the donor country. Transportation will be coordinated with the German Democratic Republic.

Handal proceeds to Bulgaria from June 27 to June 30, 1980. He is received by Dimitir Stanichev, member of the Central Committee Secretariat. The Bulgarians agree to supply German-origin weapons and other supplies, again in an apparent effort to conceal their sources.

In Hungary, from June 30 to July 3, 1980, Handal is received by Communist Party General Secretary János Kádár and "Guesel" (probably Central Committee Secretary for Foreign Affairs Andras Gyenes). The latter offers radios and other supplies and indicates Hungarian willingness to trade arms with Ethiopia or Angola in order to obtain Western-origin arms for the Salvadoran guerrillas. "Guesel" promises to resolve the trade with the Ethiopians and Angolans himself, "since we want to be a part of providing this aid." Additionally, Handal secures the promise of 10,000 uniforms to be made by the Hungarians according to Handal's specifications.

Handal then travels to Ethiopia, July 3 to July 6. He meets Chairman Mengistu and receives "a warm reception." Mengistu offers "several thousand weapons," including: 150 Thompson submachineguns with 300 cartridge clips, 1,500 M-1 rifles, 1,000 M-14 rifles, and ammunition for these weapons. In addition, the Ethiopians agree to supply all necessary spare parts for these arms.

Handal returns to Moscow on July 22, 1980 and is received again by Mikhail Kudachkin. The Soviet official asks if 30 Communist youth currently studying in the U.S.S.R. could take part in the war in El Salvador. Before leaving Moscow, Handal receives assurances that the Soviets agree in principle to transport the Vietnamese arms.

Further Contacts in Nicaragua. On July 13, representatives of the DRU arrive in Managua amidst preparations for the first anniversary celebration of Somoza's overthrow. The DRU leaders wait until July 23 to meet with "Comrade Bayardo" (presumably Bayardo Arce, member of the Sandinista Directorate). They complain that the Sandinistas appear to be restricting their access to visiting world dignitaries and demanding that all contacts be cleared through them. During the meeting, Arce promises ammunition to the guerrillas and arranges a meeting for them with the Sandinista "Military Commission." Arce indicates that, since the guerrillas will receive some arms manufactured by the Communist countries, the

Sandinista Army (EPS) will consider absorbing some of these weapons and providing to the Salvadorans Western-manufactured arms held by the EPS in exchange. (In January 1981 the Popular Sandinista Army indeed switched from using U.S.-made weapons to those of Soviet and East European origin.)

The DRU representatives also meet with visiting Palestine Liberation Organization (PLO) leader Yasir Arafat in Managua on July 22, 1980. Arafat promises military equipment, including arms and aircraft. (A Salvadoran guerrilla leader met with FATAH leaders in Beirut in August and November, and the PLO has trained selected Salvadorans in the Near East and in Nicaragua.)

On July 27, the guerrilla General Staff delegation departs from Managua for Havana, where Cuban "specialists" add final touches to the military plans formulated during the May meetings in Havana.

Arms Deliveries Begin. In mid-August 1980, Shafik Handal's arms-shopping expedition begins to bear fruit. On August 15, 1980, Ethiopian arms depart for Cuba. Three weeks later the 60 tons of captured U.S. arms sent from Vietnam are scheduled to arrive in Cuba.

As a result of a Salvadoran delegation's trip to Iraq earlier in the year, the guerrillas receive a $500,000 logistics donation. The funds are distributed to the Sandinistas in Nicaragua and within El Salvador.

By mid-September, substantial quantities of the arms promised to Handal are well on the way to Cuba and Nicaragua. The guerrilla logistics coordinator in Nicaragua informs his Joint General Staff on September 26 that 130 tons of arms and other military material supplied by the Communist countries have arrived in Nicaragua for shipment to El Salvador. According to the captured documents, this represents one-sixth of the commitments to the guerrillas by the Communist countries. (Note: To get an idea of the magnitude of this commitment, the Vietnamese offer of only 60 tons included 2 million rifle and machinegun bullets, 14,500 mortar shells, 1,620 rifles, 210 machineguns, 48 mortars, 12 rocket launchers, and 192 pistols.)

In September and October, the number of flights to Nicaragua from Cuba increased sharply. These flights had the capacity to transport several hundred tons of cargo.

At the end of September, despite appeals from the guerrillas, the Sandinistas suspend their weapons deliveries to El Salvador for 1 month, after the U.S. Government lodges a protest to Nicaragua on the arms trafficking.

When the shipments resume in October, as much as 120 tons of weapons and materiel are still in Nicaragua and some 300–400 tons are in Cuba. Because of the difficulty of moving such large quantities overland, Nicaragua—with Cuban support—begins airlifting arms from Nicaragua into El

Salvador. In November, about 2.5 tons of arms are delivered by air before accidents force a brief halt in the airlift.

In December, Salvadoran guerrillas, encouraged by Cuba, begin plans for a general offensive in early 1981. To provide the increased support necessary, the Sandinistas revive the airlift into El Salvador. Salvadoran insurgents protest that they cannot absorb the increased flow of arms, but guerrilla liaison members in Managua urge them to increase their efforts as several East European nations are providing unprecedented assistance.

A revolutionary radio station—*Radio Liberación*—operating in Nicaragua begins broadcasting to El Salvador on December 15, 1980. It exhorts the populace to mount a massive insurrection against the government. (References to the Sandinistas sharing the expenses of a revolutionary radio station appear in the captured documents.)

On January 24, 1981, a Cessna from Nicaragua crashes on takeoff in El Salvador after unloading passengers and possibly weapons. A second plane is strafed by the Salvadoran Air Force, and the pilot and numerous weapons are captured. The pilot admits to being an employee of the Nicaraguan national airline and concedes that the flight originated from Sandino International Airport in Managua. He further admits to flying two earlier arms deliveries.

Air supply is playing a key role, but infiltration by land and sea also continues. Small launches operating out of several Nicaraguan Pacific ports traverse the Gulf of Fonseca at night, carrying arms, ammunition, and personnel. During the general offensive on January 13, several dozen well-armed guerrillas landed on El Salvador's southeastern coast on the Gulf of Fonseca, adjacent to Nicaragua.

Overland arms shipments also continue through Honduras from Nicaragua and Costa Rica. In late January, Honduran security forces uncover an arms infiltration operation run by Salvadorans working through Nicaragua and directed by Cubans. In this operation, a trailer truck is discovered carrying weapons and ammunition destined for Salvadoran guerrillas. Weapons include 100 U.S. M-16 rifles and 81mm mortar ammunition. These arms are a portion of the Vietnamese shipment: A trace of the M-16s reveals that several of them were shipped to U.S. units in Vietnam, where they were captured or left behind. Using this network, perhaps five truckloads of arms may have reached the Salvadoran guerrillas.

15.
ASSISTANT SECRETARY OF STATE THOMAS ENDERS: POLICY ON EL SALVADOR (JULY 1981)

...Contrary to the insurgents' expectations, the Salvadorans contained the immediate January offensive on their own. Our assistance since has enabled the Duarte government to prevent the insurgents from turning their continuing outside support to new military advantage. Even more importantly, our assistance gives the Salvadoran people a chance to defend their right to self-determination by developing a political solution to the conflict....

And that is what I would like to talk about today: a political solution. For just as the conflict was Salvadoran in its origins, so its ultimate resolution must be Salvadoran.

For more than 18 months, El Salvador has had a government with a consistent and stable policy, one that emphasizes domestic reform, closer trade and diplomatic relations with neighboring nations, and firm resistance to outside intervention.

El Salvador, however, remains a divided country. It is divided between the insurgents and a great majority that opposes the extreme left's violent methods and foreign ties. It is divided between an equally violent minority on the extreme right that seeks to return El Salvador to the domination of a small elite and a great majority that has welcomed the political and social changes of the past 18 months.

The insurgents are divided within their own coalition—between those who want to prolong their ill-starred guerrilla campaign and those who are disillusioned by their failure to win the quick military victory their leaders had proclaimed inevitable; between those who despise democracy as an obstacle to their ambitions to seize power and those who might be willing to engage in democratic elections.

Finally, the vast majority of Salvadorans in the middle are also divided —over whether to emphasize the restoration of the country's economic health or the extension of the country's social reforms; between those who honor the army as one of the country's most stable and coherent institutions and those who criticize it for failing to prevent right-wing violence; between those who see the need to develop participatory institutions and those who maintain that there is no alternative to the old personalistic politics.

Address before the World Affairs Council, Washington, July 16, 1981.

Only Salvadorans can resolve these divisions. Neither we nor any other foreign country can do so. It is, therefore, critical that the Salvadoran Government itself is attempting to overcome these divisions by establishing a more democratic system. We wholeheartedly support this objective. Not out of blind sentiment, not out of a desire to reproduce everywhere a political system that has served Americans so extraordinarily well, and certainly not because we underestimate the difficulties involved. Rather we believe that the solution must be democratic because only a genuinely pluralistic approach can enable a profoundly divided society to live with itself without violent convulsions, gradually overcoming its differences.

PROPOSED STEPS

How can a country beset by so many troubles get from here to there? *The first thing to say is that promises must be kept.*

One can debate endlessly about El Salvador's land reform—whether the takeover of the big farms might have a high penalty in lost production for export, whether one can really give clear titles to over 200,000 individual peasant workers, and so forth. But the changes that have already taken place are real. The issue is no longer whether land reform is advisable or not. The issue now is how to consolidate and perfect what has been done. Individual titles are a practical necessity if peasants are to know that their new opportunities to work their own way out of subsistence poverty are fully legitimate. There is no other choice if economic and social chaos and an eventual guerrilla victory are to be avoided. . . .

Second, there must be demonstrable progress in controlling and eliminating violence from all sources. Violence of the left and violence of the right are inextricably linked. Since the failure of the January offensive, the tragic cycle of violence and counter-violence has been most evident in Chalatenango and Morazán, the remote areas where guerrilla forces are concentrated, and where most of the violent incidents recently attributed to the far right and to government forces have taken place. Elsewhere, the violence has tended to fall as the level of nationwide insurgent activity has declined. The investigations into the murders of the four American Catholic women and the two AIFLD [American Institute of Free Labor Development] experts, though still unfortunately incomplete, have led to detentions.

But more needs to be done. Cuban and Nicaraguan supplies to the guerrillas must stop. There is no doubt that Cuba was largely behind the arms trafficking that fueled the guerrilla offensive this winter. In April, when Socialist International representative Wischnewski confronted Castro with our evidence of Cuban interference, Castro admitted to him that Cuba had shipped arms to the guerrillas—just as we had said.

After their arms trafficking was exposed, Cuba and Nicaragua reduced the flow in March and early April. Recently, however, an ominous upswing has occurred, not to the volume reached this winter but to levels that enable the guerrillas to sustain military operations despite their inability to generate fresh support.

The other side of the coin is that more Salvadoran Army leadership is needed, both to fight rightist death squads and to control security force violence. This is a primary objective of our training effort. There must be improvement. The basic reality, however, is that violence will likely be countered by violence until a rational and legitimate political process is devised to break this vicious circle.

This brings me to my third point, that all parties that renounce violence should be encouraged to participate in the design of new political institutions and the process of choosing representatives for them. The Government of El Salvador has announced that it will hold presidential elections in 1983. Prior to that, a constituent assembly to be elected in 1982 will develop a new constitution.

The parties already legally registered include two groups associated with the insurgent political front: the National Revolutionary Movement led by Guillermo Ungo and the Democratic National Union, the electoral vehicle of the traditional Communist party. These parties, and any others that may wish to do so legally, now have before them the opportunity to test their strength against reformist and conservative parties according to the ultimate test of democracy: ballots, not bullets.

Before developing this critical point further, let me note that the value and importance of elections as a means for resolving and overcoming differences should not be underestimated in Central America today. Costa Rica has been able to resolve its political differences peacefully largely because elections have been held uninterruptedly since 1948—and are scheduled again next February.

Honduras elected a constituent assembly in April 1980 and will elect a president and a legislative assembly this coming November. The courage of Honduran leaders in standing by their election commitments despite regional turmoil and economic difficulties deserves recognition as an important contribution to the advancement of peaceful political processes in their country and in the region as a whole.

Guatemala this month began a campaign that is to lead to constitutionally mandated presidential elections next March. All of Guatemala's friends hope the campaign will evolve in a climate free of violence and contribute to the resolution of Guatemala's serious problems.

In all of Central America, only Nicaragua has no elections scheduled in the months ahead. The government has reneged on its promises to the people who overthrew Somoza 2 years ago and has said only that elections may be possible sometime in the future—maybe in 1985. What an extraordinary contrast between this clear lack of self-confidence on the part of the new revolutionary rulers of Nicaragua and the invitation from the embattled Salvadoran revolutionary junta to the political parties of El Salvador to organize for free elections. . . .

Nonetheless, before elections could take place, all parties would want to know how campaign security will be assured, and whether extremists might ultimately permit an actual election campaign without violence. If elections are held, would the results be respected? The government's intentions are clear. El Salvador's new military leaders have made the reform process possible. An army confident that its integrity will be respected, and that elections will be fair, can also be effective in curbing violence from the right as well as from the left. But it is only realistic to recognize that extremists on both left and right still oppose elections, and that an army suspicious that its institutional integrity might not be respected could itself become a destabilizing element. In this regard, we should recognize that El Salvador's leaders will not—and should not—grant the insurgents, through negotiations, the share of power the rebels have not been able to win on the battlefield. But they should be—and are—willing to compete with the insurgents at the polls. . . .

I have one more thing to say. *That is that the search for a political solution will not succeed unless the United States sustains its assistance to El Salvador.* . . .

16.
ENDERS-ORTEGA CORRESPONDENCE (1981)

On August 12, 1981 Assistant Secretary of State for Inter-American Affairs Thomas Enders met with Nicaraguan Comandante Daniel Ortega to discuss a possible normalization of bilateral relations. A follow-up letter by Enders, printed here, restates the U.S.'s prime concern over Nicaraguan support for Salvadoran guerrillas and notes that the U.S. will submit to Nicaragua several draft proposals that could provide a basis for normalized relations. The Nicaraguan government found the U.S. proposals unacceptable, and the failure of Enders' initiative led the administration to adopt in November 1981 the "two-track" policy of sup-

---

Letters of August 31, 1981, and September 16, 1981, from U.S. Assistant Secretary of State Thomas Enders to Comandante Daniel Ortega, Coordinator of the Junta of the Nicaraguan Government of National Reconstruction.

porting rebels to pressure the Nicaraguan government while continuing to press for negotiations.

Dear Comandante Ortega:

. . . Let me reiterate what I said in Managua. . . . The continued use of Nicaraguan territory to support and funnel arms to insurgent movements in the area would pose an insurmountable barrier to the development of normal relations between us. Unless this rapport is ended now, I can see no way that our proposed dialogue can bear fruit. A halt to the use of Nicaraguan territory for these purposes is, in fact, the sine qua non of a normal relationship. . . .

As I had mentioned to you, we and others are deeply preoccupied with apparent moves to build up Nicaragua's armed forces beyond traditional levels. As I understood, Nicaragua is concerned with the possibility of U.S. aggressive acts and of U.S. acquiescence to, or sponsorship of, groups opposed to the Government of Nicaragua. You had also expressed your view that U.S. economic assistance to Nicaragua should be resumed.

Over the next few weeks we will be passing to you, through our Chargé in Managua, a series of illustrative drafts designed to meet these concerns. . . .

[What follows is an excerpt from the second of these draft proposals, included in a Enders letter dated September 16, 1981.]

. . . The United States and Nicaragua reaffirm that their relations are guided by certain fundamental principles of the international legal order, exemplified in particular by their rights and obligations as set forth in the charters of the United Nations and the Organization of American States, the Inter-American Treaty of Reciprocal Assistance, and other conventions and treaties promoting inter-American cooperation to which both countries are party.

These mutual commitments include:

— Settlement of all disputes by peaceful means;
— Condemnation of the threat or use of force aimed against the territorial integrity or political independence of any other state;
— The inadmissibility of intervention by any state, to undermine the political independence of another state or the self determination of its people; and
— The commitment of each state to refrain from assisting or acquiescing in terrorist or armed activities from its own territory directed toward the commission of violent acts against another state.

Acts of aggression or other acts that threaten the stability of the region or the territorial integrity, sovereignty or independence of any state in the region will be resisted consistent with the UN and OAS charters and the Inter-American Treaty of Reciprocal Assistance and their procedures for collective self-defense.

Nicaragua and the United States intend to continue to consult closely on matters of mutual interest, and to seek expanded opportunities for cooperation in the interests of promoting peace, security, and the process of economic development both in Nicaragua and the neighboring states of Central America.

Sincerely,

Thomas O. Enders

17.
RONALD REAGAN: CARIBBEAN BASIN INITIATIVE (FEBRUARY 1982)

The Caribbean region is a vital strategic and commercial artery for the United States. Nearly half of our trade, two-thirds of our imported oil, and over half of our imported strategic minerals pass through the Panama Canal or the Gulf of Mexico. Make no mistake: The well-being and security of our neighbors in this region are in our own vital interest.

Economic health is one of the keys to a secure future for our Caribbean Basin and to the neighbors there. I'm happy to say that Mexico, Canada, and Venezuela have joined in this search for ways to help these countries realize their economic potential. Each of our four nations has its own unique position and approach. Mexico and Venezuela are helping to offset energy costs to Caribbean Basin countries by means of an oil facility that is already in operation. Canada is doubling its already significant economic assistance.

We all seek to ensure that the peoples of this area have the right to preserve their own national identities, to improve their economic lot, and to develop their political institutions to suit their own unique social and historical needs. The Central American and Caribbean countries differ widely in culture, personality, and needs. Like America itself, the Caribbean Basin is an extraordinary mosaic of Hispanics, Africans, Asians, and Europeans, as well as Native Americans.

At the moment, however, these countries are under economic siege. In 1977, 1 barrel of oil was worth 5 pounds of coffee or 155 pounds of sugar. To buy that same barrel of oil today, these small countries must provide five times as much coffee (nearly 26 pounds) or almost twice as much sugar

Speech to the Organization of American States, February 24, 1982. *Department of State Bulletin,* April 1982.

(283 pounds). This economic disaster is consuming our neighbors' money, reserves, and credit, forcing thousands of people to leave for other countries—for the United States, often illegally—and shaking even the most established democracies. And economic disaster has provided a fresh opening to the enemies of freedom, national independence, and peaceful development.

PROPOSED ECONOMIC PROGRAM

We've taken the time to consult closely with other governments in the region, both sponsors and beneficiaries, to ask them what they need and what they think will work. And we've labored long to develop an economic program that integrates trade, aid, and investment—a program that represents a long-term commitment to the countries of the Caribbean and Central America to make use of the magic of the marketplace, the market of the Americas, and to earn their own way toward self-sustaining growth.

At the Cancún summit last October, I presented a fresh view of a development which stressed more than aid and government intervention. As I pointed out then, nearly all of the countries that have succeeded in their development over the past 30 years have done so on the strength of market-oriented policies and vigorous participation in the international economy. Aid must be complemented by trade and investment.

The program I'm proposing today puts these principles into practice. It is an integrated program that helps our neighbors help themselves, a program that will create conditions under which creativity and private entrepreneurship and self-help can flourish. Aid is an important part of this program because many of our neighbors need it to put themselves in a starting position from which they can begin to earn their own way. But this aid will encourage private sector activities but not displace them.

First. The centerpiece of the program that I am sending to the Congress is free trade for Caribbean Basin products exported to the United States. Currently, some 87% of Caribbean exports already enter U.S. markets duty-free under the generalized system of preferences. These exports, however, cover only the limited range of existing products, not the wide variety of potential products these talented and industrious peoples are capable of producing under the free trade arrangement that I am proposing. Exports from the area will receive duty-free treatment for 2 years. Thus, new investors will be able to enter the market knowing that their products will receive duty-free treatment for at least the pay-off lifetime of their investments. Before granting duty-free treatment, we will discuss with each country its own self-help measures.

The only exception to the free trade concept will be textile and apparel products because these products are covered now by other international agreements. However, we will make sure that our immediate neighbors have more liberal quota arrangements.

This economic proposal is as unprecedented as today's crisis in the Caribbean. Never before has the United States offered a preferential trading arrangement to any region. This commitment makes unmistakably clear our determination to help our neighbors grow strong. The impact of this free trade approach will develop slowly. The economies that we seek to help are small. Even as they grow, all the protections now available to U.S. industry, agriculture, and labor against disruptive imports will remain. And growth in the Caribbean will benefit everyone, with American exports finding new markets. . . .

Second. To further attract investment, I will ask the Congress to provide significant tax incentives for investment in the Caribbean Basin. We also stand ready to negotiate bilateral investment treaties with interested basin countries.

Third. I'm asking for a supplemental fiscal year 1982 appropriation of $350 million to assist those countries which are particularly hard hit economically. Much of this aid will be concentrated in the private sector. These steps will help foster the spirit of enterprise necessary to take advantage of the trade and investment portions of the program.

Fourth. We will offer technical assistance and training to assist the private sector in the Basin countries to benefit from the opportunities of this program. This will include investment promotion, export marketing, and technology transfer efforts, as well as programs to facilitate adjustments to greater competition and production in agriculture and industry. I intend to seek the active participation of the business community in this joint undertaking. The Peace Corps already has 861 volunteers in Caribbean Basin countries and will give special emphasis to recruiting volunteers with skills in developing local enterprise.

Fifth. We will work closely with Mexico, Canada, and Venezuela, all of which have already begun substantial and innovative programs of their own, to encourage stronger international efforts to coordinate our own development measures with their vital contributions, and with those of other potential donors like Colombia. We will also encourage our European, Japanese, and other Asian allies as well as multilateral development institutions to increase their assistance in the region.

Sixth. Given our special valued relationship with Puerto Rico and the U.S. Virgin Islands, we will propose special measures to ensure that they also will benefit and prosper from this program. With their strong traditions of democracy and free enterprise, they can play leading roles in the development of the area.

18.
U.S. CONGRESS: CERTIFYING DEMOCRATIC PROGRESS IN EL SALVADOR (1981)

ASSISTANCE FOR EL SALVADOR

SEC. 727. (a) It is the sense of the Congress that assistance furnished to the Government of El Salvador, both economic and military, should be used to encourage—

(1) full observance of internationally recognized human rights in accordance with sections 116 and 502B of the Foreign Assistance Act of 1961;
(2) full respect for all other fundamental human rights, including the right of freedom of speech and of the press, the right to organize and operate free labor unions, and the right to freedom of religion;
(3) continued progress in implementing essential economic and political reforms, including land reform and support for the private sector;
(4) a complete and timely investigation of the deaths of all United States citizens killed in El Salvador since October 1979;
(5) an end to extremist violence and the establishment of a unified command and control of all government security forces in this effort;
(6) free, fair, and open elections at the earliest date; and
(7) increased professional capability of the Salvadoran Armed Forces in order to establish a peaceful and secure environment in which economic development and reform and the democratic processes can be fully implemented, thereby permitting a phased withdrawal of United States military training and advisory personnel at the earliest possible date.

(b) It is the sense of the Congress that the United States' economic assistance to El Salvador should put emphasis on revitalizing the private sector and supporting the free market system. The Congress recognizes that the lack of foreign exchange to buy imported raw materials and intermediate goods is a major impediment to the ability of the Salvadoran economy to provide jobs. The Congress also recognizes that the funds budgeted for economic assistance are only a fraction of the foreign exchange needed, and United States economic aid should be used, wherever possible, to stimulate

Sections 727–731 of the Foreign Assistance Act of 1981, which became Public Law 97–113 on December 29, 1981.

private sector lending. Therefore, the Congress urges the President to set aside a portion of the economic support funds to provide guarantees to private United States banks willing to give credits to the Salvadoran private sector.

RESTRICTIONS ON MILITARY ASSISTANCE AND SALES TO EL SALVADOR

SEC. 728. (a)(1) The Congress finds that peaceful and democratic development in Central America is in the interest of the United States and of the community of American States generally, that the recent civil strife in El Salvador has caused great human suffering and disruption to the economy of that country, and that substantial assistance to El Salvador is necessary to help alleviate that suffering and to promote economic recovery within a peaceful and democratic process. Moreover, the Congress recognizes that the efforts of the Government of El Salvador to achieve these goals are affected by the activities of forces beyond its control.

(2) Taking note of the substantial progress made by the Government of El Salvador in land and banking reforms, the Congress declares it should be the policy of the United States to encourage and support the Government of El Salvador in the implementation of these reforms.

(3) The United States also welcomes the continuing efforts of President Duarte and his supporters in the Government of El Salvador to establish greater control over the activities of members of the armed forces and government security forces. The Congress finds that it is in the interest of the United States to cooperate with the Duarte government in putting an end to violence in El Salvador by extremist elements among both the insurgents and the security forces, and in establishing a unified command and control of all government forces.

(4) The United States supports the holding of free, fair, and open elections in El Salvador at the earliest date. The Congress notes the progress being made by the Duarte government in this area, as evidenced by the appointment of an electoral commission.

(b) In fiscal year 1982 and 1983, funds may be obligated for assistance for El Salvador under chapter 2 or 5 of part II of the Foreign Assistance Act of 1961, letters of offer may be issued and credits and guarantees may be extended for El Salvador under the Arms Export Control Act, and members of the Armed Forces may be assigned or detailed to El Salvador to carry out functions under the Foreign Assistance Act of 1961 or the Arms Export Control Act, only if not later than thirty days after the date of enactment of this Act and every one hundred and eighty days thereafter, the President makes a certification in accordance with subsection (d).

(c) If the President does not make such such a certification at any of the specified times then the President shall immediately—

(1) suspend all expenditures of funds and other deliveries of assistance for El Salvador which were obligated under chapters 2 and 5 of part II of the Foreign Assistance Act of 1961 after the date of enactment of this Act;

(2) withhold all approvals for use of credits and guarantees for El Salvador which were extended under the Arms Export Control Act after the date of enactment of this Act;

(3) suspend all deliveries of defense articles, defense services, and design and construction services to El Salvador which were sold under the Arms Export Control Act after the date of enactment of this Act; and

(4) order the prompt withdrawal from El Salvador of all members of the Armed Forces performing defense services, conducting international military education and training activities, or performing management functions under section 515 of the Foreign Assistance Act of 1961.

Any suspension of assistance pursuant to paragraphs (1) through (4) of this subsection shall remain in effect during fiscal year 1982 and during fiscal year 1983 until such time as the President makes a certification in accordance with subsection (d).

(d) The certification required by subsection (b) is a certification by the President to the Speaker of the House of Representatives and to the chairman of the Committee on Foreign Relations of the Senate of a determination that the Government of El Salvador—

(1) is making a concerted and significant effort to comply with internationally recognized human rights;

(2) is achieving substantial control over all elements of its own armed forces, so as to bring to an end the indiscriminate torture and murder of Salvadoran citizens by these forces:

(3) is making continued progress in implementing essential economic and political reforms, including the land reform program;

(4) is committed to the holding of free elections at an early date and to that end has demonstrated its good faith efforts to begin discussions with all major political factions in El Salvador which have declared their willingness to find and implement an equitable political solution to the conflict, with such solution to involve a commitment to—

(A) a renouncement of further military or paramilitary activity; and

(B) the electoral process with internationally recognized observers.

Each such certification shall discuss fully and completely the justification for making each of the determinations required by paragraphs (1) through (4).

(e) On making the first certification under subsection (b) of this section, the President shall also certify to the Speaker of the House of Representatives and the chairman of the Committee on Foreign Relations of the Senate that he has determined that the Government of El Salvador has made good faith efforts both to investigate the murders of the six United States citizens in El Salvador in December 1980 and January 1981 and to bring to justice those responsible for those murders.

REPORTING REQUIREMENT RELATING TO EL SALVADOR

SEC. 729.(a) Not later than ninety days after the date of enactment of this section, the President shall prepare and transmit to the Speaker of the House of Representatives and to the chairman of the Committee on Foreign Relations of the Senate a report setting forth—

> (1) the viewpoints of all major parties to the conflict in El Salvador and of the influential actors in the Salvadoran political system regarding the potential for and interest in negotiations, elections, and a settlement of the conflict; and
>
> (2) the views of democratic Latin American nations, Canada, the Organization of American States, and European allies of the United States regarding a negotiated settlement to such conflict.

(b) It is the sense of the Congress that the President shall, as soon as possible, send a special envoy or use other appropriate means to consult with and gather information from appropriate representatives of the parties to the Salvadoran conflict, democratic governments of Latin America, Canada, and European allies of the United States regarding the attainment of a negotiated settlement in El Salvador.

RESTRICTIONS ON AID TO EL SALVADOR

SEC. 730. None of the funds authorized to be appropriated by this Act may be made available for the provision of assistance to El Salvador for the purpose of planning for compensation, or for the purpose of compensation, for the confiscation, nationalization, acquisition, or expropriation of any agricultural or banking enterprise, or of the properties or stock shares which may be pertaining thereto.

EL SALVADORAN REFUGEES

SEC. 731. It is the sense of the Congress that the administration should continue to review, on a case-by-case basis, petitions for extended voluntary departure made by citizens of El Salvador who claim that they are subject to persecution in their homeland, and should take full account of the civil strife in El Salvador in making decisions on such petitions.

19.
HOUSE OF REPRESENTATIVES COMMITTEE ON INTELLIGENCE: U.S. INTELLIGENCE PERFORMANCE ON CENTRAL AMERICA (SEPTEMBER 1982)

VALUE AND DIFFICULTY OF INTELLIGENCE ON CENTRAL AMERICA

From 1978, when the Sandinista-led revolution against Anastasio Somoza in Nicaragua gained momentum, until El Salvador became a major focus for East-West relations under the newly-elected U.S. administration in 1981, Central American issues increased dramatically as subjects demanding the attention and resources of the intelligence community. Throughout this period and into the present, the Committee has monitored intelligence performance closely, partly to ensure the availability of the necessary resources for collection and analysis, but primarily to evaluate and reinforce the quality of analysis and the integrity of the intelligence process.

Several factors have contributed to both the difficulty and the importance to the United States of intelligence on this region. Foremost among these is that capabilities for collection and analysis had to be expanded rapidly, as a region which had been of low policy interest became a focus for concern. The rapid prominence of the conflict in El Salvador as a policy issue, and the change of U.S. administrations while the region was in upheaval, have made intelligence more important to the policy process than it might otherwise be.

Adding to the difficulty of intelligence in this region are the shifts in policy emphasis that have occurred over the last few years. As policies change, so do the kinds of questions that policymakers ask, and the kind of data required. The region has many historical and economic ties to the United States, and Americans have traditionally viewed it as a special area of interest. However, the exact nature of U.S. interests and objectives in revolutionary Central America is not always self-evident. Rather, the definition of U.S. interests in each of the particular circumstances facing the United States throughout Central America is shaped to a large extent by intelligence—by the way it analyzes and presents the causes of conflict, the nature of the governments in the region, the actions and

Staff Report, Subcommittee on Oversight and Devaluation, Permanent Select Committee on Intelligence, September 22, 1982.

goals of the Soviet Union, the capabilities of guerrilla forces, and the objectives and popular support of other political groups. Finally, the job of intelligence is made difficult because apparent similarities across the region often serve to mask substantial differences from country to country.

Whom to aid and how; whether to focus on intercepting arms to guerrillas; how to promote economic development; whether and with whom to negotiate; and how to reinforce positive developments and respond to negative ones—these are among the policy issues that confront the United States. To address them properly, intelligence must meet especially high standards of accuracy, objectivity, and sensitivity to the full range of local and global factors, and to the political, military, and socio-economic dimensions of a given situation.

ACHIEVEMENTS AND WEAKNESSES

The intelligence community has contributed significantly to meet the needs of policymakers on Central America. Over the last two years perhaps its greatest achievement lies in determining with considerable accuracy the organization and activities of the Salvadoran guerrillas, and in detecting the assistance given to them by Cuba and other communist countries. Although amounts of aid and degrees of influence are difficult to assess, intelligence has been able to establish beyond doubt the involvement of communist countries in the insurgency. On March 4, 1982, the Chairman of this Committee publicly recognized these achievements of the intelligence community by issuing a press release, which said in part:

> The insurgents are well-trained, well-equipped with modern weapons and supplies, and rely on the use of sites in Nicaragua for command and control and for logistical support. The intelligence supporting these judgments . . . is convincing.
> There is further persuasive evidence that the Sandinista government of Nicaragua is helping train insurgents and is transferring arms and support from and through Nicaragua to the insurgents. They are further providing the insurgents with bases of operation in Nicaragua. Cuban involvement— in providing arms—is also evident.

In monitoring the voluminous production of written and oral intelligence on Central America, the staff has also found good performance in many other areas. These include CIA predictions in mid-1978 of Somoza's downfall; insightful descriptions of Guatemala's increasingly polarized society; detailed reporting on the attitudes, structure, capabilities and needs of various military services in Central America; valuable background papers compiled on major Central American political leaders; careful analyses of the effects upon the economies of the region of worldwide economic problems and of disruption caused by terrorism and guerrilla warfare.

The contribution of intelligence in these and other areas testifies to the strengths of the intelligence community. These include careful analysis, sometimes conducted by personnel who have lived in the region, and honed by vigorous debate among analysts; successful exploitation of multiple sources of intelligence; the skillful allocation of collection assets; and the dedicated and painstaking processing of many small items of information, which, taken together, provide significant insights.

Notwithstanding the strengths described above, when intelligence is held against the high standards required of it, certain weaknesses appear. These sometimes lie in analysis or in the management of collection, or sometimes simply in their presentation. The weaknesses, which the report identifies in particular instances of intelligence on El Salvador and Nicaragua, include:

- Suggestion of greater certainty than is warranted by the evidence;
- Reliance on some unquestioned and sometimes contradictory assumptions;
- Acceptance of descriptions given by the Salvadoran government when intelligence analysts recognize grounds for skepticism; and
- Resistance to examining objectively information from non-intelligence sources—a tendency to view such information simply as material to be countered.

AREAS OF PARTICULAR CONCERN—INTELLIGENCE PERFORMANCE ON:

A. External Support to Salvadoran Insurgents

The intelligence community has devoted considerable effort to identifying support to the Salvadoran insurgents from other countries. Information on arms trafficking was growing when, in September 1980, President Carter's certification that Nicaragua was not aiding the insurgents focused major attention on the subject. In late 1980 documents were captured from the guerrillas which showed that a substantial amount of arms and other supplies had been obtained from communist countries. They showed Cuba, with Nicaraguan participation, to be heavily involved in the coordination, control, and movement of the materiel.

In early 1982 Secretary Haig asserted that the Salvadoran insurgency was controlled by non-Salvadorans. A major intelligence briefing, based primarily on an analysis of sensitive intelligence, was provided by the intelligence community to select audiences in the Congress and executive branch. This Committee received that briefing on March 4, and the Chairman issued the press release quoted earlier in this report. This statement confirmed the existence of convincing intelligence that the insurgents rely on the use of sites in Nicaragua for certain headquarters and logistical operations, and of persuasive evidence of Cuban and Nicaraguan support. The statement did not address the extent of control of the insurgency by non-Salvadorans, a point which remained subject to differing interpretations.

The briefing was based on a skillful and professional examination of data obtained from various sources. The analysis was impressive and of definite value to policymakers. Yet the presentation was flawed by several instances of overstatement and overinterpretation. Clearly these inaccuracies were of little intrinsic importance. However, they detracted somewhat from the credibility of the presentation. . . .

The briefing stated that "lots of ships have been traced" from the Soviet Union, through various other countries, and on to Nicaragua, but when the Committee asked how many ships had been traced along this route and when, the written response indicated that intelligence could show only a very few examples. Another statement was that, "You don't plan an operation like what is being run in El Salvador if you haven't gone to somebody's command and general staff college." Subcommittee staff understood this statement to mean that the insurgency was being commanded by graduates of schools comparable to the U.S. Army Command and General Staff College—presumably in the Soviet Union or bloc countries. The Committee asked about the evidence, and the written response explained the comment as "a figure of speech meant simply to emphasize the greater sophistication and training of the Salvadoran insurgents compared to the Sandinistas at the time that they overthrew Somoza."

A slide titled "Guerrilla Financing (Non-Arms)" indicated that Salvadoran guerrillas were receiving money in addition to weapons, showing a total of some $17 million annually. This resulted from an extrapolation which, as outlined by the briefer, seemed particularly tenuous. It was based on a single piece of evidence indicating the monthly budget for the commander of one faction on one front. The extrapolation would have required that figure to be representative of the budgets of the other four factions, and all five factions to be equally active on each of the five fronts. In a question for the record, the Committee asked about these assumptions. In its response, the intelligence community said it was unable to comment on whether the original monthly figure was representative, and instead explained that the bottom line of $17 million which appeared in the briefing slide was "not an estimate," but was intended only to indicate that "relatively large sums of currency" were going to the guerrillas. . . .

B. Extremist Elements of the Salvadoran Right

Rightist violence—as distinct from lawful political activities of the right—has been recognized as a necessary subject for reporting. The problem of death squad activity, the involvement of security forces in political killings, and the reputed attitudes of Salvadoran officials toward these problems have all been treated in reporting from the U.S. Embassy over the past two years. In interviews with staff, officials have emphasized that they recognized that rightist violence and its relationship to the security forces was a priority for their reporting.

Despite this, intelligence has provided little firm information about the subject of violence by the right and the security forces. The entire subject of political killings—whether by the right or the left—is often described as unknowable. Although educated guesses are sometimes made on the basis of the identity of the victim—murders of government informants and soldiers' families attributed to leftist killers, and murders of labor organizers and refugee workers attributed to rightists—other information about political killings that might permit such attribution is not systematically collected or analyzed.

The large number of unexplained murders, witnesses' fear of retaliation, and the danger of travel in El Salvador make the investigation of individual killings extremely difficult. Nevertheless, relatively more is known about the organization and whereabouts of the insurgents in their conduct of both guerrilla operations and of terrorist killings than about the circumstances or lines of authority resulting in abductions of alleged leftist sympathizers or in the depositing of bodies along Salvadoran highways during curfew hours. . . .

In its various statements about political violence, the Embassy study indicates fundamental uncertainty about the level at which decisions are made concerning the political killings by the right or by security forces. It reports that "armed civilians who ostensibly form part of the state's security net" but who have "become a law unto themselves in many areas, operating within loosely defined boundaries, . . . are judged responsible for a fair share of anonymous murders. . . .

20.
INTELLIGENCE AUTHORIZATION ACT FOR FISCAL YEAR 1984

. . . **SEC. 109. (a)** The Congress finds that—

(1) the Government of National Reconstruction of Nicaragua has failed to keep solemn promises, made to the Organization of American States in July 1979, to establish full respect for human rights and political liberties, hold early elections, preserve a private sector, permit political pluralism, and pursue a foreign policy of nonaggression and nonintervention;

(2) by providing military support (including arms, training, and logistical, command and control, and communications facilities) to groups seeking to overthrow the Government of El Salvador and other Central American governments, the Government of National Reconstruction of Nicaragua has violated article 18 of the Charter of the Organization of American States which declares that no state has the right to intervene, directly or indirectly, for any reason whatsoever, in the internal or external affairs of any other state;

(3) the Government of Nicaragua should be held accountable before the Organization of American States for activities violative of promises made to the Organization and for violations of the Charter of that Organization; and

(4) working through the Organization of American States is the proper and most effective means of dealing with threats to the peace of Central America, of providing for common action in the event of aggression, and of providing the mechanisms for peaceful resolution of disputes among the countries of Central America.

(b) The President should seek a prompt reconvening of the Seventeenth Meeting of Consultation of Ministers of Foreign Affairs of the Organization of American States for the purpose of reevaluating the compliance by the Government of National Reconstruction of Nicaragua—

(1) with the commitments made by the leaders of that Government in July 1979 to the Organization of American States; and

(2) with the Charter of the Organization of American States.

Public Law 98-215, 98th Congress.

(c) The President should vigorously seek actions by the Organization of American States that would provide for a full range of effective measures by the member states to bring about compliance by the Government of National Reconstruction of Nicaragua with those obligations, including verifiable agreements to halt the transfer of military equipment and to cease furnishing of military support facilities to groups seeking the violent overthrow of governments of countries in Central America.

(d) The President should use all diplomatic means at his disposal to encourage the Organization of American States to seek resolution of the conflicts in Central America based on the provisions of the Final Act of the San José Conference of October 1982, especially principles (d), (e), and (g), relating to nonintervention in the internal affairs of other countries, denying support for terrorist and subversive elements in other states, and international supervision of fully verifiable arrangements.

(e) The United States should support measures at the Organization of American States, as well as efforts of the Contadora Group, which seek to end support for terrorist, subversive, or other activities aimed at the violent overthrow of the governments of countries in Central America. . . .

21.
REP. MICHAEL BARNES AND OTHERS: DEMOCRATIC ALTERNATIVES (DECEMBER 1982)

The Reagan Administration's extreme approach is fostering not peace and democracy, but increased polarization and radicalization.

Since January 1981, brutal civil wars have intensified in El Salvador and Guatemala, the threat of war between Nicaragua and Honduras has increased partly because of U.S. actions, and moderate and democratic elements have lost influence in Nicaragua and throughout the region. Neither "quiet diplomacy" with respect to human rights nor massive doses of military aid have accomplished their intended purpose.

The ability to make a free and open choice of political allegiance is the essence of democracy, but it is becoming less and less possible to make such a choice in Central America. Those seeking to rule by coercion rather than consent reside on both extremes of the region's political spectrum. These extremes are not opponents, but rather allies; they gather strength from each other, and they must equally be opposed.

Position Paper of eighteen Democratic senators and representatives, December 9, 1982.

The Reagan Administration has chosen a policy which lends confidence to the terrorist right; which motivates and strengthens the terrorist left; . . .

- After two years and hundreds of millions of dollars of aid, the United States is further than ever from achieving its goals in El Salvador. Although the elections last March confirmed the deep desire of the Salvadoran people for participatory democracy, the electoral initiative was too narrowly based to move El Salvador toward national reconciliation. Rather, it weakened those advocating a moderate course, and left competition for power in the hands of brutal and historically undemocratic military cliques. The Reagan Administration has failed dismally to demonstrate strength or seriousness of purpose in pushing for economic reforms and respect for human rights in El Salvador, and has explicitly opposed a dialogue without preconditions between the government and opposition groups.

- The Administration's support for covert military action against Nicaragua has produced a propaganda bonanza for the radical left, an excuse for a military build-up by Managua, and a growing threat of regional war. It has also shifted the focus of world attention from Nicaragua's errors in policy to ours, and contributed to a political atmosphere inside that country within which moderate and democratic elements may not long survive.

- The Administration has persisted in viewing Honduras as a convenient staging ground for regional military initiatives rather than a fragile democracy needing insulation from the conflicts engulfing its neighbors. The result is an increasingly divided and fearful country, unable to derive internal confidence from its recent transition to civilian democratic rule. . . .

The Administration has refused to recognize the nature and source of the tensions which threaten to destroy all of Central America. It has sought to apply a simplistic economic and political world view. . . .

1. We urge the Administration to join with Mexico and Venezuela in encouraging the prompt initiation of discussions between and among our own government and the governments of Honduras, Nicaragua and El Salvador for the purpose of ending all acts of subversion and aggression and achieving a just and lasting peace in the region.

2. We urge the Administration to lend its full support to negotiations without pre-conditions, aimed at resolving peacefully the internal political disputes presently existing between the populations and the governments of El Salvador and Guatemala. Additionally, we believe that an effort to reconcile Nicaraguan opposition groups, including democratic exile groups, with the government of that country through a negotiating process or other mutually acceptable means should be strongly encouraged. In each of these countries our purpose should be to facilitate the creation of an open democratic electoral process and genuine political pluralism;

3. The U.S. should cease assisting covert military activities directed at Nicaragua. Any accusations concerning Nicaragua's alleged support for subversive activities in El Salvador, Costa Rica, or Honduras, should—if private discussions fail to resolve the matter—be made public and brought promptly to the attention of the United Nations or the Organization of American States.

4. We reiterate our belief that respect for internationally recognized human rights, including the rights of indigenous peoples, should be a cornerstone of American foreign policy, both in Central America and around the globe. . . .

Security assistance may not be provided to governments—such as that currently in power in Guatemala—which are engaged in a consistent pattern of gross violations of internationally recognized human rights. Nor may military aid to El Salvador continue unless a series of legal conditions are met concerning human rights, economic reforms and investigations into the cases of murdered Americans.

5. We propose a new and expanded inter-American development program aimed at encouraging multilateral efforts in behalf of economic and agricultural self-sufficiency, and at providing emergency aid to democratic governments such as those of Costa Rica, Honduras, and the Dominican Republic. This program will be designed to build on and improve upon the Caribbean Basin Initiative of 1982.

We will take into account the fact that in countries where serious political and military repression exists, no amount of economic assistance will, in itself, be sufficient to produce meaningful social development or reform.

We believe the time has come to stop the killing and start the talking in Central America. We reject the view that violence is inevitable or endemic to the region's culture. We have witnessed—and place great faith in—the courage, the persistence, and the wisdom of those in each of these countries who have been working for peace, democracy and social justice.

22.
AMBASSADOR DEANE HINTON: JUSTICE IN EL SALVADOR (OCTOBER 1982)

Reflecting today on my experiences in El Salvador, I would no doubt be well advised to talk of other things—perhaps to talk of the economy, of the private sector's determined efforts to keep working despite everything, including the sad practice of some Salvadorans blowing up the economic infrastructure and other Salvadorans keeping desperately needed capital outside the country; of what I consider to be, in war economy conditions, sound governmental policy; and of American economic assistance—over $230 million this year. Or perhaps I should analyze basic issues posed by enormous population pressure and rapid population growth. Another subject, for another day, might be reflections on educational requirements to prepare citizens for their critical role in a functioning democracy.

But, for better or worse, today I want to talk of a subject so many of you, because of indifference or shame or fear or for what other reason I know not, leave in eloquent silence.

CRIMINAL SYSTEM ISSUE

Neither internal confidence nor external support can long survive here in the absence of an effective system of criminal justice. Until all are protected by the law, until all are subject to the law, El Salvador will lack a fundamental prerequisite for a healthy society and, I might add, for a healthy economy.

In the first 2 weeks of this month, at least 68 human beings were murdered in El Salvador under circumstances which are familiar to everyone here. Every day we receive new reports of disappearances under tragic circumstances. American citizens in El Salvador have been among the murdered, among the disappeared. Is it any wonder that much of the world is predisposed to believe the worst of a system which almost never brings to justice either those who perpetrate these acts or those who order them? The "Mafia" must be stopped. Your survival depends on it. The guerrillas of this Mafia, every bit as much as the guerrillas of Morazán and Chalatenango, are destroying El Salvador.

The battle has been joined. Both the civilian and military authorities of the Government of El Salvador have spoken out unequivocally against the abuses of basic human rights. They have backed up their words with action. They have begun the process of bringing to justice those who commit crimes under whatever banner—no matter who they might be.

Are there anywhere near enough properly trained and rewarded prosecutors to deal with the violence in the society as to make successful prosecution virtually impossible for any but a self-confessed criminal? Are judges sufficiently protected and isolated so as to assure verdicts based neither on bribery nor on fear? Can the prison system absorb and control those who should be convicted?

These are questions with which all civilized societies must deal, but it is sad to see a society in which the answers are so painfully and consistently inadequate.

If you are not convinced that I am talking about a fundamental and critical problem, consider these facts. Since 1979 perhaps as many as 30,000 Salvadorans have been killed illegally; that is, not in battle. Less than 1,500 cases of "crimes against the person"—that is, homicide, assault, and battery—have been prosecuted before your courts. Most striking of all, there have been less than 200 convictions for these crimes.

. . . as the representative of the United States in El Salvador, I can try to communicate as clearly and honestly as I can the sentiments of the American people, the Congress, and the Administration on this subject. The message is simple: El Salvador must have substantial progress on bringing the murders of our citizens, including those who ordered the murders, to justice; in advancing human rights; and controlling the abuses of some elements of the security forces. If not, the United States, despite our other interests and our commitment to the struggle against communism, could be forced to deny assistance to El Salvador.

23.
SECRETARY OF STATE GEORGE P. SHULTZ:
STRUGGLE FOR DEMOCRACY (APRIL 1983)

. . . But just as no amount of reform can bring peace so long as guerrillas believe they can win a military victory, no amount of economic help will suffice if guerrilla units can destroy roads, bridges, power stations, and crops again and again with impunity. So we must also support the security of El Salvador and the other threatened nations of the region. . . .

Faced with a grave regionwide crisis, we must seek regional, peaceful solutions. We are trying to persuade the Sandinistas that they should come to the bargaining table, ready to come to terms with their neighbors and with their own increasingly troubled society.

EL SALVADOR

Let's now look at how this strategy works in practice, and let me turn first to El Salvador. The basic fact about El Salvador today is that its people want peace. Because they do, they have laid the essential groundwork for national reconciliation and renewal. Let me give you some details.

U.S. Department of State, Current Policy Paper 478.

First. Even in the midst of guerrilla war, respect for human rights has grown. Violence against noncombatants is still high, but it has diminished markedly since our assistance began 3 years ago. The criminal justice system does remain a major concern. . . .

Second. In 3 short years and despite determined guerrilla opposition, El Salvador's Government has redistributed more than 20% of all arable land. Some 450,000 people—about 1 Salvadoran in every 10—have benefited directly and have acquired a personal stake in a secure future.

Third. The general economic situation is poor. Just to stay even this year, El Salvador will need substantial economic assistance to import seed, fertilizer, and pesticides for its farms and raw materials for its factories. . . .

Fourth. This brings me to a fourth point. The three government battalions we have trained conduct themselves professionally, both on the battlefield and in their relations with civilians. But only 1 Salvadoran soldier in 10 has received our training—fewer than the many guerrillas trained by Nicaragua and Cuba.

Fifth. And, finally, what is at issue in El Salvador is the cause of democracy. I cannot stress this point enough, and here the progress has been substantial. The Constituent Assembly, elected a year ago, has drafted a new constitution, sustained a moderate government of national unity, and extended land reform. . . .

We will not support negotiations that short circuit the very democratic process El Salvador is trying to establish. We will not carve up power behind people's backs as happened in Nicaragua. I'm shocked at the suggestions I sometimes hear when I'm testifying that what we ought to do, having observed these people try by violence to prevent an election from happening, is to allow them by violence and with our agreement to shoot their way into the government. No dice. We will not support that kind of activity. . . .

24.
VICE-PRESIDENT GEORGE BUSH: DEATH SQUADS IN EL SALVADOR (DECEMBER 1983)

A guerrilla war is a long, arduous effort fought on many fronts: military, economic, social, and political. But the crucial battle is not for territory;

Speech at a dinner hosted by President Álvaro Borja Magaña in San Salvador.

it is for men's minds. The guerrillas never lose sight of that objective. They know the government is responsible for protecting the people. So their goal is to cripple the government, distort its priorities, and sow doubt about its legitimacy.

For a government to survive a guerrilla challenge, it must continue to protect its citizens even as it fights to defend itself from those who play by other rules—or no rules at all. As it does, it must continue to respect the rule of law and the rights of the individual. And it must honor basic human decencies. If it does not, it will lose that crucial battle for the support and approval of the people.

Mr. President, you and many other Salvadorans have demonstrated extraordinary personal courage in the struggle against tyranny and extremism, but your cause is being undermined by the murderous violence of reactionary minorities.

Tom Pickering's [U.S. Ambassador to El Salvador] remarks—which I greatly admire and which the President and I both fully endorse—were right on the mark. These rightwing fanatics are the best friends the Soviets, the Cubans, the Sandinista *comandantes,* and the Salvadoran guerrillas have. Every murderous act they commit poisons the well of friendship between our two countries and advances the cause of those who would impose an alien dictatorship on the people of El Salvador. These cowardly death squad terrorists are just as repugnant to me, to President Reagan, to the U.S. Congress, and to the American people as the terrorists of the left.

Mr. President, I know that these words are not those of the usual dinner toast. My intention is not to abuse your hospitality nor to offend you and your other guests. I speak as a friend, one who is committed to your success —the success of democracy in El Salvador. And I owe it to you as a friend to speak frankly.

We in the U.S. have never asked that others be exactly like us. We're a nation that is constantly debating its own shortcomings. But on certain fundamental principles, all Americans are united.

I ask you as a friend not to make the mistake of thinking that there is any division in my country on this question. It is not just the President, it is not just me or the Congress. If these death squad murders continue, you will lose the support of the American people, and that would indeed be a tragedy.

25.
PRESIDENT RONALD REAGAN: ADDRESS TO JOINT SESSION OF THE CONGRESS (APRIL 27, 1983)

. . . Central America's problems do directly affect the security and well being of our own people. And Central America is much closer to the U.S. than many of the world trouble spots that concern us. As we work to restore our own economy, we cannot afford to lose sight of our neighbors to the South.

El Salvador is nearer to Texas than Texas is to Massachusetts. Nicaragua is just as close to Miami, San Antonio, San Diego, and Tucson as those cities are to Washington where we are gathered tonight.

But nearness on the map does not even begin to tell the strategic importance of Central America, bordering as it does on the Caribbean—our lifeline to the outside world. Two-thirds of all our foreign trade and petroleum pass through the Panama Canal and the Caribbean. In a European crisis, at least half of our supplies for NATO would go through these areas by sea. . . .

For several years now, under two administrations, the U.S. has been increasing its defense of freedom in the Caribbean Basin. And I can tell you tonight, democracy is beginning to take root in El Salvador, which, until a short time ago, knew only dictatorship. The new government is now delivering on its promises of democracy, reforms, and free elections. It was not easy and there was resistance to many of the attempted reforms with assassinations of the reformers. Guerrilla bands and urban terrorists were portrayed in a worldwide propaganda campaign as freedom fighters representative of the people. Ten days before I came into office, the guerrillas launched what they called a "final offensive" to overthrow the government. Their radio boasted that our new Administration would be too late to prevent their victory. They learned democracy cannot be so easily defeated.

President Carter did not hesitate. He authorized arms and ammunition to El Salvador. The guerrilla offensive failed, but not America's will. Every President since this country assumed global responsibilities has known that those responsibilities could only be met if we pursued a bipartisan foreign policy.

As I said a moment ago, the government of El Salvador has been keeping its promises, like the land reform program which is making thousands of

The White House, Office of the Press Secretary.

farm tenants, farm owners. In a little over 3 years, 20 percent of the arable land in El Salvador has been redistributed to more than 450,000 people. That is about one in ten Salvadorans who has directly benefitted from this program.

El Salvador has continued to strive toward an orderly and democratic society. The government promised free elections. On March 28th, little more than a year ago, after months of campaigning by a variety of candidates, the suffering people of El Salvador were offered a chance to vote—to choose the kind of government they wanted. Suddenly the so-called freedom fighters in the hills were exposed for what they really are—a small minority who want power for themselves and their backers, not democracy for the people. The guerrillas threatened death to anyone who voted. They destroyed hundreds of busses and trucks to keep the people from getting to the polling places. Their slogan was brutal: "Vote today, die tonight." But on election day, an unprecedented 80 percent of the electorate braved ambush and gunfire, and trudged for miles to vote for freedom. That is truly fighting for freedom. We can never turn our backs on that. Members of this Congress who went there as observers told me of a woman who was wounded by rifle fire on the way to the polls, who refused to leave the line to have her wound treated until after she had voted. Another woman had been told by the guerrillas she would be killed when she returned from the polls, and she told the guerrillas, "You can kill me, you can kill my family, kill my neighbors, but you can't kill us all." The real freedom fighters of El Salvador turned out to be the people of that country—the young, the old, the in-between—more than 1 million of them out of a population of less than 5 million. The world should respect this courage, not allow it to be belittled or forgotten. Again I say in good conscience, we can never turn our backs on that.

The democratic political parties and factions in El Salvador are coming together around the common goal of seeking a political solution to their country's problems. New national elections will be held this year and they will be open to all political parties. The government has invited the guerrillas to participate in the election and is preparing an amnesty law. The people of El Salvador are earning their freedom and they deserve our moral and material support to protect it.

Yes, there are still major problems regarding human rights, the criminal justice system, and violence against non-combatants. And, like the rest of Central America, El Salvador also faces severe economic problems. But, in addition to recession-depressed prices for major agricultural exports, El Salvador's economy is being deliberately sabotaged.

Tonight in El Salvador—because of ruthless guerrilla attacks—much of the fertile land cannot be cultivated; less than half the rolling stock of the railways remains operational: bridges, water facilities, telephone and electrical systems have been destroyed and damaged. In one 22-month period, there were 5,000 interruptions of electrical power. One region was without electricity for a third of a year.

I think Secretary of State Shultz put it very well the other day: "Unable to win the free loyalty of El Salvador's people, the guerrillas are deliberately and systematically depriving them of food, water, transportation, light, sanitation, and jobs. And these are the people who claim they want to help the common people."

They do not want elections because they know they would be defeated. But, as the previous election showed, the Salvadoran people's desire for democracy will not be defeated.

The guerrillas are not embattled peasants armed with muskets. They are professionals, sometimes with better training and weaponry than the government's soldiers. The Salvadoran battalions that have received U.S. training have been conducting themselves well on the battlefield and with the civilian population. But, so far, we have only provided enough money to train one Salvadoran soldier out of ten, fewer than the number of guerrillas trained by Nicaragua and Cuba.

And let me set the record straight on Nicaragua, a country next to El Salvador. In 1979, when the new government took over in Nicaragua, after a revolution which overthrew the authoritarian rule of Somoza, everyone hoped for the growth of democracy. We in the U.S. did, too. By January of 1981, our emergency relief and recovery aid to Nicaragua totalled $118 million—more than provided by any other developed country. In fact, in the first 2 years of Sandinista rule, the U.S. directly or indirectly sent five times more aid to Nicaragua than it had in the 2 years prior to the revolution. Can anyone doubt the generosity and good faith of the American people?

These were hardly the actions of a nation implacably hostile to Nicaragua. Yet, the government of Nicaragua has treated us as an enemy. It has rejected our repeated peace efforts. It has broken its promises to us, to the Organization of American States, and, most important of all, to the people of Nicaragua.

No sooner was victory achieved than a small clique ousted others who had been part of the revolution from having any voice in government. Humberto Ortega, the Minister of Defense, declared Marxism-Leninism would be their guide, and so it is.

The government of Nicaragua has imposed a new dictatorship; it has refused to hold the elections it promised; it has seized control of most media and subjects all media to heavy prior censorship; it denied the bishops and priests of the Roman Catholic Church the right to say Mass on radio during Holy Week; it insulted and mocked the Pope; it has driven the Miskito Indians from their homelands—burning their villages, destroying their crops, and forcing them into involuntary internment camps far from home; it has moved against the private sector and free labor unions; it condoned mob action against Nicaragua's independent human rights commission and drove the director of that commission into exile.

In short, after all these acts of repression by the government, is it any wonder opposition has formed? Contrary to propaganda, the opponents of the Sandinistas are not die-hard supporters of the previous Somoza regime. In fact, many are anti-Somoza heroes who fought beside the Sandinistas to bring down the Somoza government. Now they have been denied any part in the new government because they truly wanted democracy for Nicaragua and still do. Others are Miskito Indians fighting for their homes, lands, and lives.

The Sandinista revolution in Nicaragua turned out to be just an exchange of one set of autocratic rulers for another, and the people still have no freedom, no democratic rights, and more poverty. Even worse than its predecessor, it is helping Cuba and the Soviets to destabilize our hemisphere.

Meanwhile, the government of El Salvador, making every effort to guarantee democracy, free labor unions, freedom of religion, and a free press, is under attack by guerrillas dedicated to the same philosophy that prevails in Nicaragua, Cuba, and, yes, the Soviet Union. Violence has been Nicaragua's most important export to the world. It is the ultimate in hypocrisy for the unelected Nicaraguan government to charge that we seek their overthrow when they are doing everything they can to bring down the elected government of El Salvador. . . . But let us be clear as to the American attitude toward the government of Nicaragua. We do not seek its overthrow. Our interest is to ensure that it does not infect its neighbors through the export of subversion and violence. Our purpose, in conformity with American and international law, is to prevent the flow of arms to El Salvador, Honduras, Guatemala, and Costa Rica. We have attempted to have a dialogue with the government of Nicaragua but it persists in its efforts to spread violence.

We should not—and we will not—protect the Nicaraguan government from the anger of its own people. But we should, through diplomacy, offer an alternative. And, as Nicaragua ponders its options, we can and will—with all the resources of diplomacy—protect each country of Central America from the danger of war.

Even Costa Rica, Central America's oldest and strongest democracy, a government so peaceful it does not even have an army, is the object of bullying and threats from Nicaragua's dictators.

Nicaragua's neighbors know that Sandinista promises of peace, non-alliance, and non-intervention have not been kept. Some 36 new military bases have been built—there were only 13 during the Somoza years.

Nicaragua's new army numbers 25,000 men supported by a militia of 50,000. It is the largest army in Central America supplemented by 2,000 Cuban military and security advisors. It is equipped with the most modern weapons, dozens of Soviet-made tanks, 800 Soviet-bloc trucks, Soviet 152-MM howitzers, 100 anti-aircraft guns, plus planes and helicopters. There are additional thousands of civilian advisors from Cuba, the Soviet Union, East Germany, Libya, and the Palestine Liberation Organization. And we are attacked because we have 55 military trainers in El Salvador.

The goal of the professional guerrilla movements in Central America is as simple as it is sinister—to destabilize the entire region from the Panama Canal to Mexico. If you doubt me on this point, just consider what Cayetano Carpio, the now-deceased Salvadoran guerrilla leader, said earlier this month. Carpio said that after El Salvador falls, El Salvador and Nicaragua would be "arm-in-arm and struggling for the total liberation of Central America."

Nicaragua's dictatorial junta, who themselves made war and won power operating from bases in Honduras and Costa Rica, like to pretend they are today being attacked by forces based in Honduras. The fact is, it is Nicaragua's government that threatens Honduras, not the reverse.

It is Nicaragua who has moved heavy tanks close to the border, and Nicaragua who speaks of war. It was Nicaraguan radio that announced on April 8th the creation of a new, unified revolutionary coordinating board to push forward the Marxist struggle in Honduras.

Nicaragua, supported by weapons and military resources provided by the Communist bloc, represses its own people, refuses to make peace, and sponsors a guerrilla war against El Salvador. . . .

Some people talk as though the U.S. were incapable of acting effectively in international affairs without risking war or damaging those we seek to help.

Are democracies required to remain passive while threats to their security and prosperity accumulate?

Must we just accept the destabilization of an entire region from the Panama Canal to Mexico on our southern border?

Must we sit by while independent nations of this hemisphere are integrated into the most aggressive empire the modern world has seen?

Must we wait while Central Americans are driven from their homes, like the more than 4 million who have sought refuge out of Afghanistan or the 1½ million who have fled Indochina or the more than 1 million Cubans who have fled Castro's Caribbean utopia? Must we, by default, leave the people of El Salvador no choice but to flee their homes, creating another tragic human exodus?

I do not believe there is a majority in the Congress or the country that counsels passivity, resignation, defeatism, in the face of this challenge to freedom and security in our hemisphere.

I do not believe that a majority of the Congress or the country is prepared to stand by passively while the people of Central America are delivered to totalitarianism and we ourselves are left vulnerable to new dangers. . . .

Now, before I go any further, let me say to those who invoke the memory of Vietnam: There is no thought of sending American combat troops to Central America; they are not needed—indeed, they have not been requested there. All our neighbors ask of us is assistance in training and arms to protect themselves while they build a better, freer life. . . .

We will pursue four basic goals in Central America:

- First: In response to decades of inequity and indifference, we will support democracy, reform, and human freedom. This means using our assistance, our powers of persuasion, and our legitimate "leverage" to bolster humane democratic systems where they already exist and to help countries on their way to that goal complete the process as quickly as human institutions can be changed. Elections—in El Salvador and also in Nicaragua—must be open to all, fair and safe. The international community must help. We will work at human rights problems, not walk away from them.

- Second: In response to the challenge of world recession and, in the case of El Salvador, to the unrelenting campaign of economic sabotage by the guerrillas, we will support economic development. By a margin of two-to-one, our aid is economic, not military. Seventy-seven cents out of every dollar we will spend in the area this year goes for food, fertilizers, and other essentials for economic growth and development. And our economic program goes beyond traditional aid: The Caribbean Basin Initiative introduced in the House earlier today will provide powerful trade and investment incentives to help these countries achieve self-sustaining economic growth without exporting U.S. jobs. Our goal must be to focus our immense and growing technology to enhance health care, agriculture, industry; to ensure that we who inhabit this interdependent region come to know and understand each other better, retaining our diverse identities, respecting our diverse traditions and institutions.

- Third: In response to the military challenge from Cuba and Nicaragua— to their deliberate use of force to spread tyranny—we will support the security of the region's threatened nations. We do not view security assistance as an end in itself, but as a shield for democratization, economic development, and diplomacy. No amount of reform will bring peace so long as guerrillas believe they will win by force. No amount of economic help will suffice if guerrilla units can destroy roads, bridges, power stations, and crops again and again with impunity. But, with better training and material help, our neighbors can hold off the guerrillas and give democratic reform time to take root.

- Fourth: We will support dialogue and negotiations—both among the countries of the region and within each country. The terms and conditions of participation in elections are negotiable. Costa Rica is a shining example of democracy. Honduras has made the move from military rule to a democratic government. Guatemala is pledged to the same course. The U.S. will work toward a political solution in Central America which will serve the interests of the democratic process.

To support these diplomatic goals, I offer these assurances:

- The U.S. will support any agreement among Central American countries for the withdrawal—under fully verifiable and reciprocal conditions—of all foreign military and security advisors and troops.
- We want to help opposition groups join the political process in all countries and compete by ballots instead of bullets.
- We will support any verifiable, reciprocal agreement among Central American countries on the renunciation of support for insurgencies on neighbors' territory.
- And, finally, we desire to help Central America end its costly arms race, and will support any verifiable, reciprocal agreements on the non-importation of offensive weapons.

26.
UNDER SECRETARY OF DEFENSE FRED IKLE:
TOWARD VICTORY (SEPTEMBER 1983)

To begin with, you should know that the President's policy for Central America has not yet been given a chance to work: the blocking votes in Congress have denied the President the means to succeed.

Indeed, members of Congress have involved themselves in the management of U.S. policy for Central America more than for any other region of the world.

- While Congress has quickly and easily approved some four and a half billion dollars in Security Assistance for nations in the Mediterranean region, it slashed nearly in half the much smaller allocation for nations in the Caribbean region—so much closer to home.

Speech to the Baltimore Council on Foreign Affairs, September 12, 1983.

- While Congress has been generally supportive of the deployment of some 1200 U.S. Marines to Lebanon, it fought fiercely to limit the number of U.S. trainers in El Salvador to 55. . . .

Another piece of fiction is the charge that the Reagan Administration is "militarizing" the problems of Central America and is bringing the East-West conflict to the region. Well, the East is already here. The Soviets are giving ten times as much military assistance to Cuba and Nicaragua as we are providing to all of Latin America. And Soviet military advisors in Cuba and Nicaragua outnumber U.S. military advisors in the Caribbean region twenty to one.

Since Congress is so deeply involved in our day-to-day policy towards Central America, our key objectives need to be clear to the American people. Moreover, Congress must share with the Administration an understanding of our basic strategy.

On one thing we can all agree: We do not want the United States to fail. We must succeed. . . .

Equally important is what we want to prevent. We want to prevent the expansion of totalitarian regimes—particularly Leninist ones, since they will import Stalinist police systems, bring in Soviet arms, and even invite Soviet military bases. There are two more reasons why Leninist regimes are particularly dangerous: once entrenched, they tend to become irreversible and they usually seek to export their totalitarianism to other nations.

Given these objectives, what should be our strategy? . . .

. . . The resources needed to succeed are small compared to our investment for security in other regions of the world. Once those in Congress who are now blocking adequate assistance give us the means to succeed, the capability and determination of the United States will become clear. This will make the Soviet Union more cautious, which in turn will help our success. On the other hand, if we signal that we are afraid of victory over the forces of violence, if we signal that we have opted for protracted failure, we will only encourage the Soviets to redouble their effort. We will be inviting ever-increasing difficulties.

The third requirement of U.S. strategy for Central America is least well understood. We should seek to prevent the partition of Central America, a division of this region into two spheres, one linked to the Soviet bloc and one linked to the United States. Such a partition would inexorably lead to a hostile confrontation of large military forces, a confrontation that could last for decades. . . .

The Sandinista regime in Nicaragua is determined to create a "second Cuba" in Central America. Ever since they seized power, the Sandinistas embarked on a major military buildup. Today, they have a much larger army than Somoza ever had, and they have expressed the intention to build the largest force in Central America. Nicaragua is building new military airfields, and is importing Soviet tanks, helicopters, armored vehicles, and other equipment.

This "second Cuba" in Nicaragua would be more dangerous than Castro's Cuba since it shares hard to defend borders with Honduras and Costa Rica. The Sandinistas have already started terrorist activities in both these countries. In addition, Nicaragua provides essential support for the insurgency in El Salvador.

Even after the insurgency in El Salvador has been brought under control, Nicaragua—if it continued on its present course—would be the bridgehead and arsenal for insurgency for Central America. . . .

Let me recapitulate.

Our basic objectives for Central America are clear: we want to strengthen democracy; we want to prevent in this hemisphere the expansion of totalitarian regimes, especially those linked to the Soviet Union.

To this end, we extend economic support and promote democratic development. But given forces of violence that will not accept the democratic will of the people, we also have to provide military assistance—enough to succeed. In addition, we must prevent consolidation of a Sandinista regime in Nicaragua that would become an arsenal for insurgency, a safe haven for the export of violence. If we cannot prevent that, we have to anticipate the partition of Central America. Such a development would then force us to man a new military front-line of the East-West conflict, right here on our continent.

To prevent such an outcome, the Administration and Congress must work together with a strategy that can succeed.

27.
KISSINGER COMMISSION: REPORT ON CENTRAL AMERICA (JANUARY 1984)

MAJOR THEMES

—The crisis in Central America is acute. Its roots are indigenous—in poverty, injustice and closed political systems. But world economic reces-

From the summary of the report by the National Bipartisan Commission on Central America in *Briefing Book: Central America: Democracy, Peace and Development Initiative* (Washington, 1984). Portions adapted from *The Report of the President's National Bipartisan Commission on Central America* (New York, 1984), pp. 100–101, 109–11, 115, 124.

sion and Cuban-Soviet-Nicaraguan intervention brought it to a head. . . .

Indigenous reform movements, even indigenous revolutions, are not themselves a security concern of the United States. History holds examples of genuinely popular revolutions, springing wholly from native roots. In this hemisphere Mexico is a clear example. But during the past two decades we have faced a new phenomenon.

The concerting of the power of the Soviet Union and Cuba to extend their presence and influence into vulnerable areas of the Western Hemisphere is a direct threat to U.S. security interests. This type of insurgency is present in Central America today. . . .

POLITICAL AND ECONOMIC DEVELOPMENT

—Central American economies grew substantially during the 60's and early 70's. But income distribution was highly inequitable, except in Costa Rica and Panama.

—Trend toward more pluralistic political systems in El Salvador, Guatemala and Nicaragua reversed in early 70s.

—World recession and rising political violence had catastrophic effect on region's economies in late 70's, early 80's. All have declined dramatically. El Salvador's gross domestic product is off 25% since 1978.

—Even with successful stabilization programs and restored political stability, per capita wealth in 1990 would only be three-quarters of what it was in 1980.

—There must be substantial increase in outside assistance.

—Commission believes economic development cannot be separated from political and social reform. Objective must be parallel development of pluralistic societies and strong economies with far more equitable distribution of wealth.

—We propose a program of U.S. assistance designed to promote economic growth, democratization and greater social equity.

—We encourage the greatest possible involvement of the U.S. private sector in the stabilization effort. Recommend the formation of an emergency action committee of private sector personalities to provide advice on new private-public initiatives to spur growth and employment.

RECOMMENDATIONS: AN EMERGENCY STABILIZATION PROGRAM

—Leaders of U.S. and Central America should meet to initiate a comprehensive approach to economic development of the region and reinvigoration of the Central American Common Market.

—A $400 million supplemental in FY84 over and above the $477 million now in the budget for the seven countries. There is urgent need to stabilize economies now going downhill very fast.

—Focus this assistance on labor-intensive infrastructure projects and housing. Unemployment is a critical problem—politically and economically.

—Establish a program to provide U.S. Government guarantees for short-term trade credits. External credit has dried up. Without it economies cannot be reactivated.

—Provide an emergency loan to the Central American Common Market to permit the reactivation of this vital organization. Lack of resources in the Market to settle trade accounts among the countries has stalled it.

—U.S. Government should take an active role in the efforts to resolve the external debt problems of Central America . . .

RECOMMENDATIONS: MEDIUM AND LONG-TERM

—Commission estimates $4 billion in net external exchange inflows needed to 1990 to foster a growth rate of 3 percent per capita, returning these countries to pre-recession levels of per capita wealth. About half—$12 billion—is expected to come from international institutions, other donor countries and loans and investments from private sector sources.

—U.S. Government will have to provide as much as $12 billion if these financing needs are to be met. . . .

—Urge that Congress authorize multi-year funding of this program. Commission believes firm, long-term commitment is essential.

—To give form and structure to the development effort suggest establishment of the Central American Development Organization (CADO). Perhaps ¼ of U.S. aid could be channelled through CADO.

—CADO would consist of the United States and those countries of the seven willing to commit themselves to internal democracy and reform. Continued membership would depend on demonstrated progress toward those goals. Adherence to regional security pact also required.

—Nicaragua could participate by meeting these conditions. . . .

—Urge extension of duty-free trade to Central America by other major trading nations.

—Review non-tariff barriers to imports from Central America with a view toward using whatever flexibility that exists within the framework of multilateral agreements, to favor Central American products. . . .

HEALTH AND EDUCATION . . .

—Goals should include a reduction of malnutrition, elimination of illiteracy, expanded education health, and housing opportunities. . . .

—Commission calls for formation, under direction of the Peace Corps, of a Literacy Corps and a Central American Teachers Corps.

—To meet needs in higher education, U.S. Government scholarships should be raised to approximately 10,000 over 4–6 years, a level comparable to Cuban and Soviet Union efforts. . . .

—Judicial systems in Central America can be strengthened by providing resources for training judges, judicial staff, and public prosecutors. . . .

—U.S. Government should provide more resources to meet critical problem of refugees and displaced persons—more than one million of them need help.

SECURITY ISSUES

—In El Salvador there are two separate conflicts: (1) between those seeking democratic reform and those seeking to retain their privileges; (2) between Marxist-Leninist guerrillas and those who oppose Marxism-Leninism.

—In discussing the latter we identify three general propositions about such guerrilla movements:

(1) They depend on external support. Without it they are unlikely to succeed.
(2) They develop their own momentum which reform alone cannot stop.
(3) Victorious, they create totalitarian regimes, even though they have enlisted support of democratic elements in order to project democratic, reformist image.

—External support comes from Soviet Union, Cuba and now Nicaragua. Cuba has developed into a leading military power through Soviet assistance. Since Sandinista victory, Soviets have come around to support Cuba's strategy of armed road to power in Central America. . . .

The ability of the United States to sustain a tolerable balance of power on the global scene at a manageable cost depends on the inherent security of its land borders. This advantage is of crucial importance. It offsets an otherwise serious liability: our distance from Europe, the Middle East, and East Asia, which are also of strategic concern to the United States. Security commitments in those areas require the United States to supply its forces overseas at the far end of transoceanic lines of communication whose protection can be almost as costly as the forces themselves.

At the level of global strategy, therefore, the advance of Soviet and Cuban power on the American mainland affects the global balance. To the extent that a further Marxist-Leninist advance in Central America leading to progressive deterioration and a further projection of Soviet and Cuban power in the region required us to defend against security threats near our borders, we would face a difficult choice between unpalatable alternatives. We would either have to assume a permanently increased defense burden, or see our capacity to defend distant troublespots reduced, and as a result have to reduce important commitments elsewhere in the world. From the standpoint of the Soviet Union, it would be a major strategic coup to impose on the United States the burden of defending our southern approaches, thereby stripping us of the compensating advantage that offsets the burden of our transoceanic lines of communication.

Such a deterioration in Central America would also greatly increase both the difficulty and the cost of protecting these lines of communications themselves. Under present plans, some 50 percent of the shipping tonnage that would be needed to reinforce the European front, and about 40 percent of that required by a major East Asian conflict, would have to pass from the Gulf of Mexico through the Caribbean–Central American zone. These same sea routes also carry nearly half of all other foreign cargo, including crude oil, shipped to this country.

The Soviets have already achieved a greater capability to interdict shipping than the Nazis had during World War II, when 50 percent of U.S. supplies to Europe and Africa were shipped from Gulf ports. German U-boats then sank 260 merchant ships in just six months, despite the fact that Allied forces enjoyed many advantages, including a two-to-one edge in submarines and the use of Cuba for resupply and basing operations. Today this is reversed. The Soviets now have a two-to-one edge overall in submarines and can operate and receive aircover from Cuba, a point from which all 13 Caribbean sea lanes passing through our choke points are vulnerable to interdiction.

The Soviet ability to carry out a strategy of "strategic denial" is further enhanced by the presence near Havana of the latest Soviet-managed electronic monitoring complex outside the Soviet Union, as well as by the regular deployment of TU-95 naval reconnaissance aircraft.

Nowhere is the added threat of an entire new set of problems posed by Nicaragua. It already serves as a base of subversion, through overland infiltration of people and supplies, that can affect the entire region, Panama included. Panama is gradually assuming full responsibility for the security of the Canal; this means that any threat to the political security of that country and to the maintenance of its friendly relations with the United States automatically constitutes a strategic threat.

As Nicaragua is already doing, additional Marxist-Leninist regimes in Central America could be expected to expand their armed forces, bring in large numbers of Cuban and other Soviet bloc advisers, develop sophisticated agencies of internal repression and external subversion, and sharpen polarizations, both within individual countries and regionally. This would almost surely produce refugees, perhaps millions of them, many of whom would seek entry into the United States. Even setting aside the broader strategic considerations, the United States cannot isolate itself from the regional turmoil. The crisis is on our doorstep.

Beyond the issue of U.S. security interests in the Central American Caribbean region, our credibility worldwide is engaged. The triumph of hostile forces in what the Soviets call the "strategic rear" of the United States would be read as a sign of U.S. impotence. . . .

EL SALVADOR

—The war is stalemated, a condition to the ultimate advantage of the guerrillas. . . .

In the Commission's view it is imperative to settle on a level of aid related to the operational requirements of a humane anti-guerrilla strategy and to stick with it for the requisite period of time. . . .

With respect to El Salvador, military aid should, through legislation requiring periodic reports, be made contingent upon demonstrated progress toward free elections; freedom of association; the establishment of the rule of law and an effective judicial system; and the termination of the activities of the so-called death squads, as well as vigorous action against those guilty of crimes and the prosecution to the extent possible of past offenders. These conditions should be seriously enforced. . . .

THE SEARCH FOR PEACE . . .

—Commission calls for negotiations in El Salvador between guerrillas and the government to be elected in March to establish conditions for later legislative and municipal elections in which all could participate: electoral commission with FMLN-FDR representation, cease-fire and end to all violence; international observation of elections.

—Adequate economic and military assistance from U.S. can help to achieve such a settlement. . . .

—Commission proposes comprehensive regional settlement based on:

(1) Respect for sovereignty and non-intervention.
(2) Verifiable commitments to non-aggression and an end to all attempts at subversion—covert or overt.
(3) Limitations on arms and sizes of armed forces. Prohibition of foreign forces, bases and advisers.
(4) No military forces, bases or advisers of non–Central American countries would be permitted.
(5) Commitment to internal pluralism and free elections in all countries.
(6) Provision for verification of all agreements.

(7) Establishment of an inter-government council to meet regularly to review compliance.

(8) Adherence to the overall agreement would be required for membership in the Central American Development Organization.

—U.S. would support the agreement and provide assistance; and would commit itself to respect results of elections within countries as long as principles of pluralism at home and restraint abroad observed.

—Commission's proposal based on and amplifies 2 points of the Contadora Group.

—Commission fully endorses Contadora efforts.

—Finally, majority of Commission opposes dismantling existing incentives and pressures for the regime in Managua to negotiate seriously. . . .

—As for Soviet Union, establishment of Soviet military base in Nicaragua is not the major concern. Before that could have happened the crisis would have reached proportions not containable in Central American dimensions.

—There is little promise in negotiating with the Soviet Union over Central America. Soviets would seek to cast such negotiations in terms of sphere of influence, an unacceptable concept for the U.S.

28.
ROBERT WHITE: U.S. POLICY AND THE SALVADORAN RIGHT (FEBRUARY 1984)

STATEMENT OF HON. ROBERT E. WHITE, FORMER U.S. AMBASSADOR TO EL SALVADOR

. . . For 50 years El Salvador was ruled by a corrupt and brutal alliance of the rich and the military. The young officers' revolt of 1979 attempted to break that alliance. It was the Reagan renewed tolerance and acceptance of the extreme right which led to the emergence of the National Republican Alliance, ARENA, and the rise of ex-Major Roberto D'Aubuisson.

ARENA is a violent Fascist party modeled after the Nazis and certain revolutionary Communist groups. ARENA has not only a civilian party structure, but also a military arm obedient to the party. The founders and chief supporters of ARENA are rich Salvadoran exiles headquartered in

---

Hearings before the Committee on Foreign Affairs, House of Representatives, February 6, 1984.

Miami and civilian activists in El Salvador. ARENA's military arm comprises officers and men of the Salvadoran Army and security forces.

I have here a series of brilliant reports by Craig Pyes of the *Albuquerque Journal* and Laurie Bechland of the *Los Angeles Times,* which I recommend to the committee.

SALVADORAN EXILES IN MIAMI

My Embassy devoted considerable resources to identifying the sources of rightwing violence and their contacts in Miami, Fla. Information on the Salvadoran exiles residing in Miami proved particularly difficult to develop.

However, in January 1981, we located a source who was regarded by the Miami group as one of them. The source said he had talked to wealthy people in San Salvador who have been interrogated and threatened in Miami.

These men have been called to Miami and seated at the end of a long table, facing the "Six," and made to answer such questions as "Why are you contributing to the Communist victory by keeping your business open?" or "Why do you do the work of the Communist agents White and Bowdler?" The reference is to former Assistant Secretary William Bowdler.

According to the source, the Miami Six explained to him that to rebuild the country, it must first be destroyed totally, the economy must be wrecked, unemployment must be massive, the junta must be ousted and a "good" military officer brought to power who will carry out a total cleansing—*limpieza*—killing 3 or 4 or 500,000 people.

Last, the "Six" made the following threat: "Unless you close down your factory/business, get out of the country, stop working for Alianza Productiva, INCAFE, American Embassy, et cetera, you will be sorry."

MIAMI SIX

Who are these madmen and how do they operate? According to the source, the principal figures are six enormously wealthy former landowners. He continued that central power was exercised by the Miami Six, noting that others among the emigrés and their wealthy allies here have some role from time to time but the top leadership is Enrique Viera Altimirano, Luis Escalante, Arturo Muyshondt, the Salaverria Brothers—probably Julio and Juan Ricardo—and Roberto Edgardo Daglio. All are in Miami. They hatch plots, hold constant meetings and communicate instructions to D'Aubuisson.

BACKGROUND ON D'AUBUISSON

Let us review a few of the items from the record of Roberto D'Aubuisson and his organization, formerly called the Broad National Front, now ARENA.

October 1979: D'Aubuisson is expelled from the Salvadoran military for human rights abuses. Christian Democrat leader Napoleón Duarte later charges that he has turned his office into a "torture chamber and death house."

March 1980: D'Aubuisson plans and orders the assassination of Archbishop Oscar Romero. I will return to this.

May 14: A gang of D'Aubuisson supporters assault the U.S. Embassy residence. Mario Raedello, a D'Aubuisson aide and now a leader of ARENA, using a loudspeaker calls on U.S. Marines guarding our Embassy to desert. During the attack, Raedelli drove a car registered to D'Aubuisson against the gates of the Embassy in order to blockade me inside. His stated intention was to hold me hostage until D'Aubuisson was released from prison.

I had Raedello barred from the United States for attacking the U.S. Embassy. The Reagan administration has since found him eligible to enter our country.

November 27, 1980: Six members of the executive committee of the Revolutionary Democratic Front are kidnapped and assassinated. Their bodies show signs of torture, dismemberment, and strangulation. The Maximiliano Hernández Martínez Anti-Communist Brigade publicly takes credit for the murders.

In a May 12, 1981, letter to Representative Lee Hamilton of this committee, Richard Fairbanks, then Assistant Secretary of State for Congressional Relations for the Reagan administration, stated that "Ex-Major Robert D'Aubuisson reportedly leads a rightwing terrorist group called the Maximiliano Hernández Brigade."

March 11, 1981: Four men fire on the Chancery of the U.S. Embassy from a truck. Ambassador Frederick Chapin later identifies Roberto D'Aubuisson as the author of the attack. "This incident has all the earmarks of a D'Aubuisson operation," he said.

EVIDENCE LINKING D'AUBUISSON TO ARCHBISHOP ROMERO'S MURDER

Subsequent to the murder of Archbishop Romero, several events occurred which link D'Aubuisson and his organization to the death of Archbishop Romero.

On or about May 1, D'Aubuisson circulates a videotape in which he calls for the overthrow of the U.S.-backed Government. In the videotape,

D'Aubuisson implicitly takes credit for the murder of Archbishop Romero. In his presentation, D'Aubuisson refers with contempt to the revered Archbishop as "The Ayatollah who has left us." My Embassy submitted a copy of this videotape to the Department of State.

On May 7, a group of young officers arrest D'Aubuisson for coup plotting and discover documents which lead competent observers to conclude that D'Aubuisson and his group carried out the execution of Archbishop Romero.

The civilian judge in charge of trying Roberto D'Aubuisson is driven from El Salvador by threats from death squads. As soon as he arrives in Costa Rica, he states publicly that the evidence points to D'Aubuisson as the author of the murder of the archbishop.

MURDER OF AIFLD WORKERS

January 4, 1981: Two Salvadoran enlisted men kill Rodolfo Viera, head of the Agrarian Reform Institute, Michael Hammer and Mark Pearlman, both of the American Institute for Free Labor Development, AIFLD. These men have testified that two members of D'Aubuisson's organization, Lt. Rodolfo López Sibrian and Capt. Eduardo Ernesto Alfonso Avila, ordered them to kill Viera and the two Americans.

Any doubt about the guilt of these two Salvadoran military officers may be resolved by reading the AIFLD investigation report.

The Salvadoran military has rebuffed the Reagan administration's requests to try López Sibrian and Avila. López Sibrian is on active duty. Avila is under detention for leaving his post without permission. I can state with moral certainty that as soon as the Congress acts on the aid package for El Salvador, Avila will be released.

In conformity with the evidence, the administration of President Carter classified Roberto D'Aubuisson as a terrorist, a murderer, and a leader of death squads. As ambassador, I denied him access to the U.S. Embassy and succeeded in having him barred from our country.

Shortly after President Reagan took office, this administration overturned this policy and began the process of rehabilitating ex-Major D'Aubuisson. No longer was he a pariah. Today he is one of the leading Presidential candidates in the election scheduled for March 25. In a very real sense, the Reagan administration created Roberto D'Aubuisson, the political leader.

Yet from the first days in office, the Reagan White House knew, beyond any reasonable doubt, that Roberto D'Aubuisson, in addition to other crimes, planned, and ordered the assassination of Archbishop Oscar Arnulfo Romero.

According to an eyewitness account, Roberto D'Aubuisson summoned a group of about 12 men to a safe house, presided over a meeting, announced the decision to assassinate the Archbishop and supervised the drawing of lots for the honor of carrying out the plot.

The officer who won the lottery was Lt. Francisco Amaya Rosa, a D'Aubuisson intimate, Amaya Rosa chose a military hanger-on and sharp-shooter named Walter Antonio Álvarez to fire the single bullet which ended the life of Archbishop Romero as he said mass in the Orphanage of the Good Shepherd.

Another cable contains the information that some months later, as ARENA's political campaign was getting under way, D'Aubuisson decided that Álvarez could not be trusted. He pronounced another death sentence. A four-man death squad went into action and executed Walter Álvarez as he stood watching a soccer game.

All of the above information was reported to Washington.

The Reagan White House took on a great responsibility when it chose to conceal the identity of Archbishop Romero's murderer and not to use the evidence gathered by the Embassy to write "finis" to the political fortunes of ARENA and the ambitions of Roberto D'Aubuisson.

Did the Kissinger Commission have access to Embassy reports detailing the systematic murder of Salvadoran moderates by ARENA and the intimate collaboration which exists between high military commanders and death squads?

President Reagan has advocated free elections as the solution to the problems of El Salvador. Yet in El Salvador the press is controlled by ARENA. We can all be certain that the government and ARENA will do its best not to permit any news of D'Aubuisson's guilt to reach the people of El Salvador. How can people cast a free vote if vital information is denied them?

I have one last point, Mr. Chairman.

I have charged that there exists a coverup of vital information. The validity of this charge is not affected by passing a few telegrams before several legislators and insisting that the information is too sensitive for the public. In the elegant parlance of Watergate, this is known as a limited hangout.

The obligation of any administration is to draw obvious conclusions from information in the best interests of the United States. Concerned citizens of the United States and other countries will eagerly await the Reagan White House explanation of how the objectives of democracy and human rights are served by:

Refusal of the Reagan administration to act on evidence linking the Miami exiles to ARENA and the death squads; rehabilitation of Roberto D'Aubuisson, the ultra-rightist, death squad leader; certification of progress on human rights: By affirming as true what is known to be false, the White House has undermined its own reputation; suppression of the report by

Judge Harold Tyler on the investigation into the circumstances surrounding the death squads' role in the murder of the American churchwomen.

I earnestly hope, Mr. Chairman, that the Reagan administration will change their policy, and begin to work for a negotiated peace, and make a real beginning to rooting out the terror which is institutionalized into the Salvadoran Government.

29.
U.S. CONGRESS: DEBATE ON SALVADORAN AID
(APRIL-MAY 1984)

Mr. STUDDS [D—Mass.]. The amendment before us at the moment, the amendment offered by myself, would condition all U.S. military aid to El Salvador on the ability and willingness of that Government to meet a series of conditions and on the willingness of the President of the United States and the Congress of the United States to concur that those conditions had been met.

Think about the three conditions, I say to my colleagues. They are not particularly difficult if one is so inclined. Not only that, but they are precisely what Mr. Duarte, the apparently newly elected President of El Salvador, says he seeks to achieve. Those involved in death squad activity are well known. Prisoners need not be tortured and killed, and the negotiating process must be initiated if the people of El Salvador are ever again to know peace. The standard for compliance is not absolute, but it must be sufficient to convince both the President and this Congress that the purpose of the conditions has been achieved.

And let me suggest to my colleagues that there is nothing inconsistent with the fundamental goals of U.S. security policy, with the desire to avoid a military takeover by the forces of the extreme left in El Salvador and throughout Central America, there is nothing inconsistent with this Congress in the name of the people whom we represent insisting that the people who are to be recipients of U.S. military aid respect minimal norms of civilized behavior in dealing with their own people.

Mr. BROOMFIELD [R—Mich.]. Mr. Chairman, if you want America to pull out completely from El Salvador, then cast your vote for the Studds amendment. If you want to turn that country over to the Marxists, and Cuban-Nicaraguan dominance, vote for this approach. You will be casting

Congressional Record, April 30 and May 11, 1984. Selections from pp. H3131–3781, S5011–5674, E1815–2117.

a vote for a program which will push El Salvador off the cliff.

If you are thinking of supporting the Studds amendment, you should ask, What happens if the guerrillas win?

What kind of society will they build in El Salvador?

Will human rights be respected?

Will opposition parties exist?

Will a future Marxist-Leninist government permit voting?

Will the Salvadorans be allowed to practice their faith?

Will future generations of Salvadoran children grow up in a democratic nation assured of peace?

What is beyond El Salvador if communism triumphs in that country?

Will the exporters of the revolution without frontiers take it to the Rio Grande?

If that happens, democracy in the entire region will be lost and America's national security will be in jeopardy. The world has become too dangerous and too complex for us to simply drop out. We cannot just hope that all will be well in the world.

There are many reasons why I oppose the Studds amendment. It is completely unacceptable. In essence, it severely restricts the administration's flexibility in pursuing U.S. foreign policy objectives in Central America.

Although some conditions are appropriate, and realistic, overconditioning will kill any effort. A certain amount of pressure can be exerted by our Government on other countries. We can encourage them to make progress in certain areas. Unrealistic demands, however, will not be met.

The amendment before us conditions El Salvador to death and severely restricts the President's options. The President must have flexibility in conducting foreign policy. Tying both of his hands behind his back is foolish and dangerous. This proposal would take away all of his flexibility.

Is this the way Congress helps promote our foreign policy interests in our own backyard? I agree with responsible congressional oversight, but not with irresponsible meddling. The legislative branch should help the President conduct a successful foreign policy, not hinder him.

Mr. STUDDS. There are so many ways in which this debate takes us back to the debates that took place during the Vietnam war. What we decide today may ultimately determine whether the United States of America becomes involved directly with our own military forces in Central America.

We have at this point perhaps a last chance to exercise leverage in Central America and especially in El Salvador to have the new President elect get the support from the military forces to deal with that society in such a fashion as to make the government of El Salvador capable of receiving the support both of its own people and that of the American people.

When it is said as the President has that the solution is more and more military involvement in Central America, we ignore the history of the United States in relation to Central America and go back to the worst day of our relationship with the nations of that region. What we ought to be doing is working with the Contadora nations in helping us bring a negotiated resolution to the present conflict in Central America.

There has been discussion on the floor already about how it is all the fault of the Communists and the Marxists and the Leninists that such serious problems exist in Central America. Costa Rica has been pointed to as an example of how aggressive the Nicaraguans are and how they are now in the process of preparing to wage war on Costa Rica.

What we ought to note is that we, the United States of America, have placed Costa Rica in the untenable position of serving as the haven for counter revolutionary forces which we built and now fund to fight against Nicaragua. It is a perfect example of how we are both Americanizing the conflict and spreading it throughout the region.

As in Honduras, where we have, in essence, built one, gigantic American military base out of that country. It is filled with military camps, runways and landing strips, military hospitals, training camps for the Salvadoran Army, radar stations and hundreds of ships off the coast. In El Salvador our pilots are flying surveillance missions and are accompanying observers of bombing missions with the Salvadoran forces. Our military advisers have already found themselves fired upon.

The American people have said to us quite clearly, in every poll that has been taken, "Do not let the United States become involved in combat in Central America," and yet the President's policies inexorably take us down that path.

The gentleman from Massachusetts offers us a way of avoiding that awful prospect. The choice this body makes today is a historic one. It is a choice between whether this country will be drawn into a prolonged and bloody war in Central America, or whether we will seek a negotiated resolution to the region's conflicts.

Congress will also decide whether it will exercise its constitutional right to influence U.S. foreign policy, or whether, as it did in the early days of the Vietnam conflict, abdicate its responsibilities and give sole authority to the President. In Vietnam we witnessed the tragic consequences of a President acting alone, without congressional involvement and approval. I hope today that we will choose a different course from the one made 20 years ago.

The President has clearly staked out his course. It is one based on military force and covert action, not negotiations and peace. It pays lipservice to the goals of the Contadora nations, while steadily increasing the numbers of U.S. military trainers, troops, and arms in the region.

In the past year, U.S. Armed Forces have edged dangerously close to a direct combat role in Central America. Senior administration officials now acknowledge that contingency plans are being prepared for use of American troops in the region. American advisers in El Salvador, who now carry automatic weapons, have been exposed to hostile fire. U.S. aircraft provide combat support for Salvadoran troops in battle zones. American advisers on training missions with Salvadoran pilots participate in bombing runs against guerrilla units.

Off the coasts of Nicaragua, ships operated by the Central Intelligence Agency have served as control centers for the mining of Puerto Corinto and Puerto Sandino.

Now may be our best and perhaps last chance to reach a negotiated settlement to the conflicts in El Salvador and the rest of Central America. We should use our power, leverage, and persuasion to bring the contending parties to the negotiating table, not draw them closer to war.

In El Salvador, the guerrillas and government security forces are at a stalemate. Neither side is certain of the degree of America's future military involvement, and it seems that now we have the conditions for bringing about a negotiated solution. Shipment of additional U.S. military aid or more American troops would only provoke both sides into continuing the war.

The Studds amendment would go a long way toward bringing about a peaceful resolution of the conflict in El Salvador. By tying military aid to negotiations, we will strengthen Mr. Duarte in his pledge to halt the war and bring the warring factions to the negotiating table. By linking aid to elimination of the death squads, we will send an unambiguous message that the Salvadoran military must comply with basic human rights conditions.

The reforms we are asking are not extraordinary, nor impossible to achieve. We are simply expecting of the Salvadorans behavior that we expect of all our allies.

Congress must act now to change the course of current U.S. policy in Central America before it is too late. U.S.-funded Contras along Nicaragua's southern border now threaten to draw Costa Rica into a war with Nicaragua. A helicopter carrying two U.S. Senators has been downed along the Salvadoran border. A U.S. trainer has been shot and killed in San Salvador.

In poll after poll the American people have demonstrated that they do not want American military involvement in Central America. It is time that the House join the American people and cast its vote for peace, and against the militaristic policies of this administration.

Mr. LAGOMARSINO (R—Calif.) Critics of administration policy in El Salvador say they do not want a military solution applied to that country. But that is what you will have if you restrict military aid as the Studds amendment proposes—a military solution by the left. Limiting military aid will not force the democratically elected Government of El Salvador to negotiate. It will make the Salvadoran military feel less secure and less likely to support any proposal for dialog with the armed opposition in El Salvador. Restricting military aid will only give the leftist guerrillas every reason to believe they will achieve their objectives by continuing to fight rather then having to dialog with the government.

Neither the administration nor those of us who support the administration's policy in El Salvador is seeking a military solution to the problems of Central America. Newly elected President Duarte has said that he will engage in a dialog with the leftist opposition to find a peaceful settlement through the electoral process to the crisis in his country.

Mrs. BOXER [D—Calif.]. Mr. Chairman, I support the Studds amendment because it helps us achieve our goal in El Salvador.

So now it becomes necessary to ask the question: What is this goal for El Salvador? I believe people on all sides of the issue would say the goal for El Salvador is true democracy and a government which gains the support of its own people.

To do this it seems to me the government must do the following: One, put an end to the death squads which terrorize the people and killed four American nuns. And I might add to my colleague from this side of the aisle, who said that the guerrillas don't fool around, that death squads do not fool around either. Two, they must make real progress on social and land reform to bring economic justice to the people of El Salvador. Three, they must engage in meaningful, peaceful negotiations to end the civil war.

If these three improvements are accomplished I believe true democracy in El Salvador is possible, without these reforms the civil war will worsen because the people in El Salvador will not support their government. They will not be in sympathy with their government.

Mr. BONIOR [D—Mich.]. Last night, President Reagan delivered a speech to the American people that dangerously distorted the situation in Central America. A policy that is based on this view is destined for disaster. If we ignore the complexities of the struggle for democracy in El Salvador as the President did last night, I believe we will place the people of the region and our own Nation in great danger.

Since 1979, the El Salvadoran Army security forces and paramilitary squads allied with them have been responsible for the deaths of nearly 40,000 noncombat and civilians, according to documentation supplied by the Catholic Church in that country.

In the final 3 months of 1983, the civilian death toll at the hands of the government forces averaged 120 per week.

To suggest on this floor that murders in Chicago, Boston, New York, and other cities are comparable to this is just pure rubbish.

The corruption, the incompetence, and the brutality of the Salvadoran military, itself, has been a major cause of the insurgency in El Salvador, just as such grievances were a major cause of the rebellion that overthrew Anastasio Somoza. To ally ourselves unequivocally with such forces is not only morally repugnant, it is contrary to our national best interests.

If the Government of El Salvador cannot meet the minimum standards for human rights and political reform that we are proposing today, if it cannot control the death squads and reach out to embrace the prospects for negotiations, it will never win the support of the people of El Salvador or stem the rising tide of violence.

If we tie our Nation's prestige to a government that cannot meet these basic conditions, if we commit ourselves to massive military aid without asking whether that aid is being used in support of realistic policies, then we are endangering ourselves indeed.

Mr. LIVINGSTON [R—La.]. One would have to be blind not to see what is going on in Central America. I daresay that many of our blind citizens understand very well and see very clearly the fact that the leaders of the communist government there are fulfilling the promises that they themselves made to us over the last 4 years. They have said, and they are following through with their declarations, that they are bent on revolution without borders throughout Central America. They will not be content until communism has prevailed in all of the countries, not just Nicaragua, but Costa Rica, Honduras, Guatemala, El Salvador, ultimately Mexico, and throughout Central America. Yet, they have offered nothing, even in Nicaragua, despite their promises, other than totalitarian repression.

They have repressed the Catholic Church, they have not followed through with the promised elections, they have eliminated the free press, they control the private economy, they have overwhelmingly increased the militarization of that country. In fact, they have got an armed services in Nicaragua that is larger than all of the military in all of the other countries in Central America put together.

They have discriminated and repressed and exiled and even imprisoned members of the ethnic populations of their country, and yet we close our eyes, our ears, and we close our hearts and our minds to what is going on in Nicaragua and what they intend for our neighbors in the rest of Central America.

Mr. Chairman, my home in New Orleans is closer to San Salvador in El Salvador than it is to New York or to Los Angeles. The United States of America is dependent upon the sealanes going through Central America for 50 percent of all of our imports and our exports. Thirty percent of all of our exports go to Latin America. We are vitally dependent on everything that happens down there. And yet we ignore the fact that what is happening to our neighbors to the south may someday soon, very soon, happen to us. We choose to ignore that fact.

Mr. FRANK [D—Mass.]. Mr. Chairman, people listening to this debate might be excused for some confusion as to what is in the amendment offered by the gentleman from Massachusetts. It is not an amendment to cut off all aid. One Member said, "Well, what about the death squads on the left?" This amendment would, if it is carried out, provide $132 million, a substantial part of which would go toward shooting at the death squads on the left. It is not an effort to cut off all military aid. It is an effort to provide conditions under which military aid could be provided in a manner that would be useful.

One of the most conspicuous facts about this administration's current policy in El Salvador is its lack of success. They have had much of what they have asked for. And through no fault of the people of the United States, the Salvadoran Government and army have been unable to organize itself, to appeal to its people sufficiently to put down its armed rebellion.

Some of the reasons it has failed to do so are reasons the gentleman from Massachusetts is addressing. This says, "Yes, the full amount of military aid will go if the death squads on the government side are stopped."

Does this say that we have no confidence in the new president? Quite to the contrary. He is the one to whom it is addressed. If people had no confidence that Mr. Duarte could do this, then the amendment would not have had any purpose. It says that we want negotiations which aim at full participation and free elections. What we are saying is that the effort to date has been notably unsuccessful through no fault of anyone in the United States. There has been an inability in El Salvador itself to pull this together.

We are saying these are the conditions which we think are the minimum necessary if this effort is to succeed, and if these conditions are met, then we are prepared to provide military assistance.

So the effort to portray this as some total withdrawal, some unilateral abstention, is simply wrong. The failures, the problems, the gains that the rebellion has had so far are the result of current policy. Current policy has been here dismally unsuccessful, and the amendment of the gentleman from Massachusetts is trying to create conditions under which it could succeed.

Mr. DOWNEY [D—N.Y.]. My colleagues, the overwhelming number of Central Americans have been in rebellion at one point or another over the last 80 years because their children starved, not because they knew or cared anything about Marxism. And the only criticism that comes from our Republican colleagues is: that we here on the Democratic side, who are supporting the Studds amendment, are overly concerned with poverty and deprivation in Central America, and care too little about the advance of communism.

I am concerned about the advance of communism and it seems to me that the one sure-fire method for communism to continue in El Salvador is for us to give unfettered military aid for the death squads to continue; for the people who might want to be in the center, whatever that is, to move further to the left.

So it seems to me that if we are serious about communism, we should be worried both about poverty and deprivation in Central America and about the illegal forces on the right. And that is what the Studds amendment addresses.

We also appear to be trapped by our failure to understand the history of this region. Now, because of mistakes that have been made on both sides, we are left with very few options in El Salvador. One of those options is to do nothing, to allow the revolution to work its will and to suffer the consequences, whatever they may be. Both sides reject that option.

The other option is to recognize that negotiations can work, that our leverage which we will be handing Mr. Duarte over the military is the condition that the Studds amendment requires for military aid, to ask our friends in the Contadora countries to use their influence with the left to bring them to the table. That is the option that I believe will work. That is an option that is serious.

The third option offered by our President and supported by the members of his party is to continue to do what we are doing, provide the aid, ignore the fact that there is a serious problem with hunger and malnutrition, to speak against the death squads but really do nothing about them, because once you have given the aid you have bought their argument, you have been sucked into their agenda. You hold nothing over their head. They will continue unabated the slaughter of their own people.

Ronald Reagan and American power can win this conflict if we choose to. There is no doubt about that. And we will have an opportunity to vote on the modern Gulf of Tonkin resolution offered by the gentleman from Michigan [Mr. Broomfield], a little later this afternoon. It may require American troops but we will ultimately prevail.

What we fail to understand is, that Presidents Taft, Wilson, and Coolidge won against the revolutionaries in Nicaragua from 1911 through 1933. We won those revolutions, and what are the consequences of winning there? The consequences of continuing to use American force and to continue to eschew the notion that diplomacy works better than force are clear and inevitable.

First of all, millions of people who know little and care less about Marxism or democracy will die. We will polarize the situation in Central America and in El Salvador. We will have contentious arguments with our allies divert our attention from more serious goals, and lastly and most importantly we will have failed to solve anything because we will have won against the revolutionaries only to allow them 5 to 10 years in the future to regroup and fight again.

We cannot ultimately win this war. We cannot win a peace without bringing both sides to the table. We cannot win a peace unless we are prepared to be tough with the people who are sowing the seeds of communism.

So I urge you, I urge you to understand the lessons of history, to support the Studds amendment and begin to bring the bloodshed which has run in rivers over the last 80 years in Central America to a halt.

Mr. OBEY [D—Wis.]. The issue is not whether the United States has legitimate interests to defend in Central America. It obviously has. The issue is, simply, whether we are going to defend those interests in a manner which is effective, or whether we are going to defend them in a manner which is ineffective.

The issue is not whether Marxism is suffocating to freedom or antithetical to the legitimate interests of the United States in that part of the world. It is. And if you have any doubts about it, all you have to do is visit the Soviet Union, as a number of us did last July.

The issue is not whether El Salvador has a decent record on human rights; I would submit, it does not. But neither do a number of other countries with whom we find it necessary to do business because we are a great world power.

Human rights is not the only consideration, but it is a very important consideration, for two basic reasons: Morally, because as God's creatures we have some responsibility to every human being in this world, including people who are not lucky enough to be born in a country like the United States; and, second, tactically, because abuse of human rights by our so-called allies can weaken our own ability to defend our national interests.

I do not like the committee provision which we are voting on today. I have great doubts about the requirement that the Congress ought to pass a resolution after Presidential certification, in fact, certifying whether or not the President is truthful and accurate in his certification.

I think that that process could give us significant executive-legislative problems long term, and I do not welcome those problems. But I think the Broomfield amendment is even more dangerous, for three fundamental reasons:

First, because it risks Americanizing that war because it removes effective limits on the number of advisers, and as those with clear memories will recall, that is how we eventually fell, slowly but surely, into Vietnam.

Second, the Broomfield amendment sends the wrong message to Mr. Duarte's opponents in the Army. It sends them a message that they can afford to ignore the needs for reform which are crucial if the rebels are not to, in the last analysis, win in that country.

Third, and most importantly, I believe, it delays changes in American policy which are needed to give American policy a chance of success and which are needed to achieve broad-based agreement in this country on a policy that could be sustainable, not just through one administration, but through a number of administrations.

What are those changes that are needed? I would suggest in the main there are two: No. 1, we need to aggressively support the Contadora negotiation initiatives, and right now I submit we are not doing that, public statements to the contrary.

No. 2, I think we need an intensification and a clarification of the administration's position on the death squads.

Right now, despite administration claims to the contrary, our allies in Central America simply do not believe that we are pursuing anything but a military option. If you doubt that, I invite you to read the testimony made by former Ambassador Sol Linowitz, I trust, regarded as a distinguished American on both sides of the aisle. He makes quite clear that our allies in Central America have grave doubts about our willingness to follow the Contadora process aggressively.

Second, the administration's policy on human rights is at best cloudy. The Vice President and Ambassador have made very constructive statements in El Salvador on the need to clean up the death squad operation. But the President himself has left doubt about the policy of this government because of his now famous statement that he was not at all sure that, in fact, the rightwing was responsible for the activities of the death squads. They probably are not responsible for the total activity of the death squads. But, as the Ambassador said, without control of those rightwing death squads, we are handicapped in dealing a blow to the ability of the rebels to survive.

If American policy is not changed, America will lose in Central America, and that is the issue before us today.

30.
REP. EDWARD BOLAND: THE BOLAND AMENDMENT
(MAY 1983)

TITLE VIII—PROHIBITION ON COVERT ASSISTANCE FOR MILITARY OPERATIONS IN NICARAGUA; AUTHORIZATION OF OVERT INTERDICTION ASSISTANCE

PROHIBITION ON COVERT ASSISTANCE OR MILITARY OPERATIONS IN NICARAGUA

Sec. 801. (a) None of the funds appropriated for fiscal year 1983 or 1984 for the Central Intelligence Agency or any other department, agency, or entity of the United States involved in intelligence activities may be obligated or expended for the purpose or which would have the effect of supporting, directly or indirectly, military or paramilitary operations in Nicaragua by any nation, group, organization, movement, or individual.

AUTHORIZATION OF OVERT INTERDICTION ASSISTANCE

Sec. 802. (a) The Congress finds that—

(1) in the absence of a state of declared war, the provision of military equipment to individuals, groups, organizations, or movements seeking to overthrow governments of countries in Central America violates international treaty obligations, including the Charter of the United Nations, the Charter of the Organization of American States, and the Rio Treaty of 1949; and
(2) such activities by the Governments of Cuba and Nicaragua threaten the independence of El Salvador and threaten to destabilize the entire Central American region, and the Governments of Cuba and Nicaragua refuse to cease those activities.

(b) The President is authorized to furnish assistance, on such terms and conditions as he may determine, to the government of any friendly country in Central America in order to provide such country with the ability to prevent use of its territory, or the use of international territory, for the transfer of military equipment from or through Cuba or Nicaragua or any other country or agents of that country to any individual, group, organiza-

---

Intelligence Authorization Act for Fiscal Year 1983, introduced on May 13, 1983.

tion, or movement which the President determines seeks to overthrow the government of such friendly country or the government of any other country in Central America. Assistance under this section shall be provided openly, and shall not be provided in a manner which attempts to conceal United States involvement in the provision of such assistance.

(c) Assistance may be provided to a friendly foreign country under this section only if that country has agreed that it will not use any assistance provided by the United States under this section, the Foreign Assistance Act of 1961, or the Arms Export Control Act to destabilize or overthrow the government of any country in Central America and will not make any such assistance available to any nation, individual, group, organization, or movement which seeks to destabilize or overthrow any such government. . . .

31.
ASSISTANT SECRETARY OF STATE LANGHORNE MOTLEY: ENDS AND MEANS OF U.S. POLICY (JANUARY 1985)

There are two things that the vast majority of the American people do *not* want in this region so close to home: They do *not* want a second Cuba, and they do *not* want a second Vietnam.

By a second Cuba, I mean the institutionalization of another well-armed Communist state, this time on the mainland, supported by the Soviet Union and working actively against U.S. interests and friends who depend on us.

And by a second Vietnam, I mean a prolonged conflict involving U.S. combat troops with no clear goal and no end in sight consistent with the protection of strategic American interests.

It is true that some Americans are concerned with one and not the other: some would risk another Vietnam to prevent another Cuba, while others are so concerned with any sign of a second Vietnam that they ignore the threat of a second Cuba. But the majority of our fellow citizens seek and will support a policy which serves our interests while preventing *both* a new Cuba *and* a new Vietnam. . . .

In recent years the sheer number of our "friends" has multiplied throughout the hemisphere. The people, and now the elected government,

Speaking before the Western Hemisphere Subcommittee, House of Representatives, January 29, 1985.

of Grenada. The giants, Brazil and Argentina, rejoining the family of democracies. The economically beleaguered governments and peoples of countries like Peru, Ecuador, Jamaica, Bolivia and Uruguay. All are friends, with whom we can and should stand proudly.

The people of Central America are also our friends. They feel acutely the tension between their democratic aspirations and the discredited but powerful extremisms of left and right. And they share an abiding concern with what *they* perceive as the ultimate extremism: the interference in their internal affairs by the Sandinistas and their Soviet and Cuban mentors.

Political polling in Costa Rica, El Salvador and Honduras has consistently revealed a consensus: that Nicaragua is a direct threat, that measures against Nicaragua must be sustained in the defense of the rest of Central America, and that the United States is the only country capable of carrying out such a policy. . . .

The evolution of Central America can usefully be measured against benchmarks offered one year ago. *Events have demonstrated that the report of the National Bipartisan Commission was right in its analysis and sound in its recommendations.* In so complex and divisive a situation, this record commands attention.

El Salvador illustrates the point. As recently as a year ago, many in the United States, in Western Europe, and even in Latin America believed El Salvador was caught in an endless war between guerrillas of the left and death squads of the right. But Dr. Kissinger and his colleagues insisted that electoral democracy and political dialogue—*not* externally imposed "power sharing"—would provide a workable foundation for attacking the "seamless web" of political, economic, social and security problems.

1984 in Nicaragua confirmed different but equally important lessons from the Bipartisan Commission's report. The key lesson: that dictatorship, no matter the rhetoric, leads to repression, civil war, and foreign entanglements. (That in 1984 Ortega had himself "elected" as Somoza had had himself "elected" in 1974 only underscores the point.)

But 1984 also confirmed another critical lesson: that the Sandinistas can change their ways if the pressure to do so is clear. Throughout 1983 and into 1984, a variety of pressures—military exercises, naval maneuvers, internal opposition (both armed and unarmed), falling international prestige—*did* produce some change, at least rhetorically, in Sandinista behavior. There were renewed promises of free elections and continued negotiations within the Contadora process. But then something happened. . . .

There is nothing mysterious about diplomatic negotiations. Commonsense rules apply as much to the multilateral "Contadora" talks on Central America as, for example, to a labor-management dispute in the United States. But many have *not* applied common sense. When it comes to Central America, some take at face value things they would never accept at home.

First, in any negotiation, the *agenda has to have something in it for each side.* Otherwise, why negotiate? Fidel Castro, for example, often says "let's negotiate," but it always turns out that the only important item *he* wants on the agenda is the U.S. economic boycott; anything *we* might want—as elimination of Cuban support for guerrillas—he rejects. In the first years of their rule, the Sandinistas obviously saw no advantage in "negotiating away" their support for Salvadoran and other guerrillas, or their military build-up and ties to the USSR and Cuba. They took our money but ignored attempts to discuss our concerns. But by 1983 they had an incentive. The strength of their internal democratic resistance, armed and unarmed, their neighbors' military exercises with the U.S., and their own plummeting international prestige gave the Sandinistas *something to bargain for.* That's when Contadora started rolling.

Second, *nobody bargains for something he expects to get free.* If the Nicaraguans in the armed resistance are abandoned, why should the Sandinistas negotiate with them? If the World Court makes decisions without considering the concerns of other Central Americans, why should Nicaragua compromise with its neighbors?

Third, *pressure outside of the formal negotiation is a normal part of the process.* What some call "coercive diplomacy" has been part of history since the first diplomats and the first soldiers. People and nations do not move to the negotiating table simply because it's a nice piece of furniture. If anyone knows of a more effective way to create a bargaining situation with the Sandinistas, let us know.

Fourth, *it takes at least two to negotiate.* If one side practices the theory that "what's mine is mine, what's yours is negotiable," then the parties might as well be a thousand miles apart rather than sitting around a green felt table—whether in Geneva or Contadora or Manzanillo. An announcement by one party that one of several contending texts "must" be signed immediately without further conversation is a declaration of unwillingness to negotiate further.

Fifth, *balance must be maintained. If one side gets what it wants first, it will lose its incentive to compromise.* That's like a labor union agreeing to postpone consideration of pay raises without first trying to get them. Or the September 7 draft for a Contadora *acta,* which would have satisfied Nicaragua's basic demands but left issues fundamental to others for "future" discussion.

Sixth, *what negotiators say publicly is part of the negotiating process.* Nicaragua's statement that it was ready to sign the September 7 draft *act* "as is" was a transparent ploy aimed at resisting the balancing changes sure to be insisted upon by the other participants. To see why, just carefully read the timetable and ground rules under which the draft *acta* was tabled.

Seventh, *an unenforceable, unverifiable agreement is worse than no agreement at all.* A mere announcement of "adherence" or a signature mean nothing without a means to ensure compliance. And if an agreement fails, a solution will become even more difficult.

Eighth, *what is important is the practical end result. Not* the fact of a ceremonial meeting or a frameable document, *not* self-satisfying statements to the press, but whether or not the "deal" really does bring results —whether higher wages for workers in the local plant or peace to Central America.

And, finally, *if pressure and negotiations fail and the problem continues—* as is possible, if not necessarily likely, in the case of Nicaragua's Sandinistas—*then the alternatives will surely be less desirable and far more expensive.* Let us be specific:

— the Sandinistas have global ties and plans for Nicaragua and the rest of Central America that are contrary to U.S. interests;

— they will not modify or bargain away their position unless there is some incentive for them to do so;

— the only incentive that has proved effective thus far has been opposition from other Nicaraguans (remember what happened after the 1980 emergency supplemental for Nicaraguan reconstruction?);

— if pressure is taken away, the Sandinistas will have no reason to compromise;

— if the Sandinistas have no reason to compromise, Contadora will surely fail; and

— if Contadora fails, the long-run costs to the U.S. in terms of money and lives will be much greater.

The perceived U.S. relationship to the Nicaraguans who have taken up arms against those who cheated them of the goals of their revolution against Somoza has been controversial. However, the fact that the Nicaraguan armed resistance has been able to sustain, and in some respects even increase, its operations in recent months reflects its substantial indigenous as well as hemispheric support. Realistically, part of the debate over the future should focus on what Nicaragua would be like without pressure from the armed opposition, which short of changes in Sandinistas behavior is the only internal obstacle to consolidation of an undemocratic regime at home providing military support to Marxist revolutions throughout Central America.

U.S. policies must also consider the consequences of any failure to induce the Sandinista government to allow political pluralism. Contrary to their own pronouncements, the Sandinistas may be content to be left alone to build Marxism in one country. But the burden of proof should lie on those who proclaim that the Sandinistas are interested in doing their thing totally within Nicaragua. Neither the Cuban precedent nor the Sandinistas' behavior to date fit that proposition. And if a long-term policy of containment were to become necessary, both the U.S. and its friends in Central America would pay the price, in resources dearly needed for other purposes.

Nicaragua's freedom fighters deserve the solidarity of the West no less —some would say more, because of the imperative of proximity—than the Afghan rebels or the Polish Solidarity movement. Shall we always wring our hands when a country suffers from Soviet or Marxist dictatorship but fail to help those who resist it?

The identity of the resistance fighters has been clouded by Sandinista propaganda denunciations of them as "murderers, marauders, and rapists." They are said to be mercenaries and mostly former National Guardsmen who remain loyal to Somoza. In fact, all you have to do is count the numbers through; there are far more resistance fighters than there ever were members of the National Guard, even at its peak in Somoza's last days. The freedom fighters are peasants, farmers, shopkeepers, and vendors. Their leaders are without exception men who opposed Somoza. And what unites them to each other and to the thousands of Nicaraguans who resist without arms is disillusionment with Sandinista abuse, corruption, and fanaticism. The myth that if Somoza was bad the Sandinistas have to be good was exploded long ago for most Nicaraguans.

Let us be clear: It is partly *because* our adversaries are intervening on behalf of totalitarianism in Central America that so many of our friends are involved in internal opposition to dictatorship. The Nicaraguan resistance was labeled "contras" by the people who wanted to deny them legitimacy. But the historical fact is that they are more "for" than "against": They are *for* democracy, *for* national independence and *for* the original promises of the anti-Somoza revolution. What they are *against* are the subverters of those ideals. The Nicaraguan democratic resistance clearly has a principled claim on our support. These are friends who merit our standing with them—and indeed can be frustrated if they are denied our help.

32.
SECRETARY OF STATE GEORGE P. SHULTZ: AMERICA AND THE STRUGGLE FOR FREEDOM (FEBRUARY 1985)

A revolution is sweeping the world today—a democratic revolution. This should not be a surprise. Yet it is noteworthy because many people in the West lost faith, for a time, in the relevance of the idea of democracy. It was fashionable in some quarters to argue that democracy was culture bound; that it was a luxury only industrial societies could afford; that other institutional structures were needed to meet the challenges of development; that to try to encourage others to adopt our system was ethnocentric and arrogant.

In fact, what began in the United States of America over two centuries ago as a bold new experiment in representative government has today captured the imagination and the passions of peoples on every continent. The Solidarity movement in Poland; resistance forces in Afghanistan, in Cambodia, in Nicaragua, in Ethiopia and Angola; dissidents in the Soviet Union and Eastern Europe; advocates of peaceful democratic change in South Africa, Chile, the Republic of Korea, and the Philippines—all these brave men and women have something in common: they seek independence, freedom, and human rights—ideals which are at the core of democracy and which the United States has always championed.

Proxies, like Cuba and Vietnam, have consistently supplied money, arms, and training in efforts to destabilize or overthrow noncommunist governments. "Wars of national liberation" became the pretext for subverting any noncommunist country in the name of so-called "socialist internationalism."

At the same time, any victory of communism was held to be irreversible. This was the infamous Brezhnev doctrine, first proclaimed at the time of the invasion of Czechoslovakia in 1968. Its meaning is simple and chilling: once you're in the so-called "socialist camp," you're not allowed to leave. Thus the Soviets say to the rest of the world: "What's mine is mine. What's yours is up for grabs."

In recent years, Soviet activities and pretensions have run head on into the democratic revolution. People are insisting on their right to independence, on their right to choose their government free of outside control.

Commonwealth Club, San Francisco, California, February 22, 1985. U.S. Department of State, Bureau of Public Affairs, Current Policy No. 659.

Where once the Soviets may have thought that all discontent was ripe for turning into communist insurgencies, today we see a new and different kind of struggle: people around the world risking their lives against communist despotism. We see brave men and women fighting to challenge the Brezhnev doctrine. . . .

In the Western Hemisphere, over 90% of the population of Latin America and the Caribbean today live under governments that are either democratic or clearly on the road to democracy—in contrast to only one-third in 1979. In less than 6 years, popularly elected democrats have replaced dictators in Argentina, Bolivia, Ecuador, El Salvador, Honduras, Panama, Peru, and Grenada. Brazil and Uruguay will inaugurate civilian presidents in March. After a long twilight of dictatorship, this hemispheric trend toward free elections and representative government is something to be applauded and supported.

THE CHALLENGE TO THE BREZHNEV DOCTRINE

Democracy is an old idea, but today we witness a new phenomenon. For many years we saw our adversaries act without restraint to back insurgencies around the world to spread communist dictatorships. . . .

In Africa, as well, the Brezhnev doctrine is being challenged by the drive for independence and freedom. In Ethiopia, a Soviet-backed Marxist-Leninist dictatorship has shown indifference to the desperate poverty and suffering of its people. . . .

In the face of this Soviet invasion, the Afghans who are fighting and dying for the liberation of their country have made a remarkable stand. Their will has not flagged; indeed, their capacity to resist has grown. The countryside is now largely in the hands of the popular resistance, and not even in the major cities can the Soviets claim complete control. Clearly, the Afghans do not share the belief of some in the West that fighting back is pointless, that the only option is to let one's country be "quietly erased," to use the memorable phrase of the Czech writer Milan Kundera.

In Cambodia, the forces open to democracy, once all but annihilated by the Khmer Rouge, are now waging a similar battle against occupation and a puppet regime imposed by a Soviet ally, communist Vietnam. . . .

Armed insurgencies continue, while the regime persists in relying on military solutions and on expanding the power and scope of the police and security apparatus. . . .

In Angola, UNITA [National Union for the Total Independence of Angola] has waged an armed struggle against the regime's monopoly of power and in recent years has steadily expanded the territory under its control. Foreign forces, whether Cuban or South African, must leave. At some point there will be an internal political settlement in Angola that reflects Angolan political reality, not external intervention.

Finally, an important struggle is being waged today closer to home in Central America. Its countries are in transition, trying to resolve the inequities and tensions of the past through workable reforms and democratic institutions. But violent antidemocratic minorities, tied ideologically and militarily to the Soviet Union and Cuba, are trying to prevent democratic reform and to seize or hold power by force. The outcome of this struggle will affect not only the future of peace and democracy in this hemisphere but our own vital interests.

In Nicaragua, in 1979 the Sandinista leaders pledged to the Organization of American States (OAS) and to their own people to bring freedom to their country after decades of tyranny under Somoza. The Sandinistas have betrayed these pledges and the hopes of the Nicaraguan people; instead, they have imposed a new and brutal tyranny that respects no frontiers. Basing themselves on strong military ties to Cuba and the Soviet Union, the Sandinistas are attempting, as rapidly as they can, to force Nicaragua into a totalitarian mold whose pattern is all too familiar. They are suppressing internal dissent; clamping down on the press; persecuting the church; linking up with the terrorists of Iran, Libya, and the PLO [Palestine Liberation Organization]; and seeking to undermine the legitimate and increasingly democratic governments of their neighbors.

This betrayal has forced many Nicaraguans who supported the anti-Somoza revolution back into opposition. And while many resist peacefully, thousands now see no choice but to take up arms again, to risk everything so that their hopes for freedom and democracy will not once again be denied.

The Sandinistas denounce their opponents as mercenaries or former National Guardsmen loyal to the memory of Somoza. Some in this country seem all too willing to take these charges at face value, even though they come from the same Sandinista leaders whose word has meant so little up to now. But all you have to do is count the numbers: more people have taken up arms against the Sandinistas than ever belonged to Somoza's National Guard. In fact, most of the leaders of the armed resistance fought in the revolution against Somoza; and some even served in the new government until it became clear that the *comandantes* were bent on communism, not freedom; terror, not reform; and aggression, not peace. The new fighters for freedom include peasants and farmers, shopkeepers and vendors, teachers and professionals. What unites them to each other and to the other thousands of Nicaraguans who resist without arms is disillusionment with Sandinista militarism, corruption, and fanaticism.

Despite uncertain and sporadic support from outside, the resistance in Nicaragua is growing. The Sandinistas have strengthened their Soviet and Cuban military ties, but their popularity at home has declined sharply. The struggle in Nicaragua for democracy and freedom, and against dictatorship, is far from over, and right now may well be a pivotal moment that decides the future.

AMERICA'S MORAL DUTY

This new phenomenon we are witnessing around the world—popular insurgencies *against* communist domination—is not an American creation. In every region the people have made their own decision to stand and fight rather than see their cultures and freedoms "quietly erased." . . .

But America also has a moral responsibility. The lesson of the postwar era is that America must be the leader of the free world; there is no one else to take our place. The nature and extent of our support—whether moral support or something more—necessarily varies from case to case. But there should be no doubt about where our sympathies lie.

It is more than mere coincidence that the last 4 years have been a time of both renewed American strength and leadership and a resurgence of democracy and freedom. As we are the strongest democratic nation on earth, the actions we take—or do not take—have both a direct and an indirect impact on those who share our ideals and hopes all around the globe. If we shrink from leadership, we create a vacuum into which our adversaries can move. Our national security suffers, our global interests suffer, and, yes, the worldwide struggle for democracy suffers.

The Soviets are fond of talking about the "correlation of forces," and for a few years it may have seemed that the correlation of forces favored communist minorities backed by Soviet military power. Today, however, the Soviet empire is weakening under the strain of its own internal problems and external entanglements. And the United States has shown the will and the strength to defend its interests, to resist the spread of Soviet influence, and to protect freedom. Our actions, such as the rescue of Grenada, have again begun to offer inspiration and hope to others. . . .

HOW TO RESPOND?

The question is: How should we act? What should America do to further both its security interests and the cause of freedom and democracy? A prudent strategy must combine different elements, suited to different circumstances.

First, as a matter of fundamental principle, the United States supports human rights and peaceful democratic change throughout the world, including in noncommunist, pro-Western countries. Democratic institutions are the best guarantor of stability and peace, as well as of human rights.

Therefore, we have an interest in seeing peaceful progress toward democracy in friendly countries.

Such a transition is often complex and delicate, and it can only come about in a way consistent with a country's history, culture, and political realities. We will not succeed if we fail to recognize positive change when it does occur—whether in South Africa, or the Republic of Korea, or the Philippines. Nor will we achieve our goal if we ignore the even greater threat to the freedom of such countries as South Korea and the Philippines from external or internal forces of totalitarianism. We must heed the cautionary lessons of both Iran and Nicaragua, in which pressures against rightwing authoritarian regimes were not well thought out and helped lead to even more repressive dictatorship. . . .

Second, we have a moral obligation to support friendly democratic governments by providing economic and security assistance against a variety of threats. . . .

Americans have always responded with courage when overwhelming danger called for an immediate, all-out national effort. But the harder task is to recognize and meet challenges before they erupt into major crises, before they represent an immediate threat, and before they require an all-out effort. We have many possible responses that fall between the extremes of inaction and the direct use of military force—but we must be willing to use them, or else we will inevitably face the agonizing choice between those two extremes.

Economic and security assistance is one of those crucial means of avoiding and deterring bigger threats. It is also vital support to those friendly nations on the front line—like Pakistan, Thailand, or Honduras and Costa Rica—whose security is threatened by Soviet and proxy efforts to export their system.

Third, we should support the forces of freedom in communist totalitarian states. We must not succumb to the fashionable thinking that democracy has enemies only on the right, that pressures and sanctions are fine against rightwing dictators but not against leftwing totalitarians. We should support the aspirations for freedom of peoples in communist states just as we want freedom for people anywhere else. For example, without raising false hopes, we have a duty to make it clear—especially on the anniversary of the Yalta conference—that the United States will never accept the artificial division of Europe into free and not free. This has nothing to do with boundaries and everything to do with ideas and governance. Our radios will continue to broadcast the truth to people in closed societies.

Fourth, and finally, our moral principles compel us to support those struggling against the imposition of communist tyranny. From the founding of this nation, Americans have believed that a people have the right to seek freedom and independence—and that we have both a legal right and a moral obligation to help them.

In contrast to the Soviets and their allies, the United States is committed to the principles of international law. The UN and OAS Charters reaffirm the inherent right of individual and collective self-defense against aggression—aggression of the kind committed by the Soviets in Afghanistan, by Nicaragua in Central America, and by Vietnam in Cambodia. Material assistance to those opposing such aggression can be a lawful form of collective self-defense. . . .

In those few cases where national security requires that the details are better kept confidential, Congress and the President can work together to ensure that what is done remains consistent with basic American principles.

Do we really have a choice? In the 1970s, a European leader proposed to Brezhnev that peaceful coexistence should extend to the ideological sphere. Brezhnev responded firmly that this was impossible, that the ideological struggle continued even in an era of détente, and that the Soviet Union would forever support "national liberation" movements. The practical meaning of that is clear. When Soviet Politburo member Gorbachev was in London recently, he affirmed that Nicaragua had gained independence only with the Sandinista takeover. The Soviets and their proxies thus proceed on the theory that any country not Marxist-Leninist is not truly independent, and, therefore, the supply of money, arms, and training to overthrow its government is legitimate.

Again: "What's mine is mine. What's yours is up for grabs." This is the Brezhnev doctrine.

So long as communist dictatorships feel free to aid and abet insurgencies in the name of "socialist internationalism," why must the democracies, the target of this threat, be inhibited from defending their own interests and the cause of democracy itself?

How can we as a country say to a young Afghan, Nicaraguan, or Cambodian: "Learn to live with oppression; only those of us who already have freedom deserve to pass it on to our children." How can we say to those Salvadorans who stood so bravely in line to vote: "We may give you some economic and military aid for self-defense, but we will also give a free hand to the Sandinistas who seek to undermine your new democratic institutions."

Some try to evade this moral issue by the relativistic notion that "one man's freedom fighter is another man's terrorist." This is nonsense. There is a self-evident difference between those fighting to impose tyranny and those fighting to resist it. In El Salvador, pro-communist guerrillas backed by the Soviet bloc are waging war against a democratically elected government; in Nicaragua and elsewhere, groups seeking democracy are resisting the tightening grip of totalitarians seeking to suppress democracy. The essence of democracy is to offer means for peaceful change, legitimate political competition, and redress of grievances. Violence directed against democracy is, therefore, fundamentally lacking in legitimacy. . . .

Nowhere are both the strategic and the moral stakes clearer than in Central America.

The Sandinista leaders in Nicaragua are moving quickly, with Soviet-bloc and Cuban help, to consolidate their totalitarian power. Should they achieve this primary goal, we could confront a second Cuba in this hemisphere, this time on the Central American mainland—with all the strategic dangers that this implies. If history is any guide, the Sandinistas would then intensify their efforts to undermine neighboring governments in the name of their revolutionary principles—principles which Fidel Castro himself flatly reaffirmed on American television a few weeks ago. Needless to say, the first casualty of the consolidation of Sandinista power would be the freedom and hopes for democracy of the Nicaraguan people. The second casualty would be the security of Nicaragua's neighbors and the security of the entire region.

I do not believe anyone in the United States wants to see this dangerous scenario unfold. Yet there are those who would look the other way, imagining that the problem will disappear by itself. There are those who would grant the Sandinistas a peculiar kind of immunity in our legislation—in effect, enacting the Brezhnev doctrine into American law.

The logic of the situation in Central America is inescapable.

- The Sandinistas are committed Marxist-Leninists; it would be foolish of us and insulting to them to imagine that they do not believe in their proclaimed goals. They will not modify or bargain away their position unless there is compelling incentive for them to do so.

- The only incentive that has proved effective thus far comes from the vigorous armed opposition of the many Nicaraguans who seek freedom and democratic government.

- The pressures of the armed resistance have diverted Sandinista energies and resources away from aggression against its neighbor El Salvador, thus helping to disrupt guerrilla plans for a major offensive there last fall.

- If the pressure of the armed resistance is removed, the Sandinistas will have no reason to compromise; all U.S. diplomatic efforts—and those of the Contadora group—will be undermined.

Central America's hopes for peace, security, democracy, and economic progress will not be realized unless there is a fundamental change in Nicaraguan behavior in four areas.

First, Nicaragua must stop playing the role of surrogate for the Soviet

Union and Cuba. As long as there are large numbers of Soviet and Cuban security and military personnel in Nicaragua, Central America will be embroiled in the East-West conflict.

Second, Nicaragua must reduce its armed forces, now in excess of 100,-000, to a level commensurate with its legitimate security needs—a level comparable to those of its neighbors. The current imbalance is incompatible with regional stability.

Third, Nicaragua must absolutely and definitively stop its support for insurgents and terrorists in the region. All of Nicaragua's neighbors, and particularly El Salvador, have felt the brunt of Sandinista efforts to destabilize their governments. No country in Central America will be secure as long as this continues.

And fourth, the Sandinistas must live up to their commitments to democratic pluralism made to the OAS in 1979. The internal Nicaraguan opposition groups, armed and unarmed, represent a genuine political force that is entitled to participate in the political processes of the country. It is up to the Government of Nicaragua to provide the political opening that will allow their participation.

We will note and welcome such a change in Nicaraguan behavior no matter how it is obtained. Whether it is achieved through the multilateral Contadora negotiations, through unilateral actions taken by the Sandinistas alone or in concert with their domestic opponents, or through the collapse of the Sandinista regime is immaterial to us. But without such a change of behavior, lasting peace in Central America will be impossible.

The democratic forces in Nicaragua are on the front line in the struggle for progress, security, and freedom in Central America. Our active help for them is the best insurance that their efforts will be directed consistently and effectively toward these objectives.

But the bottom line is this: those who would cut off these freedom fighters from the rest of the democratic world are, in effect, consigning Nicaragua to the endless darkness of communist tyranny. And they are leading the United States down a path of greater danger. For if we do not take the appropriate steps now to pressure the Sandinistas to live up to their promises—to cease their arms buildup, to stop exporting tyranny across their borders, to open Nicaragua to the competition of freedom and democracy, then we may find later, when we can no longer avoid acting, that the stakes will be higher and the costs greater.

33.
PRESIDENT RONALD REAGAN: PEACE PROPOSAL
(APRIL 4, 1985)

I want to announce today a proposal for peace in Central America that can enable liberty and democracy to prevail in this troubled region and that can protect the security of our own borders, economy, and people.

On March 1, in San José, Costa Rica, the leaders of the Nicaraguan democratic resistance met with a broad coalition of other exiled Nicaraguan democrats. They agreed upon and signed a historic proposal to restore peace and democracy in their country.

The members of the democratic resistance offered a cease-fire in return for an agreement by the Nicaraguan regime to begin a dialogue mediated by the Bishops' Conference of the Roman Catholic Church with the goal of restoring democracy through honest elections. To date, the Nicaraguan regime has refused this offer.

The Central American countries, including Nicaragua, have agreed that internal reconciliation is indispensable to regional peace. But we know that, unlike President Duarte of El Salvador, who seeks a dialogue with his opponents, the communists in Nicaragua have turned, at least up until now, a cold shoulder to appeals for national reconciliation from the Pope and the Nicaraguan bishops. And we know that without incentives, none of this will change.

For these reasons, great numbers of Nicaraguans are demanding change and taking up arms to fight for the stolen promise of freedom and democracy. Over 15,000 farmers, small merchants, whites, blacks, and Miskito Indians have united to struggle for a true democracy.

We supported democracy in Nicaragua before, and we support democracy today. We supported national reconciliation before, and we support it today. We believe that democracy deserves as much support in Nicaragua as it has received in El Salvador. And we're proud of the help that we've given to El Salvador.

You may recall that in 1981, we were told that the communist guerrillas were mounting a final offensive, the government had no chance, and our approach would lead to greater American involvement. Well, our critics were wrong. Democracy and freedom are winning in El Salvador. President Duarte is pulling his country together and enjoys wide support from the people. And all of this with America's help kept strictly limited.

The formula that worked in El Salvador—support for democracy, self-defense, economic development, and dialogue—will work for the entire region. And we couldn't have accomplished this without bipartisan support in Congress, backed up by the National Bipartisan Commission on Central America, headed by Henry Kissinger. And that's why, after months of consulting with congressional leaders and listening carefully to their concerns, I am making the following proposal: I'm calling upon both sides to lay down their arms and accept the offer of church-mediated talks on internationally supervised elections and an end to the repression now in place against the church, the press, and individual rights.

To the members of the democratic resistance, I ask them to extend their offer of a cease-fire until June 1.

To the Congress, I ask for immediate release of the $14 million already appropriated. While the cease-fire offer is on the table, I pledge these funds will not be used for arms or munitions. These funds will be used for food, clothing, and medicine and other support for survival. The democratic opposition cannot be a partner in negotiations without these basic necessities.

If the Sandinistas accept this peace offer, I will keep my funding restrictions in effect. But peace negotiations must not become a cover for deception and delay. If there is no agreement after 60 days of negotiations, I will lift these restrictions, unless both sides ask me not to.

I want to emphasize that consistent with the 21 goals of the Contadora process, the United States continues to seek:

1. Nicaragua's implementation of its commitment to democracy made to the Organization of American States;
2. An end to Nicaragua's aggression against its neighbors;
3. A removal of the thousands of Soviet-bloc, Cuban, PLO [Palestine Liberation Organization], Libyan, and other military and security personnel; and
4. A return of the Nicaraguan military to a level of parity with their neighbors. . . .

Democracy can succeed in Central America, but Congress must release the funds that can create incentives for dialogue and peace. If we provide too little help, our choice will be a communist Central America with communist subversion spreading southward and northward. We face the risk that 100 million people from Panama to our open southern border could come under the control of pro-Soviet regimes and threaten the

United States with violence, economic chaos, and a human tidal wave of refugees.

Central America is not condemned to that dark future of endless violence. If the United States meets its obligations to help those now striving for democracy, they can create a bright future in which peace for all Americans will be secure.

34.
REP. LEE HAMILTON: THE BARNES-HAMILTON AMENDMENT (APRIL 1985)

SECTION 1. UNITED STATES SUPPORT FOR PEACE IN CENTRAL AMERICA

THE CONGRESS FINDS AND DECLARES THE FOLLOWING:

(1) The United States desires peace in Nicaragua and throughout Central America. United States policy toward Nicaragua should encourage all combatants to establish a ceasefire and come together in peace negotiations in order to resolve the internal Nicaraguan conflict, nurture democratic institutions in that country, and promote peace and stability, as part of a regional settlement through the Contadora process or the Organization of American States.

(2) The countries of Central America, working through the Contadora process, have agreed to 21 principles (set forth in the Contadora Document of Objectives issued on September 9, 1983) which provide an appropriate framework for achieving peace and security in the region.

(3) Combatants on both sides of the conflict in Nicaragua have expressed in words their goals for peace and democracy in Nicaragua and throughout the region. United States policy should be designed to encourage these goals, including through the resumption of bilateral talks between the United States and Nicaragua.

(4) There are disturbing trends in Nicaragua's foreign and domestic policies, including—

    (A) the Sandinista government's curtailment of individual liberties, political expression, freedom of worship, and the independence of the media;

    (B) the subordination of military, judicial, and internal security functions to the ruling political party;

(C) the Sandinista government's close military ties with Cuba, the Soviet Union, and its Warsaw Pact allies, and the continuing military buildup that Nicaragua's neighbors consider threatening; and

(D) the Sandinista government's efforts to export its influence and ideology.

(5) The Congress will continue to monitor developments in Nicaragua to determine whether progress is being made to curtail these disturbing trends. Such progress will be a key element in congressional consideration of future economic and security assistance requirements in the region.

(6) If the Congress determines that progress is being made toward peace and development of democratic institutions in Nicaragua, consideration will be given to initiating a number of economic and development programs, including but not limited to—

(A) trade concessions,

(B) Peace Corps programs,

(C) technical assistance,

(D) health services, and

(E) agricultural development.

(7) Should Nicaragua not address the concerns described in paragraph (4), the United States has several means to address this challenge to peace and stability in the region, including political, diplomatic, and economic means. In addition, the United States—

(A) should through appropriate regional organizations, such as the Organization of American States, seek to maintain multilateral pressure on Nicaragua to address the concerns;

(B) should, if called upon to do so, give serious consideration to supporting any sanctions adopted by such an organization; and

(C) should consider the imposition of trade sanctions.

(8) In assessing whether or not progress is being made toward achieving these goals the Congress will expect, within the context of a regional settlement—

(A) the removal of foreign military advisers from Nicaragua;

(B) the end to Sandinista support for insurgencies in other countries in the region including the cessation of military supplies to the rebel forces fighting the democratically elected government in El Salvador;

(C) restoration of individual liberties, political expression, freedom of worship, and the independence of the media; and

(D) progress toward internal reconciliation and a pluralistic democratic system.

(9) The Congress is deeply concerned about human rights violations by both the Sandinista government and the armed opposition groups.

SEC. 2. PROHIBITION OF FUNDING FOR MILITARY OR PARAMILITARY OPERATIONS IN NICARAGUA.

The prohibition contained in section 8066(a) of the Department of Defense Appropriations Act, 1985 (as contained in section 101 of Public Law 98-473), shall continue in effect without regard to fiscal year until the Congress enacts a joint resolution repealing that prohibition.

SEC. 3. ASSISTANCE FOR IMPLEMENTATION OF CONTADORA AGREEMENT AND HUMANITARIAN ASSISTANCE FOR REFUGEES.

(a) IMPLEMENTATION OF CONTADORA AGREEMENT.—During fiscal year 1985, the President may allocate $4,000,000, which shall remain available until expended, for payment to the Contadora nations (Mexico, Panama, Colombia, and Venezuela) for expenses arising from implementation of an agreement among the countries of Central America based on the Contadora Document of Objectives of September 9, 1983, including peacekeeping, verification, and monitoring systems.

(b) HUMANITARIAN ASSISTANCE FOR REFUGEES.—During fiscal year 1985, the President may make available up to $10,000,000 for the provision of food, medicine, or other humanitarian assistance for Nicaraguan refugees who are outside of Nicaragua, regardless of whether they have been associated with the groups opposing the Government of Nicaragua by armed force. Such assistance may be provided only through the International Committee of the Red Cross or the United Nations High Commissioner for Refugees, and only upon its determination that such assistance is necessary to meet humanitarian needs of those refugees. To the maximum extent feasible, such assistance should be provided to those organizations in kind rather than in cash. Assistance may not be provided under this subsection with the intent of provisioning combat forces. . . .

(d) SOURCE OF FUNDS.—Funds used pursuant to this section shall be derived from the funds appropriated to carry out chapter 1 of part I (relating to development assistance) or chapter 4 of part II (relating to the economic support fund) of the Foreign Assistance Act of 1961 or section 2(b) (relating to the "Migration and Refugee Assistance" account) or section 2(c) (relating to the Emergency Refugee and Migration Assistance Fund) of the Migration and Refugee Assistance Act of 1962.

SEC. 4. REPORTS TO THE CONGRESS.

No less frequently than once every 3 months, the President shall submit to the Congress a written report—
(1) describing any actions by the Sandinista government, and the groups opposing that government by armed force, which have contributed to or hindered efforts to establish a political dialogue in Nicaragua, to find a peaceful solution to the conflict, and to nurture democratic institutions in Nicaragua;
(2) describing the status of the Contadora process and United States efforts to begin the political dialogue in Nicaragua and to find a peaceful solution to the conflict;
(3) containing an accounting of any funds used under section 3 for implementation of a Contadora agreement or for humanitarian assistance for refugees; and
(4) containing such recommendations as the President deems appropriate with respect to future United States policies regarding Nicaragua.

SEC. 5. PRESIDENTIAL REQUEST FOR AUTHORITY WITH RESPECT TO NICARAGUA.

(a) PRESIDENTIAL REQUEST.—On or after October 1, 1985, the President may submit to the Congress a request for authority to take specified actions with respect to Nicaragua.
(b) CONGRESSIONAL ACTION ON PRESIDENTIAL REQUEST.—A joint resolution which grants the President the authority to take those actions specified in the request submitted pursuant to subsection (a) shall be considered in accordance with the procedures contained in section 8066(c) of the Department of Defense Appropriations Act, 1985 (as contained in section 101 of Public Law 98-473), except that references in that section to the Committee on Appropriations of each House shall be deemed to be references to the appropriate committee or committees of each House. For purposes of this subsection, the term "joint resolution" means only a joint resolution introduced after the Congress receives the President's request pursuant to subsection (a), the matter after the resolving clause of which is as follows: "That the Congress hereby authorizes the President, notwithstanding any other provision of law, to take those actions with respect to Nicaragua which are specified in the request submitted to the Congress pursuant to Public Law 99- ," with the public law number of this joint resolution inserted in the blank. . . .

Mr. HAMILTON [D—N.Y.]. Mr. Chairman, I rise in support of this amendment. This amendment seeks to move toward a negotiated solution which will protect the national interests of the United States in Central America:

It deemphasizes a military approach. It encourages a ceasefire.

It prohibits military aid to the Contras, until Congress acts otherwise.

It encourages a regional approach to peace. It encourages the Contadora process and the use of the OAS.

It encourages diplomacy. It encourages bilateral talks between the United States and Nicaragua.

It offers incentives to Nicaragua if it conducts itself in a way which promotes peace and development.

It promises sanctions if it does not.

It makes available humanitarian aid for the refugees of the conflict through international groups.

It provides for a Presidential report, congressional monitoring, and an assured reconsideration of policy in light of changing circumstances.

All of us in the House share common goals. We want peace in Central America. We want national reconciliation in Nicaragua. We want the removal of Soviet and Cuban military advisers. We want Nicaragua to stop its excessive military buildup, and its destabilization of the region.

The question before us is how best to achieve these goals. Until recently, the President has favored military assistance to the Contras. Now the President has changed his views and favors U.S. assistance for economic and humanitarian aid to the Contras. That is a significant change and the President is to be commended for it. That change has altered the entire nature of the debate, and, in my judgment, for the better.

The question before us today, thus, is no longer about continuing military assistance, it is about what form this economic and humanitarian assistance will take:

What agencies will administer this aid;

What kinds of oversight and accountability provisions will exist to insure that this assistance is for truly humanitarian purposes; and

Whether funds shall be available for the Contadora process.

These are narrower questions than the previous issue before us concerning whether the United States would continue to fund a covert action against Nicaragua.

The $14 million under discussion today is a relatively small sum of money, but the shift in policy by the President away from military and toward economic and humanitarian assistance, can be a key signal of the future direction of U.S. policy.

This amendment would:

Provide $4 million for expenses arising from the implementation of a Contadora agreement, such as expenses for peacekeeping, verification, and monitoring systems;

Provide $10 million humanitarian assistance for refugees who are out-side of Nicaragua, regardless of whether they are associated with the contras. This assistance may be provided only through the International Committee of the Red Cross or the U.N. High Commissioner for Refugees upon the determination of such organizations that the assistance is neces-sary for humanitarian purposes and may not be provided for the provision-ing of combat units;

Require that the President must report to the Congress every 3 months on progress made in achieving the objectives of the resolution and on any expenditure of funds under the resolution and may, under expedited proce-dures, request further action by the Congress any time after October 1, 1985;

Continue in effect the prohibition of funding for military or paramilitary operations in Nicaragua;

Support a cease-fire in Nicaragua, peace negotiations and a regional settlement of the conflicts in Central America through the Contadora process or the Organization of American States;

Notes the disturbing trends in Nicaragua's domestic and foreign policies, set up a procedure for monitoring those trends and make curtailment of them a key element in future congressional decisions;

Call for consideration of economic and development programs for Nicaragua and technical and trade assistance should progress be made in bringing peace and democracy to that troubled nation; and

Call for consideration of political, diplomatic, and economic steps by the United States unilaterally and through the OAS should progress not be made by Nicaragua in addressing these concerns.

Mr. Chairman, this amendment, embodying a constructive new policy for peace in Central America, deserves strong support for several reasons:

First, this proposal is a bipartisan proposal. It is cosponsored by three Democrats and four Republicans. We contend today over the one major aspect of U.S. policy toward Central America on which there is no consen-sus. But that obscures the progress that has been made in recent months toward a consensus on Central American policy. Following the construc-tive contribution of the Kissinger Commission and of others, there is today a growing recognition of the importance of Central America to the United States, of the social and economic deprivation which has existed there, of the external threat, and of the need to provide both economic and security assistance to friends in the area.

Yet, on Nicaragua there are deep divisions.

This amendment is sponsored by Members with a variety of views and approaches to the problems of Central America in an effort to get beyond the deep divisions which have plagued Central American policy and get the United States behind regional peace efforts and negotiations aimed at national reconciliation in Nicaragua. It is an effort to help build on the emerging consensus on policy toward Central America.

Second, this amendment emphasizes the importance of a regional peace settlement.

U.S. efforts alone will not bring peace and stability to Central America. We must work with, and have the support of, our friends in the area. U.S. policy should be directed toward promoting regional peace and stability through the Contadora process. This amendment is based on the premise that the best way to achieve U.S. goals in Central America is through close coordination with the Contadora countries and the other friendly governments in the region.

The Contadora countries believe that they are now close to achieving a regional peace settlement, according to President Betancur of Colombia. As a sign of our additional commitment to the diplomatic process, this resolution provides $4 million for expenses arising from implementation of an agreement among the countries of Central America based on the Contadora principles.

There does not exist, at present, an established Contadora administrative unit capable of receiving funds to implement such an agreement, but the Contadora nations have over 100 diplomats working on a Central America agreement. Costs will be associated with peacekeeping, verification and monitoring provisions of any regional peace settlement.

We do not now know the precise costs associated with implementing agreements or how much of them the United States will be expected to pay. However, we believe we should be prepared to support and encourage Contadora diplomacy. The $4 million is seed money for peace. It is a tangible demonstration of our commitment to support regional diplomatic efforts toward a peace agreement.

Third, this proposal shifts the emphasis of U.S. policy away from military options to the pursuit of nonmilitary, diplomatic, political and economic strategies.

The amendment is based on the view that we have not fully pursued available diplomatic, economic and political options.

The amendment provides for tough-minded diplomacy. It encourages the United States to take its case and its evidence to the OAS, the United Nations, and the Contadora nations. It encourages a regional settlement with the involvement of the Contadora countries and other friendly governments in the region.

By deemphasizing military options and allowing time for negotiations, the amendment tests the stated desire of the Government of Nicaragua to pursue negotiations with the Contadora countries and the resumption of bilateral talks with the United States. Negotiations among the parties to the internal conflict in Nicaragua will not be easy, but that is the whole point of negotiations. If there were no disagreements, negotiations would not be necessary.

If negotiations do stall or if Nicaragua's disturbing policies continue, the United States has several policy options it can pursue which can make life difficult for the Sandinistas. These include:

Strengthening the defense capabilities of Nicaragua's neighbors;

Taking political and economic steps against Nicaragua in conjunction with our allies in Europe and Japan; and

Acting through regional security mechanisms and in cooperation with our friends in the region.

To date, the United States has been unable to pursue these alternatives effectively because our friends and allies are reluctant to support our efforts while we support the covert war against Nicaragua.

The amendment does not preclude, at a later date, the consideration and pursuit of military options against Nicaragua. Those military options should be a choice of last resort, not the means early employed, in U.S. policy.

It is my view that measured nonmilitary policies to protect and promote U.S. interests, in conjunction with the broad-based regional diplomatic process, offer the best hope to achieve regional peace and stability in Central America.

Fourth, this amendment is balanced. It seeks to put equal pressures on all parties to the conflict in Nicaragua.

This amendment:

Puts equal pressure on all sides of the internal Nicaraguan conflict to enter a negotiating process to achieve national reconciliation in Nicaragua and promote a pluralistic, democratic system in that nation;

It expresses our deep concern about the disturbing external influences in Nicaragua and the conduct of the Nicaraguan Government;

It criticizes both the Sandinistas and the groups opposing the Sandinistas on human rights; and

It provides incentives for Nicaragua if its conduct changes in ways the United States considers important for the peace and stability of the area, and sanctions if it does not.

Because this balanced approach puts pressure on all parties, it has a more realistic chance of promoting a negotiating process. No government wants to negotiate with a gun at its head or when its opponents have incentives for negotiations to fail.

We must be both fair—and tough—in our approach. That balance is in this amendment and that combination is more likely to win the respect and support of other states in the region and around the world. The military action denied us that respect and support.

We all have our objections to Nicaragua's policies and doubts about dealing with the Sandinista government. But if pressures and incentives are to work on that government, there must be time to begin a negotiating process and the absence of undue and unbalanced pressure on the parties. This resolution provides that time and balance.

It also tells the Nicaraguan Government, that if they do not grasp the opportunity offered, the United States will pursue policies that will make life even more difficult for them.

Fifth, this proposal provides for the humanitarian relief of refugees.

There are growing numbers of refugees outside of Nicaragua, and these people need help.

People who are in need of food, clothing, and shelter should be helped, and that aid should be provided on a nonpolitical basis. The $10 million in this proposal is not intended to help carry on a war. It does not provide food and medicine and clothing to the Contras so the assistance they receive from other sources can be used to carry on the war. It is intended to help those who have been victims of the war. This aid is to be provided regardless of whether refugees have been associated with the groups opposing the Government of Nicaragua by armed force.

To insure that this humanitarian assistance reaches those in need, the vehicles for its provision are the U.N. High Commissioner for Refugees and the International Committee of the Red Cross. Both of these organizations have long experience in refugee assistance and in this region. This assistance would be provided according to the standard procedures under which these organizations normally operate. These procedures include that aid cannot be provided to armed groups or individuals.

Sixth, this proposal provides for Executive reporting and congressional review of policy to determine what additional steps are necessary, as circumstances change.

Should the diplomatic process not move forward, the Congress will weigh that fact heavily. The Congress will consider carefully which parties have been helpful in advancing peace and which parties have been a hindrance.

Congressional ability to reopen this issue at a later date is an important signal, and incentive, to all parties to the conflict.

The Sandinistas would know that if they did not participate in such a dialogue, they will have strengthened the case for aid to the Contras.

The Contras would know that their own good faith efforts, as well as their willingness to address human rights violations, would be carefully monitored by Congress.

35.
REP. LEE HAMILTON AND REP. ROBERT MICHEL:
DEBATE ON CONTRA FUNDING (APRIL 1985)

Mr. HAMILTON [D—N.Y.]. Mr. Chairman, I rise in opposition to the resolution (H.J. Res. 239), a joint resolution to approve the obligation of funds available under Public Law 98-473 for supporting military or paramilitary operations in Nicaragua.

The issue before Congress is not whether we like the Sandinista government. Most of us have serious problems with that government and its policies. The question before us is: How can we best achieve our common goals of peace, internal reconciliation in Nicaragua, and democracy in the region?

I oppose House Joint Resolution 239 for several reasons:

1. THIS POLICY SHOULD BE REJECTED BECAUSE THERE ARE BETTER ALTERNATIVES TO ACHIEVE OUR OBJECTIVES WHICH SHOULD BE PURSUED FIRST BEFORE ANY RESORT TO THE APPLICATION OF MILITARY FORCE

The President's statement of the problem we confront in Nicaragua is to either fund the Contras or accept an expansive communism in Central America. He suggests that those of us who oppose the funds for the Contras really favor the spread of communism. May I respectfully suggest that the question that divides us is not whether to oppose communism in that area, but how best to do it.

Let me try to state the elements of a better alternative.

In brief, I believe we can move toward a negotiated solution which will protect the American national interest through the application of a vigorous, consistent, and tough diplomacy, conducted with the advice and support of our friends in the area, and backed up by a willingness to apply maximum economic pressure. If Nicaragua tries to destabilize the region, our strategy should include political, diplomatic, and economic sanctions, which should be used before military options, such as covert actions, are used.

First, the United States clearly does have legitimate security interests in Nicaragua. These interests include:

Prohibition of Soviet bases; reduction, if not the elimination, of Cuban and Soviet influence; removal of foreign troops; and cessation of efforts to promote revolution.

Second, if the threat is as great as the President says, let us deal with it openly and straightforwardly—not by a nonsecret secret war, or an overt-covert war.

Third, I favor a tough diplomacy. We should act to put international law on our side. We should take our evidence and our case to the OAS, to the Contadora nations, and to the UN.

Our diplomacy should make clear that we can live with a Sandinista government that stops threatening U.S. national interests and moves toward an open political system.

Our diplomacy and our policy should reflect our values and traditions. Mining harbors, rejecting the jurisdiction of the World Court, preparing manuals which suggest approval of assassination, and financing others to fight to protect our national security interests is not the preferred way for the United States to act.

Our diplomacy must recognize the centrality of a regional effort.

Regional security mechanisms, regional organizations, and other Latin American states can be mobilized to bring heavy pressure on the Managua government. Legal, overt containment of Nicaragua is possible with the support of the states in the region through the Contadora process and the OAS.

The Sandinista government took a more flexible stand in 1983, when it agreed to multilateral negotiations through the Contadora process. The pressure to do so was not from the Contras but from Mexico and Cuba. Castro urged the Sandinistas not to become isolated, and that the refusal to negotiate multilaterally was isolating them from the region. Hence, their change in position.

The U.S. commitment to resist communism in Central America must be consistent with the goals of other countries in the region. Those states support the Contadora process, and do not support military intervention in Nicaragua. If the United States does not support and give high priority to the Contadora process, the United States is jeopardizing the single process most likely to bring peace to the region and to form a bulwark against Communist infiltration.

Today the United States is the single largest trading partner with Nicaragua. We buy almost 20 percent of their total exports.

Fourth, I favor an aggressive use of U.S. economic power.

Our policy in the region will be strengthened as we give high priority not to fighting a war, but to strengthening the economic and political development of the nations of the area;

Our ability to resist communism in the region will hinge not on covert activity, but on our ability and the ability of governments in the region to address the basic problems of social and economic development and participation in the political process;

If regional pressures fail, the United States has several economic and diplomatic measures available to it to isolate Nicaragua, should this prove necessary. We should be prepared to cut trade and investment to Nicaragua and to employ economic sanctions, and to urge our allies to do the same.

These measures include:

Denying Nicaragua World Bank, IMF, and private bank loans. Nicaragua's substantial arrearages can help us get allied cooperation in this regard;

Stopping Nicaraguan airline from flying to the United States;

Denying visas to Nicaraguan citizens;

Imposing a partial or full economic embargo on trade with Nicaragua in conjunction with our allies;

Breaking diplomatic relations with Nicaragua; and

Strengthening the military and intelligence capabilities of the states in the region.

We all know that there are tough non-military steps we could take against Nicaragua that have not been taken.

Fifth, I do not reject the military option.

If diplomatic, political and economic pressures on the Sandinista government do not work, United States, as opposed to Contra, military action is likely to have a far greater impact on the Sandinista government.

I do not support such military action at this time, but I remember that the Sandinistas were and are deeply concerned, even panicky, about U.S. intervention. If a demonstration of strength is needed, military maneuvers and U.S. seapower are likely to have more of an impact than the covert war.

I recognize that the military option in defense of U.S. interests is sometimes required. I do not claim the United States should never use that option. I say at this point in time we should try harder to resolve the conflicts in the area through political, diplomatic, and economic means. If those means fail, and if the Government of Nicaragua threatens U.S. national interests in the area and it becomes necessary to exercise the military option, let us do so openly, and not ask someone else to fight our battles for us.

2. THE ADMINISTRATION'S PROPOSAL PUTS US ON THE PATH TOWARD MILITARY INTERVENTION

The President has elevated the struggle to change the Sandinista government through military force to one of the highest priorities of his administration. On February 21, President Reagan said that it was U.S. policy to seek to remove the Sandinista government unless it changed its goals and present structure and allowed the Contras into the government. He said, "You can say we're trying to oust the Sandinistas by what we're saying."

On April 15, he said, "To do nothing in Central America is to give the first Communist stronghold on the North American continent a green light to spread its poison through this free and increasingly democratic hemisphere."

The Secretary of State does not equivocate: Nicaragua is now behind the Iron Curtain.

But, General Paul Gorman, the retiring Commander of the U.S. Southern Command—and a supporter of aid to the Contras—stated in February 1985 that a Contra overthrow of the Sandinista government was not "feasible in the near future" even with U.S. financial assistance, and that such military pressure would take years to produce results. The CIA has consistently arrived at this same conclusion.

So, the President now wants to overthrow the Sandinistas; his top military commander says that the Contras cannot do it. The question, then, is how do you achieve the President's objective.

The President says Nicaragua is vital to U.S. interests and the Sandinistas are a threat to the United States. The U.S. military and the CIA say that what we are now doing will not succeed. The President insists on the removal of the Sandinista government. Clearly, the Sandinistas will not accept that they step aside. With that condition there really is no chance for diplomacy to work.

Thus, the conclusion follows that greater application of U.S. military force is the next option. A close examination of the President's own report confirms this.

The $14 million in the President's request is as a down payment on deeper U.S. military involvement. As reported in the press, the President anticipates the deployment of from 20,000 to 25,000 Contras in the north and 5,000 to 10,000 Contras in the south of Nicaragua—a total of 35,000 Contras. This new commitment is to enlarge the Contras to a force over twice its present size.

As reported in the press, the President's own report then states: "Direct application of U.S. military force . . . must realistically be recognized as an eventual option, given our stakes in the region, if other policy alternatives fail."

Make no mistake, the $14 million request is the next step on the slippery slope to further major U.S. intervention in Nicaragua.

3. THIS PROPOSAL REQUESTS MONEY FOR OBJECTIVES THAT ARE NOT CLEAR

Throughout the long involvement of the CIA in Nicaragua, we have seen tactics in search of an objective.

The United States simply has not been able to decide what it wants from the Sandinistas;

Since 1981, various purposes have been advanced for the covert action against Nicaragua;

First, the United States sought to interdict the flow of arms from Nicaragua to El Salvador;

Then, to force Nicaragua to turn inward;

Then, to bring Nicaragua to the negotiating table;

Then, to bring pluralism and free elections to Nicaragua;

Then, to oust the Sandinistas.

Today, U.S. policy statements on Nicaragua, especially those by the President, no longer emphasize the external conduct of Nicaragua but the removal of the Sandinistas. The President says we do not advocate the overthrow of the Sandinistas if they "would turn around and . . . say uncle." That phraseology is surely tantamount to requiring their removal.

But what does overthrow mean, and how do we propose to achieve this?

The administration wants to use the Contras to apply pressure on the Sandinistas, but that is a tactic—not an objective, not a policy.

Until recently, you could take your choice of administration policy.

Secretary Shultz wrote on February 6 that we do "not seek to destabilize or overthrow the Government of Nicaragua; nor to impose or compel any particular form of government there."

Fred Ikle, the Under Secretary of Defense, has said that our goal is military victory.

On April 15, the President said that "We will do everything we can to win this great struggle."

At the very least, these differing statements by the President and other administration officials suggest a lack of precision in defining U.S. policy goals, confusion about those objectives and a failure to articulate a clear policy objective.

4. THE PRESIDENT'S PROPOSAL CONTINUES TO ALLOW THE CIA TO MANAGE THE WAR IN NICARAGUA—AND THE CLEAR RECORD OF THE PAST SEVERAL YEARS IS THAT THE CIA CANNOT CONTROL THIS OPERATION WITH PRECISION

The most spectacular and objectionable CIA excesses of the recent past include:

The mining of Nicaragua's harbors;

Air and maritime attacks on Nicaraguan ports and other installations; and

The publication of the CIA manual, which clearly sought an objective that the administration rejected.

The CIA and the United States have become tarred with Contra atrocities and other Contra human rights violations. These acts of misconduct are probably no better and no worse than the conduct of the Sandinistas. The difference is that the U.S. is financing the Contras.

Since we depend on the Contras to carry out our policies, we must also answer for their actions. Their objective to overthrow the Government of Nicaragua has not, throughout most of this operation, been our objective. In recent weeks the President has adopted their objective. The Contras have dictated American policy, at least as much as the United States has dictated their policy.

The United States has always supported the Contadora process, but this weekend Commander Bermúdez said, "We don't have to respect any Contadora process."

The President now proposes that the CIA have less control over the Contras than in the past. The CIA's role would be to provide money, arms, and intelligence to the Contras, but not involve itself in day-to-day operations, planning, or oversight. The result of the President's proposal will be even greater identification of the United States with Contra activities, but less U.S. control over them.

5. THIS PROPOSAL MAKES IT MORE DIFFICULT TO OBTAIN REGIONAL SUPPORT FOR UNITED STATES POLICIES AND FOR INITIATIVES TO BRING PEACE TO THE REGION

It is inconsistent for the United States both to support the Contadora process and to seek military support for the Contras. Support for the Contras flagrantly violates one of the Contadora's principles that seeks to guarantee "that the territory of one state is not used to conduct acts of aggression against the territory of another state." U.S. policy should make unmistakably clear its support of the Contadora process. Our friends in the area do not support U.S. military intervention in the area, whether direct or through surrogates;

President Betancur of Colombia reinforced this on April 16 when he said that he and other Latin American leaders: "Firmly believe that any foreign support to guerrilla groups, whatever the origin, is clearly in opposition to the prevailing doctrine in Latin America regarding foreign intervention in the internal affairs of our continent."

He also said of the President's plan that tying negotiations to aid for the rebels made it "no longer a peace proposal, but a preparation for war."

U.S. financial assistance to the Contras is a violation of U.S. treaty obligations under article 18 of the OAS Charter, which provides as follows: "No state or group of States has the right to intervene, directly or indirectly, for any reason whatever, in the internal or external affairs of any other State."

We should note the impact of any decision at this moment to increase military involvement. The Contadora peace negotiations for Central America are close to reaching full agreement, according to President Betancur and others. The United States should, without equivocation, support those negotiations. When we support renewed funding of the Contras for covert war, we undercut the Contadora process;

Because of its efforts to promote the covert war, the United States has also not been consistent in its support for negotiations with Nicaragua. Direct negotiations with Nicaragua should precede any resort to the military option. As the last few years would indicate, the two cannot be dovetailed successfully.

6. THE PRESIDENT'S PROPOSAL CONTINUES A CIA POLICY WHICH HAS NOT WORKED

The Contras are simply not in a position to achieve the goals the United States seeks in Nicaragua. They cannot defeat the Sandinista forces.

The Contras have never been able to seize and hold territory in Nicaragua. They operate only in the mountains. They have never developed urban support. They haven't even been able to sustain operations in Nicaragua without supply from the outside. They depend heavily on their sanctuaries in Honduras and Costa Rica, without which they could not continue their fight.

They have never fared well in direct confrontation with Sandinista units of appreciable size.

Three years of U.S. support and $80 million in U.S. funding have not produced an insurgency capable of sustaining itself among the population of Nicaragua.

7. THE PRESIDENT'S PROPOSAL CONTINUES A COUNTERPRODUCTIVE POLICY. THERE ARE BETTER WAYS TO CONTAIN COMMUNISM IN CENTRAL AMERICA INSTEAD OF THE COVERT WAR

The covert activity has provided the Sandinistas with a convenient external threat which they have used to justify a host of repressive measures against opposition parties, the press, the church, and the people of Nicaragua. They have used this external threat to justify a military buildup, an unpopular draft, and large scale reliance on Cuban, Soviet, and other Eastern bloc military allies;

The Sandinista government will have no incentive to moderate its position or its behavior internally or externally as long as a covert action continues which seeks its overthrow. No government willingly submits to such military pressure from a foreign source. The covert action only encourages more extreme positions by the Sandinistas;

Attempts by the United States to renew funding for paramilitary operations against the Sandinista government are undermining the consensus that is developing in this country and in this Congress over our policy toward Central America;

The successful ability of the U.S. Government to deny its involvement in covert operations has always been a criterion for their success. We can no longer deny our involvement in the Contra war. The United States has suffered from the propaganda burden of this covert war in Latin America generally, and in Europe and throughout the Third World. A willingness to defend U.S. legitimate national security interests by military actions is not displayed by this war, just as it was not displayed by the Bay of Pigs invasion in 1961. Ineffective and counterproductive military action is interpreted throughout the world as a sign of weakness, not of strength.

8. THE PRESIDENT'S PROPOSAL CONTINUES A POLICY WHICH AMERICAN PEOPLE DO NOT SUPPORT

By a margin of 70 to 18 percent, Americans oppose the policy of U.S. involvement in attempts to overthrow the Sandinista government in Nicaragua. This poll is based on a February 1985 *Washington Post*–ABC News poll and shows a higher level of opposition to the Contra war than recorded in any of the three previous surveys conducted over the last 18 months;

This poll reflects the deep fears of the American people that current policies are leading to U.S. intervention;

There is a growing consensus in the United States in favor of increased levels of economic and security assistance for friendly and democratic states in Central America at the same time there is growing opposition to the Contra war. U.S. policy should not let the Contra war dominate the U.S. agenda in the region. Rather, it should build on the important emerging consensus.

9. CONCLUSIONS

Mr. Chairman, we, as a nation, are surely capable of arriving at a policy toward this small, desperately poor Central American country, and addressing the threat that it represents to us, and our friends, without military intervention.

In my view, we have not tried as hard as we could to use other than military means to achieve regional peace and security.

The fundamental question is whether the United States can rise to the challenge of leading the countries of Central America toward peace and development. We cannot do that by promoting war.

We cannot expect to impose democracy by force. There is a better way to deal with our problems in Nicaragua than by fighting this nasty little war. We cannot make peace by making war; we cannot preserve peace by destroying it.

I urge you to oppose further military aid to the Contras.

Mr. BROOMFIELD [R—Mich.]. Mr. Chairman, I yield 7 minutes to the distinguished gentleman from Florida [Mr. Mica].

[Mr. Mica asked and was given permission to revise and extend his remarks.]

Mr. MICA [D—Fla.]. Mr. Chairman, I take this opportunity with a great deal of personal concern over the direction of our Nation and what history will record our actions to be in these coming moments with regard to Nicaragua. Being from Florida and being raised in a situation where I saw firsthand a situation develop in Cuba that has come to be most difficult, one of the most if not the most difficult situations we deal with on a day-to-day basis in this hemisphere, having gone to high school with young men who went home to fight in Cuba, in that ill-fated Bay of Pigs mission, and have them come back and tell me the reports of what was going on in their country, and seeing the results, I cannot help but urge my colleagues to take a new look at this entire situation and, based on this thought: We Democrats should remember that it was a combined committee of Democrats and Republicans that approved covert aid in Nicaragua, and we approved it at a preliminary level and we approved it at a secondary level and we approved it at a tertiary level. Only until that level got to a point where there was concern did we recoil and say maybe we should reconsider. But why did we do it? Why? Because there was a major change, not just in this administration but in the previous administration, in what the Sandinistas were doing and what the tenets of their original revolution were.

Ortega had said publicly,

Costa Rica will be the jewel for our plucking, once we are in place.

Before this administration, as I recall, even came to power, the statement was made around the world that,

We, Nicaragua, will build the largest standing army ever to be seen in this Hemisphere outside of the United States.

These were concerns of Democrats and Republicans. These were concerns of Americans.

Now we do differ, and I do have concerns with some of the actions of the Contras and the politics that go back and forth, but I think we ought to understand that, had we not expressed some sensitivity, where would we be even today? Would there be any willingness on the part of Nicaragua to enter into minor agreements like they did today? Would there be any willingness on the part of Nicaragua to enter into minor agreements like they did today? Would there be any actions of reciprocity or willingness to deal with the Contadora group?

Recall that I sponsored the Mica amendment 3 years ago on this floor that lost by one vote that said, "Let's all stop, let's all stop at once," and our side, my side, did not agree with that approach at that time, that maybe we should not do anything.

There were 21 original tenets, and we agree with those—freedom of religion, freedom of the press, a pluralistic system for business, all of these tenets published around the world in documents in colleges and universities and in their own revolution that they would adhere to if they took over. And these were the concerns that Democrats and Republicans addressed when they said yes, we need to do something to swing that Sandinista revolution a little more back to its original cause. But not only did they not move back toward their original cause, not only have they not proceeded as quickly as we had hoped, they simply turned their backs and said that that was not the case at all.

Mr. MICHEL [R—Ill.]. . . . The issue is this: Do you want to help the forces of democratic pluralism in Nicaragua or do you want to consolidate the power of the Marxist-Leninist dictatorship?

Recently, the Sandinista leader Mr. Ortega insulted the Congress by holding out a carrot. He promised a ceasefire if we would just do his bidding and abandon the democratic forces in his country.

This is the kind of cynicism one expects from such a source. I can understand Ortega saying it; what I can't understand is anyone in the Congress believing it.

If you have a sense of déjà vu about all this, so do I. Today we are repeating a ritual that we have gone through many times.

It goes something like this:

The United States goes to the aid of a group or country that is fighting Communists. The cry is raised that our side isn't good enough to support. It is corrupt. It is immoral. It commits atrocities. A propaganda campaign is mounted against the allies of the United States.

Then the critics of the administration tell us the Communists are open to change if only we would be more generous in our treatment of them.

When the true facts of Communist tyranny become inescapably clear, the administration's critics tell us they oppose what the Communists are doing. But they don't like the means the administration has chosen to stop it. They offer no realistic alternative themselves.

Does this sound familiar? It should. We have been through this scenario over and over again in the past 30 years. And in every case the Communists proved to be worse than forces we had originally supported but then abandoned. Millions of innocent men, women, and children have paid the price of our refusal to acknowledge that communism is the worst form of tyranny.

In the present case, we even have some critics of the President who do not want to call the Sandinistas Communists.

But the Sandinistas are self-proclaimed Marxist-Leninists. And if someone can point out the substantive differences between Marxist-Leninists and Communists I'd sure like to hear it.

Gertrude Stein said, "A rose is a rose is a rose." I say a Sandinista is a Marxist-Leninist is a Communist. So I'm going to call them what they are.

They believe in their ideology the way religious people believe in God. They will ultimately sell their nation to the Soviet Union the same way Castro sold Cuba if we give them the chance.

We will hear a lot today about the real and alleged sins of the democratic forces of Nicaragua.

I'll let other Members correct these distortions.

As for myself, I don't care if the democratic forces of Nicaragua are good enough to go to Heaven. I'm interested in seeing that they are strong enough to save their country from a Communist hell.

We are told we should not be supporting a group that wants to overthrow the Government of Managua.

Overthrow the Communists in Nicaragua? Fat chance, the way we're providing aid.

Fourteen million dollars worth of aid isn't going to help them overthrow an armed force of 62,000 active duty personnel, a total force of 119,000, including reserves and militia.

This Sandinista force has Soviet MI-24 Hind attack helicopters. It has 150 tanks, 200 other armored vehicles and some 300 to 400 surface-to-air missiles. The Sandinistas have nearly completed a runway long enough to service any aircraft in the Soviet or Cuban inventory.

But, we are told that if we give $14 million worth of aid—in any form —to the democratic forces, they will suddenly run into Managua and take over.

What nonsense! I for one wish this country could make a decision to give the democratic forces what they really need to make a difference in Nicaragua. But the political facts dictate we argue about $14 million to help those engaged in a struggle with the largest standing army in Central America.

We are not faced with a choice between force and dialogue. We are faced with a choice between a mixture of force and dialogue on one hand and inevitable Marxist-Leninist consolidation of power on the other.

Saying you are against the Sandinistas but don't want to help the democratic forces is not enough. That's like saying you are against a disease but unwilling to treat it. It's like saying you are against arson but don't want to fund the fire department. It's like saying you are against crime in the streets but want to provide the police with food stamps and not weapons.

The bishops of Nicaragua, in their Easter pastoral letter, condemned the Sandinistas and asked them to enter into negotiations with the democratic forces.

Those religious groups closest to the scene recognize the true character of the Sandinistas. Listen to Jews whose synagogue was closed and were forced to leave the country. They'll tell you about freedom of religion in this new Communist state. Listen to the Miskito Indians whose clergy were killed by the Sandinistas.

One newspaper columnist recently wrote that the Sandinistas can't be all bad because they like baseball and they even jog.

This is the same kind of argument that we heard when Andropov became head of the Soviet Union. He drank scotch and liked jazz.

Sometimes you wonder how these scotch-drinking jazz-loving baseball-playing, jogging, lovable Communists ever find the time to read Karl Marx and to do away with dissenters.

Let me read to you one of their goals as outlined in the definitive statement of principles of the Sandinistas, in 1969. They have never repudiated this goal.

> Struggle for a true union of the Central American peoples within one country beginning with support for national liberation movement in neighboring states.

Stripped of the Communist jargon that means the ongoing revolution. They said it themselves.

We should at least pay them the tribute of acknowledging they believe deeply in their own principles.

If the United States doesn't believe we have the moral and political right to aid the democratic force fighting communism, then God help the future of freedom in this hemisphere.

The Communists have no legitimacy. Their legitimacy comes through the barrel of a gun. Why do critics of the President insist that they are legitimate rulers? The people didn't give them power. They took power from the people.

Let me read to you the report of the Bipartisan Commission on Central America, still the most definitive and objective study of the current tragedy in Central America. This is what the Commission had to say about Nicaragua:

> The consolidation of a Marxist-Leninist regime in Managua would be seen by its neighbors as constituting a permanent security threat. Because of its secretive nature, the existence of a political order on the Cuban model in Nicaragua would pose major difficulties in negotiating, implementing, and verifying any Sandinista commitment to refrain from supporting insurgency and subversion in other countries.

Let me now tell you what I believe the real issues are:

I believe, with the bipartisan commission, that the current Communist government in Nicaragua is a threat to peace and stability in the region. I believe the Communists are ideologically committed to human rights violations as matter of Marxist-Leninist principles. I believe they will aid the Soviet Union in establishing an enclave in this hemisphere.

Because of that threat I believe the United States, along with its democratic allies in the region, has the moral, diplomatic, and geopolitical right and duty to aid Nicaraguans who wish to have a pluralistic, democratic society in Nicaragua.

I believe that to abandon the signers of the San José Declaration would constitute a grave historic and irrevocable error that we will pay for dearly in the years ahead.

I believe it is not enough for Members of this House to state they don't like what the Communists are doing, but are unwilling to take action against them. This is de facto handing over of Nicaragua to allies of the Soviet Union.

Spare us the stale, ritualistic, generalized criticisms of the Communists. We'll believe you are sincere about them when you do something about them.

I am reminded of an old saying:

Things are what they are. The consequences of them will be what they will be. Why then do we seek to delude ourselves?

I hope the debate that follows discusses some of the points I have raised, for I sincerely believe that if all the facts are taken into consideration, a bipartisan majority in this House will do the right thing and continue to help those democratic forces of Nicaragua.

36.
PRESIDENT RONALD REAGAN: LETTER TO REP.
DAVE MCCURDY (JUNE 1985)

THE WHITE HOUSE,
Washington, DC.

Hon. DAVE MCCURDY,
House of Representatives, Washington, DC.

DEAR CONGRESSMAN MCCURDY:

I am writing to express my strongest support for your bipartisan proposal to assist the forces of democracy in Nicaragua. It is essential to a peaceful resolution of the conflict in Central America that the House of Representatives pass that proposal, without any weakening amendments.

My administration is determined to pursue political, not military, solutions in Central America. Our policy for Nicaragua is the same as for El Salvador and all of Central America: to support the democratic center against the extremes of both the right and left, and to secure democracy and lasting peace through national dialog and regional negotiations. We do not seek the military overthrow of the Sandinista government or to put in its place a government based on supporters of the old Somoza regime.

Just as we support President Duarte in his efforts to achieve reconciliation in El Salvador, we also endorse the unified democratic opposition's March 1, 1985 San José Declaration which calls for national reconciliation through a church-mediated dialog. We oppose a sharing of political power based on military force rather than the will of the people expressed through free and fair elections. That is the position of President Duarte. It is also the position of the Nicaraguan opposition leaders, who have agreed that executive authority in Nicaragua should change only through elections.

It is the guerrillas in El Salvador—and their mentors in Managua, Havana, and Moscow—who demand power sharing without elections. And it is the Sandinistas in Nicaragua who stridently reject national reconciliation through democratic processes. Our assistance has been crucial to ensuring that democracy has both the strength and will to work in El Salvador. In Nicaragua, our support is also needed to enable the forces of democracy to convince the Sandinistas that real democratic change is necessary. Without the pressure of a viable and democratic resistance, the Sandinistas will continue to impose their will through repression and military force, and a regional settlement based on the Contadora principles will continue to elude us.

I understand that two "perfecting" amendments will be offered that will seek to nullify the intent of your proposal. One, supported by Ed Boland, would prohibit the exchange of information with the democratic resistance and permanently deny even humanitarian assistance because it would "have the effect" of supporting "directly or indirectly" the military efforts of the resistance. The other, supported by Dick Gephardt, would prohibit humanitarian assistance for at least 6 months and then continue the prohibition until Congress votes yet again.

The Boland amendment is clearly intended to have the same effect as the Barnes amendment that was rejected by the House in April. If the Boland prohibitions are enacted, the only way humanitarian assistance could be provided would be for the recipients to abandon their struggle and become refugees. The Gephardt proposal, guaranteeing the Sandinistas six additional months without effective pressure, would send a signal of irresolution to friends and adversaries, while denying the democratic resistance help that it so desperately needs. These amendments would prevent us from providing humanitarian assistance and exchanging information to sustain and preserve the democratic resistance. They would effectively remove the resistance as a source of pressure for dialog and internal reconciliation. If those struggling for democracy are not supported, or worse, forced to become refugees, the Sandinistas will be encouraged to press their military advantage and the prospects for a peaceful resolution will be diminished.

I take very seriously your concern about human rights. The U.S. condemns, in the strongest possible terms, atrocities by either side. We are committed to helping the democratic resistance in applying strict rules regarding proper treatment of prisoners and the civilian population. And we urge their leaders to investigate allegations of past human rights abuses and take appropriate actions to prevent future abuses.

I recognize the importance that you and others attach to bilateral talks between the United States and Nicaragua. It is possible that in the proper circumstances, such discussions could help promote the internal reconciliation called for by Contadora and endorsed by many Latin American leaders. Therefore, I intend to instruct our special Ambassador to consult with the governments of Central America, the Contadora countries, other democratic governments, and the unified Nicaraguan opposition as to how and when the United States could resume useful direct talks with Nicaragua. However, such talks cannot be a substitute for a church-mediated dialog between the contending factions and the achievement of a workable Contadora agreement. Therefore, I will have our representative meet again with representatives of Nicaragua only when I determine that such a meeting would be helpful in promoting these ends.

Experience has shown that a policy of support for democracy, economic opportunity, and security will best serve the people of Central America and the national interests of the United States. If we show consistency of purpose, if we are firm in our conviction, we can help the democratic center prevail over tyrants of the left or the right. But if we abandon democracy in Nicaragua, if we tolerate the consolidation of a surrogate state in Central America responsive to Cuba and the Soviet Union, we will see the progress that has been achieved in neighboring countries begin to unravel under the strain of continuing conflict, attempts at subversion, and loss of confidence in our support.

There can be a more democratic, more prosperous, and more peaceful Central America. I will continue to devote my energies toward that end, but I also need the support of the Congress. I hope the House will support your legislation.

Sincerely,

RONALD REAGAN.

37.
REP. DAVE MCCURDY: SPEECH ON CONTRA AID
(JUNE 1985)

Mr. MCCURDY. Mr. Speaker, after the defeat of the bipartisan package to provide humanitarian assistance to the democratic resistance in Nicaragua on April 24, many Democratic and Republican Members gathered together that evening on this floor to develop a package that we could support. We developed a package that we believe stated policy for the first time that made sense in Nicaragua.

The Michel-McCurdy-McDade amendment moves clearly to the center to help support the democratic elements within the resistance forces in Nicaragua. We modeled this amendment after the successful bipartisan policy toward El Salvador.

In El Salvador, we heard the same arguments that we have heard today; that is, you could not break with the extreme right or left, and that the

Congressional Record, June 12, 1985, p. H4137.

course of the policy inevitably led to a military invasion by the United States.

My colleagues, those critics were wrong. They were wrong then and they are wrong today.

The issue is not whether we are for negotiated settlement or military intervention. This amendment provides for a cease-fire, for negotiations, for the suspension of maneuvers, and the lifting of the boycott.

The issue is not whether we support Contadora. We provide $2 million for the Contadora nations and support the regional settlement.

The issue is not whether the CIA will be involved in distributing humanitarian assistance inside Nicaragua. Our amendment specifically prohibits the CIA and the DOD from doing so.

The issue is not over the protection of human rights inside Nicaragua by both the left and the right. Our amendment requires changes, requires progress, and U.S. monitoring on the improvement of human rights conditions inside that country.

My colleagues, the only real issue today is whether we provide real incentives for both sides and particularly the Sandinistas to negotiate with their people. . . .

CHAPTER
SEVEN

Latin America, Europe, the USSR, and Cuba

One of the symptoms and causes of the current Central America crisis is the change in the region's place in the international order. For much of its modern history, the area was generally an unchallenged U.S. sphere of influence. Today, relatively strong local countries like Mexico, Venezuela, and Cuba, as well as the Soviet bloc and Western Europe, have an important role in shaping Central America's fate.

I. Latin America

The 1979 Nicaraguan revolution illustrates this interaction between internal and international forces. Assistance from foreign supporters was of vital importance for the Sandinista victory. Cuba trained the guerrillas; Costa Rica allowed them training and base facilities; Panama's strongman, President Omar Torrijos, allowed Cuban military supplies to pass through his territory. The Sandinistas' prospects were further enhanced in May 1979 when Mexico broke relations with Somoza. A month later, the Andean Pact nations recognized the rebels as belligerents (Document 1), and delegates to the meeting of the Organization of American States that same month called for Somoza's resignation (Document 2).

In El Salvador the Mexican government as well as Latin American and

European social democrats at first supported the Marxist-led insurgents. By 1981, however, social democrats in Costa Rica, Venezuela, and the Dominican Republic, as well as Torrijos's Panamanian regime, took a more neutral stance—as did the Socialist International—in advocating a compromise political solution (Document 3). This change was in large part due to the growing control of El Salvador's Christian Democratic President, José Napoleón Duarte, particularly affecting his fellow Christian Democratic rulers in Venezuela.

One approach was that taken by France and Mexico, which recognized the FDR-FMLN as a "representative political force" in August 1981, called for negotiations, and advocated restructuring the army prior to the 1982 elections (Document 4). The Franco-Mexican stance, deemed as a pro-FMLN tilt, was answered with the Caracas Declaration, signed by foreign ministers from Argentina, Bolivia, Chile, Colombia, the Dominican Republic, Guatemala, Honduras, and Venezuela. The statement denounced the Franco-Mexican statement as intervention in Salvadoran internal affairs (Document 5). Uruguay, Brazil, Ecuador, Costa Rica, and Peru later added their signatures.

While Nicaragua's 1979 revolution was celebrated worldwide, developments following the Sandinista takeover began to arouse more concern. Within a week of Somoza's ouster, one hundred Cuban security and personnel advisers entered Managua, and the number steadily increased thereafter. This disturbed Sandinista backers like Torrijos. He gave Managua "friendly warnings" over the course it was pursuing (Document 6) and pulled out Panamanian military advisers in protest.

Speaking in Managua in February 1982, after the United States had begun training and equipping anti-Sandinista forces on the Honduran border, Mexican President López Portillo proposed a plan for détente between Nicaragua and Honduras, a dialogue in El Salvador between government and guerrillas, and a U.S.-Cuba rapprochement (Document 7).

In September 1982, Venezuela and Mexico urged President Reagan to stop arming anti-Sandinista rebels and restart a dialogue with Managua (Document 8). But when the U.S. met with several regional states, including Colombia, El Salvador, Honduras, and Costa Rica, in October 1982 the meeting only called for "truly democratic government institutions, based on the will of the people as expressed in free and fair elections," as the cornerstone to a regional peace (Document 9). Nicaragua, Mexico, and Venezuela were conspicuously absent from the gathering.

Clearly, for these often contradictory Latin American efforts to make any progress, the activist states had to coordinate their moves. Colombia, Mexico, Venezuela, Costa Rica, and Panama had first met at Panama's Contadora island in 1976 to support the U.S.-Panama treaty on the Pan-

ama Canal. These countries met again in 1979 and 1981 urging the Sandinistas to commit themselves to political pluralism, nonalignment, and a
mixed economy. In January 1983, the foreign ministers of Colombia, Mexico, Panama, and Venezuela met at Contadora to agree on a common front.
"Contadora" soon came to stand for that group's diplomatic initiative.

There were three fundamental issues behind the beginning of the Contadora group. An overriding worry was that the crisis would escalate to
involve direct U.S. intervention. A second problem was the potential for
increasing Soviet-Cuban involvement. Finally, the participants wanted to
promote democracy. On all these points, the fear was that a spreading crisis
and instability might destroy the security of all states in the region.

The basis of the Contadora process was its Document of Objectives
(Document 10) which called for regional détente, political pluralism, "national reconciliation" to end internal conflicts, reduction of arms and troop
levels, dismantling of foreign military bases, withdrawal of foreign military
advisers, and elimination of cross-border subversion. Formulating these
goals proved easier than agreeing on how to implement them or even to
produce a final treaty, but a revised provisional draft, the Contadora Act
for Peace and Cooperation in Central America (the Acta), was finally
presented on September 7, 1984 (Document 11). Two weeks later, Nicaragua unexpectedly announced it would sign this version but only on the
condition that it not be amended.

The United States, along with Costa Rica, El Salvador, and Honduras,
however, had objections to the Acta, and on October 19, 1984, these three
Central American nations offered a "counterdraft," the Tegucigalpa draft
agreement (Document 12). From that time on, Contadora met numerous
times to try to reconcile these two drafts, as in a proposed 1985 compromise draft (Document 13).

As a comparison between the original Acta and the Tegucigalpa drafts
suggests, the dispute between Nicaragua on the one hand and El Salvador,
Costa Rica, and Honduras on the other hinges on the timing, verification,
and enforcement of the security and political provisions.

The September Acta, for example, would end foreign military exercises
thirty days and foreign bases in the region six months after being signed.
Thus, U.S. facilities and exercises in Honduras would quickly cease.
Nicaragua, of course, felt threatened by the North American activities and
wanted them to end before it agreed to limiting the size of its troops and
quantity of its arms, and sending home its Soviet-bloc and Cuban advisers.
But from the point of view of the U.S. administration and its regional allies,
the training and military facilities provided were intended to balance the
stronger Nicaraguan forces. Each side wanted to time the implementation
of treaty commitments to ensure that the other side carried out its promises. Consequently, the Tegucigalpa version would negotiate the schedule

for closing down foreign bases, suspending military exercises, withdrawing foreign advisers, and limiting troop and equipment levels at the same time.

As for verification, the Acta designated an oversight committee from the Contadora group, that is from non-Central American states. The Tegucigalpa revision would include Central American representatives. To the Nicaraguans, this latter version would allow their enemies to "unite" against them; to Costa Rica, Honduras, and El Salvador, direct participation would help them guarantee the carrying out of the accord. In a similar vein, the September Acta said that matters of dispute over the treaty's application would be settled by a consensus of the Central American and Contadora foreign ministers; the counterdraft provided for a unanimous vote. While the Tegucigalpa group felt that unanimity would be so difficult to achieve that it would paralyze the implementation process, the Sandinistas felt they would always be outvoted with their three neighbors voting as a bloc.

In addition to the disputes over the proper treaty provisions, there were also differences in perceptions among the Contadora members. Venezuela was highly critical of Nicaragua, concerned that Managua was becoming militarized and Sovietized. In contrast, Mexico—which resented U.S. domination over the region—was the Sandinistas' largest noncommunist benefactor, arguing that this support would limit Nicaragua's dependence on the Soviets and Cuba.

Divisions among the five Central American states were sharper than those between Venezuela and Mexico. Costa Rica, El Salvador, and Honduras were wary of the Sandinistas' growing military power and espousal of "revolutionary internationalism." Thus, these three governments wanted more guarantees from the Contadora process and were critical of Mexico's policy. In addition, all three gave material aid or bases to the Contras just as Nicaragua performed similar services for Salvadoran, Honduran, and Costa Rican guerrillas.

II. Western Europe

Western European leaders consistently gave wholehearted support to Contadora, as in the June 1983 meeting of European leaders (Document 14). Socialists like French President François Mitterrand, Spanish Prime Minister Felipe González, and former West German Chancellor Willi Brandt (president of the Socialist International) criticized U.S. policy in Central America as exacerbating international tensions and regional problems. Like Mexico, they saw their role as countering both U.S. escalation and Soviet influence.

Not all the participants in the Socialist International agreed with this perspective. A radical caucus including the Cuban Communist Party,

Sandinistas, and Grenada's New Jewel Movement tried to mobilize support for their cause; the Italian and Portuguese socialists were quite suspicious of the Salvadoran guerrillas and the Sandinistas (Document 15). Over time, a number of European leaders, including González, moved closer to the latter perspective.

Many European Christian Democrats were more sympathetic to the U.S. analysis of the situation. Alois Mertes, a West German Christian Democrat, represents such a stance (Document 16) but is also worried lest a hard-line U.S. position antagonize European groups and endanger regional stability. The desire to avoid an international East-West crisis centered in Central America is a common theme among Europeans of both left and right. The accord between the European Common Market and Central American states in September 1984 demonstrates this consensus and European willingness to provide aid for all the states in the area (Document 17).

III. The USSR and Cuba

Both Moscow and Havana had close relations with—although they did not control—the Nicaraguan government and the Salvadoran guerrillas. The Soviets were constrained by their own overextended economic situation and by the realities of geography. Central American revolutionaries looked to Havana and Moscow for ideological inspiration and assistance.

The Soviet-Cuban connection with the Sandinistas was of long standing. FSLN founder Carlos Fonseca Amador visited the USSR in the mid-1950s and propagated an idealized view of the Soviet system (see Chapter 2). In 1959, Cuba encouraged the Sandinistas to wage a guerrilla struggle in Nicaragua, and FSLN leaders like Tomás Borge, Humberto and Daniel Ortega, and Moscow-educated Henry Ruiz received asylum and military training in Cuba.

Only in the late 1970s, however, did the Soviets and the Cubans perceive the situation as more favorable for activism. With Somoza's position weakening in 1977, Cuban Premier Fidel Castro told the three Sandinista factions they must unite in order to receive more aid. During the peak of the fighting, Cuba sent the Sandinistas arms and made contacts on their behalf with international arms dealers (Document 18). The operation was monitored and supervised for Havana by Julian López Díaz, who became Cuba's first ambassador to Nicaragua after the Sandinista victory.

The Nicaraguan government and Sandinista organizations like the press, the bureaucracy, and the neighborhood defense committees were set up along lines paralleling those in Cuba and the Soviet bloc. Bulgarian, Czech, Soviet, Cuban, and East German advisers in Nicaragua divided intelligence, counterintelligence, police training, and ideological indoctrination tasks among themselves. By 1981, the Sandinista army, equipped with Soviet-bloc arms and equipment, outnumbered the combined forces of its neighbors.

At the same time, Soviet ideology was revised to conclude that revolution in Central America could be attained through armed struggle led by politico-military fronts like the Sandinistas rather than by the more traditional communist parties (Document 19). The Kremlin's acceptance of the Sandinistas as a Soviet-style vanguard party was indicated by a mutual support agreement between the Soviet Communist Party and the FSLN in March 1980 (Document 20). Castro gave strong endorsement to the Sandinistas in his Managua speech marking the first anniversary of their victory (Document 21).

In El Salvador, Communist Party General Secretary Shafik Handal reflected these new ideas, calling for armed revolution. In an article carried by the official Soviet party journal *Kommunist* in November 1980, Handal wrote that the revolution "will be victorious by the armed road . . . there is no other way" (Document 22). As a leader in the FMLN guerrilla movement, Handal visited Moscow twice and Vietnam once to secure arms. Soviet media coverage of the FMLN's "final offensive" was optimistic, and *Pravda* reported that the "future of suffering El Salvador belongs" to the guerrillas (Document 23).

After this offensive failed, however, Soviet-bloc arms shipments dropped sharply and the FMLN adopted more cautious tactics. A secret Soviet Communist Party letter to Central American revolutionaries urged them to support Soviet foreign policy and implied more limited aid for their own local struggles (Document 24). Though the Sandinista leadership expressed a deep ideological commitment to the Soviet bloc in both private (see document 25) and public declarations, Daniel Ortega's trip to Moscow seeking hard currency to meet the country's deficits was unsuccessful. Nicaraguans were trained to fly and service MIG fighter planes but never received any of them.

Soviet General Secretary Leonid Brezhnev's response to Ortega's request reminded Ortega of the geographical distance between the USSR and Nicaragua (Document 26). In a 1983 interview with *Der Spiegel*, Brezhnev's successor, Yuri Andropov, saw Nicaragua as being in the U.S. sphere of influence (Document 27). Following the U.S. military intervention in Grenada in October 1983, Castro asserted he would not send troops to Nicaragua if it was invaded (Document 28).

Yet Moscow's support increased steadily, if slowly, over the years. By late 1985, the Soviets supplied close to 90 percent of Nicaragua's oil and the Soviet bloc provided over half of the country's foreign assistance. Nicaragua was an observer in the Soviet-led CMEA economic group. Soviet and East European personnel occupied high-level positions in Nicaraguan security, military, and intelligence bureaus. Cuban military advisers helped train the Sandinista army, militia, and defense committees. Soviet-bloc shipments of military materiel to Nicaragua were at about the same level, per capita, as those provided to Cuba. Counterinsurgency equipment included Hind-24 helicopter gunships used in Afghanistan. During Ortega's April 1985 trip to Moscow, economic links were tightened further (Document 29).

I
LATIN AMERICA

1.
ANDEAN PACT: CRITICISM OF SOMOZA (JUNE 1979)

Considering that the chiefs of state of the Andean group countries decided during their recent meeting in Cartagena to declare themselves in a state of permanent consultation in order to promote, in solidarity, all actions necessary to help put an end to the bloodshed in Nicaragua, reestablish peace and guarantee respect for human rights in that sister nation;

That in keeping with that decision the governments of the Andean countries entrusted the foreign ministers of Ecuador and Venezuela with an international mission which led to their meeting with Gen Anastasio Somoza in Nicaragua;

That during their visit to Nicaragua and their meeting with General Somoza, the two foreign ministers confirmed that the situation there is one of serious and profound deterioration of that country's social and political structure;

And that, unfortunately, General Somoza's personal statements do not leave room for any immediate or reasonable hope that that country's current government will make the necessary decisions so that peace and fraternity can once more reign in the Nicaraguan fatherland;

In the names of their respective governments and acting in accordance with the Cartagena presidential declaration, in an effort to safeguard the peaceful and fraternal coexistence which should prevail among the Latin American states, the foreign ministers of Bolivia, Colombia, Ecuador, Peru and Venezuela declare:

Their fervent hope that peace will be restored in Nicaragua as soon as pos-

Declaration of June 16, 1979. Translation from Foreign Broadcast Information Service, June 17, 1979.

sible on the basis of respect for the fundamental rights of every human being;

Their willingness to make all necessary efforts in accordance with international law and the basic principles which rule the inter-American system so that that sister nation can achieve that precious objective.

Nonetheless, the armed struggle currently being waged between the present government and vast sectors of the Nicaraguan population has already assumed such characteristics of permanence, scope and open warfare that it represents a true state of belligerency.

Objectively considered, this war situation forces one to regard the popular forces currently fighting the Nicaraguan Government as belligerents. We have officially communicated this so that these forces may enjoy the treatment and prerogatives to which they are entitled, in keeping with international law, and so that the obligations that this international law imposes on legitimate combatants may be fulfilled.

2.
OAS: RESOLUTION CONDEMNING SOMOZA (JUNE 1979)

WHEREAS:

The people of Nicaragua are suffering the horrors of a fierce armed conflict that is causing grave hardships and loss of life, and has thrown the country into a serious political, social, and economic upheaval;

The inhumane conduct of the dictatorial regime governing the country, as evidenced by the report of the Inter-American Commission on Human Rights, is the fundamental cause of the dramatic situation faced by the Nicaraguan people and;

The spirit of solidarity that guides Hemisphere relations places an unavoidable obligation on the American countries to exert every effort within their power to put an end to the bloodshed and to avoid the prolongation of this conflict which is disrupting the peace of the Hemisphere;

THE SEVENTEENTH MEETING OF CONSULTATION OF MINISTERS OF FOREIGN AFFAIRS

DECLARES:

That the solution of the serious problem is exclusively within the jurisdiction of the people of Nicaragua.

Resolution of the Seventeenth Meeting of Foreign Affairs Ministers, June 23, 1979.

That in the view of the Seventeenth Meeting of Consultation of Ministers of Foreign Affairs this solution should be arrived at on the basis of the following:

1. Immediate and definitive replacement of the Somoza regime.
2. Installation in Nicaraguan territory of a democratic government, the composition of which should include the principal representative groups which oppose the Somoza regime and which reflects the free will of the people of Nicaragua.
3. Guarantee of the respect for human rights of all Nicaraguan without exception.
4. The holding of free elections as soon as possible, which will lead to the establishment of a truly democratic government that guarantees peace, freedom, and justice.

RESOLVES:

1. To urge the member states to take steps that are within their reach to facilitate an enduring and peaceful solution of the Nicaraguan problem on the bases set forth above, scrupulously respecting the principle of non-intervention and abstaining from any action that might be in conflict with the above bases or be incompatible with a peaceful and enduring solution to the problem.
2. To commit their efforts to promote humanitarian assistance to the people of Nicaragua and to contribute to the social and economic recovery of the country.
3. To keep the Seventeenth Meeting of Consultation of Ministers of Foreign Affairs open while the present situation continues.

3.
SOCIALIST INTERNATIONAL: COMMUNIQUÉ ON EL SALVADOR (MARCH 1981)

THE SOCIALIST INTERNATIONAL COMMITTEE FOR LATIN AMERICA AND THE CARIBBEAN:

1. Expresses its deep concern with recent events aimed at converting the Salvadorean people's struggle for liberation into an East-West confrontation which ignores the fact that the nature and causes of the conflict lie in

Socialist International Committee for Latin America and the Caribbean, Panama, March 1, 1981.

unjust economic and social structures and in the long-standing denial of democratic life to that people.

2. Considers that the Salvadorean people are alone entitled to decide on their own destiny and that today more than ever we should insist upon and uphold this inalienable right of Salvadoreans to self-determination free from any foreign interference.

3. Reaffirms the aims expressed in the September 1980 Declaration of Caracas, which means working actively to achieve a political settlement of the crisis which the Salvadorean people are currently undergoing and to bring about a democratic and pluralistic regime.

4. Calls upon the contending parties to work actively for a peaceful solution which can bring the enjoyment of a genuinely democratic regime as well as peace, justice and freedom to the Salvadorean people and stability to the Central American and Caribbean area. . . .

7. Lastly, we reiterate our solidarity with the Frente Democrático Revolucionario (FDR) of El Salvador, which we regard as the legitimate representative of the Salvadorean people and a valid interlocutor for the peaceful settlement we are advocating.

4.
FRANCO-MEXICAN DECLARATION (AUGUST 1981)

The Minister for Foreign Affairs of France, Mr. Claude CHEYSSON, and the Minister for Foreign Affairs of Mexico, Mr. Jorge CASTANEDA, have held exchanges of views on the situation in Central America.

The two Ministers wish to express the deep concern of their Governments over the sufferings of the Salvadoran people in the present situation, which is a source of potential danger for the stability and peace of the region as a whole, in view of the risks that the crisis may become international.

They are therefore making the following declaration:

[The Ministers]

Convinced that it is for the Salvadoran people alone to find a just and durable settlement of the profound crisis through which the country is passing, thus bringing to an end the plight of the population,

Aware of their responsibility as members of the international community and guided by the purposes and principles of the United Nations Charter,

Taking into account the extreme gravity of the current situation and the need for fundamental social, economic and political changes,

Recognize that the alliance of the Farabundo Martí Front for National Liberation and the Revolutionary Democratic Front constitutes a representative political force, prepared to assume obligations and to exercise the rights that derive therefrom. Consequently, it is legitimate that the alliance should participate in instituting the mechanisms of rapprochement and negotiation required for a political settlement of the crisis,

Recall that it is for the Salvadoran people to initiate a global political settlement process in which a new internal order will be established, the armed forces will be reorganized, and conditions will be created for ensuring compliance with the popular will, as expressed through genuinely free elections and other mechanisms of a democratic system,

Appeal to the international community to work, particularly in the framework of the United Nations, to ensure the protection of the civilian population according to the applicable international norms and to facilitate the rapprochement of the representatives of the conflicting Salvadoran political forces, in order that there may be reconciliation in El Salvador and any intervention in its internal affairs may be averted.

5.
CARACAS DECLARATION (SEPTEMBER 1981)

The undersigned foreign ministers, representing their respective governments:

Considering that the governments of Mexico and France have decided to interfere in the internal affairs of El Salvador by making political statements designed to favor one of the subversive extremes trying to seize power in that country, express their surprise over such an attitude, which sets a very serious precedent.

Note with great distress that the pronouncement of those two governments in favor of one of the subversive extremes, which through violence is trying to thwart the democratic destiny and self-determination of the Salvador people, tacitly invites other foreign entities to voice their support for the extremist elements involved in the crisis; therefore, far from contributing to a solution of the problem, its internationalization will tend to exacerbate it.

Recall that we in Latin America, from the South of the Rio Grande on downward, have on various occasions suffered painful and bitter experiences of foreign interventions by regional and extraregional powers.

Ratify the support of their governments for the effort being made by the people of El Salvador and their democratic civilian and military leaders to achieve peace and social justice within a pluralistic and democratic system.

Affirm that it is up to Salvadorans themselves to find a political and democratic solution to the conflict, without any sort of direct or indirect foreign intervention.

CARACAS, 2 September, 1981

[Signed] OSCAR CAMILION, Argentina
MARIO ROLÓN ANAYA, Bolivia
CARLOS LEMOS SIMMONDS, Colombia
RENÉ ROJAS GALDAMES, Chile
RAFAEL CASTILLO VALDÉS, Guatemala
CÉSAR ELVIR SIERRA, Honduras
ALBERTO NOGUES, Paraguay
MANUEL ENRIQUE TAVARES, the Dominican Republic
JOSÉ ALBERTO ZAMBRANO VELASCO, Venezuela

6.
PANAMA AND THE SANDINISTAS: A REVOLUTIONARY FRIENDSHIP TURNS SOUR (DECEMBER 1979)

During the visit earlier this month by a high-level Nicaraguan delegation to Panama, both sides found it necessary to deny that relations between the two countries had deteriorated. The Nicaraguan minister of the interior, Tomás Borge, even described reports of a cooling of relations as "mythical." But Omar Torrijos, head of the Panamanian National Guard, was a little less dismissive. Relations were "fraternal," he said, but recently Panama had handed out some "friendly warnings" to the Sandinistas, particularly on the subject of Cuba. Over recent weeks the Panamanian National Guard has been leaking to the press its "concern" over the level of Cuban activities in Nicaragua. Its discontent, not to mention fury, reached such a pitch as to lead to the withdrawal of the Panamanian advisers sent to Nicaragua after the overthrow of Somoza to train the Sandinista police force. At the beginning of December, the Nicaraguan ambassador to Panama, José Pasos, was heard to remark that there were no longer any Panamanians advising the Sandinista po-

Latin America Weekly Report, December 21, 1979, p. 92.

lice because "their mission has been completed."

The Panamanian National Guard was none too enamored of its "mission" in the first place. As perhaps the most militant of the Sandinistas' allies during the civil war, the Panamanians had expected to play a leading role in the post-war reorganization; they offered help especially in the field of setting up a military intelligence network. According to the leaks by the Panamanian general staff, however, they arrived in Managua to find that the Cubans had filled all the important military advisory positions, leaving Panama with only the police. . . .

At a meeting with Fidel Castro, [Panama's deputy chief of staff] Colonel Paredes was reported to have asked, or demanded, that other countries, particularly friends of Nicaragua such as Panama and Costa Rica, be allowed to participate actively in helping to organize the new Nicaraguan army. Castro replied that he had no objection to others joining in but that Cuba would not reduce its role since it had been "on the side of the Sandinistas for 20 years."

Paredes also visited Venezuela, together with the Costa Rican interior minister, Juan José Echeverría, the Panamanian head of intelligence, Colonel Manuel Antonio Noriega, and Torrijos's personal adviser, Marcel Salamín. Panama and Costa Rica asked the Venezuelan government to send advisers for the Sandinista air force; according to a Panamanian general staff source, they wanted to prevent the Cubans from running the show.

On 17 November, three or four days after Paredes's visit to Havana, Tomás Borge made his remark, believed then to have been prompted mainly by Nicaragua's tense relations with Honduras, that Nicaragua did not stand alone and had "excellent friends, such as Cuba." His reference, however, to Nicaragua being "flexible in its alliances with foreign governments" was interpreted, in Panama City at least, as reflecting the growing unease in relations between Nicaragua and Panama.

7.
JOSÉ LÓPEZ PORTILLO: SPEECH IN MANAGUA
(FEBRUARY 1982)

We reiterate here what we have said publicly and in private to one party and the other: Central American and even Caribbean revolutions are above

February 22, 1982. Speech given at a ceremony in his honor, Carlos Fonseca Amador Plaza of the Revolution, Managua.

all the struggles of poor and oppressed people to live better and with more freedom. To describe them as something else and act as if they were otherwise is counterproductive. This in the end brings about that which one sought to avoid. Hopes should not be cancelled and people and their rights should not be hemmed in.

Mexico's posture with regard to the Sandinist revolution is based on this assessment. Our support for the struggle of the Nicaraguan people against the Somozist tyranny was not a last-minute affair. Our support for the Junta of National Reconstruction and the FSLN, during the equally difficult struggle to reconstruct a country that was destroyed, and to consolidate a young state, was extended from the very beginning, and I believe that I can confirm that it has been unfailing. Today, now that time has passed, I can say loudly and with pride, and I am sure with the agreement of all Mexicans: our solidarity with the Nicaraguan revolution is a source of pride to Mexico.

For the aforementioned reasons, and because I fully share the authentic and supportive sympathy that struggles like this one have always generated in Mexican sensibilities; this support has become a true cornerstone of our foreign policy. It is not and will not be afflicted with the vicissitudes of repentance or disillusion and it will certainly not yield to terror or threats.

Neither foreign pressure and provocations nor the natural internal impatience and demands have altered the Nicaraguan leaders' commitment to their people. They have made no changes in the position that they have outlined to the international community on many occasions. I pay tribute here to such constancy and honesty in political conduct and to their firm determination to avoid bloodying the postrevolution.

To my Sandinist friends I say: Continue on your path, which is the one chosen by the people. Mexico has been and will always be at your side. Always at your side.

It has been there in times of joy and it is there now in times of difficulty, in times when the horizon is darkened by the clouds of foreign threat, not only to Nicaragua, but also to the entire region.

An intervention in Central America and the Caribbean would represent a gigantic historic error, in addition to constituting a return to phases that sought to give rights by force. It would provoke a continental upheaval and the resurgence of a deep anti-U.S. feeling in the best men of all Latin America. I can assure . . . [interrupted by applause] I can assure my good friends in the United States that what is occurring here in Nicaragua, what is happening in El Salvador and the wind that is blowing throughout the entire region does not represent an intolerable danger to the basic interests and the national security of the United States. However, they do imply a risk of historic condemnation if there is a violent curtailment of the rights that the U.S. people undoubtedly demand for themselves: self-determination with independence, dignity and the exercise of sovereignty.

I am happy to have heard from Commander Ortega the five points that the junta has proposed and that have been publicly and openly accepted here by the Nicaraguan people. The fact that I also dare to say this publicly in front of these people means only that it is time for reason to prevail. The fact that we all agree to seek peace requires that we all adhere to peaceful reasoning. That is why I dare to outline my proposal to the people here, to the region and to the United States.

It is not an overall peace for the region, since as such it could hardly be successful. It is a matter of proposing—through channels that are separate, if close and possibly convergent over the medium term—means for negotiation, for the exchange of concessions and formalization of these concessions that could lead to a climate of detente, peace, democracy, stability and development.

This option necessarily implies two premises. Each interested party must make real concessions, and second, no one should be obliged to renounce his basic principles or his vital interests.

There are three thorny points in the region's conflict: Nicaragua, El Salvador and, if one wishes to look at things directly, the relationship between Cuba and the United States. I believe that if these last two countries were to follow the path opened by the talks between the U.S. secretary of state and the vice president of the Cuban Councils of State and Ministers, there would be real possibilities for dialogue to be converted into negotiations.

The present detente in southern Africa allows for predicting certain real possibilities in this regard. I do not wish to go into detail at this point; however, we emphatically accept the possibility that Mexico may play a more active role in this regard. We have some useful ideas which we think are effective on the subject. They are based essentially on the complex, but not unresolvable, system of mutual concessions by each party.

With every consideration, I dare to refer to El Salvador. It is obvious that the aggravation of the war, of violence and of tragedy have reached extreme levels. Mexico, which for some time has advocated a political and negotiated solution to the Salvadoran conflict, sees with great concern the increasingly limited possibility that negotiation will put an end to the bloodbath suffered by those people, who are subject to the risks of unbearable victories or intolerable intervention. Between elections without negotiation and negotiation without elections, there is undoubtedly a solution consisting of a commitment to a constituent assembly. I do not wish to go into this in detail at this time. I will say only that this solution could be one formula submitted to all the interested parties for discussion. Similarly, I believe that the main U.S. concerns regarding the possible consequences of a negotiated resolution of the Salvadoran crisis should be resolved. Mexico and other countries that are friends and even allies of the United States could be in a position to provide guarantees in this regard.

Finally, and I wish to be more specific in this case, I propose here a number of steps and ideas that fortunately coincide with those that have been expressed about Nicaragua's situation in the region. There are three basic points for a possible relaxation of tensions in the area.

First the U.S. Government must rule out all threat or use of force against Nicaragua. It is dangerous, unworthy and unnecessary. Invoking the close relationship between Mexico and its neighbor to the north, I reiterate from here my direct and respectful call to President Reagan, who fortunately has already made statements in this regard: no armed intervention in Central America and certainly not in Nicaragua.

Second, I say this with reflection and with the greatest consideration to these threatened people. It is possible and indispensable to begin a process of balanced reduction of military troops in the area. If the bands of Somozist guardsmen who are operating along the border between Honduras and Nicaragua are disarmed and if the training of similar groups within the United States is brought to an end, thus eliminating a real threat to this country's safety, once could believe that the Nicaraguan Government will simultaneously give up both the purchase of weapons and airplanes and the use of its scarce resources to maintain military troops on a scale that worries bordering and nearby countries. This is what I consider to be the truth, with all respect, Nicaraguans.

The third and last point is: I believe that it is feasible and desirable to draft a system of nonaggression pacts between Nicaragua and the United States, on the one hand, and between Nicaragua and its neighbors on the other. Such instruments would formalize previously reached agreements and, to the extent that they were not directed against any particular party, they would contribute significantly to the establishment of a lasting peace in the region.

I have no doubts that if this system of pacts became a reality, the main points of dispute in relations between Nicaragua and the United States could be resolved by negotiations immediately afterward.

8.
PRESIDENT LUIS HERRERA CAMPÍNS AND PRESIDENT JOSÉ LÓPEZ PORTILLO: LETTER TO PRESIDENT REAGAN (SEPTEMBER 1982)

Dear Mr. President and Friend:

Concerned over the events which seriously threaten the peace between Nicaragua and Honduras, and furthermore peace in Central America, we have addressed ourselves to the leaders of those countries emphasizing the need to abstain from undertaking any action that would imperil the situation, and also bearing in mind the need for sponsoring a constructive dialogue that would permit the necessary rapprochement and cooperation between the parties. . . .

We see with . . . concern the deterioration of the Central American situation endangered by a conflict that could extend to the whole region. The situation between Honduras and Nicaragua is grave and has reached the levels of armed encounters. . . .

Mexico and Venezuela, linked to the region by geographic considerations, cannot be indifferent to the problems that take place there. . . . Our countries feel that, in a most fraternal way, they should express points of view that could contribute to the solution of these problems and, in that manner, keep the continent as a reserve of peace. . . . We would wish to address for your consideration the convenience of undertaking a joint exploration of the paths still open to us in order to stop the actual and worrying escalation, the increasing tensions and the general and dangerous expectations generated by its outcome.

In the same way that we have encouraged the Nicaraguan government to adopt measures directed to avoid military engagement in its border with Honduras, we also consider it useful to put an end to the support, organization, and emplacement of former Somocista guards.

We have knowledge that conversations are underway between the representatives of the United States and Nicaragua for solving the pending problems.

We express our conviction that, in that way, progress can be attained. In congratulating ourselves for such progress, at the same time, we sincerely invite you to strengthen the dialogue so that it may facilitate a genuine negotiation able to overcome the difficulties.

Likewise, we present to you the need to effectively advance in the conclusion of a global agreement that may provide true peace between Nicaragua and Honduras, and which will bear a positive result in a framework of world tensions and confrontations.

To this effect, allow us to recall the proposals for peace in Central America in relation with the possibility of limiting armaments in the region under international control.

As stated in the Declaration of San José, Costa Rica, of May 8, 1982, adopted during the inauguration of the Costa Rican President, Luis Alberto Monge, six leaders of the region concerned over the arms race in the area, expressed the need to "adjust military personnel and equipment to levels strictly necessary for the defense of national sovereignty, territorial integrity and the maintenance of public order, subject to the requirements universally accepted in any democratic society ruled by law."

We hope, Mr. President, that these ideas find a favorable reception and serve as a basis for peace and stability in the region.

Signed,
José López Portillo
and
Luis Herrera Campíns

9.
SAN JOSÉ DECLARATION (OCTOBER 1982)

The representatives of the Governments of the Republics of Belize, Colombia, El Salvador, the United States of America, Honduras, Jamaica, and Costa Rica, and the observer representative of the Government of the Dominican Republic, convinced that direct dialogue among democratic countries is the appropriate way to review the situation in their states and, therefore, to search for solutions to common problems, . . .

DECLARE:

I. Their faith in and support for the principles of representative, pluralistic, and participatory democracy which, when properly understood, constitutes a way of life, of thinking, and of acting which can accommodate within its scope different social and economic systems and structures having a common denominator, which is respect for life, for the security of

---

Final Act of the Meeting of Foreign Ministers Interested in the Promotion of Democracy in Central America and the Caribbean. Signed by the United States, Colombia, El Salvador, Honduras, and Costa Rica.

the individual, for freedom of thought, and for freedom of the press, as well as the right to work and to receive proper remuneration, the right to fair living conditions, to the free exercise of suffrage, and of other human, civil, political, economic, social, and cultural rights.

II. Their concern about the serious deterioration of the conditions of the present international economic order and international financial system, which gives rise to a process of destabilization, anguish, and fear, affecting, in particular, those countries that have a democratic system of government. . . .

III. Their conviction that, in order to promote regional peace and stability, it is necessary to support domestic political understandings that will lead to the establishment of democratic, pluralistic, and participatory systems; to the establishment of mechanisms for a continuing multilateral dialogue; to absolute respect for delimited and demarcated borders, in accordance with existing treaties, compliance with which is the proper way to prevent border disputes and incidents, observing, whenever applicable, traditional lines of jurisdiction; to respect for the independence and territorial integrity of states; to the rejection of threats or the use of force to settle conflicts; to a halt to the arms race; and to the elimination, on the basis of full and effective reciprocity, of the external factors which hamper the consolidation of a stable and lasting peace.

In order to attain these objectives, it is essential that every country within and without the region take the following actions:

a) Create and maintain truly democratic government institutions, based on the will of the people as expressed in free and regular elections, and founded on the principle that government is responsible to the people governed;

b) Respect human rights, especially the right to life and to personal integrity, and the fundamental freedoms, such as freedom of speech, freedom of assembly, and religious freedom, as well as the right to organize political parties, labor unions, and other groups and associations;

c) Promote national reconciliation where there have been deep divisions in society through the broadening of opportunities for participation within the framework of democratic processes and institutions;

d) Respect the principle of non-intervention in the internal affairs of states, and the right of peoples to self-determination;

e) Prevent the use of their territories for the support, supply, training, or command of terrorist or subversive elements in other states, end all traffic in arms and supplies, and refrain from providing any direct or indirect assistance to terrorist, subversive, or other activities aimed at the violent overthrow of the governments of other states;

f) Limit arms and the size of military and security forces to the levels that are strictly necessary for the maintenance of public order and national defense;

g) Provide for international surveillance and supervision of all ports of entry, borders, and other strategic areas under reciprocal and fully verifiable arrangements;

h) On the basis of full and effective reciprocity, withdraw all foreign military and security advisers and forces from the Central American area, and ban the importation of heavy weapons of manifest offensive capability through guaranteed means of verification. . . .

The signing countries call on all the peoples and governments of the region to embrace and implement these principles and conditions as the basis for the improvement of democracy and the building of a lasting peace. . . .

THEY RESOLVE

IV. To create a democratic organization to provide development assistance and advisory services for elections, the purpose of which organization will be to maintain the electoral system and to develop, strengthen, and stimulate its utilization in the inter-American area, providing advice to countries that request it about its practice and implementation.

V. . . . to participate in a Forum for Peace and Democracy, the purpose of which will be to contribute to the implementation of the actions and the attainment of the objectives contained in this document, and, within the framework of this declaration, to study the regional crisis and analyze the various peace proposals or initiatives aimed at solving it. The Forum may be broadened by the inclusion of the collaboration of other democratic States.

10.
CONTADORA: DOCUMENT OF OBJECTIVES
(SEPTEMBER 1983)

The signatory states, considering:
The situation prevailing in Central America. . . . is characterized by an atmosphere of tension that threatens security and peaceful coexistence in the region . . .

DECLARE THEIR INTENTION OF ACHIEVING THE FOLLOWING OBJECTIVES:

To promote detente and put an end to situations of conflict in the area, restraining from taking any action that might jeopardize political confi-

Signed by Colombia, Mexico, Panama, and Venezuela.

dence or obstruct the achievement of peace, security and stability in the region;

To ensure strict compliance with the aforementioned principles of international law, whose violators will be held accountable;

To respect and ensure the exercise of human, political, civil, economic, social, religious and cultural rights;

To adopt measures conducive to the establishment and, where appropriate, improvement of democratic, representative and pluralistic systems that will guarantee effective popular participation in the decision-making process and ensure that the various currents of opinion have free access to fair and regular elections based on the full observance of citizens' rights;

To promote national reconciliation efforts wherever deep divisions have taken place within society, with a view to fostering participation in democratic political processes in accordance with the law;

To create political conditions intended to ensure the international security, integrity and sovereignty of the States of the region;

To stop the arms race in all its forms and begin negotiations for the control and reduction of current stocks of weapons and on the number of armed troops;

To prevent the installation on their territory of foreign military bases or any other type of foreign military interference;

To conclude agreements to reduce the presence of foreign military advisers and other foreign elements involved in military and security activities, with a view to their elimination;

To establish internal control machinery to prevent the traffic in arms from the territory of any country in the region to the territory of another;

To eliminate the traffic in arms, whether within the region or from outside it, intended for persons, organizations or groups seeking to destabilize the Governments of Central American countries;

To prevent the use of their own territory by persons, organizations or groups seeking to destabilize the Government of Central American countries and to refuse to provide them with or permit them to receive military or logistical support;

To refrain from inciting or supporting acts of terrorism, subversion or sabotage in the countries in the area;

To establish and co-ordinate direct communication systems with a view to preventing or, where appropriate, settling incidents between States of the region;

To continue humanitarian aid aimed at helping Central American refugees who have been displaced from their countries of origin, and to create suitable conditions for the voluntary repatriation of such refugees, in consultation with or with the co-operation of the United Nations High Commissioner for Refugees (UNHCR) and other international agencies deemed appropriate;

To undertake economic and social development programs with the aim of promoting well being and an equitable distribution of wealth;

To revitalize and restore economic integration machinery in order to attain sustained development on the basis of solidarity and mutual advance;

To negotiate the provision of external monetary resources which will provide additional means of financing the resumption of intra-regional trade, meet the serious balance-of-payments problems, attract funds for working capital, support programs to extend and restructure production systems and promote medium- and long-term investment projects;

To negotiate better and broader access to international markets in order to increase the volume of trade between the countries of Central America and the rest of the world, particularly the industrialized countries, by means of a revision of trade practices, the elimination of tariff and other barriers, and the achievement of price stability at a profitable and fair level for the products exported by the countries of the region;

To establish technical co-operation machinery for the planning, programming and implementation of multi-sectoral investment and trade promotion projects.

The Ministers for Foreign Affairs of the Central American countries, with the participation of the countries in the Contadora Group, have begun negotiations with the aim of preparing for the conclusion of the agreements and the establishment of machinery necessary to formalize and develop the objectives contained in this document, and to bring about the establishment of appropriate verification of monitoring systems. To that end, account will be taken of the initiatives put forward at the meetings convened by the Contadora Group.

11.
THE CONTADORA ACT FOR PEACE AND COOPERATION IN CENTRAL AMERICA (SEPTEMBER 1984)

CHAPTER II
COMMITMENTS WITH REGARD TO POLITICAL MATTERS

SECTION 2. COMMITMENTS WITH REGARD TO NATIONAL RECONCILIATION

Each PARTY recognizes *vis-à-vis* the other Central American States the commitment assumed *vis-à-vis* its own people to ensure the preservation of domestic peace as a contribution to peace in the region, and they accordingly resolve:

7. To adopt measures for the establishment or, as the case may be, the further development of representative and pluralistic democratic systems guaranteeing effective participation by the people, through political organizations, in the decision-making process, and ensuring the different currents of opinion free access to honest and periodic elections based on the full observance of the rights of citizens;

8. Where deep divisions have come about within society, urgently to promote actions of national reconciliation which will make it possible for the people to participate, with full guarantees, in genuine democratic political processes on the basis of justice, liberty and democracy, and, towards that end, to create mechanisms making possible, in accordance with the law, dialogue with opposition groups;

9. To adopt and, as the case may be, endorse, broaden and improve legal measures for a genuine amnesty which will enable their citizens to resume full participation in political, economic and social affairs, and similarly, to guarantee the inviolability of life, the liberty and the security of person of those to whom such amnesty is granted. . . .

SECTION 4. COMMITMENTS WITH REGARD TO ELECTORAL PROCESSES AND PARLIAMENTARY CO-OPERATION

Each PARTY shall recognize *vis-à-vis* the other Central American States the commitment assumed *vis-à-vis* its own people to guarantee the preservation of internal peace as a contribution to peace in the region and to that end shall resolve:

14. To adopt the appropriate measures that guarantee the participation of political parties in electoral processes on an equal footing, ensuring that they have access to the mass communication media and enjoy freedom of assembly and freedom of expression. . . .

CHAPTER III
COMMITMENTS WITH REGARD TO SECURITY MATTERS

. . . the PARTIES assume the following commitments:

SECTION 1. COMMITMENTS WITH REGARD TO MILITARY MANEUVERS

16. To comply with the following provisions as regards the holding of military maneuvers:

   (a) When national or joint military maneuvers are held in areas less than 30 (thirty) kilometers from the frontier, the appropriate prior notification to the neighboring countries and the Verification and Control Commission, mentioned in Part II of this Act, shall be made at least 30 (thirty) days beforehand. . . .

Invitations shall be issued to observers from neighboring countries.

17. To prohibit the holding of international military maneuvers in their respective territories. Any maneuver of this kind which is currently under way shall be suspended within a period of not more than thirty days after the signing of this Act.
18. To halt the arms race in all its forms, and begin immediately negotiations on the control and reduction of the current inventory of weapons and the number of troops under arms;
19. Not to introduce new weapons systems that alter the quality or quantity of current inventories of war *matériel;*
20. Not to introduce, possess or use chemical, biological, radiological or other weapons which may be deemed to be excessively injurious or to have indiscriminate effects;
21. To send to the Verification and Control Commission their respective current inventories of weapons, installations and troops under arms within a period of not more than 30 (thirty) days from the date of the signing of this Act. The inventories shall be prepared in accordance with the definitions and basic criteria agreed on in the Annex and in paragraph 21 of this section. On receiving the inventories, the Commission shall carry out within a period of not more than 30 (thirty) days the technical studies that will be used for the purpose of setting maximum limits for the military development of the States of the region, taking into account their national security interests, and of halting the arms race.

On the basis of the foregoing, the PARTIES agree on the following implementation stages:

First stage: Once they have submitted their respective inventories, the PARTIES shall acquire no more military *matériel.* The moratorium shall continue until limits are agreed on in the following stage.

Second stage: The PARTIES shall establish within a maximum period of thirty days limits for the following types of armaments: fighter aircraft and helicopters, tanks and armored vehicles, artillery, short-, medium- and long-range rockets and guided missiles and launching equipment, ships or vessels that are of a military nature or can be used for military purposes.

Third stage: Once the preceding stage has been completed and within a period of not more than thirty days, the PARTIES shall establish limits for military forces and for installations that can be used in military actions.

Fourth stage: The PARTIES may begin negotiations concerning those matters with which it is considered essential to deal. Notwithstanding the foregoing, the PARTIES may, by mutual agreement, change the periods set for the negotiation and establishment of limits. . . .

SECTION 3. COMMITMENTS WITH REGARD TO FOREIGN MILITARY BASES

24. Not to authorize the installation in their respective territories of foreign bases or foreign military schools.
25. To close down any foreign bases or foreign military schools in their respective territories within six months of the signing of this Act.

SECTION 4. COMMITMENTS WITH REGARD TO FOREIGN MILITARY ADVISERS

26. To provide the Verification and Control Commission with a list of any foreign military advisers or other foreign elements participating in military and security activities in their territory, within 30 days of the signing of this Act. In the preparation of the list, the definitions contained in the annex shall be taken into account.
27. With a view to the removal of foreign military advisers and other foreign elements, to set a timetable for phased withdrawals, including the immediate withdrawal of any advisers performing operational and training functions. To that end, the studies and recommendations of the Verification and Control Commission shall be taken into account.
28. As for advisers performing technical functions related to the installation and maintenance of military equipment, a control register shall be maintained in accordance with the terms laid down in the respective contracts or agreements. On the basis of that register, the Verification and Control Commission shall seek to set reasonable limits on the number of such advisers.

SECTION 5. COMMITMENTS WITH REGARD TO THE TRAFFIC IN ARMS

29. To stop the flow of arms, within and outside the region, towards persons, organizations, irregular forces or armed bands trying to destabilize the Governments of the States Parties.

30. To establish for that purpose internal control mechanisms at airports, landing strips, harbours, terminals and border crossings, on roads, air routes, sea lanes and waterways, and at any other point or in any other area likely to be used for the traffic in arms.

31. On the basis of presumption or established facts, to report any violations to the Verification and Control Commission, with sufficient evidence to enable it to carry out the necessary investigation and submit such conclusions and recommendations as it may consider useful. . . .

SECTION 6. COMMITMENTS WITH REGARD TO THE PROHIBITION OF SUPPORT FOR IRREGULAR FORCES

32. To refrain from giving any political, military, financial or other support to individuals, groups, irregular forces or armed bands advocating the overthrow or destabilization of other Governments, and to prevent, by all means at their disposal, the use of their territory for attacks on another State or for the organization of attacks, acts of sabotage, kidnappings or criminal activities in the territory of another State.

33. To exercise strict control over their respective borders, with a view to preventing their own territory from being used to carry out any military action against a neighboring State.

34. To disarm and remove from the border area any group or irregular force identified as being responsible for acts against a neighboring state.

35. To dismantle, and deny the use of, installations, equipment and facilities providing logistical support or serving operational functions in their territory, if the latter is used for acts against neighboring Governments.

SECTION 7. COMMITMENTS WITH REGARD TO TERRORISM, SUBVERSION OR SABOTAGE

36. To refrain from giving political, military, financial or any other support for acts of subversion, terrorism or sabotage intended to destabilize Governments of the region.

37. To refrain from organizing, instigating or participating in acts of terrorism, subversion or sabotage in another State, or acquiescing in organized activities within their territory directed towards the commission of such acts. . . .

PART II
COMMITMENTS WITH REGARD TO EXECUTION AND FOLLOW-UP

The PARTIES decide to establish the following mechanisms for the purpose of executing and following up the commitments contained in this Act:

1. *Ad Hoc Committee for Evaluation and Follow-up of Commitments concerning Political and Refugee Matters*

(a) Composition

The Committee shall be composed of five (5) persons of recognized competence and impartiality, proposed by the States members of the Contadora Group and accepted by common agreement by the Parties. The members of the Committee must be of a nationality different from those of the Parties.

(b) Functions

The Committee shall receive and evaluate the reports which the Parties undertake to submit on the ways in which they have proceeded to implement commitments with regard to national reconcilation, human rights, electoral processes and refugees.

In addition, the Committee shall be open to any communications on these subjects, transmitted for their information by organizations or individuals, which might contribute useful data for evaluation.

On the basis of the aforesaid data, the Committee shall prepare a periodic report which, in addition to the evaluation, shall contain proposals and recommendations for improving implementation of the commitments. This report shall be submitted to the Parties and to the Governments of the Contadora Group. . . .

2. *Verification and Control Commission for Security Matters*

(a) Composition

The Commission shall be composed of:

— Four Commissioners, representing States of recognized impartiality and having a genuine interest in contributing to the solution of the Central American crisis, proposed by the Contadora Group and accepted by the PARTIES, with the right to participate in decisions of the Commission. Co-ordination of the work of the Commission shall be by rotation.

— A Latin American Executive Secretary appointed by the Contadora Group by common agreement with the PAR-

TIES, with the right to participate in the decisions of the Commission, who shall be responsible for its ongoing operation.

— A representative of the Secretary-General of the United Nations and a representative of the Secretary-General of the Organization of American States, as observers.

(b) Establishment

The Commission shall be established not more than thirty (30) days after the signing of this Act.

(c) Functions

— To receive current inventories of armaments, installations and troops under arms of the PARTIES, prepared in accordance with the provisions of the Annex.

— To carry out technical studies to be used to establish maximum limits for the military development of the PARTIES in the region in accordance with the basic criteria established in commitment 22 of this Act.

— To verify that no new weapons are introduced which would qualitatively and quantitatively alter current inventories, and to verify the non-use of weapons prohibited in this Act.

— To verify compliance with this Act with regard to irregular forces and the non-use of their own territory in destabilizing actions against another State, and to consider any reports in that connection.

— To verify compliance with the procedures for notification of national or joint military maneuvers provided for in this Act.

(d) Rules and procedures

— The Commission shall receive any duly substantiated report concerning violations of the security commitments assumed under this Act, shall communicate it to the PARTIES involved and shall initiate such investigations as it deems appropriate.

— The Commission shall carry out its investigations by making on-site inspections, gathering testimony and using any other procedure which it deems necessary for the performance of its functions.

— In the event of any reports of violations or of non-compliance with the security commitments of this Act, the Commission shall prepare a report containing recommendations addressed to the PARTIES involved. . . .

PART III
FINAL PROVISIONS

1. The commitments made by the PARTIES in this Act are of a legal nature and are therefore binding.
2. This Act shall be ratified in accordance with the constitutional procedures established in each of the Central American States. The instruments of ratification shall be deposited with the Governments of the States members of the Contadora Group.
3. This Act shall enter into force when the five Central American signatory States have deposited their instruments of ratification.
4. The PARTIES, as from the date of signature, shall refrain from any acts which would serve to frustrate the object and purpose of this Act.
5. Thirty (30) days after the date of signature of this Act, the machinery referred to in Part II shall enter into operation on a provisional basis. The Parties shall take the necessary measures, before the end of that period, to ensure such provisional operation.
6. Any dispute concerning the interpretation or application of this Act which cannot be settled through the machinery provided for in Part II of this Act shall be referred to the Ministers for Foreign Affairs of the PARTIES for consideration and a decision, requiring a unanimous vote in favor.
7. Should the dispute continue, it shall be referred to the Ministers for Foreign Affairs of the Contadora Group, who shall meet at the request of any of the PARTIES. . . .

12.
TEGUCIGALPA DRAFT OF THE CONTADORA ACT
(OCTOBER 1984)

PREAMBLE

The Governments of the Republics of Costa Rica, El Salvador, Guatemala, Honduras, and Nicaragua:

1. Aware of the urgent need to strengthen peace, cooperation, trust, democracy, and economic and social development among the peoples of the region through the observance of principles and measures that will permit greater understanding between the Central American governments;

Signed by Costa Rica, El Salvador, and Honduras, as a counterdraft to the September 1984 version.

2. Concerned by the situation in Central America, which is characterized by a serious erosion of political trust, the profound economic and social crisis, the grave situation of refugees and displaced persons, border incidents, the arms race, arms trafficking, the presence of foreign advisers and foreign military presence in other forms, and the use by irregular forces of the territory of certain States for activities aimed at destabilizing other States of the region. . . .

5. That it is important to create, develop, and strengthen participatory and pluralistic democratic systems in all countries of the region. . . .

8. That the national security interests of the Central American States must be taken into account in the adoption of measures for halting the arms race, with a view to establishing military equilibrium in the region. . . .

CONVINCED, FURTHERMORE:

24. Of the need to perfect just economic and social structures that will consolidate a genuine democratic system and allow their peoples full access to the right to work, education, health, and cultures. . . .

34. Reaffirming, without prejudice to the right to appeal to appropriate international fora, their desire to resolve their conflicts within the framework of this Act. . . .

Have agreed as follows: . . .

CHAPTER II
COMMITMENTS RELATING TO POLITICAL MATTERS . . .

SECTION 2. COMMITMENTS RELATING TO NATIONAL RECONCILIATION. . . .

9. Issue and, if appropriate, ratify, expand, and improve laws and regulations that offer true amnesty and allow their citizens, whenever necessary, to become fully reincorporated in political, economic, and social life. In like manner, guarantee the inviolability of life, liberty, and personal security for those who accept amnesty. . . .

CHAPTER III
COMMITMENTS RELATING TO SECURITY MATTERS

In accordance with the obligations they have assumed under international law, the Parties undertake the following commitments:

SECTION 1. COMMITMENTS RELATING TO MILITARY MANEUVERS.

16. Comply, when conducting military maneuvers, with the following provisions which shall take effect upon the entry into force of this Act:

(a) In the event that national, joint, international, or combined, military exercises are being conducted in zones within a distance of thirty (30) kilometers from the border, the required prior notification referred to in Part II of this Act shall be given to the neighboring countries and to the Verification and Control Commission at least thirty (30) days in advance. **18.** Stop the arms race in all its forms and negotiate immediately the establishment of maximum limits for arms and military strength, and their control and reduction, so that no country will have the military capability to establish its hegemony or impose its will on another country in the region, in order to establish a military balance in the area.

On the basis of the foregoing, the Parties agree on the following stages of implementation:

First Stage

(a) (Freeze) The Parties will suspend all procurement of war material while the maximum limits of military development are being established during the second stage:
(b) (Delivery of inventories) The Parties will deliver to the Ad Hoc Group on Disarmament their inventories of existing arms and military installations, and a list of military strength within thirty (30) days after signing this Act.

The inventories shall be prepared in conformity with the criteria given in paragraphs 7, 8, 9, and 18 of the Annex to this Act, using the definitions contained therein, and in conformity with the criteria and factors set forth in paragraph 22 of this section.
(c) (Technical studies for the negotiation of limits) The Ad-Hoc Group on Disarmament shall conclude the aforementioned technical studies for negotiations on the maximum limits of the Parties' military expansion within thirty (30) days after the signature of this Act.

Second Stage

(Maximum limits of arms, military personnel strengths, and military installations) Thirty (30) days after signature of this Act the Parties shall meet to establish, within the next thirty (30) days, the following:
(a) Maximum limits for the types of arms covered by paragraphs 7, 8, 9, and 18 of the annex to this Act and schedules for their reduction.
(b) Maximum limits for military personnel strengths and military installations that each Party may have at its disposal and the schedules for their reduction or dismantling.

The maximum limits referred to in paragraphs (a) and (b) above, as well as the schedules for reduction, shall form an integral part of this Act and shall have the same legally binding force. . . .

Section 3. Commitments Relating to Foreign Military Bases

24. Refrain from authorizing the establishment of foreign military bases or military schools in their territories.

25. Close existing foreign military bases or military schools in their territories according to the schedule agreed upon by the Parties, which shall appear as an integral part of this Act, with the same binding legal effects for all the Parties. The schedule shall be agreed upon by the Parties within ninety (90) days after signing the Act.

Section 4. Commitments Relating to Foreign Military Advisers

26. Submit to the Ad Hoc Disarmament Group a list of foreign military advisers and other foreign personnel participating in military, paramilitary, and security activities in their territories within thirty (30) days after signing this Act. The list referred to in this paragraph shall be prepared in conformity with the definitions contained in the Annex.

27. The Parties agree to the reduction, with a view to the withdrawal, of foreign military advisers and other foreign personnel capable of participating in military, paramilitary, and security activities, according to the agreed schedule that is an integral part of this Act, with the same binding legal effects for all the Parties.

The schedule shall be agreed upon by the Parties within ninety (90) days after signing the Act.

28. With respect to advisers performing technical duties relating to the installation and maintenance of military equipment, a control list shall be established in conformity with the terms set forth in their contracts or agreements. The Ad Hoc Disarmament Group shall use the control list to establish reasonable limits on the number of such advisers within the same time period established in paragraph 27. The agreed limits shall be an integral part of the Act with the same binding legal effects for all the Parties.

Section 6. Commitments Relating to the Prohibition of Support for Irregular Forces. . . .

35(a). Once they (the irregulars) have been disarmed, the Verification and Control Commission shall endeavor, with financial and logistical assistance from the international organizations and governments involved in restoring peace of Central America, to relocate outside the Central American area irregulars using for their purposes the territory of a State that is not their own, independently of whether they may later wish to avail themselves of the amnesty provided for in the following paragraph.

Irregular forces which lay down their arms in their own country shall receive the broadest unconditional amnesty from their government, under the supervision of the Verification and Control Commission.

SECTION 7. COMMITMENTS RELATING TO TERRORISM, SUBVERSION, OR SABOTAGE

36. Refrain from lending political, military, financial, or other support to subversive, terrorist, or sabotage activities attempting to destabilize or overthrow the governments of the region.

37. Refrain from organizing, encouraging, or participating, in acts of terrorism, subversion, or sabotage in another State, and from permitting activities to be organized within their territories for the purpose of committing such criminal acts. . . .

SECTION 8. COMMITMENTS RELATING TO DIRECT COMMUNICATION SYSTEMS

42. With a view to preventing incidents, establish a regional communications system ensuring . . . timely contact between the appropriate governmental, civilian, and military authorities and the Verification and Control Commission.

43. Establish mixed security commissions in order to prevent or resolve incidents between neighboring States. . . .

PART II
COMMITMENTS RELATING TO IMPLEMENTATION

The Parties shall establish the following mechanisms for the implementation of the commitments contained in this Act.

1. AD HOC COMMITTEE FOR THE EVALUATION AND IMPLEMENTATION OF COMMITMENTS IN POLITICAL AND REFUGEE MATTERS. . . .

The Committee or any of its members or support personnel representing it may conduct such on-site investigations as are considered necessary and appropriate, for which purpose the governments of the Contracting Parties agree to grant them, immediately and unreservedly, every facility.

The States Party and the Contadora Group shall evaluate this report jointly and submit to the Party or Parties in question the appropriate recommendations.

If the recommendations are not followed, the Parties and the Contadora Group may jointly resort to various persuasive procedures through diplomatic channels within the time period indicated in the respective regulations, and as a last resort, bring the report publicly to the attention of the Organization of American States and the United Nations.

Ad Hoc Disarmament Group

(a) Purpose: An Ad Hoc Disarmament Group shall be established to implement the procedures designed to verify and clarify the Commitments Relating to Arms and Military Strength, contained in Part I, Chapter III, Section 2 of this Act.

(b) Composition: The Ad Hoc Disarmament Group shall be composed of representatives of the five Central American States and by representatives of four States that have not participated in the Contadora Group negotiating process, are recognized for their impartiality, technical and financial capability, and the political will to cooperate for peace in the region.

Non-Central American countries shall be proposed for membership in the Ad Hoc Disarmament Group by the Contadora Group and shall be accepted by consensus following consultations among the Central American countries.

(c) Term: The Ad Hoc Disarmament Group shall be constituted at the time of signature of this Act and shall continue to function until the latter enters into force.

2. VERIFICATION AND CONTROL MECHANISMS IN SECURITY MATTERS

(a) Membership: The Verification and Control mechanism shall be composed of:

1. A Permanent Commission composed of representatives of the five Central American States and of representatives of four States that have not participated in the Contadora negotiation process, recognized for their impartiality, technical and financial capability, and the political will to cooperate for peace in Central America.

2. An International Inspectorate composed of units of inspectors and adequate administrative personnel from the four States to be selected as prescribed in the following paragraph. Non-Central American member countries of the Permanent Commission and the International Inspectorate shall be proposed by the Contadora Group and accepted by consensus by the Central American countries.

13.
PROPOSED COMPROMISE DRAFT OF THE CONTADORA ACT (SEPTEMBER 1985)

CHAPTER II
COMMITMENTS WITH REGARD TO POLITICAL MATTERS

SECTION 1. COMMITMENTS WITH REGARD TO REGIONAL DETENTE AND CONFIDENCE-BUILDING

The Parties undertake:

3. To promote mutual trust by every means at their disposal and to refrain from any action which might disturb peace and security in the Central American region;

4. To refrain from issuing or promoting propaganda in support of violence or war, and hostile propaganda against any Central American Government, and to abide by and foster the principles of peaceful coexistence and friendly co-operation; . . .

6. Join together in seeking a regional settlement which will eliminate the causes of tension in Central America by safeguarding the inalienable rights of its peoples from foreign pressure and interests.

SECTION 2. COMMITMENTS WITH REGARD TO NATIONAL RECONCILIATION

Each Party recognizes *vis-à-vis* the other Central American States the commitment assumed *vis-à-vis* its own people to ensure the preservation of domestic peace as a contribution to peace in the region, and they accordingly resolve:

7. To adopt measures for the establishment or, as the case may be, the further development of representative and pluralistic democratic systems guaranteeing effective participation by the people, through political organizations, in the decision-making process, and ensuring the different currents of opinion free access to honest and periodic elections based on the full observance of the rights of citizens;

8. Where deep divisions have come about within society, urgently to promote actions of national reconciliation which will make it possible for the people to participate, with full guarantees, in genuine democratic political processes on the basis of justice, liberty and democracy, and, towards that end, to create mechanisms making possible, in accordance with the law, dialogue with opposition groups;

9. To adopt and, as the case may be, endorse, broaden and improve legal measures for a genuine amnesty which will enable their citizens to resume full participation in political, economic and social affairs, and similarly, to guarantee the inviolability of life, the liberty and the security of person of those to whom such amnesty is granted. . . .

SECTION 4. COMMITMENTS WITH REGARD TO ELECTORAL PROCESSES AND PARLIAMENTARY CO-OPERATION

Each Party shall recognize *vis-à-vis* the other Central American States the commitment assumed *vis-à-vis* its own people to guarantee the preservation of internal peace as a contribution to peace in the region and to that end shall resolve:

14. To adopt measures that guarantee the participation of political parties in electoral processes on an equal footing, and ensure that they have access to the mass communication media and enjoy freedom of assembly and freedom of expression;

15. They likewise commit themselves to take the following measures:

(1) Promulgate or revise the electoral legislation with a view to the holding of elections that guarantee effective participation by the people;
(2) Establish independent electoral organs that will prepare a reliable voting register and ensure the impartiality and democratic nature of the process;
(3) Formulate or, where appropriate, update the rules guaranteeing the existence and participation of political parties representing various currents of opinion;
(4) Establish an electoral timetable and adopt measures to ensure that the political parties participate on an equal footing. . . .

CHAPTER III
COMMITMENTS WITH REGARD TO SECURITY MATTERS

In conformity with their obligations under international law and in accordance with the objective of laying the foundations for effective and lasting peace, the Parties assume commitments with regard to security matters relating to the prohibition of international military maneuvers; the cessation of the arms build-up; the dismantling of military foreign bases, schools or other installations; the withdrawal of foreign military advisers and other foreign elements participating in military or security activities; the prohibition of the traffic in arms; the cessation of support for irregular forces; the denial of encouragement or support for acts of terrorism, subversion or sabotage; and lastly, the establishment of a regional system of direct communication.

To that end, the Parties undertake to take specific action in accordance with the following:

SECTION 1. COMMITMENTS WITH REGARD TO MILITARY MANEUVERS

16. To comply with the following provisions as regards the holding of national military maneuvers, with effect from the signing of this Act:

(a) When national military maneuvers are held in areas less than 30 kilometers from the territory of another State, the appropriate prior notification to the other States Parties and the Verification and Control Commission, mentioned in Part II of this Act, shall be made at least 30 days beforehand. . . .

17. To comply with the following provisions as regards the holding of international military maneuvers in their respective territories:

1. They shall reduce, with the aim of totally halting, maneuvers involving the participation of the armed forces of other States. . . .
2. The holding of international military maneuvers in their respective territories shall be subject to the following provisions from the date of the signing of this Act until such maneuvers are prohibited:

(a) The Parties shall ensure that maneuvers involve no form of intimidation against a Central American State or any other State;
(b) They shall give at least 90 days' notice of the holding of maneuvers to the States Parties and to the Verification and Control Commission referred to in Part II of this Act. . . .

SECTION 2. COMMITMENTS WITH REGARD TO ARMAMENTS AND TROOP STRENGTH

18. To halt the arms race in all its forms, and begin immediately negotiations on the control and reduction of the current inventory of weapons, as well as on the number of troops under arms;
19. On the basis of the foregoing, the Parties agree on the following implementation stages:

First Stage:

(a) The Parties undertake not to acquire, after the signing of the Act, any more military *matériel,* with the exception of replenishment supplies, ammunition and spare parts needed to keep existing *matériel* in operation, and not to increase their military forces, pending the establishment of the maximum limits for military development within the time-limit stipulated for the second stage.

(b) The Parties undertake to submit simultaneously to the Verification and Control Commission their respective current inventories of weapons, military installations and troops under arms within 15 days of the signing of this Act.

The inventories shall be prepared in accordance with the definitions and basic criteria contained in the Annex to this Act;

(c) Within 60 days of the signing of this Act, the Verification and Control Commission shall conclude the technical studies and shall suggest to the States Parties, without prejudice to any negotiations which they have agreed to initiate, the maximum limits for their military development, in accordance with the basic criteria laid down in paragraph 22 of this section and in accordance with the respective timetables for reduction and dismantling.

Second Stage:

Within a period of 60 days from the signing of this Act, the Parties shall establish within the following 30 days:

(a) Maximum limits for the types of weapons classified in the annex to this Act, as well as timetables for their reduction;

(b) Maximum limits for troops and military installations which each Party may have, as well as timetables for their reduction or dismantling.

(c) If the Parties do not reach agreement on the above-mentioned maximum limits and timetables within such period, those suggested by the Commission in its technical studies shall apply provisionally. The Verification and Control Commission shall assist the Parties in continuing the negotiations with a view to concluding an agreement.

The maximum limits referred to in subparagraphs (a) and (b) and the timetables shall be regarded as an integral part of this Act and shall have the same legally binding force.

20. In order to satisfy the requirements of peace, stability, security and economic and social development of the countries of the region, no State shall have as an objective the pursuit of the hegemony of its armed forces over those of other States considered individually. . . .

SECTION 3. COMMITMENTS WITH REGARD TO FOREIGN MILITARY BASES

24. To close down any foreign military bases, schools or installations in their respective territories, as defined in paragraphs 11, 12 and 13 of the annex, within 180 days of the signing of this Act. For that purpose, the parties undertake to submit simultaneously to the Verification and Control Commission, within 15 days of the signing of this Act, a list of such foreign military bases, schools or installations, which shall be prepared in accordance with the criteria set forth in the above-mentioned paragraphs of the annex.

25. Not to authorize in their respective territories the establishment of foreign bases, schools or other installations of a military nature.

SECTION 4. COMMITMENTS WITH REGARD TO FOREIGN MILITARY ADVISERS

26. To submit to the Verification and Control Commission a list of any foreign military advisers or other foreign elements participating in military, paramilitary, and security activities in their territory, within 15 days of the signing of this Act. In the preparation of the list, account shall be taken of the definitions set forth in paragraph 14 of the annex.

27. To withdraw, within a period of not more than 180 days from the signing of this Act and in accordance with the studies and recommendations of the Verification and Control Commission, any foreign military advisers and other foreign elements likely to participate in military, paramilitary and security activities.

28. As for advisers performing technical functions related to the installation and maintenance of military equipment, a control register shall be maintained in accordance with the terms laid down in the respective contracts or agreements. On the basis of that register, the Verification and Control Commission shall propose to the Parties reasonable limits on the number of such advisers, within the time-limit established in paragraph 27 above. The agreed limits shall form an integral part of the Act.

SECTION 5. COMMITMENTS WITH REGARD TO THE TRAFFIC IN ARMS

29. To stop the illegal flow of arms, as defined in paragraph 15 of the annex, towards persons, organizations, irregular forces or armed bands trying to destabilize the Governments of the States Parties.

30. To establish for that purpose control mechanisms at airports, landing strips, harbors, terminals and border crossings, on roads, air routes, sea lanes and waterways, and at any other point or in any other area likely to be used for the traffic in arms.

31. On the basis of presumption or established facts, to report any violations to the Verification and Control Commission, with sufficient evidence to enable it to carry out the necessary investigation and submit such conclusions and recommendations as it may consider useful.

SECTION 6. COMMITMENTS WITH REGARD TO THE PROHIBITION OF SUPPORT FOR IRREGULAR FORCES

32. To refrain from giving any political, military, financial or other support to individuals, groups, irregular forces or armed bands advocating the overthrow or destabilization of other Governments, and to prevent, by all means at their disposal, the use of their territory for attacks on another State or for the organization of attacks, acts of sabotage, kidnappings or criminal activities in the territory of another State.

33. To exercise strict control over their respective borders, with a view to preventing their own territory from being used to carry out any military action against a neighboring State.

34. To deny the use of and dismantle installations, equipment and facilities providing logistical support or serving operational functions in their territory, if the latter is used for acts against neighboring Governments.

35. To disarm and remove from the border area any group or irregular force identified as being responsible for acts against a neighboring State. Once the irregular forces have been disbanded, to proceed, with the financial and logistical support of international organizations and Governments interested in bringing peace to Central America, to relocate them or return them to their respective countries, in accordance with the conditions laid down by the Governments concerned.

36. On the basis of presumption or established facts, to report any violations to the Verification and Control Commission, with sufficient evidence to enable it to carry out the necessary investigation and submit such conclusions and recommendations as it may consider useful.

SECTION 7. COMMITMENTS WITH REGARD TO TERRORISM, SUBVERSION OR SABOTAGE

37. To refrain from giving political, military, financial or any other support for acts of subversion, terrorism or sabotage intended to destabilize or overthrow Governments of the region.

38. To refrain from organizing, instigating or participating in acts of terrorism, subversion or sabotage in another Stage, or acquiescing in organized activities within their territory directed towards the commission of such criminal acts. . . .

41. To prevent in their respective territories the planning or commission of criminal acts against other States or the nationals of such States by terrorist groups or organizations. To that end, they shall strengthen cooperation between the competent migration offices and police departments and between the corresponding civilian authorities.

42. On the basis of presumption or established facts, to report any violations to the Verification and Control Commission, with sufficient evidence to enable it to carry out the necessary investigation and submit such conclusions and recommendations as it may consider useful. . . .

CHAPTER IV
COMMITMENTS WITH REGARD TO ECONOMIC AND
SOCIAL AFFAIRS

SECTION 1. COMMITMENTS WITH REGARD TO ECONOMIC AND SOCIAL
MATTERS

With a view to strengthening the process of Central American economic integration and the institutions representing and supporting it, the Parties undertake:

45. To reactivate, perfect and restructure the process of Central American economic integration, harmonizing it with the various forms of political, economic and social organization of the countries of the region. . . .

PART II
COMMITMENTS WITH REGARD TO EXECUTION AND
FOLLOW-UP

1. The Ministers for Foreign Affairs of the Central American States shall receive the opinions, reports and recommendations presented by the execution and follow-up mechanisms provided for in this part II and shall take unanimously the appropriate decisions to ensure full compliance with the commitments contracted in the Act. Any dispute shall be submitted to the procedures provided for in this Act.

2. In order to ensure the execution and follow-up of the commitments contained in this Act, the Parties decide to establish the following mechanisms:

    A. *Ad Hoc* Committee for Evaluation and Follow-up of Commitments concerning Political and Refugee Matters;

    B. Verification and Control Commission for Security Matters; and

    C. *Ad Hoc* Committee for Evaluation and Follow-up of Commitments concerning Economic and Social Matters.

3. The mechanisms established in the Act shall have the following composition, structure and functions:

    A. *Ad Hoc* Committee for Evaluation and Follow-up of Commitments concerning Political and Refugee Matters.

    (a) Composition
        The Committee shall be composed of five (5) persons of recognized competence and impartiality, proposed by the Contadora

Group and accepted by common agreement by the Parties. The members of the Committee must be of a nationality different from those of the Parties. . . .

The Committee shall elicit the information which it deems relevant; to that end, the Party to which the communication refers shall permit the members of the Committee to enter its territory and shall accord them the necessary facilities.

The Committee shall prepare a periodic report on compliance with the commitments, which may include conclusions and recommendations.

The Committee shall send its reports to the Parties and to the Governments of the Contadora Group. When the period established by the rules for the submission of observations by the States Parties has expired, the Committee shall prepare final reports, which shall be public unless the Committee itself decides otherwise.

(c) Rules of procedure

The Committee shall draw up its own rules of procedure, which it shall make known to the Parties.

B. Verification and Control Commission for Security Matters

(a) Composition

The Commission shall be composed of

— Four Commissioners, representing four States of recognized impartiality having a genuine interest in contributing to the solution of the Central American crisis, proposed by the Contadora Group and accepted by the Parties.

— A Latin American Executive Secretary, proposed by the Contadora Group and accepted by common agreement by the Parties, who shall be responsible for the ongoing operation of the Commission.

(b) Functions

For the performance of its functions, the Commission shall have an International Corps of Inspectors, provided by the member States of the Commission and co-ordinated by a Director of Operations.

The functions of the International Corps of Inspectors shall be established in the rules of procedure of the Commission.

— For the purpose of collaborating in the performance of the functions of the Commission, the latter shall have an Advisory Body consisting of one representative of each Central American State. . . .

II
WESTERN EUROPE

14.
EUROPEAN COMMUNITY: JOINT COMMUNIQUÉ AT STUTTGART (JUNE 1983)

The Heads of State and Government confirmed their close interest in developments in Central America. They are deeply concerned at the economic and social conditions in many parts of the region, at the tensions which these create and at the widespread misery and bloodshed.

They are convinced that the problems of Central America cannot be solved by military means, but only by a political solution springing from the region itself and respecting the principles of non-interference and inviolability of frontiers. They, therefore, fully support the current initiative of the Contadora Group. They underlined the need for the establishment of democratic conditions and for the strict observance of human rights throughout the region.

They are ready to continue contributing to the further development in the area, in order to promote progress towards stability.

15.
MINUTES OF A SECRET CAUCUS WITHIN THE SOCIALIST INTERNATIONAL (1982)

EUROPE IN RELATION TO LATIN AMERICA

a. There are sharp divisions among the European parties in their outlook on Latin America.

This strong statement was instigated by the Dutch. Four Dutch journalists were killed in El Salvador in 1982.

Those attending were the Sandinistas, Cuban Communist Party, Grenada New Jewel Movement, Salvadoran Revolutionary National Party, Chilean Radical Party, and Jamaican People's National Party. From *World Affairs*, Vol. 147, No. 1 (Summer 1984).

b. Our friends in this area are prepared to accept the Latin American Revolutionary process as being palatable if restricted to the Latin American context.

c. There is a great amount of misunderstanding about Latin America both among our friends and our enemies—some amount of fear and uncertainty.

d. Many of the European SI parties expect us to understand the concept of "the Soviet Menace."

e. Some European parties are concerned that, by the Latin American presence in SI, they have let in a [text missing]

f. Many European Parties are willing to hold discussions with us at levels which indicate the contradictions among themselves—the difference between Kryski [Bruno Kreisky, former Chancellor] of Austria and Braudl [Willy Brandt, President of the SI] of Germany on the PLO question.

g. Our strongest allies in Europe are the Nordic SI parties and that of Holland. There is also good potential with the UDP [New Democratic Party] of Canada.

h. Our principal enemies are to be found among the parties of Soares and Horgo [Pietro Longo, Secretary Italian Social Democratic Party] in Portugal and Italy respectively—the Social Democrats of the U.S.A. are also our sworn enemies.

i. The reason why the European parties did not allow WPA and PLP to get beyond the consultative membership status is because of their fear of the growth of membership with parties that they do not control.

j. A Mission to Europe comprising of our most trusted forces in Latin America and the Caribbean can be strategically valuable before the Sydney Congress. It can help to assure our friends and confuse our enemies.

16.
ALOIS MERTES: EUROPE'S ROLE IN CENTRAL AMERICA: A WEST GERMAN CHRISTIAN DEMOCRATIC VIEW (SPRING 1985)

In recent years, European critics of nuclear deterrence have also been critics of the United States' Central America policy and supporters of the Sandinistas and the Salvadoran guerrillas. Despite its influence in the media, however, this group represents a minority, at least in the Federal Republic of Germany.

From Andrew J. Pierre, ed., *Third World Instability: Central America as a European-American Issue* (New York: Council on Foreign Relations, 1985), pp. 106ff.

Central America's strategic location as a bridge between the North and South American continents, as well as between the Atlantic and the Pacific Oceans, makes the United States particularly sensitive to developments in this region. . . .

[I]n Europe . . . there is no uniform assessment on how best to deal with the economic, social and political developments in Central America . . . not only because of the pluralistic nature of public opinion-forming in our open societies, but also because assessments are made according to varying national experiences and political philosophies. . . .

It is somewhat irrelevant for policymakers to ask which aspect of the Central American case—North-South or East-West—is of greater importance. Whether in the United States or Europe, those who neglect either one of these aspects are on the wrong path: they disregard the legitimate concerns of the peoples in question; hinder the genuine nonalignment of Central America; and abet the Soviet Union's global strategy to the long-term detriment of the United States and Western Europe, as well as the rest of Latin America. It seems to me that with respect to the Central American case, the European socialist parties differ from the conservative, Christian Democratic, and (in the European sense) liberal parties in the same way that their answers diverge on two fundamental questions relating to disarmament and security in Europe: (1) Is Soviet foreign policy pursuing static-defensive or dynamic-expansionist aims?; and (2) How concerned should the West be about the Soviet buildup of its military capabilities and its quest for political allies outside its own sphere of influence?

Soviet global policy is determined by two clearly recognizable impulses:

—an insatiable notion of security, which views the free trade unions in Poland, the Dubček reforms in Czechoslovakia, the desire for freedom of the entire German people, and the common defense determination of Western Europe and the United States as threats; and

—a global-revolution ideology, which asserts that the world must become communist in order to be peaceful and just. Whether or not Soviet foreign policymakers are true believers in communism is of little relevance for they believe that "proletarian internationalism" and "active solidarity" with countries like Nicaragua and with guerrillas like those in El Salvador are important instruments in furthering Soviet influence and expanding Soviet power. . . .

Europe's essential solidarity with the United States is an act of self-preservation. Every manifestation of anti-Americanism in Europe, in failing to recognize the basic mutuality of the interests of the Western democracies and thereby weakening the trans-Atlantic relationship, is a boon to Soviet diplomacy.

The 1962 Cuban missile crisis made clear to Europe that a crisis of the security of the Western Hemisphere has direct repercussions for Europe.

Until now, the Soviet Union has not viewed Latin America—with the exception of Cuba, which is a special case—as a region in which it has special interests. But it lies within the logic of the Soviet Union's efforts to discredit and weaken the United States in Europe, the Middle East, and Latin America, as well as in Soviet ideological pretensions to systematically exploit every instability and crisis outside its own sphere of influence. In Central America it is obviously pursuing the goal of promoting sources of unrest on the U.S. southern flank. While Soviet actions in the region avoid a direct military provocation against the security of the United States, they are still politically virulent enough to divert U.S. vigilance away from Europe. A dissipation of U.S. strength with regard to Central America, combined with an intensification of the Central American debate within the United States itself, would be very convenient to the Soviet Union. . . .

In the dialogue between the Christian Democrats of Europe and Latin America, the theme "equidistance" from both superpowers plays an important role. The CDU and Christian Social Union have attempted to show their friends in Latin America how unacceptable it is for them to equate the USSR and the United States. While the Soviet Union tried twice to undermine the freedom of Berlin and suppressed all political and trade-union freedoms in its sphere of influence, the United States has for decades proved itself to be a reliable guarantor of the freedom of West Berlin, the Federal Republic of Germany and Western Europe. Christian Democrats and liberals in the FRG consider it wholly inappropriate to place the constitutionally democratic United States on a par with the totalitarian USSR At the same time, prominent Latin American politicians have said to me: particularly in Central America, we urgently need the United States —not only its economic strength, but also its deterrence capability to guard against all expansionist incursions. . . .

But, as these same persons emphasize, to say this openly would be detrimental to them domestically. . . .

As for the West European countries, their own credibility is at stake in Central America (and in the rest of Latin America as well) with respect to their being able to make independent political and material contributions to the elimination of economic and social injustice. Purely verbal declarations by Europeans do not help; they only lead to embittering the North Americans, disappointing the Central Americans, and encouraging the Cubans and Soviets. . . . the Central Americans and the Contadora nations expect a concrete European contribution. . . .

Europe's contribution should enable the Central American states to achieve the diversification they desire in their foreign policy and external economic relations. . . .

Highest priority must be given to avoiding positions and situations that would leave the United States no alternative but that either of losing credibility as the leading Western power or of resorting to a military intervention. We Europeans, in the interest of the indivisibility of the security of all members of the Atlantic Alliance, must do everything possible to prevent our chief ally from being put in such a position. Were Central America to distract the United States psychologically, politically or militarily from the focal point of the Soviet threat and of Western security—namely Europe—the consequences for the cohesion of the Atlantic Alliance would be incalculable. . . .

An important, specifically German contribution to European policy in Central America is the work of the foundations of four of the Federal Republic's major political parties—the CDU, CSU, SPD, and FDP (Free Democratic Party). These foundations try to find partners in Central American countries, particularly among political parties, trade unions and cooperatives. They also carry out projects financed by the Federal Ministry for Economic Cooperation. Their aim is to strengthen the parties at the center of the political spectrum in order to overcome the extreme polarization under which many Central American countries operate. . . .

I often hear, that Americans, due to inadequate historical and political knowledge of Europe, do not differentiate sufficiently between totalitarian communism and democratic socialism, and that it is particularly the latter that is so attractive to Central Americans. On the other hand, I must unfortunately conclude that young Europeans, lacking an appropriate knowledge of history since 1917, consider dogmatic Marxist revolutionaries to be democrats, and, by contrast, see Americans as sinister imperialists who are insensitive to the peoples of Central America.

In his book, *Del Buen Salvaje al Buen Revolucionario,* the Venezuelan Carlos Rangel Guevara accurately describes how many in Europe even today fall victim to the legend of the "noble savage," except that they now apply this image to the revolutionary, who is seen in a romantic light. They contrast the "realm of light" of revolution to the "realm of darkness of U.S. imperialism," the sole purported aim of which is to liquidate the Sandinista regime in Nicaragua and to completely reestablish the hegemony it formerly held over Central America.

Judicious simplifications are necessary in politics in order to make things clearer to millions of people who are unable to grasp the multilayered complexities of political problems and yet who want to know from those in charge "what it's all about." But let us beware, both in Europe and America, of the *terribles simplificateurs,* especially when they presume to judge others. In an alliance that is so vital to the world, to pose as a self-righteous judge does not help; rather to act as an understanding friend, who shares the same problems, does.

17.
COMMON MARKET: ACCORD WITH CENTRAL
AMERICAN STATES (SEPTEMBER 1984)

. . . **6.** The Ministers reaffirmed their commitment to the objectives of peace, democracy, security and economic and social development, and political stability in Central America and were united in the view that the problems of that region cannot be solved by armed force, but only by political solutions springing from the region itself. In this conviction they affirmed their support for the pacification measures which are being developed in the Contadora process. They expressed their conviction that this process represents a genuinely regional initiative and the best opportunity to achieve a solution to the crisis through political undertaking aimed at the achievement of the aims set out in the "document of objectives" approved by all the Governments of the region on 9 September 1983. They noted with satisfaction the progress achieved so far towards such a solution, and that the revised draft Contadora Act for Peace and Cooperation in Central America is a fundamental stage in the negiotiating process for the attainment of peace in the region. They called on the States concerned to continue to make every effort to bring the Contadora process rapidly to final fruition through the signature of a comprehensive agreement which would bring peace to the region. They were agreed on the necessity for a practical commitment to the implementation of any such agreement by all the states in the region and all other countries which have interests there. . . .

15. Taking account of the importance of economic development for the countries of the Central American region, the Community will do everything possible, within the context of its present and future programs in support of developing countries, towards the development of the region. These actions should be identified by common agreement, based on the priorities and objectives of the region and should be multilateral in character. The Community declared itself willing to exploit to the full the institutional infrastructure existing in the region.

In addition to aid given on a bilateral basis by Member States of the Community to the countries of the region, the Community will provide

Joint Communiqué of Foreign Ministers' Conference in San José, Costa Rica; comments by Edgard Pisani, speaking as the representative of the Common Market Commission, September 29, 1984.

technical and financial assistance to Central America, in particular for agricultural, agro-industrial and rural projects. With the aim of promoting regional economic integration and the development of intra-regional trade, it is the intention of the Community to give priority assistance to projects of a regional nature and to help the countries of Central America and their regional institutions through sharing with them the Community's specific experience acquired in matters of integration. . . .

Mr. Edgard Pisani, Member of the Common Market Commission, stated:

The presence of 12 European Ministers and a European Commissioner will take on its true significance only if the countries of Central America adopt clearly and irrevocably a pact of the same type and spirit, and with the same democratic basis, as that adopted by the European countries themselves. For there can be no doubt that it is only if this Central American solidarity asserts and organizes itself that the danger of external intervention feared by all can really be removed. It is by progressively building up a system of mutual security and support that Central America will be able to render impossible, and above all pointless, any external intervention. . . .

Moreover, it is when the common market of the five countries of Central America is revived and thriving politically, that the European Community will be able to demonstrate its support most naturally and start making its unique experience available. . . .

We can do nothing for you unless you make the necessary effort yourselves, but as soon as you do so we will be there to back you up. The Community institutions, in particular the Commission, are standing by.

First of all, the Community can help promote your countries' products both on its own market and on the world market. In spite of what people say about it, the Common Market remains the biggest importer in the world, because it is the most liberal . . . , but you must be helped to gain a place which you do not yet have. . . .

Should this idea be taken further? Should your products be granted more generous tariff facilities than apply to them at present? We do not think so. This is not a matter of principle, but the arrangements applied to you are already favourable, and any tariff improvements, if they are indeed possible, would not really improve trade, as the problem between yourselves and us is not basically about tariffs, but trade. . . . Naturally, it will be through its firms that Europe will make its presence felt. We can encourage them and even design a specific guarantee system for private investment in this area. But development requires financial support of a special kind. . . .

Europe knows what you expect of it and what contribution it can make towards greater equilibrium in the region. It also knows whence you hail, the idea which drives and unites you through the vicissitudes of history. This Central American identity which you are striving to assert today is your business, your responsibility. But today Europe declares itself willing to work alongside you in order to turn a necessity into a reality. . . .

III
THE USSR AND CUBA

18.
CIA: CUBAN SUPPORT FOR CENTRAL AMERICAN GUERILLA GROUPS (MAY 1979)

MEMORANDUM

May 2, 1979.

SUBJECT: Cuban Support for Central American Guerrilla Groups.

KEY JUDGMENTS

The Castro regime apparently concluded by at least last fall the prospects for revolutionary upheaval in Central America over the next decade or so had markedly improved largely because of the weakened position of Nicaragua's Somoza and the ripple effect his removal would have on other countries in Central America. As a result Cuba has intensified its attempts to unify insurgent groups not only in Nicaragua—where Cuba has concentrated its efforts—but in Guatemala and El Salvador as well.

While tailoring the extent of its support to the realities of the situation in each country, Cuba has stepped up its on-island training of guerrillas from each of these countries and—in the case of Nicaragua—has on at least two and probably three occasions supplied arms—for the first time in many years—to the Sandinista National Liberation Front (FSLN). Cuba has also made a concerted effort to persuade leftist movements and parties in the region to increase their assistance to the FSLN and has used these groups to funnel aid to the Sandinistas.

Havana's approach to events in Central America, however, reflects a far more sophisticated and selective revolutionary doctrine than that which guided Cuba's actions during the 1960s. Cuba clearly believes it has a stake

From *Congressional Record,* May 19, 1980.

in preserving its improving image with many governments in the hemisphere and wants to avoid provoking a U.S. counterresponse. As a result, Cuba has used third country intermediaries to deliver its assistance to the Sandinistas and has taken care that its aid not differ in kind from the material support suplied to the FSLN by several other governments in the region.

While optimistic that trends in Central America favor the left, Havana has counseled patience and has urged its friends to prepare for a protracted struggle, even in Nicaragua. Cuba support, therefore, can be expected to continue to be geared toward helping the Sandinistas and other regional guerrilla groups develop the military and political infrastructure necessary to win a war of attrition, and the widespread grass roots support necessary to consolidate the victory.

Given the low-key approach Cuba has employed in Central America, Havana is likely to do its best to avoid being placed in a situation where it might be called upon to intervene directly with its own military units and thus risk a military confrontation with the U.S. . . .

As Somoza's position appeared to grow shakier last year, Havana intensified its effort to strengthen his opponents by urging unity among the various Sandinista National Liberation Front (FSLN) factions. By early fall Cuba was sufficiently satisfied that this had been accomplished to increase significantly its support to the Sandinistas. . . .

Reporting from several sources indicates that in late September Cuba shipped eight crates of arms—including .50-caliber machine guns designed to serve as an anti-aircraft weapon—to Panama via a Panamanian air force plane for later transshipment to FSLN forces in Costa Rica. . . .

According to a reliable source, during the week of 5–11 November three Panamanian air force planes returned to Panama from Cuba carrying crates that contained AK-47 rifles, .50-caliber machine guns, and hand-held mortars. By the end of the month the Panamanians had flown these arms to Liberia, Costa Rica, where they were given to the FSLN.

Circumstantial evidence indicates that the Cubans were involved in the recent reactivation of the Panama–Costa Rica resupply route to the FSLN. Members of the FSLN "General Staff" reportedly stated at a meeting on 13 April that their inventory included an undisclosed number of antitank rockets of Soviet and French manufacture that Cuba had provided via Panama. Although the "General Staff" members did not specify when Cuba had supplied the arms, other information indicates that Panama delivered arms to FSLN forces in Costa Rica about the time of the meeting. . . .

Training in Cuba of FSLN guerrillas—which has continued at low levels for years—has apparently been on the upswing, especially since January. Early that month a Panamanian emissary reached an agreement with Fidel

Castro to send to Cuba FSLN exiles who formerly would have been granted safe haven in Panama. On 10 March a subordinate of Noriega's said that Panama is serving as a bridge to transport FSLN personnel to Cuba, where they undergo training before returning to Nicaragua.

Evidence on the total number of FSLN guerrillas who have received training in Cuba is spotty. Members of the FSLN "General Staff" reportedly said on 13 April that Cuba has trained 300 of the FSLN combatants currently in the field. In early April an official of the FSLN Terciario faction reportedly said that half of his faction's regular combatants have received training in Cuba.

. . . The Cubans in early February promoted a meeting in San José, Costa Rica, that was attended by the Communist parties from the Central American countries as well as from Mexico and Panama. Cuban delegates used the occasion to urge their counterparts to bolster their assistance to the FSLN by creating safe havens in their countries, providing facilities for military training, and supplying arms and other equipment. Plans were also discussed for a follow-up meeting later this spring probably in Havana that would prepare a strategy for assisting revolutionary activity throughout Central America.

. . . Late last summer at Havana's direction the Honduran Communist Party established a support apparat that has been responsible for finding sites in Honduras to train FSLN guerrillas. The apparat has relied on sporadic Cuban financial aid to purchase arms, radios, and other equipment for the FSLN, and Honduran Communists have assisted the Sandinistas in border crossings. . . .

Cuba reportedly also funnels assistance to the FSLN through two groups in Costa Rica. A member of the Central Committee of the Costa Rican Communist party—the Popular Vanguard Party—said in early March that Cuba had begun to channel limited financial assistance to the FSLN through his party. The Cubans may also be helping to fund a "Committee of Solidarity with the Sandinista Front" headed by self-professed FSLN member Ernesto Cardenal, a Nicaraguan priest who resides in Costa Rica. . . .

In early March, leaders of the three major FSLN factions traveled to Cuba to meet with Castro. The Cuban leader is said to have spent nearly 48 hours over a four-day period helping to hammer out a basis for cooperation. As a result of the meeting a unified FSLN directorate was established containing three members from each faction. In return, Castro reportedly promised that Cuba would increase its assistance in the form of money, arms, and ammunition. Havana has repeatedly urged leaders of the disparate Sandinista factions to cooperate in a unified effort against Somoza; their failure to do so has been a major deterrent to increased Cuban assistance. . . .

Castro . . . in early December . . . reportedly urged two Terciario leaders to abandon plans for a large scale military offensive because he did not believe that the FSLN had the necessary logistical and organizational capability to sustain conventional operations against the Guard. Moreover, in mid-January two diplomats assigned to the Cuban embassy in Panama stated that Cuba no longer believed the the FSLN would be able to topple Somoza before his term expires in 1981.

Cuban support, therefore is likely to continue to be intended to help the Sandinistas develop the military and political infrastructure necessary to triumph in a war of attrition. The Cubans probably expect that—as was the case with the Batista army—popular sentiment will gradually turn against the National Guard and eventually render it ineffective. . . .

The Cubans have urged the Sandinistas to combine their efforts to intensify the guerrilla struggle with a highly pragmatic political approach designed to broaden the FSLN's base of popular support for a movement to oust Somoza. For example, during Castro's meeting with FSLN leaders in March, he reportedly urged them to play down the Marxist nature of their programs at this point and to offer to join with non-Marxists in forging a broad coalition. FSLN leaders have taken steps to comply with his request.

Given the low-key approach Cuba has pursued regarding the Nicaraguan situation, it is likely that Havana will do its best to avoid being placed in a situation where it might be called upon to intervene directly with Cuban military units. . . .

Cuban contacts with Guatemalan leftists have also increased in recent months. The main thrust of Cuban policy at this point—as it has been for several years—is to encourage the various insurgent groups to join together in a common effort to undermine the government. . . .

Havana's closest links are to the Guerrilla Army of the Poor (EGP), and the Cubans used it as a hub to broaden their ties with other insurgent groups. According to a reliable Guatemalan source, on 12 January a Cuban official met in Guatemala with leaders of the EGP, the Rebel Armed Forces (FAR), and the dissident wing of the Guatemalan Communist Party (PGT) to urge these three action-oriented groups to unify. The Cuban official counseled them to coordinate plans of actions, to integrate training of their respective members, and to make a greater effort to infiltrate labor movements. Stressing the importance of a united front, he implied that if the three groups improved their level of cooperation then Cuba would provide financial and material assistance.

According to the same Guatemalan source, in later January a follow-up meeting was held in which two Cuban advisers offered to provide training in Cuba for PGT dissidents and FAR members. For some years the Cubans have trained EGP guerrillas in Cuba, and—impressed with that group's initial success in recruiting members of Guatemalan Indian population—Havana began early this year to train some of these recruits. The Cubans may also plan to train members of a new guerrilla group, which is located in western Guatemala and led by Rodrigo Asturias, a former FAR member. Asturias reportedly has visited Cuba on several occasions and his group was invited to attend Cuba's revolutionary celebrations in January.

There is some evidence to suggest that the Cubans may be willing to take a more direct role in counseling Guatemalan insurgents. According to a reliable source, in late February representatives of the EGP offered the services of three Cuban "experts" to work in Guatemala with the FAR and PGT dissidents to "coordinate" the assassinations of several government security officials. The source said that some Guatemalan insurgent leaders opposed this plan, and we have no evidence to confirm that the Cuban have attempted to follow through on the reported offer. . . .

The Cubans have . . . worked hard to encourage the orthodox faction of the Guatemalan Communist Party (PGT) to lend its support to local insurgent groups. In early January Ricardo Rosales, the Secretary-General of the PGT, visited Cuba, where he met with Vice President for Foreign Affairs Carlos Rafael Rodríguez—who speaks for a group within the Cuban leadership that tends to take a softer line on the primacy of guerrilla warefare. Rodríguez blamed divisions among the PGT, the EGP, and the FAR for weakening the Guatemalan revolutionary effort and asked Rosales to coordinate his party's activities with those of the insurgents. Stating that he agreed with the PGT's promotion of the peaceful route to power by organizing the workers and students and by participating in elections, Rodríguez also emphasized the need for Guatemalan leftists to employ all form of activity to achieve a successful revolution.

The Cubans clearly feel no urgency in promoting revolutionary activity in Guatemala; rather, their efforts seem designed to prepare local insurgent groups for the long haul. At the meeting in Guatemala City in late January the Cubans reportedly urged the EGP, FAR, and PGT dissidents to have patience and not expect immediate progress in the struggle against the government. The nature of Cuban training of Guatemalan guerrillas also reflects a lack of urgency. For example, according to an EGP document captured in January 1978, members of guerrilla teams who are trained in Cuba live and work together for as long as a year before reentering Guatemala, to ensure that they will be able to cooperate effectively once they are in the field. . . .

Cuban activities with Salvadoran insurgents have recently been on the upswing. The Castro regime's interest in El Salvador has doubtless quickened as it has observed the spiraling violence and growing political polarization there, and Cuba's willingness to lend support has presumably increased because of the demonstrated willingness of the various guerrilla groups to cooperate in at least an informal alliance.

In February an untested Salvadoran source reported that about 60 members of the military army of the Popular Liberation Forces (FPL)—the group with which Cuba has maintained the closest ties—were in Cuba receiving four months of military and ideological training. The source said that upon returning to El Salvador these guerrillas were slated to serve as leaders for a force of 2,000 newly trained Salvadorans representing the "Popular Militia" of the FPL-dominated Popular Revolutionary Bloc. By late March, half of the FPL guerrillas sent to Cuba had returned home and were working with units of the "Popular Militia."

Cuba has also had links with at least one of the two smaller Salvadoran terrorist groups, the Armed Forces of the National Resistance (FARN). Eduardo Sancho Castaneda—reportedly the FARN's leading strategist—has apparently been his organization's chief conduit to the Cubans. He has maintained regular contact with Cuban officials in Costa Rica and Mexico and has occasionally traveled to Cuba.

For some time the Cubans have also been pushing for greater cooperation between the El Salvadoran Communist Party and the various insurgent groups. For example, in October 1977 Raul García Pelaes—at that time the member of the Secretariat of the Cuban Communist Party in charge of relations with foreign Communist Parties—reportedly said that Cuba was trying to promote the unification of the El Salvadoran Communist Party and the Popular Liberation Forces and to induce the Communists to adopt a policy of open insurrection against the government. Personal antipathy between the leaders of the FPL and the local Communist Party, as well as disagreements regarding the means and timing of staging a revolution in El Salvador, have continued to prevent any meaningful cooperation between these two groups, however.

19.
SERGEI MIKOYAN: THE PARTICULARITIES OF THE NICARAGUAN REVOLUTION (1980)

There is no doubt that the Nicaraguan Revolution is one of those events that compel us to reexamine and abandon certain preconceptions but it also allows us to prepare for the central tasks presented by reality. Although the saying that "the new is only something old and long-forgotten" rarely contains a grain of truth, in this case, everyone agrees on one thing:

América Latina, 3 (1980).

the victory of Nicaragua's patriots has colossal international importance. . . .

We have carried out a serious and comprehensive analysis of everything
new that this victory contributes to the treasures of revolutionary theory
and practice. . . .

For the fourth time in the course of the twentieth century (Mexico,
1910–1917; Bolivia, 1952; Cuba, 1959; Nicaragua, 1979) and the second
time over the last two decades, an armed people have defeated an oligarch-
ical regime and the domination of the most reactionary elements of society.

In addition to this, there is not a single example of a victorious revolution
on the continent that has been achieved by the peaceful road (there are only
the successful, peaceful forms of evolutionary development). In a number
of countries where patriotic military governments took power (Peru, Panama, etc.), there was no bloodshed, but there was action by the armed
forces, a fact that puts these events also in the category of armed action.

In view of this we can draw a clear conclusion: until now only the armed
road has led to the triumph of the revolution in Latin America. And the
experience of Nicaragua confirms the notion that, after the death of Che
Guevara and the defeat of a series of other guerrilla movements, some
people used to consider this idea had been refuted.

Nevertheless, it would be inappropriate to make this conclusion absolute; that is, to apply it to all countries, ignoring their peculiarities and
without taking into account different stages in their development.

20.
JOINT NICARAGUAN-SOVIET COMMUNIQUÉ (MARCH 1980)

A delegation of the Republic of Nicaragua's Government of National
Reconstruction and the Sandinist National Liberation Front (SNLF)
headed by Moses Hassan Morales, member of the Governing Council of
the Government of National Reconstruction, and Tomás Borge Martínez,
Henry Ruiz Hernández and Humberto Ortega Saavedra, members of the
SNFL's national leadership, was in the Soviet Union March 17 through
22 on an official friendly visit at the invitation of the CPSU Central Committee and the Soviet government. . . .

Soviet-Nicaraguan talks were held. A. P. Kirilenko, member of the

From *Pravda,* March 23, 1980, p.4, in *Current Digest of the Soviet Press* 32:12, pp.
10–11.

Politburo and Secretary of the CPSU Central Committee; B. N. Ponomarev, candidate member of the Politburo and Secretary of the CPSU Central
Committee; I. V. Arkhipov, Vice-Chairman of the USSR Council of Ministers; and G. M. Korniyenko, USSR First Deputy Minister of Foreign
Affairs, took part in the talks on the Soviet side. . . .

Both sides agreed to develop bilateral relations on the basis of a strict
observance of the principles of equality, sovereignty, mutual respect and
noninterference in each other's internal affairs.

The Soviet Union and Nicaragua agreed on practical steps for establishing trade and economic ties with a view to the capabilities and needs of both
countries' economies.

A trade agreement, a protocol on the establishment of a USSR trade
mission in the Republic of Nicaragua and a trade mission of the Republic
of Nicaragua in the USSR, a protocol on deliveries of goods, an agreement
on economic and technical cooperation, an agreement on cultural and
scientific cooperation, a consular convention, an agreement on air travel
between the two countries, and an agreement on cooperation in the area
of planning were signed between the USSR and Nicaragua during the visit.

Participants in the talks noted with satisfaction that they held common
views on the most important international problems. . . .

The Soviet Union and Nicaragua believe that the total elimination of the
practice of hegemonism from international relations is an extremely important area of the struggle for lasting peace and international security. They
also condemn attempts by some states to dominate others by arbitrarily
declaring entire regions of the world to be spheres of their "vital interests"
and by exerting direct military, political and economic pressure. . . .

Both sides reaffirm their support for the idea of creating nuclear-free
zones in various regions of the world, and they regard them as one means
of strengthening the nonproliferation of nuclear arms, achieving regional
military detente, and reducing the threat of nuclear war. They support the
strict observance of Latin America's status as a nuclear-free zone. . . .

Both sides favor the firm establishment of the principles of equality,
respect for sovereignty and territorial integrity, and repudiation of the use
of force or threat of force in relations among states in both Latin America
and other regions of the world. The USSR and Nicaragua resolutely condemn the imperialistic policy of interference in the internal affairs of the
Latin American peoples. Both sides oppose the preservation of colonial
ownership in the Western Hemisphere. They resolutely condemn the fascist dictatorship in Chile. . . .

The Soviet Union and Nicaragua resolutely condemn the campaign that
the imperialist and reactionary forces have launched of building up international tension in connection with events in Afghanistan, a campaign
aimed at subverting the inalienable right of the people of the Democratic

Republic of Afghanistan and other peoples of the world to follow the path of progressive transformations.

Both sides declare their solidarity with the Iranian people's struggle for their country's political and economic independence. They resolutely condemn any and all forms of pressure and threats against the Islamic Republic of Iran.

The Soviet Union and Nicaragua resolutely condemn the policy of building up tension in Southeast Asia, and they demand an end to threats, blackmail and provocations, whatever their source, against the Socialist Republic of Vietnam, the Lao People's Democratic Republic and the People's Republic of Kampuchea, and an end to interference in these countries' internal affairs. The sides declare their support for the just struggle of the peoples of Vietnam, Laos and Kampuchea for the strengthening of their independence and for the right to build a new life in conditions of peace and security. . . .

The Soviet and Nicaraguan representatives discussed the questions of friendly ties between the CPSU and the SNLF. They expressed a mutual desire to develop these ties in the interest of further deepening bilateral cooperation between the Soviet Union and Nicaragua for the good of the Soviet and Nicaraguan peoples and for the good of peace and social progress. A plan for ties between the CPSU and the SNLF in 1980–1981 was signed. . . .

An agreement on cooperation, in the area of planning, between the USSR State Planning Committee and the Republic of Nicaragua's Ministry of Planning was signed March 22 in Moscow. . . .

21.
PRESIDENT FIDEL CASTRO: SPEECH IN MANAGUA ON THE FIRST ANNIVERSARY OF THE REVOLUTION (JULY 1980)

Comrade leaders of the Sandinist National Liberation Front (FSLN) and of the Government of National Reconstruction, distinguished invited delegations and personalities, courageous Sandinist soldiers and militamen, dear Nicaraguan brothers: Some will perhaps think that I am going to make . . . an ardent and revolutionary harangue. But . . . It would not be proper for me not to take into consideration the fact already noted by former President Carlos Andrés Pérez of the presence on this platform of

From Havana Domestic Service, July 19, 1980, in *FBIS: Latin America,* July 21, 1980.

delegations and personalities from the most diverse countries, of the most diverse systems and ideologies, of the most diverse political beliefs.

However, there is something that unites us all. I would even say North Americans and we are united today and that is because of this event, this tribute and this recognition to the heroic Nicaraguan people and their historic victory of 19 July 1979. . . . I will not hide the fact that deep emotion overwhelmed me yesterday at noon when I arrived in this country. . . .

Today, I have felt the magnitude of this event, the martialism of the troops, the organization, the discipline, the impressive silence in this plaza where not even the buzzing of a mosquito is heard. . . . We could not forget our sister republic because it was precisely Nicaraguan territory, Puerto Cabezas, from which the mercenary Girón invasion departed. It has been said that the tyrant Somoza, when bidding farewell to the troops, asked them to at least bring him a hair from Castro's beard. I have come here with a full beard to offer it to the victorious Nicaraguan people, even if only symbolically.

The embrace with which our delegation and the front and government leaders greeted each other yesterday is only a symbol of these times, and of the changes of these times. When I observe you here, I must confess, it reminds us a lot of our people, our own people, our own events, our own masses. Because you are a profoundly revolutionary people, we the Cuban visitors feel as if we were in our own fatherland. . . .

The page of heroism written by you will be recorded in history. But this spirit, this heroism was not by chance. Over a period of many years Sandino fought in defense of the fatherland's independence and showed the path to be followed. The Sandinists fought for 20 years to overthrow the tyranny and set free their people. This took 20 years. That is why on a day like today the heroes cannot be forgotten, the leaders cannot be forgotten. The extraordinary merits of that indefatigable fighter Fonseca Amador will never be forgotten.

There were men who from very far away saw and prepared the path. . . . But there were men who, when the hour of liberty appeared to be the farthest away, thought, organized and prepared a strategy of struggle. Those men are the Sandinists and the members of the Government of National Reconstruction. They prepared the strategy. They prepared the tactics of struggle and gradually improved them. They were able to lead all the people. They are not vanguards because they want to call themselves vanguards. They are vanguards because they knew how to gain the place of vanguards in history and in the struggle of their people. And they were wise. Here we have them. They were wise. They were wise in the struggle and in the decisive moment of the struggle. They had the supreme wisdom of unity. That unity, as you have seen, is greater today than ever before.

They were wise in the struggle and they were wise in victory. They have continued to be wise throughout this first year because, in our judgment, the scheme prepared by the FSLN for the period of national reconstruction, that call, that appeal to all the people, that appeal to the various social sectors to rebuild the country, that scheme which includes pluralism and opposition is one of the wisest things that could have been done by any political movement under these circumstances. We are not saying this only now. Almost a year ago on 26 July 1979, when, a few days after victory, we received a large and prestigious Sandinist delegation on our anniversary, we said that Nicaraguans had all our sympathy and all our support for that project, that concept. There are many who harbored and still harbor fears about the Sandinist revolution. There are some who presume to tell the Sandinists what to do. We will never presume to tell the Sandinists what they should do, giving and offering them uncalled-for advice.

We are ready to give all our support, all the solidarity of our people without any conditions—without any conditions—and without any advice. And we are not here to teach or influence. We are here to humbly learn and to be influenced. And we are certain that the Sandinist revolution will teach us many things. That the Sandinist revolution will influence us greatly, just as we are certain that its example will greatly influence the rest of Latin America.

I have deliberately refrained from mentioning names that you and us Cubans carry deep in our hearts, and we have not mentioned conflictive matters because of the reasons I mentioned at the beginning, so that no one would accuse us of coming to Nicaragua to try to set Central America on fire or to try to set Latin America on fire. It is impossible to bring the torch of the revolution. As one of you said recently, your best, most fundamental and decisive aid to the revolutionary movement is your example. Because peoples are like volcanoes. No one inflames them. They erupt by themselves, and the mountain ranges of Central America and the Andes are volcanic.

Dear Nicaraguan brothers, what you have done in a single year is impressive. What you have done in all areas, including the very difficult area of the economy, is impressive. . . . What other country has done so much in so little time, in the first year? What other country has been able to organize a disciplined, martial army as this one in just the first year?

But despite all these impressive things . . . it pains us to see that now, a year later, the effective aid received to date by Nicaragua is only some tens of millions of dollars. We proposed almost a year ago that an emulation among all the countries was needed to see which helped Nicaragua the most. We take advantage of this occasion, this anniversary, to reiterate this challenge and to appeal for that emulation to assist Nicaragua.

These noble people need that aid, and they deserve that aid. We hail cooperation with Nicaragua regardless of its source. We even hail the aid the U.S. Government is reportedly to give. I only truly and sincerely regret that it is too little considering the wealth of the United States. It is a small amount for the richest country in the world. It is a small amount for a country that spends $160 billion on military expenditures, for a country that according to estimates is going to spend $1 trillion in the next 5 years on military things. How much more fruitful and beneficial it would be if those useless expenditures, those expenditures for the arms race, were to be used to help the underdeveloped countries of the world, were used to help countries that need so much, such as Nicaragua.

The experts, statesmen, economists and analysts know what the real problem in the world is at this time. . . .

Concern is very deep all over the world, among the most serious and sensible people in the world, especially after hearing the agreements and platform of the U.S. Republican Party—a terrible platform that is a threat to peace. A terrible platform that threatens to apply once more the big stick to Latin America. A terrible platform that speaks of reversing as much as possible the Panama Canal accords; that speaks of annexing the brother Puerto Rican people; that speaks of backing this hemisphere's genocidal governments; and that speaks of withdrawing all aid to Nicaragua. The concern is great all over the world, and that is why it behooves all to do everything within our reach to confront those policies and to fight to safeguard peace. We find ourselves in a situation such that we have to practically fight to safeguard peace. This is the situation at present in the world. . . .

22.
JORGE SHAFIK HANDAL: THE ONLY WAY . . . IS ARMED REVOLUTION (JANUARY 1980)

The fact that there are victims of the repression, that there are dozens of people machinegunned to death in the streets of San Salvador during peaceful demonstrations is really not news. What is news is that this new massacre has occurred after the establishment of a second reformist government in which the Christian Democratic Party takes part and after a huge international publicity campaign has been made regarding this gov-

From Radio Havana, January 29, 1980, Feb. 7, 1980, No. 75086, pp. 137–138.

ernment. This shows what is occurring in El Salvador. This highlights the truth that the Salvadoran revolutionaries have repeated so many times. We have stressed that the only way to truly end repression, to achieve the peace to which the Salvadoran people have a right, the only way to achieve this, the only path to achieve this is armed revolution. It is the overthrow of this reactionary power which is the instrument of the oligarchy and imperialism, of this old military dictatorship which has lasted half a century. It is the destruction of its repressive machinery which has been constantly used against the Salvadoran people during the past 50 years. It is the establishment of a new power truly based on the people's will and headed by a truly democratic and revolutionary government capable of undertaking changes in this society and of establishing freedoms and improving the lives of the Salvadoran people who are above all hard-working. [End recording]

PART TWO

PA300247 HAVANA INTERNATIONAL SERVICE IN SPANISH 0000 GMT 30 JAN 80 PA

[Text] Here is the second part of an interview with Jorge Shafik Handal, secretary general of the Communist Party of El Salvador [PCES]. This interview was held somewhere in El Salvador by a Latin American newsman and it reached Radio Havana through friendly hands. Here is Jorge Shafik Handal referring to the current political situation in El Salvador and the Salvadoran revolutionaries' view regarding the reformists and the militarymen:

[Begin recording] We do not doubt that there are still reformists in our country who honestly believe in the path of reforms despite the fact that a first attempt at this failed and that most of the reformists have decided to firmly march alongside the revolutionary movement—alongside the largest revolutionary masses of El Salvador. I say this despite the fact that the great majority of the reformists of the various political and social sectors have already made that decision following the experience with the first reformist government which began with the 15 October coup and which resigned late last year and early this year. We do not doubt that the few reformists who still support the path of reforms are honest. We believe that they too will soon understand that our path is the path of the Salvadoran people. I am specifically referring in this case to the Christian Democrats. We have traveled together many years. We know each other well. That is why I can state what I am saying. Most of the masses of the Christian Democratic Party are participating in the vast popular revolutionary movement. Among the 150,000 people in the demonstration [on 22 January] there were surely thousands of Christian Democrats. We hope that those Christian Democrats who are leaders of their party or who hold government posts will know how to react.

We also do not doubt that there are military men who support the reformist path. These do not include those who are maneuvering, such as Defense Minister Colonel García, the chiefs of the repressive agencies and many others who are used to repression and who continue to hold commands in the army, particularly in the security forces. There are still many members of the army who support a reformist path. We believe in their good faith and in their good intentions. We also believe that they are going to react.

Despite the constant propaganda against us and the constant warnings of the reactionary chiefs that the revolutionaries want to physically and morally destroy the militarymen, I think that at this stage those honest, patriotic and well-intentioned members of the army know that when we revolutionaries say they have an assured place alongside the Salvadoran people if they adopt the correct and opportune positions, we are saying the truth. This is clear to us; it is clear to the Salvadoran people and I think it is also clear to them. The revolution in our country is going to be successful. This will occur even if these militarymen to whom I referred do not decide to take the correct path because of blindness or confusion. When we say that the revolution is going to be victorious here despite all the difficulties and against all enemies we are basing our statement on that proven spirit, determination and heroic attitude of the working masses of our country. The Salvadoran people currently need great international solidarity, support and understanding. Our country is ripe for the revolution. [End recording]

23.
PRAVDA: ON THE FINAL OFFENSIVE (DECEMBER 1980)

Reports are coming in from El Salvador that detachments of the Farabundo Martí National Liberation Front have begun a major offensive. Particularly fierce fighting between the insurgents and the junta forces has developed in the north of the country. The patriots' offensive is gathering strength. The liberation struggle of El Salvador's people is entering a new phase. We are faced with yet further evidence that the sociopolitical crisis

Pravda, "El Salvador: The Struggle Sharpens," Dec. 30, 1980, in *FBIS: Soviet Union,* Jan. 5, 1981, p. K19.

in Central America has become extremely acute. In its attempts to reverse the inexorable development of this process the United States is using every means. Special attention is being paid to El Salvador, which occupies an important strategic position in the region.

The Salvadoran military junta's treasury is forever being filled thanks to American financial aid. In 1980 alone the injections have topped $95 million. In view of the increased scale of the violence in El Salvador Washington made an abortive propaganda gesture: It suspended economic and military aid to the junta. But just a fortnight later the State Department announced the "immediate resumption" of the aid program for El Salvador, under which the country will get another $20 million before the end of this year. Of course, the United States is not confining itself to merely financing the junta. The weapons Salvadoran reaction is using to kill patriots are also American.

The attempts by certain American press organs to make out that the genocide is being implemented only by extreme rightwing Salvadoran forces are futile. What are the 200 American military specialists in the country doing? Isn't it on the "advice" that villages are burned, napalm is used and poisonous herbicides and defoliants are sprayed? Is it without their knowledge that aircraft and tanks are being used against the peaceful population? And it is not for nothing that the *Wall Street Journal* for 9 December made the characteristic admission: "The Carter administration is the junta's main supporter." But the atrocities of the punitive detachments are not achieving their aim, despite comprehensive assistance from their Washington patrons. The process of the unification of El Salvador's revolutionary, progressive forces is increasing. The Salvadoran people's strengthening unity is personified by the Farabundo Martí National Liberation Front, which unites the military-political progressive organizations, and the Revolutionary Democratic Front, which represents the broad democratic and patriotic forces. The National Liberation Front recently called on El Salvador's patriots to stage a general uprising and to create a revolutionary democratic government. It is to these forces that the future of suffering El Salvador belongs.

24.
COMMUNIST PARTY OF THE SOVIET UNION: SECRET LETTER TO THE FMLN (SUMMER 1980)

TO THE FARABUNDO MARTÍ NATIONAL LIBERATION FRONT (FMLN)
COMRADES:

We must write you on some pending international problems. The bilateral struggle in the international arena has become more acute and tense. The current North American government has done everything within its power to eliminate socialist countries, the working class, workers of capitalist countries, and liberation movements; assuming that it can achieve change regionally and globally in favor of imperialism.

As a countermeasure to this line of action the Communist Party of the Soviet Union (CPSU) has increased its efforts not only to diminish the military hazard produced by U.S. imperialist ambitions, but also to clear the road toward the solution of major international problems in the interest of the people. This is the motivating force behind the latest Soviet peace initiatives and comrade Leonid Brezhnev's message to the second special session of the UN's General Assembly. Therefore, we call on you, specifically because of the imperialist media propaganda, which is meant to undermine our initiative, or distort its true meaning. . . .

Now we must take advantage of the new possibilities, focus the efforts of those who are willing to take a stance against the hazardous course of war mongers. . . .

The "crusade" announced by Reagan is not a slogan, but a reality. This is a massive counter-offensive strategy using all methods against the International Communist Movement, against true socialism, against the revolutionary and democratic parties and organizations, against the world-wide anti-militarist coalition, now reaching new levels of political influence and prestige. In this situation the Soviet Communist Party proposes as a top priority the following tasks:

- Raising everyone's consciousness about the catastrophic consequences of nuclear war;
- Explaining the causes of growing international tension and unmasking the aggressive force of imperialism;
- Pointing out concrete approaches to stop the arms race, reduce the military threat, and clarify the socialist countries' foreign policy;

- Actively countering the intentions of military circles directed against the anti-war and anti-missile movement with the aid of anti-Soviet propaganda and lies about "the Soviet military threat";
- Developing peace-keeping solidarity efforts and explaining the need for dialogue and coordination between the different currents and movements.

It is obvious that success can be achieved carrying out a campaign not against imperialism in general, but against U.S. imperialism, against the policies of the United States government, which threatens to end the existence of humanity and is the main enemy of peace and of social progress.

We must act now. An unimaginable threat looms over the world. The responsibility and relevance of all progressive parties and organizations is on the rise, as is the meaning of their actions, their initiatives, their mutual understanding, and their cohesion.

Cordially yours,
The Central Communist Party of the Soviet Union.

25.
HUMBERTO ORTEGA, NICARAGUAN DEFENSE MINISTER: SPEECH TO A CLOSED SESSION OF ARMY SPECIALISTS (AUGUST 1981)

... our internal class enemies, imperialism in general, and the United States in particular, have not accepted, nor will they accept the defeat that our victory signified for them in their principal strategic salient: Latin America.

North American imperialism, our internal class enemies, the traitorous bourgeoisie, the reactionary clergy, the bourgeois political parties like the MDN, the right wing organizations and other reactionary and counter-revolutionary forces that express themselves through *La Prensa* or through radios controlled by these sectors never rest. They work daily to destroy our process and North American imperialism does not rest either. . . .

We do not fool ourselves. Our Revolution has a profoundly anti-imperialist, profoundly revolutionary, profoundly class character. We are anti-Yankee, we are against the bourgeoisie. We are inspired by the historical traditions of our people. We are inspired by Sandinismo, the most beautiful

Translated by Robert S. Leiken.

tradition of our people kept alive by Carlos Fonseca. We are guided by the scientific doctrine of revolution, by Marxism–Leninism.

Marxism–Leninism is the scientific doctrine that guides our revolution, the instrument of analysis of our vanguard to understand the historical process and to make the Revolution. Sandinismo is the concrete expression of the historical development of the struggle in Nicaragua. Without Sandinismo we cannot be Marxists–Leninists and Sandinismo without Marxism–Leninism cannot be revolutionary. Thus, they are indissolubly united and thus our moral force is Sandinismo, our political force is Sandinismo and our doctrine is Marxism–Leninism. . . .

Capitalism developed the productive forces enormously and made technology and economics advance but preserved the exploitation of one class by another. In the twentieth century for the first time, humanity was to make a reality of Marx and Engels' theory, to create a society without classes, in which the exploitation of man by man could be eliminated. And that is the great revolution of October: the Bolshevik revolution led by Lenin.

Humanity has gone on advancing and at the moment of the triumph of the popular Sandinista revolution, of July 19, 1979, the historical development of society was polarized into two great camps: on one side the camp of imperialism, the camp of capitalism, led by the United States and the rest of the capitalist countries of Europe and of the world. And on the other side the socialist camp, composed of different countries of Europe, Asia and Latin America, with the Soviet Union in the vanguard.

[Costa Rica] is the democracy that Robelo wants. That they should have the army, the power, and we, the Sandinistas, be what the Left is in Costa Rica, a sector, an organization that is active, that puts out a newspaper, but they, the bourgeoisie, control power. Here it's the reverse. Here in Nicaragua, Sandinismo wields the power, the people wield it and they (the bourgeosie) are, must be, what we believe they should be and want them to be: a political force that is active within the limits of the Revolution under the laws imposed on it. That is how it has to be. . . .

It is therefore vital that political–ideological work in our Armed Forces be strengthened, proceeding in the first place from a clear consciousness of the content of our Revolution, proceeding in the second place from a clarification of current problems and from there the necessity of Marxism–Leninism as an instrument to analyze problems. . . .

It is not that now we are going to explain to our people: look Marxism–Leninism is good. No, not that. Marxism is borne in the heart. It is not to be sold like merchandise. . . . Marxism is an instrument of analysis. Sandinismo must be promoted within our people: support for the Sandinista Front, explaining problems from a revolutionary point of view, that the capitalists are decapitalizing and forming a black market, not contributing to reconstruction; that the government has given them so many millions and instead of using them for reconstruction they are using them to enrich themselves, make all the money they can; that they do not want revolutionary Christians to participate in the revolution. That is what must be explained. That ENABAS is working poorly because it is a new institution. That there still are corrupt elements there. Because in the government, in the ministry, we cannot substitute new people for everybody. There are still opportunists, Soamocistas, etc. . . .

To make revolution is difficult. The socialist camp after sixty years still has many problems. When it was born, it was born bombarded, blockaded by Yankee imperialism. You have the example of Cuba, that has resisted an imperialist blockade for twenty years. At the international level, the socialist camp has problems, but historically it is making the revolution. It is struggling to help humanity. It had to develop a military force, because without military force, Yankee imperialism and world reaction would have crushed all those countries. If there were no imperialism and no worldwide reaction, all those immense resources—all those immense resources of men, of the efforts of technology, of science—that the socialist camp devotes to arms would be devoted to homes, housing, schools, and welfare.

The socialist camp has to sacrifice an important part of its economy to develop its defense and to help other people that defend themselves. There's the case of Cuba, for example, that without the aid of the Soviet Union would not have the arms to defend its process. And the case of Nicaragua, too. We have had the unconditional support, the unrestricted support, in the first place, of Cuba with Fidel Castro in the vanguard.

La Prensa a few days ago made big headlines about Poland and now imperialism; the local reaction and the reactionary clergy want to raise the case of Poland like a flag to strike at the socialist camp, to strike at the Revolution, to rob it of its prestige. Today we are not going to explain the whole problematic of Poland. But we can say that there was weakness, an excess of liberalism, too much toleration for that type of counterrevolutionary sector, an excess of liberalism which permitted an obsolete ideology to gain too much space. Imperialism has taken advantage of these problems of the Polish process. It has incited them and given money and resources, and there is a difficult situation there. Nonetheless we cannot at any moment put ourself on the same side of imperialism and one must be very careful. We must point out that there has been permanent counterrevolutionary labor just as with Allende in Chile and as they wish to do here in Nicaragua. They wish to force us, they wish to tie our hands into sustaining a totally liberal system. Here there are many foreign reactionaries that want to influence our internal politics. They meet with the bourgeois parties. The gringo embassy is just as active here as it wishes. They want us to maintain that type of model. They want to imprison us in that type of model so that we do not impose revolutionary laws. They want to create anarchy, provoke scarcity; that there be fewer grains, less food, all this to create a destabilized situation of unhappiness to justify intervention.

We must be clear. Yankee imperialism can take advantage of what happens in Poland to intervene in Nicaragua. . . .

Our problem is the struggle against imperialism, the struggle against the traitorous bourgeiosie, the struggle against the reactionary clergy. But that does not mean that we are going to attack an old lady because she believes in God and carries a rosary. That is not the point. There is no need to bother about that now. What's important now is whether you are with the Revolution or whether you are against it; with imperialism or against it; with the socialist camp or against the socialist camp. What is important is to understand the historical role that the Revolution must play, to be part of the dynamic of the class struggle, the dynamic of the Revolution. . . .

26.
PRESIDENT LEONID BREZHNEV: REPLY TO ORTEGA AT KREMLIN DINNER (MAY 1982)

Allow me to cordially greet the delegation of the Republic of Nicaragua led by Comrade Daniel Ortega. You have come here from afar, from the other hemisphere of the earth. Your visit to Moscow and the fruitful talks which have taken place graphically emphasize, in our view, one of the more important law-governed processes of the present-day world development. The peoples and countries are drawn nearer not so much by geography as by politics, and distances are no impediment to mutual understanding and friendship. This is borne out by the development of relations between our countries.

The people of Nicaragua are upholding a just cause, their vital cause. The small state in Central America is making every effort to protect its independence and to live under conditions of peace, so that all acts of provocation against it should be ended. In accordance with the will of the people, that state, led by the Sandinist National Liberation Front, has set about restructuring social relations on the principles of democracy and social progress.

Nicaragua is pursuing a policy of non-alignment in international affairs, contributing as much as it can towards improving the international situa-

From Tass, May 4, 1982, in *FBIS: Soviet Union,* May 5, 1982, p. K3.

tion. We, like many other states, are in solidarity with you in all this.

Vast oceanic expanses separate us from the Western Hemisphere. The American Continent was not engulfed—at least directly—in the flames of the two world wars which devastated Europe, Asia and Africa.

But peace is cherished everywhere and all the peoples want peace. And nowadays there is no higher responsibility for a statesman than that of safeguarding peace. This holds true for South America, for the United States and for Canada alike. The distance between American and the other continents, which were the theatre of the world wars, is in no way longer than the distance from them to America.

We understand perfectly well the persevering striving of the leadership of Nicaragua to remove through talks difficulties and tension in relations with its neighbors and with the United States.

The constructive initiatives of other Latin American countries as well, such as Mexico and Cuba, that point in the same direction are in accord with the goals of our policy.

History and the present-day are yielding further proof of the fact that the freedom movement is going on and mounting amidst the mass of the people of Latin America. The peoples want to be masters of their land, of their homes, be it in Central America or in the southern Atlantic.

And if in the Western Hemisphere, too, there emerge dangerous complications and conflict situation, it is precisely because there are forces which are trying to preserve or restore their positions of dominance and to impose foreign oppression on the peoples. They do not stop at threats and pressure, blackmail and blockade, or the use of arms, and resort to actions hailing back to the time of colonial brigandage.

Here, as in other parts of the globe, the Soviet Union follows its principled policy, that of removing the existing seats of tension and preventing new ones, preventing interference in the internal affairs of states and peoples, and settling disputes by peaceful ways, at the negotiating table. We have one policy on all continents, the Leninist policy of peace and friendship among nations."

In conclusion, Leonid Brezhnev raised a toast to the health of Comrade Ortega and all the Nicaraguan guests, to the strengthening of friendship and cooperation between the Soviet Union and the Republic of Nicaragua, and to world peace.

27.
GENERAL SECRETARY YURI ANDROPOV: ON NICARAGUA AND AFGHANISTAN (APRIL 1983)

Rudolf Augstein: . . . Are they in the Soviet Union aware of the extent to which the question of Afghanistan spoils the international atmosphere—and are there any plans for doing away with such a situation?

Yuri Andropov: . . . Yes, they are aware of it. Our plans for a political settlement of the Afghan problem are no secret. . . . We consider that as soon as outside interference in the affairs of Afghanistan has been terminated and non-resumption of such interference guaranteed, we shall withdraw our troops. Our troops are staying in that country at the request of the lawful Afghan Government. . . . We are not after anything for ourselves there. . . . It is, however, necessary to bear in mind that this happens in our corner of the world, along the border. We have a long common border, and it does make a difference to us what kind of Afghanistan it will be. To make this better understood, let us put it this way, for example: as if it would not make any difference to the United States what kind of government Nicaragua would have. . . .

28.
PRESIDENT FIDEL CASTRO: IF NICARAGUA WERE INVADED (OCTOBER 1983)

Commander, would you give your opinion on the Central American crisis. For example, if Nicaragua were invaded, to what extent would Cuba support Nicaragua?

[Castro] We would try to do whatever we could for Nicaragua, but we would be facing the same problem as with Grenada. We have no naval or air means of sending direct aid to Grenada. We do not have an option here. However, this does not worry me. The Nicaraguan situation is quite differ-

---

Der Spiegel, April 24, 1983.

From Havana Television Service, Oct. 26, 1983, in *FBIS: Latin America,* October 26, 1983, p. Q14.

ent from that of Grenada. Grenada has 120,000 inhabitants; Nicaragua has 3.5 million inhabitants. Nicaragua has extensive fighting experience; it has tens of thousands of fighters. That is, the United States would have to face an armed people there. It would be an impossible struggle in which neither 1 nor 10 airborne divisions would be sufficient. This is a reality. People should not be underestimated. Nicaragua should not be underestimated.

I believe that it would be an error multiplied a hundred times to attempt invading Nicaragua, because the Nicaraguan people are courageous and combative. I believe that all the aggression sustained by Nicaragua has strengthened, rather than weakened, the revolution. It has given them experience. I' believe that Nicaragua is [word indistinct] a country that could not be occupied and could not be ruled by the United States. There is no technology or sophisticated weaponry that can solve the problems posed by an entire nation in arms.

This was not the situation in Grenada because, as a result of the domestic problems, the Army itself collected the weapons from the militias and could not muster an armed people for the resistance. This is not the case in Nicaragua. Let us hope that this great mistake will be helpful in preventing greater mistakes in Nicaragua.

29.
TASS: REPORTAGE ON SOVIET-NICARAGUAN ECONOMIC AGREEMENT (APRIL 1985)

The signing in Moscow today of an agreement on setting up a Soviet-Nicaraguan inter-governmental commission on economic, trade and scientific-technical cooperation has been a new step on the way of a further development and deepening of mutually beneficial and equal trade and economic relations between the Soviet Union and Nicaragua. From the Soviet side the agreement was signed by Mikhail Sergeychik, chairman of the USSR State Committee for Foreign Economic Relations, and from the Nicaraguan side by Henry Ruiz, minister for foreign economic cooperation.

The setting up of an inter-governmental commission will enable the sides to improve the coordination of bilateral cooperation in the economy and broaden its field. As Henry Ruiz pointed out in his address to the signing ceremony, the work of the commission will enable Nicaragua to resolve

From Tass, April 29, 1985, in *FBIS: Soviet Union,* April 29, 1985, p. K2.

successfully in cooperation with the USSR the tasks facing the Republic in the field of economic development.

No few important economic projects have been built or are under construction in Nicaragua with the USSR's technological assistance. Among them, in particular, are light industry and transport enterprises, educational centers and communication facilities. The organizations of the two countries also cooperate in geological prospecting.

Bilateral trade is also successfully developing. In 1984 its volume grew by almost 90 million rubles as compared with the preceding year to reach 138.1 million rubles.

The agreement signed today on setting up an inter-governmental commission, Mikhail Sergeychik said, will make it possible to realize the great potentialities of the USSR and Nicaragua in the field of economic, trade and scientific-technical cooperation and will serve towards the cause of strengthening friendship between the peoples of the two countries.

Index